Windows 2000 Active Directory

Windows 2000 Active Directory

Alistair G. Lowe-Norris

O'REILLY®

Beijing · Cambridge · Farnham · Köln · Paris · Sebastopol · Taipei · Tokyo

Windows 2000 Active Directory
by Alistair G. Lowe-Norris

Published by O'Reilly & Associates, Inc., 101 Morris Street, Sebastopol, CA 95472.

Editor: Robert Denn

Production Editor: Maureen Dempsey

Cover Designer: Hanna Dyer

Printing History:

> January 2000:   First Edition.

ISBN: 1-56592-638-2   [6/01]

[M]

To my partner Vicky Launders and to my parents, Pauline and Peter Norris.

Table of Contents

Preface

The Windows 2000 Active Directory is a significant improvement on the Windows NT 4.0 domain model, and it's possibly the most important new feature of the operating system. Essentially, Active Directory is the repository for information about all objects related to the network (such as users and groups, computers and printers, or applications and files). Access Control Lists and other object properties are stored in Active Directory as well to allow you to specify and maintain who can do what on the system and when they can do it. Having a single source for this information makes the network more secure and easier to manage.

Active Directory supports the Lightweight Directory Access Protocol (LDAP), which is the standard implemented in other directory service products including Novell Directory Services (NDS), Netscape Commerce Server, and Microsoft's own Exchange Server 5.0. This means that Active Directory can integrate and interoperate with the major directory services on the market today. The standard Active Directory Services Interfaces (ADSI) enables third-party vendors to integrate with Active Directory, and, as you will see later in the book, ADSI offers system and network administrators a programmatic way to manage and maintain their directories.

Windows 2000 Active Directory describes Active Directory in depth but not in the traditional way of going through the graphical user interface screen by screen by screen. Instead the book sets out to tell administrators exactly how to design, manage, and maintain a small, medium, or enterprise Active Directory on a Windows 2000 Server, Windows 2000 Advanced Server, or Windows 2000 Datacenter Server. To this end, the book you are holding has a split personality. Part I introduces you to much of how Active Directory works in general terms, so that you gain a thorough grounding in its operation. Part II moves to the single most important issue, the proper design of the directory hierarchy. Topics in the second section include in-depth looks at integration between Domain Name System (DNS) implementations, replication, enterprise-wide policies for locking down client settings, auditing, permissions, and customizing Active Directory to your own requirements. The third section is all about managing Active Directory via scripting with Active Directory Service Interfaces. Part III covers how to create and manipulate users, groups, computers, printers, and other objects that you may need in your everyday management of Active Directory and in some cases Windows NT. The last part is quite distinct from the other two.

If you're looking for in-depth coverage of how to use the Windows 2000 consoles or Resource Kit tools, then look elsewhere. However, if you're looking for a book that lays bare the design and management of an enterprise or departmental Windows 2000 Active Directory, then you need look no further.

Intended Audience

This book is for all Windows 2000 server administrators, whether you manage a single-server service or a global multi-national with a farm of thousands of servers. The departmental administrator will find a lot of useful information on how to make his job easier by centralizing authority on distributed resources.

Because the book covers the principles behind Active Directory rather than the use of the tools, you should need no real experience of Windows 2000. However, to get the most out of the book, you probably will find it useful to have a Windows 2000 server and the Resource Kit tools available so that you can check out various items as I point them out.

If you have no experience with VBScript, the scripting language I use in the book, don't worry. The syntax is straightforward, and you should have no difficulty grasping the principles of scripting with ADSI from the VBScript examples. For those who want to learn more about VBScript, I do point to various Internet sites and other books as appropriate.

Contents of the Book

This book is split into three parts:

Part I, *The Basics*

- Chapter 1, *A Brief Introduction*, sketches the major features and benefits of Active Directory and provides a high-level look at how objects are stored in the hierarchy.

- Chapter 2, *Active Directory Overview*, acts as a primer in explaining how Active Directory works by looking at its internal structures and the building blocks that it relies on.

- Chapter 3, *Active Directory Schema*, gives you information on how the blueprint for each object and each object's attributes are stored in Active Directory.

- Chapter 4, *Active Directory Replication*, details how the actual replication process for individual data items takes place between two servers.

- Chapter 5, *TCP/IP and DDNS*, describes how TCP/IP and the Domain Name System (DNS) underpin the workings of Active Directory.

Part II, *Designing the Directory Hierarchy*

- Chapter 6, *Designing the Namespace*, introduces the steps and techniques involved in properly preparing a design that reduces the number of domains and increases administrative control through the use of Organizational Units.

- Chapter 7, *Sites and Replication Topologies*, shows you how to design a representation of your physical infrastructure within Active Directory in order to gain very fine grained control over intrasite and intersite replication.

- Chapter 8, *Profiles and Group Policy Primer*, gives you a detailed introduction into the capabilities of both user profiles and Group Policy Objects.

- Chapter 9, *Designing Organization-Wide Policies*, explains how Group Policy Objects function in Active Directory and how you can properly design an Active Directory structure to make the most effective use of them.

- Chapter 10, *Active Directory Security: Permissions and Auditing*, describes how you can design effective security for all areas of your Active Directory, both in terms of access to objects and their properties, plus it includes information on how to design effective security access logging to any areas you choose.

- Chapter 11, *Designing Schema Changes*, covers procedures for extending the classes and properties in the Active Directory Schema.

- Chapter 12, *Windows NT 4.0 Migration*, gives very basic guidelines on areas to think about when conducting a Windows NT 4.0 migration. This is only an introduction to the subject; readers looking for step-by-step guides or detailed studies of migration will need to look elsewhere.

- Chapter 13, *Directory Interoperability*, looks into what methods exist now and will exist in the future for integrating Active Directory with other directories and data stores. While it goes into detail on Active Directory Connector for connecting Active Directory to Microsoft Exchange, the rest of the chapter is an overview of the options available rather than a detailed analysis.

Part III, *Scripting the Active Directory with ADSI*

- Chapter 14, *Scripting with ADSI*, introduces how to ADSI scripting by leading you through a step-by-step example involving groups.

- Chapter 15, *IADs and the Property Cache*, delves into the concept of the property cache used extensively by ADSI and shows you how to properly manipulate any attribute of any object within it.

- Chapter 16, *Users*, gives you the lowdown on how to rapidly create users, giving them whatever attributes you desire. I also show you how to create an Exchange mailbox programmatically at the same time you create a user.

- Chapter 17, *Manipulating Persistent and Dynamic Objects*, explains how other persistent objects such as services, shares, and printers may be manipulated, as well as looks at dynamic objects like print jobs, user sessions, and resources.

- Chapter 18, *Permissions and Auditing*, describes how each object contains its own list of permissions and auditing entries that govern how it can be accessed and how that access is logged. The chapter then details how you can create and manipulate the entire lists or individual entries as you choose.

- Chapter 19, *Extending the Schema and the GUI*, covers how you can create new classes and attributes programmatically in the schema and also how you can modify the existing Active Directory GUI tools that ship with Windows 2000.

- Chapter 20, *Enhancing ADSI via an ASP or VB Interface*, goes into how you can extend the scripts that have been written up to now by incorporating them into web pages or even converting them into simple VB programs.

- Chapter 21, *Scripting Fast Searches Using ADO*, demonstrates how to make use of a technology normally reserved for databases and now extended to allow rapid searching for any property of any object in the entire Active Directory.

Conventions in This Book

The following typographical conventions are used in this book:

`Constant width`
: Indicates command-line elements, computer output, and code examples.

`Constant width italic`
: Indicates variables in examples and in registry keys.

`Constant width bold`
: Indicates user input.

Italic
: Introduces new terms and URLs, commands, file extensions, filenames, directory or folder names, and UNC pathnames.

Indicates a tip, suggestion, or general note. For example, we'll tell you if you need to use a particular version or if an operation requires certain privileges.

Indicates a warning or caution. For example, we'll tell you if Active Directory does not behave as you'd expect or if a particular operation has a negative impact on performance.

We'd Like Your Feedback!

The information in this book has been tested and verified to the best of our ability, but mistakes and oversights do occur. Please let us know about errors you may find, as well as your suggestions for future editions, by writing to:

O'Reilly & Associates, Inc.
101 Morris Street
Sebastopol, CA 95472
800-998-9938 (in the U.S. or Canada)
707-829-0515 (international or local)
707-829-0104 (fax)

You also can send us messages using email. To be put on our mailing list or to request a catalog, send email to:

info@oreilly.com

To ask technical questions or comment on the book, send email to:

bookquestions@oreilly.com

For corrections and amplifications to this book, check out O'Reilly & Associates' online catalog at:

http://www.oreilly.com/catalog/win2000ads

To find links to the author's web site and email address, you can visit:

http://www.daynotes.com

Acknowledgments

Many people have encouraged me in the writing of this book, principally Vicky Launders, my partner, friend, and fountain of useful information, who has been a pinnacle of understanding during all the late nights and early mornings. Without you my life would not be complete.

My parents Pauline and Peter Norris also have encouraged me at every step of the way; many thanks to you both.

For keeping me sane, my thanks go to my good friend Keith Cooper, a natural polymath, superb scientist, and original skeptic; to Steve Joint, for keeping my enthusiasm for Microsoft in check; to Dave and Sue Peace for "Tuesdays," and the ability to look interested in what I was saying and how the book was going no matter how uninterested they must have felt; and to Mike Felmeri for his interest in this book and his eagerness to read an early draft.

I had a lot of help from my colleagues at Leicester University. To Lee Flight, a true networking guru without peer, many thanks for all the discussions, arguments, suggestions, and solutions. I'll remember forever how one morning very early you took the first draft of my 11-chapter book and spread it all over the floor to produce the 21 chapters that now constitute the book. It's so much better for it. Chris Heaton gave many years of dedicated and enjoyable teamwork; you have my thanks. Brian Kerr, who came onto the fast-moving train at high speed, managed to hold on tight through all the twists and turns along the way, and then finally took over the helm. Thanks to Paul Crow for his remarkable work on the Windows 2000 client rollout and GPOs at Leicester. And thanks to Phil Beesley, Carl Nelson, Paul Youngman, and Peter Burnham for all the discussions and arguments along the way. A special thank-you goes to Wendy Ferguson for our chats over the past few years.

To the Cormyr crew: Paul Burke, for his in-depth knowledge across all aspects of technology and databases in particular, who really is without peer, and thanks for being so eager to read the book that you were daft enough to take it on your honeymoon; Simon Williams for discussions on enterprise infrastructure consulting and practices, how you can't get the staff these days, and everything else under the sun that came up; Richard Lang for acting as a sounding board for the most complex parts of replication internals, as I struggled to make sense of what was going on; Jason Norton for his constant ability to cheer me up; Mark Newell for his gadgets and Ian Harcombe for his wit, two of the best analyst programmers that I've ever met; and finally, Paul "Vaguely" Buxton for simply being himself. Many thanks to you all.

To Allan Kelly, another analyst programmer par excellence, for various discussions that he probably doesn't remember but that helped in a number of ways.

At Microsoft: Walter Dickson for his insightful ability to get right to the root of any problem, constant accessibility via email and phone, and his desire to make sure that any job is done to the best of its ability; Bob Wells for his personal enthusiasm and interest in what I was doing; Daniel Turner for his help, enthusiasm, and key role in getting Leicester University involved in the Windows 2000 RDP; Oliver Bell for actually getting Leicester University accepted on the Windows 2000 RDP and taking a chance by allocating free consultancy time to the project; Brad Tipp whose enthusiasm and ability galvanized me into action at the U.K. Professional Developers Conference in 1997; Julius Davies for various discussions but among other things telling me how the auditing and permissions aspects of Active Directory had all changed just after I finished the chapter; Karl Noakes, Steve Douglas, Jonathan Phillips, Stuart Hudman, Stuart Okin, Nick McGrath, and Alan Bennett for various discussions.

To Tony Lees, director of Avantek Computer Ltd., for being attentive, thoughtful, and the best all-round salesman I have ever met, many thanks for taking the time to get Leicester University onto the Windows 2000 RDP.

Thanks to Amit D. Chaudhary and Cricket Liu for reviewing parts of the book.

I also would like to thank everyone at O'Reilly but especially my editor Robert Denn for his encouragement, patience, and keen desire to get this book crafted properly.

I

The Basics

This section of the book discusses the basics of Active Directory in order to provide a good grounding in the building blocks and how they function together.

- Chapter 1, *A Brief Introduction*, sketches the major features and benefits of Active Directory and provides a high-level look at how objects are stored in the hierarchy.

- Chapter 2, *Active Directory Overview*, acts as a primer in explaining how Active Directory works by looking at its internal structures and the building blocks that it relies on.

- Chapter 3, *Active Directory Schema*, gives you information on how the blueprint for each object and each object's attributes are stored in Active Directory.

- Chapter 4, *Active Directory Replication*, details how the actual replication process for individual data items takes place between two servers.

- Chapter 5, *TCP/IP and DDNS*, describes how TCP/IP and the Domain Name System (DNS) underpin the workings of the Active Directory.

1

A Brief Introduction

Windows 2000 Active Directory is Microsoft's entry into the directory services arena and provides administrators with the ability to manage enterprise-wide network objects efficiently from a central location. Information about users and groups, computers and printers, applications and files—once specified in Active Directory—is available for use throughout the network. The structure of the information matches the structure of your organization, and your users can query Active Directory to find the location of a printer or the email address of a colleague.

This book is an introduction to Active Directory, but an introduction with a difference. Instead of presenting the information inside out and feature by feature, Active Directory is viewed here from two outside-in perspectives. Part II of the book focuses on the various design issues and methodologies to enable you to map your organization's business requirements into Active Directory hierarchy. Getting the design right is critical to a successful implementation. The second perspective, presented in Part III, is a discussion of how to set up and manage Active Directory programmatically through Active Directory Services Interfaces (ADSI) scripts. If you understand how to create efficient designs and how to carry out those design decisions in scripts, you will be well on your way to building and managing a directory structure populated with the right objects at the right levels of the hierarchy.

Before turning to the details of designing and scripting, however, Part I introduces Active Directory at the conceptual level.

Major Features

Active Directory extends the Windows NT 4 domain model to provide a more efficient approach, and it provides a number of important new features as well. Of particular interest are the following:

New domain model

Domains in Windows were flat structures limited to about 40,000 objects, and this had some unfortunate consequences. For one thing, the assigning of privileges tended to be an all-or-nothing matter at the domain level; there was no delegation or inheritance within the domain. For another, the resource limitation often meant that the number of domains in an organization would grow into an unmanageable network over time. Active Directory domains are hierarchical and virtually without resource limitation. This means that administrators can delegate authority within a smaller number of more manageable domains.

Transitive trusts

Under Windows NT 4, managing trust relationships could easily become a nightmare. All trusts were manual and unidirectional, and they had to be individually specified. If domain A trusted domain B, it was still necessary to separately specify that domain B trusted domain A, if that was your desire. Moreover, if A trusted B and B trusted C, A did not trust C without a separate specification. Active Directory domains include automatic bidirectional trusts and transitive trusts to rationalize and simplify trust management.

Group policies

Using new group policies, you can specify roles complete with configuration information within the domain hierarchy. This means that you can define things so that, whenever you add a new user to a group, you can trigger automatic configuration and software installation for that user.

Multimaster replication

Each domain controller automatically propagates all the objects defined on it to every other participating domain controller. Because each controller contains all the data for the domain, Active Directory access will continue should one domain controller fail.

Global catalog

To facilitate efficient searching of Active Directory, all the objects and their frequently used attributes are stored in a partial replica of each Windows 2000 domain in a directory. This is the Global Catalog, and it is built automatically during Active Directory replication.

Standards compliance

Because Active Directory is based on the Lightweight Directory Access Protocol (LDAP) and other standards, it is possible for you to integrate Active

Directory with other directory services and for third-party vendors to integrate their components with Active Directory.

I will be discussing these and many other features in great detail in later chapters.

How Objects Are Stored in Active Directory

When you create objects in Active Directory, you create them in a hierarchical structure you have control over. The structure is made up of two types of objects: containers and noncontainers, or *leaves*. A series of containers branch downward from a root container, just as the roots of a tree do. Each container may contain noncontainers or further containers. A noncontainer, however, may not contain any other objects.

Consider the parent-child relationships of the containers and leaves in Figure 1-1. The root of this tree has two children, Finance and Sales. Both of these are containers of other objects. Sales has two children of its own, Presales and Postsales. Only the Presales container is shown as containing child leaf objects. The Presales container holds user, group, and computer objects as an example.* Each of these noncontainers is said to have the Presales container as its parent.

Figure 1-1 is what is known in Windows 2000 as a *domain.*

The most common type of container you will create in your Active Directory is the *Organizational Unit,* but there are others as well, such as *DomainDNS* and even one called *Container.* Each of these has its place, as I'll show later, but the one that you will be using most frequently is the Organizational Unit.

Uniquely Identifying Objects

When you are potentially storing millions of objects in Active Directory, each object has to be uniquely locatable and identifiable. To that end, objects have a *Globally Unique Identifier* (GUID) assigned to them by the system at creation. This 128-bit number is guaranteed to be unique by Microsoft. However, there is another way to reference an object: the AdsPath.

ADsPaths

Hierarchical paths in Active Directory are known as *ADsPaths* and can be used to uniquely reference an object. In fact, ADsPath is a slightly more general term, and

---

* Computer objects are actually containers, as they can contain printers and other items normally associated with a specific device. However, they are not normally drawn as containers in domain diagrams such as this.

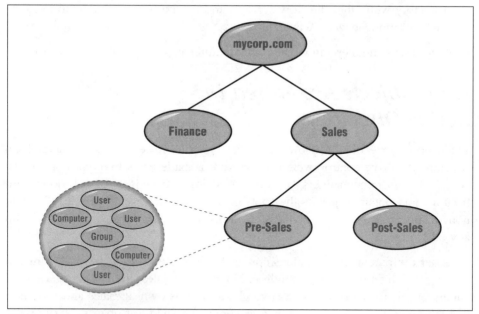

Figure 1-1. A hierarchy of objects

is used by Microsoft to apply to any path to any of the major directories: Windows 2000's Active Directory, Windows NT, Novell's NDS, Netscape's Commerce Server, and many others.

ADsPaths to Active Directory are normally represented using the syntax and rules defined in the LDAP standards. Let's take a look at how a path to the root of Figure 1-1 looks:

```
LDAP://dc=mycorp,dc=com
```

Here you can see that the path starts with a progID of LDAP followed by a colon (:) and a double forward slash (//). All LDAP paths start this way.

 You probably noted that I said that an ADsPath is *normally* represented by an LDAP path; that isn't always the case. ADsPaths to other directories can use other progIDs. I go into these other progIDs in more depth in Chapter 14, *Scripting with ADSI.*

In the previous ADsPath, after the progID, you represent the domain root, *mycorp. com,* by separating each part by a comma and prefixing each part with the letters dc. If the domain had been called *mydomain.windows.mycorp.com,* the ADsPath would have looked like this:

```
LDAP://dc=mydomain,dc=windows,dc=mycorp,dc=com
```

DC stands for Domain Component; dc is used only when specifying domain roots.

Distinguished Names and Relative Distinguished Names

A *Distinguished Name* (DN)* is the name used to uniquely reference an object in an entire *Directory Information Tree* (DIT). A *Relative Distinguished Name* (RDN) is the name used to uniquely reference an object within its parent container in a DIT. For example, this is the ADsPath for the default Administrator account in the Users Container in the *windows.mycorp.com* domain:

```
LDAP://cn=Administrator,cn=Users,dc=windows,dc=mycorp,dc=com
```

This is the DN of the same user (note the absence of the progID):

```
cn=Administrator,cn=Users,dc=windows,dc=mycorp,dc=com
```

This is the RDN of the user:

```
cn=Administrator
```

These paths are made up of names and prefixes separated by the equals sign (=). Another prefix that will become very familiar to you is ou, which stands for *Organizational Unit*. Here is an example:

```
cn=Keith Cooper,ou=Northlight IT Ltd,dc=windows,dc=mycorp,dc=com
```

All RDNs, DNs, and ADsPaths use a prefix to indicate the class of object that is being referred to. Only a few were defined as standard in March 1995 when RFC 1779, "A String Representation of Distinguished Names," was written.† Any object class that does not have a specific letter code uses the default of cn, which stands for *Common Name*. All Active Directory objects have a common name anyway, no matter what their class, but the system will be able to uniquely identify the object only by using its appropriate prefix code. Table 1-1 provides the complete list from RFC 1779. The full text can be found at *http://www.faqs.org/rfcs/rfc1779.html*.

While Microsoft Exchange uses the O prefix, Active Directory uses only DC, CN, and OU, which makes things very simple.

---

* For more information about DNs, go to *http://www.faqs.org/rfcs/rfc1484.html*.

† Request for Comments (RFCs) are computing standards documents that are published on the Internet and go through a rigorous analysis, discussion, and rejection/adoption procedure by open standards committees.

Table 1-1. Key Codes From RFC 1779, "A String Representation of Distinguished Names"

Key	Attribute
CN	Common Name
L	Locality Name
ST	State or Province Name
O	Organization Name
OU	Organizational Unit Name
C	Country Name
STREET	Street Address

Examples

Let's take a look at Figure 1-1 again. The ADsPath to the Finance container could be in one of two forms:

```
LDAP://ou=Finance,dc=mycorp,dc=com
LDAP://cn=Finance,dc=mycorp,dc=com
```

You can see that the only real difference is the two-letter prefix indicating the type of container that Finance is. In the former, Finance is defined as an Organizational Unit. In the latter, Finance is any other sort of container. So if all the containers in Figure 1-1 are Organizational Units, then the ADsPaths for Presales and Postsales are as follows:

```
LDAP://ou=Presales,ou=Sales,dc=mycorp,dc=com
LDAP://ou=Postsales,ou=Sales,dc=mycorp,dc=com
```

And if you wanted to specify a user named Richard Lang, a group called My Group, and a computer called Moose in the Presales Container, then you would do it like this:

```
LDAP://cn=Richard Lang,ou=Presales,ou=Sales,dc=mycorp,dc=com
LDAP://cn=My Group,ou=Presales,ou=Sales,dc=mycorp,dc=com
LDAP://cn=Moose,ou=Presales,ou=Sales,dc=mycorp,dc=com
```

This uses the default cn prefix, as there is no special prefix for any of these objects.

Summary

This chapter has been a brief introduction to Active Directory and to this book. The chapters in Part I will complete the conceptual introduction to Active Directory's technology and equip you to get the most out of Parts II and III.

2

Active Directory Overview

This chapter aims to bring everyone up to speed on the terminology and functionality surrounding Active Directory. I cannot stress enough how important it is that you understand the parlance of Microsoft's terminology and how each component of Active Directory fits into the whole before considering a design; if you do not know what the component items of a design do, you cannot design properly with them.

A Simple View of How It All Works

Let's start off with a simple look at how an Active Directory namespace is structured in terms of domains, trees, forests, and Organizational Units.

Domains

Windows 2000's logical structure is built around the concept of domains introduced by Windows NT 3.x and 4.x. However, in Windows 2000, the term *domain* has been updated somewhat. A domain is now made up of the following components:

- An X.500-based hierarchical structure of containers and objects

- A DNS domain name as a unique identifier; DNS names have taken over from NetBIOS names in Windows 2000, and NetBIOS is not necessary in a pure Windows 2000 environment

- A security boundary run by a security service and managed by an administrator of that domain, which authenticates any access to resources via accounts in the domain or trusts with other domains

- One or more policies that dictate how functionality is restricted for users or machines within that domain

A domain is the smallest component of Active Directory that can be reproduced on a single domain controller (DC). For example, Mycorp Company has already been allocated a DNS domain name for their company called *mycorp.com,* so they decide that the first Windows 2000 domain that they are going to build is to be named *mycorp.com.* However, this is only the first domain in a series that needs to be created, and *mycorp.com* is in fact the root of a domain tree.

Domain Trees (Trees)

The *mycorp.com* domain itself, ignoring its contents, is automatically created as the root node of a hierarchical structure called a *domain tree.* This is literally a series of domains connected together in a hierarchical fashion, all using a contiguous naming scheme. So, when Finance, Marketing, and Sales each wants its own domain, the names become *finance.mycorp.com, marketing.mycorp.com,* and *sales.mycorp.com.* Each domain tree is called by the name given to the root of the tree; hence, this domain tree is known as the *mycorp.com* tree; this is illustrated in Figure 2-1. You can also see that I have added further domains below sales, for presales and postsales work.

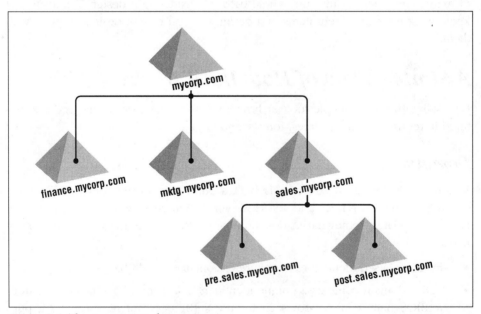

Figure 2-1. The mycorp.com domain tree

You can see that in Mycorp's setup, we now have a contiguous set of domains that all fit into a neat tree. Even if we had only one domain, it would still be a domain tree, albeit with only one domain. The term *domain tree* normally is shortened to just *tree*; that it is made up of domains is a given in Windows 2000.

Trees ease management and access to resources, as all the domains in a domain tree trust one another implicitly. Put much more simply, the administrator of *finance.mycorp.com* can allow *any* user in the tree access to any of the resources in the finance domain that he wishes. The object accessing the resource does not have to be in the same domain. This is equivalent to Windows NT 4.0's complete trust model.

This set of trust relationships, in which each domain trusts every other domain, is established automatically by Windows 2000 every time a new domain is added to the tree.

Trust relationships do not compromise security, as this is only setting up the *potential* to allow access to resources. Actual access permissions still have to be granted by administrators.

Forests

Mycorp also has a subsidiary business called Othercorp. The DNS domain name allocated and used by Othercorp is *othercorp.com*. Remember that when the *mycorp.com* domain was first created, a domain tree was also created with *mycorp.com* as the root. In fact, a new forest was also automatically created with one tree as a member: the *mycorp.com* domain tree. A forest consists of a number of discontiguous domain trees that all trust one another in the same manner that domains in a tree do. In other words, the trusts are transitive: if A trusts B and B trusts C, this implies that A trusts C as well. Forests are named after the first domain tree that they contain. This first domain is known as the *Forest Root Domain*, even though the forest is not a hierarchical structure. The Forest Root Domain is important because it has special properties.

In Windows 2000, you can never remove the Forest Root Domain. If you try to do so, the forest is irretrievably destroyed. Future versions of Windows 2000 may remove this restriction.

In Othercorp's case, all you would need to do is create the root of the *othercorp.com* tree as a member of the existing forest; thus, *othercorp.com* and *mycorp.com* can exist together and share resources. Obviously in this example, I wanted *othercorp.com* to be able to access *mycorp.com*'s resources and vice versa. This doesn't have to be the case; each could have domain trees in its own separate forest with no communication between them. Thus, the forest containing the *mycorp.com* and *othercorp.com* domain trees is known as the *mycorp.com* forest, in which *mycorp.com* is the forest root.

Organizational Units

Having covered the large-scale (domains, trees, and forests) view of Active Directory, I'll now talk about the small scale. When you look inside an Active Directory domain, you will see a hierarchical structure of objects. This hierarchy is made up of objects that can act as containers and objects that cannot. The major building block that you will create to contain objects is called the Organizational Unit. The second most common container is mainly created by the operating system and is actually called a Container (uppercase C).

Organizational Units have domainlike properties, whereas Containers do not. While both can contain huge hierarchies of containers and objects, an Organizational Unit has a security boundary (and can have multiple policies applied to it). This makes Organizational Units the most significant component of the internals of your domain.

Let me illustrate this with an example. Imagine that you are the administrator of the *pre.sales.mycorp.com* domain from Figure 2-1. You have 500 users and 500 computer accounts in the domain. Most of the day-to-day account and machine management is very simple, but the presales engineers section is currently undergoing restructuring and an extensive recruitment program; people keep being transferred in or hired. You would like to be able to give that group autonomy, by allowing one of the senior engineers to manage its own section of the tree, but it isn't a large enough requirement to justify creating another domain to manage. You can create an Organizational Unit in your hierarchy called Presales Engineers. You then nominate the senior engineer and give him autonomy over that Organizational Unit to create and delete accounts, change passwords, and create other Organizational Units and hierarchies. Obviously, the permissions that the senior engineer would be given would be properly tailored so that he had control only over that Organizational Unit and not on the *pre.sales.mycorp.com* domain tree as a whole. You could do this manually or delegate control using the Delegation-of-Control wizard, discussed in more depth in Chapter 10, *Active Directory Security: Permissions and Auditing.*

When you install a Windows 2000 domain, a number of default Containers (and one Organizational Unit) are created automatically. The Containers have names like Users, Computers, and so on. If you try to create a new Container, you will find that there is no option to do so from within the GUI tools. This is intentional; Containers normally are used by the operating system to hold hierarchies when an Organizational Unit just isn't necessary. It is possible from within scripts to create Containers if you like, but in almost every case it makes much more sense to create an Organizational Unit. So, throughout this book whenever I advocate creating hierarchies within domains, I *always* use Organizational Units. After all, since an Organizational Unit is just a superset of a Container, there is nothing a Container can do that an Organizational Unit cannot.

Each domain has a child Container called Configuration, which itself has a child container called Schema. Both the Configuration and Schema Containers are actually hidden from view by default when you open up Active Directory and view the contents. However, you can view a container by specifically connecting to it directly. The same applies to the Schema Container, which is a child of the Configuration Container. You can do this because both Containers actually represent Naming Contexts, which I'll go into in the next section.

A More Detailed View of How It All Works

Having introduced the four major components of a Windows 2000 network, let me now drill down into these concepts further.

The Building Blocks

There are three building blocks that make up Active Directory itself:

- Domain Naming Contexts
- Configuration Naming Context
- Schema Naming Context

Active Directory is split into a number of parts, which Microsoft calls *Partitions* or *Naming Contexts* (NCs). Each of these parts represents a different aspect of Active Directory. One NC is known as the Configuration and holds data representing the entire configuration of the forest, e.g., the list of NCs, how the physical network of sites and servers are configured, and so on. Another NC is known as the Schema and is responsible for maintaining data on the entire set of object and attribute types that can be created in Active Directory. The rest of the NCs are known as domain NCs, as one NC exists for each domain in the forest.

Domain Naming Contexts

The domain NCs are the part of Active Directory that hold the information on users, groups, and Organizational Units for a domain. The NCs are considered separate for the purposes of replication. However, while they are considered separate, in order to be able to reference and manipulate data in all the NCs, Active Directory joins them together into one complete structure so that you can use LDAP to reference any naming context from a tree. Active Directory is a contiguous hierarchical structure that has certain parts that, while they are joined under the hierarchy and can be accessed in the same manner as any other part of Active Directory, are in fact considered as separately replicating parts of it. In a forest, there is never but one Schema NC and one Configuration NC, but you can have as many domain NCs as you like.

Configuration Naming Context

The Configuration is a Naming Context whose name is:

```
LDAP://cn=Configuration, dc=forest-root-domain, dc=domain-component, . . .
```

So, for example, the configuration in the *windows.mycorp.com* forest would look like this:

```
LDAP://cn=Configuration, dc=windows, dc=mycorp, dc=com
```

The actual subtree starts from this item named Configuration, which is actually a Container (uppercase C). This Container and its children, normally referred to as just *The Configuration*, are replicated to every domain controller in the forest.

The Configuration holds the following information:

The physical site layout
   This is the representation of all the sites, subnets, and replication connections that make up your physical network and how they interconnect. This includes all DCs, site links, site-link bridges, replication connection objects (i.e., replication partners) for each DC, and so on. These terms are explained in more detail in Chapter 7, *Sites and Replication Topologies*, but for now imagine a series of sites with a number of intrasite and intersite connections. All of this is stored here.

The structure of the trees in the forest
   In the Partitions Container of the Configuration, an entire layout of all the domains is held. This is a complete list of all domains that make up each domain tree and all trees that make up each forest. Coupled with this, information is stored on every domain external to the forest that has had manual trusts between the forest and the domain set up. (You set up manual trusts when you want to allow access between two domains that do not reside in the same forest.)

Global configuration information for services
   Configuration information for such services as Active Directory service, the File Replication Service (FRS), the Microsoft Exchange Server services, and those of third-party products are stored in the Configuration.

Schema Naming Context

Like the Configuration, the Schema is also an independently replicated subtree or Naming Context, whose name is:

```
LDAP://cn=Schema, cn=Configuration, dc=forest-root-domain, dc=domain-component...
```

For example, the configuration in the *windows.mycorp.com* forest would look like this:

```
LDAP://cn=Schema, cn=Configuration, dc=windows, dc=mycorp, dc=com
```

The Schema, which is also a Container, and its contents, normally referred to simply as "The Schema," are replicated to every domain controller in the forest.

Although the Schema container appears to be a child of the Configuration container, it is actually a separate Naming Context in its own right. When I refer to the Configuration, I do not mean the Schema as well.

The Schema of Active Directory is the complete list of definitions of objects that can be created in Active Directory. For example, as the Organizational Unit, User, and Group objects exist in the Active Directory Schema, they can all be created in Active Directory itself. If you want to create a new type of object or property, you need to create a Schema entry first, prior to being allowed to create the objects of that type. Chapter 3, *Active Directory Schema* and Chapter 11, *Designing Schema Changes* deal with this subject in depth.

Global Catalog

The Global Catalog (GC) is a very important part of Active Directory and is used to help in rapidly responding to searches. As its name implies, the Global Catalog is a catalog of a selection of the properties from every object in Active Directory that will be useful in global searches. In fact, the GC is defined as a partial replica of every domain in the forest used for a forest-wide search.

The GC is not a Naming Context in its own right. It is not contiguous to the ordinary Active Directory tree, and is accessed separately by LDAP using its own progID (GC://).

Whenever a query comes into Active Directory, the first repository searched is the GC. This is why the GC holds only the properties of objects that will be relevant to searches. If the GC does not contain the property of the object being searched for, the query is referred automatically to Active Directory. In this manner, Active Directory is hit only by queries for lesser-used properties of objects.

One of the critical points to remember with the GC is that searching for a property in the GC will be forest wide as the GC is a forest-wide catalog; however, if you are searching for a property that is not in the GC, then the search will be conducted only in the current domain.

The properties that are stored in the GC are customizable using tools such as the Schema Manager, which allows administrators to clear or check the checkbox that dictates which properties of each class go in the GC. Certain properties, such as the Access Control Lists to objects, however, will always be stored in the GC. This ensures that should a search come in from a user for a property that exists in the GC, but to which the user has no read permission, the property will not be returned.

Which DC Holds Which Forest Components?

The forest is made up of the three main NC building blocks plus the Global Catalog. Table 2-1 describes where these components reside.

Table 2-1. Where the Building Blocks of Active Directory Reside

Name of the Building Block	Where It Resides
The domain NC	Every DC in that domain.
The Schema NC	Every DC in the entire forest.
The Configuration NC	Every DC in the entire forest.
The Global Catalog	By default, one DC per site hosts the GC. This is completely customizable by administrators.

Domains

According to Table 2-1, every DC in a domain definitely has a copy of the domain's hierarchy and the forest's Schema and Configuration. It may also have a copy of the forest's GC.

The DCs that make up a domain can all be in the same site or in separate sites; in other words, domains can span sites. As mentioned earlier, the domain is the smallest component of Active Directory that can be reproduced on a single DC. In Active Directory parlance, we say that the domain is the smallest unit of partitioning.

 A news flash to administrators of previous versions of NT: domains can now *reliably* span sites along slow links. More on this in Chapter 7.

This means that while all of the domains in the *mycorp.com* tree can be placed on separate DCs, Organizational Units within each domain cannot be partitioned and must reside on all the DCs for their Organizational Units parent domains. As an example, consider the *mycorp.com* domain tree. Say that the users in the *pre.sales.mycorp.com* domain were split into two: presales engineers and salesmen.

Most of the time the salesmen are located in offices at site A, while the engineers are at site B. I nevertheless cannot specify that only OU=Salesmen is at the DC in site A and that only OU=Engineers is at the DC in site B. Instead, I have to place the entire domain in both sites, just as in Figure 2-2.

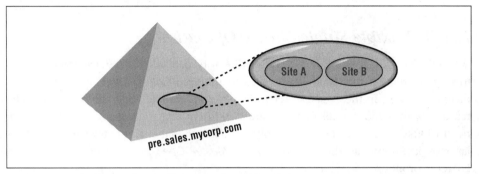

Figure 2-2. A domain is the smallest unit of partitioning

The fact that each DC in a domain keeps all the Configuration and Schema information can help speed up the response times of your clients by redirecting queries to resources in a local rather than a remote site. A specific example would be when you move an individual client workstation from site A in your organization to site B. When that client workstation boots up in the new location, it will contact the DC in site A that it last knew about in order to authenticate and process requests. However, that DC in site A may be down at the end of a very slow link, and even if it isn't, the chances are that the link between site A and site B is slower than if the client workstation had contacted a local DC in site B in the first place. The point is that when the client workstation in site B contacts the DC in site A, this DC now knows that the client workstation is not in the same site any more. So rather than authenticating the client, the DC uses the copy of the site and domain layout it has to send a referral back to the client informing it of a local DC in site B. The client workstation then contacts the DC in site B. In this way, the client gets a faster service and DCs do not get bogged down authenticating requests from remote machines.

If the DC in site A were unavailable when the client in site B tried to contact it, or if the DC in site B that the client was referred to were unavailable, then the client would then have issued a query request to the network stating that it had no DC and that it wanted one. The client would then pick the fastest response from the list of responses it received and authenticate with that DC.

It is possible to have sites that contain no DCs. In this specific case, once the DC in site A has been contacted and it knows no DC exists in site B, it will authenticate the client in site B.

FSMO (Flexible Single Master Operation)

While Active Directory is a multimaster directory database, there are some aspects to its construction that lend themselves to multiple DCs potentially making conflicting changes. In these cases, Active Directory nominates one server to act as the master. With Windows 2000, there are five such functions, known as *roles*, that need to take place on one server only. The server that is the master for a particular role is known as the *Flexible Single Master Operation* (*FSMO*) role owner; FSMO is pronounced *fizz-moe*.

Of the five roles, three exist domain wide, and two are unique enterprise wide (forest wide). If there are 12 domains in your forest, there will be 38 FSMO role owners: 12 lots of three domain-wide FSMOs and 2 single enterprise-wide FSMOs.

Any role can be transferred between servers using Active Directory Users and Computers MMC or the NTDSUTIL utility from the Windows 2000 Resource Kit. NTDSUTIL is an archaic utility that has been built with a deliberately slow and unusual interface to discourage people from damaging their Active Directory.

 NTDSUTIL allows the administrator to manage the FSMO roles and modify certain key LDAP policies that represent global configuration data for LDAP and Active Directory.

While the initial LDAP policy values are set via the *schema.ini* file during installation, they can be viewed or changed later using NTDSUTIL. They can also be viewed and changed directly from this location: cn=Default Query Policy, cn=Query-Policies, cn=DirectoryService, cn=WindowsNT, cn=Services, cn=Configuration, dc=mycorp, dc=com.

While the MMC and NTDSUTIL can trivially transfer a role from one server to another while both servers are available (and this is the normal method before taking a FSMO role owner down for maintenance), there will be some cases in which a FSMO role owner becomes unavailable without previously transferring the role. In this case, you have to use NTDSUTIL to force an ungraceful transfer of the role to a server. When you do this, bring the original FSMO role owner back, and for a while you will have two competing FSMO role owners on the network until replication takes place.

If a server with a role becomes unavailable, another server is not automatically promoted to assume the role. The administrator must move the role to a new owner manually.

The FSMO roles are the following:

Schema Master (enterprise-wide)
> The Schema Master role owner is the server that is allowed to make changes to the Schema. The default FSMO Schema Master is the first server ever to be installed in the forest. You can change the Schema Master via the Schema Manager MMC or NTDSUTIL.

Domain Naming Master (enterprise-wide)
> The Domain Naming Master role owner is the server that controls changes to the namespace. This server is allowed to add Naming Contexts to the Partitions Container for new subdomains and remove existing domains. In future versions of Windows 2000, this owner also will allow domain renaming and moving of domains between different portions of the tree. Like the Schema Master, this role owner defaults to the first DC you ever install in a forest.

PDC Advertiser (domain-wide)
> For backward-compatibility purposes, one Windows 2000 DC has to act as the Windows NT Primary Domain Controller (PDC). This role owner signifies which server has that honor. This server acts as the Windows NT master browser, and it also acts as the PDC for downlevel clients and Backup Domain Controllers (BDCs). While doing this, it replicates the Windows NT SAM database to Windows NT 4.0 and Windows 3.51 BDCs and propagates password changes and account lockout requests it receives as a normal DC down to those BDCs, in addition to propagating password changes and account lockout requests passed to it from downlevel clients out to the other DCs via multi master replication. While a domain is running in mixed mode (explained in the next section), any password changes to any object are automatically passed to the PDC for transmission to downlevel BDCs. When the domain converts to native mode, no more downlevel BDCs exist and this process stops.

RID Master (domain-wide)
> One Relative-Identifier (RID) Master exists per domain. Every security principal* in a domain has a Security Identifier (SID) that the system uses to uniquely identify that object for security permissions and authentication issues.

---

* A security principal is a security-enabled object, like a user, group, or computer.

In a way, this is similar to the Globally Unique Identifier (GUID) that every object has, but the SID is given only to security-enabled objects and is used only for security authentication and verification purposes. While you may log on or authenticate using the Common Name to reference an object, the system will always obtain and authenticate using the SID corresponding to that name.

Unique SIDs are created for standalone users, groups, and computers on Windows NT/2000 workstations and Windows NT/2000 servers in workgroups by the server or workstation hosting those objects. In a domain, the SIDs must be unique across the entire domain. As each DC can create security-enabled objects, some mechanism has to exist so that two identical SIDs are never created.

So that conflicts never occur, the RID Master maintains a large pool of unique RID values. When a DC is added to the network, it is allocated a subset of 512 values from the RID pool for its own use. Whenever a DC needs to create a SID, it takes the next available value from its own RID pool in order to create the SID with a unique value.

In this way, the RID Master makes sure that all SIDs in a domain are unique RID values. When a DC's RID pool drops to 100 free values, the DC contacts the RID Master for another set of RID values. The threshold is set to 100 and not 0 to ensure that the RID master can be unavailable for a brief time without immediately impacting object creations. The RID Master itself is in charge of generating and maintaining a pool of unique values across the entire domain.

Infrastructure Master (domain-wide)

The Infrastructure Master (a.k.a. Infrastructure Daemon) is used to maintain references to objects in other domains, known as *Phantoms*. So, if three users from Domain B are members of a group in Domain A, the Infrastructure Manager on Domain A is used to maintain references to the Phantom Domain B user members.

The Infrastructure Daemon FSMO role owner is used to continually maintain the links to Phantoms, whenever they are changed or moved on the other domain. When an object in one domain is referenced by an object in another domain, it represents that reference by the GUID, the SID (for references to security principals), and the DN of the object being referenced. The infrastructure FSMO role holder is the DC responsible for updating an object's SID and Distinguished Name in a cross-domain object reference.

In a single-domain scenario, the Infrastructure Daemon has nothing to do, so it makes no difference whether the FSMO role owner exists on a server running the GC. As soon as you introduce a second domain, the FSMO role owner should be moved to a non-GC-hosting DC.

The Infrastructure Daemon is responsible for fixing up stale references from objects in its domain to objects in other domains (*stale* means references to objects that have been moved or renamed so that the local copy of the remote object's name is out of date). It does this by comparing its (potentially stale) naming data with that of a GC, which automatically receives regular replication updates for objects in all domains and hence has no stale data. The Infrastructure Daemon writes any updates it finds to its objects and then replicates the updated information around to other DCs in the domain. However, if a GC also holds the Infrastructure role, then by definition, that server hosting the GC will always be up to date and will therefore have no stale references. If it never notices that anything needs changing, then it will never update any non-GC servers with Infrastructure updates.

If, of course, all DCs in the domain are also GCs, then no server will have stale references, and no Infrastructure Daemon is needed for that domain.

One final word of warning: keep NTDSUTIL and other tools nearby on floppies or a mastered CD of utilities in case of problems. Become familiar with the tools on a working network. If you lose one of the FSMO masters for a domain, then you should always make sure that you are in control of the situation and are promoting a new DC to be the relevant master or bringing the DC that is the relevant master back swiftly. The last thing that you will want to do is to lose one of these masters and not notice. While at Leicester University on an earlier beta of Windows 2000, I lost the entire set of FSMO Masters and couldn't get all of them back or fix the problem due to a bug. Loss of the FSMO RID Master meant that after each DC had exhausted its pool of RIDs, no more users could be created. Now, while I'm not suggesting that this will happen to you, you need to have the tools on hand and be familiar with their usage before a disaster occurs. NTDSUTIL and its quirky interface should be very familiar to you as an administrator. You should certainly get familiar with using it to move FSMO role owners around.

Mixed Mode and Native Mode

Each Windows 2000 domain is said to have one of two modes: mixed mode (the default) or native mode. A mixed-mode domain allows servers running previous versions of Windows NT to exist as part of the domain. A native-mode domain

---

The fSMORoleOwner Attribute

The FSMO role owners are stored in Active Directory in different locations depending on the role concerned. The DN of the server holding the role is actually stored as the fSMORoleOwner attribute of various objects. For the *mycorp.com* domain, here are the containers that hold that attribute in the following order: PDC Role Owner, Infrastructure Master, RID Manager Owner, Schema Master, and Domain Naming Master:

```
LDAP://dc=mycorp,dc=com
LDAP://cn=Infrastructure,dc=mycorp,dc=com
LDAP://cn=RID Manager$,cn=System,dc=mycorp,dc=com
LDAP://cn=Schema,cn=Configuration,dc=mycorp,dc=com
LDAP://cn=Partitions,cn=Configuration,dc=mycorp,dc=com
```

The information in the attribute is stored as a DN, a path to a location in Active Directory, while representing a specific server. I've already mentioned that the Configuration NC holds an entire list of all the sites and DCs forest wide, so it uses this fact to reference the known server within the Configuration Container. So, example contents for this attribute are:

```
CN=NTDS Settings, CN=MYSERVER1, CN=Servers, CN=My Site, CN=Sites,
CN=Configuration, DC=mycorp, DC=com
```

---

supports only Windows 2000 servers. This is done very simply. Remember that with previous versions of Windows NT, networks of servers used to have a Primary Domain Controller (PDC) for a domain that held a writeable copy of the accounts database, and zero or more Backup Domain Controllers (BDCs) that held a read-only accounts database copied from the PDC. Well, for a Windows 2000 network to support older NT servers, one (and only one) of the Windows 2000 servers has to act as a PDC. That way, the old servers that look for a PDC will find one. We've seen this in the preceding FSMO PDC Master discussion.

Later on in Chapter 5, *TCP/IP and DDNS*, I show you how Windows 2000 generates DNS records for Active Directory. One of these records for the *mycorp.com* domain looks like this (while this looks complicated now, I will explain it all later):

```
_ldap._tcp.pdc._msdcs    SRV    priority=0, weight=0, port=389, moose.mycorp.com
```

I'm showing it to you now so that you can see **pdc** embedded in the lefthand side and a server name on the far right. This entry states that the DC called *moose* is the current PDC, so any Windows NT BDCs or member servers* looking for a PDC will be directed to *moose*, the current FSMO PDC Master. The older BDCs that periodically request a copy of the accounts database get the relevant user, group, and computer accounts from Active Directory. While all accounts will be passed out, the total attributes for each object will be a much smaller subset of the total attributes that Active Directory now holds for these types of objects. When requests from member servers come in for authentication, the Windows 2000 DC acting as the PDC does the authentication and passes a response back in a manner that the older server would understand (i.e., using Windows NT LAN Manager (NTLM) authentication).

Going from mixed mode to native mode is a very trivial operation and is known as *upgrading*. You simply connect to a DC with the Directory Manager tool and change the properties of the domain you wish to upgrade from mixed mode to native mode. You wait for a while for the changes to replicate to all partners, and then reboot all the DCs in that domain. That's all there is to it.

However, going from mixed mode to native mode is a one-way change. Once you have done this, the only way to go back is to wipe the domain and restore from a backup made prior to the upgrade. Never upgrade to native mode unless you are certain that you will not require any Windows NT BDCs† to exist anywhere in that domain any more.

Moving any domain from mixed mode to native mode has no bearing in any way on any other domain. It doesn't matter if it is the root domain you are converting or a subdomain, because you are only removing the ability of that domain to replicate data to older Windows NT servers within the domain, not affecting its ability to replicate and interact with Windows 2000 servers in other domains.

The specific differences between mixed mode and native mode are shown in Table 2-2. When you upgrade to native mode, the DCs stop using NTLM protocols to authenticate, the RID pool becomes distributed, and you are allowed for the first time to have special groups in your Active Directory. The change may be simple to do, but its ramifications are quite wide ranging.

I've mentioned that upgrading to native-mode allows you to use extra groups, so I'll now go into groups from both modes in much more detail.

---

* A member server in a domain is a server that maintains its own personal accounts database and acts autonomously from the domain accounts database. However, as the member server is part of the domain, local resources also may be allocated to domain objects if desired.

† Windows NT member servers can still exist in native-mode domains; it's BDCs that can't.

Table 2-2. The Differences Between Mixed Mode and Native Mode

Action	Mixed Mode	Native Mode
Replication	Single-FSMO-master DC sends updates to NT4 BDCs; same DC acts like ordinary Windows 2000 DC when communicating with other Windows 2000 DCs. All Windows 2000 DCs use multi-master replication between themselves.	Only Windows 2000 servers allowed, so all DCs use multi-master replication.
Authentication	NT LAN Manager (NTLM) authentication used for communication with Windows NT downlevel servers and Kerberos authentication for Windows 2000 servers.	Kerberos only.
RID Allocation	Forced centralized.	Distributed.
NetBIOS	Can't turn off.	Can turn off.
Group definitions	Forced, i.e., global groups don't nest and local groups can exist on individual NT servers.	Allow administrators to create Windows 2000-only group definitions, i.e., universal groups and security distribution groups.

Groups

Windows 2000 supports three types of group: domain local, domain global, and universal. Each of these groups behaves differently when it is in mixed mode than when it is in native mode. To compound matters further, each type of group can have two *scopes*, distribution and security.

The scope is the easiest bit to define. If the scope is distribution, the group can effectively be considered a mailing list (a set of users that you can mail all at once). These are known as Distribution Lists in Exchange and the concept is identical. Security groups can also act as mailing lists. However, security groups can also have Access Control Lists (ACLs) applied to them for Active Directory objects or files and directories. Distribution groups do not support ACLs. Distribution groups are ignored during a user logon, while security groups that a user is a member of are enumerated and checked during logon. So you can add a user to as many mailing lists as you like without affecting speed of logon.

The three different types of mailing lists and three different types of security groups result from the legacy of Windows NT and the introduction of the GC. Global groups and local groups are the direct descendants of Windows NT groups and are stored in the domains they are created in. Universal groups are the new Windows 2000 groups. Universal groups are held in the GC. Universal groups are forest wide and global/local groups are domain wide.

In order to fully understand how groups work in Windows 2000, I will explain the following items in this section:

- How Windows NT groups have a bearing on Windows 2000

- Which groups are available in mixed mode and which are available in native mode

- Which groups each group may contain in mixed mode and native mode

- How you can nest groups across domain boundaries

- What options are available to you for converting between different group types in both native mode and mixed mode

So to start with, let's take a look at how Windows NT handles groups.

Groups in Windows NT

Back in Windows NT, domains could have two types of groups: domain local and domain global. Both were security groups. The domain local group could contain users and domain global groups. The domain global group could contain only users. Both could have permissions assigned to them. Administrators typically took advantage of the fact that global groups could nest in local groups. Users went into global groups, and local groups were given access to resources on local machines. Then you simply put the global groups in the appropriate local groups to assign the permissions.

Windows NT groups are important in Windows 2000 mixed-mode domains, as downlevel Windows NT BDCs will need to replicate these groups from the Windows 2000 FSMO PDC role owner. During an upgrade of a PDC from Windows NT to Windows 2000, Windows NT local and global groups will be migrated to Windows 2000 local security groups and global security groups, although they will still appear as local and global groups to any Windows NT BDCs.

Group availability in different modes

Table 2-3 shows the groups that you can have in mixed and native modes.

Table 2-3. The Different Groups Available in Mixed Mode and Native Mode

Type of Group	Scope of Group	Available in Mixed Mode	Available in Native Mode
Domain local	Security	Yes	Yes
Domain global	Security	Yes	Yes
Universal	Security	No	Yes
Domain local	Distribution	Yes	Yes
Domain global	Distribution	Yes	Yes
Universal	Distribution	Yes	Yes

At first, the only difference appears to be that Universal Security groups are available only in native mode. Every other group is available in either mode. The complexity comes in what each group may contain, and this varies depending on the mode of your domain and which domain the group you wish to add comes from.

Group nesting in mixed mode and native mode

You have a mixed-mode domain and you want to create and then nest some groups. Table 2-4 is the easiest way to describe what options are available.

Table 2-4. Mixed-Mode Restrictions on Group Membership Based on Group Type

Type	Scope	Can Contain Domain Local		Can Contain Domain Global		Can Contain Universal	
		Distri-bution Groups	Security Groups	Distri-bution Groups	Security Groups	Distri-bution Groups	Security Groups
Domain local	Distribution groups	Yes	Yes	Yes	Yes	Yes	No group access
	Security groups	No	No	Yes	Yes	Yes	No group access
Domain Global	Distribution groups	No	No	Yes	Yes	No	No group access
	Security groups	No	No	No	No	No	No group access
Universal	Distribution groups	No	No	Yes	Yes	Yes	No group access
	Security groups	No group access	No group access	No group access	No group access	No group access	No group access

Two points need noting: First, universal security groups are evidently not available in mixed mode, which corresponds with Table 2-4. Second, domain global security groups can contain only users in mixed mode.

When you convert a domain to native mode, certain groups become available, but you do not lose any group nesting options that you had in mixed mode. The new options in native mode can be summarized quite easily as follows:

- Domain local security groups can contain domain local security and domain local distribution groups.

- Domain global security groups can contain domain global security and domain global distribution groups.

- Universal security groups become available.

Let's look at that using the same table structure. Consider Table 2-5, with the extra options available only in native mode emphasized in italic.

Table 2-5. Native-Mode Restrictions on Group Membership Based on Group Type

Type	Scope	Can Contain Domain Local		Can Contain Domain Global		Can Contain Universal	
		Distri-btion Groups	Security Groups	Distri-bution Groups	Security Groups	Distri-bution Groups	Security Groups
Domain local	Distribution groups	Yes	Yes	Yes	Yes	Yes	*Yes*
	Security groups	*Yes*	*Yes*	Yes	Yes	Yes	*Yes*
Domain global	Distribution groups	No	No	Yes	Yes	No	No
	Security groups	No	No	*Yes*	*Yes*	No	No
Universal	Distribution groups	No	No	Yes	Yes	Yes	*Yes*
	Security groups	No	No	*Yes*	*Yes*	*Yes*	*Yes*

While these tables are fine, there is one other complicating factor that needs to be taken into account: cross-domain group membership.

Group membership across domain boundaries

If universal groups are held in the GC, then you should be able to add universal groups from one domain to universal groups from another domain. Restrictions are shown in Tables 2-6 and 2-7.

Table 2-6. Restrictions on Group Membership Based on Group Type

Group type	Can Contain Users and Computers from		Can Contain Domain Local Groups from	
	Same Domain	Different Domain	Same Domain	Different Domain
Domain local groups	Yes	Yes	Special	No
Domain global groups	Yes	No	No	No
Universal groups	Yes	Yes	No	No

Table 2-7. Restrictions on Group Membership Based on Domain

Group type	Can Contain Domain Global Groups from		Can Contain Universal Groups from	
	Same Domain	Different Domain	Same Domain	Different Domain
Domain local groups	Yes	Yes	Yes	Yes
Domain global groups	Special	No	No	No
Universal groups	Yes	Yes	Yes	Yes

Tables 2-6 and 2-7 work in conjunction with Tables 2-4 and 2-5. You would normally check to find out what groups may be members from either Table 2-4 or Table 2-5 (if any) and then cross reference with Tables 2-6 and 2-7 to identify what options you have across domain boundaries. Two items are listed as special, which means distribution only in mixed mode and distribution and security in native mode.

Also, the User and Computer object classes are derived from the Principal object class in the Schema. Groups may contain nonsecurity members that are not derived from the Principal class. These members are not subject to the preceding restrictions. For example, a domain global group may contain a Contact object without any restrictions.

Converting groups in native mode

The final ability with groups in native-mode only is that you can convert them from one sort to another. There are limits on what groups can be converted based on the existing members of the group and the current type and scope of the group. The former should be fairly obvious based on the existing restrictions that I've shown in Table 2-5. The conversion process cannot work if the existing group members would not be valid members of the new group type once the conversion had taken place. However, when you upgrade to native mode, you gain the ability to convert between groups based on these restrictions:

- Security groups can be converted to distribution groups.
- Distribution groups can be converted to security groups.

- A domain local group can be converted to a universal group provided that the domain local group is not already a member of another domain local group.

- A domain global group can be converted to a universal group provided that the domain global group does not contain any other domain global groups.

Wrap-up

While this all looks complicated, using the tables helps a lot. Ultimately you need to decide how long you will be staying in mixed mode before going native so that you can decide what sort of groups you are looking for. You also have to consider in native mode that the more universal groups that you add, the larger the GC, and the longer members of those groups will take to log on. Chapter 6, *Designing the Namespace*, and Chapter 9, *Designing Organization-Wide Policies*, explain more about when and how to use groups in your designs.

Windows NT Versus Windows 2000

Those of you who have been Windows NT administrators will already have noticed many differences between Windows 2000's Active Directory and Windows NT's SAM. Table 2-8 briefly covers the major differences.

Table 2-8. A Comparison Between Windows NT and Windows 2000

Windows NT	Windows 2000
Single-master replication is used via PDCs and BDCs.	Multimaster replication is used via DCs.
Domain is the smallest unit of partitioning.	Domain is the smallest unit of partitioning.
Domain is the smallest unit of authentication.	OU is the smallest unit of authentication.
Domain is the smallest unit of policy (system policies).	OU is the smallest unit of policy (group policy objects).
Domain is the smallest unit of security delegation/administration.	A property of an object is the smallest unit of security delegation/administration.
NetBIOS broadcasts as primary browsing and connection mechanism.	TCP/IP connections to Active Directory as primary browsing and connection mechanism.
WINS or LMHOSTS required for effective browsing.	DNS and Active Directory required for effective browsing WINS required for older clients.
Object is the smallest unit of replication.	Property is the smallest unit of replication.
Maximum recommended database size for SAM is 40 MB.	Maximum database size for Active Directory is 70 TB.

Table 2-8. A Comparison Between Windows NT and Windows 2000 (continued)

Windows NT	Windows 2000
Maximum effective number of users is 40,000 (if you accept the recommended 40 MB maximum).	Maximum number of users (objects) in one domain is between one and two million Maximum number of users (objects) in one forest is 10 million.
Four domain models (single, single-master, multimaster, complete-trust) required to solve admin-boundary and user-limit problems being per domain.	No domain models required as the complete-trust model is implemented. One-way trusts can be implemented manually.
Schema is not extensible.	Schema is fully extensible.

First, as explained earlier in the section on mixed mode and native mode, PDCs and BDCs have been replaced by DCs. It is now possible to promote member servers to DCs and demote DCs to ordinary member servers, all without needing a reinstallation of the operating system. Now, when you go to install any type of Windows 2000 server, the operating system installs initially as an ordinary member server rather than a DC. If you want the newly installed member server to be a DC, then you *promote* it using the *DCPROMO.EXE* wizard. If you choose to promote the server to a DC, DCPROMO asks you a number of questions such as whether you are creating the first-ever domain in a domain tree or joining an existing tree, whether this new tree is part of an existing forest or a new forest to be created, and so on.

As with Windows NT, domains still exist and are basically unchanged. Under both operating systems, the domain is still the smallest unit of partitioning. However, while Windows NT and Windows 2000 domains are still a unit of authentication and a unit of policy, Organizational Units now are the smallest unit of both authentication and policy. Organizational Units are an important change. Under Windows NT, administration was delegated on a per-domain basis, while under Windows 2000, both Organizational Units and domains can be used as administration boundaries. This can significantly reduce the number of domains you require.

Windows NT used NetBIOS as its primary network communication mechanism, whereas Windows 2000 is tightly integrated with DNS and uses TCP/IP. Whereas under previous versions, administrators ended up maintaining two computer lookup databases—DNS for TCP/IP name resolution and WINS for NetBIOS name resolution. Windows 2000 no longer does traditional NetBIOS name resolution. Instead, it relies on DNS. You still can install and run a WINS server, but this would be only for backward compatibility until all your machines were upgraded.

The significant difference in replication is that Windows 2000 will replicate at the attribute rather than object level. Under Windows NT, if you changed the surname of a user object, then the whole object had to be replicated out; under Windows

2000, only the surname will be replicated. This, coupled with some very clever changes to the way replication works, means that you replicate less data for shorter periods, thereby reducing the two most important factors in replication. See Chapter 4, *Active Directory Replication* and Chapter 7, *Sites and Replication Topologies* for more on replication.

The suggested maximum Windows NT SAM was 40 MB, which was roughly equivalent to about 40,000 objects depending on what proportion of computer, user, and group accounts you had in your domain. I know of one major global petrochemical organization that had a 75-MB SAM for one domain due to the huge number of groups that they were using, so this rule was never hard and fast as long as you understood the problems you would be likely to experience if you went past the limit. However, Windows 2000's Active Directory is based on the Jet Blue database used for Exchange and developed to hold up to 10 million objects per forest (1 to 2 million per domain) with a maximum database size of 70 TB. This should be enough for most people's needs and is also only a recommended maximum limit. Remember, however, that this new database holds all classes of objects, not just the users, groups, and computers of the previous version's SAM. As more and more applications are developed, more classes of objects will be added to the schema, and more objects will be added to the directory. Whether Microsoft in its next version or two will be able to ratchet the capacity up again before anyone comes close to 10 million objects is another thing entirely. To bring this into perspective, imagine that one of the world's largest aerospace companies has around half a million computers. Assuming an equivalent number of staff, this still uses only 10% of the maximum database capacity. However, when you begin to consider all the other objects that will be in Active Directory, including file shares, printers, groups, organizational units, domains, contacts, and so on, you can see how that percentage will increase.

This actually makes an important point for me. The one to two million object limit is for a *single domain*. I'll say that again. The 1,000,000–2,000,000 object limit is for one single domain. For administrators of Windows NT this may be the most significant change of all. It was extremely easy to hit the 40 MB SAM limit within an NT domain, forcing you to split the domain into two or more. You ended up managing multiple domains when you really didn't want to. It was frustrating. None of the domains were organized into a domain tree or anything of the sort, so they had no automatic trusts between them. This meant that NT administrators had to set up manual trusts between domains, and these had to be initiated at both domains in order to set up a single one-way trust. As you added more domains, you ended up managing even greater numbers of trusts. To counter this problem, Microsoft introduced four *domain models* that you could use as templates for your Windows NT design: the single-domain model, the single- master domain model, the multimaster domain model, and the complete-trust domain model. All four are shown in Figure 2-3. The most common model after the single-domain model is probably the multimaster domain model.

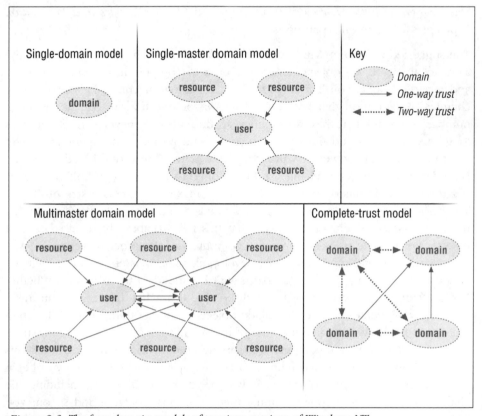

Figure 2-3. The four domain models of previous versions of Windows NT

Stated very simply, the single-domain model was, as the name implied, where you had only one domain with a SAM smaller than 40 MB and no trusts. Where multiple domains were needed for resource access but the SAM was still less than 40 MB, the single-master domain model was used. The single-master domain model was made up of one user and multiple resource domains. The important point was that the resource domains had one-way trusts with the user domain that held all the accounts. Due to the one-way trusts, the administrators of the resource domains could set permissions as they wished to their own resources for any accounts in the user domain. This meant that one central set of administrators could manage the accounts, while individual departments maintained autonomy over their own resources. When the SAM was going to grow past 40 MB a multimaster came into play. The administrators of the user domain split the user accounts into two or more domains, giving them two-way (i.e., complete) trust between each other, and then each resource domain had to have a one-way trust with each user domain. Scaling this up, for a multimaster domain with 10 user domains and 100 resource domains, that's 90 trusts to make up the intrauser trusts and 1,000 separate resource-to-user trusts that must be manually set. Finally, in some cases, the complete-trust model was used where any domain could create accounts and allocate resources to any other domain.

Windows 2000 now acts like a single-master domain model in which the Organizational Units function as the resource domains. As you can see, this eliminates the need for maintaining separate Windows NT resource domains any more, as these can be converted to Organizational Units in what was the user domain. As Windows 2000 trees and forests all have complete trust with one another, and as all the trusts are transitive, trees and forests are like multimaster domains tending toward the complete-trust model.

Finally, the Windows NT Schema was not extensible. No new object types could be added to it. When Microsoft products that extended Windows NT—like Terminal Server and File and Print for NetWare—were released, each had to store any attribute data that it wanted all together within one existing attribute. Under Windows 2000, the Schema is fully extensible, so any new products can instantly extend the Schema and add in objects and attributes as required.

 For more information on moving from Windows NT to Windows 2000, take a look at Chapter 12, *Windows NT 4.0 Migration.*

Summary

In this chapter, I've gone over the groundwork for some of the main internals of Active Directory. While I started by going over the easier domains, trees, forests, and Organizational Units, I soon moved on to some of the more detailed parts of how Active Directory works, notably the structuring of Active Directory in terms of Naming Contexts. I also covered the use of the Global Catalog and the roles of the Flexible Single Master Operators. All of these items should give you a better understanding of how Active Directory functions.

Finally, I took some time to cover how Windows NT's interoperability affects Active Directory, by explaining the two different modes that a domain can exist in. I went through some fundamental differences and delved heavily into group objects; these are the objects most affected by the two different modes.

With this information under our belts, let's now take a look at the blueprint that defines all the objects in Active Directory.

3

Active Directory Schema

Active Directory Schema is the blueprint for all classes, attributes, and syntaxes that can potentially be stored in Active Directory. Each object in Active Directory is an *instance* of one or more classes in the Schema. The user cn=LeeFlight, for example, exists as an instance of the User class. Schema attributes define the pieces of information that a class, and thus an instance of that class, can hold. Syntaxes define the type of data that can be placed into an attribute. If an attribute is defined with a syntax of Boolean, it can store True and False data.

Microsoft designed Active Directory to hold the most common objects and attributes that users of a server system would require. It was understood that any good schema would never hold every class of object or every specific attribute (languages spoken, professional qualifications) that a company would like, so it was designed to be extensible. In fact, extending the schema is not a difficult task at all; it is more difficult to design the changes that you would like to incorporate. Design issues are covered in Chapter 11, *Designing Schema Changes*; in this chapter, we're concerned only with how the schema operates.

The Structure of the Schema

The Schema Naming Context (NC) is contained in Active Directory under the Configuration NC. You can look at the contents directly by pointing a raw Active Directory viewer like ADSIEDIT or LDP at the container and viewing the contents. However, it is much easier to view the contents using the built-in Active Directory Schema Manager MMC snap-in. The MMC snap-in separates the classes and attributes for you, whereas in reality all the objects are held together within the single Schema container; that is how the raw tools will actually view the data.

The Schema itself is made up of two types of Active Directory objects: Classes and Attributes. In Active Directory, these are respectively known as Class-Schema/classSchema and Attribute-Schema/attributeSchema objects. The two distinct forms of the same names result from the fact that the Common-Name/cn attribute of a class contains the hyphenated easy-to-read name of the class, and the LDAP-Display-Name/lDAPDisplayName attribute of a class contains the concatenated string format that we're used to using when querying Active Directory with ADSI. In the Schema, the lDAPDisplayName attributes of each object are *normally** made by capitalizing the first letter of each word in the Common-Name and then removing the hyphens and concatenating all the words together. Finally, the first letter is made lowercase. This creates simple names like *user,* as well as the more unusual *sAMAccountName* and *lDAPDisplayName.* I'll use the Common-Name version from now on, as it is easier on the eyes.

Whenever you need to create new types of objects in the Schema, you must first create a Class-Schema object defining that class of object. Once the class is properly designed and added to the Schema, Active Directory extended so that objects of that type can be stored. Alternatively, if you want to add a new type of attribute to a particular class of object in the Schema, then you must first create the Attribute-Schema object in the Schema and then associate that attribute with whatever object classes were to use it.

Before I delve into what makes up an Active Directory Class, I need to explain how each class that you create is unique not just within your Active Directory but also potentially throughout the world.

X.500 and the OID Namespace

The Windows 2000 Active Directory is based on the X.500 standard, created by the ISO-ITU (International Organization for Standardization-International Telecommunications Union) in 1988. In order to properly understand how the Active Directory Schema works, you really need to understand the basics of X.500; I'll run through them here.

The X.500 standard itself specifies that individual object classes in an organization can be uniquely defined using a special identifying process. The process has to be able to take into account the fact that classes can inherit from one another, as well as the potential need for any organization in the world to define and export a class of their own design.

---

* Names defined by the X.500 standard don't tend to follow this method. For example, the Common-Name attribute has an LDAP-Display-Name of cn; the Surname attribute has an LDAP-Display-Name of sn.

To that end, the X.500 standard defined an Object Identifier (OID)* to uniquely identify every object. This OID is composed of two parts:

- One to indicate the unique path to the branch holding the object in the X.500 treelike structure

- Another to indicate the object uniquely in that branch

OID notation uses integers for each branch and object, so an example OID for an object could be:

```
1.3.6.1.4.1.3385.12.497
```

This would uniquely reference object 497 in branch 1.3.6.1.4.1.3385.12. The 1.3.6. 1.4.1.3385.12 branch would be contained in a branch whose OID was 1.3.6.1.4.1. 3385 and so on.

 Each branch within an OID number also corresponds to a name. This means that the dotted notation 1.3.6.1.4.1, for example, is equivalent to iso.org.dod.internet.private.enterprise. As the names are of no relevance to us with Active Directory, I don't cover them in this book.

This notation continues today and is used in the Windows 2000 Schema. If you wish to create an object, you need to obtain a unique branch for your organization. Using this as your root, you can then create further branches and leaf objects within the root, as your organization requires.

The Internet Assigned Numbers Authority (IANA) maintains the main set of root branches. The IANA is "the central coordinator for the assignment of unique parameter values for Internet protocols. The IANA is chartered by the Internet Society (ISOC) and the Federal Network Council (FNC) to act as the clearinghouse to assign and coordinate the use of numerous Internet protocol parameters. The Internet protocol suite, as defined by the Internet Engineering Task Force (IETF) and its steering group (the IESG), contains numerous parameters, such as Internet addresses, domain names, autonomous system numbers (used in some routing protocols), protocol numbers, port numbers, management information base object identifiers, including private enterprise numbers, and many others. The common use of the Internet protocols by the Internet community requires that the particular values used in these parameter fields be assigned uniquely. It is the task of the IANA to make those unique assignments as requested and to maintain a registry of

---

* Network administrators who are familiar with SNMP will already have seen OIDs in use. For more information on SNMP under Windows NT, take a look at *Windows NT SNMP: Simple Network Management Protocol*, by James D. Murray (O'Reilly).

the currently assigned values. The IANA is located at and operated by the Information Sciences Institute (ISI) of the University of Southern California (USC)." You can find the IANA web page at *http://www.iana.org/.*

You can request an OID namespace, i.e., a root OID number from which you can create your own branches, directly from the IANA if you like. These numbers are known as Enterprise Numbers. The entire list of Enterprise Numbers assigned by the IANA can be found at *ftp://ftp.isi.edu/in-notes/iana/assignments/enterprise-numbers.* This list of numbers changes every time a new one is added. At the top of the document you can see that the root that the IANA uses is 1.3.6.1.4.1. If you look down the list, you will see that Microsoft has been allocated branch 311 of that part of the tree, so Microsoft's OID namespace is 1.3.6.1.4.1.311. Leicester University's OID namespace is 1.3.6.1.4.1.3385. As each number also has a contact email address alongside it in the list, you can search through the file for any member of your organization that has already been allocated a number. It is likely that large organizations that already have an X.500 directory will have obtained values so that they can create X.500 classes.

In addition to Enterprise Numbers, country-specific OIDs can be purchased as well. An organization's Enterprise Number registration has no bearing on whether it has obtained a country-based OID namespace to use. If you don't see the company listed in the Enterprise Numbers list, don't be fooled; the organization could still have a number.

For example, Microsoft has been issued the Enterprise Number 1.3.6.1.4.1.311, yet all of its new schema classes use a U.S.-issued OID namespace of 1.2.840.113556 as their root. The 1.2.840 part is uniquely allotted to the United States. In other words, Microsoft has obtained two OID namespaces that it can use but is choosing to use only the U.S.-issued namespace.

If you do want to obtain an Enterprise Number, fill in the online form at *http://www.isi.edu/cgi-bin/iana/enterprise.pl.* If this URL changes, then you can navigate to it from the main IANA web page.

Once an organization has an OID namespace, it can add unique branches and leaves in any manner desired under the root. For example, Leicester University could decide to have no branches underneath and just give any new object an incrementing integer starting from 1 underneath the 1.3.6.1.4.1.3385 root. Alternatively, they could decide to make a series of numbered branches starting from 1, each corresponding to a certain set of classes or attributes that they wish to create. So, the fifth object under our third branch would have an OID of 1.3.6.1.4.1.3385.3.5.

The range of values in any part of an OID namespace goes from 1 to 268,435,455, i.e., from 2^0 through $2^{28}-1$.

To reinforce this point, let's look at a couple of examples directly from the Active Directory Schema. If you open up the Schema Manager in Windows 2000, you can look at the Active Directory Schema class OIDs very easily. Navigating through the classes when I open up the property page for the Print-Queue class, I get Figure 3-1.

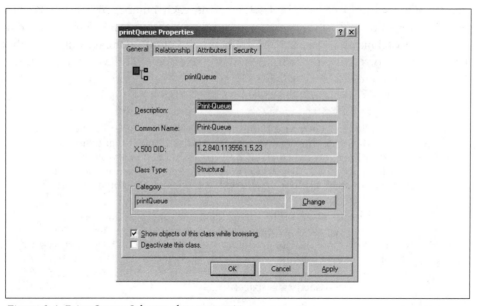

Figure 3-1. Print-Queue Schema class properties

You can see that the unique OID is 1.2.840.113556.1.5.23. This tells us that the number is part of Microsoft's object class hierarchy that it has defined. If I now navigate to the Organizational-Person class and open up the property page for that, Figure 3-2 is displayed.

Here, you can see that the unique OID 2.5.6.7 is very different, because within the original X.500 standard, a set of original classes was defined. One of these was Organizational-Person, and this is an exact copy of that class. Microsoft has included the entire base X.500 specified classes within Active Directory, and that's why Active Directory is said to be X.500-based. It is not a native X.500 directory, as it allows and uses some objects that are nonstandard, but it is based on X.500 classes, so they are included and can be inherited from.

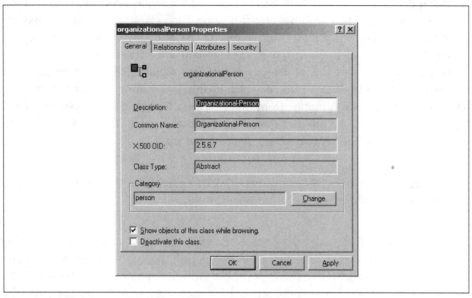

Figure 3-2. Organizational-Person Schema class properties

 This numbering notation has nothing to do with inheritance. Just because you number a set of objects a certain way does nothing other than create a structure for you to reference the objects. It does not indicate how objects inherit from one another.

Object Class Types and Inheritance

The special part about object classes is that they can inherit from one another. For example, let's say that I wanted to store two new types of objects in the Schema representing a marketing user and a finance user, respectively. These users both need all of the attributes of the existing User class as a base. However, the finance user needs seven special attributes while the marketing user needs three special attributes. The extra attributes required by both users do not match in any way. In this example, I can create a Marketing-User class, a Finance-User class, and 10 distinctly new attributes. However, rather than having to specify that the Marketing-User and Finance-User classes have all the attributes of the original User class one by one, all I need to do is specify that the new classes inherit from the User class. When I do this, both the new classes inherit every single attribute that the User class had. I can then add the extra attributes to each class and I have my two new classes. It really is that simple.

You can think of the Active Directory Schema as a treelike structure, with multiple classes branching down or inheriting from one base class at the top that has the attributes all objects need to begin with. This class, unsurprisingly enough, is called Top. Top is defined in the X.500 standard and is not a Microsoft-defined standard. Some classes inherit directly from Top, while others exist much lower down the tree. While each class may have only one parent in this layout, each class also may inherit attributes from other classes. This is possible because there are three categories of Class Schema object, known as the Object-Class-Category, that you can create: Structural, Abstract, and Auxiliary.

Structural

> If a class is Structural, then you can directly create objects of its type in Active Directory. The User and Group classes are Structural.

Abstract

> It is possible that you would want to create a class that inherits from other classes and has certain attributes but that is not one you will ever need to create instances of directly. This type of class is known as Abstract. For example, let's say that the Marketing-User and Finance-User were to be the first of a number of Structural classes that had a common structure. In that case, you could create an Abstract class to be used as the basis of other Structural classes. Abstract classes can inherit from other classes, can have attributes defined on them directly, and in all other ways act like Structural classes, except that instances of them cannot directly be created as objects in Active Directory.

Auxiliary

> An Auxiliary class is used to store sets of attributes that other objects can inherit. Auxiliary classes are a way for Structural and Abstract classes to inherit collections of attributes that do not have to be defined directly within the classes themselves.

The X.500 specifications indicate that an Auxiliary class cannot inherit from a Structural class, and an Abstract class can *only* inherit from another Abstract class.

> There are actually four types of Object-Class-Category in order to comply with the X.500 standards. While objects are required to be classified as one of Structural, Abstract, or Auxiliary by the 1993 X.500 specifications, objects defined before 1993 using the 1988 specifications are not required to comply with these categories. Such objects have no corresponding 1993 category and so are defined in the Schema as having a special category known as the 88-Class by Microsoft.

For example, let's look at the User and Computer classes. The User class is used to create users in Active Directory, and the Computer class is used to create computer accounts for Windows NT Workstation and Windows 2000 Professional clients. The Computer (OID: 1.2.840.113556.1.3.30) and User (OID: 1.2.840.113556.1.5.9) classes are Structural, which means that you can create objects of class User and Computer directly in Active Directory. The Computer class inherits from the User class. So, the Computer class is a special type of user in a way. The User class inherits from the Abstract Organizational-Person class (OID: 2.5.6.7). This means that the total attributes available to objects of class Computer include not only the attributes defined specifically on the Computer and User classes themselves but also all the attributes that are inherited from the Organizational-Person class. The Organizational-Person class is a subclass of the Abstract Person class (OID: 2.5.6.6), which is a subclass of the Abstract Top class (OID: 2.5.6.0). There are no classes above Top; it is the root class.

The User class that Microsoft needed to define in Active Directory had to be more than just the sum of the X.500 standard parts. After all, Microsoft uses Security Identifiers (SIDs) to identify users, and these were not contained in the original X.500 standards. So in order to extend the attributes that make up a user, Microsoft defined some Auxiliary classes and included these in the User class makeup. The Auxiliary classes are Mail-Recipient and Security-Principal. Mail-Recipient is a collection of attributes that allow a user to hold information relating to the email address and mail account associated with that user. Security-Principal is used to hold the SID and other security attributes that Microsoft needed that relate to the user. Figure 3-3 indicates how the Computer class is made up from a number of other classes.

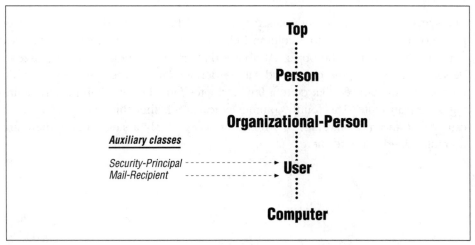

Figure 3-3. The Computer class

If you were to use a tool to look at Active Directory in raw mode, you could see the inheritance and class relationships quite clearly. For example, looking at the Object-Class attribute of any User object, you would see that the values held in this attribute were Top, Person, Organizational-Person, and User. In other words, this attribute indicates that each User object inherits attributes from all these classes. Similarly for any Computer object, the Object-Class attribute holds Top, Person, Organizational-Person, User, and Computer. If you were to look at the Subclass-Of attribute on the Computer class object itself in the Schema, you would see the User class. The User class has a Subclass-Of attribute that indicates Organizational-Person and so on.

Let's dissect an example attribute and class to see what they contain. With that information, you will be able to see what is required when you create a new object.

Attribute Classes (Attribute-Schema Objects)

Just as object class information is stored in Active Directory as instances of the class called Class-Schema, attributes are represented by instances of the object class called Attribute-Schema. When defining a new attribute, you are effectively defining a new instance of the Attribute-Schema object. As with all objects, this one has a number of attributes that can be set. The Attribute-Schema object inherits attributes from the class called Top. However, most of the Top attributes are not really relevant here. Table 3-1 shows the defining attributes of an instance of the Attribute-Schema object (i.e., an attribute) that can be set.

The syntax of an attribute indicates the type of data that it holds, which I'll cover in a moment. The mandatory column indicates whether the attribute *must* be set when initially creating the object. Attributes that are not mandatory do not have to be set when creating the object and can be defined later, if they are needed at all. From here you can see that quite a few attributes must be set when initially defining a new attribute. The fourth column indicates whether this particular attribute can accept an array of values or whether it accepts only a single value; there are no multivalued attributes here.

The tables in this chapter have been assembled by examining the Schema.

Table 3-1. The Defining Attributes of an Attribute-Schema Object Instance

Attribute	Syntax	Mandatory	Multi-valued	Description
Attribute-Id	OID	Yes	No	The OID that uniquely identifies this attribute.
Common-Name	Unicode	Yes	No	The descriptive Relative Distinguished Name (RDN).
Is-Single-Valued	Boolean	Yes	No	Whether this attribute is multivalued.
LDAP-Display-Name	Unicode	Yes	No	The name by which LDAP clients identify this attribute.
Attribute-Syntax	OID	Yes	No	Half of a pair of properties that define the syntax of an attribute. This one is an OID.
OM-Syntax	Integer	Yes	No	Half of a pair of properties that define the syntax of an attribute. This one is an integer.
Schema-ID-GUID	Octet string	Yes	No	Globally Unique Identifier (GUID) to uniquely identify this attribute.
Object-Class	OID	Yes	Yes	This will hold the values "Attribute-Schema" and "Top" to indicate that the value is an instance of those classes.
Access-Category	Integer	No	No	Used by the system.
Attribute-Security-GUID	GUID	No	No	GUID used by Windows 2000 to identify the security of this attribute.
Class-Display-Name	Unicode string	No	No	The name that is displayed when viewing instances of the attribute.
Default-Hiding-Value	Boolean	No	No	Whether the object is to be hidden or displayed within tools by default.

Table 3-1. The Defining Attributes of an Attribute-Schema Object Instance (continued)

Attribute	Syntax	Mandatory	Multi-valued	Description
Description	Unicode String	No	No	A description of the attribute.
Extended-Chars-Allowed	Boolean	No	No	Whether extended characters are allowed in the value of this attribute.
Is-Defunct	Boolean	No	No	Whether the attribute is marked as disabled (i.e., unusable) in Active Directory.
Is-Ephemeral	Boolean	No	No	Used by the system.
Is-Member-Of-Partial-Attribute-Set	Boolean	No	No	Whether the attribute is held in the GC.
Link-ID	Integer	No	No	Used by the system.
MAPI-Display-Type	Integer	No	No	The integer by which MAPI clients identify this attribute.
OID-Type	Integer	No	No	Used by the system.
OM-Object-Class	Octet string	No	No	Used by the system.
Range-Lower	Integer	No	No	For strings, this is the minimum character length; for integers, it is the minimum value; otherwise, it is unused. It must be less than Range-Upper.
Ranger-Upper	Integer	No	No	For strings, this is the maximum character length; for integers, it is the maximum value, otherwise, it is unused.
SchemaFlags	Integer	No	No	Used by the system.
SchemaFlagsEx	Integer	No	No	Used by the system.
Search-Flags	Integer	No	No	Whether this attribute is indexed: 0=Not Indexed, 1=Indexed.[a]

Table 3-1. The Defining Attributes of an Attribute-Schema Object Instance (continued)

Attribute	Syntax	Mandatory	Multi-valued	Description
System-Only	Boolean	No	No	If true, once the initial value has been set, only the system can create instances of this attribute. Administrators cannot create instances of the attribute if this is set, but they can add this attribute to new or existing classes as required. The default is false.

[a] Indexing an object allows you to locate instances of the object or objects containing a particular value of an attribute by consulting the index rather than looking at each object. Index-aided searches run much faster than other searches.

Dissecting an Example Attribute

The User-Principal-Name (UPN) attribute on the User object represents what amounts to a unique method of identifying each user across a forest. Users can log on to any workstation in any domain in the forest using the UPN if they so desire. The UPN attribute, in fact, accepts valid RFC 822 (email) addresses, so the norm for a UPN for user *tpood* in the *europe.windows.mycorp.com* domain would be either *tpood@mycorp.com* or *tpood@europe.windows.mycorp.com*. The only requirement is that the UPN is unique across all users in the forest.

The UPN is a mandatory attribute on the User class. In order to dissect the attribute, I needed to find out what values had been set for it. I used a simple ADSI script to iterate through the property cache and display all entries with a value. This code will be demonstrated in the ADSI section of the book.

The result was 26 values in the property cache, and of these 26 values, 16 are inherited attributes from the Top class and 10 are attributes defined directly on User-Principal-Name; Table 3-2 shows the values. I have used the LDAP-Display-Name rather than the Common-Name in the first column to distinguish from the actual values contained in the attributes in the third column.

Table 3-2. User-Principal-Name's Property Cache

UPN Attribute's LDAP-Display-Name	UPN Attribute's Syntax	Value Contained in UPN's Attribute	Attribute Defined on Which Class?
adminDescription	CASE_IGNORE_STRING	User-Principal-Name	Top
adminDisplayName	CASE_IGNORE_STRING	User-Principal-Name	Top

Table 3-2. User-Principal-Name's Property Cache (continued)

UPN Attribute's LDAP-Display-Name	UPN Attribute's Syntax	Value Contained in UPN's Attribute	Attribute Defined on Which Class?
cn	CASE_IGNORE_STRING	User-Principal-Name	Top
distinguishedName	DN_STRING	cn=User-Principal-Name, cn=Schema, cn=Configuration, dc=mycorp,dc=com	Top
instanceType	INTEGER	4	Top
name	CASE_IGNORE_STRING	User-Principal-Name	Top
nTSecurityDescriptor	SECURITY_DESCRIPTOR	The SID	Top
objectCategory	DN_STRING	cn=Attribute-Schema, cn=Schema, cn=Configuration, dc=mycorp,dc=com	Top
objectClass	CASE_IGNORE_STRING	Top; Attribute-Schema (2 values of a multivalued attribute)	Top
objectGUID	OCTET_STRING	A GUID	Top
showInAdvanced-ViewOnly	BOOLEAN	True	Top
systemFlags	INTEGER	18	Top
uSN_Changed	LARGE_INTEGER	USN when last changed	Top
uSN_Created	LARGE_INTEGER	USN when created	Top
when_Changed	UTC_TIME	Time when last changed	Top
when_Created	UTC_TIME	Time when created	Top
attributeID	CASE_IGNORE_STRING	1.2.840.113556.1.4.656	User-Principal-Name
attributeSecurityGUID	OCTET_STRING	A GUID	User-Principal-Name
attributeSyntax	CASE_IGNORE_STRING	2.5.5.12	User-Principal-Name
isMemberOfPartialAttributeSet	BOOLEAN	True	User-Principal-Name
isSingleValued	BOOLEAN	True	User-Principal-Name
lDAPDisplayName	CASE_IGNORE_STRING	userPrincipalName	User-Principal-Name

Table 3-2. User-Principal-Name's Property Cache (continued)

UPN Attribute's LDAP-Display-Name	UPN Attribute's Syntax	Value Contained in UPN's Attribute	Attribute Defined on Which Class?
oMSyntax	INTEGER	64	User-Principal-Name
schemaIDGUID	OCTET_STRING	The GUID that uniquely identifies this class	User-Principal-Name
searchFlags	INTEGER	1	User-Principal-Name
systemOnly	BOOLEAN	False	User-Principal-Name

Let's take a look at some of the key Top values. We can see that the name that the UPN attribute is to be known by is User-Principal-Name (Admin-Description, Admin-Display-Name, CN, Name), that it is an instance of the Attribute-Schema class (Object-Category and Object-Class), that it inherits attributes from both Top and Attribute-Schema (Object-Class), and that the UPN attribute is not visible to casual browsing (Show-In-Advanced-View-Only).

The User-Principal-Name attributes show that it:

- Is to be stored in the GC (Is-Member-Of-Partial-Attribute-Set)
- Is to be indexed (Search-Flags)
- Has an OID of 1.2.840.113556.1.4.656 (Attribute-ID)
- That when binding to it with ADSI we should use userPrincipalName (LDAP-Display-Name)
- Instances can be created by anyone (System-Only)
- It stores single (Is-Single-Valued) Unicode strings (Attribute-Syntax and OM-Syntax).

Figure 3-4 shows the UPN attribute as viewed by the Schema Manager console.

Here you can see many of the values for the UPN attribute. I have indicated which Boolean attributes are changed by checking or unchecking each checkbox.

The Syntax of Attributes

Microsoft defines the syntax of an attribute as meaning the kind of data it can hold; everyone else in computing calls it a datatype. In Windows 2000, Microsoft decided not to include the actual 18 provided syntaxes in Active Directory as objects. Instead, Microsoft has coded these syntaxes internally into Active Directory itself. Consequently, you cannot extend the Schema by defining your own

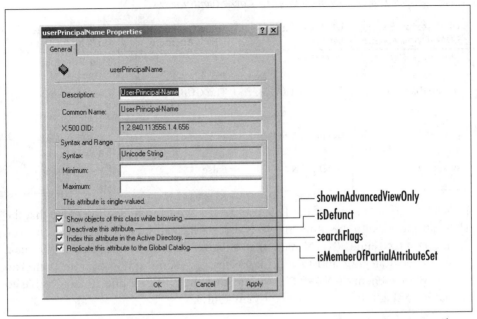

Figure 3-4. The User-Principal-Name attribute viewed using the Schema Manager console

syntaxes for the attributes of objects you create. This is a limitation on Active Directory, but extending Active Directory with user-designed syntaxes is likely to be on the list of modifications to go into the next release after Windows 2000.

Whenever you create a new attribute, you must specify its syntax. To uniquely identify the syntax among the total set of 21 syntaxes, you must specify two pieces of information: the OID and a so-called OM-Syntax. This pair of values must be set together and correctly correlate with Table 3-3. More than one syntax has the same OID, which may seem strange, and in order to distinguish between different syntaxes uniquely, you thus need a second identifier. This is the result of Microsoft requiring some syntaxes that X.500 could not provide. Table 3-3 shows the 21 expanded syntaxes, including the X.500 name of the syntax with any special Microsoft-chosen name following it in parentheses.

Table 3-3. Syntax Definitions

Syntax	OID	OM-Syntax	Description
Undefined	2.5.5.0	Not applicable	Not a valid syntax
Distinguished Name	2.5.5.1	127	The Fully Qualified Domain Name (FQDN) of an object in Active Directory
Object ID	2.5.5.2	6	OID

Table 3-3. Syntax Definitions (continued)

Syntax	OID	OM-Syntax	Description
Case-sensitive string	2.5.5.3	20	A string that differentiates between uppercase and lowercase
Case-insensitive string	2.5.5.4	20	A string that does not differentiate between uppercase and lowercase
Print Case String (Printable-String)	2.5.5.5	19	A normal printable string
Print case string (IA5-String)	2.5.5.5	22	A normal printable string
Numeric string	2.5.5.6	18	A string of digits
OR name	2.5.5.7	127	An X.400 email address
Boolean	2.5.5.8	1	True or False
Integer (integer)	2.5.5.9	2	A 32-bit number
Integer (enumeration)	2.5.5.9	10	A 32-bit number
Octet string (octet-String)	2.5.5.10	4	A byte string
Octet string (object)	2.5.5.10	127	A byte string
Time	2.5.5.11	23	The number of seconds elapsed since 1 January 1970
Unicode	2.5.5.12	64	A wide string
Address	2.5.5.13	127	Used internally by the system
Distname-Address	2.5.5.14	127	Used internally by the system
NT Security Descriptor	2.5.5.15	66	A Security Descriptor (SD)
Large integer	2.5.5.16	65	A 64-bit number
SID	2.5.5.17	4	A Security Identifier (SID)

Most of these are standard programming types. If you're not sure which syntax to use, take a look at some other similar attributes and see if you can find an appropriate syntax for the attribute you wish to create.

The User-Principal-Name attribute has an Attribute-Syntax of 2.5.5.12 and an OM-Syntax of 64, so it must store Unicode strings.

Object Classes (Class-Schema Objects)

All classes of objects are instances of the Class-Schema object, which is a subclass of Top. Table 3-4 shows the most-used attributes that you may wish to set, from both the Top and User classes, when defining a new class.

The Governs-Id, LDAP-Display-Name, Schema-ID-GUID, and MAPI-Display-Type are all representations of how this class can be referenced by various methods.

Table 3-4. The Defining Attributes of a Class-Schema Object Instance

Attribute	Syntax	Mandatory	Multi-valued	Description
Common-Name	Unicode	Yes	No	The descriptive Relative Distinguished Name (RDN).
Governs-Id	OID	Yes	No	The OID that uniquely identifies objects of this class.
LDAP-Display-Name	Unicode	No	No	The name by which LDAP clients identify this class.
Schema-ID-GUID	Octet string	Yes	No	Globally Unique Identifier (GUID) to uniquely identify this class.
MAPI-Display-Type	Integer	No	No	The integer by which MAPI clients identify this class.
RDN-ATT-ID	OID	No	No	The attribute that indicates what two-letter-prefix (cn=, ou=, dc=) is used to reference the class. You should use only cn here unless you have a very solid idea of what you are doing and why.
Description	Unicode string	No	No	A description of the attribute.
Sub-Class-Of	OID	Yes	No	The class that this one inherits from; the default is Top.[a]
Must-Contain	OID	No	Yes	The list of attributes that are mandatory for this class.
System-Must-Contain	OID	No	Yes	System version of the previous attribute.
May-Contain	OID	No	Yes	The list of attributes that are optional for this class.
System-May-Contain	OID	No	Yes	System version of the previous attribute.
Poss-Superiors	OID	No	Yes	The list of Auxiliary (or 88-Class) classes that this object can be created within; i.e., User objects can be created within Organizational Unit objects.
System-Poss-Superiors	OID	No	Yes	System version of the previous attribute.
Auxiliary-Class	OID	No	Yes	The list of Auxiliary (or 88-Class) classes that this object inherits attributes from.
System-Auxiliary-Class	OID	No	Yes	System version of the previous attribute.

Table 3-4. The Defining Attributes of a Class-Schema Object Instance (continued)

Attribute	Syntax	Mandatory	Multi-valued	Description
Default-Secu-rity-Descriptor	Octet string	No	No	The Security Descriptor to assign to new instances of this class. Note that this SD is applied only to new instances of the class if and only if an SD is not specifically provided and set during the creation of the instance.
Object-Class-Category	Integer	Yes	No	0 = 88-Class 1 = Structural 2 = Abstract 3 = Auxiliary
System-Only	Boolean	No	No	If True, once the initial value has been set, only the system can create and modify instances of this class. The default is False.
Object-Class	Object	Yes	Yes	The class that this object is an instance of; i.e., Class-Schema.
NT-Security-Descriptor	NT-Security-Descriptor	Yes	Yes	Security Descriptor on the Class-schema object itself. For example, setting an SD allows you to govern who can actually create instances of the object and who cannot.
Default-Hiding-Value	Boolean	No	No	Whether the object is to be hidden or displayed within tools by default.

[a] Remember that the X.500 specifications indicate that an Auxiliary class cannot inherit from a Structural class, and an Abstract class can inherit only from another Abstract class.

If the class inherits from only one other class, then that class's OID is entered into the Sub-Class-Of attribute. The Sub-Class-Of attribute is not multivalued, so if you want the class to inherit from multiple classes, you inherit from one Sub-Class-Of as before and make use of the Auxilary-Class/System-Auxiliary-Class attributes to contain the list of OIDs that point to the rest of the inherited classes.

A number of the attributes have duplicates prefixed with the word *System*. When you define a class for the first time, any initial contents of Must-Contain, May-Contain, Auxiliary-Class, and Poss-Superiors are copied into the corresponding system attribute and then the contents of the nonsystem attributes are erased. This enables you to create a class that has set values that can never be removed. The system attributes cannot ever be changed after the initial creation of the class. However, the nonsystem attributes can be changed as you wish. This allows anyone to later modify the class and add extra Must-Contain, May-Contain, Auxiliary-Class, and Poss-Superiors items without being able to erase the original set values. This is explained further in the following User class dissection under "How inheritance affects Must-Contain, May-Contain, Poss-Superiors, and Auxiliary-Class."

Using the System-Only attribute allows you to create a class that applications and services running on the system can create, but your administrators cannot. This is very useful if you wish to store information in Active Directory for a class without having administrators play with the schema and possibly corrupt your Active Directory by creating invalid instances of objects. For example, if you were writing an application or service to roll out on all your Windows 2000 servers, you could get the system to register objects of your own application-specific class in order to keep track of the deployment. This would contain all of the data specific to the application on that server, such as the version number. You could then query those objects whenever you wished—a great way to maintain a centralized link to the information you need from these services. If you ever roll out an upgrade, you can instantly query the object type to find the version number of the service or application that is running, allowing you to immediately see who has and has not upgraded. Your application that queries this information will always be stable because no invalid objects can be created external to your application.

 According to the strict X.500 standard, RDN-Att-ID is a multivalued object, but Microsoft has sensibly chosen to make it single-valued here to minimize confusion.

Dissecting an Example Class

The User class is a good example of an object, and I used a slightly modified version of the same script that I used for the UPN attribute in order to obtain the list of values that have been set for the User class. Again, I could just as easily have used a tool like ADSIEDIT or LDP.

The result gives 29 values in the property cache. Of these 29 values, 17 are inherited attributes from the Top class and 12 are attributes defined directly on User. Table 3-5 shows the values.

Table 3-5. User's Property Cache

User Attribute's LDAP-Display-Name	User Attribute's Syntax	Value Contained in User's Attribute	Attribute Defined on Which Object?
adminDescription	CASE_ IGNORE_ STRING	User	Top
adminDisplayName	CASE_ IGNORE_ STRING	User	Top
cn	CASE_ IGNORE_ STRING	User	Top
defaultHidingValue	BOOLEAN	False	Top
distinguishedName	DN_STRING	cn=User, cn=Schema, cn=Configuration, dc=mycorp, dc=com	Top
instanceType	INTEGER	4	Top
name	CASE_ IGNORE_ STRING	User	Top
nTSecurityDescriptor	SECURITY_ DESCRIPTOR	The SID	Top
objectCategory	DN_STRING	cn=Class-Schema, cn=Schema, cn=Configuration, dc=mycorp, dc=com	Top
objectClass	CASE_ IGNORE_ STRING	Top; classSchema (2 values of a multivalued attribute)	Top
objectGUID	OCTET_ STRING	A GUID	Top
showInAdvancedViewOnly	BOOLEAN	True	Top
systemFlags	INTEGER	16	Top
uSN_Changed	LARGE_INTEGER	USN when last changed	Top
uSN_Created	LARGE_INTEGER	USN when created	Top
when_ Changed	UTC_TIME	Time when last changed	Top

Table 3-5. User's Property Cache (continued)

User Attribute's LDAP-Display-Name	User Attribute's Syntax	Value Contained in User's Attribute	Attribute Defined on Which Object?
when_Created	UTC_TIME	Time when created	Top
governsID	CASE_ IGNORE_ STRING	1.2.840.113556.1.5.9	User
defaultObject-Category	DN_STRING	cn=person, cn=schema, cn=configuration, dc=mycorp, dc=com	User
defaultSecuri-tyDescriptor	CASE_ IGNORE_ STRING	Long text-encoded representation of a SID	User
rDNAttID	CASE_ IGNORE_ STRING	cn	User
lDAPDis-playName	CASE_ IGNORE_ STRING	User	User
schemaID-GUID	OCTET_ STRING	The GUID that uniquely identifies this class	User
subClassOf	CASE_ IGNORE_ STRING	organizationalperson	User
systemAuxilia-ryClass	CASE_ IGNORE_ STRING	securityPrincipal; mailRecipient	User
systemMay-Contain	CASE_ IGNORE_ STRING	Various attributes[a]	User
objectClassCat-egory	INTEGER	1	User
system-PossSuperiors	CASE_ IGNORE_ STRING	builtinDomain; organizationalUnit; domainDNS	User
systemOnly	BOOLEAN	False	User

[a] userCertificate; userWorkstations; userSharedFolderOther; userSharedFolder; userPrincipalName; userParameters; userAccountControl; unicodePwd; terminalServer; servicePrincipalName; scriptPath; pwdLastSet; profilePath; primaryGroupID; preferredOU; otherLoginWorkstations; operatorCount; ntPwdHistory; networkAddress; msRASSavedFramedRoute; msRASSavedFramedIPAddress; msRASSavedCallbackNumber; msRADIUSServiceType; msRADIUSFramedRoute; msRADIUSFramedIPAddress; msRADIUS-CallbackNumber; msNPSavedCallingStationID; msNPCallingStationID; msNPAllowDialin; mSMQSignCertificatesMig; mSMQSignCertificates; mSMQDigestsMig; mSMQDigests; maxStorage; logonWorkstation; logonHours; logonCount; lockoutTime; localeID; lmPwdHistory; lastLogon; lastLogoff; homeDrive; homeDirectory; groupsToIgnore; groupPriority; groupMembershipSAM;gPOptions; gPLink; dynamicLDAPServer; desktopProfile; defaultClassStore; dBCSPwd; controlAccessRights; codePage; badPwdCount; badPasswordTime; adminCount; aCSPolicyName; accountExpires

Let's take a look at some of the key Top values. You see that the name of the class is to be known by the name User (Admin-Description, Admin-Display-Name, CN, Name), that the class is defined at a specific place in the Schema NC (Distin-guished-Name), that it is an instance of the Class-Schema class (Object-Category and Object-Class), that it inherits attributes from both Top and Class-Schema (Object-Class), that this object class has a SID governing who can access and manipulate it (NT-Security-Descriptor), that the instances of the User class are visi-ble in normal browsing (Default-Hiding-Value), and that the User class itself is to be hidden from casual browsing (Show-In-Advanced-View-Only).

From the User attributes, you can see that the User has an OID of 1.2.840.113556. 1.5.9 (Governs-ID), can have instances created by anyone (System-Only), that when binding to it with ADSI you should use User (LDAP-Display-Name), that it inherits attributes not only from Top and Class-Schema but also from Security-Prin-cipal and Mail-Recipient (Object-Class [Top] and System-Auxiliary-Class), that when connecting to instances of the class via LDAP, the two-letter prefix used should be cn= (RDN-Att-ID), that the User class is a direct subclass of the Organizational-Per-son class (Sub-Class-Of), that there are a large number of attributes that instances of the User class can have values for (System-May-Contain), that this class can be created directly under only three different parents in Active Directory (System-Poss-Superiors), that the class is Structural (Object-Class-Category), and the default Security Descriptor to apply to new instances of the User class if one is not speci-fied on creation (Default-Security-Descriptor).

How inheritance affects Must-Contain, May-Contain, Poss-Superiors, and Auxiliary-Class

Let's look at the Must-Contain, May-Contain, Auxiliary-Class, Poss-Superiors, and their system attribute pairs. You can see that the only values that are set are Sys-tem-Poss-Superiors, System-May-Contain, and System-Auxiliary-Class. These were the values set on the initial creation of the User class and cannot be changed. Note that there were no mandatory attributes set at the creation of the original class as the System-Must-Contain attribute is not listed. If you later wished to add an extra set of attributes or add a new optional attribute to the User class, you could use Auxiliary-Class or May-Contain and modify the base definition. This occurs if, for example, you use the Active Directory Connector (ADC) to link your Active Direc-tory and a Microsoft Exchange 5.5 Schema. When you install the ADC for the first time in a forest, it modifies the Schema to extend it to include new Exchange objects and attributes, as well as modifying existing Active Directory objects to include new Exchange-relevant attributes. If you were to do this, the User class would be directly modified to include three of these Exchange-relevant Auxiliary classes in the Auxiliary-Class attribute: msExchMailStorage, msExchCustomAt-tributes, and msExchCertificateInformation. The ADC is discussed more fully in Chapter 13, *Directory Interoperability.*

The attributes that are required when you create a new user are not listed in the Must-Contain attribute. That's because Object-SID, SAM-Account-Name, and the others are inherited from other classes that make up this one. The Must-Contain attributes can be defined either directly on the Auxiliary-Class, System-Auxiliary-Class, or Sub-Class-Of classes, or they can be defined on the classes inherited from further up the tree. Both SAM-Account-Name and Object-SID, for example, are defined on the Security-Principal class.

The same principle applies to the May-Contain attribute. The entire set of these attributes is available only when you recurse back up the tree and identify all the inherited May-Contain attributes on all inherited classes.

Poss-Superiors, on the other hand, can be made up of only those items defined directly on the class, those defined on the class in the Sub-Class-Of attribute, or any inherited classes defined on any other Sub-Class-Of attributes up the Sub-Class-Of tree. If that was too confusing, try this: an instance of the User class can have Poss-Superiors from itself, from the Organizational-Person class defined in the Sub-Class-Of attribute, from the Person class (the Organizational-Person class's Sub-Class-Of attribute), and from Top (the Person class's Sub-Class-Of attribute).

Viewing the User class with the Schema Manager MMC

Take a look at Figure 3-5. This shows the User class viewed with the Schema Manager MMC. You can see the relevant general User data shown here.

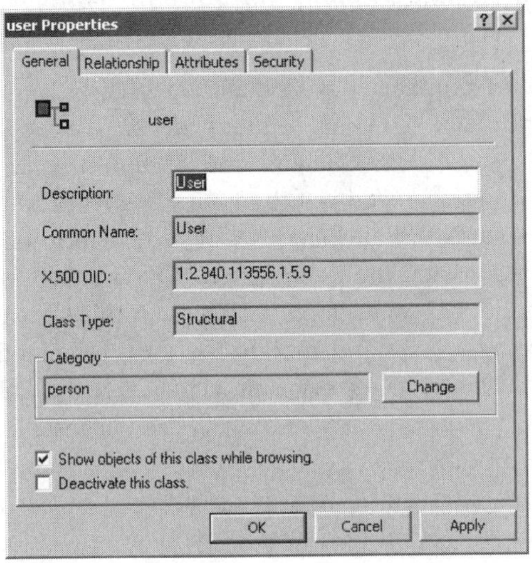

Figure 3-5. User Class Schema entry general settings

Notice that quite a bit of it is not configurable after the initial configuration. That includes Governs-ID, Schema-ID-GUID, RDN-Att-ID, Object-Class-Category, System-Only, Object-Class, Sub-Class-Of, System-Must-Contain, System-Poss-Superiors, System-May-Contain, and System-Auxiliary-Class.

To see the so-called relationship settings (Sub-Class-Of, Auxiliary-Class, System-Auxiliary-Class, Poss-Superiors, System-Poss-Superiors), look at Figure 3-6. In this screen, you can see that the User class in this Schema is inheriting attributes from the normal auxiliary classes as well as the three extra Exchange classes incorporated into the Schema by installing the ADC.

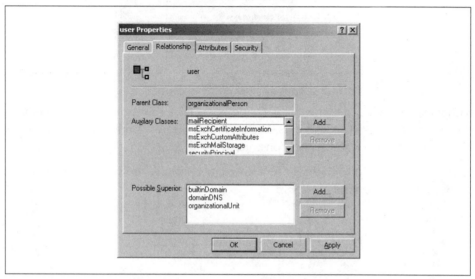

Figure 3-6. User Class Schema entry relationship settings

The third and final screen is displayed in Figure 3-7. This shows the Must-Contain, System-Must-Contain, May-Contain, and System-May-Contain attributes of the User class. Here the accountExpires attribute is highlighted, and the text underneath indicates that this is a system attribute, and thus it must be held in System-May-Contain.

Summary

In this chapter I've introduced you to how the internal blueprint for all objects in Active Directory, known as the Schema, was derived from the X.500 directory service. I explained that X.500 classes and attributes do exist in the schema and that the OID numbering system is still followed. I then detailed how an attribute and its syntax was structured in the Schema, as Attribute-Schema objects, using the User-Principal-Name of the User object as an example. I then showed how

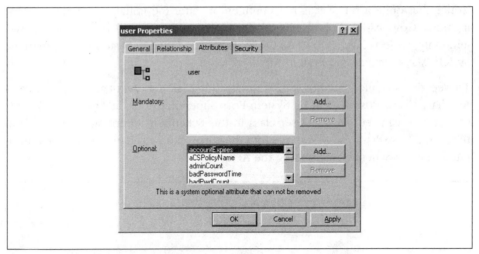

Figure 3-7. User Class Schema entry attribute settings

attributes are added to classes by detailing how classes are stored in the Schema as instances of Class-Schema objects. To make this clearer, I dug into the details of the User class to see how it was constructed.

Chapter 11 builds on what you've learned here to see how you would design changes in an enterprise environment.

4

Active Directory Replication

This chapter introduces a major feature of Windows 2000: replication of the data in Active Directory. There are two aspects to replication:

- How data gets replicated around an existing network of links between DCs

- How the Knowledge Consistency Checker (KCC) generates and maintains the replication links between servers, both intrasite and intersite

This chapter looks at the former, how a number of servers with already existing links replicate data among themselves. I'll defer discussion of how the links are created and managed until Chapter 7, *Sites and Replication Topologies*. That describes the physical infrastructure of a network layout using sites, how the KCC sets up and manages the site links, and then details how to effectively design and tailor sites, site links, and replication in Active Directory.

Sites

Windows 2000 uses the term *site* to mean a collection of machines (servers, workstations, or both) that coexist on a fast network, i.e., a physical network in a particular location with good connectivity between all sections of that network. In TCP/IP terms, this would be a collection of well-connected IP subnets. Windows 2000 uses sites to replicate the logical namespace around the physical network.

Windows 2000 replication is very efficient. Only changed properties, rather than entire objects, are replicated, as was the case in Windows NT. Replication also can take place over multiple TCP/IP transports, so that you can find a replication protocol to suit the environment a particular site requires.

The recommended minimum speed for a well-connected network is 1.5MBps (i.e., a T1 link). You will see this actual value vary from article to article and book to book, as different people will find that their network will run fine over a slower connection speed. We'll cover this later, but the absolute true minimum is around 128KBps of available replication bandwidth out of a 256KBps total available bandwidth. Your mileage may vary; you would need to do your own testing to see for yourself. Microsoft's final recommendations should be the main arbiter here.

Administrators do the actual creation of sites, as the process is not automatic. Once you've set up a site, a Windows 2000 process automatically creates and dynamically manages a replication schedule and a set of *intrasite* replication links among DCs in the site. As you add more DCs, more intrasite links are added automatically. If you were to do nothing more, data would be effectively replicated by Windows 2000 around your site. When you add your second site, the same automatic intrasite creation mechanisms spring into action creating links and a replication schedule among the various DCs in this second site. The algorithm that is used adapts as more sites and DCs are added so that certain built-in criteria are never breached; this assures that the network is always properly replicated. Note, however, that creating a second site does *not* trigger the system to also automatically create *intersite* replication links and a replication schedule. Instead, these have to be created manually as required by administrators.

The process that automatically creates and manages links is called the Knowledge Consistency Checker (KCC). I'll cover the KCC in greater depth later in Chapter 7.

Site and WAN Management Tools

Obviously, as more sites and connections are created, the system can get very large. You need tools to manage this sort of system and Windows 2000's Active Directory Sites and Services Management Console (SSM) takes care of this. This tool is a lot more than a simple management system, however. It actually allows you to get right into the guts of Active Directory's sites and site connections in order to tinker with the setup that was created by default. You can create new sites and new links, break other links, set replication schedules for each link, change the criteria that the system uses as its defaults for setting up links and replication, and so on. Basically, the SSM allows you to directly manipulate part of the Configuration Naming Context of your Active Directory. The SSM is a very useful tool with a large scope that will become very important to you in your management of sites and replication.

When you open the SSM, you actually open a window directly onto an area of Active Directory. If you use a special Active Directory tool, such as ADSIEDIT, to connect directly to the cn=Configuration Naming Context, you will see the cn=Sites and cn=Services child containers within. These containers are the roots of the data that you manipulate directly with the SSM.

Other tools available in the Windows 2000 Resource Kit:

RepAdmin

A command-line tool for administering replication.

ReplMon

A graphical utility for managing and monitoring replication.

Why Have Windows 2000 Sites?

Sites exist to allow clients to find the closest DC, GC, DFS share point, or even an application distribution point (via SMS). If you take a laptop to a new site in a domain, the laptop needs to be able to determine where the nearest DC is; it uses sites to do that. Sites don't even have to have any servers at all in them; a site can be composed entirely of workstations. In this case, clients need to find a DC, preferably in the nearest site. The client actually queries both Active Directory (for cost-based selection of the nearest site) and the DNS (using site records that I will go through in Chapter 5, *TCP/IP and DDNS*). Sites are published in the DNS as well as being part of Active Directory namespace structure. While the details on sites are held in the DNS, the actual topology is held in Active Directory. This topology uses costs to determine the proximity of other sites.

With cost-assigned ratings to links and the fact that Windows 2000 replicates only updated properties rather than entire objects, Windows 2000 has improved Windows NT's attempts to span domains across WAN links. While under Windows NT, creating a domain across very slow links was next to impossible; Windows 2000 it possible to span domains across very slow links or even links that do not have synchronous connections at all but instead receive and send changes asynchronously via email. In fact, while Windows 2000 domains can easily be defined to span sites, sites also can hold multiple domains. Remember that a site literally represents an area of good connectivity, but it doesn't dictate how you arrange your domains; the connections between sites do that.

The First Site

When you create the first domain controller of the first domain in a new forest, a default site called Default-First-Site-Name is created and the domain controller is assigned to it. Subsequently, installed domain controllers are added to this site automatically. Even if you then create multiple sites, new servers are always added to the first site. In order to change that, you need to assign one or more IP subnets to each site. That way, any server or workstation on a specified subnet is automatically added to the appropriate site.

The Default-First-Site-Name site can be renamed if you wish, but note that site names cannot exceed 63 characters or contain dot (.) or space characters.

Adding Subnets to a Site in the SSM

When adding subnets to sites via the SSM, you must enter the name of the subnet in the form `network/bits masked`, e.g., 10.186.149.0/24 would be network 10.186.149.0 with subnet mask 255.255.255.0.

The `bits masked` in the subnet name is the number of bits set in the subnet mask for that subnet. It can be between 0 and 31. The subnet mask is made up of 4 octets or bytes (4 sets of 8 bits). To convert the subnet mask to bits, convert each octet from the subnet mask to binary. So, the subnet mask 255.255.255.0 would be 11111111.11111111.11111111.00000000 in binary, which uses 8+8+8 bits (i.e., 24) to define the subnet mask. A subnet mask of 255.255.248.0 would be 11111111.11111111.11111100.00000000, which is 8+8+6 or 22.

If TCP/IP subnets and addresses mean very little to you, check out Chuck Semeria's article on "Understanding IP Addressing: Everything You Ever Wanted To Know" at *http://www.3com.com/nsc/501302.html.*

Data Replication

Microsoft has introduced a number of new terms for Windows 2000 replication, and most of them will be completely unfamiliar to anyone new to Active Directory. In order to properly design replication, you need to understand how replication works, but more to the point you need to understand how replication works using these new terms, which are used throughout both Microsoft's documentation and its management tools. Here is the list of the terms that you'll encounter as I explain replication. These definitions will make more sense later.

Naming Context (NC)

The objects replicated within Active Directory.

Update Sequence Number (USN)

This 64-bit value, which is assigned to each object, increments every time a change takes place.

Originating write/update and replicated write/update

A change made to an object on a specific DC is an originating write; replication of that change to all other DCs is a replicated write.

High-Watermark Vector

This USN represents the maximum number of changes ever to occur on a particular NC.

Up-to-date vector

This is the USN on a specific server that represents the last originating write for an NC on that server.

Tombstone

Because of the complex replication available in Windows 2000 and Active Directory, simply deleting an object potentially would result in it being re-created at the next replication interval. So deleted objects are *tombstoned* instead. This basically marks them as deleted. Objects marked as tombstoned are actually deleted 60 days after their original tombstone status setting; however, this time can be changed by modifying the tombstonelifetime property of cn=DirectoryServices,cn=WindowsNT,cn=Services,cn=Configuration,dc=mycorp,dc=com.

Property version number

This number indicates how often this particular property has been updated.

Timestamp

This time and date are stored on an object for comparison checking.

Globally Unique Identifier (GUID)

This system-generated alphanumeric string represents a unique identifier for an object within an enterprise.

Flexible Single Master Operator (FSMO)

This term designates a server that performs one of the following roles: PDC Master, Infrastructure Master, RID Manager, Schema Manager, or Domain Naming Master.

A Background to Metadata—Data That Governs the Replication Process

Active Directory replication enables data transfer between NCs on different servers without either ending up in a continuous replication loop or leaving any data out. In order to make this process work, each NC holds a number of pieces of information that specifically relate to replication within that particular NC. So the replication data for the Schema NC is held in the Schema NC and is separate from the replication data for the Configuration NC, which is held in the Configuration NC.

To minimize the use of abbreviations, I will refer to DCs from now on simply as *servers*. The terms *property* and *attribute* are used interchangeably.

The High-Watermark Vector and orginating/replicated updates

Each server has a separate Update Sequence Number (USN) for each NC. The USN is stored as a 64-bit value in the Active Directory database indexed for rapid searching. This value is used to indicate how many updates have actually taken place to an NC on a particular server and is known as the High-Watermark Vector. Each server also maintains a record of the updates that it made to its NC for a particular USN. This allows other servers to request individual changes based on particular USNs. Replication distinguishes between two types of update:

Originating update
> Occurs when the server itself or an application connected to that server makes a change to its own copy of the NC.

Replicated update
> Occurs when the server receives a change it needs to make to its own NC from another server.

So if you use the Active Directory Users and Computers console to create five users on Server A, Server A's USN is incremented five times, once for each originating update. If Server A receives six more changes from Server B, then Server A's USN is incremented six more times, once for each of the six replicated updates.

If an Active Directory database transaction is aborted, i.e., fails to complete, then the associated USN value is ignored from then on by Active Directory. It is not assigned to any object or reused in any way. The USN continues incrementing as changes occur, but that value is considered unusable.

To summarize, each server in a forest holds three NCs (domain, Configuration, and Schema), and each of these has a High-Watermark Vector USN.

High-Watermark Vector table

Each server also maintains a list of the High-Watermark Vectors for all of its replication partners. This table is updated only during replication. If I have a server with two partners, then each partner maintains the High-Watermark Vector for my server. If a change occurs on my server, the High-Watermark Vector on my server is updated, but the High-Watermark Vectors on my partners are not updated until the next replication cycle.

Up-To-Date Vector

Each server also maintains the USN that represents the last originating write for the NC on itself. This is known as the Up-To-Date Vector. If the USN on a server for a particular NC was 2000, and the server made an originating-write to that NC, both the High-Watermark Vector and the Up-To-Date Vector USN would become 2001. If, subsequently, the server received five replicated writes, then the Up-To-Date Vector would stay at 2001, while the High-Watermark Vector became 2006. Obviously, if a server never has an originating-write, then the Up-To-Date Vector USN is never set for that server.

Up-To-Date Vector table

Each server also maintains a list of the Up-To-Date Vectors for every server that has ever made an originating-write. This is known as the Up-To-Date Vector table. If Server A makes an originating write, it creates an Up-To-Date Vector for itself and adds it to the Up-To-Date Vector table. Then when it next replicates with all of its partners, it passes its Up-To-Date Vector table to those partners. The highest originating write value for a server is thus passed around to all servers in an NC.

If you are replicating a domain NC, the maximum number of entries in an Up-To-Date Vector table has to be the total number of servers that make up the domain. If you are replicating the Configuration or Schema NCs, which are replicated enterprise wide, the maximum number of entries in the table would be the number of servers in the entire forest.

As the tables have to uniquely identify the server in addition to the USN, each entry in both sets of tables stores the GUID of the server along with the USN value.

Summary

The following list summarizes the important points of this section:

- Active Directory is split into separate parts, each of which replicates independently. These parts are known as Naming Contexts (NCs) or Partitions. (Normally the only time that you see the term *Partitions* used is actually within Active Directory itself; almost everyone refers to them as *NCs*.)

- Within each NC, a variety of metadata is held:

  — Each NC on a server has a unique USN for itself. This USN is incremented whenever a change occurs on that server by any means. This is known as the High-Watermark Vector for that server within this NC.

  — For each NC on a server, the server records the USN of the last originating write that was made to the NC and the server's identifying GUID. This is known as the Up-To-Date Vector for that server within this NC.

  — For each NC on a server, the server maintains a High-Watermark Vector table that contains one entry for each of its replication partners within this NC. The values a server holds for its replication partners are updated only during a replication cycle.

  — For each NC on a server, the server maintains an Up-To-Date Vector table that contains one vector entry for every server that has ever made an originating write within this NC. Each entry consists of two values: an Originating-DC-GUID and an Originating-USN. These values are updated only during a replication cycle.

While each server has a GUID, so does the Active Directory database (*NTDS.DIT*). This latter GUID is used to identify the server's Active Directory database in replication calls. The GUID is initially the same as the server GUID but changes if Active Directory is restored on that server.

This change of GUID makes sure that the other DCs on the network do not immediately replicate all the missing changes to this newly restored version of Active Directory. As the GUIDs are different, the change is detected and Active Directory is left alone.

How an Object's Metadata Is Modified During Replication

In order to see how the actual data is modified during replication, consider a four-stage example:

Step 1

An object (a user) is created on Server A.

Step 2

That object is replicated to Server B.

Step 3

That object is subsequently modified on Server B.

Step 4

The new changes to that object are replicated back to Server A.

This four-step process is shown in Figure 4-1. The diagram depicts the status of the user object on both Server A and Server B during the four time periods that represent each of the steps.

Now use Figure 4-1 to follow a discussion of each of the steps.

Step 1—Initial creation of a user on Server A

When you create a user on Server A, then Server A is the originating server. During the Active Directory database transaction representing the creation of the new user on Server A, a USN (1000) is assigned to the transaction. The user's uSNCreated and uSNChanged properties are automatically set to 1000 (the USN of the transaction corresponding to the user creation). All of the user's properties are also initialized with a set of data as follows:

- The property's value(s) is/are set according to system defaults or parameters given during user creation.
- The property's USN is set to 1000 (the USN of this transaction).

- The property's version number is set to 1.

- The property's timestamp is set to the time of the object creation.

- The property's originating-server GUID is set to the GUID of Server A.

- The property's originating-server USN is set to 1000 (the USN of this transaction).

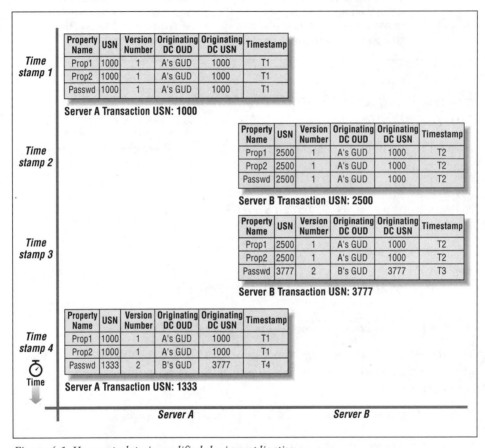

Figure 4-1. How metadata is modified during replication

This tells you that the user was created during transaction 1000 on this server (uSNCreated = 1000). It also tells you that the user was last changed during transaction 1000 (uSNChanged = 1000). You know that the properties for the user have never been modified from their original values (property version numbers = 1), and these values were set at transaction 1000 (property's USN = 1000). Finally, you know that each property was last set by the originating-server Server A during transaction 1000 (originating-server GUID and originating-server USN).

The preceding example showed two per-object values and five per-property values being changed. While uSNChanged and uSNCreated are real properties on each object in the AD, properties of an object can only have values and cannot hold other properties, like a version number.

In reality, all of the per-property replication metadata (Property Version Number, Time-Changed, Originating-DC-GUID, Originating-USN, Property-USN) for every property of any object is encoded altogether as a single byte string and stored as replPropertyMetaData, a nonreplicated property of the object.

A property's metadata can be seen by using the RepAdmin, ADSIEDIT, or LDP tools provided in the Resource Kit.

Step 2—Replication of the originating write to Server B

Later, when this object is replicated to Server B, Server B adds the user to its copy of Active Directory as a replicated-write. During this transaction, USN 2500 is allocated, and the user's uSNCreated and uSNChanged properties are modified to correspond to Server B's transaction USN (2500).

This tells you that the user was created during transaction 2500 on this server (uSNCreated = 2500). It also tells you that the user was last changed during transaction 2500 (uSNChanged = 2500). You know that the properties for the user have never been modified from their original values (property version numbers = 1), and these values were set at transaction 2500 (property's USN = 2500). Finally, you know that each property was last set by the originating-server Server A during transaction 1000 (originating-server GUID and originating-server USN).

Step 3—Password change for the user on Server B

Now an originating-write (a password change) occurs on Server B's replicated-write user. Some time has passed since the user was originally created, so the USN assigned to the password change transaction is 3777. When the password is changed, the user's uSNChanged property is modified to become 3777. In addition, the password property (and only the password property) is modified in the following way:

- The password value is set.
- The password's USN is set to 3777 (the USN of this transaction).
- The property's version number is set to 2.
- The property's timestamp is set to the time that transaction 3777 occurred.

- The property's originating-server GUID is set to the GUID of Server B.

- The property's originating-server USN is set to 3777 (the USN of this transaction).

Now looking at the user object, you can see that the object was last changed during transaction 3777 and that that transaction represented a password change that originated on Server B.

Step 4—Password change replication to Server A

This step is similar to Step 2. When Server A receives the password update during replication, it allocates the change transaction a USN of 1333.

 Remember that updates occur at the property level and not the object level, so only the password is sent and not the whole user.

During transaction 1333, the user's uSNChanged property is modified to correspond to Server A's transaction USN.

This tells you that the user was created during transaction 1000 on this server (uSNCreated = 1000). It also tells you that the user was last changed during transaction 1333 (uSNChanged = 1333). You know that all but one of the properties for the user have retained their original values (property version numbers = 1), and these values were set at transaction 1000 (property's USN = 1000). Finally, you know that all but one of the properties were last set by the originating-server Server A during transaction 1000 (originating-server GUID and originating-server USN). The password was modified for the first time since its creation (password version number = 2) during transaction 1333 (password's USN = 1333), and it was modified on Server B during transaction 3777 (originating-server GUID and originating-server USN).

That's how object and property metadata is modified during replication. Let's now take a look at exactly how replication occurs.

The Replication of a Naming Context Between Two Servers

In the following examples, there are five servers in a domain: Server A, Server B, Server C, Server D, and Server E. It doesn't matter what NC they are replicating or which servers replicate with which other servers (as they do not all have to interreplicate), as the replication process for any two servers will be the same nonetheless. Replication is a five-step process:

Step 1

Replication with a partner is initiated.

Step 2

The partner works out what updates to send.

Step 3

The partner sends the updates to the initiating server.

Step 4

The initiating server processes the updates.

Step 5

The initiating server checks whether it is up to date.

Step 1—Replication with a partner is initiated

Replication occurs between only two servers at any time, so let's consider Server A and Server B, which are replication partners. At a certain point in time indicated by the replication schedule on Server A, Server A initiates replication for a particular NC with Server B and requests any updates that it doesn't have. This is a one-way update transfer from Server B to Server A. No new updates will be passed to Server B in this replication cycle, as this would require Server B to initiate the replication.

Server A initiates the replication by sending Server B a request to replicate along with five pieces of important replication metadata, i.e., data relating to the replication process itself. The five pieces are:

- The name of the NC that Server A wishes to receive updates for

- The maximum number of object updates that Server A wishes to receive during this replication cycle

- The maximum number of values that Server A wishes to receive during this replication cycle

- Server A's High-Watermark Vector for Server B in this NC

- Server A's Up-To-Date Vector table for this NC

The maximum object updates and property values are very important in limiting network bandwidth. If one server has had a huge volume of updates since the last replication cycle, limiting the number of objects replicated out in one go means that network bandwidth is not inordinately taken up by replicating those objects in one huge sweep. Instead, the replication is broken down into smaller chunks over multiple replication cycles.

This step is illustrated in Figure 4-2, which shows that while the initiation of the replication occurs from an NC denoted as xxxx on Server A (where xxxx could represent the Schema, the Configuration, or any domain), the actual replication will occur later from Server B to Server A. High-Watermark Vector is abbreviated to HWMV and Up-To-Date Vector to UTDV.

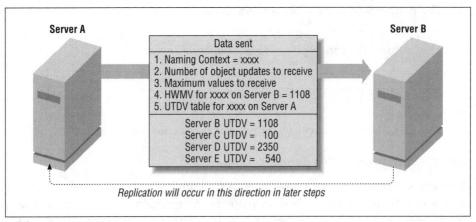

Figure 4-2. Initiating replication with Server B for NC xxxx

Step 2—The partner works out what updates to send

Server B receives all of this metadata and works out which updates it needs to send back for this NC. First, Server B finds its own High-Watermark Vector for its copy of the NC and then compares the two High-Watermark Vectors. Assuming that there have been some updates, then Server B instantly knows how many updates have happened since Server A last replicated with Server B. This has to be true, as Server A would have been updated with Server B's High-Watermark Vector during the last replication cycle. So, any difference between the two vectors now must represent changes on Server B since the last replication, and Server B knows which individual USNs Server A is missing. Assuming also for now that the number of updates does not exceed the maximums specified by Server A in its metadata, Server B can supply all of the missing updates to Server A.

However, this entire set of updates may not need to go to Server A if Server A has had some of them replicated already from other servers. Server B now needs some way of knowing which updates Server A has already seen, so that it can remove those items from the list of updates to send. That's where the Up-To-Date Vector table comes in. For each update that could potentially be sent, Server B checks two pieces of data attached to the object that was updated: the GUID of the server that originated the update (the Originating-DC-GUID) and the USN associated with that update on the originating server (the Originating-USN). For example, a password change to a user may have been replicated to Server B and recorded as USN

1112 but in fact may have originated on Server D as USN 2345. Server B cross references the originating server's GUID with Server A's Up-To-Date Vector table to find Server A's Up-To-Date Vector for the originating server. If the Up-To-Date Vector recorded in the table for the originating server is equal to or higher than the USN attached to the update on Server B, then Server A must have already seen the update. This has to be true, because Server A's Up-To-Date Vector table is used to indicate the highest originating-writes that Server A has received.

Let's say that Server B has four updates for Server A: one originating-write (Server B USN: 1111) and three replicated-writes (Server B USNs 1109, 1110, and 1112). The reason there are four is that 1112 is the last update made on Server B in this example, and Server A's HWMV for xxxx on Server B from Figure 4-1 is 1108. So, look for updates starting at 1109 up to the last update on Server B, which is 1112. The first two replicated-writes (Server B USNs 1109 and 1110) originated on Server E (Server E USNs 567 and 788), and one (Server B USN 1112) originated on Server D (Server D USN 2345). This is shown in Table 4-1.

Table 4-1. Potential Updates to Be Sent

Server B USN	Originating DC GUID	Originating DC USN
1109	Server E's GUID	567
1110	Server E's GUID	788
1111	Server B's GUID	1111
1112	Server D's GUID	2345

According to Figure 4-2, Server A already has Sever-D's 2345 update because Server A's Up-To-Date Vector for Server D is 2350. So, both Server A and Server B already have Server D's 2345 update, and there is no need to waste bandwidth sending it over the network again. The act of filtering updates that have already been seen from being continually sent between the servers is known as *propagation dampening.*

Now that you know how the High-Watermark Vector table and Up-To-Date Vector table help Server B to work out what updates need sending, let's look at the exact process that Server B uses to work out what data is required.

When Server B receives a request for updates from Server A, it starts by making a copy of its Up-To-Date Vector table for Server A. Having done that, it puts the table to one side, so to speak, and does a search of the entire NC for all objects with a uSNChanged value greater than Server A's High-Watermark Vector for Server B. This list is then sorted into ascending uSNChanged order.

Next, Server B initializes an empty output buffer to which it will add update entries for sending to Server A. It also initializes a value called Last-Object-USN-Changed. This will be used to represent the USN of the last object sent in that particular replication session. This value is not an attribute on any particular object, just a simple piece of replication metadata. Server B then enumerates the list of objects in ascending uSNChanged order and uses the following algorithm for each object:

- If the object has already been added to the output buffer, Server B sets Last-Object-USN-Changed to the uSNChanged property of the current object. Enumeration continues with the next object.

- If the object has not already been added to the output buffer, Server B tests the object to see if it contains changes that need to be sent to the destination. For each property of the current object, Server B takes the Originating-DC-GUID of that property and locates the Up-To-date Vector entry that corresponds to that GUID from Server A's Up-To-Date Vector table. From that vector entry, Server B looks at the Up-To-Date-Vector Originating-USN. If the property's Originating-USN on Server B is greater than Server A's Up-To-Date-Vector Originating-USN, the property needs to be sent.

  If changes need to be sent, then an update entry is added to the output buffer. Server B sets Last-Object-USN-Changed to the uSNChanged property of the current object. Enumeration continues with the next object.

  If no changes need to be sent, Server B sets the Last-Object-USN-Changed to the uSNChanged of the current object. Enumeration continues with the next object.

During the enumeration, if the requested limit on object update entries or values is reached, the enumeration terminates early and a flag known as More-Data is set to TRUE. If the enumeration finishes without either limit being hit, then More-Data is set to False.

Step 3—The partner sends the updates to the initiating server

Server B identifies the list of updates that it should send back based on those that Server A has not yet seen from other sources. Server B then sends this data to Server A. In addition, if More-Data is set to FALSE, then one extra piece of metadata is sent back as well. The returned information from Server B is:

- The output buffer updates from Server A
- Server B's Last-Object-USN-Changed value (i.e., its own High-Watermark Vector)
- The More-Data flag
- Server B's Up-To-Date Vector table for this NC (sent only when More-Data set to FALSE)

This is shown in Figure 4-3.

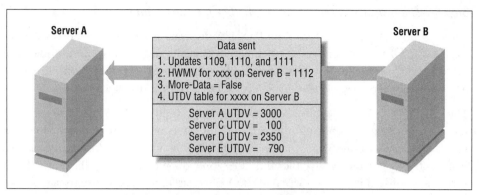

Figure 4-3. Server B sends the updates to Server A for NC xxxx

---

 If Server B calculates that Server A is already up to date and requires no updates, then only the last two pieces of metadata are returned to Server A. This can occur if Server B's High-Watermark Vector is identical to that passed by Server A, i.e., no updates have occurred since the last replication cycle. This also can occur if Server B's High-Watermark Vector has changed but all the updates have already been seen by Server A. In both cases, just the metadata is returned.

Step 4— The initiating server processes the updates

Server A receives the data. For each update entry it receives, Server A allocates a USN and starts a database transaction to update the relevant object in its own copy of the Active Directory database. If this update represents a change to an object (rather than an object deletion, for example), the object's uSNChanged property is set to the USN of this transaction. The database transaction is then committed. This process continues for each update entry that was received.

After all the update entries have been processed, Server A's High-Watermark Vector for Server B is set to the Last-Object-USN-Changed received from Server B. In other words, Server A now knows that it is up to date with Server B, up to the last change just sent over.

The Last-Object-USN-Changed Server A receives allows it to know the last update that Server B has made. This will be used in the next replication cycle. In the previous example, the highest update sent across to Server A is USN 1111. Server B's USN 1112 update is not actually sent since Server A has already seen it. However, the Last-Object-USN-Changed returned by Server B with the data would still be 1112 and not 1111.

Step 5—The initiating server checks whether it is up to date

Server A now checks the More-Data flag. If More-Data is set to True, Server A goes back to step 1 to start replication with Server B again and request more updates. If More-Data is set to False, every update must have been received from Server B, and so finally Server A's Up-To-Date Vector table is itself updated.

The Up-To-Date Vector table allows Server A to identify which updates Server B has seen and thus by replication which updates it has now seen. Server A does not replace its Up-To-Date Vector table with the one it was sent. Instead, it checks each entry in the received table and does one of two things. If the entry for a server is not listed in its own Up-To-Date Vector table, it adds that entry to its own table. This allows Server A to know that it has now been updated to a certain level for a new server. If the entry for a server is listed in Server A's Up-To-Date Vector table and the value received is higher, it modifies its own copy of the table with the higher value. After all, it has now been updated to this new level by Server B, so it had better record that fact.

Table 4-2 shows Server A's Up-To-Date Vector table and High-Watermark Vector for the xxxx Naming Context before step 1 and after step 5.

Table 4-2. State of UTDV Table and HWMV for Server A Before and After Updates

	HWMV for Server B	Server B UTDV	Server C UTDV	Server D UTDV	Server E UTDV
Before step 1	1108	1108	100	2350	540
After step 5	1112	1112	100	2350	790

Summary

The following main points summarize replication between Naming Contexts:

- The High-Watermark Vector table is used to detect updates that need to be sent from replication partners.

- The Up-To-Date Vector table is used in propagation dampening to filter the updates so that only updates that the initiating server has not seen are transmitted from a partner.

- The uSNChanged property on each object is used to identify which objects potentially need sending out as updates to the initiating server.

You can force manual replication of a particular NC on a DC if you choose, using SSM.

How Replication Conflicts Are Reconciled

While the replication process is fine on its own, there are times when conflicts can occur because two servers perform irreconcilable operations between replication cycles. For example, Server A creates an object with a particular name at roughly the same time that Server B creates an object with the same name. Both can't exist at the same time in Active Directory, so what happens to the two objects? Does one get deleted or renamed? Do both get deleted or renamed? What about an administrator moving an object on Server D to a new Organizational Unit while at the same time on Server B that Organizational Unit is being deleted? What happens to the soon-to-be orphaned object? Is it deleted along with the Organizational Unit or moved somewhere else entirely? Consider a final example: if an admin on Server B changes a user's password while the user himself changes his password on Server C, which password does the user get?

All of these conflicts need resolving within Active Directory during the next replication cycle. The exact reconciliation process and how the final decision is replicated back out depends on the exact conflict that occurred.

Conflict due to identical property change

In this case, the server starts reconciliation by looking at the version numbers of the two properties. Whichever property has the higher version number wins the conflict. If the property version numbers are equal, the server checks the timestamps of both properties. Whichever property was changed at the later time wins the conflict. If the property timestamps are equal, then the originating server GUIDs are checked for both properties. As GUIDs must be unique, these two values have to be unique, so the server arbitrarily takes the property change from the originating server with the higher GUID of the two as canon.

Conflict due to a move of an object under a now deleted parent

This is a fairly easy conflict to resolve. In this case, the parent is deleted, but the object is moved to the Lost and Found Container, which was specially set up for this scenario. The ADsPath of the Lost and Found Container for Mycorp is:

```
LDAP://cn=LostAndFound,dc=mycorp,dc=com
```

Conflict due to creation of objects with names that conflict

The server starts reconciliation by looking at the version numbers of the two objects. Whichever object has the higher version number wins the conflict. If the object version numbers are equal, then the server checks the timestamps of both objects. Whichever object was changed at the later time wins the conflict. If both object timestamps are equal, then the originating server GUIDs are checked for both objects. The server simply takes the object change from the originating server with the higher GUID of the two as canon.

In this case, however, the object that failed the conflict resolution is not lost or deleted. Instead, the offending name is renamed on the object that failed to a unique value, which is basically a GUID. That way, at the end of the resolution, both objects exist, with one having its conflicting name changed to a unique value.

Replicating the conflict resolution

Let's say that Server A starts a replication cycle. First it requests changes from Server B and receives updates. Then Server A requests changes from Server C and receives updates. However, as Server A is applying Server C's updates in order, it determines that a conflict has occurred between the updates recently applied by Server B. Server A resolves the conflict according to the preceding guidelines, and finds in Server C's favor. Now, while Server A and Server C are correct, Server B still needs to be updated with Server C's value.

To do this, when Server B next requests updates from Server A, it receives, among others, the update that originated on Server C. Server B then applies the updates it receives in sequence, and when it gets to the update that originated on Server C, it detects the same conflict. Server B then goes through the same conflict resolution procedure that Server A did and comes to the same result. So, Server B then modifies its own copy of the relevant NC to accommodate the change.

Additional problems occur when changes are made on a server and it goes down prior to replicating the changes. If it never comes back up to replicate changes, those changes are lost.

Alternatively, if it comes back up much later and attempts to replicate those changes back to Active Directory, there is a much greater chance of conflict resolution with that server failing the conflict, if many of the changes that were made on that server have subsequently been made in Active Directory more recently on other servers. This isn't a problem but is something you need to be aware of.

Summary

We've now looked at how the physical infrastructure of an organization is represented in Active Directory—using sites. We've also considered the metadata that governs the replication process, how the system keeps track of changes to objects and properties automatically, how data is replicated around between servers including propagation dampening, and how conflicts are reconciled.

Later on, in Chapter 7, I take this knowledge further and show you how Active Directory manages and automatically generates the replication links that exist both within and between sites. With that knowledge, we can move on to the design principles for sites and links in Active Directory.

5

TCP/IP and DDNS

TCP/IP underpins Windows 2000 and thus Active Directory itself. Active Directory communicates solely over TCP/IP and requires support for a specific DNS feature set in order to work. The Domain Name System consists of the servers that translate TCP/IP names into numeric addresses throughout the Internet.

This chapter looks at how Active Directory uses the DNS (more specifically DDNS, or Dynamic DNS) by investigating the records it sets up for domains. After covering the basics of how Windows 2000 makes use of the DDNS, I also explain how to implement a Windows 2000 design based on if you have an existing domain name/IP address. I finish off by explaining what value-added benefits you could use within your organization when you integrate Windows 2000's DNS with Active Directory. However, I do not discuss Microsoft's DNS offering that ships with Windows 2000 in any real depth or how to correctly install, configure, and make use of it. I explain only how DNS impacts your Windows 2000 designs.

How TCP/IP and DDNS Are Used

Simply stated, any communication that Windows 2000 needs to make with any resource on your network is likely to be done over TCP/IP unless you specifically configure it otherwise. Windows 2000 lives and breathes TCP/IP, which by implication requires a DNS Server, so if your company doesn't have an Internet domain name—such as *microsoft.com, leicester.ac.uk,* or *oreilly.com*—you're about to need one. Even if you have a small network with no Internet connectivity or domain name, you still will need to fake an internet domain name (like *mycorp. com* or *othercorp.com* that I use in my examples) in order to create your domains.

Throughout this section I use the term *domain* to mean two things: an Internet domain name used with the DNS and a Windows 2000 domain name. The DNS domain name and the Windows 2000 domain name do not have to be the same, but having different ones can cause management headaches as your brain tries to think in too many directions at once. By and large, they end up being the same in most Windows 2000 networks. I'll cover this in greater depth in the sections on how your DNS setup affects your design.

When queries for resources in DNS are made, they will more than likely be entered as hostnames rather than actual addresses. This means that somewhere a DNS server receives queries about those hostnames and returns responses having resolved them to proper addresses. So almost all network access to Windows 2000 resources is going to route through DNS.*

As mentioned earlier in Chapter 2, *Active Directory Overview*, DNS routing can be seen in the following scenario:

1. A client moves from Site A to Site B.

2. When the client boots for the first time, it thinks it is still in Site A, so it proceeds to contact a DC in Site A.

3. The DC in Site A receives the request and realizes that the client should now be talking to any DC that is available in Site B.

4. The server does a lookup for a DC in Site B. If there is no local DC in that new site, the server will authenticate the client anyway. However, if there is a DC in Site B, the server responds with the address of a DC in Site B using a message like "Don't use me; use this DC local to you instead."

5. The client then contacts the suggested DC in Site B. Three things can happen: the DC responds and authenticatse the client; the DC fails to respond (it could be down) and the client searches, finds, and authenticates with another DC in Site B; or the DC fails to respond and the client searches and fails to find another DC in Site B, instead turning back to the DC in Site A and authenticating with the original server.

This all happens via DNS lookups.

---

* Those in the know realize this effectively signals a death knell for WINS, the NetBIOS name to address resolver service. More information on how WINS has changed can be found in an article I wrote for *Windows 2000 Magazine* (formerly *Windows NT Magazine*) entitled "Tombstones Mark the Coming of the End for WINS." The article can be accessed from *http://www.winntmag.com/Magazine/Author. cfm?AuthorID=306&Action=Author.*

For more information on how DNS works, I would suggest you get a copy of *DNS on Windows NT* by Paul Albitz, Matt Larson, and Cricket Liu (O'Reilly).

Give Me Facts!

Windows 2000 uses and expects to communicate with a name server that understands dynamic updates when it is installed for the first time. This is actually in an effort to ease your workload. Effectively, if you have a DNS server that supports dynamic updates, your clients can update the server with any records that it may need about those clients. *DNS* refers to a standard server and *DDNS* to a DNS server that supports dynamic updates.

The text of RFC 2136 that defines dynamic DNS can be found at *http://src.doc.ic.ac.uk/computing/internet/rfc/rfc2136.txt.*

Microsoft jumped quickly onto this bandwagon and adopted the standard with Windows 2000. Whenever a Windows 2000 server or client is installed, it will try to contact the DNS server that it is configured with to place entries in the database. A workstation or member server requires only a single entry to be added to the DNS, that of its name and IP address. However, during promotion of a DC, making changes to an existing DC, or demoting (i.e., removing) a DC, a number of entries will need to be added to or removed from the DNS. A sizable number definitely need adding for the promotion of a DC that is creating a new domain.

Your clients, servers, and domains definitely need the DNS in order to intercommunicate, so you have two choices:

- You can install a DDNS server on the network so that your workstations, servers, and domains can all update the DDNS automatically with any records that they require.

- You can update any other DNS on your network manually or via any programmatic methods that you've developed, adding in the data that each client, server, and domain requires.

Let me elaborate with an example. Let's say that Mycorp wants to create the first domain in the *mycorp.com* domain tree but does not choose to use a DDNS. Whether this domain is a Windows NT upgrade to Windows 2000 or a brand new Windows 2000 installation makes little difference here. Mycorp's administrator has chosen to name the domain using the Internet domain name that Mycorp owns, and the *mycorp.com* zone[*] is created on an ordinary DNS. The server is first installed as a member server in a workgroup with a static TCP/IP address and other details including the name *moose.mycorp.com*.

At this point, errors will appear in the event log about name registration. These errors indicate that the server is trying to automatically update the *mycorp.com* DNS, with its *moose.mycorp.com* name and IP address. However, the *mycorp.com* zone is being hosted by a DNS, not a DDNS, so it will not accept these updates. In fact, errors are likely to appear for the *mycorp.com* domain on the primary DNS server for that zone as well. The administrators can happily ignore these errors, but they should add the required data manually.

These error messages will continue to be generated at regular intervals because the Windows 2000 system still tries to update the DNS *even if the data already exists in an identical fashion*. All Windows 2000 knows is that it hasn't succeeded in the update, so it keeps on trying. The solution is to change a registry flag on the server so that it does not participate in dynamic updates.

The administrators then run DCPROMO and try to promote the server to a DC. The promotion succeeds, but the DC complains that it cannot update the DNS with new entries and asks if they want to write the changes to a file (*%Systemroot%\System32\Config\Netlogon.dns*) for them to attempt a manual update at a later date. Mycorp's administrators agree and the DC is up and running. Event log errors are now starting to stack up about name registration, and DNS errors are mounting on the primary DNS server. While the server appears to be up, many administrators who do not understand how DDNS works may be wondering how stable the DC is. In fact, we now know that the server is perfectly stable, but the problem lies in its ability to contact other machines and vice versa.

Effectively, the server hosting the domain is trying to update a DDNS that obviously isn't available. Again these updates are continually attempted until they either succeed or the registry value is altered.

Now let's assume that I have an isolated network segment with no access available to the existing *mycorp.com* DNS servers wherever they may be. This way, I can put in a DDNS server that hosts the *mycorp.com* zone without affecting the existing DNS servers for *mycorp.com*.

I install Windows 2000 Server as a member server of a workgroup called *workgroup*, with a machine name of *moose.mycorp.com* and a valid TCP/IP address of

---

[*] A *zone* is a part of the Internet hierarchy that has been delegated. For example, if *mycorp.com* were owned and managed by Mycorp's own DNS servers, then Mycorp would be said to manage its own domain name from its own zone.

10.1.1.1. This is no different than before. However, after the installation of the initial member server (with the appropriate "cannot add DNS entries" errors), I deviate from the previous Mycorp setup and install Microsoft's Windows 2000 DNS service onto it. Initially I set up no zones on the DNS service, but I do modify the TCP/IP information for *moose* so that the DNS that it references is the one it is running. I now have a member server that sends all DNS name resolution queries to itself but that manages no zones. No entries can be added to the DNS yet, as no zones have been created. In other words, the server cannot auto-register its own name yet, so it will still generate those errors.

I now create a forward lookup zone for *mycorp.com* hosted on the DDNS on that server. In order to make the server auto-register itself with the DDNS, I find the Local Area Connection icon, which resides inside the My Network Places folder available from the Settings option on the Start menu. I can right-click on that icon and disconnect the local LAN. Once it's disconnected, I can then right-click on the icon and select the Reconnect option. This is the same as the system starting the network services on boot up after a reboot, but without needing the reboot. Bringing up a command prompt (or using the Run box from the Start menu) and typing `ipconfig /registerdns` does the same thing. If I then open up the *mycorp. com* zone in the DNS Manager MMC, and use the Refresh button a few times, I should now be able to see the host entry added for this server.

Although I discuss only forward lookup zones here, reverse lookup zones are also automatically updated if they exist.

At this point, I promote the server to be the first domain of a new tree in a new forest. The DC will then automatically register entries in the DDNS for the domain. When it has finished, the DNS will look something like this:

```
mycorp.com.        SOA    moose.mycorp.com administrator. (42 900 600 86400 3600)
mycorp.com.        NS     moose.mycorp.com
moose              A      10.1.1.1

mycorp.com.        A      10.1.1.1

ee032e19-aa13-11d2-b2a4-00104b62b635            CNAME  moose.mycorp.com
ee032e19-aa13-11d2-b2a4-00104b62b635._msdcs CNAME  moose.mycorp.com

gc._msdcs          A      10.1.1.1

_gc._tcp           SRV    priority=0, weight=0, port=3268,
    moose.mycorp.com
_gc._tcp.default-first-site-name._sites SRV    priority=0, weight=0, port=3268,
    moose.mycorp.com
```

```
_kerberos._tcp                    SRV     priority=0, weight=0, port=88, moose.mycorp.com
_kerberos._tcp.dc._msdcs          SRV     priority=0, weight=0, port=88, moose.mycorp.com
_kerberos._tcp.default-first-site-name._sites SRV  priority=0, weight=0, port=88,
    moose.mycorp.com
_kerberos._tcp.default-first-site-name._sites.dc._msdcs SRV priority=0, weight=0,
    port=88, moose.mycorp.com
_kerberos._udp                    SRV     priority=0, weight=0, port=88, moose.mycorp.com

_kpasswd._tcp                     SRV     priority=0, weight=0, port=464, moose.mycorp.com
_kpasswd._udp                     SRV     priority=0, weight=0, port=464, moose.mycorp.com

_ldap._tcp                        SRV     priority=0, weight=0, port=389, moose.mycorp.com
_ldap._tcp.dc._msdcs              SRV     priority=0, weight=0, port=389, moose.mycorp.com
_ldap._tcp.default-first-site-name._sites SRV  priority=0, weight=0, port=389,
    moose.mycorp.com
_ldap._tcp.default-first-site-name._sites.dc._msdcs SRV priority=0, weight=0,
    port=389, moose.mycorp.com
_ldap._tcp.default-first-site-name._sites.gc._msdcs SRV priority=0, weight=0,
    port=3268, moose.mycorp.com
_ldap._tcp.ee032e1a-aa13-11d2-b2a4-00104b62b635.domains._msdcs SRV   priority=0,
    weight=0, port=389, moose.mycorp.com
_ldap._tcp.gc._msdcs              SRV     priority=0, weight=0, port=3268, moose.mycorp.com
_ldap._tcp.pdc._msdcs             SRV     priority=0, weight=0, port=389, moose.mycorp.com
```

While it may look complicated, it isn't. Let's go through what these records actually mean, splitting the records up into sections for ease of understanding.

To start with, you have three records that dictate the *mycorp.com* zone information in the DNS:

```
mycorp.com.       SOA     moose.mycorp.com administrator. (42 900 600 86400 3600)
mycorp.com.       NS      moose.mycorp.com
moose             A       10.1.1.1
```

First a standard start-of-authority (SOA) record for the *mycorp.com* zone is now installed on *moose*. We also have an address (A) or hostname record in order to resolve the name *moose* and a name server (NS) record indicating that *moose* hosts the *mycorp.com* zone on its DNS server. If you add another DNS server in the future, more NS records are added in here as usual.

 The trailing dots on some of the names indicate that these are Fully Qualified Domain Names (FQDNs) and do not need the domain name of *mycorp.com* concatenated onto them.

For example, *moose* (no dot) should be converted to *moose.mycorp.com* whereas *mycorp.com* (dot) should not be converted to *mycorp.com.mycorp.com*.

Next you have another A record:

```
mycorp.com.       A       10.1.1.1
```

This is the record for the domain itself. Whenever a query comes in to request a list of DCs for that domain, this value is passed back in response. If you later added two more DCs, the three values in the DNS would look something like this:

```
mycorp.com.      A      10.1.1.1
mycorp.com.      A      10.1.1.2
mycorp.com.      A      10.1.1.3
```

Then if a query came in again, all three would be returned. If you want to test this, simply do an **nslookup** on any domain for yourself. Here I have issued four separate queries, one after the other:

```
> nslookup mycorp.com
Server:   moose.mycorp.com
Address:  10.1.1.1

Name:     mycorp.com
Addresses:  10.1.1.1, 10.1.1.2, 10.1.1.3

> nslookup mycorp.com
Server:   moose.mycorp.com
Address:  10.1.1.1

Name:     mycorp.com
Addresses:  10.1.1.2, 10.1.1.3, 10.1.1.1

> nslookup mycorp.com
Server:   moose.mycorp.com
Address:  10.1.1.1

Name:     mycorp.com
Addresses:  10.1.1.3, 10.1.1.1, 10.1.1.2

> nslookup mycorp.com
Server:   moose.mycorp.com
Address:  10.1.1.1

Name:     mycorp.com
Addresses:  10.1.1.1, 10.1.1.2, 10.1.1.3
```

The addresses are being issued on what is known as a *round-robin* basis, i.e., the addresses returned are rotated with each query. Earlier in the chapter when I mentioned that a new workstation on the network would issue a query requesting a list of DCs to authenticate with, this is the method that it uses. So with 3 DCs and 300 new workstations needing to authenticate, 100 of the workstations should authenticate with each DC.

Next you have two addresses registered that look like this:

```
5f580a42-7582-11d2-9682-de30b96fb799          CNAME   moose.mycorp.com
5f580a42-7582-11d2-9682-de30b96fb799._msdcs CNAME   moose.mycorp.com
```

These are alias or canonical name (CNAME) entries created for the GUID unique to the server called *moose*. The first is an alias to the server itself. If a query comes in for *5f580a42-7582-11d2-9682-de30b96fb799.mycorp.com* (zone appended as noted earlier), the DNS knows that this is actually a reference to *moose.mycorp. com* and refers the query to that address. If more DCs were added, extra entries would be added to the DNS for the corresponding GUIDs like this:

```
5f580a42-7582-11d2-9682-de30b96fb799        CNAME moose.mycorp.com
b32590db-61d2-11d2-ad0d-a7f09a611580        CNAME frasier.mycorp.com
c38677f5-432e-11d2-bd0e-fd1e4e64068e        CNAME niles.mycorp.com
```

The second alias resolves a query from a DC for *5f580a42-7582-11d2-9682-de30b96fb799._msdcs.mycorp.com* to the DC called *moose. msdcs* refers to Microsoft's Domain Controller Services and these addresses are used by the DCs to intercommunicate.

Next we have this A record:

```
gc._msdcs          A      10.1.1.1
```

This is a reference to a server that is holding a copy of the Global Catalog. So whenever a Global Catalog query comes in, the referral is to our *moose* server, which, being the only DC at present must have a copy of the GC. If later when we have three DCs, we decide we want a second GC server, during the modification to keep a copy of the GC on an extra DC, a record is automatically added with an identical name but a different address.

```
gc._msdcs          A      10.1.1.1
gc._msdcs          A      10.1.1.3
```

This means that global catalog queries now have an equal chance of hitting either server, as both addresses are returned in a round-robin fashion when requests for a valid GC come in to the DNS.

The last two sections hold a series of server resource records (SRVs) like this:

```
_gc._tcp                                 SRV    priority=0, weight=0, port=3268,
   moose.mycorp.com
_gc._tcp.default-first-site-name._sites SRV    priority=0, weight=0, port=3268,
   moose.mycorp.com

_kerberos._tcp            SRV    priority=0, weight=0, port=88, moose.mycorp.com
_kerberos._tcp.dc._msdcs  SRV    priority=0, weight=0, port=88, moose.mycorp.com
_kerberos._tcp.default-first-site-name._sites SRV priority=0, weight=0, port=88,
   moose.mycorp.com
_kerberos._tcp.default-first-site-name._sites.dc._msdcs SRV priority=0, weight=0,
   port=88, moose.mycorp.com
_kerberos._udp            SRV    priority=0, weight=0, port=88, moose.mycorp.com

_kpasswd._tcp             SRV    priority=0, weight=0, port=464, moose.mycorp.com
_kpasswd._udp             SRV    priority=0, weight=0, port=464, moose.mycorp.com
```

```
_ldap._tcp                 SRV     priority=0, weight=0, port=389, moose.mycorp.com
_ldap._tcp.dc._msdcs       SRV     priority=0, weight=0, port=389, moose.mycorp.com
_ldap._tcp.default-first-site-name._sites SRV priority=0, weight=0, port=389,
   moose.mycorp.com
_ldap._tcp.default-first-site-name._sites.dc._msdcs SRV priority=0, weight=0,
   port=389, moose.mycorp.com
_ldap._tcp.default-first-site-name._sites.gc._msdcs SRV priority=0, weight=0,
   port=3268, moose.mycorp.com
_ldap._tcp.ee032e1a-aa13-11d2-b2a4-00104b62b635.domains._msdcs SRV   priority=0,
   weight=0, port=389, moose.mycorp.com
_ldap._tcp.gc._msdcs       SRV     priority=0, weight=0, port=3268, moose.mycorp.com
_ldap._tcp.pdc._msdcs      SRV     priority=0, weight=0, port=389, moose.mycorp.com
```

That's a lot of records of type SRV with some very strange names littered with underscores. They were suggested in October 1996 in "Experimental" RFC 2052 "A DNS RR for Specifying the Location of Services (DNS SRV)." The full text can be found at *http://src.doc.ic.ac.uk/computing/internet/rfc/rfc2052.txt*. Simply put, SRV records allow you to specify server(s) on your network that should be used for specific protocols. These records also allow you to remap the port numbers for individual protocols if you want to.

Take an example of a web server and browser. If I want my browser to connect to *www.mycorp.com* over the HTTP protocol, I would type in *http://www.mycorp. com*. This would then transmit a request out to talk to port 80 on *www.mycorp. com*. Mycorp can put up an ftp server called *ftp.mycorp.com* that is a different machine than the web server. However, when I fire up my browser and type *ftp:// www.mycorp.com*, the command fails, as a port 20 query is redirected to the wrong machine. Mycorp wants to get every piece of traffic that they can, but they cannot use an alias (CNAME) entry from ftp to www and vice versa, as these records already exist. There was frankly little they could do before SRV RRs of RFC 2052. SRVs allow clients to query for which server(s) in an organization will serve a particular protocol and on which port number. So for the web/ftp example, with SRV resource records, Mycorp can put in the following records:

```
_www._tcp          SRV     priority=0, weight=0, port=80, www.mycorp.com
_ftp._tcp          SRV     priority=0, weight=0, port=20, ftp.mycorp.com
```

Now a newer client that supports the use of SRV records can query which Mycorp server will serve an ftp tcp request (*_ftp._tcp.mycorp.com*) and will be told to connect to the relevant server. Use of these SRV records is up to the individual applications and the resolver in the TCP/IP stack. Older stacks won't know anything, but newer software and stacks will, and their use will become more widespread.

There are three sets of entries for SRV RRs. The following relate to the GC:

```
_gc._tcp                                    SRV     priority=0, weight=0, port=3268,
   moose.mycorp.com
_gc._tcp.default-first-site-name._sites SRV         priority=0, weight=0, port=3268,
   moose.mycorp.com
```

TCP/IP Port Numbers

This viewpoint on TCP/IP is a good representation of traffic into a server's ports. When a server receives packet traffic from an application with a certain type of protocol, that traffic is designated to a particular port. If the traffic's contents need security, then it can be redirected to a secure port for that protocol instead. Each port has a unique number that identifies it.

Take web traffic for example. When you connect to a web site, you connect to port 80 using the HTTP protocol from a web browser. A web browser can also download files remotely using the FTP protocol. However, this protocol uses port 20 instead.

In Windows 2000, many protocols are used. However, some new ones may be unfamiliar to you. Here are some examples:

```
kerberos        88      Kerberos Secure Authentication
ldap            389     Lightweight Directory Access Protocol
kpasswd         464     Kerberos Passwords
msft-gc         3268    Microsoft Global Catalog
msft-gc-ssl     3269    Microsoft Global Catalog with LDAP/SSL
```

This information is gathered from a complete list of the Internet Assigned Numbers Authority (IANA) port numbers at *http://src.doc.ic.ac.uk/rfc/iana/ assignments/port-numbers.html.*

These will resolve queries asking which server will serve GC requests in the *mycorp.com* domain. The response will point the machine querying to *moose* on the standard 3268 GC port. Note that the second one is allowing queries based on specific sites. For a domain spanning multiple sites, you would have many different entries for each site here.

The next are for Kerberos authentication:

```
_kerberos._tcp            SRV    priority=0, weight=0, port=88, moose.mycorp.com
_kerberos._tcp.dc._msdcs  SRV    priority=0, weight=0, port=88, moose.mycorp.com
_kerberos._tcp.default-first-site-name._sites SRV  priority=0, weight=0, port=88,
   moose.mycorp.com
_kerberos._tcp.default-first-site-name._sites.dc._msdcs SRV priority=0, weight=0,
   port=88, moose.mycorp.com
_kerberos._udp            SRV    priority=0, weight=0, port=88, moose.mycorp.com

_kpasswd._tcp             SRV    priority=0, weight=0, port=464, moose.mycorp.com
_kpasswd._udp             SRV    priority=0, weight=0, port=464, moose.mycorp.com
```

These items point to port 88 or port 464, depending on the protocol, and some include the site information. The last sets are here:

```
_ldap._tcp                SRV    priority=0, weight=0, port=389, moose.mycorp.com
_ldap._tcp.dc._msdcs      SRV    priority=0, weight=0, port=389, moose.mycorp.com
_ldap._tcp.default-first-site-name._sites SRV  priority=0, weight=0, port=389,
```

```
moose.mycorp.com
_ldap._tcp.default-first-site-name._sites.dc._msdcs SRV priority=0, weight=0,
    port=389, moose.mycorp.com
_ldap._tcp.default-first-site-name._sites.gc._msdcs SRV priority=0, weight=0,
    port=3268, moose.mycorp.com
_ldap._tcp.ee032e1a-aa13-11d2-b2a4-00104b62b635.domains._msdcs SRV   priority=0,
    weight=0, port=389, moose.mycorp.com
_ldap._tcp.gc._msdcs      SRV     priority=0, weight=0, port=3268, moose.mycorp.com
_ldap._tcp.pdc._msdcs     SRV     priority=0, weight=0, port=389, moose.mycorp.com
```

These are for LDAP queries to ports 389 (pure LDAP) and 3268 (GC protocol). Note the last one hiding in the shrubbery. This points the user to which DC is acting as the current PDC in a mixed-mode domain.

When servers need to do lookups, replicate, or perform many other tasks, they all route through the DNS via queries. The DNS has to be continually queried, since the server entries themselves can be dynamic. There is no point in a client caching which DC is the FSMO PDC Master right now, in case the server crashes and an administrator forces the FSMO PDC Master on another DC, changing the DNS entry to point to the new server in the process. The DNS is always queried for this reason. Active Directory holds all the replication connections, site layouts, and so on, as shown earlier. Yet when it comes time to communicate, the DC queries the DNS for the GUID entries or whatever it requires and then establishes communication with the server and port number supplied in the result of the query.

How You Already Use TCP/IP and DNS

While this book is on Windows 2000's Active Directory, many readers will have little experience with TCP/IP and the DNS. This section is aimed at helping the TCP/IP beginner understand what is required to set up a Windows 2000 network.

Your organization is likely to fall into one of five categories:

- An organization without any Internet domain name of its own.

- A smaller organization with an already purchased and in-use Internet domain name. An ISP manages the domain for you at a cost and it has its own DNS servers for this domain. The clients in your organization do not have IP addresses allocated to them by your organization. If the clients wish to access the internet, possibly to modify your organization's web pages, then the client dials up an ISP through a modem and is allocated an IP address from the ISP's IP address pool after dialing up.

- A smaller organization with an already purchased and in-use Internet domain name. Either an ISP manages the domain for you remotely at a cost using its own DNS servers or you buy time from an agency that comes in and configures your own domain, TCP/IP data, and DNS servers. Your organization's clients have their own IP addresses managed by the ISP or the outsource company.

- An organization with an already purchased and in-use Internet domain name. Someone in your company manages the domain and uses DNS servers that *are* running one of Microsoft's DNS servers.

- An organization with an already purchased and in-use Internet domain name. Someone in your company manages the domain and uses DNS servers that *are not* running one of Microsoft's DNS servers, i.e., they are using Unix-based BIND DNS servers or similar.

These five distinctions will dictate how you approach the naming scheme and layout of your design to some extent (more on this in the actual design sections later in the chapter).

No Domain Name or IP Addresses

If your organization matches the first category, then you have no domain name or set of IP addresses that you are allowed to allocate to your machines. You have two options open to you. You can purchase a domain name and IP address range, thus moving your organization into one of the other categories, or you can fake a domain name and set of IP addresses. No, I'm not kidding. If you are the proud administrator of Alfie's Chip Shops, a medium-size organization that has never needed an Internet presence and in your mind won't gain anything from the organization getting one, there is nothing to stop you using *alfies.com, alfiesfishshops. com, mygreatnet.com, windows2000.com,* or even *microsoft.com,* confusing as that might be. Similarly with IP addresses, you can use whatever you like, although you might as well use one of the three networks designated specifically for use internally by organizations. I use Class A Network 10, with addresses like 10.1.1.1, throughout the book as that is my preference.

 If you want to read more about obtaining TCP/IP addresses for your network or about the three pools of addresses that are for internal use, look at RFC 1918 at *ftp://src.doc.ic.ac.uk/rfc/rfc1918.txt.* This document describes the adoption of TCP/IP in organizations that have no need of Internet connectivity, such as airport departure/arrival displays, cash registers connected via IP in banks, and so on.

All you will need is a single DNS server, and you can configure your domain. This is a possible solution and one that will work. Even if you have clients on your network that have modems or share a modem from a pool and dial up an ISP to access the Internet using a standard ISP account, you do not have any problems. In this case, the ISP will allocate IP addresses and names from a dynamic pool for the modem connection when you dial up and the name *fishclient.alfieschipshop. com* that you are using on your Windows 2000 LAN will be used only within the

LAN and never across the Internet. However, if you ever decide that you need an Internet presence, you will run into trouble if someone else has registered the name you have been using in the meantime. In that case, you will need to wipe out your entire Windows 2000 organization and start all over again because you cannot rename the root of domain trees.

The times of being able to easily acquire a Class B or C address space are long gone. Most new companies rent their pool of IP addresses from an ISP. ISPs obtain large numbers of addresses, and as long as you use the ISP and send your traffic through them, you can have the numbers. If you change ISPs, your organization will need to get new addresses via the new ISP that you move to.

If you want to obtain a set of addresses for your own personal use irrespective of ISP, you need to find an ISP that is also an Internet Registry (IR) provider. Many ISPs can sell you a domain name, but only those that are IRs can sell you various sizes of address pools. Of these IRs, some will host your addresses only as mentioned earlier, some will sell you addresses outright, some will sell you the addresses and then host them for you. It takes much more justification than ever before for organizations to acquire an address space for their use. You may find it all but impossible to do anything but rent a set of addresses from your ISP.

A Domain Name but No IP Addresses

In the second category, you have less of a problem. This time you have a domain name but no dedicated set of IP addresses that you are allowed to allocate to your machines on your Windows 2000 LAN. Regarding the domain name for your tree, assuming a simple scenario where you only want one domain tree and you want to use the IP domain that you already have, you still will need a DNS server on your network for Windows 2000 to work. However, if your ISP already hosts *mycorp.com* on the Internet, there is nothing to stop you hosting it internally on your own DNS as well. The LAN-based DNS server will serve your Windows 2000 network, and your ISP's DNS servers will host the internet version of the same name. As mentioned earlier, your dial-up IP addresses are separate from the ones you use on the LAN, so you can choose whatever IP addresses that you want if you wish, although again I suggest using one of the three available pools for an internal network. If you expect that at some point in the future your desktop PCs will all have direct Internet access whenever they need it, you really should think long and hard about purchasing a pool of TCP/IP addresses now.

An Externally Managed Domain Name and Set of IP Addresses

When you get to the next category, you begin to have a need to actually talk to your outsource supplier or ISP. At this point, you need a DNS that supports the Windows 2000 DNS requirements. If you have an ISP-managed domain, get in touch with your technical contact and ask him to find the answer to the following questions:

Q: We would like to install a Windows 2000 server network. In order to install the first Windows 2000 Server, it requires configuration with a TCP/IP domain name, and will then want to add a series of records to the corresponding DNS zone. I will be using the *mycorp.com* domain, and I will need some records added to the *mycorp.com* zone. Among the records Windows 2000 will want to add are some SRV Resource Records. Does your DNS server support these SRV Resource Records as detailed in RFC 2052? If it does not support SRV Resource Records, when will you be updating your DNS to support these records?

If the ISP responds that it will not be supporting SRV RRs, find another ISP to accommodate your requirements and move your business. Frankly, if your ISP is not willing to move with the times, it doesn't deserve your business. As SRV RRs are a requirement of the DNS that supports Windows 2000, you have to make sure that the DNS you are using supports them.

If you outsource, ask them a similar question about your own DNS. If they say that it doesn't, then you'll need to pay for an upgrade or replacement to the software. Assuming that your own DNS or the one provided by your existing ISP supports SRV RRs or will do soon, move on to the next question:

Q: Windows 2000 supports dynamic updates as specified in RFC 2136. Does your DNS support dynamic updates? If the DNS server does support dynamic updates, then is the dynamic update option turned on? Put another way, if our organization puts a Windows 2000 network in place, does the primary DNS server for our domain allow dynamic updates?

Let's be clear here. The DNS may *support* dynamic updates, yet have it turned off for any number of reasons. This isn't a problem, but you need to understand the implications. If the DNS for your domain name does not support dynamic updates (or the dynamic update option is turned off) your ISP or outsource supplier will have to do more work, which *they may charge you for.* Every time a new client or server is put on the network, the DNS will need to be updated. This could be done automatically if the DNS supported dynamic updates (and has the option turned on). Once you promote the first DC of your new Windows 2000 domain, the promotion process will complain. You will be asked whether you want to output the DNS information into a file for manual input later. Once you do this, you will need to pass the information to your technical contacts, and they will manually update the DNS with this information. You will also need to alter a registry setting on the DC to make sure that it doesn't keep trying to use dynamic update to the DNS. Then, for every other client and server that you install, DNS information will need to be added manually and the registry change made so that your event logs do not keep filling up.

Securing Your Dynamic Updates

The Internet Network Working Group that devised RFC 2136 did not advocate allowing it on a network in the absence of any security measures. This is because dynamic update makes it possible for anyone who can reach an authoritative name server to alter the contents of any zones on that server. This is obviously a serious increase in vulnerability from the previous technological standpoint of DNS.

What is recommended is an implementation of RFC 2137 (known generally as Secure Dynamic Update) or an equivalent technology of strong security measures, such as the TSIG Internet Draft, to secure your servers from wanton updates.

As this book is being written, Windows 2000's DNS does not support the TSIG security enhancements for two reasons. First, RFC 2137 is only currently in draft. Second, when you select to have an Active Directory integrated primary (more on this later) in the GUI, you allow the use of Active Directory's strong security.

Once the DNS is stored in Active Directory, it is represented as a series of objects in a hierarchy. These objects have ACLs the same as any other object, allowing you to restrict access to that hierarchy if you require. This is normally done through enabling Secure Dynamic Update, which allows only the computers that you specify to make new entries or modify existing entries in a zone. By default, all authenticated computers in a forest can make new entries in a zone, and only the computer that created an entry is allowed to modify the data associated with that entry.

Finally, while RFC 2137 security doesn't fit into this model at present, I expect Microsoft will issue more information on this matter as the RFC goes through later stages and Windows 2000's security begins to be heavily documented.

RFC 2137 can be found at *ftp://src.doc.ic.ac.uk/rfc/rfc2137.txt.*

An Internally Managed Domain Name and Set of IP Addresses Using a Microsoft DNS

This is fairly simple. If the DNS server is the one supplied with Microsoft Windows NT 4.0, then it needs an upgrade since this DNS does not support SRV RRs or dynamic updates. The easiest solution is to upgrade and use the DNS server supplied with Windows 2000. You just have to make sure that all the DNS servers for the zone are compliant prior to attempting to install the first DC of your domain.

One problem comes to mind when the server hosting the domain you want to use is not among the first servers that you want to update. Your only recourse in this case is to bring up two (or more) Windows 2000 servers as members of a workgroup, not a domain, and install the new DNS server software on them. Make these servers secondaries to the zone that you need. Then once the zone is fully updated and the clients in this zone are fully happy with the new setup, promote one of these secondary DNS servers to a primary and remove the zone from the original NT DNS. Now you have the zone running on a compliant DNS for your new domain. If that was too quick for you, look at it like this: *MOOSE* and *NILES* are two NT servers running a DNS hosting the *mycorp.com* zone. *MOOSE* is the primary and *NILES* is the secondary. Bring up *MARTIN* and *DAPHNE* as two Windows 2000 servers in a workgroup and install the DNS service on them. You now make *MARTIN* and *DAPHNE* additional secondaries for the *mycorp.com* zone and wait for all the zone transfers to take place. Next, promote *MARTIN* to be the primary for the zone and demote *MOOSE* to be a secondary. Then remove *mycorp.com* from *MOOSE* and *NILES*. Whether *MOOSE* and *NILES* hold other zones is immaterial; you have solved the problem of obtaining a Windows 2000–capable DNS.

An Internally Managed Domain Name and Set of IP Addresses Using a Non-Microsoft DNS

Without wishing to enter into a holy war with any DNS gurus who happen to be reading this, the simple truth of the matter is that if you set the system up as Microsoft would like you to, i.e., with proprietary Windows 2000 DNS servers, it will work. However, that will not be possible for many sites. Most large organizations that I talk to have Unix servers hosting their DNS domains. They have hosted domains for a number of years, with many DNS server software upgrades under their belts and in-house scripts for registering and manipulating the databases. Before Windows NT 4.0 was released in 1996, Microsoft didn't provide a DNS server. Neither did Novell with NetWare 3.x and early versions of NetWare 4.x. Unix was the obvious choice for a DNS server. A simple purchase of a Sun Unix box and a copy of the freeware Unix BIND software would run a DNS for your organization happily enough.

Now, with the advent of Windows 2000, you can change all that, with the emphasis on *can*. While Microsoft would love you to change over and use Windows 2000's DNS, there is no definite need to do so. If you have a dependent infrastructure of scripts and utilities that will take time to migrate, then you can happily stay as you are as long as you have a DNS that meets the following minimum requirements according to Microsoft's current thinking:

- Support for SRV RRs (RFC 2052)

- Support for dynamic update (RFC 2136)

- Support for incremental zone transfer (RFC 1995)

Let's look at these further. We know that we need SRV RRs for the service to work properly, so that is an accepted requirement. We also know that you don't need to have dynamic update if you are satisfied to manually register all your machines. So, that really isn't a requirement, providing you are willing to accept the consequences.

What about incremental zone transfer? In the old days when a change occurred in a DNS zone, the whole DNS zone file was passed across the network to the secondary servers. Now, using the RFC 1995 standard, individual records can be sent across the network when zone transfer needs to take place. If your DNS uses incremental zone transfer, it can negotiate with all versions of DNS and use the lowest common format that they both understand to transfer data.

If you're running a DNS on Unix, you are almost certainly running BIND as your DNS software. If so, then Unix BIND v8.1.2 is the minimal review for SRV RR and dynamic updates.

Dynamic Updates and Windows 2000's DHCP Server

It's time to bring up the subject of clients. It's all very well to go on about how Windows 2000 and Unix DNS servers can service domain names for your servers, but the clients are important too. If you allow only Windows 2000 and Windows 98 clients in your organization to access your new shiny Windows 2000 network, everything will work perfectly well. If, however, you have a mixture of what are termed *downlevel clients*, i.e., clients that are at a previous version of the operating system such as Windows 95, Windows 3.x, Windows NT 3.x, and Windows NT 4.x, you need to be aware that the TCP/IP component of these clients is not DDNS-aware. This means that these clients won't update your new sparkly Microsoft DDNS automatically.

To complicate matters, Microsoft's Windows 2000 DHCP server has been configured to be DDNS-aware. Windows 2000's DHCP server can register and update reverse lookup (PTR) and hostname (A) resource records on behalf of its

DHCP-enabled clients. To complicate matters further, the DHCP specification allows vendor-specific extensions to be defined. Microsoft decided to include Option-81, originally suggested by Cisco in October 1996, which relates to the return of a client's Fully Qualified Domain Name (FQDN) to the DHCP server.

When a client using DHCP is booted up, it requests its IP address, zone name, DNS server and also Option-81—the Fully Qualified Domain Name of the client, *and* the zone. By default, the Windows 2000 client will update forward and DHCP will update reverse lookup. This can be configured on the client. To restate:

- Windows 98 and Windows 2000 clients can update the DDNS.

- Downlevel clients cannot register their own data in the DDNS.

- Downlevel clients can make use of a DHCP server as a proxy to register their addresses in the DDNS for them, since the DHCP server itself is DDNS-aware.

- Option-81 allows the DHCP server to register more information than just the PTR and A. It allows dynamic configuration of the FQDN on the client.

This is effectively illustrated in Table 5-1.

Table 5-1. The Default Actions of Dynamic Update for a Variety of Clients

	Uses Microsoft's DHCP server for TCP/IP without Option-81	Uses Microsoft's DHCP server for TCP/IP with Option-81	Uses statically configured TCP/IP data or DHCP server that does not support DDNS
DDNS-aware (i.e., Windows 2000 or Windows 98)	Client registers all forward lookup zone entries, and the DHCP server registers reverse lookup PTR entries.	Client registers all forward lookup zone entries (including FQDN), and the DHCP server registers reverse lookup PTR entries.	Client registers all info in DDNS.
Downlevel client	DHCP server registers all forward lookup zone entries and all reverse lookup PTR entries.	DHCP server registers all forward lookup zone entries (including FQDN) and all reverse lookup PTR entries.	No automatic registration.

As you can see, the DHCP server can do different things depending on the client to which it is talking. You can also manually modify the DHCP server to operate in one of three ways:

- DHCP server updates both A and PTR records for clients always.

- DHCP server updates only PTR records.

- DHCP server updates both A and PTR records when client requests it.

The next section addresses the design considerations for running the DNS for your Windows 2000 network using Microsoft's DNS Server as opposed to any other DNS server.

Integrated DNS

If you have decided not to use Microsoft's Windows 2000 DNS software, then this section explains what value-added capabilities you will be unable to make use of. On the other hand, if you've seen the light or are undecided, let me explain what integrated DNS is all about.

In the normal world of DNS, you have two types of name servers: primary masters and secondary masters (a.k.a. secondaries or slaves). The primary master name server for a zone holds the data for the zone in a file on the host and reads the entries from there. Each zone has only one primary master. A secondary master gets the contents of its zone from the primary master that is authoritative for the zone. Each primary master name server can have multiple secondary master name servers. When a secondary master starts up, it contacts its primary master and requests a copy of the relevant zone via zone transfer. The contents of the secondary masters file are then dynamically updated over time according to a set scheme. This is normally either a periodic update or triggered automatically by a message from the primary master stating that it has experienced an update. This is a very simplified picture, as each name server can host multiple zones, allowing each server to have a primary master role for some zones and a secondary master for others.

 Sorry, DNS aficionados, caching DNS servers are not relevant here so I'm not covering them.

Each type of server can resolve name queries that come in. However, if a change has to be made to the underlying contents of the DNS file, it has to be made on the primary master name server for that zone. Secondary master name servers cannot accept updates.[*]

If you have a Windows 2000 network and use Windows 2000's DNS server, then you can optionally integrate your DNS server into Active Directory. Effectively, this means that you can store the contents of the zone file in Active Directory as a

---

[*] This isn't strictly true. While slaves cannot process updates, they can and do forward updates that they receive to their master name server.

hierarchical structure. Integrating the DNS into Active Directory will mean that the DNS structure is replicated among all DCs. From that moment on, all DCs will be able to respond and resolve name lookup requests. In effect, this makes all the DCs like secondary masters. This makes the DNS much more fault tolerant instantly, since you have so many more secondary masters on the network. Not bad in itself, but there's more. Each DC also will allow updates to the DNS. Each DC holds a writeable copy of the DNS. This effectively makes the entire set of DCs act like primary master name servers, where each DC can write to the zone and can issue authoritative answers for the zone. This automatically applies to all DCs when you integrate. This is a far cry from the standard model of one primary master name server and one or more secondary master name servers.

Leveraging the Integration

Let's say that I have 10 DCs running *mycorp.com*, with one acting as the primary DNS and one acting as the secondary. I have 300 clients that point to these two DNS servers. I now integrate the DNS into Active Directory. When all 300 clients want to issue DNS queries, they still do so to the primary master as they would have done before the integration. If the primary master fails, the secondary will still resolve queries in the same way. When the clients boot and perform dynamic update, they all update the primary master DNS. However, if the primary master fails, the secondary now can receive and will accept dynamic updates to the DNS. Dynamic update is fault tolerant after the primary master fails.

This doesn't seem particularly thrilling so far. After all, if a client comes along and needs to update the DNS via dynamic update, in theory it can pick any server to do so. Yet if the client will update only the DNS servers that it knows about starting with the first in its list, what was the point of integrating the DNS? You can now use any or all of the 10 servers in any order as the DNS list for the client. You could provide an order of 6,7,8,9,10,1,2,3,4,5 for half the machines and 1,2,3,4,5,6,7,8,9,10 for the other half. This means that the queries would at least get load-balanced, so that while DC1 and DC6 stayed up and working, they would only receive half the query traffic.

Interraction can also help when your clients are down at the end of a slow link where you have placed a DC to help them authenticate. If you had no DNS/Active Directory integration, you would have to install and run a secondary master at that location or accept that TCP/IP resolution would be slower down that link. Alternatively, if you had integrated the DNS with Active Directory, your clients at that location could use that DC on their site as their primary contact for DNS. Other off-site DNS servers would be configured second, third, and so on down the clients list. Doing this would mean that you would not have to run a separate DNS server at that site and would receive fast DNS query resolution.

How DNS Affects Design

Microsoft understands that many organizations setting up Windows 2000 networks will already have a DNS infrastructure. Consequently, you don't have to run Microsoft's DNS server, integrate DNS with Active Directory, or anything fancy like this at all. However, if you do use TCP/IP heavily on your network, then the layout of that infrastructure will have a bearing on your design of your network.

I think the easiest way to look at how DNS affects design is with a series of guidelines. I'll go through each one in turn, explaining its relevance:

- Don't make the NetBIOS name and the DNS hostname different.

- Name your domains appropriately.

- Don't have conflict with an existing DNS infrastructure.

- If you integrate DNS with Active Directory, you still need a nominated primary DNS server.

- Larger zones that span sites will generate more replication within Active Directory if their DNS is integrated.

Don't Make the NetBIOS Name and the DNS Hostname Different

Windows 2000 still incorporates the NetBIOS naming scheme as well as TCP/IP. Microsoft hasn't completely shed the shackles of NetBIOS naming, even if it isn't used much in Windows 2000. So, as both are used, each can be distinctly named, although I don't recommend it. Windows 2000 is complex enough without adding to it by introducing complexities where a host is named one way for NetBIOS and another for TCP/IP.

Name Your Domains Appropriately

You cannot rename a domain once it is created. Make sure you name it right on the first try. At Leicester University, we named our first domain, the forest root domain, *ntservice.le.ac.uk*. Unfortunately, the Windows NT 5.0 operating system was renamed Windows 2000. The operating system now didn't have NT in the name any more, so *ntservice* made no sense at all. Consequently, when we decided on a new name, we had to wipe our existing network out of existence and create a structure based on our new name.

Also remember that if your domain is called *bunny.mycorp.com*, your Windows 2000 client logon dialog box will ask for a username and password to *bunny*. The name that you choose for your domain is visible, so be careful to choose an appropriate one.

Be careful naming your network around the current name of the operating system, i.e., *windows2000.mycorp.com*, or *win2k.mycorp. com*. When you upgrade in 2002 to a new operating system, the name will not be appropriate any more, and you may have quite a job on your hands to change the existing name at that time. The name *Windows* seems fairly static, so *windows.mycorp.com* may be appropriate, but who can say?

You Don't Have To Conflict Existing Infrastructures

If you have a large organization with multiple workstations and many machines, with Windows 2000 being only a small subset, you probably have no desire to let your Windows 2000 network demand to be in the root of your existing domain.

For example, let's say that *mycorp.com* had tens of thousands of Mac, Unix, and PC clients on IntraNetware, Unix, and NT networks. The DNS administrator may not want the Windows 2000 network to sit at the root of the existing domain. Instead he may wish to make a subdomain, say *windows.mycorp.com*, for your network infrastructure to sit under. This isn't a problem. Leicester University's Windows 2000 network has been set up this way. The university already had an existing DNS infrastructure running on Unix BIND servers, and we saw no need to go in and break up the party. Various departments and sections had their own servers as subdomains, so we created a new zone for the Windows 2000 network.

We did put a Windows 2000 DNS server in as being authoritative for the subdomain, with all clients in this subdomain dynamically updating the DNS. We did this because we wanted the Windows 2000 subdomain clients to be capable of supporting dynamic updates to the DNS, but the main campus servers in other subdomains and the main domain do not have this facility.

If You Integrate DNS with Active Directory, You Still Need a Nominated Primary DNS Server

We know that the Internet DNS structure is hierarchical. These superiors further up the hierarchy need to communicate with our name servers, specifically through our primary name server that is authoritative for the *mycorp.com* zone, for example. For this to work, you still need a primary name server to which to refer name servers above you in the hierarchy. Referring them to a DC will not do.

This is true even if you are using a subdomain for your Windows 2000 network. You still need to refer the DNS server for your Windows 2000 network to its superior. Take Leicester University as an example; the subdomain that we set up still needs a primary name server that talks to the main campus primary name server that allocated it the zone in the first place.

Larger Zones That Span Sites Will Generate More Replication Within Active Directory if Their DNS Is Integrated

No matter how global or how many sites your organization covers, if it is very decentralized, you are likely to have a larger number of DNS zones than a centralized organization would. Obviously for two companies of similar size, this also means that the centralized organization has zones that are a lot larger, as each zone needs to contain more hosts in a smaller number of zones. In a centralized organization, these large zones are likely to span sites, requiring much more traffic over a wider area than if you had a decentralized organization.

So, with a centralized organization with larger zones that span sites, if you set up your DNS as an Active Directory integrated primary master name server (what a mouthful!), then your Active Directory replication between DCs across WAN links will include the DNS entries. As I'll show in Chapter 7, *Sites and Replication Topologies*, Active Directory replication has been optimized across WAN links. So while it may not be too much of a problem to include DNS updates in the replication traffic, you need to be aware that such traffic will exist.

Summary

Microsoft's Windows 2000 operating system can initially look complex with Organizational Units, forests, domain trees, and domains. In fact, each one is fairly straightforward, and I hope these first five chapters have helped you to get a clearer picture of the way that things work.

You do not need to have a domain name for your organization to make Windows 2000 work, providing that you never need to communicate with the Internet from your network. You also do not need your own IP address pool; even the Internet Network Working Group acknowledges that. If you don't have a set of IP addresses, just use one of the three available unassigned pools for internal networks. If this chapter has encouraged your organization to get a domain name, then all is well and good.

With Windows 2000, Microsoft incorporated some of the latest enhancements to TCP/IP and DNS. Windows 2000's support for dynamic updates in its own Dynamic DNS, allowing Windows 2000 clients to update the DNS server automatically, is quite a step forward for administration of complex networks. If introduced organization wide, manual registrations are consigned to obsolescence. Choosing to integrate your DNS into Active Directory gives you the fault tolerance of secondary master name servers while actually giving you the capabilities of many multiple master name servers, without needing to actually install them on each server.

II

Designing the Directory Hierarchy

Because Active Directory is so intricately linked with Windows 2000, these chapters effectively cover how to design a Windows 2000 network. Chapter 6 details how to tailor a design that fits your organization. Chapter 7 covers how to represent your physical network infrastructure inside the Active Directory, so that replication and bandwidth are used effectively. Although the designs will be separate projects, they do intertwine and to some extent each can have a bearing on the other in certain areas.

You should start your design with the namespace. However, you will not be able to complete the logical namespace design until you have the physical design sketched out. It's very much a chicken and egg situation. You should plan to go through and complete a rough draft of the namespace design, then make a rough draft of the physical design, and then consider modifications to both.

Then you can consider the Group Policy Object (GPO) design. Group Policy Objects control such things as user-environment lockdown, forced registry changes, application availability, and so on to sets of machines or users. Because these relate to sites, domains, Organizational Units, users, computers, and groups in your Active Directory, it makes sense in my experience to incorporate these changes into a namespace and site design that already exist.

You can then take a look at security and at tailoring Active Directory to your own requirements by modifications to the Schema. Finally, this section takes a brief look at the present and the future of integrating and interoperating Active Directory with other directories and operating systems and of migrating to Active Directory.

- Chapter 6, *Designing the Namespace*, introduces the steps and techniques involved in properly preparing a design that reduces the number of domains and increases administrative control through the use of Organizational Units.

- Chapter 7, *Sites and Replication Topologies*, shows you how to design a representation of your physical infrastructure within Active Directory in order to gain very fine grained control over intrasite and intersite replication.

- Chapter 8, *Profiles and Group Policy Primer*, gives you a detailed introduction into the capabilities of both user profiles and Group Policy Objects.

- Chapter 9, *Designing Organization-Wide Policies*, explains how Group Policy Objects function in Active Directory and how you can properly design an Active Directory structure to make the most effective use of them.

- Chapter 10, *Active Directory Security: Permissions and Auditing*, describes how you can design effective security for all areas of your Active Directory, both in terms of access to objects and their properties, it includes information on how to design effective security access logging to any areas you choose.

- Chapter 11, *Designing Schema Changes*, covers procedures for extending the classes and properties in the Active Directory Schema.

- Chapter 12, *Windows NT 4.0 Migration*, gives very basic guidelines on areas to think about when conducting a Windows NT 4.0 migration. This is only an introduction to the subject; readers looking for step-by-step guides or detailed studies of migration will need to look elsewhere.

- Chapter 13, *Directory Interoperability*, looks into what methods exist now and will exist in the future for integrating the Active Directory with other directories and data stores. While it goes into detail on the Active Directory Connector for connecting the Active Directory to Microsoft Exchange, the rest of the chapter is an overview of the options available rather than a detailed analysis.

6

Designing the Namespace

The basic emphasis of this chapter is to reduce the number of domains that you require for Windows 2000 while gaining administrative control over sections of the namespace using Organizational Units. This chapter aims to help you create a domain namespace design. That includes all the domains you will need, the forest and domain-tree hierarchies, and the contents of those domains in terms of Organizational Units and even groups.

There are a number of restrictions that you have to be aware of when creating Active Directory designs. I will introduce you to them in context as I go along, but here are the most important:

- Too many Group Policy Objects (GPOs) means a long logon time as the group policies are applied to sites, domains, and Organizational Units. This obviously has a bearing on your Organizational Unit structure, as a 10-deep Organizational Unit tree with GPOs applying at each branch will incur more GPO processing than a 5-deep Organizational Unit tree with GPOs at each branch.

- You cannot rename a domain tree once it has been created. Leicester University had to go through a complete domain wipe and rebuild to change a domain name, and at that time, the service wasn't large and it was fairly easy to manage. I wouldn't fancy doing the same thing with a huge domain, though.

- You can never remove the forest root domain without destroying the whole forest in the process. The forest root domain is the cornerstone of your forest.

- The Schema Admins group will exist only in the forest root domain. So if you are migrating from a previous version of NT, you have to make sure that the first domain that you migrate is the one that you want to be in charge of Schema changes.

- Schema changes are not reversible. If you add an object called Shopfitterk, but the letter *k* is a mistake, the object is created for good. You can disable it so that it can never be used, but you can never remove it from the underlying directory.

- During the course of the writing of this book, the successor to Exchange 5.5 has been called Exchange 6.0, Exchange Platinum, and Exchange 2000. I'll use the latter. Fully functioning clients of Exchange 2000, such as Microsoft Outlook 2000, are not designed to use LDAP to access the Exchange directory, and instead use the Messaging API (MAPI) to intercommunicate. While the Exchange 2000 directory is potentially accessible via LDAP, the Exchange 2000 message store is accessible only via MAPI, so pure LDAP would not give you full functionality anyway. So when you put your Exchange 2000 server into your new Windows 2000 domain, you will find that the GC is the total scope of the Exchange data that can be searched and Active Directory cannot. This drastically limits what Exchange can see within Active Directory. When you use Outlook to examine the contents of the Contacts or Address-Book, you cannot access the phone number by default, since that is not a property stored in the GC. Of course, you can add the phone number to the GC, but that means that you end up with more data in the GC than you would normally choose to have.

- This leads to another problem with the GC: the lack of a regional catalog. Imagine that you have 20 printers in your office in Sweden and 12 printers in your office in Brazil. The users in Sweden will never need to print to the printers in Brazil, and the users in Brazil will never need to print to the printers in Sweden. However, by default, details of all printers are published in the GC. So, whenever changes are made to printers in Sweden, all the changes get replicated to the GCs on the Brazil servers because the GC replicates all of its data everywhere. You have two options. You can decide not to replicate any printer data and force printer searches to hit Active Directory each time, or you can replicate all printer data everywhere.

- Multiple domains cannot be hosted on a single DC. Imagine three domains, off a root located in the United States, which correspond to three business units. Now imagine a small office of 15 people in Eastern Europe or Latin America with a slow link to the main site. The 15 users are made up of three sets of five; each set of five users uses one of the three business units/domains. If you as an administrator decide that the slow link is too slow and you would like to put in a DC for the three domains at the local server and to ease replication, then the small office will have to install three DCs. Hosting multiple domains will not be introduced until at least the next version of the operating system after Windows 2000.

The Complexities of a Design

Active Directory is a complex beast, and designing for it isn't easy. Take a look at a fictitious global company called PetroCorp depicted in Figure 6-1.

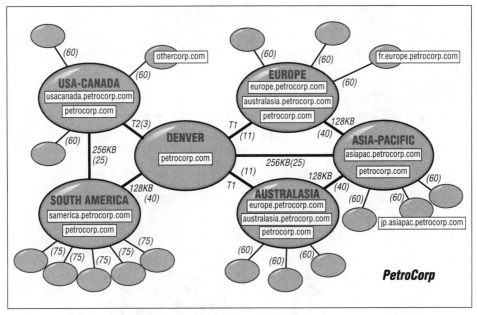

Figure 6-1. The sites and servers of a company called PetroCorp

Here you can see a huge network of sites linked with various network connections across wide area networks. A variety of domains seem to exist for *othercorp. com* and *petrocorp.com*, and as each one of those square boxes represents a single domain controller (the servers that host Active Directory in an organization), you can see that some of the servers will need to replicate data across those WAN links. *petrocorp.com*, for example, seems to need to replicate to all of the major sites, since it has domain controllers (DCs) in each of those sites.

Take a look at Figure 6-2, which shows a much more complex hierarchy.

It's possible to see the users and computers in all the Organizational Units in this view, and the structure seems to be set up so that Group Policy Objects (GPOs, represented by trapezoids) can act on various portions of the tree. These GPOs could be anything from what menus appear on the screen to what applications can be run to what hardware is available for each user.

Following is a discussion of the principles and processes that will help you create complicated designs like these to mirror the complexities in your own organization.

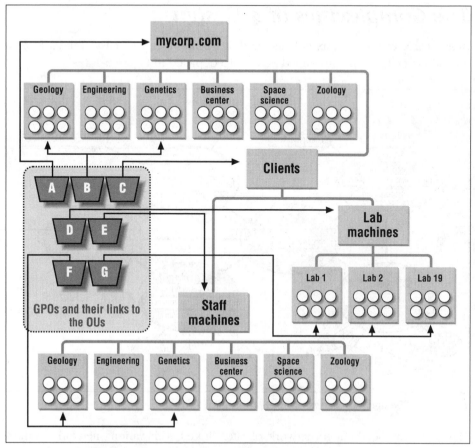

Figure 6-2. A complex domain tree showing GPOs

Where to Start

Before you sit down to make your design, you will need to obtain some important pieces of information. You will need a copy of your organizational structure. This is effectively the document that explains how your organization's business units fit together in the hierarchy. Next you will need a copy of the geographical layout of your company. This includes the large-scale picture in continents and countries and also the individual states, counties, or areas in which you have business units. Third, you will need a copy of the network diagram, indicating the speeds of connection between the various sites. Finally, you need a copy of any diagrams and information on any systems that will need to interface to Active Directory, like existing X.500 databases, so that you can take them into account. Once you've gathered the information, you can sit down and plan your design.

Overview of the Design Process

The namespace design process takes place in three stages:

Design of the Domain Namespace
During the first stage, you actually deal with the namespace design itself. That means calculating the number of domains that you need, designing the forest and tree structure, and defining the naming scheme for workstations, servers, and the network as a whole.

Design of the Internal Domain Structure
During the second stage, you need to concentrate on the internal structure of each domain that you have previously noted. Here you also need to use your business model as a template for the internal structure and then move on to consider how administration and other rights will be delegated. The internal structure can also be modified depending on how you intend to use Group Policy Objects; this will be covered in Chapter 9, *Designing Organization-Wide Policies.*

Global Catalog Design
During the third stage, you work out your designs for the global catalog (GC).

 When you are finished with your design, you can implement the design by setting up a test forest in a lab environment. This will enable you to get a better feel for how the design actually works and whether there is anything you have failed to consider. I can't stress the use of a test environment enough.

Domain Namespace Design

The first stage in your design is to work out the domain, domain-tree, and forest configuration of your network. The best way to do this is to make a first pass at designing the domains and then structure them together into a series of trees. Before we start, however, let's take a look at our objectives for this part of the design.

Objectives

There are two objectives for the design of the domain namespace:

- Designing Active Directory to represent the structure of your business
- Minimizing the number of domains by making much more use of the more flexible Organizational Units

Represent the structure of your business

You need to make Active Directory look as much like your business structure, geographical or organizational, as possible. With geographical structure, your business runs itself as self-contained units within each geographical site. In this model, people at those sites handle administration for each site. Under the organizational or political model, the business is based on a series of departments that have members from a number of different geographical sites. Normally, with this structure, the organization has a head office for all departments at one location, but that is not always the case.

In the former model, finance units based in France and Australia would be separate finance departments. In the latter model, France and Australia would have geographical finance branches of a larger finance department controlled from a head office.

It doesn't matter to Active Directory which model you choose, except that the intention is to mirror the structure of your business in the Active Directory design. If your business crosses both of these boundaries, then it becomes less clear-cut. In order to make your design simpler to understand, you should choose to go with one model or the other. I would not suggest a mix-and-match approach unless you can definitely rationalize it, adequately represent it on paper, and delegate administration effectively.

If you already have a large investment in a TCP/IP infrastructure with business/organization- or geographic-centered DNS zones or you have a large existing Exchange organization, then you can use this as the basis of your design. Simply stated, if your DNS or Exchange setup is based on one model, then go with that model for your Active Directory design. It should be obvious that it will be easier for an administrator to think about both areas if the designs are based on the same model.

Minimize the number of domains

Remember that Windows 2000 emphasizes reducing the number of domains that you need. Each forest can store 10 million objects, with a recommendation that no more than 1 to 2 million* go in any one domain, which is more than enough for all the users, groups, and computers in most organizations. So size isn't a consideration. Each domain can also be partitioned using Organizational Units, allowing you to delegate different administrators for each Organizational Unit in a domain if

---

* The upper limit recommendation is still being worked out at present. This is why there is such a large span.

you so desire. You do not have to create a new domain if you wish to delegate administration over a part of the system. These two aspects of Active Directory tend to eliminate a number of sizing and permission problems associated with traditional NT installations.

If you're an experienced NT domain designer, start trying to push the tendency to create multiple domains from your mind. Think in terms of multiple Organizational Units instead.

Step 1—Decide on the Number of Domains

Start by imagining that every object is to be stored in one domain. This will give you a much simpler layout for administration. It doesn't matter what the domain is called for now; just label it as your organization's main/sole domain.

Now expand the number of domains that you have by adding other domains that you can give specific justification for. While the number of objects and delegation of administration are not good reasons for creating new domains, there are three main reasons that would require more domains:

- The need to isolate replication
- A requirement for a unique domain policy
- A requirement for keeping a Windows NT domain

If you can match any of these criteria, then write down a new domain for that area.

Isolated replication

While replication is mainly discussed in the next chapter, it does have a bearing here on domain design. If you have a headquarters and a branch office connected via a slow link, and you don't want to use up any bandwidth at all in replicating domain directory data from the main domain to the branch offices, you need to consider creating a separate domain for the branch office.

A slow link in an ideal case is defined as a 256-KB link with 128-KB spare capacity. However, each organization will need to make its own decision about what it will accept as a minimum for a slow-link; the value could be 64 KB or 1 MB. As we are only drafting the namespace and physical site/replication designs and then coming back to revise both using the combined data, the exact figure for a slow link in your organization is not important right now.

This will ensure that only limited traffic is replicated between both offices. In fact, this will be limited to the GC, configuration, and Schema information only.

So if you want to really minimize traffic down a link, create a new domain for the remote office. In most cases, this isn't necessary.

Unique domain policy

In Chapter 8, *Profiles and Group Policy Primer* and Chapter 9, *Designing Organization-Wide Policies*, I will explain the basics of Group Policy Objects (GPOs) and how to properly design them. For now the important thing to understand is that policies are Active Directory objects that reference a number of settings that can be applied to users or computers. These settings are things like a fixed desktop, a certain core set of applications, the ability of users to perform a shutdown, and so on. If you're coming from a Windows NT background, these are Windows NT system policies on a much grander scale. GPOs can be applied to various parts of your Active Directory structure. If you create an Organizational Unit called Finance and then decide that OU=Finance needs special settings, you can create a GPO and assign it to OU=Finance. Then all the computer settings in the GPO will be applied to all computers in OU=Finance, and all the user settings in the GPO will be applied to the users in OU=Finance.

For my exercise, we need to look at what settings have to be applied on a domain-by-domain basis. Here's a list of what types of settings can be set only on a domain-wide basis:

- Password policies, such as password length, password expiry interval, and so forth. This is effectively the same as for Windows NT 4.0.

- Account lockout policies, such as lockout threshold, lockout duration, and so forth. Again this is the same as for NT 4.0.

- Kerberos policies.

- Encrypted file system recovery policies.

- IP security policies.

- Public key encryption policies.

- Certificate authorities.

If you know that your organization already has three different password schemes that have to be maintained, you will need three domains. If a special department or geographical area needs special encryption, security safeguards, certificates, and so on, you may have another candidate for a domain.

In-place upgrade of current domain

Many organizations have large existing Windows NT infrastructures and will be planning to migrate at some point. During the design of your migration to Windows 2000, you will need to consider the option of merging old Windows NT domain hierarchies into single domains. This is known as *collapsing* old domain structures. However, even though Windows 2000 usually requires fewer domains than Windows NT, as it can accommodate more objects and allow delegation of administration without domains, organizations may wish to retain some of their current domains.

If your organization has a domain that you feel should not be removed for some reason, you need to indicate it on the list of domains. Then when it comes time to implement your Windows 2000 rollout, you can do an in-place upgrade on the existing domain, rather than bringing it into an existing Windows 2000 domain.

Final notes

You now should have your first draft of the list of domains that you think you will need. There is one more very important point on this subject. Domains are very inflexible and unforgiving. They don't rename and once they're created, you tend to be stuck with them. My advice is to make sure that you have extremely static top-level (tier-1) domains.

Make sure that these domains will never need to be renamed and will not become obsolete. If either of these may occur, you would be better off making them Organizational Units or at the very least low-level domains so changes will not impact domains at a higher level.

Step 2—Design and Name the Tree Structure

Now you have the domains listed. Next you need to consider what sort of hierarchy to put them in. The easiest place to start is with one domain, the one that will become the forest root.

Choose the forest root domain

The forest root domain is normally the largest domain left after you split off the smaller ones using the preceding domain design process, but it doesn't have to be. The key here is that this domain needs to be centrally managed by an IT group, capable of making solid policy and naming decisions. This domain will have special properties. For example, the Schema Admins group will exist only in the forest root domain. The administrators of this forest root domain have control over who is added to the Schema Admins group and thus allowed to modify the Schema. While the administrators of the forest root domain can add any user from anywhere in the entire forest to the group (due to hierarchical and transitive trusts between all domains), it is the administrators of the forest root domain that call the shots. So, this domain is special. Its administrators dictate how the network expands, who can and cannot add domains and where they should go. This group has the grand vision for the design and operation of the network.

Whichever domain corresponds to this is the one that should be the forest root domain. If you are having difficulty choosing, pick one of the likely candidates for now. If it becomes obvious later that it was the wrong choice, you can come back and readjust then. Then grab a blank piece of paper and draw the forest root domain at the top of the sheet in a triangle. The triangle is the symbol that Microsoft uses to indicate a domain in Windows 2000.

Design the namespace naming scheme

As each domain has a DNS name to identify it, you need to consider what names you are going to choose. You can use any of the Internet RFC 1123 standard characters:

- A–Z

- a–z

- 0–9

- – (dash character)

Microsoft's DNS supports a wider range of characters, such as the Unicode character set, but if you need compatibility with other DNS flavors, be very careful allowing these.

There are currently two schools of thought on how to pick the DNS names for your Windows 2000 network: root zone or subzone. The root zone method says that you name your Windows 2000 network based on the root zone for your organization. For Mycorp, this would be *mycorp.com*. The subzone method suggests that you pick a new subdomain from your root zone and make that the Windows 2000 network. For Mycorp, this could be *windows.mycorp.com* or *msnetwork. mycorp.com*. If you choose the root zone method and wish to have a non-Windows 2000 DNS, you will either need to turn on dynamic update or manually plant a number of records in the DNS as shown in Chapter 5, *TCP/IP and DDNS*. If you choose the root zone method and wish to have a Windows 2000 DNS at your root, you will need to migrate your existing entries, if you have any, to it. Both methods are fine, but require configuration or migration at the root. A less-invasive procedure would be to choose a new subzone for your Windows 2000 network and run your network from that. With this setup you still have two choices, but they are less disruptive to any existing structure and you won't have to affect the main root zone. Arguably, the easiest solution is to let two Windows 2000 servers on your network run a DNS server and manage this DNS zone. This allows you to have a root that doesn't allow dynamic updates and a subdomain that does. The alternative would allow a non-Windows 2000 DNS to manage the zone.

Leicester University had a very large existing DNS infrastructure branching down from the root domain that we didn't want to affect with this new Windows 2000 infrastructure. The main DNS servers, while being dynamic update capable, did not have dynamic update turned on for specific reasons. So we set up two Windows 2000 servers to run a DNS service and gave them a subdomain to host. We then delegated that subdomain on the main DNS servers and told them which Windows 2000 servers had authority for the new zone. We then modified DHCP to point all new client workstations at the two Windows 2000 DNS servers and configured the DNS servers to pass any queries that they could not resolve back to the main campus DNS servers. Clients could update the dynamic DNS servers on Windows 2000 without affecting the main campus servers. However, external queries were still resolved by passing them to the main campus servers for resolution.

Start with forest root and assign a DNS name to the domain, writing the name inside or beside the triangle on the paper. You should pick it very, very carefully for two reasons: First, renaming a domain is impossible in this version of Windows 2000. Second, you can never remove the forest root domain from your network. You would have to wipe your entire setup and start again.

Create additional trees

Having created and named your forest root, you need to consider your other domains. If you have two distinct business units that will require discontiguous names, then you need two trees coming from a domain root. Draw all the other root domains that you think you will need as separate triangles at the same horizontal level on the paper and assign them valid DNS names. These domains are all root domains. A real-world example is the Microsoft brand name and the MSN brand name. Both *msn.com* and *microsoft.com* could be separate trees in the same forest. They couldn't be in the same tree, without giving them a hierarchical link, i.e., *msn.microsoft.com*.

If I think that Mycorp's finance department needs a separate domain, I will make a subdomain and call it *finance.mycorp.com*. Within Windows 2000 I could make *finance.mycorp.com* a separate tree in its own right, but as hierarchical and transitive trusts exist throughout a forest I gain absolutely nothing by doing this. The only differences come in choosing finance to be a new domain (which I did) or a new forest in itself. Making it a new tree gains me absolutely nothing.

Create additional forests

So far, I've been considering domains that will exist in the same forest. You may have business units that will require two separate forests entirely. So, how do you know if that is the case?

The first and most common reason may be political; certain business units may decide that they want to be as autonomous as possible. From the previous tip, it may be that the finance department has to politically be completely separate, so you would end up making a second forest with *finance.mycorp.com* as the second forest's forest root domain. In effect, you are treating this business unit as a separate, autonomous, and discontiguous part of the tree.

The second reason involves having two businesses that must be separately maintained. This also requires two forests.

The third reason is one born out of necessity. Remember from Chapter 2, *Active Directory Overview*, that certain aspects of a namespace are forest wide in scope. If you want to isolate a separate schema, configuration, or GC, then your only solution is to create a separate forest.

If any of these reasons is true, you need to create a second forest root domain and give it a unique DNS name, as you did for the first forest root domain. In effect, you need to separate your designs and do each individually. The best thing to do now would be to figure out how many forests you need, which domains from your list are going to be the forest root domains, name these roots, and then use separate pieces of paper for each forest. Draw separate forests on separate sheets of paper, and maintain separate lists of domains for each forest. You're now doing x designs, where x is the number of forests you have.

There is one other important point that you need to be aware of. While domains and trees in a forest maintain automatic trust relationships, it is possible to set up manual trust relationships with domains external to a forest. You are therefore able to set up manual trust relationships between forests. These relationships can be one-way trusts (A trusts B but B does not trust A) or two-way trusts (A trusts B and B trusts A).

If you require a limited trust (in the Windows NT/2000 sense) situation, in which you wish to give access to your forest to vendors and partners, you can do this manually. If you have two forests that you wish to link, you have two options: establish an explicit one-way trust or distribute a public Kerberos ticket.

The former allows other domains that are either members of another domain tree in a different forest or that do not support Kerberos authentication to have limited access to a domain in the forest. Only resources in the domain will be visible; no other resources in the tree are available for access.

The latter allows a Kerberos negotiation to start with a client that is not already a trusted member of the domain. A public Kerberos ticket allows a user that is not a member of the domain at all to be authenticated by using an explicitly distributed and dated Kerberos ticket.

One other method to allow access to Active Directory is via a *digital certificate*. Effective use of digital certificates allows secure communication between two machines. A digital certificate is used for public-key encryption applications, mostly seen on the internet where pages need a special certificate installed on the client to allow authentication over Secure Sockets Layer (SSL). A certificate server, such as the Microsoft Certificate Server that ships with Windows 2000, can be set up to issue, renew, and revoke digital certificates that will allow access to Active Directory. The certificates are used to authenticate connections via specific computers and users. Active Directory has extensions that allow individual user and computer accounts to have digital certificates assigned to them, allowing authentication over this mechanism. While these concepts aren't difficult, they are outside the scope of this book.

Arrange subdomain hierarchy

You now have a forest root domain with a valid DNS name. You possibly have other some other domains that will act as the roots of separate trees in the same forest or even extra forest root domains representing separate forests entirely. Now you need to lay out the domain tree hierarchies. If you have a number of remaining domains listed on your sheet of paper from Step 1, these are the subdomains that will form your domain-tree hierarchy.

Start with the first forest. Representing each domain with a triangle on the paper, lay it out in a hierarchical fashion beneath one of the domain tree roots in that forest. Name the domain appropriately, according to its position in the hierarchy. Continue doing this for all the domains in that forest. Now move on to the next forest and repeat.

For example, if I had *mycorp.com* as a tree root, and finance, marketing, and sales all needing separate domains, I would make them *finance.mycorp.com*, *marketing.mycorp.com*, and *sales.mycorp.com*. If the sales domain needed separate domains for presales and postsales, I would arrange these two domains beneath sales, as *pre.sales.mycorp.com* and *post.sales.mycorp.com*.

Each subdomain can manage its own accounts and data, or its parent in the hierarchy can manage them. That's the reason the hierarchy exists.

Worldwide Standards on Naming Conventions for Subdomains

If you want some guidelines for naming your subdomains, the International Standards Organization (ISO) has published a series of alphabetical codes for countries and U.S. states. If you wanted to use what could be considered an official standard, then ISO 3166 defines two-letter country codes and two-letter U.S. state codes (mostly) for your use.

The relevant information can be found on the following web pages:

http://www.nsrc.org/codes/country-codes.html

http://www.theodora.com/country_digraphs.html

http://iso3166.styx.net/?searchfor=%25&submit=Go+fetch&searchin=country

http://www.unicode.org/unicode/onlinedat/countries.html

Step 3—Design the Workstation and Server Naming Scheme

You now have one or more forests of domain trees. Each tree is uniquely named in a hierarchical fashion. You now have to consider the naming scheme for the servers and workstations that make up that scheme.

 While I am considering the naming scheme here, the exact placement of machines in Active Directory is covered in Chapter 9 on designing GPOs. This is because GPOs have a definite impact based on machine location.

Each Windows NT and Windows 2000 client or server in a Windows 2000 network has to have a computer account somewhere in the forest in order to let users log on via that client. When a workstation is added to a domain in a forest, the computer account is created in Active Directory and a trust relationship is set up between the client and the domain, so that the client is recognized as a valid member of the domain.

Where a client is placed in the forest determines part of the name. Standalone servers and DCs will be placed in the individual domains that they host. Clients can be placed anywhere, but usually are placed in the domain that the users of that client normally will log on to.

Under Windows NT 4.0, if you had a single-master or multimaster domain model in which multiple resource domains had one-way trusts to one or more master user domains that held the accounts, the workstations normally were placed in the resource domains. This enabled the workstations to log on to both the resource domain and the user domain. Putting the clients in the user domain only would have meant that the clients could not be used to access the resources in the resource domains, as no trust existed in that direction.

Cast this completely out of your mind in Windows 2000. Each domain has a hierarchical and transitive trust between it and every other domain, so it doesn't make any difference where the clients are located any more.

All hosts are named *computer.domain*. For example, a server called *moose* in *mycorp.com* would be called *moose.mycorp.com*; a server called *moose* in the finance domain would be called *moose.finance.mycorp.com*.

While deploying Windows 2000 does not force you to change the names of any existing hosts that you have, if you are due to amalgamate a series of domains and have clients with identical names, you need to make modifications so that host-names are unique throughout the entire forest. You can easily make use of ADSI (discussed later in Part III) to script a query for a list of computers from every one of your domains and then check the lists via a second script for duplicate names.

If you don't already force a naming scheme, now is the time. Fully Qualified Domain Names must be unique across the entire forest. This is achieved by appending the domain component onto the computer name. That leaves you to worry about the prefix, meaning that computer names have to be unique only domain wide.

Hostnames, like DNS domain names, can be formed from any of the following characters:

- A–Z

- a–z

- 0–9

- – (dash character)

Names cannot be longer than 15 characters. This is because Windows 2000 still has some legacy support for NetBIOS names, and the hostname that you choose will be incorporated as the NetBIOS name on the client. NetBIOS names are limited to 15 characters.

You need to work out a forest-wide naming scheme, determining how you will name the clients within the 15-character limit using only the characters from the previous list. I can't help you much here; the choice of your naming scheme is up to you.

Remember that Windows 95 and Windows 98 devices do not require computer accounts in the domain. However, if you do deploy these clients and anticipate upgrading them later to Windows NT Workstation or Windows 2000 Professional, the names of these clients will become an issue. It would be better to designate a name now to facilitate an easier upgrade later.

Design of the Internal Domain Structure

Having designed the domain namespace, you can now concentrate on the internals of each domain. The design process itself is the same for each domain, but the order is mostly up to you. The first domain that you should design is the forest root domain. After that, you iterate through the tree, designing subdomains within that first tree. Once the tree is finished, you go on to the next tree and start at the root as before.

In a tree with three subdomains under the root called Finance, Sales, and Marketing, you could either design the entire tree below Finance and then the entire tree below Sales and so on, or you could design the three tier-2 domains first, then do all the subdomains immediately below these three, and so on.

When designing the internals of a domain, you need to consider both the hierarchical structure of Organizational Units and the users and groups that will sit in those Organizational Units. Let's look at each of those in turn.

 When I refer to a *hierarchy*, a *tree*, or the *directory tree*, I mean the hierarchical Organizational Unit structure within a domain. I am not referring to the hierarchy of domain trees in a forest.

Step 4—Design the Hierarchy of Organizational Units

Earlier when I discussed how to design domains, I spoke of how to minimize the number of domains you had. The idea was to represent most of your requirements for a hierarchical set of administrative permissions using Organizational Units instead.

Organizational Units are the best way to structure your data because of their flexibility. They can be renamed and easily moved around within and between domains and placed at any point in the hierarchy without affecting their contents. These two facts make them very easy for administrators to manage.

There are four main reasons to structure your data in an effective hierarchy:

To represent your business model to ease management
Partitioning your data into an Organizational Unit structure that you will instantly recognize will make managing it much more comfortable than with every user and computer in one Organizational Unit.

To delegate administration
Windows 2000 allows you to set up a hierarchical administration structure that hasn't been possible with Windows NT. If you have three branches, and the main administrator wants to make one branch completely autonomous with its own administrator but wants to continue to maintain control over the other two, it's easy to set up. In a way, most of the limitations that you come up against when structuring Active Directory will be ones that you set: political necessities, organizational models, and so on. Active Directory really won't care how you structure your data. Your Organizational Unit's flat or triangular structure will make no real difference.

To replace Windows NT resource domains
If you have a previous Windows NT installation with a master or multimaster domain model, you can replace your resource domains with Organizational Units in a single domain. This will allow you to retain all of the benefits of having resource domains (i.e., resource administration by local administrators who do not have account administration rights) without forcing you into having multiple domains that you don't really want or need.

To apply policies to subsets of your users and computers
As policies can be applied to each individual Organizational Unit in the hierarchy, you can specify that different computers and users get different policies depending on where you place them in the tree. For example, let's say that you want to place an interactive touch-screen client in the lobby of your headquarters and allow people to interact with whatever applications you specify, such as company reports, maps of the building, and so on. To lock this down in Windows NT (so that the client could not compromise your network in any way) required time and may have required that the client be in a separate domain or even standalone. Now with Active Directory, if you lock down a certain Organizational Unit hierarchy using policies, you can guarantee that any computer and user accounts that you create or move to that part of the tree will be so severely restricted that hacking the network from the client won't be possible. That's why Organizational Unit structure matters to policies.

Let's take Leicester University as an example. The university is a large single site with mostly 10/100-MB links around campus and 2-MB links to some outlying areas a couple of miles away. Our domain model was multimaster under Windows NT, but under Windows 2000 we can move to a single domain (i.e., the only domain in the only tree in the only forest). So it is much simpler than before. Administration is centrally managed, which means that delegation of administration was of little concern during design. That meant we could structure the data in any way we liked. We have a departmental organizational model for our Organizational Unit structure holding our accounts. We created a flat structure with more than a hundred Organizational Units directly off the root and almost no lower Organizational Units at all. Each Organizational Unit corresponded to one department, and that held all the users from that department. We also had an Organizational Unit hierarchy for the computer accounts separate from the department Organizational Units. This was due to our requirement for group policies; I'll come back and discuss this in more detail in Chapter 9.

When you are creating Organizational Units, you need to ask:

- How will the Organizational Units be used?

- Who are the administrators and what sets of administrator permissions should they have?

- What policies will be applied?

The hierarchy is to organize information in a manner pleasing to your administration that allows you to delegate administration to various parts of the tree.

You should not nest user or computer accounts in an Organizational Unit structure in such a way that the polices that apply to the accounts constitute a slowdown. Microsoft recommends nesting no more than 10 Organizational Units deep, but in fact, it's the actions of policies that impact how deep you go to a much greater extent. This is to prevent slowdown on booting (policies applied to the computer account on boot up) or logon (policies applied to the user account on logon). If your users were in a 10-tier structure but only four policies were applied to the users, you shouldn't have a problem with logons. You can break this rule, but boot up and/or logon will slow down as a result. By how much is a very relative question and the easiest answer is to test it on your network to get your own feel for the delay if this becomes a problem. I cover this item in much more depth in Chapter 9 on GPOs. All you need to be aware of here is that this can be a problem.

Recreating the business model

The easiest way to start a design is to consider the business model that you sat down with when starting these designs. You now need to recreate that structure in Active Directory using Organizational Units as the building blocks. Create a complete Organizational Unit structure that exactly mirrors your business model as represented by that domain. In other words, if the domain you are designing is the Finance domain, then implement the finance organizational structure within the Finance domain; you don't create the entire organization's business model within each Organizational Unit, you create only the part of the model that would actually apply to that Organizational Unit. Draw this structure out on a piece of paper. Figure 6-3 shows the Organizational Unit structure of *mycorp.com*'s domain. I've expanded only the Finance Organizational Unit here for the example.

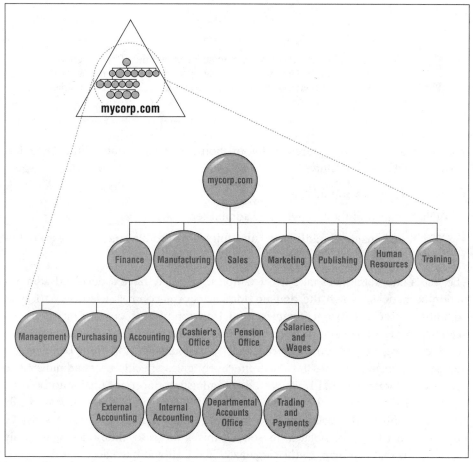

Figure 6-3. The Mycorp domain's internal Organizational Unit structure

Once you have drawn an Organizational Unit structure as a template for your Active Directory hierarchy within the domain, you can begin to tailor it to your specific requirements. The easiest way to tailor the initial Organizational Unit design is to consider the hierarchy that you wish to create for your delegation of administration.

Delegating full administration

First, identify any areas of your hierarchy where you will need to grant administrators autonomous access over their branch of the tree. These Organizational Units will need to have at least two administrators that will look after that Organizational Unit. These administrators will look after the structure below that Organizational Unit, creating whatever Organizational Units, users, groups, shares and so on that they desire. They will not, however, have administrator access to any other part of the tree.

 You need two administrator accounts in case one of the accounts ever gets locked. That way, you can use the second account to unlock the first. Having the second account as the domain administrator is perfectly fine.

You need to note three pieces of information about each one of the Organizational Units that you identify:

- Who will be the administrators?

- Which branch of the tree will they administer?

- Will the domain administrator have full or no administrative access to this branch?

The last is important. Let's take two examples. You may have a devolved administration scenario in which the domain administrator account is used only to grant administrator access to an Organizational Unit for two accounts. Once the two accounts have administrator access to the Organizational Unit, the administrator account's access is subsequently blocked by deliberate action from being inherited at that Organizational Unit. That effectively gives specific users administrative access over Organizational Units with the administrator account unable to be used to organize that data. In the second example, the domain administrator normally has access inherited throughout the tree, except at a number of key sensitive Organizational Units for political reasons. If this is the case, then once again, only the accounts that can manage the Organizational Unit will have access to it.

You must ensure that delegated users take responsibility and can be held accountable. This cannot be stressed too strongly. It is possible for an administrator of a low-level Organizational Unit to corrupt a tree and affect other people. The best way to highlight this is with user accounts. Remember, user accounts are visible forest wide and so in some sense must be unique forest wide. In much the same way as with computers, the domain component normally is used here in an attribute of the user object called the User-Principal-Name (UPN). So while the normal username only has to be unique domain wide, the UPN attribute ensures forest wide uniqueness. Let's concentrate on the domain wide part.

If a low-level Organizational Unit administrator creates a user with a username that someone else wants to create in another Organizational Unit, that's tough. Only one account of any name can exist. I deal with creating a naming scheme for administrators to follow later in Step 5.

If you do not have a company policy in this area, you need to create one and document what delegation you set up.

Delegating other rights

Having noted the three pieces of information for all Organizational Units that need full administrative access, you next need to identify those Organizational Units that require some users to have a more restricted set of permissions. You may want to set up account administrators that have the ability to create and delete user accounts, as well as setting passwords and account details. You may want accounts that can create and publish printers. We're only interested in rights in general terms at the moment. So just note:

- What the access rights are
- Which branch of the tree the access rights are to be applied to
- Which users or groups (in general terms) will have these access rights

I ought to explain that it is possible to set access rights of any sort down to the individual property level on a specific object if you require. That means you can allow a user named Richard Lang to change the password or telephone number of a user named Vicky Launders (and only that user) if you wish. Obviously the more minute the access, the more complex things can get, especially as permissions are inherited down a tree by default. To make things easier, Microsoft provides a simple Delegation-Of-Control wizard that allows you to set these access rights in a fairly easy manner. All this information on permissions to Active Directory is covered in much greater depth in Chapter 10, *Active Directory Security: Permissions and Auditing*. However, all we're concerned with at this stage in the design is delegation of control at the Organizational Unit level. From experience, I can tell you that assigning access rights at the Organizational Unit level is actually a lot simpler to manage than tracking permissions to individual objects and properties.

Step 5—Design of Users and Groups

Before starting this section, I must make the distinction between groups and Organizational Units clear. Organizational Units are containers for objects that allow the objects to be represented in a hierarchical structure within a domain. Placing objects in such a hierarchy allows delegation of administration to those Organizational Units on a selective basis. We've seen all this already. Groups, on the other hand, have only users or computers as members and can be used in assigning permissions or rights to the members collectively. Let's say that I have 50 users contained in an Organizational Unit called FinanceOU and also have the users as members of a group called FinanceGrp. When I want to grant these 50 users read permissions to a share or restricted access to certain parts of a domain's hierarchy, I assign the permissions to the FinanceGrp. The fact that they are in the Organizational Unit makes no difference when you wish to assign permissions to objects contained inside the Organizational Unit. However, if I wish to delegate someone to have permission to manage those 50 accounts, then I place the administrative delegation onto the Organizational Unit. Here I'll be talking about how to effectively design user accounts and the groups those users belong to.

Naming and placing users

When you are designing users, the only thing you really have to worry about is the username or user identifier that the client logs on with. Each username (the SAM-Account-Name property of a user object) must be unique throughout each domain. Arguably, if you have decided to delegate administration within your organization, then you need to create a naming scheme to which each administrator will adhere so that unique usernames are generated for all users throughout your forest. That way, if you ever collapse the existing domains, you never need to rename the users if there are any conflicts. Naming groups is important, too.

Another name that you must give to all Windows 2000 users is known as the *user principal name* (the User-Principal-Name property of the user object). This property looks like an RFC 822 email address, i.e., *username@here.there.somewhere. com*. In fact, this property is not the email address, but is a unique identifier for the user in the entire forest. It has to be unique as it is stored in the GC. So while the users *AlistairGLN* in *mycorp.com* and *AlistairGLN* in *finance.mycorp.com* are perfectly valid, their UPNs (as the attribute is more commonly called) must be different. The normal way to create a UPN is simply to append an @ symbol and the domain onto the end of the username. This ensures uniqueness because the username was unique in the domain, appending the domain forces a unique forest-wide UPN. This makes *AlistairGLN@mycorp.com* and *AlistairGLN@finance. mycorp.com* the UPNs for the two users in the example.

However, while it is conventional to construct the UPNs in this way, you can in fact make the UPN of a user anything you wish. I could, for example, append the *domain@mycorp.com* to all my users, eliminating the need to rely on domains at all. If I do that though, I need to make sure that my usernames (SAM-Account-Name) in each domain are unique not only domain wide but also forest wide. So in my previous example, I can't have two users with the username AlistairGLN. In order for such a scheme to work, a central database or allocating authority needs to be set up to uniquely generate and allocate names. Leicester University has maintained a separate database from the early 1980s for this purpose, as have many other universities and companies. If this database or authority can generate unique usernames via a reliable algorithm, then you can make use of a much simpler UPN.

 Just because I chose *@mycorp.com* as the suffix does not mean I am limited to a forest or domain name. I could just as easily have chosen *@moosebanana.com,* which has no relation to the domains or the forest. The UPN simply has to be unique for every user in the forest.

UPNs are very important. Imagine a user sitting down at a client anywhere in a forest and being presented with the logon dialog box. Here he can type in his username (SAM-Account-Name), password, and domain and be authenticated to the forest. However, it is perfectly valid to authenticate with the UPN. If the user, presented with the same logon dialog box, instead types in a UPN in the first field, the domain box becomes grayed out and inaccessible. In other words, a UPN and a password are all that is needed to authenticate to the tree. This makes sense, since the UPN is unique forest wide, so apart from a password, nothing else should be needed. You now should be able to see that even with a very large and complex set of domains in a forest, you can use a simplified UPN form that does not contain a domain component and simply instruct users to log on with a UPN and a password. This means that users never need to care about what domain they are in.

Your choice of where you place the user accounts in each domain's hierarchy really is affected only by who is to administer the accounts and what GPOs will be applied on the Organizational Unit the account is in. Other than that, it makes little difference.

Naming and placing groups

Groups (especially universal groups that get stored in the GC) need unique names, too. A naming scheme for groups should be laid out in the design. Where you put groups is less important. In effect, groups can go almost anywhere in the hierarchy. The GPOs that determine your placement of users, for example, do not apply to groups. However, as the groups available to you will differ based on the mode of your network, the only way you can do a proper design is to know roughly how long you intend to stay in mixed mode before upgrading. If you have no previous Windows NT infrastructure and do not require any applications that run on NT, you can go native immediately. Even some Microsoft BackOffice applications, such as Microsoft Systems Management Server 2.0 (in its unpatched state as it was initially released), recommend that you don't install them under Windows 2000, while Microsoft Exchange Server 5.5 and SQL Server will happily install. If you will have to spend the next year or so upgrading your Windows NT infrastructure to Windows 2000, then you'll be running with a mixed mode domain for a while. Running in mixed mode is not a problem, by the way; it's the best method for migrating your servers piecemeal and makes the whole migration process easier. This sort of migration is covered in Chapter 12, *Windows NT 4.0 Migration*.

If you are planning to wait a while on mixed mode before upgrading, for whatever reasons, then you need to do two sets of group designs: what the groups will be prior to the upgrade and what you will convert them to after the upgrade. Of course, the two designs may be the same.

Going native in one domain does not have to affect the mode of another domain. There is nothing wrong with *admin.windows. mycorp.com* going native while *windows.mycorp.com* is mixed mode or vice versa. Remember that mixed mode and native mode only affect the use of BDCs in a domain, not the use of Windows NT clients or member servers.

Understanding the problems with universal groups

Universal groups are great. They can contain users and groups from any domain, and they can have access to resources. Surely the best solution is to use just this one type of group and make your life easier. Unfortunately, it's not that simple. As I said in Chapter 2, universal groups and their list of members are contained in the GC as well as Active Directory. So when membership of any universal group changes, those changes need to be replicated out to the GCs and Active Directory. The more often the membership of those groups changes, the more replication that takes place. And the more universal groups that you have, the larger the

GC will become. As more Universal groups are added, there is thus a larger chance that membership changes (and thus replication) will occur with more frequency. It's a sort of vicious circle. However, while the size of the GC and replication is important, there are also implications when computing membership permissions.

If a user wishes to log on, the permissions for both the user and any groups that the user is a member of must be determined. First, the list of groups that the user is a member of is checked. Then the groups are checked to see which universal groups the user is a member of. Then those universal groups are checked for group membership and so on. The point is that with many Universal groups nested together, the logon process can take longer as the security *tokens* on each group are expanded. This is known as *token explosion*. The idea is to reduce this as much as you can by reducing the group membership via universal groups.

Creating proper security group designs

If your organization is based on a single site (in the Windows 2000 sense of being a "fast interconnected set of subnets," which is detailed in the next chapter), you can use universal security groups entirely. You don't have to, but for the purposes of design it will make very little difference in the long run which you choose.

Assuming, however, that your organization has multiple, then you should make use of domain local security and domain global security groups as well as universal security groups. If you wish to use Universal Security groups, do not put individual users into them as members. Remember that the Universal Security group and its members are held in the GC, so if you only add other groups as members you are unlikely to create as many group memberships as you would using individual users. That will limit the size of the GC and thus the impact of replication.

Based on the tables in Chapter 2, for large complex organizations with many different sets of permissions to many individual resources, I still would suggest using two sets of security groups. One set of Security groups has permissions to local resources on a particular server, and the other set of Security groups contains the users. You then can add one set of Security groups to another to control access. In this manner, you are maintaining a fine-grained control over the access permissions for groups while not having to add users many times over to multiple groups.

In mixed mode, I would use Domain Local Security groups for access to local resources and add users to Domain Global Security groups or even Universal Distribution groups. In native mode I would do one of three things:

- Continue as before, but now allow Universal Security groups to be members of Domain Local Security groups

- Convert the Domain Local Security groups to Universal Security groups with the same membership since before as this is now allowed under native mode

- Convert the Domain Local Security groups and Domain Global Security groups to Universal Security groups, understanding the impact this will have on the GC and the potential for token explosion

Step 6—Global Catalog Design

The GC is part friend part enemy. When it comes to aiding searches, it is very useful. Queries can be resolved much faster in the Global Catalog than in Active Directory itself. As Active Directory is optimized for searches, you can get some idea that the GC must be supercharged. In fact, the reason searches can be conducted quickly mostly comes down to the fact that the data contained in the GC is a much, much smaller subset than that in Active Directory. But the GC can be a real problem if it starts replicating data everywhere. If you properly design the GC and understand its limitations, you are unlikely to have problems.

The GC design is dependent partially on the namespace and partially on the replication design. On the namespace side, designing its contents is important in order to properly respond to searches, and on the replication side, designing the GC to interact using a reasonable amount of your bandwidth is important. I'll consider only half the picture in this chapter and do a draft design, coming back and revising the draft design in the next chapter.

By default, Windows 2000 will manage however many GC servers you have per site (normally one). While Windows 2000 gives you a default server to host the GC, you don't have to stay with that. You have the choice of adding multiple GC servers or not even hosting the GC on a site at all if you wish.

 If you decide to use universal groups and the server holding the GC goes down at a site, access to the universal groups will not be possible. If a universal group denies or allows a user access, and the user performs a logon while the GC is down, the universal groups will be ignored. If this is unacceptable, you definitely need to make sure each site uses multiple GCs for fault tolerance.

The namespace of the GC is also highly configurable. Each property of every object in the Windows 2000 Schema has a modifiable attribute that is used to indicate whether the attribute is to be contained in the GC. Most objects store at least one property in the GC, even if it is only their Common-Name (cn) attribute.

Examples of properties that are held in the GC include the password for all user objects (so that authentication is rapid) and the access permissions for each object (so that details on objects are not given out in responses if the requester does not have the relevant permissions).

You can access the GC and look at its contents via any raw Active Directory viewer tools using the following progID: GC://

If an attribute is being placed in the GC that you specifically do not want included, you can exclude it. You can do this either by unchecking the box in the Schema Manager or programmatically via ADSI. If you want an attribute included in the GC, the process is the reverse.

Obviously, the more data that you specify to be stored in the GC, the larger the GC will get. If the attribute that you include is for a class that contains only a handful of objects, the impact will be negligible. If you specify an attribute for a class of object that has tens of thousands of instances, you will impact the size of the GC.

The larger the GC gets, the longer each search will take and the more bandwidth will be taken up as these extra attributes replicate every time they change.

This doesn't mean that you should not change anything. You just have to be aware of the potential impact. The time taken for searches is not immediately easy to measure. Every administrator knows that network bandwidth utilization is never the same twice and fluctuates every second with different numbers of users doing different tasks. This will affect your query times.

What you need to consider in this stage of namespace design is what attributes you wish to include and which default ones you wish to exclude. This decision is affected by the fact that searches for properties that are contained in the GC are conducted forest wide, while searches for properties not contained in the GC are conducted only domain wide.

Only members of the schema administrators group in the forest root domain can modify whether schema attributes are included in or excluded from the GC. This group can have members from any domain, but the group itself is contained in the forest root domain.

Including and Excluding Attributes

Microsoft has decided that a certain core set of attributes should go in the GC. If you wish to remove attributes from the GC, any searches on the attributes that you remove will be conducted only within the domain that generated the query. To make that point completely clear: Consider a query coming from *windows.mycorp. com* looking for all available printers. Assume *windows.mycorp.com* is part of a larger tree with *mycorp.com* as its root and *othercorp.com* as another tree in the forest. Also assume that a number of printers exist in those domains that the query could potentially find. With all the default printer attributes held in the GC, a query would find every printer throughout the forest. Conversely, if I remove all printer attributes from the GC, a query from *windows.mycorp.com* for the names of all printers available would return only printers from *windows.mycorp.com*.

The best way to approach this part of the design is to decide whether any objects should be hidden in a domain. For example, should printers be restricted to be visible only domain wide or do some people need to print to printers forest wide? Even if they do need this, will they need to *search* for these printers forest wide, or should you create multiple instances of the same printer, one per domain? Both are valid solutions. Do you want shares published domain wide or forest wide?

Start by working out which classes of object you might want to hide attributes from outside of the domain. There may even be some classes you wish to exclude altogether from the GC. Next, for each object class look in the Schema and determine what attributes for that class are currently included in the GC. Then decide if any of the attributes indicated there are ones that you wish to remove.

 A script to write out a list of those attributes of a class that are included in the GC alongside a list of those that are excluded is contained in Chapter 19, *Extending the Schema and the GUI*.

If you decide that you want some instances of an object to be visible and some objects not to be visible, then you are stuck. An attribute is either included or excluded from the GC. It's the same sort of impossibility as being "a little bit pregnant." You have to make a choice as to whether you want the attribute of the class visible. If you exclude all attributes of a class from the GC, the class by implication is itself entirely excluded.

Finally, a word of caution: you must be careful when excluding attributes from the default set. It's fine to exclude attributes that seem to make little difference to the overall picture, but restricting security descriptor or cn attributes can cause problems with your GC.

Other Design Considerations

In many cases you may need to revise your namespace designs a number of times. Certainly GPOs will make a difference as to how you structure your users and computer objects, so I would not assume that one pass through a design process will be enough.

Once you have a basic design down, there is nothing stopping you from putting that design to one side and working on identifying a perfect design for your Windows 2000 network, one that you would like to implement in your organization ignoring all Windows 2000–imposed design constraints. You then can work out how difficult it will be to move to that perfect design from the practical one that you worked out using the preceding steps. You can look at the feasibility of the move from one to the other and then rationalize and adjust your final design to take into account the factors that you have listed. You then can use this as an iteration tool so that your final design is much closer to the perfection that you are aiming for.

Apart from GPOs, which I cover in Chapters 8 and 9, there are other aspects of Active Directory design that I have not and will not be covering. For example, you are quite likely to want printers advertised in Active Directory so that they can be accessed easily using a simple search of Active Directory (which the Add Printer wizard now uses as the default option). You may want shares advertised in Active Directory, so that users can easily locate data partitions on a site nearest to them. The Distributed Filing System (DFS) that allows you to organize disjointed and distributed shares into a single contiguous hierarchy is a fine example of this in action. When you reference a share held by the DFS, the DFS will use Active Directory to automatically redirect your request to the closest share replica. There is also the matter of designing your own objects and attributes that you want to include. However, there are two points that you should consider:

- Active Directory should hold only static or relatively static data. At the very least, the lifetime of the data has to be greater than the time to replicate to all DCs throughout the organization. When considering which objects to add, don't consider adding objects with very short life spans.

- Any object that you include will have attributes that are held in the GC. For every type of object that you seek to store in Active Directory, check the schema class entry for that object to find out what attributes will be stored in the GC. Consider whether you need to add or remove items from that list by referring back to the design principles.

Design Examples

Having covered the design of the namespace, some real-world example designs are in order. I have created three fictitious companies that will serve as good models for demonstrations of the design process. I also will use these three companies in the following chapters. The companies themselves are not fully detailed here, although there is enough information to enable you to make a reasonable attempt at a namespace design. In the chapters that follow, I will expand the relevant information on each company as required for that part of the design.

I used a number of criteria to create these companies:

*   The companies were set up to represent various organizations and structures.

*   While each corporation has a large number of users and machines, the design principles will scale down to smaller organizations well.

*   In these example corporations, I am not interested in how many servers each company has or where those servers are. These facts come into play in the next chapter on sites. I am interested in users, groups, machines, domains, and the business and administration models that are used.

TwoSiteCorp

TwoSiteCorp is an organization that employs 50 thousand people using 50 thousand machines. The organization spans two sites connected with a 128-KB dedicated link. The London site has 40 thousand clients and 40 thousand employees, while the new expansion at the Leicester site has 10 thousand clients and 10 thousand employees. TwoSiteCorp's business model is based on a structure in which users are members of one of three divisions: U.K. Private Sector, U.K. Public Sector, and Foreign. No division is based entirely at one site. Various other minor divisions exist beneath these as required for the management structure. Administration is handled centrally from the major London site by a team of dedicated systems administrators.

Step 1—Set the number of domains

While TwoSiteCorp's 128-KB link between its two physical locations is slow for site purposes, there is no need to split the two sites into two domains. No particular part of the organization has a unique policy requirement, because the administrators decide that they will implement one set of policies for all users. Finally, the sites already have two Windows NT domains installed. However, management has no desire to maintain either, so both will be rationalized into one domain. Thus, TwoSiteCorp will end up with one domain.

Step 2—Design and name the tree structure

TwoSiteCorp's single domain will be the forest root domain. The designers decide to name the domain *twositecorp.com* after their DNS domain name. With only one domain, they do not have to worry about any other trees or forests or the domain hierarchy.

Step 3—Design the workstation and server naming scheme

TwoSiteCorp decides that each machine name will be made up of four strings concatenated together. The first string will be three characters representing the location of the machine (e.g., LEI or LON). The next three characters will be used to indicate the operating system (e.g., W2K, NT4, or W98). The next string will hold two or three letters indicating the type of machine (e.g., DC, SRV, or WKS). Finally, the last string will be a six-digit numeric one that will start with 000001 and continue to 999999. The following are example machine names:

- *LEIW2KDC000001*

- *LEIW2KDC000002*

- *LONNT4WKS000183*

Step 4—Design the hierarchy of Organizational Units

TwoSiteCorp needs three major Organizational Units (U.K. Private Sector, U.K. Public Sector, and Foreign) based on its business model of divisions. The second and succeeding tiers of Organizational Units can then be created according to the lower-level management structure if required. There is no necessity to do so in this scenario, although it would make the structure easier to visually manage. In fact, this domain could be completely flat with all users and machines in one Organizational Unit, but then you aren't gaining much from Active Directory's ability to structure the data in a useful manner for administration. Speaking of administration, since it is handled centrally, there is no need to delegate administration for the three top-tier Organizational Units to any specific group of administrators, although there is room for expansion should that become necessary. Nor does TwoSiteCorp need to delegate any other permissions to the Organizational Unit structure. Now TwoSiteCorp has a fairly simple hierarchy that perfectly maps their domain.

Step 5—Design the users and groups

TwoSiteCorp has two Windows NT domains at present using a variety of global groups and local groups. During the migration, the company will have a mixed-mode domain. However, their ultimate aim is to move to native mode very quickly and reap the added benefits of universal groups. The design therefore needs to cover what universal groups the company would like for its resources. The existing global and local groups can be moved to Active Directory during migration, allowing the current setup to work with the new system. Once the switchover to native mode goes ahead, either the groups can be converted to universal groups and rationalized to fit into the new design, or they can be left as they are and new universal groups created according to the design to take the place of the old groups.

Step 6—Design the Global Catalog

Central Corp has no specific GC requirements and therefore leaves the system to work out its own defaults.

Summary

This is a very simple system that maintains a good level of administration based on the structure of the organization while managing to maintain control over its expansion in the years to come.

RetailCorp

RetailCorp is a global multibillion dollar retail organization that has more than 600 stores spread throughout the world under four different store names. There are around 60 thousand staff in the company with about 25 thousand in the central office based in Leicester in the United Kingdom. Each store is connected to the central HQ via 64-KB leased lines. Each store has a number of Windows NT point-of-sale workstations running database software and one or more large database servers in the back room. The database servers replicate the day's transactions down the links each evening to the central HQ.

RetailCorp is very centralized with almost no administrators at the stores themselves. The only really special requirement that the company has is that it would like the administrators to be able to easily hide the operating environment from staff on the tills at each branch. Changes to tills should be possible on an individual branch or global level.

Step 1—Identify the number of domains

RetailCorp has no need to isolate replication or do any in-place upgrades. The part about policies is a little tricky: do they need new domains for every branch in case policy changes need to be applied to one branch specifically? The answer is no. The administrators need to be able to apply policies to certain branches or all branches, but these policies have to do with the user interface and thus fall into the area of Group Policy Objects rather than individual domains. That effectively leaves them with one domain.

Step 2—Design and Name the Tree Structure

RetailCorp, having only one domain, makes that the forest root domain. The namespace has the *retailcorp.com* global name that is already in use.

Step 3— Design the workstation and server naming scheme

RetailCorp uses a central database to register machines, which automatically produces a 15-character name based on a machine's location and purpose (i.e., client, database server, file and print server). Every time a machine is moved or its function changes, the name is updated in the central database and the machine is renamed.

Step 4—Design the hierarchy of Organizational Units

It is decided to make each store an Organizational Unit, so that central administrators can delegate control over individual stores and their objects as required. However, to make things even easier to manage and delegate on a countrywide or regional basis, RetailCorp creates a series of country Organizational Units under the base. Each of these country Organizational Units contains either the shop Organizational Units directly (for countries with only a handful of stores) or a series of regional Organizational Units that themselves contain the store OUs.

Step 5— Design the users and groups

RetailCorp uses a central database to generate its own unique usernames and group names as needed. It has done this for many years, and the database produces a changes file on an hourly basis that a script picks up and applies to Active Directory in the same manner that it does with all other systems.

Step 6—Design the Global Catalog

RetailCorp has had problems with printers before, with users printing to printers at the wrong site. To make sure that printer details are not replicated past boundaries, all printer attributes are removed from the GC. The rest of the defaults are accepted as standard, and the company intends to keep an eye on the situation to make sure that there are no problems with this in the future.

Summary

This shows the way that a geographically based company can do its own design. It's not particularly difficult, although this design does not take into account the slow links between the stores and the HQ. That is left until the next chapter, when we revisit RetailCorp from a physical-layer perspective.

PetroCorp

PetroCorp (see Figure 6-1) is a global multibillion dollar petrochemical organization that has more than a hundred thousand people and machines at about a hundred sites around the world. The business has its global headquarters in Denver. There are five major sites that link to the HQ and to which the smaller 94 branch offices link. The major sites or hubs represent Asia-Pacific, Australasia, USA-Canada, South America, and Europe. The small sites link to the five hubs via 64-KB links; the hubs connect to the HQ via T2, T1, 256-KB, and 128-KB links. Some of the hubs are also interconnected. Management structure is geographic with each geographical unit running itself as an independent business as part of the global whole. The top level of the management structure is at HQ, which sits above the five hubs. Even though Denver could be considered as being within the USA-Canada area, the organization is not structured that way. In fact, Denver oversees the hubs in terms of selecting the administrators and how the network is to be structured. Corporate policy dictates that branches that have more than 500 people have their own administrator, backup support, and helpdesk staff locally. Branches with fewer than 500 people have to be managed by the administrators of the hub to which they connect (see Figure 6-4).

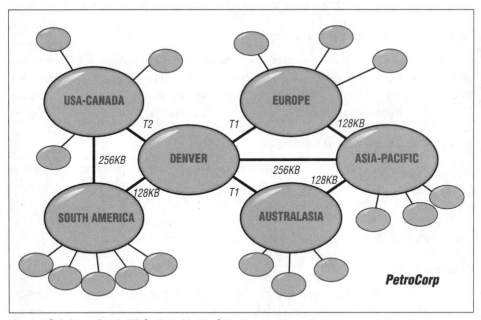

Figure 6-4. PetroCorp's Wide Area Network

Other considerations include:

- Due to special company policies, public key encryption and different language settings are used in each of the hubs (and their branches). So Europe and its branches have different settings from those in Australasia and its branches.

- Japan has a database system running on Windows NT 4.0 that must stay in its own domain.

- PetroCorp recently acquired OtherCorp, a Canadian company that has a strong brand name that PetroCorp would like to maintain. OtherCorp is solely based in a new branch in Canada.

- The links between the eight South American branches and the hub are very unreliable.

- The branch in France needs to maintain a number of Windows NT BDCs and member servers running legacy applications and services that will not run under Windows 2000. This requirement may exist for a few years.

- The Asia-Pacific 128-KB link to Europe is severely congested at all times.

- Current U.S. laws explicitly state that information in a U.S. directory can be published anywhere except in countries that are subject to American export restrictions (currently including but not necessarily limited to Cuba, the Federal Republic of Yugoslavia (Serbia and Montenegro), Iran, Iraq, Libya, North Korea, and Syria). Since Active Directory is a directory that has the United States as its origin, it cannot be exported out to those countries.

Step 1—Set the number of domains

There is a wrong way and a right way to look at PetroCorp:

The wrong way

PetroCorp starts off with five domains representing the hubs because each requires different public-key security settings.* As the branch offices are part of the domain at each hub, the hub's settings will apply to the branch offices as well because the settings are domain wide. So extra domains are not needed, although they are needed for each branch office for Japan and OtherCorp. As France cannot upgrade, whatever domain France is in must remain in mixed mode. Management could make the Europe domain mixed mode but would like it to be native mode in order to make use of the features. So a special domain for France makes a total of eight domains.

---

* That they also require different language settings is a red herring as Windows 2000 can support different language settings on a per-client basis rather than a per-domain basis like Windows NT.

The right way

> PetroCorp starts off with one domain: the one representing Denver, the HQ of PetroCorp. The organization then needs to create a separate domain for each of the five hubs for the public-key security settings. As the branch offices are part of the domain at each hub, the hub's settings will apply to the branch offices as well, due to the settings being domain wide. Now an extra domain each is needed for Japan and OtherCorp. France cannot upgrade, so whatever domain France is in must remain in mixed mode. Management could make the Europe domain mixed mode, but would like it to be native mode so that they can make use of the Windows 2000 features. A special domain for France makes a total of nine domains.

Both solutions can seem valid although you may feel that the first is not as valid as the second. The first solution would result in problems during later parts of the design process. That there are different sites with different link speeds is not really an issue here. The issue revolves around the major HQ that is separate from but oversees the five hubs in an administrative capacity. In the wrong design, one of these domains must become the forest root domain with the relevant authority that confers. USA-Canada is the natural choice. Then HQ administrators would effectively be running the USA-Canada domain, which conflicts with the initial company notes that each hub and the HQ has its own administrators. Consequently, the second design is better.

Step 2—Design and name the tree structure

PetroCorp chooses the Denver domain as the forest root domain. The forest root domain is to be called *petrocorp.com.*

When it comes to choosing a naming scheme for the domains corresponding to the hubs, the administrators choose a simple one. The domains will be called:

- *europe.petrocorp.com*
- *usacanada.petrocorp.com*
- *samerica.petrocorp.com*
- *asiapac.petrocorp.com*
- *australasia.petrocorp.com*

The domain representing OtherCorp will be called *othercorp.com.* They could have merged OtherCorp into PetroCorp's structure and just used multiple DNS names for the web servers and so on. However, the company may be sold for a profit in the future, and management wants to keep it politically separate.

There are obviously now two distinct trees. We'll put them in the same forest so that resources can be shared. The subdomain hierarchy is fairly easy to follow from now on. The domains for France and Japan will follow ISO 3166 country codes and be called *fr.europe.petrocorp.com* and *jp.asiapac.petrocorp.com.* Figure 6-5 shows the forest view of the domain trees.

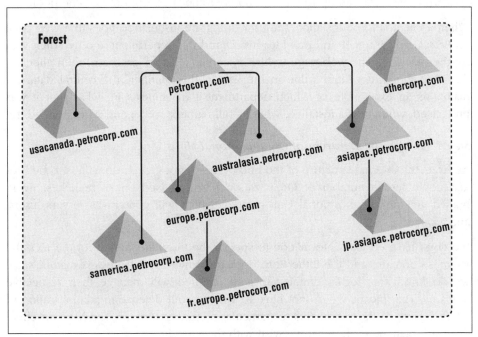

Figure 6-5. PetroCorp's forest domain tree hierarchies

Step 3—Design the workstation and server naming scheme

PetroCorp has decided that it specifically does not want to use any parts of its naming scheme to duplicate data that can be obtained elsewhere. For example, PetroCorp does not want to use country, city, or building information as this can be gathered from the exact Windows 2000 site that the client is in. For example, there's no point in including the data UK, London, Building 3 if the site that the computer resides in is called UK-London-Building3. They also do not want to include indications of the operating system or version, as they will be using Microsoft Systems Management Server (SMS) to inventory each device so the required information can be retreived directly from SMS's own database. They do, however, want to include the department that the client is installed in.

They also decide to use this name as part of the worldwide asset-registering system under development, so that they can institute a worldwide rolling update program of older devices. Thus, they need to include the year the client was purchased and when the client was introduced to the network.

To do this, they decide to take a leaf from the FSMO RID Master's book and use a central pool of values at their HQ for the naming of machines. Names of machines will start with an up-to-seven-letter department code, followed by a two-digit year code and finish with an up to six-digit number allocated from the central pool.

When a client is to be installed, the user doing the installation goes to a web page on PetroCorp's intranet and provides his ID and the department and two-digit year for the machine. The web page (which is connected to a database) then allocates that user the next central value in the list. In this manner, the central database maintains an exact note of which department a machine is in, what year it was purchased, when it was installed, what its full name is to be, and who installed it.

Step 4—Design the hierarchy of Organizational Units

As far as the internal structure of the hub domains goes, each domain is to be broken down into a number of Organizational Units based on its branches. Every branch gets an Organizational Unit created, which will contain its servers, users, and groups.

We don't have enough information to specify the internal structure of the HQ, the Japanese domain, and the OtherCorp domain. However, that doesn't matter, since we do know that local administrators at all three will manage their respective domains. That means we do not have to worry about delegating administration of internal parts of those domains to particular administrators. So, we have an effective carte blanche to do what we wish with those designs.

The company notes state that each branch with more than 500 people locally employs its own administrator, backup support, and helpdesk staff. Assuming we have identified the standard set of permissions that each of the three sets of staff require at each branch, we need to delegate administrative responsibility for the three functions to the relevant groups of staff in those branches. So, branch staff members now have administrative responsibility for their branch Organizational Unit only, and branches without any staff will be centrally managed.

Step 5—Design the users and groups

In addition to whatever other groups the organization's designers decide it needs, three groups corresponding to the three delegated jobs need to be created in every branch that is to have autonomous control. These three groups will be used when delegating responsibility.

Any domains intending to stay on Windows NT (i.e., France), can run in mixed mode, with other domains going native as soon as is feasible. Domain Global Security and Domain Local Security will be mainly used, although a scattering of Domain Universal Security groups will be used in the native-mode domains as soon as conversion takes place.

Step 6—Design the Global Catalog

Current U.S. laws explicitly state that information in a U.S. directory can be published anywhere except in countries that are subject to American export restrictions. As PetroCorp's Active Directory is a directory that has the United States as its origin, Active Directory cannot be exported to those countries. That throws a monkey wrench into PetroCorp's design, as PetroCorp has offices in several of those countries.

PetroCorp has a number of solutions open to them. They could have Europe or Australia host the PetroCorp domain and make the Denver office a subdomain, with Denver managing both. That's not particularly appropriate here. There are many other variations along those lines as well as a number of solutions that are workable. Here are two examples:

- Create entirely separate domains in separate forests in those countries. These forests, being outside the central forest, will have no Global Catalog exporting issues.

- Create one entirely new forest called something like *export.petrocorp.com*, which is not in any way related to the existing *petrocorp.com* domain even though the name appears that way. The *export.petrocorp.com* forest could contain servers from all the companies that have export restrictions, holding them together under one manageable structure. This can be hosted (have the forest root domain in another country) and be remotely managed. Manual trusts between forests can now be considered as long as these don't also break the laws.

Summary

This shows the way that a global company can do its own design and maintain a large degree of control. It also shows how laws in the real world can really wreak havoc with a good design!

Designing for the Real World

It's very easy to get bogged down in the early stages of the namespace design without actually progressing much further. The stumbling block seems to be that it feels conceptually wrong to have only one domain, yet administrators can't put their finger on what the problem is. Experienced Windows NT administrators who manage multiple domains seem to find this much more of a problem than those coming from another operating system.

Leaving behind the Windows NT model of using domains is very hard to do. It seemed comforting somehow; this group of people had this domain for this reason and that group had that domain for that reason. I'm not saying that domains were put in with no consistent strategy, just that you knew where you were with domains. It was a very similar problem when standalone NetWare 3.1x administrators contemplated the Novell Directory Services (NDS) concept of NetWare 4.x. There was terrific resistance from many NetWare administrators because of a lack of understanding about the directory and the fact that disparate departments would now have to cooperate together if all resources were to be brought under the same tree. The same applies to the Windows 2000 Active Directory now.

If you follow the guidelines in the initial steps of the namespace design, then you quite probably will end up with one domain to start with. That's the whole point of the design process, to reduce the number of domains you need. Yet NT administrators tend to feel that they have conceptually lost something very important; having only one domain and that somehow this design doesn't "feel right."

This is partly a conceptual problem: a set of domains with individual objects managed by different teams can feel more secure and complete than a set of Organizational Units in a single domain containing individual objects managed by different teams. While this isn't the case, it can *feel* that way, and NT administrators will take a while to become comfortable with the technology. Just because Microsoft say it is OK, and because I say it is OK, does not convince everyone.

It's also partly an organizational problem, and possibly a political problem. Putting in a Windows 2000 server system is a significant undertaking for an organization and shouldn't be taken lightly. This change is likely to impact everyone across the company, assuming you're deploying enterprise wide. Changes at that level are likely to have to be ratified by a person or group who may not be directly involved with the team proposing the change on a day-to-day basis. So you have to present them with a business case that explains that the benefits of moving to Windows 2000 outweigh the cost of staying where you are.

Identify the Number of Domains

Following my advice in this chapter and Microsoft's official guidelines from the White Papers or Resource Kit will lead most companies with a single internet domain name with one domain for their namespace design. Admittedly, if your business has more than one internet domain name registered, that number will be one domain per internet domain name registered. That still may seem like too few domains.

It is *your* network and you can do what you want. More domains give you better control over replication traffic but may mean more expense in terms of hardware. If you do decide to have multiple domains but have users in certain locations that need to log on to more than one domain, you need DCs for each domain that the users need in that location. This can be expensive. I'll come back to this again later, but let's start by considering the number of domains you need.

If the algorithm I use to help you determine the number of domains gives you too small a figure in your opinion, here's how you can raise it:

- Have one domain for each registered internet domain name that your company uses and that will need to be used for Windows 2000. That's basically one domain per domain tree root in a forest.

- Have one domain for every single-master and multimaster Windows NT domain that you have. If you are using the Windows NT multimaster domain model, consider the entire set of multi masters as one domain under Windows 2000 (use Organizational Units for your resource domains).

- Have one domain per geographical region, such as Asia-Pacific, Africa, Europe, and so on.

- Have one domain whenever putting data into one domain would deny you the control over replication that you would like if you used Organizational Units instead. It's all very well for me to say that Organizational Units are better, but that isn't true in all situations. If you work through the algorithm and come up with a single domain holding five Organizational Units, but you don't want any of the replication traffic from any of those Organizational Units to go around to certain parts of your network, you need to consider separate domains.

  Even Microsoft didn't end up with one domain. They did manage to collapse a lot of Windows NT domains though, and that's what you should be aiming for if you have multiple Windows NT domains.

Design to Help Business Plans and Budget Proposals

There are two parts to this: how you construct a business case itself for such a wide-reaching change and how you can show that you're aiming to save money with this new plan.

Simply stated, your business case should answer two main questions:

- Why will it be so bad if you stay where you are now?

- Why will it be so bad if you do not move to the Windows 2000 operating system?

If you can sensibly answer these two questions, you've probably solved half of your business case; the other half is cost. Here I'm talking about actual money. Will using Windows 2000 provide you with a tangible business cost reduction? Will it reduce your Total Cost of Ownership (TCO)? It sure will, but only if you design it correctly. Design it the wrong way, and you'll increase costs.

Imagine first that you have a company with two sites, Paris and Leicester, separated by a 64-KB WAN link. Now imagine you have one domain run by Leicester. You do not have to place a DC in Paris, if it is acceptable when a user logs on, the WAN link will use bandwidth for items like these:

- Roaming user profiles

- Access to resources, such as server-based home directories

- Group Policy Objects

- Application deployment via Microsoft Installer (MSI) files

If authentication across the link from Paris would represent a reasonable amount of traffic, but you do not want profiles and resources coming across the slow link, you could combat that by putting up a member server in Paris that could service those resources. You could even redirect application deployment mount points to the local member server in Paris (note that I'm saying *member server* and not *DC* here). However, if Group Policy Objects themselves were not to go across the link, then you need to consider a DC in Paris holding all the local resources. That gives you two sites, one domain, and two DCs.

Now let's expand this to imagine that you have a company with 50 WAN locations; they could be shops, banks, suppliers, or whatever. These are the Windows 2000 sites. Next, imagine that the same company has 10 major business units: Finance, Marketing, Sales, IS, and so on. You really have three choices when designing Active Directory for this environment:

- Assuming everything else is equal, create a single domain with a DC in whichever sites require faster access than they would get across any link. Now make the business units Organizational Units under the single domain.

    Pro

    Everything is in one domain.

    Pro

    You need as many DCs as you have sites with links that you consider too slow. If you want to count a rough minimum, make it one DC per site with more DCs for larger sites; that is a rough minimum of 50 DCs. This is a low-cost solution.

    Pro

    With one forest and one domain, any user can log on quickly everywhere because authentication is always to a local DC.

    Con

    Every part of the domain is replicated to every other part of the domain, so you have no granularity if you don't want objects from one business unit replicating to DCs everywhere.

- Create multiple domains representing the 10 major business units. Place DCs for each business unit in whichever sites require faster access than they would get across any link.

  Pro

  This means more domains than the previous solution, but replication can now be better controlled on a per-business unit basis between sites.

  Con

  Windows 2000 cannot host multiple domains on a single DC. It is anticipated that its successor will be able to do so. This can make for an extremely high cost due to the large number of DCs that you may need. If you need to be able to log on to each of the 10 business unit domains from every site, then you need 10 DCs per site, which makes 500 DCs. That's a much more costly solution. When the successor to Windows 2000 comes out, you would be looking only at around 50 DCs, which is the same number of DCs as the single-domain solution. Sadly, that isn't here yet, so this can be an expensive solution.

  Pro/Con

  With one forest and multiple domains, any user can log on quickly at any site that has a local DC for his domain; otherwise, he would have to span a WAN link to authenticate his logon and send down his data.

- Create multiple domains representing geographical regions that encompass the 50 sites. Make these geographical regions the domains and have each domain holding Organizational Units representing business units that contain only the users from that region.

  Pro

  Even if you end up with 10 geographic regions, the DCs for each region are placed only in the sites belonging to that region. So if there were five sites per region (to make the math simple), then each of the five needs only one DC. As the namespace model is a geographic model, you need to place a DC for Europe in the Asia-Pacific region only if the Asia-Pacific region ever has users from Europe that visit who need to authenticate faster than they would across the WAN link from Asia-Pacific to Europe. So the number of DCs that you need is going to be smaller.

  Pro

  Domain replication traffic occurs now only within a region and between regions that have DCs hosting the same domain.

  Con

  You end up duplicating the business units in all the domains... or maybe not, if some don't need all business units—you get the idea.

Pro/Con

> With one forest and multiple domains, any user can log on quickly at any site that has a local DC for his domain, otherwise he would have to span a WAN link to authenticate his logon and send down his data.

I hope this illustrates that while it is easy to map a simple and elegant design on paper, there can be limitations on the feasibility of the design based on replication issues, DC placement, and cost.

Recognizing Nirvana's Problems

Arguably, there are a number of "best" ways to design depending on whom you talk to. I propose an iterative approach with Windows 2000, and this is probably going to happen anyway due to the nature of the many competing factors that come into play. On your first pass through this chapter, you'll get a draft design in hand for the namespace. In Chapter 7, *Sites and Replication Topologies*, you'll get a draft site and replication design. Then you'll come up against the issue that your namespace design may need changing based on the new draft sites and replication design, specifically on the issues of domain replication and server placement that I have just covered. After you've revised the namespace design, you can sit down and look at the GPO design (using Chapters 8 and 9) in a broad sense as this will have an impact on the Organizational Unit structure that you have previously drafted in your namespace design. And so it goes.

While this is the way to design, you will come up against parts of your organization that do not fit in with the design that you're making. The point is to realize that your job is to identify a very good solution for your organization and then identify how to adapt that solution to the real world that your company lives in. One domain may be ideal but may not be practicable in terms of cost or human resources. You have to go through stages of modifying the design to a compromise solution that you're happy with.

Summary

In this chapter, I presented a series of six steps toward effective namespace design:

1. Decide on the number of domains

2. Design and name the tree structure

3. Design the workstation and server naming scheme

4. Design the hierarchy of Organizational Units

5. Design the users and groups

6. Design the the Global Catalog

Following these six steps allows you to solve the two main objectives of this chapter:

- To come up with an Active Directory namespace design to represent the structure of your business

- To minimize the number of domains by making much more use of the more flexible Organizational Units

While I've shown you how to start to design your Windows 2000 Active Directory, there is still a long way to go. Designing the namespace of domains, trees, and forests and the internal Organizational Unit hierarchy according to the guidelines given here means that you should have a structural template that represents your business model within the preceding restrictions. Hopefully this design makes sense in terms of your organization and will be simpler to manage.

The rest of the design still needs to be completed. You need to take a look at the low-level network links between sites and how they will affect your replication decisions. We then need to tackle the subject of how to revise the initial namespace design based on Group Policy Objects, security delegation and auditing, schema changes, and so on. Next I'll move on to designing the physical site topology that the DCs use when communicating with one another.

7

Sites and Replication Topologies

As I mentioned in Chapter 4, *Active Directory Replication*, there are two aspects to replication:

- How data gets replicated around an existing network of links between DCs
- How the Knowledge Consistency Checker (KCC) generates and maintains the replication links between servers, both intrasite and intersite

I covered the former in Chapter 4, and I'll cover the latter here, leading to an explanation of how to properly design a representation of your organization's physical infrastructure within Active Directory.

Intrasite and Intersite Topologies

Two distinct types of replication links exist with Windows 2000 sites: intrasite (within sites) and intersite (between sites). A Windows 2000 service known as the Knowledge Consistency Checker (KCC) is responsible for automatically generating the replication links between intrasite DCs. The KCC will create intersite links automatically for you but only when an administrator has specified that two sites should be connected. Every aspect of the KCC and the links that are created is configurable, so you can manipulate what has been automatically created and what will be automatically created via manipulation of the various options. You can even disable the KCC if you wish and manually create all links.

Note that there is a large distinction between the KCC (the process that runs every 15 minutes and creates the replication topology) and the replication process itself. The KCC is not involved in the regular work of replicating the actual data in any way. Intrasite replication along the links created by the KCC uses a notification process to announce that changes have occurred. If no changes occur at all within a six-hour period the replication process is kicked off automatically anyway just to make sure. Intersite replication on the other hand does not use a notification process. Instead it uses a replication schedule to transfer updates, using compression to reduce the total traffic size.

The KCC uses a fairly simple algorithm to create the topologies, and the topologies it creates work well in their default configurations. However, I don't think as a Windows 2000 administrator you should just accept the topologies it creates without examining them in detail. You should investigate and understand what has been done by the KCC. If you then look over the topology and are happy with it, you have actively, rather than passively, accepted what has been done. While letting the KCC do its own thing is fine, every organization is different, and you may have requirements for the site and link design that it is not aware of and cannot build automatically.

Other administrators will want to delve into the internals of Active Directory and turn off the KCC entirely, doing everything by hand. This approach is valid, as long as you know what you're doing, but I prefer to let the KCC do its work, helping it along with a guiding hand every now and then. I cover all these options in the design section later.

The KCC

DCs within sites have links created between them by the KCC. These links use the DC's GUID as the unique identifier. These links exist in Active Directory as connection objects and only use the Directory Service Remote Procedure Call (DS-RPC) transport to replicate with one another. No other replication transport mechanism is available. However, when you need to connect two sites, you manually create a site link via the Sites and Services Manager (SSM) and specify a replication transport to use. When you do this, intersite link connection objects are automatically created by the KCC in Active Directory. There are two replication transports to choose from: standard DS-RPC or Inter-Site Mechanism Simple Mail Transport Protocol (ISM-SMTP). The latter means sending updates via the mail system using certificates and encryption for security.

There are two reasons that the KCC cannot automatically create links between two sites. First, the KCC has no idea which sites you will want to connect. Second, the KCC does not know which replication transport protocol you will want to use.

The KCC runs locally every 15 minutes on each DC. The default time period can be changed, and it can be started manually on demand if required. If I create two servers in a new domain called Server A and Server B, the KCC will run on each server to create links. Each KCC is tasked with creating a link to define incoming replication only. The KCC on Server A will define an incoming link from Server B, and Server B's KCC will define an incoming link from Server A. The KCC creates only one incoming link per replication partner, so Server A will never have two incoming links from Server B, for example.

The KCC does not create one topology for all NCs, nor one topology per NC. The Configuration and Schema NCs share one replication topology, so the KCC creates a topology for these two together. The KCC also creates another topology on a per-domain basis. Because the Schema and Configuration are enterprise wide in scope, the KCC needs to replicate changes to these items across site links. The KCC needs to maintain a forest-wide topology spanning all domains for these two NCs together. However, unless a domain is set up to span multiple sites, the topology for a particular domain will be made up of only intrasite connections. If the domain does span sites, then the KCC needs to create a replication topology across those sites.

The GC is not a Naming Context in its own right, and so it can't really have its own replication topology. As the GC is formed from a selection of attributes on those servers that host the GC in each domain, the GC replication becomes part of the replication for each domain. As two partners replicate a domain NC, the GC is replicated as well. There is no replication of the GC between different domains.

Automatic Intrasite Topology Generation by the KCC

For each NC, the KCC builds a bidirectional ring of links between the DCs in a site. However, while upstream and downstream links are created between partners around a ring, the KCC creates links across the ring as well. It does this to make sure that it stays within the following guidelines:

- Every DC must be within three hops from any other DC. This is known as the *three-hop rule*.

- The default latency (maximum time for replication between any two DCs) for replication is five minutes.

- The maximum convergence (maximum time for an update to reach all DCs) is 15 minutes.

Technically speaking, due to the three-hop rule, when you put in your eighth DC the KCC will start adding branches across the circular ring.

Assuming you have five servers in a ring and you add a sixth, the other servers around the ring add and delete connection objects in order to accommodate the newcomer. So if Server C and Server D are linked and Server F interposes itself between them, Server C and Server D delete their interconnections and create connections to Server F instead. Server F also creates connections to Server C and Server D. Let's now take a look at this process in more detail.

Two servers

Mycorp starts off with one DC, Server A. When Server B is promoted as the second DC for the domain, the DCPROMO process uses Server A as its source for Active Directory information for the GC, Schema, and Configuration on Server B. During the promotion process, the Configuration Container is replicated from Server A to Server B, and Server B creates the relevant incoming connection object representing Server A. Server B then informs Server A that it exists, and Server A correspondingly creates the incoming connection object representing Server B. Replication now occurs for all NCs using the connection objects. While replication occurs separately for each NC, the same connection object is used for all three at this moment.

Three servers

The DCPROMO process is later started on Server C. Server C then uses a DNS lookup and picks one of the existing DCs to use as a promotion partner. For now I'll say that it picks Server B. During the promotion process, the Configuration container is replicated from Server B to Server C, and Server C creates the relevant incoming connection object representing Server B. Server C then informs Server B that it exists, and Server B correspondingly creates the incoming connection object representing Server C. Replication now occurs for all NCs using the connection objects.

At present, you have two-way links between Server A and Server B as well as between Server B and Server C. We have no links between Server A and Server C, but the KCC must create a ring topology for replication purposes. So as soon as Server B does a full replication to Server C, Server C knows about Server A from the Configuration NC. Server C's KCC then instantly creates an incoming connection object for Server A. Server A now finds out about Server C in one of two ways:

- Server A requests updates from Server B and identifies a new DC.
- Server C requests changes from Server A, and this allows Server A to identify the new DC.

Server A now creates an incoming connection object for Server C. This completes the Server A to Server B to Server C to Server A loop.

Four servers

Server D comes along, and the promotion process starts. It picks Server C to connect to. Server D ends up creating the incoming connection object for Server C. Server C also creates the incoming connection object for Server D. You now have the loop from the previous section plus a two-way link from Server C to Server D. See Figure 7-1 for this topology.

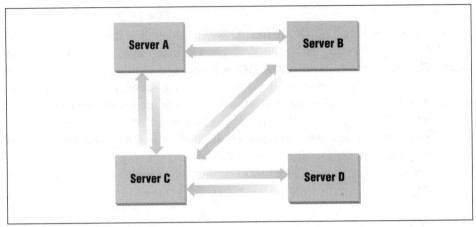

Figure 7-1. Adding a fourth DC to a site

Server D's KCC now uses the newly replicated data from Server C to go through the existing topology. It knows that it has to continue the ring topology, and as it is already linked to Server C, Server D has to create an incoming connection object for one of Server C's partners. It chooses Server B in this case. So Server D's KCC creates an incoming connection object for Server B. Server D then requests changes from Server B. The rest of the process can happen in a number of ways, so I'll just play out one scenario.

Server B now knows about Server D. Server B's KCC kicks into action and realizes that it doesn't need the link to Server C, so it deletes that connection and creates a new one directly to Server D itself. Finally, as replication takes place around the ring along the existing links, Server C notes that it has a now defunct incoming link from Server B and removes it. You now have a simple ring as depicted in Figure 7-2.

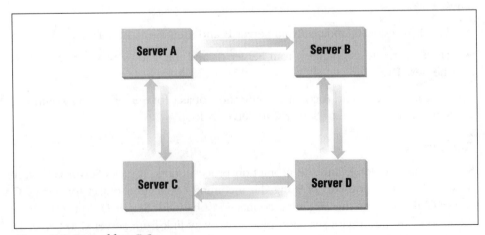

Figure 7-2. Ring of four DCs

Eight servers

Once you hit eight servers connected together, you need more links across the ring if you are to maintain the three-hop rule. If you look at Figure 7-3, you will see this demonstrated. If the cross-ring links did not exist, some servers would be four hops away from one another. The KCC figures out which servers it wishes to link by allowing the last server into the ring to make the initial choice. So, if Server H is the new server in the ring, it knows that Server D is four hops away and makes a connection to it. When Server D's KCC receives the new data that Server H has linked to it, it then reciprocates and creates a link to Server H. However, this doesn't completely solve the problem.

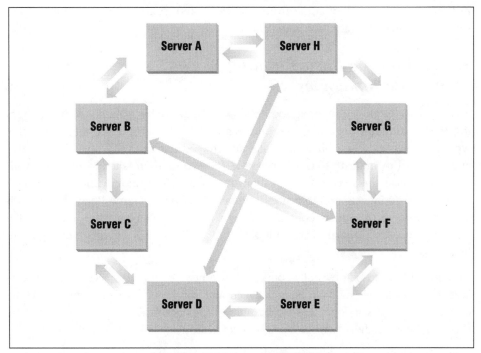

Figure 7-3. Eight servers and the extra KCC-generated links

Consider Server B and Server F, they're still four hops away from each other. So, now the KCC creates a link between these pairs in order to maintain the three hop rule.

Now what?

I've now gone through the mechanism that the KCC uses for intrasite link generation between DCs. However, that's not the whole story. Remember that Windows 2000 can have multiple domains per site, so what happens if I add *othercorp.com* (a new domain in the same forest) to the same site or even *sales.mycorp.com* (a new child domain). What happens then? The answer is the same for both, and it is based on NCs:

- The Schema and Configuration replicate enterprise wide, and they share a replication topology. Although they replicate separately, it is along the same links.

- Each domain replicates only domain wide, so the domain topologies for both domains stay in the same ring formation that they previously had.

Once the two domains integrate, the KCC-generated topology for *mycorp.com* and the KCC-generated topology for the other domain stay the same. However, the KCC-generated Configuration/Schema replication topology that exists separately on both domains will form itself into its own ring, encompassing both domains according to standard KCC rules.

To summarize, when you have multiple domains in a site, each domain will have its own KCC-generated topology connecting its DCs, but all the DCs in the site, no matter what domain they come from, will be linked in a separate topology representing Schema/Configuration replication.

Site Links—The Basic Building Blocks of Intersite Topologies

Having sites is all well and good, but you need to be able to connect them together if you are ever going to replicate any data. An intersite connection of this type is known as a site link. Site links are created manually by the administrator and are used to indicate that it is possible for two or more sites to replicate with each other. Site links connect more than two sites if the underlying physical network already connects multiple sites together using ATM, Frame Relay, MANs with T1 connections, or similar connections. For example, if a 64-KBps Frame Relay network exists and is shared by multiple sites, all those sites can share a single site link.

Sites do not have to be physically connected by a network for replication to occur. Replication can occur via multiple links between any two hosts from separate sites. However, in order for Windows 2000 to be able to understand that replication should be occurring between these two sites, you have to create a site link between them.

Figure 7-4 shows part of a network that has two site links connecting three sites.

The site links correspond to the underlying physical network of two dedicated leased-line connections, with one network having a slightly higher cost than the other (not a monetary cost, a value set by the administrator indicating the speed of the link). The Sales domain has two domain controllers that need to replicate, one in London and one in Brasilia. However, in this figure replication is broken, as the two DCs cannot directly replicate with each other over a single site link. This may seem confusing as both servers are more than likely able to see each other across the network, but you must nevertheless create a site link between sites that have DCs that need to replicate.

Consider it another way. There are three ways to fix the problem. First, you could add a new Sales DC, say Sales=DC3, to Paris. This allows Sales=DC1 to replicate with Sales=DC3 and Sales=DC3 to replicate with Sales=DC2. Second, you could

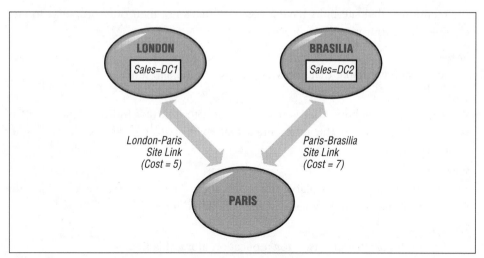

Figure 7-4. Broken Sales domain replication over site links

use a site link bridge, discussed in the next section. Third, you could create a third site link (with the combined cost of the two physical networks that will be used for the replication traffic) that indicates to the two servers that they can replicate with each other. Figure 7-5 shows that new site link in place.

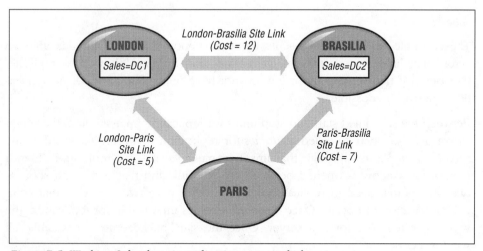

Figure 7-5. Working Sales domain replication over site links

Replication of the Sales domain is now possible between Sales=DC1 and Sales=DC2. Replication traffic will go over the existing physical links, for a total cost of 12 to use those links.

I've mentioned that site links have a cost, but that's not their only property. In fact, site links have four important properties:

Name
> An identifying name that you wish to give to the site link.

Cost
> An integer weighting that you give to the site link that indicates the speed of the link relative to the other links that exist. Lower costs are faster; higher costs are slower.

Schedule
> The times that are available for replication to occur. Replication does not occur on that site link outside of the scheduled times.

Transports
> The protocols that are used for replication along this link.

Cost

As each link has a cost, it is possible to calculate the total cost of traveling over any one route by adding up all the costs of the individual routes. If multiple routes exist between two disparate sites, then the KCC will automatically identify the lowest cost route and use that for replication.

Schedule

The schedule on a link represents the time period that replication is allowed across that link. Servers also maintain times that they are allowed to replicate. Obviously, if two servers and a link do not have times that coincide, no replication will ever be possible.

Between the scheduled start and stop times for replication on a site link, the server is available to open so-called *windows* for replication to occur. As soon as any server that replicates through that link becomes available for replication, then a replication window is opened between the site link and that server. As soon as two servers that need to replicate with each other have two windows that coincide, replication can occur. Once a server becomes unavailable for replication, the window is removed for that server. Once the site link becomes unavailable, all windows close.

> If two servers that need to replicate never have two replication windows that coincide, their connection is deemed to be unavailable

Transport

Site links can currently replicate using two transport mechanisms:

- Directory Service Remote Procedure Call (DS-RPC)
- Inter-Site Mechanism Simple Mail Transport Protocol (ISM-SMTP)

A site link using DS-RPC means that servers wishing to replicate using that site link can make direct synchronous connections using TCP/IP across the link. As the transport protocol is synchronous, the replication across the connection is conducted and negotiated in real time between two partners. This is the normal sort of connection for a real-time link. However, some sites may not be connected all the time. In fact, they may dialup only every half hour to send and receive email or be connected across the Internet or even have a very unreliable link. This sort of link is where ISM-SMTP comes into play.

The SMTP connector, as a site link using the ISM-SMTP transport, is called allows partner DCs to encrypt and email their updates to each other. In this scenario, Windows 2000 assumes that you already have an underlying SMTP-based connection mechanism between these two sites. If you don't, then you'll have to set one up for this to work. If a connection is in place, then the SMTP Connector assumes that the existing underlying mail routing structure will sort out how mail is transferred. To that end, a site link using the SMTP Connector ignores the scheduling tab, as it will send and receive updates automatically via the underlying system whenever the email system sends and receives them itself.

SMTP Connector messages are encrypted using digital signatures, so to encrypt the messages, you need to install the optional Windows 2000 Certificate Server service and obtain your own digital signature for your organization.

> The SMTP Connector cannot be used for domain NC replication. It can, however, be used to replicate GC, Schema, and configuration information. This means that multisite domains with slow links will be required to use DS-RPC for domain replication. Of course, this doesn't mean that the physical connection between sites has to be up all the time, only that it must be up when the DCs in each site communicate.

When the KCC becomes involved

When you have two sites that you want to connect, you have two options. You can manually create a site link between them, at which point the KCC will automatically connect together one DC from each site. The KCC will automatically select the DCs and create the relevant incoming connection objects for both servers. Alternatively, you can create the incoming connection objects manually in Active Directory using the SSM. The two DCs that link two sites, no matter how the connection objects are created, are known as *bridgehead servers*.

The KCC actively uses site link costs to identify which routes it should be using for replication purposes. If a stable series of site links exists in an organization, and a new route is added with a lower cost, then the KCC will switch over to use the new link where appropriate and delete the old link. The network of connections that the KCC creates is known as a *minimum-cost-spanning tree*.

Having the KCC compound your mistakes

If you make a mistake with site link costings, then you can cause network problems very quickly. For this reason you need to be aware of what the KCC is doing. If you bring up a new site link with a very high cost, say 50, and you accidentally leave off the zero, then the route cost of 5 for the new site link may cause the KCCs on all DCs to suddenly reorganize the links to route through your new slow link. Your link becomes saturated, and your servers replicate much more slowly, if at all, over the slow link.

In fact, the KCC didn't make the mistake, but it has compounded it by following its algorithm. If a real cost-5 link were introduced that represented a real cost saving over many other routes, it is the KCC's job to switch over and use that link. That's why you always need to check your data for the intersite replication topology carefully.

While it's difficult to guard against making a mistake like this sometimes, no matter how careful an administrator you are, if you understand the way that the KCC works, you will be able to use this information to debug potential problems much more rapidly.

Site Link Bridges—The Second Building Blocks of Intersite Topologies

While site links are used to indicate that replication can take place between two sites, site link bridges indicate that replication is possible between two sites that don't have a direct site link. Site link bridges can be created automatically by the KCC, or they can be manually created. When a bridge is created, certain specified site links become members of that bridge and are designated as being interconnected (or bridged) for replication purposes. The bridge knows how these sites are connected, so you would specify that this site link bridge bridged the London-Paris link and the Paris-Brasilia link. Then servers in Brasilia or London will see that a replication connection is now possible via the site link bridge, and the site link bridge will know that in order for traffic to get from London to Brasilia, it must use the London-Paris and then Paris-Brasilia links in that order. Figure 7-6 demonstrates this in action.

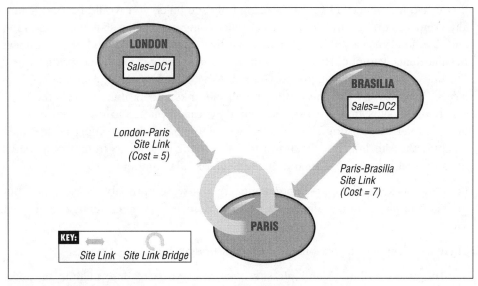

Figure 7-6. Working Sales domain replication using a site link bridge

The point here is that a site link bridge knows how the site links in its care are interconnected and thus how to route requests from one site through to another along its network of site links.

For a more complex example, consider the network of site links corresponding to physical networks in Figure 7-7.

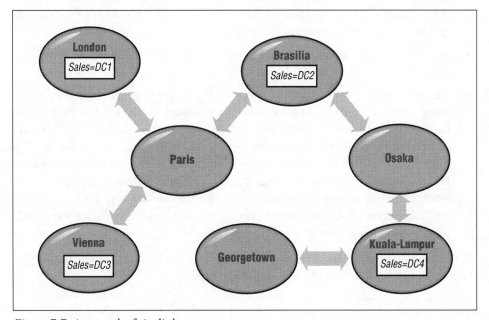

Figure 7-7. A network of site links

If you had to connect all four DCs using only site links, you would have to manually connect London and Vienna to Brasilia using something like Vienna-London and London-Brasilia (although that isn't the only solution) and then connect Brasilia-Kuala Lumpur. However, with a site link bridge you could bridge every site link except Kuala Lumpur to Georgetown (capital of the Pulau-Pinang province in Malaysia, by the way). Bridging all the links except this one tells the servers in those sites that are bridged that they can replicate to any sites that are bridged over the existing site links. So when Vienna wishes to replicate to Kuala Lumpur, the site link bridge knows that the traffic should go from Vienna-Paris, Paris-Brasilia, Brasilia-Osaka, and finally Osaka-Kuala Lumpur.

Bridging the Kuala Lumpur–Georgetown site link would probably make sense, but in this example there is no need, as no Sales domain servers currently exist in that site.

There are a number of reasons why site link bridges make great sense:

- The ability to bridge multiple site links saves you creating multiple site links that do not mirror your physical network solely for Windows 2000 replication purposes.

- If you do not have a fully routed IP network throughout your organization, using a site link bridge enables you to connect nonrouted IP networks for replication purposes.

- The KCC determines what route to use across all site links within a bridge, based on the costs of all possible links. So, if you have more than one link between sites, bridging all links will make sure that the KCC picks the best one when creating a replication connection.

- The KCC can be configured to automatically bridge all site links that use a common transport.

- Site link bridges can be used to force replication to go through certain hub sites. Look at Figure 7-7 again. Imagine you had networks directly between London and Brasilia, London and Vienna, and Vienna and Brasilia; but you did not want to use them for replication traffic under any circumstances. That means you should not create site links between these three sites, since the KCC will detect the link as available for replication purposes and create connection objects across it. Instead, use a site link bridge and force replication traffic between these three sites to be replicated across the existing site links in Figure 7-7 by routing it all through Paris.

Now that you've seen the site links and site link bridges, let's take that look at how to design your sites and their replication links.

Designing Sites and Links for Replication

There is only one really important point, which is the overriding factor when designing a replication strategy for your network: how much traffic and over what period will you be replicating across the network? However, replication isn't the only reason for creating sites. Sites also need to exist to group sets of machines together for ease of locating data, finding the nearest DC to authenticate with, or finding the nearest DFS share mount point.

Step 1—Gather Background Data for Your Network

Before you sit down to design your site and WAN topology, you need to obtain the map of your existing network infrastructure. This map should contain all physical locations where your company has computers, along with every link between those locations. The speed and reliability of each link should be noted.

If you have an existing IP infrastructure, write down all the subnets that correspond to the sites that you have noted.

Step 2—Design the Sites

From the network diagram, you need to draw your site structure and name each site, using a one-to-one mapping from the network diagram as your starting point. If you have 50 physical WAN locations, then you have 50 sites. If only 30 of these will be used for Windows 2000, you may not see a need to include the entire set of sites in Active Directory. But if you do, it is much easier to visualize your entire network and add clients or servers to those locations later.

 When drawing Windows 2000 networks, sites normally are represented by ovals.

Remember that a site is a well-connected set of subnets (*well-connected* tends to mean about 10-MBps LAN speed). A site does not have to have a server in it; it can be composed entirely of clients. If you have two buildings, or an entire campus, that is connected over 10/100-MBps links, your entire location is a single site.

This is not a hard-and-fast rule. By the normal rules, two locations connected over a 2-MBps link represent two distinct sites. You can, however, group networks together into single sites if you want to. You have to appreciate that there will be

Active Directory Database and Traffic Sizing

I conducted a number of tests with beta 1 and onward of Windows 2000 to determine how much network bandwidth is used when replicating objects and properties. As Windows 2000 replicates at the property level, you need much less bandwidth to replicate a changed property than you do to replicate the entire object (with the changed property), as was the case under Windows NT. However, this introduces more of a problem. Under Windows NT, the number of attributes and thus the size of an object was fixed, so if you knew that you were going to make 200 user password changes a day on average, you were going to replicate 200 times the size of a user object. Under Windows 2000, I can tell you that a user is approximately 4 KB in the *NTDS.DIT* (Active Directory database). I can also tell you that one Organizational Unit is approximately 1.5 KB. So, if I make 200 password changes, how much data gets replicated? The answer is 200 times the password property size—but how much is that? We know that it is less than 4K, but how much less? It matters if the figure is 20,000 password changes or modifications to other attributes. If you couple this with creations, deletions, and other Active Directory changes, you have to start making estimates for your replication before you can actually figure out what site links that this data will use.

As each successive build was introduced, I had to redo my figures, and there were significant changes as Windows 2000 was refined. Microsoft has started publishing its own comprehensive figures. So rather than duplicate their work, I stopped producing mine and started referring to theirs. I suggest that you obtain Microsoft's current replication figures for Windows 2000 so that you can make effective decisions regarding replication. The link to Microsoft's documents on this area can be found on the web page for this book at the O'Reilly web site. I can't give you valid URLs here because Microsoft has yet to release the documents into the public domain.

These figures will allow you to gauge the total size of your Active Directory for a domain and then work out both how much replication traffic you will have to initially pass to a new DC for each NC and how much regular NC traffic you will need to pass between DCs.

In order to determine the correct size of the Active Directory database—*C:\ WINNT\NTDS\NTDS.DIT*—first force an online defragmentation and then reboot. This will report an accurate *NTDS.DIT* size. If you don't do this, the wrong size will be reported because the file is constantly held open.

more replication than if you had created two sites and a site link because DCs in both physical locations will maintain the intrasiteintrasite replication ring topology. If you had created two sites and a site link, only two Bridgehead Servers would replicate with each other.

I've also successfully used a single site to represent two networks, one with clients and one with servers, separated by a 2-MBps link. The clients at the end of the 2-MBps link successfully authenticated quickly and downloaded profiles from a server at the other end of the other link. If I'd used two sites, I'd have had to create a site link between them, but the clients still would have had to authenticate across the link anyway.

To summarize, I would suggest that, by default, you create one site per 10-MBps-or-higher location, unless you have an overriding reason not to do so.

Step 3—Design the Domain Controller Locations

Placing of DCs is fairly easy, but the number of DCs to use is a different matter entirely.

Where to put DCs

Each workstation in a domain exists in a single site that it knows about. When a user tries to log on to the domain at that workstation, the workstation authenticates to a DC from the local site, which it originally locates via a DNS query. If no DC is available in the local site, the workstation finds a remote site, and by a process of negotiation with a DC in that site, either authenticates with that DC or is redirected to a more local DC.

This consideration governs the placement of DCs. You should put at least one DC for each domain in all sites for authentication purposes. You should place one DC for authentication purposes per domain in all sites that meet any of the following criteria:

- The site has links that are not fast enough for logon purposes to a particular domain.

- The site has links that may be fast enough for logon, but you do not wish to authenticate across them for a particular domain.

- If a site has a number of workstations, and the users themselves are from a native-mode domain that makes heavy use of universal groups, you should put a DC with a GC in the same site or to a nearby one with a fast link. As universal groups exist in the GC and as all universal groups are expanded on logon, you should make sure that a DC is placed in a nearby site, so that token explosion (see Chapter 6, *Designing the Namespace*) is not propagated across a slow link.

The first and second points also need to be considered in the light of the number of users and workstations at the sites. If a branch office has a 64-KBps link, would you want users to log on using a centrally located DC at the other end of that link?

If you had 10 users in that office, it may be no problem. If you had 20 users, you may not be so sure. If you had 50 it would be impossible, so you should put in a DC at that site.

How many DCs to have

Deciding how may DCs to create is never easy, as Windows NT administrators well know. The problem is that it depends on the power of the individual server and what else the server is doing at the time as much as it does on the operating system's ability to authenticate users. If you have an Intel server that's already serving 500 heavy users and is close to its load limit, could it authenticate 100 additional users quickly enough at the same time? Powerful servers can authenticate hundreds of users simultaneously, but even these servers will balk if they are already heavily loaded.

I'm afraid that I can't answer this question for you. The only way to decide is to consider how many users will need to use DCs for authentication purposes and what pattern of logons occur throughout the day at your organization. That way, you should be able to judge for yourself how many DCs you may need for authentication purposes.

Reasons for putting a server in more than one site

By default, any server that you install or bring into a domain will belong to one site only. However, there can be instances in which you may want to configure a server to belong to multiple sites. For example, you might want to make sure that workstations from a number of sites all authenticate using one DC.

Here's an example: imagine five sites (Cairo, Delhi, Bangkok, Sydney, and Rio de Janeiro), each representing a 20-user branch office of a large centralized company. Each site has a 64-KBps link back to the main office in London. You've decided that each site can authenticate down the slow link to a central server, even though all 20 users will log on at 0900 each morning, because time zone differences effectively stagger the load. In addition, to make sure that these clients do not authenticate with any other servers, you have to provide them with their own central server that is also a member of all the remote sites. That way, when the clients attempt to log on, they will do so down the slow link, but only to that one server.

While sites are used for replication, for clients to find resources, and to cut down on traffic on intersite connections, modifying the site membership can cause performance problems. However, in this case we understand the consequences and this looks like a good decision.

Configuring a server to have multiple site membership is fairly straightforward. First, manually create the sites that the server is to be a member of if they do not already exist. Then edit the registry on the server that is to have multiple site membership and add a REG_MULTI_SZ value called SiteCoverage to the HKLM\SYSTEM\ CurrentControlSet\ServicesNetlogon\Parameters subkey. Add the names of the sites to this value. If you're using RegEdit or RegEdt32, use Shift-Enter to add the data for multiple lines.

Step 4—Plan Intrasite Replication

This is a short step. Your only requirement is to set the schedules that the replication cycles use. As to the connection objects themselves, if you don't specifically need to change the intrasite replication topologies that the KCC sets up, then don't. Leave the KCC to do its stuff by itself; it takes care of things pretty well. You could remove the default links and make a long linked list of replication partners—A to B to C to D to E—rather than a ring if you wanted to, but you have to have a very good reason to do so.

If you do want to manipulate the existing setup of replication between DCs, you'll have to stop the KCC service generating the intrasite topology for that site.

You can turn off intrasite or intersite topology generation by the KCC by using the SSM to look at the properties of the specific NTDS Site Settings object that you are interested in.

Step 5—Decide How You Will Use the KCC to Your Advantage

There are really three ways to use the KCC to your advantage over intersite links:

- Manually create all the connection objects and turn off the KCC for intersite replication. This isn't something I would recommend unless you know exactly what you're doing.

- Let the KCC generate your entire topology for you automatically. This is the default and is what Microsoft recommends as standard. You still need to create all site links manually, but if you leave site link transitiveness on by default, the KCC will not need you to create extra site links in order to replicate data via sites that do not have the relevant DCs. Site link bridges will not be used in this scenario.

You can define multiple site links between two distinct sets of Bridgehead Servers at separate sites if you wish, i.e., DC1 in Site A connects to DC3 in Site B and DC2 in Site A connects to DC4 in Site B. This will help in case one of the servers at one end of a single site link goes down, as this means that you will lose only one site link and not the intersite connectivity.

- A mixture of the two can be had by forcing the KCC to make decisions based on certain key information that you provide. For example, if you make sure that you leave site links nontransitive, the KCC will be able to replicate only across site links that do exist. You then can make use of site link bridges to force the KCC to use certain routes for replication.

If you have many connections that need to be created but don't want to use the KCC, you can use the KCC to start with, allow it to create its default objects, turn it off, and then modify the objects to whatever you choose. If you have 500 links, for example, but want to manipulate only one, this is the best way of doing things.

You can leave this step until after you have designed the site links (steps 6, 7, and 8) if you are not sure what to do. The example design for PetroCorp shows why this is useful later.

Step 6—Create Site Links for Low-Cost Well-Connected Links

Now that you have all the sites down on paper, you need to think about the links. In this step we identify those sites that are interconnected with what can be considered very fast links or backbones.

Site links should be created along 2-MBps-or-higher connections between distinct sites. For each link, you need to choose an appropriate name, cost, and transport. The name should be distinct and immediately conjure up what the link represents. The transport for low-cost links is normally DS-RPC; such a high-capacity network can cope with traffic of this nature. However, if you only want to use email across a link, then make the transport ISM-SMTP. If you set up both for some reason, you normally would set a slightly higher cost for the SMTP Connectors than you would for standard DS-RPC-based replication.

When choosing costs, the values you choose depend entirely on the different intersite link speeds that you have in your organization. If you have only 64-KBps and 1-MBps* links between sites, then you really need only two values. If you use both transport types, then you'll need four. However, if your sites have many different types of connection, such as 10 MBps, T3, T2, T1, 256 KBps, and 64 KBps, you'll need many more. The values that you use should represent in your own mind the difference in cost for using a route. The key to using costs is to realize that everything is relative. After all, if you have two routes to a site and they have a cost of 1 and 2, respectively, 2 seems twice as slow as 1. That isn't true; it is just a slower link—not twice as slow. Because the numbers are so close together, there is almost nothing between these values. However, the difference between 10 and 20 is more significant. When determining values, I suggest that as a starting point; use 1 through 10 for low-cost fast links, 11 through 20 for medium-cost links, and 21 and above for higher-cost routes.

Create all the site links along fast interconnected links between sites.

Step 7—Create Site Links for Medium-Cost Links

Having identified the fastest links and created site links for them, you now need to create any links that are interconnected with a similar transport at medium cost. These are sites such as those connected via MANs with T1 connections, interconnected via frame relay clouds, or entirely connected together. Create these sites now, and remember to use a slightly slower value for any SMTP Connectors.

Step 8—Create Site Links for High-Cost Links

Finally, you have the WAN connections that are high cost due to their slow speed or unreliability. You now need to create those site links and allocate a name, transport, and cost as before. For unreliable links, consider using an SMTP Connector with a certificate to encrypt the data. This will ensure that as soon as a link is available for email that your updates will propagate backward and forward as required. For more reliable links, use the standard DS-RPC connector; later in Step 10 you can configure the replication times to be suitable to that link.

Step 9—Create Site Link Bridges

If you chose the third option in Step 5 and turned off site link transitiveness, you now need to create site link bridgesite link bridges or more site links in order to satisfy your desire to force the KCC to create its topology along certain paths.

---

* In the U.K., 64-KBps links are known as *kilostream links* and 1-MBps links are known as *megastream links*.

Step 10—Design the Replication Schedule

Now sit down with your entire map and identify in which time windows you will allow replication along the various links. Low-cost links may allow traffic all day. Medium-cost links may allow traffic from late afternoon until early morning, and high-cost links may allow replication windows only at very specific times. It all depends on you. In my mind, there is certainly a split between the high-, medium- and low- cost link replication schedules that you create. Remember that you must have a common window for replication across all routes.

Examples

Having considered the 10 steps, let's take another brief look at the three examples from the previous chapter and see what they will need in terms of sites.

TwoSiteCorp

TwoSiteCorp has two locations split by a 128-KBps link. This means creation of two sites, separated by a single site link, with DCs for domain authentication in each site. The site link cost is not an issue, as only one route exists between the two sites. Here the only issue is scheduling the replication, which depends on the existing traffic levels of the link. Schedule replication during the least busy times for a slow link like this. If replication has to take place all the time, as changes need to be propagated rapidly, then it is time to consider increasing the capacity of the link.

RetailCorp

RetailCorp has a large centralized retail organization with 600 shops connected via 64-KBps links to a large centralized 10/100-MBps interconnected headquarters in London. In this situation, you have one site for HQ and 600 sites for the stores. RetailCorp also will use a DC in each store. They then have to create 600 high-cost site links, each with the same cost. RetailCorp decides this is one very good reason to use ADSI (discussed in Part III) and writes a script to automate the creation of the site link objects in the Configuration. The only aspect of the site links that is important here is the schedule. Can central HQ cope with all of the servers replicating intersite at the same time? Does the replication have to be staggered? The decision is made that all data has to be replicated during the times that the stores are closed; for stores that do not close, data is replicated during the least busy times. There is no need to worry about site link bridges or site link transitiveness as all links go through the central hub, and no stores need to intercommunicate. The administrators decide to let the KCC pick the Bridgehead Servers automatically.

PetroCorp

PetroCorp has 94 outlying branch offices. These branch offices are connected via 64-KBps links to five central hub sites. These five hubs are connected to the central organization's HQ in Denver via T2, T1, 256-KBps, and 128-KBps links. Some of the hubs also are interconnected. To make it easier to understand, look at PetroCorp's network again (Figure 7-8).

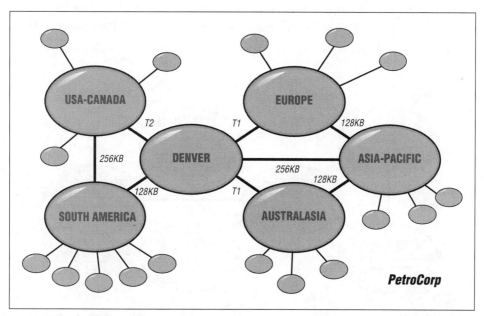

Figure 7-8. PetroCorp's network connections

Initially, you need to create 100 sites representing HQ, the hubs, and the branch offices. How many servers do you need per site? From the design I made in Chapter 6, I decided on nine domains in the forest. Each of those distinct domains must obviously have a server within it that forms part of the single forest. However, although the description doesn't say so, there is very little cross-pollination of clients from one hub needing to log on to servers from another hub. As this is the case, there is no need to put a server for every domain in every hub. If a user from Denver travels to the *asiapac.petrocorp.com* domain, the user can still log on to *petrocorp.com* from the Asia-Pacific hub, albeit much more slowly. PetroCorp sees that what little cross-pollination traffic it has is made up of two types of user:

- Senior *petrocorp.com* IT and business managers traveling to all hubs.

- Groups of Europe and Australasia users regularly staying at the alternate hub for periods during joint research. This means that *europe.petrocorp.com* users need to log on in the Australasia hub and *australasia.europe.com* users need to log on in the Europe hub.

While the senior managers' use is infrequent, these key decision makers need to log on as rapidly as possible to access email and their data. Money is found to ultimately place *petrocorp.com* servers for authentication purposes in each of the five hubs. The second requirement means that servers for each domain need to be added to the alternate hub. The ultimate intention in the next release of Windows 2000 is to allow each DC to support multiple domains; then, all five hubs plus Denver will support all of the six major domains. Until that time, only enough money is found to support *petrocorp.com* from outside its own Denver location and the Europe/Australasia hubs hosting each other's domains (see Figure 7-9).

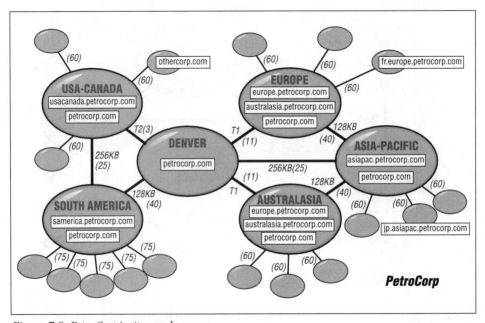

Figure 7-9. PetroCorp's sites and servers

While domains normally are represented by triangles in diagrams, here the rectangular borders around a domain name represent servers that host that domain. Each domain is hosted by multiple servers represented by a single rectangle, although you could run this structure using only one server per rectangle. You can see that *petrocorp.com* is hosted in Denver, as well as in all other hubs.

Regarding intrasite KCC topology generation: PetroCorp has decided to let the KCC automatically generate intra-domain server links. If this causes a problem, then local administrators should be able to handle it.

The site links are depicted in Figure 7-9 with parentheses to indicate the costs. They can also be described as follows:

- Create one low-cost (3) DS-RPC site link for the T2 connection.

- Create two medium-cost (11) DS-RPC site links representing the T1 connections.

- Create high-cost DS-RPC site links for the five remaining interhub connections of 256 KBps (25) and 128 KBps (40).

What about the branches? According to Chapter 6's original description, all links are stable except the links between the eight South America branches and the hub, which are very unreliable. In this case, you have two choices: you can either let the clients in those eight sites authenticate across the less-than-reliable links or you can place servers in those branches so that authentication is always possible, even when the link is down. PetroCorp opts for the latter and places servers in each of the eight branches. However, DS-RPC is not the best replication mechanism for asynchronous links like these, so instead PetroCorp creates digital certificates and rolls out a certificate server to those sites to enable the replication mechanism to use the underlying mail transport via an SMTP Connector for each link. That changes the list to include the following site links:

- Create 86 high-cost DS-RPC site links for each of the stable 64 KBps (60) links.

- Create eight high-cost ISM-SMTP site links for each of the unstable 64 KBps (75) links representing South America branches.

PetroCorp's administrators then sit back and decide that they are going to create some redundant site links of the same cost so that if a single Bridgehead server is lost in any of the major hubs, replication can still continue. Each hub has enough DCs to cope with this, so they add the redundant links.

While steps 6, 7, and 8 have been completed, I have, however, appeared to skip steps 4 and 5. Step 5 was left until now on purpose, since the administrators wanted to wait until the site links were designed to see whether site link transitiveness should be turned on or off and whether bridging routes might help. Now you can easily see that transitivity is important between the Europe and Australasia hubs. If you don't turn transitiveness on by default, then you need to create a site link bridge in Denver that allows the *europe.petrocorp.com* and *australasia. petrocorp.com* domains to replicate across the two T1 links even though they have no direct links.

Now, look at the diagram again, and consider that transitiveness is turned on. This means any site can use any connection to any other site based on the lowest cost. So if you leave site link transitiveness on and let the KCC create the intersite connection objects and Bridgehead Servers, replication traffic between Denver and

South America is likely to route through USA-Canada, as the total cost across those two links (28) is lower than the direct link (40). This also is true for Asia-Pacific to either Europe (40) or Australasia (40). All traffic is likely to route through Denver (36) because of that. All this means is that the slow 128-KBps links will not have their bandwidth used up by replication; instead, the 256-KBps links will absorb the overflow. In the eastern link you have potentially added two lots of bidirectional replication traffic across the 256-KBps link. Whether this is a problem is up to PetroCorp to decide. They have four main choices:

- Turn off transitiveness throughout the network. This forces the KCC to use only directly connected routes to replicate. This forces the use of the 128-Kbps links by default. Now add the site link bridge at Denver as mentioned previously. Now add any other site link bridges to enforce using certain routes when the directly connected routes are not to be used for replication.

- Turn off transitiveness throughout the network. This forces the KCC to use only directly connected routes to replicate. This forces the use of the 128-KBps links by default. Now add the site link bridge at Denver as mentioned previously. Now add any other site link bridges to enforce use of certain routes when the directly connected routes are not to be used for replication. Finally, turn off the KCC intersite topology generation in key sites where the Bridgehead Servers need to be handpicked from the available DCs, creating the connection objects manually.

- Leave transitiveness turned on throughout the network, automatically bridge all site links of the same DS-RPC transport, and allow the KCC to choose the lowest cost routes and accept the routes that it chooses, controlling it with schedules.

- Leave transitiveness turned on throughout the network, automatically bridge all site links of the same DS-RPC transport, and turn off the KCC intersite topology generation in key sites where the Bridgehead Servers need to be handpicked from the available DCs, creating the connection objects manually.

Which of these is chosen depends entirely on the traffic use of the links, the requirements on those links, and how much use the administrators wish to make of the KCC. PetroCorp decides that it wants the KCC to make most of the connections but still wants to retain the greatest control and the potential to force the KCC to use certain routes. To that end, they select the second option.

In the end, the company chooses to bridge South America to Denver via USA-Canada to free up the 128-KBps link for other traffic. They also choose to bridge Europe to Asia-Pacific via Denver to free up what is currently a congested link. The KCC automatically routes all traffic via Denver, as this bridge cost is lower than the single site link. Finally, the administrators allow the KCC in the Denver site to generate the eight intersite site links (four connections, each with two site links for redundancy) and then turn off intersite generation for that site. They then modify the connection objects created (deleting some and creating others), because they have a number of DCs that they do not want to use for replication purposes within Denver that the KCC picked up and used.

This is a fairly complicated site problem, but one that wasn't difficult to solve. There are many other viable solutions. I could easily have made all the redundant links that I created use the SMTP Connector with a higher cost to make sure that they were used only in an emergency. Many options are available to you as well. That's why a design is so important.

Summary

After this chapter, you should have more of an insight into creating the site and replication infrastructure for your own Windows 2000 network. Having a basic understanding of the replication process (from Chapter 4) and how the KCC operates should allow you to make much more informed judgments on how much control you want to exert over the KCC in your designs. I feel that it is always better to give free reign to the KCC if possible, while maintaining a firm grip over what it has authority to do. While this can seem contradictory, I hope that my explanations on using site link bridges and restricting transitiveness when appropriate show how this is possible in practice.

The next two chapters deal with how to update your designs to reflect your requirements for Group Policy Objects in your organizations.

8

Profiles and Group Policy Primer

Before getting to the meat of how to effectively structure your Active Directory to take Group Policy Objects into account, I need to give you a solid introduction to the subject of profiles and policies. It's a very large subject, and it's worth treating properly so that you get the most out of your system. This chapter is the introduction to the subject, and the next chapter builds on it to show how policies work in Active Directory and how to design a tree to incorporate them effectively.

The goal of policy-based administration is for the administrator to state a wish about the state of users/computer environment once, then rely on the system to enforce that wish. With Windows 2000 group policies, that state is nearly realized.

In Windows NT, system policies had a number of limitations. System policies:

- Were limited to domains
- Were not secure
- Could only apply to users, groups of users, or computers
- Tended to set values until another policy specifically unset them
- Were limited to desktop lockdown

That has really changed with Windows 2000 group policies. Group policies are the primary Windows 2000 mechanism for applying changes to computers and users throughout an organization. In contrast to system policies, group policies:

- Can be applied to individual clients, sites, domains, and Organizational Units
- Are highly secure
- Can apply to users, computers, or groups of either
- Can set values and automatically unset them in specified situations
- Can do far more than just a desktop lockdown

With group policies, an administrator can define a very large number of detailed settings that are to be enforced on users throughout the organization and be confident that the system will take care of things. Let's take a simple example from Leicester University. We administrators wanted workstation access to the Systems Administrator toolset, which normally is installed only on a server. While we could install these tools on our own PCs, we actually wanted the tools to follow us around the network and be available from any PC that we chose to log on from. However, we didn't want to leave these tools installed on that PC when we logged off and went away. Prior to Windows 2000, I would have had to arrive at that client, log on, install the toolset, do whatever was required at that client, uninstall the toolset, and finally log off again. This is a considerable chore for large numbers of machines. With Windows 2000, we were able to use group policies to specify that the toolset was to be automatically installed on any client that I logged on to before the desktop appeared. That way, I could go straight to the Start menu and use the tools I wanted. Then, when I went to log off, the same group policies would uninstall the toolset from the machine.

Let's take another example. At the university we use a central logon script for every user. This is no different than Windows NT. However, we also apply extra logon scripts for some sets of users based on which Organizational Unit they are in. So some of our users get more than one logon script depending on where in Active Directory their accounts reside. That's a significant step forward from Windows NT, but it doesn't end there. We also can specify logoff scripts that run when a user logs off the system. Similarly, we can have a central logoff script that applies to all users and a series of other logoff scripts tailored to users in certain parts of the tree. Workstations also can have scripts, but instead of executing at logon and logoff, these scripts run at startup and shutdown. Want to install a new Dynamic Link Library (DLL) on all clients? How about using a startup script to do it? Have a desire to start the (normally disabled) web service on a series of workstations for a conference that runs for a week? Why not create a startup script in Active Directory that starts those services? When the week is over, remove the script, and the workstations return to normal mode. Of course, as you've probably guessed, this startup script runs in addition to any other startup scripts such as a central one for all workstations. So, rather than a single user logon script available for Windows NT, we now have multiple user logon/logoff scripts and multiple workstation startup/shutdown scripts.

Let's take a final example. You are required to change a set of registry key values for every client in your organization so that the clients can all receive an organization-wide company video broadcast from the chairman and CEO. You set up a simple Group Policy with the customized registry changes configured and apply it to every computer in your organization. At present, this functionality may seem no different from what you could have achieved with Windows NT system policies.

You apply these changes one evening, and the next morning, 20 thousand work-stations across your network are rebooted so that they receive this policy on star-tup. The Group Policy applies and the settings are changed. However, about an hour later you realize that one of the values in the registry needs changing again. You don't want to force 20 thousand clients to reboot, and with Windows 2000 you don't have to. You can specify that this policy be reapplied every 15 minutes to all workstations after they have booted. So, you make the change to the group policies and sit back, knowing that within 15–45 minutes* every workstation will receive the policy again with the updated change.

With examples like these, it becomes quite easy to see the power of group poli-cies. While some of the examples can be accomplished under Windows NT, they require a lot more time and effort to achieve than with Windows 2000's simple Configuration tool.

The rest of the chapter goes into detail about group policies.

 Group policies are normally referred to simply as *GPOs* (pro-nounced Gee-Pee-Ohs), corresponding to the term Group Policy Objects, during normal discussions. This is the style I use for the remainder of the book.

A Profile Primer

The terms *policies* and *profiles* often are included together in documentation, yet they perform very different functions. Because they interrelate, it is easy to get confused about them. To make things clear, I'll cover the essentials of profiles so that you can understand how you can manipulate them using group policies.

Let's consider a Windows 2000 workstation with a newly created account for a user named Richard Lang with the username RLang. When Richard logs on to the client, the system creates a profile directory for him corresponding to his user-name Rlang in the *Documents and Settings* directory. If Richard were to log on to a Windows NT workstation or a Windows 2000 workstation that was upgraded from a previous version of Windows NT, the profile would be created under the *%systemroot%\Profiles†* directory.

---

* A random time interval of 0–30 minutes is added so that all workstations do not attempt to redownload the policy at the same time.

† *%systemroot%* is the system environment variable that refers to the location of the Windows NT system files. If Windows NT were installed onto drive C: in the normal way, then *%systemroot%* would be *C:\ WINNT.*

Inside this directory, the Windows NT/2000 system places a file called *NTUSER. DAT,* along with various other data files. Let's concentrate on the *NTUSER.DAT* file for a moment. This file contains what is known generally as the user portion of the registry. You see, Windows 95, Windows 98, Windows NT, and Windows 2000 all have a registry that consists of two parts: the so-called user portion represented by the file *NTUSER.DAT* (or *USER.DAT* on Windows 9x systems) and the system or computer portion of the registry, known as *SYSTEM.DAT.*[*] The user part of the registry holds information indicating what screensaver should be used for that user; what colors, background, and event sounds are set; where the user's My Documents folder points to; and so on. The system portion of the registry holds hardware device settings, installed software information, and so on. When a user logs on to a client, the combined effects of the settings for the machine held in the system portion of the registry and the settings for the user held in the user portion of the registry take effect.

When you use a tool such as *REGEDIT.EXE* or *REGEDT32.EXE* to examine the registry on a machine, both portions of the registry are opened and displayed together for you to look at within one tool.

The two registry tools have been developed with different requirements in mind and consequently have different functionality. The REGEDIT tool was developed for Windows 9x clients, and as such allows for management of the datatypes of that registry format as well as for rapid searching for any key or value that contains a given word or phrase. REGEDT32, on the other hand, is designed to support the extra Windows NT/2000 datatypes that are required within those registries. REGEDIT cannot write out those types. However, REGEDT32 has an awful search mechanism that allows searches only through keys. So, while REGEDT32 is used on Windows NT/2000 for day-to-day management of the registry, a systems administrator also knows how to use REGEDIT on those operating systems due to its superior search capabilities. REGEDIT also has a few other benefits including the ability to export registry hives in a readable format.

Figure 8-1 shows a view of the registry on a Windows 2000 client when viewed from REGEDIT. The screen shot also shows the five registry hives (as they are known) available to Windows 2000. The two important hives are HKEY_LOCAL_MACHINE, also known as HKLM, which corresponds to the system part of the registry, and HKEY_CURRENT_USER, also known as HKCU, which corresponds to the user portion of the registry.

---

[*] As the *SYSTEM.DAT* file is not specific to any particular user, but rather to the client itself, it is held in the *%systemroot%* folder on the client.

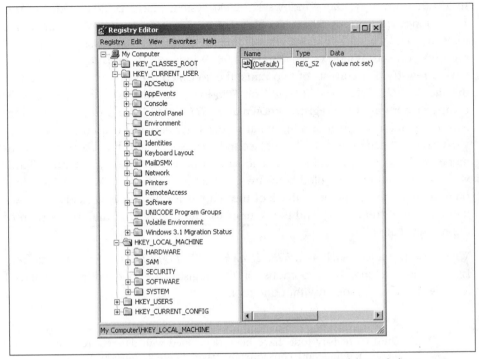

Figure 8-1. A REGEDIT view of the registry on a Windows 2000 Professional client

When Richard logs on, he gets the *NTUSER.DAT* file. In this scenario, when Richard logs on to the local client, the file is copied from the Default User profile directory that already exists on that machine under Documents and Settings. During Richard's first logon, the system also creates a series of directories underneath Richard's profile directory with names like My Documents, Start Menu, Desktop, and so on. If Richard ever places an icon on the desktop or saves a file from WordPad to the My Documents folder, the data is placed inside the relevant folders in Richard's profile. The Start Menu folder holds the Start menu structure that Richard sees when he clicks the Start button.

The Default User and All User Folders

The default contents placed inside all these folders in Richard's profile come directly from the same folders in the Default User profile. However, when Richard logs on, he may see icons or folders inside My Documents, Start Menu, and Desktop that do not appear in his own profile directories. These extra items are displayed as if they were part of Richard's profile, but in fact they are part of the All Users profile that also resides on the computer. In fact, the settings from the *All Users\NTUSER.DAT* file also are available to Richard. The All Users profile is a great way of adding new items to every user's profile on the client without having to add every item manually. During installation, NT-aware software tends to ask whether the installation is just for the user installing the software or whether it is for all users of the client. If the software is told that it is for all users, then it modifies the All Users profile by default.

To recap, when Richard logs on for the first time, a profile directory *Documents and Settings\Rlang* is created for him, and everything from the *Documents and Settings\Default User* profile is copied into it. Richard's profile now contains an *NTUSER.DAT* file that contains all of his user settings, as well as a series of folders representing his Desktop, his Start Menu, and his My Documents among others. In addition to any files or folders copied in from the Default User profile, Richard also seamlessly sees all of the items corresponding to the *Documents and Settings\ All Users* profile, although they will not exist in his own Rlang directory hierarchy. He also may not be able to remove or delete the files and shortcuts if he doesn't have the permission to do so.

Logging On Locally to the Workstation

Windows 2000 stores much more data in Richard's profile than Windows NT would. In addition, more registry keys have been added to both portions of the registry to enable much more fine grained control over what happens in a profile. I'll have more to say about this later.

If Richard logs off and then on again, the system will detect that he already has a profile folder on the workstation and so will continue to use that rather than create a new one. That is why when Richard creates a desktop file and logs off and on again, the file is still visible on Richard's desktop. If Richard logs off and an administrator logs on and installs a Windows NT/2000-conversant piece of software, this is likely to install itself into the All Users profile, adding folders and files, and changing the registry as required. So when the administrator logs off and Richard logs back on, the new software in the All Users profile will be available to him as if it were part of his own profile; this includes providing any All Users *NTUSER. DAT* HKCU registry settings that he may need for the application.

As the registry settings are held in the All Users profile, you might think that Richard cannot change them. This is not the case. As soon as he changes a setting, the system will write it out to his own registry, and this will override any future value for that setting from the All Users profile. Richard's profile will thus contain only the customizations that override the defaults passed in from the All Users profile.

Logging On to the Domain

Now let's say that Richard instead logs on to a Windows NT/2000 domain. If you set the system up in the standard manner, when Richard logs on for the first time to the domain, he is given a profile directory on the local workstation that he logs on to. In exactly the same manner as a logon to the workstation itself, this new profile is made from the Default User and All User profiles on the workstation. When Richard logs off, his profile stays at the workstation. If he then logs on to the domain from another workstation, he has a new profile created for him on that workstation. If Richard then logs off from this workstation and logs on at another, he gets a third profile created. Finally, if he logs back on to the first workstation, he will get his profile that he used there last. This default scenario is very limiting, and Windows NT and Windows 2000 provide three key profile technologies for domain usage that you need to be aware of to manipulate profiles to work in a better manner for your organization:

- Roaming profiles
- Cached profile deletion
- Relocating the Default User profile

Having profiles stored on each workstation makes little sense. What would make a lot more sense would be storing the profiles centrally and having them accessible from anywhere on the network where you log on. This is possible and uses what are called *roaming profiles.* Under Windows NT, you simply filled in the relevant profile field for a user in the User Manager for Domains and pointed the new location at a share for that user. Under Windows 2000, you use Active Directory Users and Computers tool, but the concept is the same. If you did this for Richard, when he logged on for the first time, the system would detect that he did not currently have a roaming profile, and his profile would be created on the workstation as before. However, when he logged out, his profile would be copied up to the network location to become his roaming profile. Then when he logged back on again from anywhere on the network, his new profile on the network share would roam with him and would be downloaded to the workstation for him to use. This download on logon and upload on logout continues throughout the lifetime of the account, provided the account's profile property is not deleted.

Cached Profile Deletion

One problem can come up with this scenario. First, if Richard logs on at a hundred workstations throughout the life of the account, a hundred copies of his profile at various stages of development will exist on the a hundred workstations. To combat this, administrators can set a registry key on the workstations that forces them to discard the profile after the roaming profile upload on logout. The key is

DWORD, is held in the system part of the registry, and is the same in Windows NT as in Windows 2000. Setting it to a value of 1 turns it on:

HKLM\SOFTWARE\Microsoft\WindowsNT\CurrentVersion\Winlogon\DeleteRoamingCache

This setting needs to be applied to all the computers from which you wish to delete cached profiles. The fastest way to implement such a change in Windows 2000 is to use a group policy, unless you really relish changing the registry manually on every client. You simply make this one change centrally, then have it roll out to all computers that you wish to affect. Under Windows 2000, you do not even need to know that this is the key in the registry that is being modified, as this is one of the many default computer options that are available from the GUI, which hides the actual registry keys and values that you are changing.

A Server-Based Default User Profile

If you wanted to change a setting in the user portion of the registry or add a new icon to the desktop for all new users, you ordinarily would need to modify the Default User profile on every client. This is really an unacceptable solution. The simpler solution would be to store a centrally located copy of the Default User profile that the users automatically downloaded on first logon. That way, if you needed to make a change, you would need to make it only on the centrally stored copy and not on every client. This can be achieved by placing the Default User profile in the *NETLOGON* share for Windows NT or Windows 2000. Previously I said that when the user logs on to the domain for the first time the system copies the Default User profile from the client workstation. That is, in fact, true only when a Default User profile does not exist in the *NETLOGON* share; if a central Default User profile does reside in the *NETLOGON* share, that is used in creating the user's own profile.

 The directory that *NETLOGON* actually refers to under Windows NT is *%systemroot%\system32\repl\import\scripts* and under Windows 2000 is *%systemroot%\SYSVOL\sysvol<yourdomain><yourcorp>com\SCRIPTS*.

The basic point is that while Windows 2000 profiles may be stored under different locations, may store more data, and may be more customizable than Windows NT profiles, they work on the same principles as their direct predecessors.

This is not true for policies, though, and I'm now going to cover what you can do with group policies before moving on to look at exactly how they work in Active Directory.

Capabilities of GPOs

GPOs are manipulated and changed using the Group Policy Editor, a Microsoft Management Console snap-in that graphically displays all the disparate policy settings that administrators can set. Most settings in a GPO have three states: enabled, disabled, and unconfigured. By default, all settings in a GPO are unconfigured. Any unconfigured settings are ignored during application, so the GPO comes into play only when settings have actually been set. Each setting needs to be configured as enabled or disabled before it can be used, and in some cases the option needs no other parameters. In other cases, a host of information must be entered to configure the option; it all depends on what the option itself does. All of this is done within the Group Policy Editor (GPE), the GUI tool for manipulating GPOs.

Enabling and disabling most options is fairly straightforward. However, due to Microsoft's choice for the names of certain settings for GPOs, you actually can have the choice of enabling or disabling options with names like Disable Access to This Option. By default, this setting isn't in use, but you can disable the disable option (i.e., enable the option) or enable the disable option (i.e., disable the option). Be careful and make sure you know which way the setting is applied before you actually go through with the change.

GPOs can apply a very large number of changes to computer and user objects in Active Directory. These changes are grouped together within the GPE under the three headings of Software Settings, Windows Settings, and Administrative Templates. There are two sets of these headings, one held under Computer Configuration and one held under User Configuration. The items under the three headings differ, as the settings that will apply to users and to computers are not the same.

Some of the settings under Administrative Templates would look more sensible under the other two sections. However, the Administrative Templates section holds data that is entirely generated from the Administrative Template (ADM) files in the system volume. So it makes more sense to include all the ADM data together. ADM files contain the entire set of options available for each setting, including explanations that are shown on the various property pages in the GPE.

ADM files can be added and removed by right-clicking either Administrative Template location in the GPE and choosing Add/Remove Templates. Very comprehensive information on customizing GPOs and adding in your own templates can be found in Microsoft's Windows 2000 Group Policy technical white paper on their web site.

During my work on GPOs I ended up wanting an easy-to-access list that detailed which settings were available in general terms so that I could easily open up the GPE and locate the setting I was looking for. Because such a list did not exist, I compiled one myself, which I'll now go through and enumerate, explaining what each aspect of the GPO actually does.

Software Installation Settings (Computer and User)

Windows 2000 now comes with the ability to deploy applications automatically to users or computers using GPOs. These applications can now be installed, updated, repaired, and removed simply using GPOs and their interaction with a new Windows 2000 technology called the Microsoft Installer.

To comply with the Windows 2000 logo program, where an application gets the ability to sport the "Designed for Windows 2000" logo or equivalent, each application must ship with an installation routine that uses the Microsoft Windows Installer technology. During creation of a software application, the author can now create a new MSI (Microsoft Installer) file that is the descendant of the original *SETUP.EXE* files that used to be created. The MSI contains all of the data required to fully install the application and then some. It knows about the files that are required by the application, including notes such as sizes and version numbers, and it maintains a host of other information including language settings, where to install the application, what files are critical to the functional operation of the application, and so on. On any system that has the Microsoft Windows Installer service installed, the MSI file can be run as if it were an executable, and the application will install.

The administrator has a way of customizing the defaults for the MSI file to tailor the exact settings for the application, say installing it on drive Z: rather than C: or installing Spanish and Polish support in addition to English. The process of customizing the MSI file in this manner is known as creating a *transform*. The transform is used by the installer service to make sure that the MSI file installs the appropriate items in the correctly configured way.

 Microsoft Office 2000 is the first application to ship with this technology. Prior to installing Office 2000 on any Windows 9x or NT client, Office has to install the Windows Installer service, which it does automatically. Once this is done, the MSI file for Office 2000 can be run by the new Windows Installer service.

That's not all, though; this technology has a lot more to it. First, it has the capability to self-repair applications. So let's say that a user accidentally deletes one or more of the core files required for the application to work. When the user attempts to run the application, the icon or application that the user tries to run first checks with the MSI and the transform to make sure that no critical data is missing. If it is, the data is copied to the appropriate locations, and the application is started. This effectively brings about fully functional self-repairing applications.

Applications also can be deployed using GPOs so that users get them as soon as they log on, or whenever they browse Active Directory to find the applications. You can even tell the MSI to auto-install on any client PC that attempts to open a file with an extension that an MSI-aware application can read.

 Microsoft expects to release an SMS Repackager Step-Up tool after Windows 2000 to permit conversion of an SMS package to a Windows Installer package.

While the Microsoft Installer service is very useful and its configuration will become second nature to administrators as time goes on, the actual technology itself is not really appropriate to this book. If you want to find out more on the Windows Installer service and how you can write your own MSI for both existing and new applications, check out the InstallShield web site *http://www.installshield. com/* for the newer version of the InstallShield tool that compiles MSI files, or search the Microsoft web site *http://search.microsoft.com/us/dev/default.asp* for the phrase *Windows Installer*.

Microsoft Installer files are inserted into a GPO from the Software Installation section. Figure 8-2 shows the GPE with two GPOs snapped into it, with one expanded in the scope pane to show the two Software Installation parts.

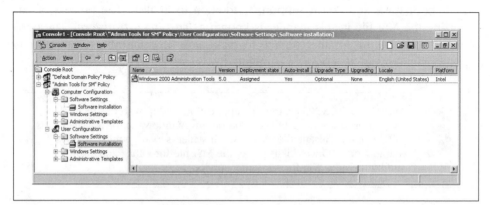

Figure 8-2. Software Installation settings for a GPO

Software Installation is listed under both the computer and user sections of the GPO, and thus you can deploy software installations to both computers and users through the two different parts of the GPO. Here, this GPO is deploying the Version 5.0 Systems Administration tools as an assigned application to all users that receive this GPO. If you remember the example from the start of this chapter, this GPO is used to auto-install the Systems Administration tools onto any client that certain systems administrators log on to. We know that it auto-installs, because that is one of the configured options that has been checked in the GPE in Figure 8-2. More information on Microsoft Installer applications can be found in the next section.

Windows Settings (Computer)

This part of a GPO holds startup and shutdown scripts as well as security settings. In Figure 8-3, the GPO being edited is the Default Domain Policy installed by default on creation of a domain. This GPO applies to all computers in the domain, so any change that I make to this GPO will affect DCs, member servers, and ordinary workstations alike.

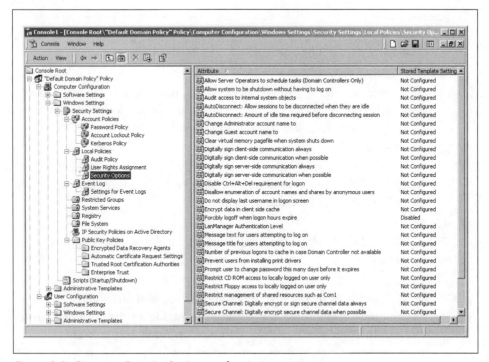

Figure 8-3. Computer Security Settings and scripts

Startup and shutdown scripts can be made to execute asynchronously or synchronously. They can use VBScript, JScript, any other ActiveX scripting host language or even plain old CMD/BAT files that you may already be familiar with. You can even pass parameters to the scripts by configuring the parameters into the GPO.

The Security Settings portion of the GPO is by far the larger of the two sections covered by the Windows Settings heading. The items displayed in Figure 8-3 cover the following areas:

Account Policies

These policies allow you to apply settings that govern how accounts on the system will work.

The settings for the following three policies can only be applied domain wide; they cannot have different values for different Organizational Units in a domain. This is why you need to consider multiple domains in the namespace design if you need to apply different settings to different sections of your organization.

Password Policy

These settings allow you to specify policy settings for passwords, such as how many days a password should exist before expiration.

Account Lockout Policy

These settings allow you to specify how many grace logons a user is allowed before he locks out his account due to bad logon attempts. You also specify how long the account should stay locked out.

Kerberos Policy

This setting is domain wide only, so it only exists in the Default Domain Policy. It allows you to configure the various Kerberos security and ticketing policies that apply to the domain.

Local Policies

These policies directly affect the operation of a local machine, be it a workstation or a DC.

Audit Policy

These policies list items that, when turned on, will write audit entries for success and/or failure to the security event log of any machine that is affected. In other words, if I were to turn on Audit Logon Events (Failure) in the Default Domain Policy, any failed logon attempts on any machine within that domain would be logged to the security event log on that same machine.

User Rights Assignment

While permissions are used to allow or deny access to an object in Active Directory or a part of a filesystem, user rights give special abilities to an account or the operating system, such as whether the machine can be accessed only locally or only across the network, whether an account can add workstations to a domain, or whether an account can act as part of the operating system and manipulate devices at a low level. These items used to be available from a menu in Windows NT's User Manager, but a few more items have been added to accommodate the changes to Windows 2000.

Security Options

These settings, which are displayed in the results pane of Figure 8-3, allow configuration of security on one or more computers throughout your organization.

Event Log → Settings for Event Logs

These settings allow you to set various properties of the three main event logs (security, application, and system), such as the maximum size, how long to retain the logs, and so on, on any computer that receives this policy.

Restricted Groups

This allows you to indicate specific groups on any computer that receives this policy and force them to be members of other groups or to have members themselves.

System Services

This setting allows you to manipulate services that may be running on any machine that receives this policy and set the permissions for access to those services, such as who can start, stop, and change properties, as well as the default state (i.e., Automatic, Manual, or Disabled).

Registry

This setting allows you to add a registry key on any computer that receives this policy and automatically set its permissions and auditing properties. If you wanted to audit successful and unsuccessful accesses to the HKEY_USERS key for computers in one specific Organizational Unit only, you would do it by adding an entry to a GPO that affected that Organizational Unit.

File System

This setting allows you to add a file or directory on any computer that receives this policy and automatically set its permissions and auditing properties. If you wanted to set read, write, and change access permissions to the *C:\WINNT* or *C:\WINNT\SYSTEM32* directory for every computer in one specific Organizational Unit only, you would do it by adding an entry to a GPO that affected that Organizational Unit.

IP Security Policies on Active Directory

This allows you to configure whether a server requires use of Internet standards on IP security (IPSec) when clients attempt to communicate with the server or whether it just requests IPSec if the client is capable. From the client side it allows you to dictate whether a client will always use IPSec of a certain form or whether it will use IPSec only when a server requests it. All aspects of IPSec can be configured from here.

Public Key Policies

This location allows you to set all manner of Public Key Infrastructure (PKI) settings that are now natively supported in Windows 2000. Administrators can specify that the system has a trusted certificate list that it considers reputable, that it will automatically pass certificates of a certain type out to users or computers without their intervention, and that key users (with the administrator as default) can be made Recovery Agents and thus gain the permission to use another user's public keys and certificates to decrypt that user's encrypted data. As these settings are specific to a GPO, and a GPO can be specific to a location in Active Directory, this allows you to set out a number of different policy settings that apply to different areas of the tree as required.

Administrative Templates (Computer)

This is the GPO location that stores changes to registry settings that affect the HKEY_LOCAL_MACHINE portion of the registry. The entire hierarchy of graphical items depicted in the list along with their settings and help descriptions has been assembled from the set of ADM template files that exist in the system volume for each GPO. This structure has not changed much since the Windows NT format, and administrators will be able to start adding their own templates as required, thus adding other branches and leaves to the hierarchy. Figure 8-4 shows the hierarchy of items.

System

This contains a few keys that don't fit under the following three headings. It will become a catchall container for any nonspecific system keys as time goes on.

Logon

This includes a number of items related to how the system is to operate during logon. For example, you can set when and how the system detects a slow link during a logon and what actions to take when a slow link is detected. Actions could include choosing a locally cached profile over the network profile or loading the network profile anyway. This area allows fairly heavy customization of how user profiles will work under Windows 2000, and you can even specify that a user who fails to find his network

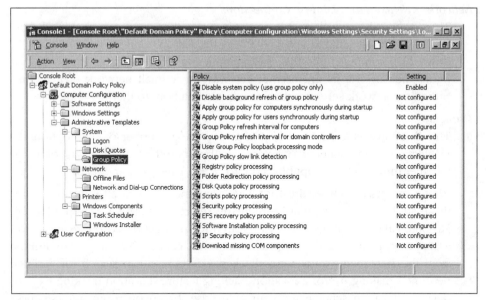

Figure 8-4. Computer administrative templates

profile is automatically logged out rather than being able to log on with a default profile or a cached profile. Couple this with the setting to delete cached copies of roaming profiles, and you instantly gain the ability to secure a workstation against keeping a user's roaming profile after he has logged out and making sure that he cannot log on with a temporary profile if the system can't find his roaming profile at any point. This is a good example of making sure that your own rules for how profiles are dealt with as far as GPOs are concerned are acted on centrally.

Disk Quotas

This section contains settings that allow you to turn disk quotas on at any machines that receive this GPO, as well as manipulate a variety of settings.

Group Policy

This is one of the most significant areas, as it contains settings that govern how computers this policy applies to are going to implement Group Policy. The contents are depicted in Figure 8-4.

Network → Offline Files

This is a large set of values that govern exactly how files and folders are to be made available on the local machine when it is offline. You can turn offline folders on and off, set the cache size to be used for such items, define how synchronization is to occur, and so on.

Network → Network and Dial-up Connections

This location has one key that determines whether users can enable, disable, and configure the shared access feature of a dial-up connection from any Windows 2000 computer that this policy applies to. Shared access lets users configure their system as an Internet gateway for a small network of machines, providing network services, such as name resolution, to that network.

Printers

This location has a series of keys that provide a number of new options for printers, dictating whether printers can be shared at all from a computer, whether they can be autopublished into Active Directory, and so on.

Printer objects in Active Directory have a number of extra attributes now, and these attributes can and will be regularly searched. Take an example like the attribute called Location; users can search for printers based on location from a simple pop up box that appears when you choose Search. . . For Printers from the Start menu on a network client. Users also can search for "printers near me," making use of a location tracking feature. Location tracking lets you design a location scheme for your enterprise, based on room number, floor number, building name, city, country, and so on and assign computers and printers to locations in your scheme. Location tracking overrides the standard method of locating and associating users and printers, which uses the IP address and subnet mask of a computer to estimate its physical location and proximity to other computers. GPO settings here allow you to force a workstation to search as if it were in a specific location (i.e., forcing your own value for location whenever that client searches for printers nearby), as well as turning on location tracking and its associated options.

Windows Components → Task Scheduler

Ordinary logged-on domain users normally can manipulate the task scheduler on a machine. As an administrator you may not want this, or you may want to set certain tasks and not allow users to delete them. These options allow you to disable creation and deletion of tasks, prevent the running or stopping of tasks on an ad hoc basis, prevent scheduling any applications that do not appear anywhere other than the user's Start menu, and so on.

Windows Components → Windows Installer

These settings allow an administrator to configure a number of Microsoft Installer options that will apply to all applications installed on this computer. These include options such as whether to disable the use of MSI files on that client, whether to install all MSI files with elevated privileges (i.e., whether to install using the local SYSTEM account which has full rights to the files and folders on the machine's disks, which the user may have no rights to), how much logging is to be done, and so on.

Windows Components → Internet Explorer

> A few settings here allow an administrator to dictate whether IE can autodetect missing components and new versions as well as what its security zone settings are.

Windows Settings (User)

While this section contains only a few settings, the contents are likely to become very familiar to you. This area holds logon and logoff scripts, allows you to redirect core system folders to network areas from the normal hard disk locations, and allows you to specify IP security policies. Figure 8-5 shows a snapshot of the contents.

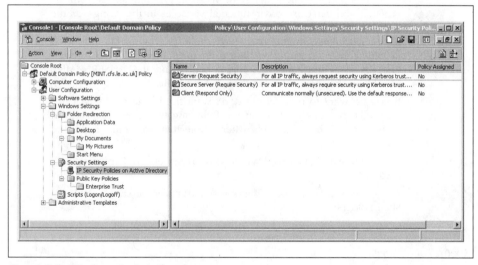

Figure 8-5. Windows Settings (user)

Folder Redirection

> This is a very useful setting that is easy to understand and manage. If an administrator wants to redirect the My Documents, My Pictures, Application Data, Desktop, and Start Menu locations from their defaults, this section allows it to be done. For example, at Leicester University we use roaming profiles, but we don't want the My Documents folder to roam with the user because of the large number of folders and files it would contain. In other words, downloading and uploading My Documents would slow down logon/logoff considerably. So instead we redirect the user's My Documents folder (and the My Pictures folder within it) to the network paths when he logs on. That way, whenever an application, such as Microsoft's Office 2000, attempts to save a document to the My Documents folder, the folder that the user sees is the My Documents folder located in his home folder.

This part of the GPO is different from the others in that it doesn't contain settings as such. Instead, the folders listed should be right-clicked and the Properties item selected from the drop-down menu that appears. This brings up the main redirection settings window for that folder. This window allows you to redirect all users who receive this GPO to one folder or allow a finer-grained control so that users who are members of a certain group get Folder A, users who are members of another group get Folder B, and so on. You can then specify other settings such as whether the existing folder is to be moved when this GPO takes effect and whether the folder is moved back when the policy stops taking effect.

I find this policy somewhat useful. Its main problem stems from the fact that you can't use environmental variables in the strings, as the GPO will take effect before environmental variables are set. So if you have a set of users who are to have their My Documents redirected to folders that correspond to their usernames, there is no way of getting the usernames into the folder path using the %USERNAME% variable in the same way that there is for profiles.

If you do want to redirect but don't want the hassle of doing it this way, edit the relevant keys in the following two user registry locations to point the folders elsewhere. Note that both must be edited for the process to take effect:

HKCU\Software\Microsoft\Windows\CurrentVersion\Explorer\Shell Folders

HKCU\Software\Microsoft\Windows\CurrentVersion\Explorer\User Shell Folders

---

Logon/Logoff scripts

This is where you can specify the logon and logoff scripts that users will execute. Whether these are executed synchronously or asynchronously is specified in the User Configuration Administrative Templates section of the GPO.

Security Settings → IP Security Policies on Active Directory

These settings correspond to those held under Windows Settings in the computer portion of the GPO. The results pane of Figure 8-5 shows the three default policies held under this location. Note the two extra icons in the top right of the MMC; the first allows you to create an IP security policy, and the second allows you to manage IP filter lists and their actions. Both are also available by right-clicking in the usual manner.

Security Settings → Public Key Policies

These settings correspond to those held under Windows Settings in the computer portion of the GPO.

Administrative Templates (User)

This is the core of the settings that will govern how the administrator controls the system's look and feel for the user. The settings here are all geared to various lockdowns that you may wish to make to a user's account; if you do not wish to lock down a user's account, most of these settings will not be of much use. If roaming profiles are turned on, these settings roam with the user's profile as he logs on at each client. Figure 8-6 shows the full branch expanded.

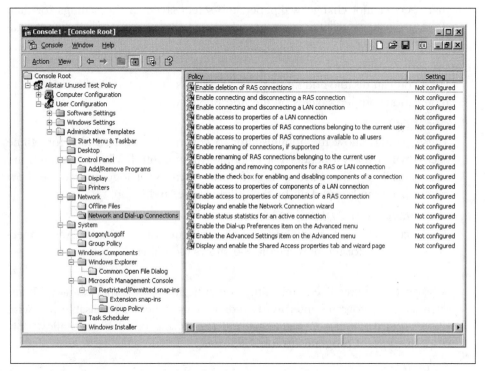

Figure 8-6. Administrative Templates (user)

Start Menu & Taskbar

This location is used when the administrator wishes to customize how the Start menu and the taskbar appear to the users this policy applies to. Here an administrator can disable various options on the Start menu, such as the control panel, printers, logoff, or the shutdown button, and also can remove various items, such as Run, Search, or Favorites, entirely if so desired.

Desktop

Like the last item, this section is used to lock down the desktop. Here you can remove the various icons, such as My Network Places, as well as configure whether the desktop settings themselves can be changed and whether they are even saved on logout. Active Desktop is configured (or disabled) from here.

Control Panel → Add/Remove Programs

This allows you to set how the new Windows 2000 Add/Remove Programs control panel is customized for an individual user. You can disable the option entirely, hide some of the options, or even force the system to bypass the addition of other software but still add official components to the system by going straight to the Components menu.

Control Panel → Display

This can be used to disable individual tabs on the Display control panel, so that users cannot change wallpaper, the screensaver, or the settings for their display (such as display drivers), which as administrators well know, can cause immense problems.

Control Panel → Printers

Here you can disable adding or deleting printers, as well as decide whether to hide various property pages on the Add Printer wizard.

Network → Offline Files

These settings allow the administrator to govern how cached files for offline access will actually operate. For example, these control whether the files are automatically synchronized at logoff, how much event logging is done, how much space can be used up by the offline cache, and so on.

Network → Network and Dial-up Connections

This section allows the administrator to configure how RAS and LAN connections will work for the user. Figure 8-6 shows the full list of options.

System

A few extra features live here, as they don't fit under any other category. Items such as how programs interpret two-digit years, whether to disable the Windows registry editors—*Regedt32.exe* and *Regedit.exe*, or whether to allow only a specified list of programs to run for a user.

Logon/Logoff

This is a useful set of keys that really should be called Logon, Logoff, and Profiles. The logon/logoff part allows the administrator to specify whether logon/logoff scripts run visibly and whether they run synchronously.* Administrators also can disable the Lock Workstation, Task Manager, Change Password, and Logoff buttons on the Windows Security screen that you get when you press Ctrl-Alt-Del while being logged on.

---

* You can't run a logon script synchronously if it needs to interact with the user's environment. Synchronous logon scripts will always finish prior to environment variables being set and prior to the user's profile being loaded. It isn't possible to query the number of new mail messages a user has in a synchronous logon script by reading the user's name from the environment variables or profile, for example, as the user is not yet fully logged on when the script runs. The solution is to run the script asynchronously.

In the profile settings you can specify whether certain directories do not roam with the user's profile. This is a very useful option if you don't want the Internet Explorer cache and history files or the My Documents files roaming with the user. Administrators also can specify whether the user's roaming profile should be limited in size to a certain value, along with various warnings that occur regularly; this is a useful addition that was first introduced in Service Pack 4 for Windows NT.

Group Policy

As it was in the Computer section of Administrative Templates, this is one of the most significant areas. It contains configuration data that governs how group policies apply to users. For example, it allows you to configure when and how a slow link is detected, how often the user section of this GPO is refreshed, and whether GPOs are downloaded only from the FSMO PDC role owner (described in Chapter 2, *Active Directory Overview*) or from any DC.

Windows Components → Windows Explorer

These settings relate to how the shell and desktop look and feel. You can customize whether specific icons (such as drives in My Computer or Entire Network in My Network Places) are displayed, decide whether certain normal modes of operation (such as whether to disable workgroup contents in My Network Places or remove the Folder Options menu from the Tools menu) are blocked, or change the default settings (such as changing the maximum number of recent documents from 15 to a lower or higher value).

Windows Components → Windows Explorer → Common Open File Dialog

This setting allows administrators to tailor the dialog box that is displayed automatically by programs whenever users need to browse to and open a file. For example, you can specify whether the Back button or the Common Places bar—which contains icons representing History, Desktop, Favorites, My Documents, and My Network Places—are displayed. If this seems confusing, run up any program on Windows 2000 and open a file to see what I mean.

Windows Components → Microsoft Management Console

While you may use the MMC to create your own consoles regularly, you may wish users to be able to use only existing consoles and not create new ones. Alternatively, you may want to allow users to create consoles but limit them to only a few snap-ins. These settings allow you to do either.

Windows Components → Microsoft Management Console → Restricted → Permitted Snap-ins

This section contains the entire set of snap-ins that are available standard. Administrators use this policy to prevent users from gaining access to individual snap-ins or explicitly permit them to use each one. As with all settings, by default these snap-ins are unconfigured, which means all users get all snap-ins.

Extension snap-ins

Some snap-ins can come with what are termed *extensions*, extra sets of configurable options that you can add to give more functionality to the snap-in. This section contains a list of all permitted extensions and allows you to enable or disable them as you wish.

Group Policy

These items correspond to the headings that I've been going through here. You can decide, for example, to allow a certain set of users access only to the Administrative Templates (User) section that I'm discussing here. Another set of users may have access to manipulate Group Policy objects, but the MMC allows them to see only the Software Installation (User) and Software Installation (Computer) parts. This effectively blocks their ability to manage parts of policies that you as the administrator don't give them rights to.

Windows Components → Task Scheduler

This contains settings to allow the administrator to configure the ability of users to use the task scheduler on clients. Administrators can disable the ability to create new tasks, prohibit viewing existing tasks, or limit certain functionality.

Windows Components → Windows Installer

This area contains configuration settings for users that relate to the software packages in MSI form that have been deployed to the user. For example, the administrator can configure whether applications are always deployed with elevated privileges, in what order locations are searched for MSI packages (used when a user requests a list of packages or a user attempts to open a file with an unknown extension), and whether the ability to roll back a failed installation is enabled or disabled.

Summary

Whew! That was a lot of settings. I've now covered the basics of what profiles can do and how modifications to a standard centralized profile make a lot of sense and are easy to manage. I've also taken a very in-depth look at the diverse sort of registry, user interface, file permission, and system changes that can be made using GPOs.

It's now time for a good look at exactly how Windows 2000 GPOs actually work from under the hood, so to speak.

9

Designing Organization-Wide Policies

This chapter takes a solid look at Group Policy Objects (GPOs) from two main perspectives:

- How Windows 2000 GPOs actually work.

- How to effectively structure your Active Directory using Organizational Units and groups so that you can make the best use of the GPOs required in your organization.

How Windows 2000 GPOs Work

Group Policies are very simple to understand, but their uses can be quite complex. Each GPO can consist of two parts: one that applies to a computer (such as a startup script or a change to the system portion of the registry) and one that applies to a user (such as a logoff script or a change to the user portion of the registry). You can use GPOs that contain only computer policies, only user policies, or a mixture of the two.

How GPOs Are Stored in Windows 2000

GPOs themselves are stored in two places: Group Policy Configuration (GPC) data is stored in Active Directory, and certain key Group Policy Template (GPT) data is stored as files and directories in the system volume. They are split because while there is definitely a need to store GPOs in Active Directory if the system is to associate them with locations in the tree, you do not want to store all the registry changes, logon scripts, and so on in Active Directory itself. To do so would fill Active Directory with a huge volume of information for every GPO, which would make the system unwieldy. To that end, each GPO consists of the object holding GPC data, which itself is linked to a companion directory in the system volume that may or may not have GPTs stored within. The GPT data is essentially a folder structure that stores Administrative Template–based policies, security settings, applications available for software installation, and script files. GPT data is stored in the *System Volume* folder of DCs in the *Policies* subfolder.

Third-party developers can extend GPOs by incorporating options that do not reside in the normal GPT location.

The GPO objects themselves are held as instances of the Group-Policy-Container class within a single container in Active Directory at this location:

```
LDAP://CN=Policies,CN=System,dc=windows,dc=mycorp,dc=com
```

Through a process known as *linking*, the GPOs are associated with the locations in the tree that are to receive the Group Policy.* In other words, one object can be linked to multiple locations in the tree, which explains how one GPO can be applied to many Organizational Units, sites, or domains as required.

Let's consider the Group-Policy-Container class objects themselves. Take a look at Figure 9-1; I am using one of the Windows 2000 Resource Kit tools, ADSIEdit, to show the view of the Policies container and its children.

Here you can see 10 Group-Policy-Container objects shown with their GUID as the Common-Name (cn) field. The Display-Name attribute of these objects holds the name that administrators of Active Directory would see when using one of the normal tools to view these objects. Each GPO also has an GPC-File-Sys-Path that holds the full path to the corresponding directory in the system volume.

If you were to look under the Policies container on a default installation, you would find only two children. These children would correspond to the Default Domain Policy† and the Default Domain Controllers Policy, the only GPOs created automatically by the system on installation. The Default Domain Policy is also associated with a special system container created on installation located at:

```
LDAP://CN=Default Domain Policy, CN=System, dc=windows,
dc=mycorp, dc=com
```

---

* The GPC data part of a GPO is an object in Active Directory. This object, like all others, has attributes. One of the attributes of a GPO is a multivalued one called gPLink that stores Active Directory ADsPaths of the containers that the GPO is linked to.

† The default settings for these two policies can be found in Microsoft's Windows 2000 Group Policy technical white paper on their web site.

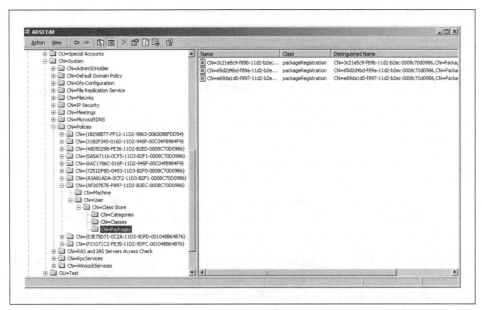

Figure 9-1. GPOs in the Policies container

Looking at Figure 9-1, you see that the eighth GPO down the list has more children within the User container than all the other GPOs. That's because it is a policy to deploy an MSI application to users. In fact, this GPO also has 80 entries under the Classes container that I haven't displayed. MSI applications tend to store large amounts of data in Active Directory. This particular policy is the one described in the introduction to the previous chapter. It applies the Administrator tools MSI file during an administrator-equivalent logon in order to install the tools on whatever workstation the administrator happens to log on. When the administrator logs off, it completely uninstalls the tools so that no subsequent users have access to them at that client computer.

How GPOs Are Used in Active Directory

Any GPO is initially created as a standalone object in Active Directory. Each object then can be linked one or more times to three different container types: Sites, Domains, and Organizational Units. GPOs for domains and Organizational Units are held in the domain relating to their application, but creating a GPO for a site stores that GPO in the forest root domain by default; administrators can change this if they wish.

Now in the normal state of affairs, what you as an administrator would do is to open up the properties of the Site, Domain, or Organizational Unit, then create a GPO and link it to that location in one go. To all intents and purposes, it appears that you have created a GPO at that location in the tree, rather than what really happened, which was that the system created the GPO as a standalone object and then linked it to that container.

To apply a GPO to a set of users or computers, you simply create a GPO in Active Directory and then link it to a Site, Domain, or Organizational Unit. Then by default, the user portion of the GPO will apply to all users in the container and its children, and the computer portion of the GPO will apply to all computers in the container and its children.

So if I were to create a policy and link it to a site or domain, all computers and users of that site or domain, respectively, would get the policy. If I were to create a policy and link it to an Organizational Unit, then all users and computers in that Organizational Unit and all the users and computers within Organizational Units beneath that Organizational Unit and so on down the tree would get the policy.

To identify the links on a GPO, you simply look at the Links tab of the GPO's properties. Figure 9-2 shows a scan for the locations in the domain Organizational Unit hierarchy to which *mycorp.com* has linked the Default Domain Policy. It seems that Mycorp has chosen to link the Default Domain Policy to a location farther down the tree as well, the Users Organizational Unit within the finance Organizational Unit, within the *mycorp.com* domain.

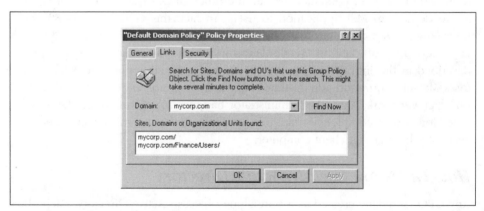

Figure 9-2. Identifying GPO links

I want to make three major points here:

- GPOs apply only to sites, domains, and Organizational Units.

- A single GPO can be linked to multiple locations in the tree.

- GPOs by default affect all of the users and computers in a container.

This generates further questions. If multiple policies apply to different locations in a tree, then can multiple GPOs apply to the same container, and if so what takes precedence? Why would you want to apply one GPO to different parts of the tree? In addition, how can we stop the GPO applying to the entire set of users and computers in the container? Let's consider each of these questions to understand policies better.

Prioritizing the Application of Multiple Policies

Let's say that I set a GPO for all users in a site to run a logon script that executes a news system local to that site. Let's also say that I set a domain GPO to set a series of Kerberos security settings for each user. Finally, I have two user logon scripts that I need to run in a specific order for specific Organizational Units in that domain. GPOs for larger containers get applied before GPOs for smaller containers. That means that any GPOs on the site get applied first, followed by any GPOs on the domain, followed by any GPOs on the Organizational Units that a user or computer resides in. This process is known as SDOU. If multiple GPOs are linked to a single site, domain, or Organizational Unit, the administrator can prioritize the order in which the GPOs are applied to that container. So in this scenario, the site news system runs first, then the Kerberos settings are applied, and finally the two logon scripts are applied in the order determined by the administrator. We know that each computer and user will exist in one site and one domain. However, while each object will exist in only one Organizational Unit as well, there is an Organizational Unit hierarchy to be considered. And there is the domain tree hierarchy as well.

To account for this, the GPOs for the site that the object resides in apply first in prioritized order. No other sites have any influence over this. Then, the GPOs for the domain that the object resides in apply in prioritized order. GPOs applied to parent domains in the domain tree have no influence on objects in domains lower down the tree. Domain trees do not impact GPO application at all. The Organizational Unit structure, however, has a significant bearing on what happens with GPOs. GPO links are inherited down the tree. So while a child Organizational Unit can have its own GPOs linked to it, it also will inherit all of its parent's GPO links. These Organizational Unit GPOs are applied in prioritized order according to the Organizational Unit hierarchy once the site and domain GPOs have been applied.

There are exceptions. You can block inheritance, force an override, and even define ACLs on objects. I'll cover all these later in this section.

For example, Paul Burke has the following ADsPath to his account (see Figure 9-3):

```
LDAP://cn=PaulBurke, ou=Databases, ou=Gurus, ou=Financial Sector,dc=mycorp,dc=com
```

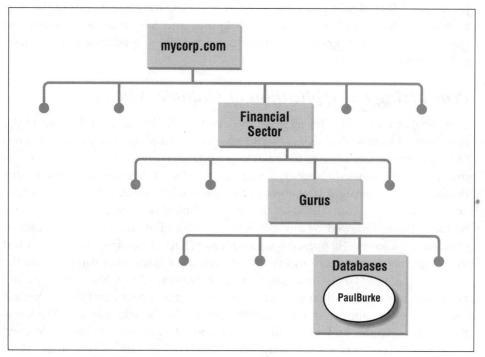

Figure 9-3. Graphical representation of the location of the Paul Burke user

The site GPOs are applied first, and the *mycorp.com* domain GPOs are applied next. Then come the GPOs on the financial sector Organizational Unit, the GPOs on the gurus Organizational Unit, and the GPOs on the databases Organizational Unit. From this, it's fairly easy to see how Organizational Unit hierarchy design has a significant effect on GPO potential.

Remember that GPOs have a computer part as well as a user part. When a computer boots, any site GPOs that have computer settings are applied in prioritized order. This is followed by any domain GPOs with computer settings and so on down the Organizational Unit hierarchy until any GPOs on the Organizational Unit that the computer resides in are applied. During boot up the user portions of these GPOs are ignored. Later, when a user logs on, the same process applies with the user settings this time. The computer settings are ignored during user logon.*

---

* This is the default case. There is a setting that you can use to force a different mode of operation. I'll explain this later when I cover loopback mode.

Standard GPO Inheritance Rules in Organizational Units

Any unconfigured settings anywhere in a GPO can be ignored since they are not inherited down the tree; only configured settings are inherited. There are three possible scenarios:

- A parent has a value for a setting, and a child does not.

- A parent has a value for a setting, and a child has a nonconflicting value for the same setting.

- A parent has a value for a setting, and a child has a conflicting value for the same setting.

If a GPO has settings that are configured for a parent Organizational Unit, and the same policy settings are unconfigured for a child Organizational Unit, the child inherits the parent's GPO settings. That makes sense.

If a GPO has settings configured for a parent Organizational Unit that do not conflict with a GPO on a child Organizational Unit, the child Organizational Unit inherits the parent GPO settings and applies its own GPOs as well. A good example of this is two logon scripts; these scripts don't conflict, so both are run.

If a GPO has settings that are configured for a parent Organizational Unit that conflict with the same settings in another GPO configured for a child Organizational Unit, then the child Organizational Unit does not inherit that specific GPO setting from the parent Organizational Unit. The setting in the GPO child policy takes priority, although there is one case in which this is not true. If the parent disables a setting and the child makes a change to that setting, the child's change is ignored. In other words, the disabling of a setting is always inherited down the hierarchy.

Blocking Inheritance and Overriding the Block in Organizational Unit GPOs

It is possible to force the settings of a GPO to be applied as the final settings for a child.

Blocking inheritance is a fairly simple concept. If you block inheritance to a specific Organizational Unit, then GPOs linked to parent Organizational Units up the tree are not applied to objects in this specific Organizational Unit or its children.

LGPOs (Local GPO, discussed shortly) are processed even when Block Policy Inheritance is checked.

Refer back to Figure 9-3. If I decide to block inheritance at the databases Organizational Unit, then Paul Burke will receive only GPOs directly defined on the databases Organizational Unit. If I decide to block inheritance at the gurus Organizational Unit, then Paul Burke will receive only GPOs on the databases Organizational Unit and those inherited from the gurus Organizational Unit. The Organizational Unit that you block inheritance at stops any higher level GPOs from applying to the branch starting at the blocked Organizational Unit. In fact, I can block inheritance on any of the Organizational Units within the *mycorp.com* domain. For example, blocking inheritance on the financial sector Organizational Unit makes sense, if I want to block site-level GPOs from applying.

This can cause problems. For example, let's say that you have delegated control over an Organizational Unit branch to a group of administrators and allowed them access to manipulate GPOs on that branch. You may be applying GPOs to Organizational Units farther up the hierarchy that you wish this delegated branch to receive. However, your branch admins have the ability to block inheritance of these parent Organizational Unit policies of yours. The branch administrators also have the ability to configure a setting that conflicts with one you set in a parent GPO; the branch administrator's child setting will take precedence in conflicts.

To prevent this, you can check the No Override box on an individual GPO. This allows administrators to force GPOs to be inherited by all children of an Organizational Unit. However, it has one further effect: it prevents GPO settings in child Organizational Units from overriding conflicting settings in a parent OU.

Let's say that I change a registry setting using a GPO on the financial sector Organizational Unit. Unfortunately, another administrator then sets the same registry setting (among many others) to a conflicting value on the gurus Organizational Unit and also blocks inheritance at the databases Organizational Unit. By default, the registry setting will be correctly applied only to the Financial Sector Organizational Unit, as the gurus Organizational Unit receives the different setting (child overrides parent on conflicts due to inheritance rules), and the databases Organizational Unit doesn't inherit either policy. To fix both problems, I could set my original financial sector Organizational Unit policy to No Override. It then prevents the specific setting on the GPO on the gurus Organizational Unit from modifying it without affecting any of the other GPO settings. My GPO also is forced down past the Block Inheritance set up at the databases Organizational Unit.

If you are making use of No Override on a policy, I suggest that you consider setting up an ACL on that policy to restrict the abilities of others to edit that GPO, leaving just a core group of administrators with the relevant permissions. This will ensure that it is not changed without the knowledge of the core group.

In summary:

- If Block Inheritance has been checked for a child-level GPO and No Override has not been checked for any parent GPOs, the child GPO will not inherit any policies from any parent GPOs farther up the hierarchy.

- If No Override has been checked for a parent-level GPO, the child-level GPO will inherit all of the parent's configured policies, even if those policies conflict with the child's policies, and even if Block Inheritance has been set for the child.

When Policies Apply

I've already said that the computer portion of a GPO applies during boot up and the user portion of a GPO applies during logon. However, that isn't the only time that a policy can apply. The policies also can be set to refresh periodically after a certain time interval. How often this occurs and what conditions are attached to this refreshing are specified under the System\Group Policy key under the Administrative Templates section of the computer and user sections of a GPO.

Set the refresh value to 0 to have the policy continually apply every seven seconds. This is very useful for a test environment but obviously not for a live service.*

You also can manually refresh policies on a client using the *SECEDIT.EXE* tool with the command `SECEDIT /refreshpolicy` option.

Refreshing is very useful for users who do not shut down their computers or log off from the system for days. In that case, GPOs will apply in the normal way, just at very irregular intervals over long periods. Consequently, setting up policy refresh means that you can manage to apply those settings to such users at whatever interval you decide.

You may think that refreshing should be fairly straightforward—a policy refreshes or doesn't refresh—but there is quite a bit more to it. The problems come when you attempt to refresh settings that could potentially affect the currently logged-on user and cause his machine to behave in an unusual or unstable manner. Let's consider a few examples:

- I decide to use a GPO to deploy Office 2000, which comes with its own MSI files for use with the Application Deployment GPOs. The deployment goes well, but I later decide that I need to change a few registry keys governing the

---

* There is a chance that this will be taken out of the final version of the product.

way Office operates. I add these into the appropriate parts of the GPO so that new users receive them and that rolling out these new registry keys to users currently running Office will not cause the running application to fail. I have to be careful as to whether I want the registry keys to apply during a refresh or during the next logon or boot up of the machine (depending on whether they are user or computer registry settings).

- I have deployed an application using an MSI file that has insinuated itself into all users' registries. Unfortunately, there is a serious problem with the application and I want to remove it, so I remove it from the list of deployable applications. Users who are not logged on now will have the application auto-uninstalled when they next log on, but what about currently logged-on users? If the policy is set to auto-refresh, the application will attempt to uninstall itself while users are logged on, even if some of them are using the application at the time.

- I decide to add a new logon script to a GPO so that users are alerted about the number of new mail messages. If this policy is set to auto-refresh, the system may detect that this logon script is new and automatically run it against any logged-on clients. Users who logged on at 0900 and receive a logon script message welcoming them to the system and telling them they have new mail at 1500 could be confused.

All of these show the problems with refresh. What if you do want refresh to occur? Consider the following example.

I decide that I want a script that alerts users about system changes. This script fires up a dialog box that explains various changes to the system during a critical upgrade, for example. It could even auto-open a browser window to an intranet web page holding important changes. I need this script to run once during logon and then every time the page changes. Every time I make a system change, I remove and re-add the logon script for the specific GPO that I wish to apply to all affected users. I then specify that the GPO should refresh periodically. The script is then run whenever I require it to do so, and all users who are logged on at the time will have an alert message pop up on their screens, generated by the script running again on their client.

All of these items and more are configurable in the GPO. The point is that if you do turn on refresh, make sure you go through both areas of the GPO thoroughly to make sure that the specific items being refreshed are sensible.

Local Group Policy Objects

It is now possible for standalone or domain-member Windows 2000 workstations and member servers to hold their own Local Group Policies, known as LGPOs.

LGPOs are applied prior to any GPOs on the site, but have restrictions in that they can contain only security settings, software policies, and scripts. File deployment and application deployment are not available in LGPOs.

LGPOs are applied first before site GPOs. This is normally represented by the string LSDOU.

While GPOs consist of two parts, the Active Directory object and the templates in the system volume, LGPOs consist of only the template portion. These templates cannot be stored in the system volume because the concept does not exist on the local machine. Instead, the LGPO templates are stored in *%systemroot%\System32\ GroupPolicy*. These ADM files can be added to and extended in the same way as with standard GPOs.

While LGPOs will be very useful in environments in which no DCs exist and Windows NT system policies really failed to deliver, their use in enterprise organizations is likely to be quite limited. In some cases, LGPOs will be useful if an administrator requires a machine-specific policy to execute before all others or if a domain client is not to execute any domain GPOs, but mostly their use will be confined to standalone environments.

LGPOs are processed even when Block Policy Inheritance is checked.

If conflicts occur on a domain client with an LGPO and subsequently applied Active Directory GPOs, then the Active Directory GPO will prevail over the original LGPO.

If you do have a requirement for a domain client not to execute domain GPOs, you need to change a setting in the LGPO that will make a registry change on that local client when it is next booted. This key is checked both when the client boots and when a user logs onto the domain. If the key is properly set, the user and computer will have only the LGPO applied, and any domain GPOs will be ignored.

How Existing Windows NT 4.0 System Policies Affect GPO Processing

Windows NT 4.0 system policies were useful in making sure that a setting was applied with a specific value somewhere in the registry. These policies dotted the registry with settings throughout its structure and was known as *tattooing* the registry. Once these settings were applied, to unset them the administrator had to either edit the registry or create another policy to force the different settings to the system. By default, ordinary users also had the ability to change registry settings in the user portion (HKCU) held in their profile, so they could easily unset values that the administrator wished to be firmly set.

In order to counteract this and bring all the policy settings under one roof, so to speak, Windows 2000 was designed so that the GPOs exist as registry keys and values in locations that are restricted to administrator access. These locations are:

* HKEY_CURRENT_USER\Software\Policies

* HKEY_LOCAL_MACHINE\Software\Policies

* HKEY_CURRENT_USER\Software\Microsoft\Windows\CurrentVersion\ Policies

* HKEY_LOCAL_MACHINE\Software\Microsoft\Windows\CurrentVersion\ Policies

The first two keys are the preferred locations for all new policies. An administrator can specify that a value be set in a user's registry, then reset on a regular basis. Any settings those users have set themselves will be overwritten by the proper administrator-set values. However, administrators still can import any ADM files and modify keys throughout the registry as they wish. It is up to administrators to make sure that the policy is re-applied regularly or is in a part of the registry to which the user has no access, unless they wish the user to be able to change it permanently.

When to Use Windows NT System Policies

During an upgrade, Windows NT system policies that reside in the *NETLOGON* share will be transferred to Windows 2000's *NETLOGON* share (now known as the system volume). However, only Windows NT and Windows 9x downlevel clients will use these policies; Windows 2000 clients will not use them. Windows 2000 GPOs do not affect downlevel clients at all..

If you have downlevel clients that need policies applied to them, whether these policies already exist or need to be created from scratch, then you need to fall back on the old system policies that were provided for use on these systems. You

Windows NT System Policies

Windows NT provided a tool called System Policy Editor (*POLEDIT.EXE*) that was installed with the resource kit. This was a very basic graphical tool that allowed you to manage three types of policies: computer, user, and group. By default, the only two policies were Default User and Default Computer.

Do not confuse the Default User policy with the Default User profile; they are not the same thing at all.

If you decided that your entire organization would have only one set of policies for everyone, you would simply modify the Default User and Default Computer policies. Whenever a client booted in your organization, it would retrieve the Default Computer Policy and lock itself down (or unlock itself) according to that policy. Whenever a user logged on to that client, the Default User policy would apply and lock or unlock the settings for that account.

The default policies basically allowed you to lock down the desktop settings of the machine based on a series of template files, also known as ADM files. It was always possible to create your own ADM files, or modify the existing ones, with settings that corresponded to registry changes you wanted to make. If you created a new file, you just imported it into the tool and could then start applying the policy.

If you did not want just one policy for every computer and user in your organization, you could create policies for individual users, computers, or groups. When a client booted or a user logged on, the system would determine, according to a set of rules, which of the policies would apply to that computer or user. Only one policy was ever applied to a user or computer.

cannot use the Windows 2000 GUI to administer these older policies, so you will need to use the old System Policy Editor (*POLEDIT.EXE*) tool that has been reissued with Windows 2000 to manipulate such policies. The POL files generated by the System Policy Editor will still need to be placed in the *NETLOGON* share as they were under previous versions of Windows NT.

There is one benefit to administrators who have been using system policies to administer downlevel clients for some time; while the system policies themselves are not transferable, GPOs can be extended using ADM files of the exact format. This means that administrators can migrate their old template files over from system policies to GPOs as required.

If you have any system policy functionality that you wish to apply to your Windows 2000 clients, you will have to reimplement your system policies as GPOs because Windows 2000 will not upgrade your system policies for use with Windows 2000.

I don't intend to cover system policies any more here since there are a number of white papers and other documents within Microsoft's Knowledge Base at *http://support.microsoft.com/support/* that can do the job very well. The best way to find them is to search for the string System Policies.

How Policies Apply to Clients with Different Operating Systems

If you have a Windows NT 4.0 client in a workgroup or a domain, the only policies that can apply are downlevel Windows NT 4.0 policy (POL) file policies.

If you have a standalone Windows 2000 client or member server, policies are evaluated in the following order:

- Downlevel Windows NT 4.0 policy (POL) file
- Windows 2000 local GPO

If you have a Windows 2000 client or member server in a mixed-mode domain, policies are evaluated in the following order:

- Downlevel Windows NT 4.0 policy (POL) file
- Windows 2000 local GPO
- Site GPOs in priority order
- Domain GPOs in priority order
- Organizational Unit GPOs in priority order, applied in a hierarchical fashion down the tree ending with the Organizational Unit that the computer or user resides in

As this extends the LSDOU process to include Windows NT 4.0 system policies, this process is commonly written as 4LSDOU.

If you have a Windows 2000 client or member server in a native-mode domain, policies are evaluated in LSDOU order.

Combating Slowdown Due to GPOs

If you apply too many policies, there will be slowdowns. But there are no good guidelines for how many policies to apply. I can tell you that in my lab environment, I saw a slowdown when I started applying more than twelve policies. *Unfortunately, that data is of absolutely no use to you.* Read on to see why.

Limiting the number of GPOs that apply

The problem with trying to test the impact of GPOs on speed of the client during boot up and logon is possible only by direct testing. *I would not advocate taking my value as a hard and fast rule.* Each policy has to be identified, opened, read to see if it applies, actually applied, and finally closed before moving on to the next policy. This process, which is done automatically by the system, will take time. So executing three policies of 20 changes each will be slower than implementing one change of 60. I arrived at the value of 12 by using a series of tests with large and small policies in my test domain in my lab environment. It was my lab environment; without knowing what settings were in my policies, the layout of my network, the specification and bandwidth capabilities of my clients and servers, and so on, that data is of no of no use to you. Even if I provided it, there is little chance that it would be similar to your layout, so you'll need to do your own testing to work out what's acceptable. Lab test simulation is really the best way to get a feel for how much the policies that you want will impact your clients.

Microsoft has its own take on designing your Active Directory for GPOs. They recommend that you should not have Organizational Unit structures more than ten deep in order that policies do not take too much time during logon. This advice is still only half helpful, and I'll come back to it in the design section later.

Block Inheritance and No Override

If you use either Block Inheritance or No Override, you incur extra processing. For this reason you should be cautious in their use.

Disabling parts of GPOs

There is another way to speed up policies. Let's say that you have an Organizational Unit that has three policies on it: a computer startup script, a computer shutdown script, and a user logon script. Let's also say that you have a need for three policies rather than one, perhaps because they are applied elsewhere in the Organizational Unit hierarchy as well. When a user in your Organizational Unit logs on, the system will attempt to apply any user settings from all three GPOs. We know that two of the policies have no relevance whatsoever to a user. Wouldn't it be a nice touch to have some way to tell the system not to bother processing the user portion for GPOs that deal only with computer data and vice versa. In fact, this is a very simple process. All you do is look at the properties of a GPO and check one box or the other in the General tab, as shown in Figure 9-4.

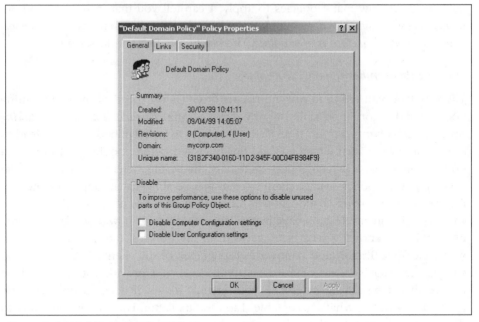

Figure 9-4. Disabling part of a GPO

With all the settings in a GPO, normally browsing both user and computer parts of the tree to see if each part was empty and whether any changes had been made would be a lengthy process. However, Microsoft has thought of this, and as Figure 9-4 shows, the revisions indicate exactly how many changes have been made to the GPO. This guides you in whether to disable or enable parts of a GPO.

GPOs with no revisions in a section are skipped; disabling part of the policy stops the need to check the revision level, thus can partially speed up the process.

Limiting cross-domain linking

It is possible for an administrator of one domain to create a GPO and for it to be applied to an SDOU in another domain. For example, if the administrator of *othercorp.com* is given access to centralized setup GPOs within *mycorp.com*, he can link the *mycorp.com* GPOs to SDOUs in the *othercorp.com* domain.

 Cross-domain linking is possible only because GPO links are held in the GC.

While this is feasible, it is not normally recommended for network bandwidth considerations, since the objects in Active Directory and the templates in the system volume need reading on the remote domain. Normally it's better to consider duplicating the GPO in the second domain instead of cross-domain linking to it. However, if the links between the domains are as fast and reliable as the links within the second domain that is to receive the policy and if the domain holding the GPO can apply it to the user or computer fast enough to make the administrator happy, then there is nothing stopping you from doing this.

Limiting GPO application across WAN links

This shouldn't be a problem if you set up your sites' configuration correctly, but you need to be aware of the implications, nonetheless.

Data on GPOs linked to site objects is copied to all DCs in a forest because site information is part of the Configuration container that is replicated to all DCs in all domains in the entire forest. So any GPO linked to a site object will be applied to all machines in that site regardless of which domain in the forest they are in.

However, while multiple domains will receive the link information, those same domains will not receive the entire GPO itself. Instead, the GPO will reside in one domain and clients in the site will read the GPO from that domain as required.

In the normal course of events, this shouldn't be a problem since a site is supposed to be an area of well-connected subnets. A site hosts three domains— Domain A, Domain B, and Domain C; Domain A holds the site GPO itself, and clients of all three domains will access the GPO from Domain A. However, if Domain B for some reason were mistakenly down a slow WAN link of some kind, the machines in Domain B would be accessing the GPO across that slow link. If you use site GPOs and the site spans slow WAN links (which it shouldn't do), you will cause GPOs to be accessed across those links.

The Power of Access Control Lists on Group Policy Objects

The real problem with all the information so far is that a policy appears to apply to all users and/or computers in whatever container it is linked to. There is a way of changing that, which is why they're now called *group policies* rather than just *policies.*

As each GPO is an object in Active Directory, and all objects have an Access Control List (ACL) associated with them; it follows that it must be possible to allow and deny access to GPOs using that ACL. With ACLs it is possible to allow and deny access to GPOs based on security group membership. It is also possible to go to an even finer-grained detail and set access control for an individual

computer or user. Take a look at Figure 9-5. This shows us that the system secu-
rity group called Authenticated Users will be able to read and apply the Group
Policy. If I unchecked the Apply Group Policy checkbox, then the Authenticated
Users group would not receive this policy.

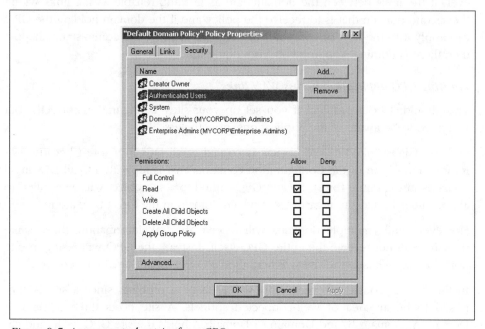

Figure 9-5. Access control entries for a GPO

This is a significant feature of GPOs and one that you can heavily use to your
advantage. Let's take a simple example in which I create a single GPO to roll out
an internal application and link it to the finance Organizational Unit and the marketing Organizational Unit in one domain. Now all users in the finance and marketing Organizational Units will receive that application via the GPO on logon.
Let's also say that a certain subset of users from both Organizational Units are not
to receive this application. All I do is create a security group to hold that user subset and set up an Access Control Entry (ACE) to the Application Deployment GPO
and check the Deny Apply Group Policy checkbox. Now, every user that I make a
member of that new security group will not receive the policy.

 Deny always overrides Allow. Let's say a user or computer is a member of four security groups. If a GPO has an ACL that contains an
ACE for the individual user or computer with Read and Apply rights,
an ACE for three of the security groups that have Read and Apply
rights and an ACE for the fourth security group that has Apply rights
denied, the GPO will not be applied.

This has practical applications, too. At Leicester University we maintain a separate Organizational Unit structure for our computer objects. On our open area lab machines, where students from anywhere around the university can log on, we maintain tight security. Each computer in that lab has a corresponding computer account object in an Organizational Unit that represents that lab. Two GPOs are created and linked to that single Organizational Unit; one GPO locks down that machine tightly, and the other GPO unlocks it. In other words, we set two completely conflicting GPOs to act on the same Organizational Unit. Normally that would be plain silly, but we then use two security groups that already exist to give one security group access only to the lockdown GPO and one security group access only to the unlock GPO. Whenever we create computer accounts in that Organizational Unit, we place the computers in the lockdown security group. That means the computers in that security group will automatically receive the lockdown policy. If we decide that we need to do work in that lab and wish a particular client, or all clients, unlocked, then all we do is make the relevant computers members of the unlocked security group and finish off by rebooting them or waiting for a refresh. As long as we never place a computer object in both groups, we have a client that is either locked or unlocked depending on its group memberships.

This is a good demonstration of how you can make use of conflicting GPOs on a single Organizational Unit based solely on permission granted by the ACLs to those GPOs, one of the most important aspects of GPOs.

Loopback Merge Mode and Loopback Replace Mode

Due to overwhelming requests from the beta test sites, Leicester University included, Microsoft extended Group Policy to cope with a particular requirement that otherwise would have been very difficult. Loopback mode is a specially configured GPO option that allows you to apply the user portion of a GPO to a user based on the computer he is logging on from. For example, imagine I have a suite of public kiosks in the foyer of my organization to give outsiders information about the company. Company employees also can use these devices if they quickly want to check email on their way in or out. Since literally anyone in the building can use the kiosks, I need a lot of security. I don't want those kiosks to allow company employees to have all the privileges and permissions that they normally would at their desktop devices; I want them to be able to use only email. What I can do is tie a set of user restrictions into the user portion of a GPO that sits on the Organizational Unit that holds the computer objects. Then employees are locked down at the kiosks, and nowhere else. This effectively allows me to restrict what employees can do to their own settings on a per-machine basis.

Many administrators can see the use of this setting in certain environments and for certain situations. Take a lab of machines in a university where staff accounts are to be locked down like student accounts while the staff members are in the lab, but not at their private machines. As a final example, consider that the finance Organizational Unit users have a lot of deployed applications specific to finance. These applications are to work only when accessed from the finance computers and not from anywhere else. So you would put them as deployed applications into the computer section of GPOs that apply to the finance Organizational Unit. However, if you also deployed applications to finance users (via the user portion of a GPO) that were supposed to roam with the users everywhere except in sales and marketing, you could use loopback mode to stop the applications being advertised specifically in those two Organizational Units.

Loopback mode can be found in the Group Policy settings of the computer portion of any GPO. If you open that item, you get Figure 9-6, which allows you to switch between the two modes of loopback operation: merge mode and replace mode.

Figure 9-6. Setting loopback mode

When a user logs on to a machine that uses loopback merge mode, the user policies are applied first as normal; then the user portion of any GPOs that apply to the computer are applied in sequence, overriding any of the previous user policies as appropriate. Replace mode, by contrast, ignores the GPOs that would apply to the user and instead applies only the user portions of the GPOs that apply to the computers. Figure 9-7 illustrates this.

In Figure 9-7, the domain *mycorp.com* spans two sites, main site and second site. Marketing computers exist in main site, and finance computers in second site. Policy A applies to main site only, Policy B applies to the entire domain, and C, D, E, and F apply to the Organizational Units as indicated. Policy G applies to the Second Site.

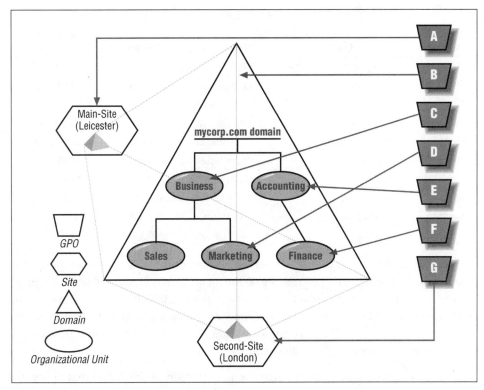

Figure 9-7. Loopback mode processing

Table 9-1 summarizes the position. When loopback is not turned on, the only real difference comes from the site policies (A or G) that are applied. When you turn replace mode on for all the GPOs, it becomes more obvious what will happen. In each case, the policy relating to the user is applied first in order, followed by the entire set of policy items that would apply to a user residing in the computer location. Take the example of a finance user logging on at a marketing computer in the main site. The finance user first has the user portion of the site policy that he is logging on from applied (A), followed by the user portion of the domain policy (B), the user portion of the accounting Organizational Unit (E), and the user portion of the finance Organizational Unit (F). After this, the user portion of the site (A) is applied again, followed by the user portion of the domain policy (B), the user portion of the business Organizational Unit (C), and finally the user portion of the marketing Organizational Unit (D).

Table 9-1. Resultant Set of Policies for Figure 9-7

Loopback Mode in Use	Organizational Unit That User Resides in	Where Computer Resides	Resultant Set of Policies
No	Marketing	OU=marketing (main site)	ABCD
No	Finance	OU=finance (second site)	GBEF

Table 9-1. Resultant Set of Policies for Figure 9-7 (continued)

Loopback Mode in Use	Organizational Unit That User Resides in	Where Computer Resides	Resultant Set of Policies
No	Marketing	OU=finance (second site)	GBCD
No	Finance	OU=marketing (main site)	ABEF
Merge	Marketing	OU=marketing (main site)	ABCDABCD
Merge	Finance	OU=finance (second site)	GBEFGBEF
Merge	Marketing	OU=finance (second site)	GBCDGBEF
Merge	Finance	OU=marketing (main site)	ABEFABCD
Replace	Marketing	OU=marketing (main site)	ABCD
Replace	Finance	OU=finance (second site)	GBEF
Replace	Marketing	OU=finance (second site)	GBEF
Replace	Finance	OU=marketing (main site)	ABCD

Remember that later policies can override earlier policies, so the user portion of the policies applying to the location of the computer will always override previous policies if there is a conflict. With policy order ABEFABCD, D can override C, which can override B, which can override A, which can override F, and so on. Also, in all these cases, if any of the computer GPOs do not have any defined settings in the user portion, the policy is ignored.

Loopback replace mode is used when the user portion of the GPOs that apply to a computer are to be the only ones set. So for the finance user logging on to a computer in marketing in the main site, the only policies that get applied to that user are ABCD, the user portions of the GPOs that apply to the marketing computer.

Administrators must be aware that loopback mode can impose a significant amount of extra load on the processing at the client, especially when using loopback in its merge mode.

How GPOs Work Across RAS and Slow Links

GPOs and even user profiles can still work across slow links, and a lot of the configuration is left in the hands of the administrator. Administrators can specify what speed is used in the definition of a slow link. For computers and users, the following policy areas need looking at:

```
Computer Configuration
    Administrative Templates\System\Group Policy\Group Policy Slow Link
    Detection
User Configuration
    Administrative Templates\System\Group Policy\Group Policy Slow Link
    Detection
```

In both cases, the default setting is 500 KBps, but administrators can set any KBps connection speed time that they wish. This speed is used against a new Windows 2000 slow-link-detection algorithm; if the speed is above the value, then the link is fast, below the value indicates a slow link.

This is the algorithm in pseudocode, as it existed for beta 3:

```
Ping server with 0KB of data : Receive response#1 as a time in
  milliseconds (ms)
If response#1 < 10ms Then
        Exit as this is a fast link
Else
        Ping server with 4KB of data : Receive response#2 as a time in
    milliseconds
        Calculate Total-speed as response#2-response#1
End If
Ping server with 0KB of data : Receive response#1 as a time in
  milliseconds
If response#1 < 10ms Then
        Exit as this is a fast link
Else
        Ping server with 4KB of data : Receive response#2 as a time in
          milliseconds
        Calculate Total-speed as Total-speed + (response#2-response#1)
End If
Ping server with 0KB of data : Receive response#1 as a time in
  milliseconds
If response#1 < 10ms Then
        Exit as this is a fast link
Else
        Ping server with 4KB of data : Receive response#2 as a time in
          milliseconds
        Calculate Total-speed as Total-speed + (response#2-response#1)
End If

'Average the total speed of (response#2-response#1)
Difference-in-milliseconds = Total-Speed/3

'If we know 4KB (32,768 bits) was moved in a certain number of
  milliseconds,
'then we need to calculate the number of bits moved per second
  (not per ms)
Bits-per-second-value = (32768 * 1000/Difference-in-milliseconds)

'Eight bits is a byte, so calculate bytes/second
bps-value = (Bits-per-second-value * 8)

'Calculate kilobytes/second to compare against GPO value
Kbps-value = bps-value / 1024
```

User profiles work in a similar manner. The following setting supports both checking the performance of the filesystem and checking the speed of the user profile server in both kilobytes per second and milliseconds. This was included by

Microsoft to get past problems where the user profile server was not IP capable; in this case, it checks the filesystem performance instead:

```
Computer Configuration\
  Administrative Templates\System\Group Policy
    Slow network connection timeout for user profiles
```

The following GPOs are applied across slow links:

- When a user dials in from a RAS connection, both computer and user GPOs are applied.

- When a user logs in using the "Logon using dial-up connection" checkbox on the logon screen, user policies are applied.

- When the computer is a member of the same domain as the RAS server or is in a domain with a trust relationship to the one the RAS server is in, both are applied.

GPOs are not applied:

- When the logon is done using cached credentials which then include a RAS connection.

- To computers that are members of a different domain or workgroup.

By default in all these cases, security settings (i.e., IP security, EFS recovery, etc.) and Administrative Template settings are the only ones to be applied by default; folder redirection, disk quotas, scripts, and software installation policies are not applied. You can't turn off registry settings you have to apply. You can, however, alter the default state of any of the others including the security settings using the relevant sections of those GPOs.

Summary of Policy Options

That's a lot of information on GPOs. Let's summarize what I've covered about the workings of GPOs so far:

- GPOs exist in a split state. The configuration data for the GPO, known in shorthand form as GPC data, is held in the object itself. The template files and settings that tell the GPO what its capabilities are, known in shorthand form as GPT data, are stored in the system volume.

- Individual GPOs can be linked to multiple sites, domains, and Organizational Units in Active Directory as required.

- GPOs can contain policies that apply to both computers and users in a container. The default operation of a GPO on a container is to apply the computer portion of the GPO to every computer in that container during boot up and to apply the user portion of the GPO to every user in that container during logon. GPOs also can be set to refresh periodically.

- Multiple GPOs linked to a particular container in Active Directory will be applied in a strict order according to a series of priorities. The default-prioritized order corresponds to the exact order in which the GPOs were linked to the container. Administrators can adjust the priorities as required.

- While GPOs exist only in a domain environment due to their dependence on Active Directory, individual domain or workgroup computers can have local GPOs, known as LGPOs, defined for them.

- Windows NT 4.0 system policies also can apply to standalone Windows NT/ 2000 clients or Windows NT/2000 mixed-mode domain clients.

- GPOs are inherited down the Organizational Unit hierarchy by default. This can be blocked using the properties of an OU, domain, or site. Administrators can also can set a checkbox that allows a policy to override all lower settings and bypass any blocks.

- Loopback mode allows the administrator to specify that user settings can be overridden on a per-machine basis. Effectively, this means that the user parts of policies that normally apply only to computers are applied to the users as well as (merge mode) or instead of (replace mode) the existing user policies.

- A number of things can slow down processing on a client, including attempting to process many policies one after the other. Use of loopback, especially in merge mode, can significantly impact this. Attempting to apply GPOs across domains can also lead to slowdowns depending on the network speed between the domains.

- Policies apply in a strict order known as 4LSDOU. This notation indicates that Windows NT 4.0 system policies apply first, followed by any LGPO policies, followed by site GPOs, domain GPOs, and finally any Organizational Unit GPOs hierarchically down the tree. At each point, the policies are applied in prioritized order if multiple policies exist at a location.

- When policies are to be applied to a client, the system identifies the entire list of policies to be applied before actually applying them in order. This is in order to determine if any blocking, overriding, or loopback has been put in place that could alter the order or application of the policies.

- ACLs can be used to limit the application of GPOs to certain individual users or computers or groups of users or computers. Specifically setting up the ACLs on a GPO to deny or allow access means that you can tailor the impact of a policy from the normal method of applying the GPO to all users or computers in a container.

- If you use the MMC interface and look at the properties of an individual GPO, three tabs are displayed on the property page. The General tab shows you summary details on the policy and allows you to disable the computer or user part of the policy if you require. The Links tab allows you to find all locations in Active Directory that have links to that GPO. The Security tab allows you to limit the scope of the GPO on a container via ACLs.

- Finally, both user profiles and policies can be applied across a slow link, but the speed that the system uses to determine whether a link is slow is configurable by the administrator within an individual GPO. In addition, while security settings and administrative templates normally are applied by default, the exact settings that will apply across a slow link when one is detected are configurable by the administrator as well. The only exception is that administrative templates will always be applied; the administrator has no control over this.

Using the Group Policy Editor Tool

Unfortunately at the present time, there is no programmatic way to manipulate GPOs via scripts. That's not to say that you can't interface to the objects using ADSI, but there has been no `IADsGroupPolicy` interface or similar to allow manipulation of the settings from a script. This isn't immediately surprising, since GPOs are quite complex and the actual interface would need to interface not only to Active Directory but also to the system volume if all GPO options were to become scriptable. Consider the introduction of ADM files and the publication of MSI-capable applications, and you have one large interface to come up with. I expect to see this rolled out in future versions of ADSI, but in the meantime, while scripting is out of the question, there is a way to programmatically add/edit/delete GPOs using fully compilable program code, such as C++. For more information, look up the `IGroupPolicyObject` interface defined in *gpedit.h* in the platform SDK for more details.

That leaves us with the GUI tool called the Group Policy Editor (GPE). This tool, however, can be accessed in a number of ways. As with all Windows 2000 tools, the GPE is an MMC snap-in that you use if you want to actually change a specific GPO or LGPO.

You can start a new or existing MMC and add the snap-in yourself if you like. If you do this, the snap-in will allow you to focus on only a particular GPO/LGPO. Each GPO/LGPO that you wish to change has to be loaded in as a separate GPE snap-in to the MMC; unfortunately, you can't tell the GPE to show you all policies in the tree, which would have been useful. However, in theory it is possible to save the console and start it from a command line with a parameter, in order to focus the GPE on a single GPO/LGPO of your choice. In practice, I've never got this to work on the beta builds that I've used, although I'm quite willing to admit that I may be getting the syntax wrong.

Managing LGPOs is done using the same GPE tool that you would use to manage GPOs. If you use the GPE from a workstation or server in a domain, then you can focus the snap-in to look at an LGPO on a local client. If you use the GPE on a standalone server or a workstation, then the GPE will automatically focus on the LGPO for that machine. No matter how the focus is shifted to look at an LGPO, the GPE will load only the extensions that are appropriate to the templates in use locally on that client. Domain-specific extensions are not loaded for LGPOs.

The GPE and Its Relationship with the PDC FSMO Role Owner

When you are editing GPOs, the GPE connects to and uses the FSMO PDC role owner. This ensures that multiple copies of the GPE on different machines are all focused on the same DC. This behavior may be overridden in two cases:

- If the PDC is unavailable for whatever reason, an error dialog will be displayed, and the administrator may select an alternate DC to use.

- Microsoft is also currently considering a GPE View menu option and/or a policy to allow the GPE to inherit from the DC that Active Directory Users and Computers MMC is focused on. This is likely to be most useful when there is a slow link to the PDC.

If GPOs are edited on multiple DCs, this could lead to inconsistencies because the last person to write to the GPO wins. For this reason, you should execute caution when multiple administrators regularly administer policies.

Starting an MMC and adding the GPE snap-in is not the normal method of accessing GPOs. In fact, there is a whole extended interface available from either Active Directory Sites and Services or Active Directory Users and Computers tool. If you open up the former, you can right-click any site and from the drop-down list select Properties, finally clicking the Group Policy tab on the resulting property page. If you open the latter, then you can right-click any domain or Organizational Unit container and follow the same steps. Ultimately, the Group Policy property page from any of these tools produces a window like Figure 9-8 with a number of options. Figure 9-8 itself is focused on the policies linked to the root of the *mycorp.com* domain. The following buttons are found on the Mycorp.com Properties menu:

New

> This button allows you to create new GPOs and automatically link them to the container for this property page. Since Figure 9-8 is the property page for the domain, any policies that are created and linked in here would be applied to the entire domain.

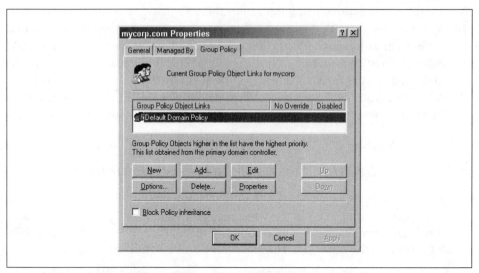

Figure 9-8. Looking at the domain policies

Add

This button allows you to link an existing GPO to the container for thisproperty page.

Edit

This button allows you to manipulate the selected policy in the display pane.

Delete

This button allows you to remove a policy. If do this, a dialog box will appear and ask if you wish to just remove the GPO's link to the container for this property page or to permanently delete the GPO.

Properties

This button allows you to bring up the properties of the GPO itself, i.e., the General, Links, and Security tabs in Figures 9-4, 9-2, and 9-5, respectively.

Options

This button allows you to set two specific options relating to the application of this GPO by bringing up a dialog box similar to that shown in Figure 9-9.

No Override

This option allows you to force the settings of this GPO to apply no matter what other GPOs later attempt to block inheritance.

Disabled

This option allows you to completely disable the GPO's application to *the current container.* If you choose this option, any ACLs that you have set on this GPO to explicitly allow or deny application of this policy to individual users, computers, or groups will be ignored. This policy will not be applied under any circumstances.

Disabling the GPO is not the same as setting an ACE with the Apply Group Policy checkbox cleared for the group Authenticated Users. Denying the ability to apply group policy for a GPO to a group via an ACE is much more restrictive, as the restriction will apply to the GPO across all containers and not just for the one container, which is what the Options button allows you to do.

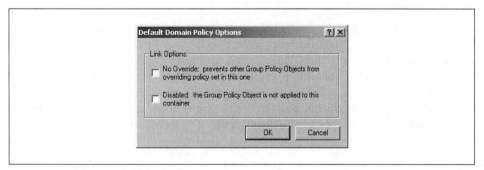

Figure 9-9. Domain Policy Options

Block Policy inheritance

This checkbox is used to indicate that policies from further up the 4LSDOU inheritance chain are not to be inherited by objects at this point and below. This is used when you want a particular level in the tree to define its own policies without inheriting previously defined ones above it. For example, a block at the site level blocks Windows NT system policies and LGPOs (i.e., 4L) from applying; a block at the domain level blocks 4LS; a block at an Organizational Unit level blocks 4LSD in addition to any other Organizational Unit parents above this level in the tree.

Up/Down arrows

These buttons allow you to prioritize multiple GPOs in the display pane. In Figure 9-8 only one GPO is displayed, so these buttons are disabled.

Using GPOs to Help Design the Organizational Unit Structure

In Chapter 6, *Designing the Namespace*, I described the design of the Active Directory Organizational Unit hierarchy. I also explained that other items have a bearing on that design. You see, there are two key design issues that affect the structure of your Organizational Units: permissions delegation and GPO placement. If you decide that your Active Directory is to be managed centrally rather

---

GPE GUI Shortcuts

Some useful shortcuts supported by Explorer have been copied over to the GPE. For example, you can highlight a branch in the GPE and press * on the numeric keypad to automatically expand the entire tree at that point. You can press + and – on the numeric keypad to expand and collapse individual highlighted branches. You can also use the cursor keys to navigate up and down the list. The Tab key switches back and forth between the scope pane and the results pane.

One last point that is very useful: If you open up the GPE and double-click on any item, it brings up a floating property page window. There is nothing to stop you going back to the GPE and highlighting any other location in the tree, navigating using the cursor keys, and using the keys in the previous paragraph. Each item that you select, however, correspondingly modifies the floating property page. You can see each item's description and options in the floating property page while navigating through the GPE as before.

---

than in a distributed fashion and that you will employ only a few GPOs that will be implemented mostly domain wide (rather than many GPOs on many Organizational Units), your Organizational Unit structure can be almost any way that you want it to be. It shouldn't make much difference whether you have 400 branches coming off the root or one container with every item inside it. However, if permissions over specific objects do need to be delegated to specific sets of administrators, then it will make more sense to structure your domain Organizational Units in a manner that facilitates that administration. This doesn't have to be the case, but it makes it much easier to use Organizational Units.

For example, if I have 1,000 users and 10 managers who each manages 100 users, I could put my 1,000 users in one Organizational Unit and then give the 10 admins permission to modify only their 100 users. This is a slow and daft way to run systems administration. What would be better would be to create 10 Organizational Units and put 100 users in each, giving each administrator permissions over his particular Organizational Unit. This makes much more sense, as the administrator can be changed very easily, it is easier to report on access, and so on. Sense and reducing management overhead are the overriding keys here; either solution is feasible, one is just easier to implement and maintain.

 Permissions delegation is covered in more detail in Chapter 10, *Active Directory Security: Permissions and Auditing.*

The same fundamental facts apply to GPOs. If you are going to need to apply multiple policies to multiple sets of users, it makes more sense and will be easier to manage if you set up multiple Organizational Units. However, this isn't always possible, for example, if the Organizational Unit structure that you have as an ideal conflicts with the one that you will need for permissions delegation, which again conflicts with the one you would like for GPO structuring.

Identifying Areas of Policy

I'm assuming that within your organization you will be writing a document that describes your plan for the security features you wish to use on your Windows 2000 system and exactly how those features will be implemented. Part of this document will relate to other security features of Windows 2000, such as Kerberos, firewalls, Active Directory permissions, and so on, but here we're concerned with GPOs.

First you need to identify the general policy goals that you wish to achieve with GPOs. There's no need to go into the exact details of each GPO setting and its value at this moment. Instead, you're looking at items like "Deploy financial applications" and "Restrict desktop settings." As you identify each general policy area, you need to note whether it is to apply to all computers or users in a site, to all computers or users in a single domain, or to a subsection of the user and computer accounts. If you aren't sure for some items, then put the items in more than one category. You end up with items like "Deploy financial applications to accountants in France" and "Restrict desktop settings in Southern Europe."

Once you have the general policy areas constructed, you need to construct an Organizational Unit structure that facilitates implementation of this policy design. At this point, you start placing computers and users in various Organizational Units, deciding if all objects in each container are to receive the policy or whether you will restrict application to the policy via ACLs. There are a number of questions you can ask yourself during this stage. To help with this, a loose set of guidelines follows the example in the next section.

Ultimately the document will need to specify exactly which GPO settings are to be applied, which groups you will set up for ACL permission restrictions, and what the Organizational Unit structure is going to be. It helps to explain justifications for any decisions you make.

To make the guidelines more meaningful, I'll show how you can structure a tree in different ways using a real-world example.

How GPOs Influenced a Real Organizational Unit Design

Leicester University needed an Organizational Unit structure that represented its user and computer population. The system needed to allow users from every department to roam anywhere on campus and log on to the system. User accounts were fairly generic across the system, with the main differences resulting only from membership in certain groups indicating the type of account the user had (staff, undergraduate, and so on). The main distinction came in the two sorts of machines that we maintain on campus: staff devices that exist in a number of staff member's offices, and open devices that exist in areas known as open area labs, which anyone could use. While staff machines always exist within a department, labs exist in certain locations and buildings throughout the university campus.

Having full Internet and drop-in access, we needed to make sure that these open area client devices were as secure as they could possibly be. This security had to extend to all users who logged on at the machines, whether they were staff or student. However, we also wanted to make sure that staff accounts were not locked down in their own departments. In other words, we wanted the user profiles of the staff users to be much more locked down only in the open area labs and nowhere else.

In terms of policies, we needed to apply quite a few. While the specifics aren't important here, we needed a number of policies to apply to different areas:

Area	Policies to Apply to
A	All computers and users in the domain
B	Users in specific departments
C	All clients (not servers)
D	All open area clients
E	All staff clients
F	Staff clients in specific departments
G	Open area clients in specific labs

With these requirements, we came up with a design. This was a lengthy process, but I'll try to break it down so that it makes sense. Let's take a look at the users themselves to start with.

Users were always members of a specific department, and this was how the university was structured in terms of its business, so it seemed logical to name the Organizational Units after the university departments. I should add, by the way, that Leicester University needed only one domain, the forest root domain in a single forest, for its organization; the Organizational Unit structure was much more important than the domain structure in this case. The overall Organizational Unit structure came out something like that shown in Figure 9-10. Each department is joined directly to the root of the domain, with the users (represented by the circles) being children of the departmental containers.

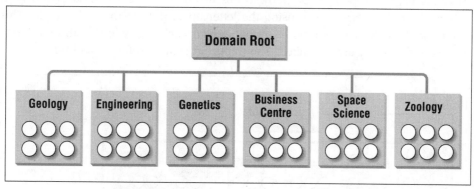

Figure 9-10. OU structure to hold user objects

Next, we needed an Organizational Unit structure that represented the distinct divisions of computers that existed throughout the university. There's no necessity to presume that your computers should go in the same Organizational Unit structure as your users, and that's how we approached the concept at Leicester. Initially, based on the policy areas, it seemed sensible to us to create an entirely new client tree that held only the machine accounts. This hierarchy ended up looking like the one in Figure 9-11.

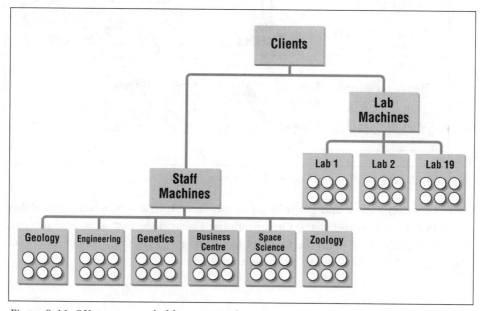

Figure 9-11. OU structure to hold computer objects

Here you can see the branch solely for the computer accounts, with two children that each hold lab locations or departments themselves. Notice how the staff machine branch of the tree looks remarkably like the user structure diagram from Figure 9-10. I'll come back to that in a minute. For now, let's see if we can successfully apply the policies properly to this hierarchy. Take a look at Figure 9-12; where the policies are shown using the letter notation from the earlier table. This screen looks very cluttered, but it simply depicts each policy area with indications of where the policy area is linked. The trapezoid is Microsoft's symbol for a GPO.

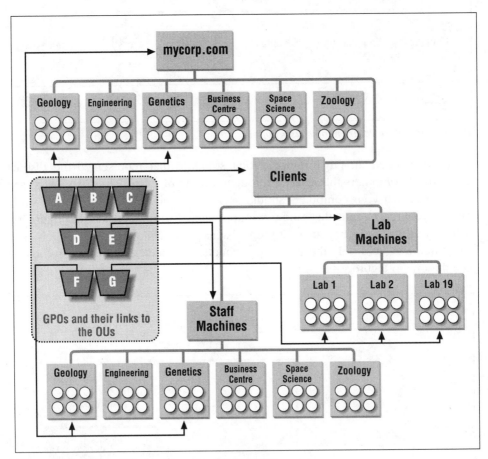

Figure 9-12. GPOs applied to the entire OU structure

Not every department and lab is listed in this screen. In a similar vein, I've linked the GPOs to only some of the Organizational Units, since that would be the case in reality. After all, if every department or lab were to receive a policy, then you might as well link the GPO to the parent.

The merits of collapsing the Organizational Unit structure

I've created a structure that is understandable and perfectly represents the business that we operate. That's a good achievement from this design. The next step is to consider whether the domain would be easier to manage if I merged the duplicated staff organizational units.

Take a look at Figure 9-13. This is the hierarchy if I do away with all the staff machine Organizational Units and put the staff computers directly into the departmental Organizational Units. Policy areas A and B stay the same. Policy area C has to apply to all clients so I can't use the clients Organizational Unit any more. I have two choices: link the policy to the domain and have it apply to all Organizational Units containing computers beneath the root or link the policy to each Organizational Unit under the root by hand. The latter solution also requires me to link the GPO to any new Organizational Units that I create under the root, if they are to receive the policy.

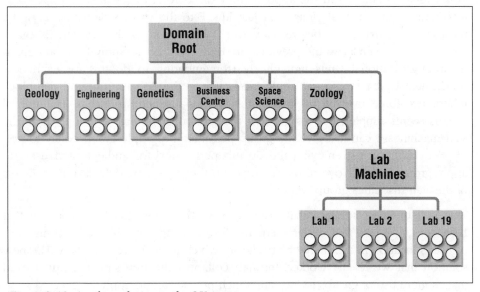

Figure 9-13. Another solution to the OU structure

The former is the easier solution to manage, so let's run with it and link policy area C to the domain root. Unfortunately, this means that the GPO is going to apply to any computer objects in the domain, including Organizational Units that we store servers in, such as the domain controllers Organizational Unit that exists under the root of the domain. We don't want this, so the only way forward here is to block policy inheritance at these server Organizational Units. You may see where this is going now. I've not only blocked policy area C from being inherited by these Organizational Units that contain servers, I've also blocked any other policies that may need to apply as part of policy area A. My only solution to fix this is to use my ability to force an override of policy area A down the tree. So much for a simpler solution. We now have at least one block in place (for the domain controllers Organizational Unit) and policies from area A overriding all blocks down the tree to make sure they get past the blocks I just set up. While this is a solution, it's starting to feel more complex than the one before. Isn't there a better way?

Yes, by making use of security groups. Forget about the blocks and inheritance for now and consider that instead I put all the computers that are not to get policy area C in a security group. I can then deny the Apply Group Policy permission to this particular security group, so that no members of the group ever have that policy applied to them. This is a much easier solution. However, it does mean that the administrators must remember that if a new computer is created that is not to receive the policy, it must be added to the group.

Policy areas D and G can still apply as they did before. Policy area F applies only to certain Organizational Units, so I just link F to the various departments under the root and carry on as before. However, I have more problems with E. Again, the choices are similar to the previous predicament: I could apply E to the department Organizational Units individually (remembering to do this for each new department I create), I could apply the policy to the domain root and use block inheritance–force override as before, or I could use groups again. The use of groups seems simpler, so let's go with that option. If I create a group for all the staff machines, I can just give the group permission to apply group policy to policy E in addition to removing the default permission for authenticated users to apply group policy. Now all users won't run the policy, by default, but members of the staff machines group will.

This is a different solution that now achieves the same goal. The solution that Leicester chose (the first design) required fewer groups and allowed a computer's or user's location in the hierarchy to dictate which policies were applied. The new solution that we've just worked through collapses the tree structure but instead makes more use of groups to indicate which policies are to apply.

In fact, this tends to be a rule: as you collapse a structure where a number of GPOs apply, you need greater control via groups or the use of block inheritance and overrides.

A bridge too far

I could go one stage further and remove the lab machines' Organizational Unit entirely. That would give me the same problems with policy area D that I had with E. The simpler solution is to add all lab machines into a group and allow only members of that group to access the policy.

You can continue on in this manner, removing Organizational Units and creating more groups until you actually end up with all objects in a single Organizational Unit under the domain. At that point, all the GPOs are applied to that Organizational Unit and you control access to the Organizational Units via groups. Prioritization of the order that the multiple GPOs would apply might be more of a nightmare in this situation.

I hope you can see that there are a number of options open to you when designing your Organizational Unit structure for GPOs. It doesn't really matter which method you choose, as long as you're happy with it. The Organizational Unit structure that Leicester adopted requires less maintenance, because you don't have to put an object in a group after creation; you just create it in the place in the tree that it is to receive policies from. That's less of an issue with the capabilities of ADSI, since the code to bind to the parent group and add the newly created object to that group is two extra lines of code.

We also created some other Organizational Units for specific functions. For example, one Organizational Unit holds all the groups that we ever created. That way, when we want to find a group, we know where it is. We also created a test Organizational Unit so that we could roll out policies and do testing with users and computers within test in the domain without affecting the existing user setup that was already in place.

It may appear that Leicester doesn't make much use of groups to control access to GPOs, but that's not the case. Just because we set the Organizational Unit structure up in a way that made sense to us doesn't mean that we shouldn't make good use of groups as well. Let me give you some examples. Look back at Figure 9-12. Policy areas D and G actually consist of a number of completely different and opposing GPOs that can affect all lab machines (D) or machines in specific labs (G). One group of settings entirely locks down the workstations in those labs from access to the hard disk and various control panels and places other security measures. Another raft of settings serves to unlock the machines entirely; in other words, this GPO is the complete opposite of the first. Further sets of GPOs allow us to put the lab into a mixture of the two states with some areas locked down and others remaining unlocked. These policies are applied as required to the specific lab Organizational Units, so that if all were to apply at the same time, it would be a complete fiasco. Instead, we use global security groups, one for access to each GPO, and make the computers from that lab members of each group.

To gain access to the policies, we move the computers from one group into another. If a client needs to be unlocked entirely, we move it to the unlocked group and reboot or wait until the policy refreshes. Similarly, if a user from zoology decides that he wants his machine locked down, we can apply the relevant GPOs to the zoology Organizational Unit, then place that machine in the global group that allows access to the GPO.

If we had a situation in which the client was either locked down or not locked down, we could have just used one group and had a lockdown state by default, with membership in the group implying an unlocked state or vice versa.

Loopback mode

I've held one important aspect of Leicester's GPO design until now, that of loop-back mode. Leicester needs to use loopback mode in order to lock down both staff and students while they are in a lab environment. To do this successfully requires that the computer policies be separate from the user policies. When you add this requirement to the equation, it makes more sense to keep the lab part of the tree separate in some way from the other part of the tree. This will ensure that the user sections of the computer policies do not apply to any user accounts except during loopback mode. Both Figures 9-11 and 9-12 have structures that will happily accommodate the requirement.

Guidelines for Designing GPOs

In this section, I provide guidelines that help you toward two critical design goals:

- All policies should be applied quickly, so that users do not feel a significant impact by their processing.

- All policies should be as easy as possible to administer and maintain.

With these two concepts in mind, let's take a look at the guidelines:

Design in a way that you feel comfortable with
As shown in the example in the last section, it can be easier to do large designs by considering the user Organizational Unit and computer Organizational Unit structures separately. If you want to do them together and have a small enough network that you can easily do them together, that's fine. If not, try it the way we first did.

Restrict the number of policies that apply as best you can
In a perfect world, this wouldn't be important. But in the real world, the more policies you have, the more processing the client has to do in addition to its normal logon/boot up, the longer it will take to complete the process.

If you have multiple policies applying to an object from the same location in a tree, consider collapsing them into a single object, since this will process faster than multiple policies will. If the number of policies you are applying during a logon/boot up is larger than you can effectively get out to the client across the network or, more importantly, get the client to process, you need to consider reducing or collapsing the policies. If you need to apply a significantly large set of policies with many settings to log on that extends logon to five minutes, but feel that is acceptable to achieve this level of policy, that's fine.

When it comes down to it, only you know what you can accept, and you will need to do your own testing in this area to satisfy your constraints. If you have to have a client logged on in less than four seconds, you have to work within that constraint. I'm sure that Microsoft will release some guidelines on the matter after the launch of Windows 2000 as well. In the meantime, consider these points: Microsoft likes to recommend no more than 10 Organizational Units deep to make sure that you don't use too many GPOs. As we know, this isn't very helpful. Having one GPO applying at a site, one at the domain, and one at each of five Organizational Units means only seven GPOs. Having 10 applying at each level is 70. So it's not only how deep you nest your Organizational Unit structure that matters, it's how many policies you can apply. The unfortunate part, of course, is that it always comes back to how many settings you are applying in each policy.

The simple answer is that a faster machine with more RAM can apply more policies in less time than a slower PC with less RAM; consequently, for a network of heterogeneous clients, you will need to do testing on your own network to see how fast application of policies is and how much bandwidth that they take up. Sorry, but that's the way it is for now.

Use security groups to tailor access

While you can set up ACLs to allow or deny application of policy to an individual user or computer, it makes more sense to use groups to do this whenever you can. If you use groups, it lets you keep all policy access in one object and can make complex systems much more manageable.

Limit the use of block/force inheritance

You should be very cautious of blocking inheritance at locations in the tree unless you are quite sure that this is the right way to solve your problem. The repercussions from a simple blocking of inheritance can spiral quickly as you encounter areas of policy that need to override the block. Your well-designed system can become quite difficult to maintain if you block and override regularly. This is not to say that you should never use them, just exercise caution in their use.

Collapse the Organizational Unit design

If you wish, you can collapse your Organizational Unit design and make more use of groups (or even block inheritance/force override) to govern access to specific policies. These are both perfectly valid solutions, and you should use whichever you are more comfortable with. Remember the axiom that the more you collapse the Organizational Unit structure while maintaining or increasing the number of GPOs, the greater need for control via groups or block inheritance/force override.

Avoid using cross-domain GPO links

If you link GPOs across domains, the entire set of *sysvol* data as well as the object information itself needs to transfer over from the source domain whenever a user or computer needs to access it. So unless you have very fast links between the two domains with enough available bandwidth, you should duplicate the functionality of the GPO in the target domain instead of cross-domain linking.

Prioritize GPOs

Remember that it is possible to prioritize applications of multiple GPOs at the site, domain, or Organizational Unit level. This ordering of the application of policies allows you to add useful options to the administrator's toolkit. For example, if you need a group of users to reverse specific settings that are being applied by default as part of a larger set, create a new GPO with ACLs for this group that apply in the priority list to unset all the previous settings. This solution allows you to override a selection of previous settings without creating two GPOs, one with settings for everyone and one for just this group. The former allows you to add in settings to the main GPO and still have them apply to everyone, without needing to add them to the second GPO of the latter solution. Prioritizing GPOs can be very useful.

Increase processing speed

The main ways to increase processing speed are to reduce the number of GPOs that you apply, disable the computer or user portion of a GPO if it is not needed, or limit the use of block inheritance, force override, cross-domain linking, and loopback mode. All of these place an extra processing load on the client to some degree. A really bad mistake would be to use combinations of them.

Be cautious with Loopback mode

Loopback mode is a very useful tool but is another technology that you need to approach with caution. As a completely different set of policies (replace mode) or a very large number of policies (merge mode) will be applied to your users and since there are no Resultant Set of Policy (RSoP) tools in existence as I write this, you need to take great care to ensure that the policy received by a user is the one you expect.

In most cases, loopback merge mode will incur significant extra processing load on the client PC and extra bandwidth on the network. That's not to say it isn't useful, but you have to be very aware of the delays that could occur after its introduction. Loopback replace mode imposes less of a processing load, but it can still be a problem. If you are contemplating loopback mode, ensure adequate stress testing of user impact.

Limit how often GPOs are updated

This relates to two specific times. You should limit your modifications to GPOs that could immediately cause a policy refresh on all clients or users, as this could impose a slowdown across the network and on the client. It would be better to make the updates during scheduled systems maintenance times. You also should carefully control the policy refresh interval. You have to ask yourself if you really need to refresh policy every 10 minutes, whether every 24 hours might be sufficient? Make the refresh interval a sensible one.

Restrict blocking of domain GPOs

You should not block domain GPOs in order to specifically use LGPOs on a domain client without very good reasons. If you do choose to apply LGPOs only to a client, you need to be aware of the management overhead because each client needs to be managed individually. If you have 20 orphaned clients using LGPOs and you need to make a change, you need to make it 20 times, one per client. The whole concept behind GPOs was to aid centralized management and administration of distributed resources, not distributed management of distributed resources. Think carefully before going down this path.

Use test GPOs

I always recommend creating test GPOs and linking them to a branch of test Organizational Units set up for this purpose. No GPO should ever be applied to users or computers unless it has been fully tested.

Choose monolithic or segmented GPOs

While I would recommend keeping similar settings, or all settings relating to a particular item, in the same GPO, there is nothing stopping you from having only a few huge GPOs as opposed to a number of smaller GPOs. If you go for the monolithic approach, you process fewer GPOs, which is obviously faster; however, delegation is not as easy due to the fact that the policy contains so many settings. Segmented GPOs allows easier delegation but can impact performance. Mix and match the two to a level that you are comfortable with and that works for your network.

Designing Delegation and Change Control

Now that you've designed a policy-based implementation for your organization, you have to work out how you will maintain firm control over GPOs once you start deploying them. Specifically, you need to consider who will be managing your GPOs and how you will keep control over the wide-ranging changes they can make.

The importance of change control procedures

The best way to keep track of GPOs in your organization is through a series of change-control procedures. These will work well whether your GPO administrators are domain administrators or not. I suggest a file such as a Word document with tables, a spreadsheet, or even a database in a central location to hold data on each GPO, the settings that it applies, whether it applies to computers and users or both, the containers in Active Directory that it applies to, and so on. You also should add extra columns/fields to the data for the proposer of the original GPO and those people who ratified the change. If you add those fields/columns, every time a new change is made, it is added by the proposer to the existing data set. Then the proposer or the system automatically contacts the rest of the GPO administrators and asks them to review and ratify the change in the data set. Discussions could continue via email if there were problems preventing ratification or if items needed clarifying. Finally, when the GPO data is ratified by all, it can be regression-tested on test systems if that hasn't already been done and then implemented within Active Directory.

Default GPO Permissions

Any user, computer, or group needs both Read and Apply Group Policy in order to apply a policy. Active Directory ships with certain permissions already in existence for GPOs. These are:

- Authenticated Users group has Read and Apply Group Policy.

- Creator Owner has Full Control without an explicit Apply Group Policy.

- Local System group has Full Control without an explicit Apply Group Policy.

- Domain Admins group has Full Control without an explicit Apply Group Policy.

- Enterprise Admins group has Full Control without an explicit Apply Group Policy.

- Group Policy Admins group has Full Control without an explicit Apply Group Policy.

Administrators in the latter two groups are also authenticated users and so inherit the Read permission from that group. If you don't want administrators to have the user parts of GPOs applied on logon, set the Apply Group Policy setting to Deny for Domain Admins, Enterprise Admins, and possibly Creator Owner as well.

Designing the delegation of GPO administration

There are three types of permission that can be considered here:

- The permission to allow sets of users to link policies to a domain or an Organizational Unit branch

- The permission to allow sets of users to create GPOs

- The permission to allow sets of users to change the GPOs themselves

Link delegation can be easily accomplished using the Delegation of Control Wizard* that you get by right-clicking an object in Active Directory and choosing Delegate Control. Here you are actually delegating read and write access to the gPLink† attribute of the GPO itself.

The other GPO attribute that can be delegated in this way is called gPOptions. As discussed earlier and shown is Figure 9-9, this deals with the area of blocking inheritance. If you're interested in how these attributes work, set up a few GPOs in your Active Directory. Then use ADSIEDIT from the Windows 2000 Resource Kit to examine the attributes of the newly created GPOs in this location:

LDAP://CN=Policies,CN=System,dc=windows,dc=mycorp,dc=com

Creation of GPOs is limited to those indicated in the sidebar by default. However, you can add users to the Group Policy Admins security group, which allows members to create new GPOs. If a member of Group Policy Admins creates a GPO, that user is set as the Creator Owner‡ of the GPO and can continue to manage it. The Creator Owner of a GPO can manage the GPO, even if the user is removed from all groups that give GPO management privileges.

The Group Policy Admins group does not give full control to all GPOs in the domain, as the name implies.

Editing can be more problematic. Due to the underlying security restrictions in force, in order to open a GPO and look at it or modify it within the GPE, users must have write access to the GPO. Users also need to be able to write to the appropriate GPT directories as well, which non-administrators will not have the ability to do.

---

* This wizard is discussed more fully in Chapter 10.

† The GPC data part of a GPO is an object in Active Directory. This object, like all others, has attributes. One of the attributes of a GPO is a multivalued one called gPLink that stores Active Directory ADsPaths of the containers that the GPO is linked to.

‡ When administrators create GPOs, the Domain Admins group becomes the Creator Owner.

GPC data in Active Directory (i.e., the actual Active Directory object itself) will *never* inherit security permissions from parents up the tree. There is a special block in place that prevents this in Active Directory, so that all GPO ACLs have to be modified from within the Group Policy tools.

You can delegate edit access to new GPOs, as long as the people creating those GPOs are the ones that will be editing them, by placing those users into the Group Policy Admins group. If you also want to delegate edit access to more people or to GPOs that a user is not the Creator Owner of, then open up the properties of each GPO in turn and give the appropriate user or group of users Full Control to the policy. There is no simple way to give a set of users the ability to manipulate all GPOs in a domain very quickly; you have to go through the GPOs one at a time.

 A word of warning before I finish up here. Correctly applied, GPOs are fundamental to the well-being of your Windows 2000 system. Policies incorrectly applied to the root of the domain could lock down the Administrator account or disallow logons at domain controllers. This is obviously a worst-case scenario, and you'd have to be a significant fool to get to that state of affairs in the GPE and then choose Save. However, there are mistakes that are much more likely to occur: a mistyped registry value that forces users to an invalid proxy server and thus stops Internet Explorer from working, forgetting to clear a checkbox and thus applying a policy down an entire branch of the tree (the default) when it was only to apply to the root of the branch, and so on. These changes have the potential to affect all users or computers throughout the tree, so I would caution you to keep the administrators of GPOs to a very select subset. If you allow nonadministrators the ability to create, change, and delete GPOs, then they have to be able to take responsibility for and be accountable for their actions. Users who are already administrator-equivalent will automatically be able to administer GPOs and should already be held accountable.

Creating customized GPEs for administrators

The GPE comes with a series of permitted snap-ins that normal administrators will get by default. These snap-ins allow administrators to manage all parts of a GPO. However, it is possible to ship customized GPEs that focus on only one GPO and load only certain permitted snap-ins. This allows you to state that Group 1 can manage this part of a policy and Group 2 that part of the same policy. This is a very useful tool that I encourage you to use when delegating administration, but you must be aware that just giving a restricted tool to certain users will not stop them from being able to manipulate other aspects of a GPO if they open up their own GPE and point it at the same policy.

To solve this problem, cast your mind back to the section when I was discussing the Administrative Templates (User) section, specifically the Windows Components → Microsoft Management Console → Restricted → Permitted snap-ins → Group Policy section. The best solution is to use the Restricted → Permitted snap-ins → Group Policy section of a GPO in order to allow and deny users or groups access to certain extensions. This covers you completely, since your users or groups can now run up only their own GPE with the extensions that you have explicitly permitted them to use.

Debugging Group Policies

If at any point you need to debug group policies, there are two mechanisms: using a checked version of a DDL to produce a special log, or setting registry settings to generate verbose information to the normal event logs. The former has worked for Windows NT for some time and is adequately described for Windows NT System Policies in Microsoft Knowledge Base article Q154120, which can be found at: *http://support. microsoft.com/support/kb/articles/q154/1/20.asp*. The next two sections cover each of these methods, and either or both may be used to solve your problem. However, you should note that the former is probably the more difficult of the two solely because you need to contact Microsoft to get hold of the checked version of the DDL you need, whereas the latter is solely a registry change.

Logging to a File Using a Checked Version of userenv.dll

The first method involves replacing the *userenv.dll* file with a checked version in order to get all policy data logged to a file. Checked versions of files have the debug options enabled and run considerably slower due to the extensive logging and checking involved in the lines of code. To start the debug process, follow these steps:

1. To enable the log file, rename the file called *userenv.dll* file in the *%windir%\ system32* directory to *userenv.orig* or a unique name of your choice.

2. Copy the checked version of *userenv.dll* (which you can find on the Windows 2000 CD or obtain from Microsoft) to the *%windir%\system32* directory of the client computer that you want to debug. The checked version of the *userenv.dll* file must match the version/build of Windows 2000 that you are using.

3. Start *regedt32.exe* and create a new value called UserEnvDebugLevel as a REG_DWORD in the HKLM\Software\Microsoft\WindowsNT\CurrentVersion\ Winlogon key.

4. Assign UserEnvDebugLevel the value 10,002 in hexadecimal format.

5. Restart the computer. From now on, log information will be recorded on this machine in the text file *c:\winnt\debug\userenv.log.*

When you are finished debugging, replace the checked version of the DLL with the normal version, remove the registry key, and reboot the client.

Verbose Logging to the Event Log

Verbose logging in the event log can be turned on by simply setting a registry key. Once the key exists with the correct value, logging is done automatically. The value, a REG_DWORD, is called RunDiagnosticLoggingGroupPolicy and needs to be created with a value of 1 in the HKLM\Software\Microsoft\WindowsNT\CurrentVersion\Diagnostics key.

The value of 1 sets the logging to verbose mode; this is similar to what you get from the checked DLL in the previous section, although the checked version may yield slightly more information. Setting the value to 0 is the same as having the key absent and is known as *normal logging,* which is the default that Windows NT used to support. In other words, the key makes a difference only when set to a value of 1. It's really as simple as that.

 This key is actually one of four currently supported keys that you can use at this location. You also can create RunDiagnosticLogging-Intellimirror, RunDiagnosticLoggingAppDeploy, and RunDiagnostic-LoggingGlobal. The last turns Application Deployment, Intellimirror, and Group Policy logging on without needing to set all three individually.

Summary

While GPOs are more advanced than Windows NT System Policies, Microsoft is not standing still in their development. There are a number of areas in which GPOs are deficient and Microsoft is working on enhancements and fixes for the future. For example:

•   Microsoft is currently working on a mechanism to expose all GPO data using a standard Schema. This will allow automation and manipulation of the data in an easier way. This Schema will interface with the Windows Management Instrumentation (WMI)[*] initiative.

---

[*] WMI is an implementation of the Desktop Management Task Force's (DMTF) Web-based Enterprise Management (WBEM) initiative, which provides standards for accessing and sharing management information in an enterprise environment.

- Various independent software vendors and Microsoft are aiming to ship tools that will enable you to see the Resultant Set of Policy on a client. Microsoft's tool will be very basic and will show such information as the policies applied to a user or computer and what policies would apply if a user logged in at that computer. The tools provided by the vendors are likely to be significantly richer.

- Cutting and pasting GPOs within and between domains is currently not possible.

Microsoft recognizes how new and difficult these GPOs may seem and is producing copious documentation to help administrators in understanding and deployment. Their current raft of documentation is already proving useful enough that I feel that I don't have to duplicate it here and can simply reference it instead.

10

Active Directory Security: Permissions and Auditing

Permissions can be set for Active Directory in the same way that they can for files. While you may not care that everyone in the tree can read all your user's phone numbers, you may want to store more sensitive information and restrict that access. Reading is not the only problem, of course. You also have create, modify, and delete privileges to worry about, and the last thing you need is a disgruntled or clever employee finding a way to delete all your users in an Organizational Unit. And inheritance increases the complexity in the normal way.

None of this should be new to system managers, who already deal with Windows NT Access Control Lists and Access Masks, IntraNetWare's Trustee Lists and Inherited Rights Masks, and Unix's access permissions in file masks. In fact, Microsoft has carried the NT terminology from file permissions forward to Active Directory in Windows 2000, so if you already know these terms, you're well ahead. If you are not familiar with them, don't worry. Microsoft has a great tradition of calling a shovel a ground-insertion–earth-management device. Terminology in permissions can seem confusing at first, so I'll go through it all in detail.

Managing the permissions in Active Directory doesn't have to be a headache. You can design sensible permissions schemes using guidelines on inheritance and complexity that will allow you to have a much easier time as a systems administrator. The GUI that Microsoft provides is fairly good for simple tasks but more cumbersome for complex multiple permissions. By design, however, Active Directory permissions are supported by ADSI which opens up a whole raft of opportunities for you to use scripts to track problems and manipulate access simply and effectively.

Yet permissions are only half the story. If you allow a user to modify details of every user in a specific branch below a certain Organizational Unit, you can monitor the creations, deletions, and changes to objects and properties within that branch using auditing entries. In fact, you can monitor any aspect of modification to Active Directory using auditing. The system keeps track of logging the auditing events and you can then periodically check them or use a script or third-party tool to alert you quickly to any problems.

Figure 10-1 shows you the basics. Each object stores a binary value called a Security Descriptor, or SD, that holds all the information describing the security for that object. Included with the information are two important collections that hold the relevant permissions called Access Control Lists, or ACLs. The first ACL, called the System-Audit ACL or SACL, defines the permission events that will trigger both success and failure audit messages. The second, called the Discretionary ACL or DACL, defines the permissions that users have to the object, its properties, and its children. Each of the two ACLs holds a collection of Access Control Entries, or ACEs, that correspond to individual audit or permission entries.

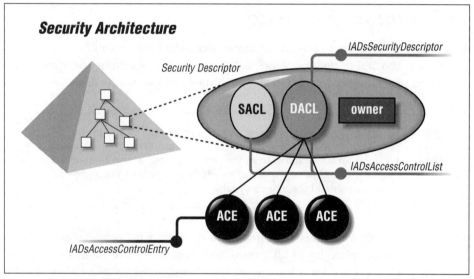

Figure 10-1. Active Directory Security Architecture

ACEs can apply to the object as a whole or to the individual properties of the object. This allows an administrator to control not just which users can see an object, but what properties those users can see. An object is never revealed to those users who do not have the permission to see the object. For example, all users might be granted read access to the telephone number and email properties for all other users, but Security Descriptors of users might be denied to all but members of a specially created security administrators group. Individual users might be granted write access to personal properties such as the telephone numbers and mailing addresses on their own user objects. The possibilities are limited only by the objects and their corresponding properties in the tree. As Active Directory Schema is extensible, organization-specific permissions can be allowed and denied for all the objects and properties your organization creates.

Deny permissions always override allow permissions.

Auditing takes place when the system logs an event in the security event log on a particular DC to indicate that an Active Directory event has taken place. You can monitor the creation, modification, or deletion of any object in Active Directory. This can, of course, be useful for maintaining records of security problems, as well as in dealing with unusual behavior by the system.

Using Windows 2000's GUI to Examine Permissions

To access the default permissions for any object, select Active Directory Users and Computers MMC and right-click on it. Choose Properties from the drop-down menu and select the Security tab of the properties window that is displayed.

To make the Security tab visible, you need to right-click in the display pane of Active Directory Users and Computers MMC, choosing View Advanced Features from the pop-up menu. If you re-open the properties window of the object to which you wish to assign permissions, you should see a Security tab.

The window in Figure 10-2 is your first point of contact for permissions. The top area contains a complete list of all groups and users who have permissions to the object whose properties I am looking at. The Permissions section below this list displays which general permissions are allowed and denied for the highlighted user or group. The general permissions listed are only those deemed to be the most likely to be set on a regular basis. Each general permission is only an umbrella term representing a complex set of actual implemented permissions hidden underneath the item. Consequently, the general permission called Read translates to specific permissions like Read All Properties and List Contents, as I will show later. Below the Permissions section are three important parts of this window:

Advanced button

> The Advanced button allows you to delve further into the object, so that permissions can be set using a more fine-grained approach.

Text display area

The second part of this area of the window is used to display a message, such as that shown in Figure 10-2. The text shows that the permissions for the current object are more complex than can be displayed here. Consequently, I would have to press the Advanced button to see them.

Inheritance checkbox

The "Allow inheritable permissions from parent to propagate to this object" checkbox allows you to *orphan* (my term) this object from the tree. When you clear the checkbox on the security properties or Access Control Settings windows mentioned later, the system pops up a Yes/No/Cancel dialog box that asks if you want to convert your inherited entries to normal entries. If you click Cancel, the operation aborts. Clicking No removes all inherited entries and orphans the object or branch. Clicking Yes converts the inherited entries to standard entries, as if you had manually applied the old inherited permissions to this object manually. All normal permission entries for the object are unchanged by whatever choice you make. I will cover this in more detail later in the book.

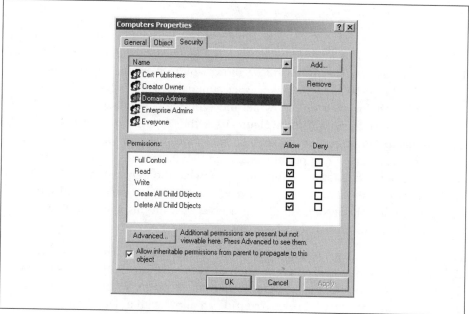

Figure 10-2. Security properties of an object

Clicking the Advanced button actually displays the same users and groups again, but in slightly more detail. Figure 10-3 shows this window, known as the Access Control Settings (ACSs) for the object.

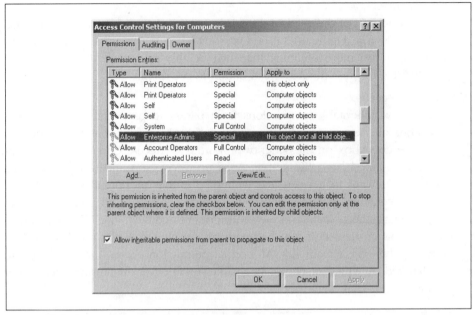

Figure 10-3. Access Control Settings for an object

While the ACS window gives only slightly more information than the previous window, it serves an important purpose; it is a gateway to the lowest, most atomic level of permissions. The ACS window allows you to view the globally set permissions from Figure 10-2, as well as a brief summary of the advanced permissions that may be set for each object. While the Name and Permission columns effectively duplicate information from Figure 10-2, the Type field shows whether the permissions to the object for this user or group are Allow or Deny. If a group has some allow and some deny permissions, then two entries are recorded in this window. The Apply To column usefully indicates what the permission applies to. This could be to *this object only, the object and all sub-objects,* or just to an individual property, say telephoneNumber, of a user object. Again this window allows you to indicate whether to orphan the object, just as Figure 10-2 does.

Permission entries that are inherited have soft-focus icons. This makes it instant and easy to spot inheritance. If you open up a Permissions Entry (PE) window for the object, the checkboxes have grayed-out check marks so that you cannot edit the permission. You can, however, override an allow with a deny from here.

You now have two choices to view the atomic permissions. You can click Add, which pops up a window allowing you to add a new user or group to those with permissions set on this object. Alternatively, you can highlight an existing user or group and click the View/Edit button. If you highlight a user or group or add one from the pop-up window, the next screens you see are the PE windows, shown in Figures 10-4 and 10-5.

Until you know exactly what you are doing with permissions, I suggest that you create a few test users and groups in order to play with permissions settings. The last thing you want to do is make a simple mistake with a built-in group or user and deny yourself access to the tree. If you create two test users and three test groups, put each user in a separate group, and then put both users in the third group, you will have the basis of a test system.

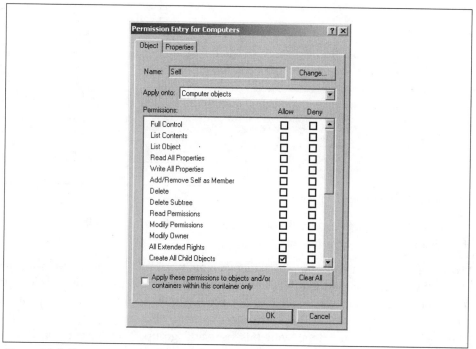

Figure 10-4. Permission Entry for an object

The PE windows are two sides of the same coin, one representing permissions to the object and the other representing permissions to the properties of that object. This is the lowest, most atomic level you can get to when setting permissions. Here is where you can really tailor a system to do exactly what you want.

The object name is displayed in the title of the PE window, with the name of the user or group which has permissions prominently displayed in the field at the top. The user or group then has permissions allowed and denied from the column entries. The entries in the window are relative and vary depending on the entry in the drop-down list under the heading of Apply Onto. What is not immediately obvious from this window is how large the drop-down box can actually get.

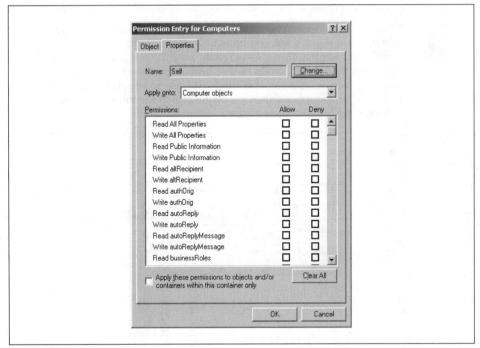

Figure 10-5. Permission Entry for an object's properties

Figure 10-6 shows this nicely. If you look at the scroll bar, you will get an idea of how many items are currently not displayed.

To set a permission from the PE window, you would pick where you want to apply the permission and then click the relevant Allow and Deny boxes, selecting OK when done. Since Microsoft has not provided an Apply button, you cannot specify a set of permissions applied onto one area, click Apply, and then repeat the cycle until you are done with this user and group. You have to click OK, which means the window closes, whereupon you then have to click Add again, and so on. This is a tiresome problem if you are implementing multiple changes from a set of preprepared designs, but one you have to live with.

Permissions Created by a Default Installation

It is interesting to see which permissions the system applies by default to a new DC server on installation. These permissions are obtained by looking at the PE windows for the properties of the domain as a whole, shown in Table 10-1. All permissions apply to the domain as a whole, i.e., this object only in the Apply Onto field.

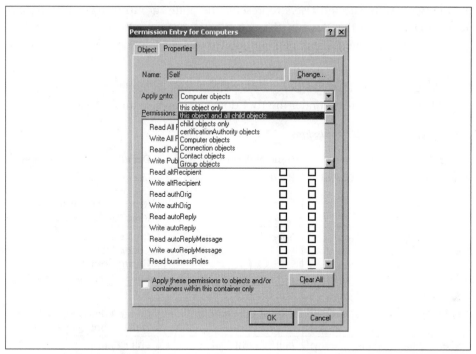

Figure 10-6. Permission Entry window showing the large number of targets to which permissions can be applied

Table 10-1. Default Domain Permissions

User or Group Name	Default Object Permissions	Default Attribute Permissions
Authenticated Users (global group)	List contents Read permissions Read All Properties	Read All Properties
Everyone	Read All Properties	Read All Properties
Administrators (local group)	List contents Read All Properties Write all Properties Add/Remove self as member Read permissions Modify permissions Modify owner Create and Delete for all objects	Read All Properties Write All Properties
System (the operating system)	List contents Read All Properties Write all Properties Add/Remove self as member Delete Read permissions Modify permissions Modify owner Create and Delete for all objects	Read All Properties Write All Properties

By the way, Authenticated Users represents the entire group of users that are currently logged onto the domain through a user account. Everyone contains the group of Authenticated Users plus all anonymous connections and logons to the domain.

Now let's take a look at the default PE permissions created for a new Organizational Unit which I create under the root domain shown in Table 10-2.

Table 10-2. Default OU Permissions

User or Group Name	General Permission Name	Default Object Permissions
Authenticated Users (Global Group)	Read	List contents List object Read permissions Read All Properties
Account Operators (Local group)	Special Permissions	Create Groups Create Users Create Computers Full Control (computers)
Administrators (Local group)	Full Control	Full Control
Print Operators (Local Group)	Special Permissions	Create Print-Queue Objects Delete Print-Queue Objects
System (the operating system)	Full Control	Full Control

The second column relates to the general permission groups shown previously in Figure 10-3. Here I can see what Read permission actually represents within Active Directory. Print Operators has been given control of printers in the domain, and Account Operators has been given account rights. Neither of these permissions has a general permission name that applies to it, so they are referred to as *Special Permissions.*

Using the Delegation of Control Wizard

To help with delegating permissions for objects in Active Directory, Windows 2000 comes with a wizard called the Delegation of Control wizard. It is intended to allow administrators to delegate management of certain types of objects to key individuals or groups in the organization. It is activated by right-clicking almost any container in the DIT and selecting the wizard from the pop-up menu. Builtin and LostAndFound are the two containers for which it does not work by default.

The wizard is useful only when you need to clearly apply general allow permissions to one or more object types below a container. It is not useful if you want to specify deny permissions (which it doesn't support), remove previously delegated control, delegate control over individual objects, or apply special permissions to branches of the tree. The wizard's great strength is its ability to set permissions and apply them to multiple users and groups at the same time. I use the wizard to set these sorts of permissions, although much less regularly than I do the standard GUI, since it is much more limited in what it can do. Scripting with ADSI also provides a solution here which is more adaptive to an administrator's own needs.

The wizard provides six screens for you to navigate through. The first is the welcome screen, which tells you what the wizard does. The second specifies the LDAP path to the container you want to delegate control for. This screen also has a Browse button, allowing you to scan through Active Directory to find the location of the object you are looking to delegate control from. The third screen allows you to specify the users or groups to whom you are going to delegate the control. The fourth screen asks what task you wish to delegate control for in that container. Figure 10-7 shows this window.

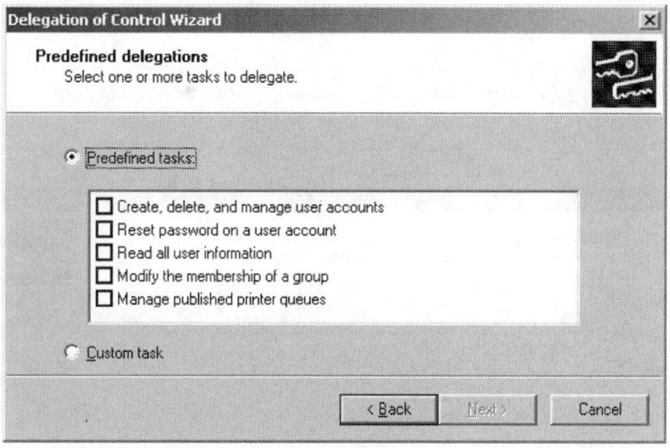

Figure 10-7. Delegation of Control wizard—object type selection

The default is to delegate control for a specific task, but if you choose the Custom radio button and click Next, then an extra page opens, allowing you to specify individual objects. Figure 10-8 shows this.

If you want to delegate certain permissions to computer or user objects in a specific container or branch, you can do it from here. The next screen of the wizard allows you to specify what permissions you wish to assign for the selected users/groups. Figure 10-9 shows this screen.

When the window opens initially, only the first checkbox is checked. As you click each of the other boxes, the list of specific permissions that you can delegate becomes very large as it encompasses all of the permissions that you could potentially delegate. Finally, the sixth screen of the wizard summarizes the previous answers and allows the user to go back, cancel, or finish and grant the permissions.

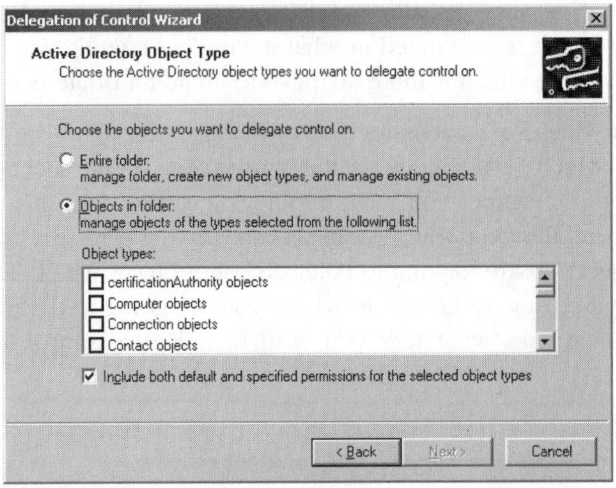

Figure 10-8. Delegation of Control wizard—choosing objects to delegate

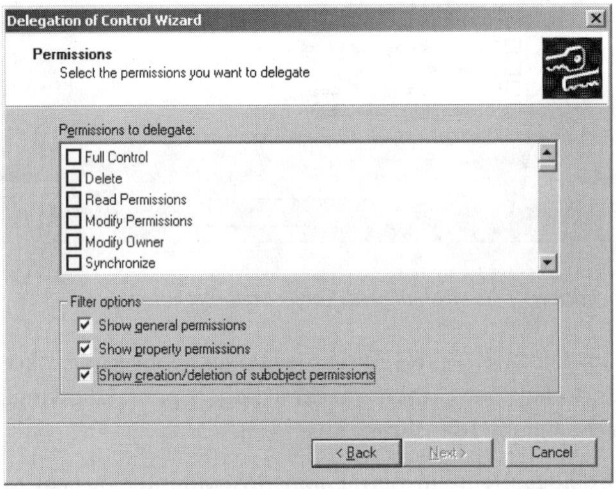

Figure 10-9. Delegation of Control wizard—access rights selection

However, just as the permissions listed in the security properties for an object (Figure 10-2) can change, so can the permissions listed in the access rights box, depending on the object(s) to which permissions are being applied. A good demonstration of this is to open up the security permissions for any user and scroll through the displayed list of permissions. Next open up the wizard on any container and specify Custom Task (see the screen shown in Figure 10-7) and only user objects (see Figure 10-8). The screen shown in Figure 10-10 should then display the same list that the screen in Figure 10-2 does. This makes sense since they should be the same; available permissions for one user should be the same as the available permissions for all users. It is still nice to see the correlation and appreciate it in the flesh so to speak.

Using Windows 2000's GUI to Examine Auditing

Examining auditing entries is almost identical to viewing permissions entries. If you go back to the screen shown in Figure 10-3 and click on the Auditing tab, an ACS screen similar to that in Figure 10-10 is displayed.

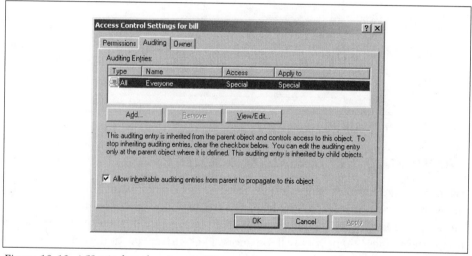

Figure 10-10. ACS window showing auditing entries

This ACS window shows the list of Auditing Entries (AEs) that have been defined on the object. This object has one AE, and it's not very helpful viewing it from here since the detail is too limited. So just as you would do with permissions, you can click the View/Edit button and drill down and view the individual AE itself.

Figure 10-11 shows the successful and failed items that are being awaited. The items are grayed out because this entry is inherited from further up the tree; i.e., it is not defined directly on this object but rather further up the hierarchy.

Figure 10-12 shows an example AE window for successful and failed auditing of properties. Here you are auditing only property writes.

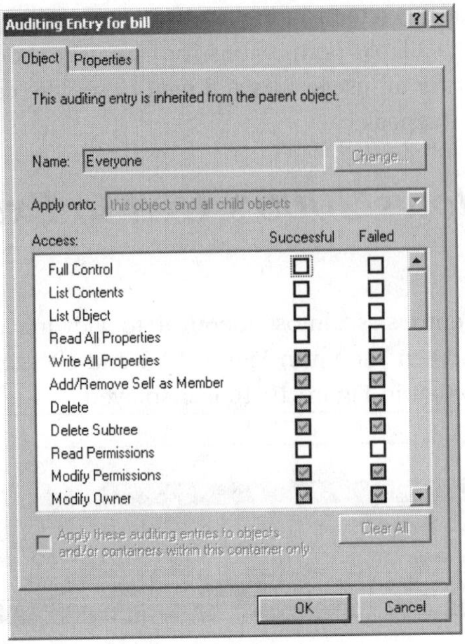

Figure 10-11. Auditing entry for an object

Designing Permission Schemes

Having worked through many designs for different domain structures, I have come up with a series of rules or guidelines you can follow in order to structure the design process effectively. The idea is that if you design your permissions schemes using these rules, then you will be more likely to create a design with global scope and minimum effort.

The Five Golden Rules of Common Sense Permissions Design

This list is not exhaustive. As soon as I finished drafting it, I realized that there was one rule I had missed. I am sure you will be able to think of others beyond these. If, however, these rules spark your creative juices and help you design more effectively, they will have done their job.

The rules are:

1. Assign object permissions to groups of users rather than individual users whenever possible.

2. Design group permissions so that you have a minimum of duplication.

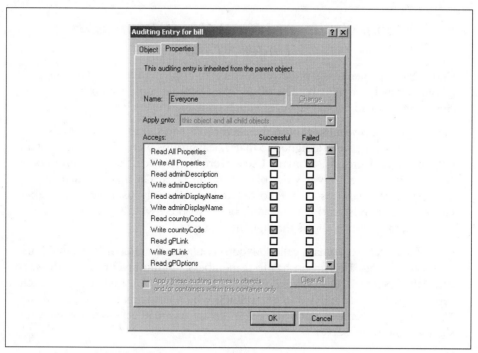

Figure 10-12. Auditing entry for an object's properties

3. Manage permissions globally from the ACL window.

4. Allow inheritance: do not orphan sections of the tree.

5. Keep a log of every unusual change that you have made to the tree, especially when you have orphaned sections of it or applied special rights to certain users.

Let's look at these rules in more detail.

Rule 1—Apply permissions to groups whenever possible

By default, you should use groups to manage your user permissions. At its simplest, this makes sense whenever you have more than one user for whom you wish to set certain permissions.

Some things need to be made very clear about how groups are different between Windows NT and Windows 2000:

Global Group and Local Group Permissions Under NT 4.0

Under NT 4.0, Microsoft's preferred method of applying file and directory permissions was to create two sets of groups: Local Groups, which had permissions and Domain Global Groups, which contained users.

The Local Group would exist on the server that had the resource, and the relevant permissions were assigned to that. Local groups were allowed to contain both users and groups. Domain Users were then placed in Domain Global Groups, which themselves were placed in the Local Groups on each server. Domain Global Groups were allowed to contain only users and not other groups. This may sound complicated, but it worked well in practice. A good way of demonstrating this is through an example.

Consider an NT 4.0 domain called Mycorp containing a Global Domain Group called Marketing. This group has four members. Within Mycorp are two servers, called Server1 and Server2, which each have published a share. Each server also has a Local Group SH_USERS, which contains the Global Group Marketing as a member. Each SH_USERS group has read access to the relevant share on the same server.

You use global groups in this scenario because it is faster to deal with a large number of users as one group than it is to deal with them individually. In a similar vein, it makes sense to keep control over permissions to resources by creating Local Groups, each with a relevant set of permissions. That way, if you ever need to modify the permissions for a particular set of users, you need to modify only the Local Group's permissions.

So if I decide that Keith and Sue should have full permissions to the share on Server1, I could create a Local Group on Server1 with full permissions and add a newly created Global Group, say MKTG_ADMIN, to it with Keith and Sue as members. Future users who need full permissions are added to this Global Group.

- Windows 2000 supports the concept of two types of group: security and distribution. A distribution group is one that contains users for mailing purposes and cannot have security rights assigned to it. Consequently, I am only dealing with security groups here.

- Mixed-mode Windows 2000 domains natively support Security groups that have two types of scope: Global or Local. These correspond to the Windows NT 4.0 Domain Global and Local groups.

- Native-mode Windows 2000 domains have access to a third scope, universal. Universal groups contain other groups and have permissions assigned to them.

More detailed information on the differences between Windows NT groups and Windows 2000 groups and how Windows 2000 groups differ in mixed mode and native mode can be found in Chapter 2, *Active Directory Overview*.

Under mixed mode, the paths you can choose are clear. You either follow the method outlined in the sidebar, or you choose to assign permissions in some other manner of your own choosing.

When you convert your domain to native mode, you have a more difficult decision: do you choose "Domain users go into universal groups, universal groups go into universal groups, universal groups are assigned resources;" or move to "Domain users go into universal groups, universal groups are assigned resources;" or do you assign permissions in a manner of your own choosing?

I'm not advocating whether you should use one group or two, as I'll explain in more detail in the next section on how to plan permissions. I am advocating that whichever way you choose to implement group permissions, you should add users to groups and apply permissions to groups, even if the group initially contains only one user. This removes organizational dependence on one particular account. Time after time I have seen organizations in which individual users with a whole raft of permissions to various objects suddenly leave or change roles. The new administrator then has to go in and unravel differing permissions settings from this account. I have even seen one administrator, who looked in anguish at the tangled mess of a recently departed administrator's account, delete his own account and rename the departed user's account just so that he could get the correct permission set without having to figure out the mess! If the old administrator had been a member of, say, five different groups, each with the relevant permissions, then the new administrator could simply have replaced the group memberships of the old account with his new account. This is a much simpler approach, and I am sure that none of the preceding common sense is very new to systems administrators.

Rule 2—Design group permissions so that you have minimum duplication

It makes much more sense to create groups with simple permission sets than it does to create multiple groups with overlapping permissions. If you decide that some of your users need, say, create and modify, while others need modify and delete, and a third set needs just modify, it makes much more sense to create three separate groups with create, delete, and modify, than it does to make three groups with the permissions sets described. Let's consider an example. I will call the three groups CRE_MOD, MOD_DEL, and MOD. Let's now say I add 10 users to each group. If the only modifications to ever happen to these groups are occasional membership changes, then this solution fits adequately. However, let's say that as with every large organization, the permissions requirements change over time. If Dave Peace, a member of CRE_MOD, now needs delete, what do I do? Do I make a special case of Dave's account and add the delete permission to his account only? Arguably, that is the simple solution, but according to Rule 1, I really should create a group to manage the permission. Do I create a DEL group and add Dave's account or create a CRE_MOD_DEL group and move his membership from CRE_MOD to the new group? Both are valid solutions.

Let's say I go with the former and create a DEL group, adding Dave as a member of that group. Things change again, and Mark Newell joins. Mark needs to be a member of groups giving him both MOD and DEL, so do I add him to MOD_DEL or MOD and DEL? Either way, I now have potential confusion. Whenever I have to check for members who can modify and delete I have to check three groups, not one.

If I'd taken the second approach and chosen to create CRE_MOD_DEL rather than the DEL group, then when Mark joins, he is added to MOD_DEL, and things seem to be working fine. Paul Burke now moves from another team and requires create only, so a CRE group is created and his account added to that. Later, three others join the CRE group, but Paul now needs create and delete, so CRE_DEL is created, and he is moved to this group. Now I have six groups: CRE, MOD, CRE_DEL, CRE_MOD, MOD_DEL, and CRE_MOD_DEL. Unfortunately, if I ever have to check who has create and modify permission, I have to check the three groups: CRE, MOD, and CRE_MOD.

This example has been heavily contrived. However, I hope it serves to show that duplication will occur whenever you have users requiring separate permissions to an object or property as well as combinations of those permissions. It is for this very reason that I suggest creating separate groups for the lowest-common-denominator permissions that you need to set.

For example, if you have users who always need read, list, and create but require different combinations of delete and modify, then it makes no sense to have three groups—one each for read, list, and create. You would instead create one group with the read, list, and create permissions assigned to it; one group for delete and one for modify. Then you would use multiple group memberships to assemble the group permissions as you require them.

The most important point to note is that I am talking about minimizing and simplifying the number of groups. If you only need CRE_MOD_DEL to an object, you do not create three groups; you create one.

If after you have created a group with multiple permissions you find that you now need groups with individual permissions, create the smaller groups and migrate the users. Then you can remove the larger group. This simplifies your workload, meaning not only do you manage fewer groups, but you also are revising and extending your permissions design to cope with changes. In fact, following this rule does allow you to create a permissions scheme you can be confident will be fully flexible and will enable you to cope with any changes in the future.

Rule 3—Manage Advanced permissions only when absolutely necessary*

Whenever you right-click an object to view its properties, the Security Properties window that appears has an Advanced button on it. This was shown in Figure 10-2 in the previous section. The Security Properties window itself has the following allow and deny options typically as General Permissions:

- Full control
- Read
- Write
- Create all child objects
- Delete all child objects

The screen also allows you to specify whether the object inherits permissions from its parent. In other words, it allows you to orphan the object from its parents.

The general permissions are not limited to those five in the previous list and indeed change depending on the object you are looking at. For example, the security properties for any user object display additional general permissions, including items such as Reset Password, Modify Web Information, and Send As. While these general permissions make sense for the user object, they are not all appropriate for other objects. This rule suggests that you manage permissions for objects from the Security Properties window as often as you can. You should choose the Advanced button only when you wish to allow or deny a permission to one aspect of an object rather than the whole object. An example would be manipulating the permission to a user object's telephone number rather than the whole account details.

While there is nothing wrong with managing atomic permissions to objects and properties, permissions are much easier to manage from a higher level. The main permissions administrators might want to set were put here for this express purpose so that users and groups could easily manage the tree, without having to worry about the large amount of individual properties if they did not need to.

---

* Please note that this says Permissions and not Auditing. Auditing entries can be accessed only from the Advanced tab, so this rule makes less sense for auditing entries.

Rule 4—Allow inheritance; do not orphan branches of the domain tree unless you have to

If you allow or deny permission for a group or user to all objects of a certain type in a container, then by default the permissions are applied recursively to all objects of that type in all the child containers down the tree. It is possible to block inheritance, but I recommend leaving inheritance in place (the default) and only orphaning other branches on an individual basis when there are good justifications for doing so. The reason is simple. If you specify that children do not inherit certain permissions from their parents, then you are setting your Active Directory up to be more complex to manage. Here is a very contrived example of when it could be appropriate to orphan a branch. Let's say you have a domain tree called *mycorp.com* that has a policy that all members of Mycorp should be able to print to all printers in the organization. Consequently, everyone has print rights to every printer down the tree by default. Now *mycorp.com* has, among others, two Organizational Units off of the root called Finance and Sales. The Finance Organizational Unit has two printers that the Finance people specifically do not want Sales staff using. Consequently, having obtained a special dispensation from management to override the policy, they specify that a domain group containing all sales staff, called SALES_GRP and contained in the Sales Organizational Unit, has no access to view or list the printers in the Finance Organizational Unit and all children. This is effectively using a PE window on the Finance Organizational Unit and setting a Deny on Full Control to apply this to Print-Queue Objects only.

Now the Finance Organizational Unit has three child Organizational Units called Loans, Borrowing, and Markets. The Sales team regularly use a legacy application which has to print results to a printer in the Borrowing Organizational Unit. Unfortunately, as SALES_GRP has no access to printers in the Borrowing Organizational Unit because of the permissions restriction, they are initially out of luck. Here are three of the many solutions to the problem:

- Create a second printer to the same device which resides in Sales and allow SALES_GRP to print to that.

- Remove the SALES_GRP restriction from the Finance Organizational Unit and its children down the tree; that brings you back to the starting point where you allow everyone to print to every printer. Now manually apply the same restrictions for SALES_GRP to the Finance, Loans, and Markets Organizational Units, but do not apply them down the tree. Of course this means that everyone in Sales can print to all printers in Borrowing, but I could further restrict this by applying restrictions on all printers to which Sales should have no access.

- Orphan the Borrowing Organizational Unit so that it does not inherit the printer permissions for SALES_GRP from its parent. This should allow print permission for the SALES_GRP to the printers in the Borrowing Organizational Unit.

Both the second and third items should allow print permission for the SALES_GRP to the printers in the Borrowing Organizational Unit. At first glance, the second and third items may appear to be identical. However, if the number of Organizational Units under Finance were 20 or 30, I would much rather choose the third method than the second. I have got better things to do than to manually assign 20 or 30 sets of permissions.

There are two other important differences between the second and the third items. First, if I add a new Organizational Unit called Payments under Finance, then in the third example Payments automatically inherits the permissions from Finance as they are applied down the tree on creation. Consequently, all the printers in Payments are restricted from SALES_GRP as per the dispensation. In the second example, the permissions are not applied down the tree and the administrator has to remember to apply restrictions to SALES_GRP for Payments if the dispensation is to be consistently applied.

The second point is that the Borrowing Organizational Unit in the third example loses *all* inherited permissions that would be applied by inheritance from its parent. This is significant if Borrowing had multiple inherited entries, and every other inherited entry should stay put. When you orphan the Organizational Unit, you could specify that the inherited permissions for the Organizational Unit be converted to normal permission entries specific to this Organizational Unit. This saves you the trouble of manually applying inherited permission entries now. However, these manual changes will have to be remembered for the day when the permissions are changed on the parent, so that the administrator can come back and manually change them on Borrowing.

Ultimately, the preceding example shows that there is nothing wrong with orphaning sections of the tree or choosing not to apply permissions down the branch of a tree. It is just important to remember that every time you do it you are creating slightly more work for yourself. As an administrator of a tree, you should keep track of these changes in a log, so that you can easily reference your special cases when required.

Rule 5—Keep a log of unusual changes

This may sound like an obvious statement, but it is surprising how many administrators overlook such a simple requirement. Simply put, it is always wise to keep a log of custom changes that you make to a default installation so that you and others have something to refer back to. There will be times when you may not be available and this sort of information is required. The following list shows the relevant fields of a basic Active Directory ACL log:

- Unique Name of Object or LDAP Location of Object in Tree

- Object Class Being Modified

- Object or Property Being Modified

- User or Group to Whom Permissions Are Being Assigned

- Permissions Being Assigned

- Notes on Reasons Why This Change Is Being Made

Let's now look at how you can put these rules into practice in your own designs.

How to Plan Permissions

There are a number of Active Directory Users and Computers structures administrators that may need to implement in their organizations. Some examples could be:

- A set of centralized teams, each with responsibility for certain areas. Users can be members of more than one area: account modifiers, printer managers, computer account managers, publishing managers, and so on.

- A manager for each individual major Organizational Unit under a domain.

- Again, a manager for each individual major Organizational Unit under a domain, but this time each manager is also able to delegate responsibility for lower Organizational Units.

- An administrator of the top-level domain is to be given permission to every subdomain by each subdomain's administrators.

While I could go through each of the preceding settings and show how to design permissions in each case, every organization is different. For that reason, it seems better to try and show what I consider to be the best way to design Active Directory permissions for all types of organizations.

First, create two documents, one called Allow and the other called Deny. On each document, label two sections, one called Global Tree Permissions and the other Specific Tree Permissions. Place two subheadings under each of the two sections, calling one General Permissions and the other Special Permissions. You should end up with three columns for each general and special heading: LDAP path, What To Set, and To whom.

The first six columns relate to permissions that will apply throughout the whole tree; the last six relate to permissions that will apply to specific locations in the tree. The latter is likely to be much the larger of the two. The General columns relate to permissions that can be set without recourse to the use of the Advanced button, such as read access to all objects below an Organizational Unit. The

Special columns relate to those permissions that you have to manually bring up a PE window for, such as allowing read access to all telephone numbers of user objects below a particular Organizational Unit. The last three columns relate to the LDAP path to the object that is to have properties set, the permissions that are being set, and the group or user to whom the permissions are being assigned.

The LDAP path under Global Tree Permissions is, strictly speaking, unnecessary, since these columns relate to permissions applied to the domain as a whole. If, however, you have a special need to apply permissions to a large number of Organizational Units directly below the root, then you could use this column for this purpose.

Now you should go through your Active Directory design and begin to populate both the Allow and Deny tables. For a first pass you should concentrate on a thorough design listing all the permissions that you think you will need. Print out a number of copies of the table. Once you have a list in front of you, you can start amalgamating identical permissions into groups. It is likely that you will need to go through many iterations of these designs until you get a pared-down list that you are happy with. As you go through the design, you will start identifying groups of users to which you need to apply permissions. When designing the groups, you have two choices as previously discussed under Rule 2. You can either create a single group to which permissions are set and which contains users, or you can create two groups, one to hold permissions and one to hold users.

The decision on whether to go for single or dual groups is not necessarily an easy one. My preference is to use single groups as often as possible, unless I need extra flexibility or have a lot of permissions to assign to many groups. I do use both in my network, and do not feel that there is a definite need for advocating using only one type. In order to help you to make a bit more sense of the decision, a few reasons why you would want to consider one or the other are shown in Table 10-3.

Table 10-3. When to Consider User Groups and Permission Groups or Combined Groups

You Should Consider One Group if	You Should Consider Two Groups if
You want to keep the number of groups to a minimum.	You want greater flexibility. Having one group for permissions and one for users, means that you are always able to manage the system with a minimum of fuss.
You have only a small or simple tree, where it would be fairly easy to track down problems.	You have a large or complex tree, where you need to be able to identify any problems quickly in the complexity that is your tree.
You need only to assign a few simple permissions.	You need to assign a large number of permissions.

Table 10-3. When to Consider User Groups and Permission Groups or Combined Groups (continued)

You Should Consider One Group if	You Should Consider Two Groups if
You have very little change in the membership of groups and very few changes to permissions.	You have regular changes in your group membership or regular changes to permissions.
You have little cross-membership of groups.	You have major cross-membership of groups, where a user could exist in more than one group with conflicting permissions. (Two groups makes it easier to debug problems in a large environment.)
You very rarely need new groups.	You regularly need new groups with subsets of your existing users who have been assigned to some task.
You very rarely have to split user groups up so that each user group subset has different permissions than the original group had.	You regularly have to split an existing group into more than one group, because each requires a differing set of permissions than the old group used to have.

One last point: if you are creating permission groups and user groups, remember to name them sensibly from the outset using something like pg_Finance and ug_Finance, for example. It makes it easier when managing and scripting if you can easily identify which type of groups are which.

Bringing Order Out of Chaos

I've had people ask what I would recommend to someone arriving at a new company where the previous directory services administrator had left a tree with no proper permissions design or consistency. In this situation, start by analyzing what the organization requires and work from there. You also should analyze what permissions Active Directory currently has assigned, although solely concentrating on this could be detrimental. After all, if the last administrator was not competent or knowledgeable enough to set up a sensible permissions scheme from the start, he may not have accurately implemented the permissions required by the organization.

When analyzing Active Directory, you need to start by identifying the members of the built-in groups on the server, such as Domain Administrators, Backup Operators, and so on. Now do the same for the other groups that are specific to the organization. Once this is done, using the previously described tables, you need to list the permissions on the root of the first domain in the tree you are responsible for. From there you should look at the permissions for the first container or Organizational Unit in that list. Then navigate the branch represented by that container, looking sequentially at the child containers, continually recursing the tree. Once this first branch of the root is mapped out for the container permissions, you may be getting an idea of what permissions are required. Now go through all the objects in that branch, including printers, users, shares, and so on. This time is consuming and annoying, but after a while you may start getting an idea of what is going on. All of this is just a sensible approach to going through Active Directory, not a quick-fix solution. You still have to continue throughout the domains you are responsible for in order to complete the process. It is also legitimate to use a script to iterate through Active Directory and print all the ACLs out to a file. For help on this, consult Chapter 18, *Permissions and Auditing.*

Your first main goal should be to move the individual user permissions to groups with users assigned to them as often as possible, thus making Active Directory simpler to manage and comprehend. These groups should be sensibly named for what they do rather than who they contain (after all, you are looking to understand Active Directory first). Hopefully, you can start consolidating users with identical permissions into the same group.

Your second goal is to remove permissions that users or your newly created groups should not have. This may of course mean that your new groups need to have their members split into two or more separate extra groups. For example, possibly a group that has Read All Properties and Write all properties to an object actually needs three groups with permissions instead: one to have Read All Properties, one to have both Read and Write All Properties, and one to have Read and selected Write rather than complete Write access. This may be evident from your Active Directory analysis, or it may come out of discussions with users or their managers, with whom you should at least confirm the changes before implementing them just to make sure your analysis is correct.

Ultimately, your third goal, having rationalized the array of Active Directory permissions, is to try and limit both the orphaning of objects and branches as well as to try and move as many advanced permissions to general permissions as you can. You might think that it makes more sense to do this earlier, and in some cases this is true, especially when the whole tree is almost a complete set of orphaned objects. However, if you complete the first two goals, you will have an Active Directory tree that you understand and that has been brought back into line with sensible rules. It is much easier to attempt to fix problems with orphaning and advanced permissions once you have a manageable and rationalized tree. You may end up going back and changing groups or permissions that you already sorted out in attaining the first two goals, but consider how much more difficult it would be to attempt to do these concurrently. After all, you are trying to make the best of an already annoying task. There is no sense in trying to do everything at once. As you go through the tree checking for orphaning, you should document the orphans, as specified in Rule 5, just as if you had set up the orphans from scratch yourself. That way, you can use the tables to analyze and keep track, crossing off those that are of no use as you rationalize the tree.

Designing Auditing Schemes

Designing auditing, in contrast to permissions, is a relatively easy process. Imagine the circumstances in which you may need to check what is happening in Active Directory, and then set things up accordingly.

 You must remember that every Active Directory event that is audited causes the system to incur extra processing. Having auditing turned on all the time at the root for every modification by anyone is a great way to get all DCs to really slow down if a lot of Active Directory access occurs on those DCs.

That point bears repeating. Auditing changes to anywhere in the domain Naming Context (NC) will propagate domain wide and cause logging to the security event log on every DC that services the Domain NC. Auditing changes to the Configuration NC or Schema NC will cause all DCs in a forest to begin auditing to their security event logs. You must have tools in place to retrieve logs from multiple DCs if you wish to see every security event that occurs. After all, if you have 100 DCs and are logging Configuration NC changes, then as changes can occur on any DC, you need to amalgamate 100 security event logs in order to gather a complete picture.*

Here are a few examples where designing auditing could come in handy:

- Someone complains that user details are being set to silly values by someone else as a joke.

- You notice new objects you weren't expecting have been created or deleted in a container.

- Active Directory hierarchy has changed and you weren't informed.

- You suspect a security problem.

In all these scenarios, you will need to set auditing options on a container or a leaf object. These auditing entries do not have to exist all the time, so you could write them up and then code them into a script that you ran at the first sign of trouble. That way, the system is immediately updated and ready to monitor the situation. This can happen only if you are prepared.

You need to analyze the scenarios that you envisage cropping up and then translate those into exact sets of auditing entry specifications. Then after you have

---

* Applications for consolidation of event logs are SeNTry by Mission Critical, Event Admin by Aelita, and AppManager by NetIQ. Also, note that Microsoft's WMI technology has excellent event logging, reporting, and notification capabilities if you wish to script such items yourself.

written each scenario up and an emergency occurs, you will be able to follow the exact instructions that you previously laid down and set up a proper rapid response, which is what auditing is all about.

Step one in a real emergency may be to turn all auditing on at the root to make sure that you capture everything to the security log. Step two may be to then turn on auditing for the specific items that you need to audit, so that with step three you can finally remove the Audit-All at the root that normally would cause a severe slowdown. That way, you slow Active Directory briefly while setting up the auditing you actually require, but you don't lose any audit entries during that time. The point is that having a properly prepared set of scripts will save you trouble in the long run as you can quickly use your "Audit all object creations and deletions below a container" or "Audit this object only for any changes" scripts to take the object or container DN as a parameter and so make the scripts generic. How to create scripts is covered later in the book in Chapter 18.

Real-World Examples

It now seems appropriate to put what I have laid out earlier into practice. I will use a series of tasks that could crop up during your everyday work as an administrator. The solutions I propose probably are not the only solutions to the problems. That is often the case with Active Directory; there are many ways of solving the same problem.

Hiding Specific Personal Details for all Users in an Organizational Unit from a Group

In this example, an Organizational Unit called Hardware Support Staff contains the user accounts of an in-house team of people whose job is to repair and fix broken computers within your organization. Whenever a user has a fault, he rings the central faults hotline to request a support engineer. An engineer is assigned the job, which is added to the end of his existing list of faults to deal with. The user is informed about which engineer will be calling and approximately when he will arrive. As with all jobs of this sort, some take longer than others, and users have discovered how to find the mobile or pager number of the engineer they have been assigned and have taken to calling him to get an arrival time update rather than ringing the central desk. Management has decided that they do not want to restrict who can ring the pager or mobile, and they also do not want to stop giving out the engineer's name as they feel it is part of the friendly service. Consequently, they have asked you to find a way of hiding the pager and mobile numbers in Active Directory from all users who should not have access.

The solution that I will use is to remove the default ability of every user to see the property of the Engineer objects by default. I can do this either from the parent OU or manually for each engineer. This ensures that only users or groups that I allow to see the properties will do so. Since this is a simple problem with a simple solution, it is easier to use the GUI than to write a script.

I start by creating that group for users who are allowed to see these properties, calling it Support Phone or something similar. Now I have to make the decision: do I select the parent Organizational Unit itself and assign permissions to hide the property for objects within the container and down the tree or do I manually apply permissions to every support engineer's account? The latter is likely to take much longer with any reasonable number of support staff, and it comes with the added problem that I will have to do the same tasks every time a new support staff member joins the team. In this instance, I will choose the former; however, it should be noted that this will hide all the mobile and pager numbers of all users under the Hardware Support Staff Organizational Unit, even if some of them are not engineers. This is covered in the next example.

I open the ACS window for the Hardware Support Staff Organizational Unit and click Add. I then locate the Support Phone group and click OK. This opens the PE window for Support Phone relating to the Organizational Unit. Now I click the Properties tab, specify to apply to this object and all sub-objects, and then click Allow for both the properties Read Phone-Pager-Primary and Read Phone-Mobile-Primary. These two items may already be allowed by default. If I now click OK, the permissions are applied down the tree, so that everyone in the Support Phone group can now read the mobile and pager properties of all user objects below that Organizational Unit.

I need to restrict the rest of the tree from viewing these two properties. From the ACS window for the Organizational Unit, I add a group in the same manner as before, this time specifying Everyone as the group. I select the Properties tab, find the Read Phone-Pager-Primary and Read Phone-Mobile-Primary properties, and remove the check marks which occur in the two allow fields. I click OK, and all members of the group Everyone have no rights to the two properties below this Organizational Unit. This differs from specifically denying all members access.

 If I had denied the Everyone group from reading the two properties as my first step, then when I opened up the PE window for the Support Phone group, it would not have had the existing check marks inside it for the two fields. This would be because Active Directory would already have realized that the members of Support Phone were obviously members of Everyone, the group containing every user on the system, and consequently would have removed the two settings.

Hiding Specific Personal Details for Some Users in an Organizational Unit from a Group

Let's extend the previous example. I now have 100 engineers and 30 admin staff members directly under this Hardware Support Staff Organizational Unit. There are no child containers splitting up the users. The support staff would like others to be able to find their pager and mobile details and not have them restricted like the engineers. Having completed the previous task, I have successfully restricted both the admin and engineers details.

The less elegant restricting inheritance solution

To allow admins' numbers to be visible, I can orphan the admin staff. This is a slow process, since I have to individually select each admin user and from the Security tab of the Properties window clear the inherit permissions from their parents' checkbox. Obviously, I could script this to speed up the process. Having done this for all 30 users, it means that the user objects do not inherit:

- The Everyone group's inability to read the Read Phone-Pager-Primary and Read Phone-Mobile-Primary properties by default

- The Support Phone group's ability to read the two properties

Consequently, the default permissions apply, which means that these two properties are visible by default.

The other important aspect to note about this solution is that any other permissions applied to the parent Organizational Unit will also not be applied to these children. This may conflict with your other permissions requirements and is covered in the example after next.

The more elegant rearrange-the-tree solution

I will solve this by creating two Organizational Units under Hardware Support Staff called Admin and Engineers. I then move all of the 30 admin users into the Admin Organizational Unit and the 100 engineers into the Engineers Organizational Unit.

I also should remove all previously applied permissions and restrictions to bring back a default set of permissions for the Hardware Support Staff Organizational Unit.

I open a PE window on the Engineers Organizational Unit for the group Everyone, then clear the check marks from the Read Phone-Pager-Primary and Read Phone-Mobile-Primary property checkboxes and click OK. I then assign the Support Phone group permissions to the Engineers Organizational Unit in a similar manner to the previous example. That effectively solves the problem in a much neater and less time consuming way.

A More Complex Hiding Problem

Now I will modify the previous problem again. The engineers' pager and mobile numbers are still to be restricted from everyone, but this time the admin staff wishes to have their pager numbers restricted while having their mobile numbers visible. Let's look at adapting both of the previous solutions to this problem.

The less elegant restricting inheritance solution

Here I have orphaned the admin staff from the tree, so they cannot inherit the pager restriction. The only solution is to manually apply the Everyone group's pager restriction to each of the 30 admin accounts.

The more elegant rearrange-the-tree solution

With users in both the child Organizational Units, this is a simple problem to solve. I just specify that the group Everyone has no permissions to access the pager property of the parent Organizational Unit for this object and all subobjects. I then apply the same sort of restriction for the Read Phone-Mobile-Primary for Everyone to the Engineers Organizational Unit only.

This elegantly solves the problem. There was originally no reason to move the admin users to their own Organizational Unit, other than conventions of balance and form with all users under the parent residing under their own child Organizational Unit according to their type. I also could have just as easily left the engineers in the parent Organizational Unit and manually applied 100 sets of identical restrictions, but why waste that sort of time, when Active Directory was designed to have containers to solve this sort of problem.

Allowing Only a Specific Group of Users to Access a New Published Resource

The Finance department has created a new share called Budget_Details and had it published in the tree. The permissions to the share itself allow only the correctly authorized staff to read and view the contents, but everyone by default can see the share in the tree. The Finance department does not want the share visible to anyone who is not a member of the Finance group.

This is a simple example due to the fact that I have recognized existing groups, Everyone and Finance, to which permissions are to be applied. This in fact is very similar to the telephone restrictions of the previous examples. All I do is open up the PE window for the share object relevant to the Everyone group and remove the allow permissions. I then open up the PE window for the share object relevant to the Finance group and assign Read and List permissions. A simple solution to a simple problem.

Restricting Users in an Organizational Unit from Viewing Properties of Users Outside That Organizational Unit

Let's say the administrator wishes to restrict the ability of users to search and view personal details of users outside their Organizational Unit. It seems like a simple request, with such a powerful Active Directory, I should be able to restrict browse rights on user object permissions up the tree for users in each Organizational Unit. This example serves to show how a request can appear to be simple on the surface, while in fact being one of the worst management nightmares. Hopefully this example will show you that you need to be very careful about what can and cannot be done with Active Directory at present.

Ultimately this may seem like a strange request, even foolish, given that Active Directory is supposed to be set up as a global information store for searching. This problem is made more difficult because it is actually many problems, all of the same type. If you have 100 Organizational Units off the root in your Active Directory, then you are looking at 100 identical problems, not one. In addition, the problem is global-deny/selective-allow not global-allow/selective-deny. As deny overrides allow, you cannot just deny globally and open up an allow when you need it as you could if the situation were reversed; you have to create denials everywhere except certain locations, which is not a simple task.

Again, at first glance, you appear to be helped toward a solution because each set of users is contained in individual Organizational Units. In fact, that will not directly help in any way. Users in ou=Finance will have to be grouped together in order to apply permissions for them to ou=Accounts, ou=Marketing, and so on. It appears that the users in Finance will benefit from being in Finance because it seems you should be able to say "All these users in ou=Finance have no rights to ou=Marketing" and so on. However, permissions can only be set *for* users and groups that *apply to* containers. First you add all the users in each Organizational Unit to a group that represents their location in their particular Organizational Unit. For example, the Finance Organizational Unit would contain users who would be members of the USER_Finance group and so on. For 100 Organizational Units, that is 100 groups. I will call these groups *user groups* for now.

Now I create 100 groups representing the deny permissions that need to be applied. For example, I would create a DRUP_Finance (Deny Read User Permissions) or similar; the name will make sense later. Each of the 100 groups would be created and assigned a deny permission entry for user object attributes of the relevant Organizational Unit and below. I will call these groups "permission groups" for now.

Now I add the user groups, rather than the individual members, as members of the permission groups. This means that I will be adding 99 user group entries to each permission group entry. That is 9,900 operations, a horrific amount. I can use a script because, while setting permissions is not possible within ADSI, here all I am doing is adding groups as members of other groups, something that can be done with ADSI.

This solution implies 100 user groups to manage and 100 permission groups with one permission each and 99 members to manage. This is the best and easiest solution to the problem. Chapter 20, *Enhancing ADSI via an ASP or VB Interface*, includes the code for this task.

What about orphaning as a solution instead? Surely I could specify that each user group has no permissions to read personal details of anyone in the root domain and below. Then I could just orphan each Organizational Unit. Unfortunately, that would work for one Organizational Unit but not for many. With each Organizational Unit orphaned, none of the Organizational Units actually inherit any of the deny restrictions. Consequently, all I end up with is a management nightmare without a solution.

You may be thinking at this point that I could apply all 100 deny restrictions at the root and then orphan each Organizational Unit specifying that the system convert inherited entries to normal entries. Then I could remove each individual restriction relating to the members of that particular Organizational Unit. This would help in implementing a lot of individual entries.

Let's assess the results of this solution. First, I apply 100 separate ACS deny entries to the root. I then perform 100 orphan operations. With each orphan operation, I convert inherited to normal and remove the offending ACS entry, implying each orphaned entry has 99 separate permission denial normal entries. This means at the end that I am looking at managing 9,900 separate permission entries on 100 Organizational Units.

These are the most important things to remember:

*   Do not assume that simply stated problems are easy to solve in Active Directory. Always consider how many users, groups, and permissions you are likely to need to implement.

*   If you are looking at a global-deny/selective-allow throughout the tree, you are looking at a complex problem.

*   When it comes to a job that looks as if you have thousands of permission operations to accomplish, create permission groups and user groups and use a script to automate the creation.

I would hate to have to implement such a system because of the ongoing management nightmare that would accompany such a decision after the initial setup. However, there may be a time when you or your boss or organization decide for security reasons that you have to restrict objects in this way.

Summary

Security is always important, and when access to your organization's network is concerned, it's paramount. I hope this chapter has given you an understanding of how permission to access can be allowed or denied to entire domains or individual properties of a single object. Auditing is also part of security and having mechanisms already designed, so that they can be constantly working or dropped in when required, is the best way to keep track of such a system.

Assigning permission and auditing entries to an object appears to be a simple subject on the surface. However, once you start delving into the art of setting permissions and auditing entries, it quickly becomes obvious how much there is to consider. Global design is the necessary first step.

While expanding your tree later by adding extra containers is rarely a problem, in a large tree it makes sense to have some overall guidelines or rules that allow you to impose a sense of structure on the whole process of design and redesign. Ideally, the golden rules and tables that I created should allow you to plan and implement sensible permissions schemes, which was the goal of the chapter.

11

Designing Schema Changes

In order for Active Directory to hold any object, such as a user, it needs to know what the attributes and characteristics of that object are. In other words, it needs a blueprint for that object. Active Directory Schema is the blueprint for all classes, attributes, and syntaxes that potentially can be stored in Active Directory.

The default schema definition is defined in the *%systemroot%\ntds\schema.ini* file that also contains the initial structure for the *NTDS.DIT* (Active Directory database). This file is a plain ASCII file and is viewed using Notepad or something similar.

The following considerations should be kept in mind when you contemplate extending your Schema:

*   Microsoft designed Active Directory to hold the most common objects and attributes that users of a server system would require. Because they could never anticipate every class of object or every specific attribute (languages spoken, professional qualifications) that a company would like, Active Directory was designed to be extensible. After all, if these objects and properties are going to be in everyday use, then the design shouldn't be taken lightly. Administrators need to be aware of the importance of the Schema and how to extend it. Extending the Schema is a useful and simple solution to a variety of problems. Not being aware of the potential means that you will have a hard time identifying it as a solution to problems you might encounter.

*   Designing Schema modifications is very important, in part because any new class or attribute that you create in the Schema is a permanent addition. While unused objects can be disabled if you no longer require them, they cannot be removed in the present version of Windows 2000.

- While it is easy to extend Active Directory, it's surprising how scarce and confusing some of the information is. This is obviously both a personal opinion and something that will change with time.

This chapter takes you through the process of extending the Schema, from the initial design of the changes through the implementation and discusses how to avoid the pitfalls that can crop up. I discuss at what point in your use of Windows 2000 you are likely to come across the need for schema extensions. I then talk about analyzing the choices available and seeing if you can obtain the required design result some other way, because schema changes are not to be undertaken lightly. I obviously cover how to implement schema changes from first principles, but before that I identify the steps in designing or modifying a class or attribute. Finally, I cover the pitfalls that could imperil an Active Directory and provide guidelines to help you avoid them.

I don't spend much time introducing a large number of specific examples. This is mainly because there's no way I can conceive of every sort of class that you will require. Consequently, for examples I use only one new generic class as well as a few attribute extensions to the default user object. When giving examples of modifying a class, I use the user object class for my modifications.

Let's look at how you would design the changes you may wish to make in an enterprise environment.

Nominating Responsible People in Your Organization

If you don't already have a central person or group of people responsible for the OID namespace for your organization, you need to form such a group. This OID Managers group is responsible for obtaining an OID namespace, designing a structure for the namespace that makes sense to your organization, managing that namespace by maintaining a diagram of the structure and a list of the allocated OIDs, and issuing appropriate OIDs for new classes from that structure as required. Whenever a new class of attribute or object is to be created in your organization's forest, the OID Managers provide a unique OID for that new class, which is then logged by the OID Managers with a set of details about the reason for the request and the type of class that it is to be used for. All these details need to be defined by the OID Managers group.

The Schema Managers, by comparison, are responsible for designing and creating proper classes in the Schema for a forest. They are responsible for actually making changes to the Schema via requests from within the organization, for making sure that now defunct objects are marked as disabled, for ensuring that redundant objects doing the same thing are not created, that inheritance is used to best effect, that the appropriate objects are indexed, and that the GC contains the right objects.

The Schema Managers need to decide on the membership of the Schema Admins universal group that resides in the Forest Root Domain of a particular forest. One possibility is that the Schema Managers wish to keep a set of user accounts as members of Schema Admins by default all the time. Another is that they may decide to remove every member of that Schema Admins group so that no unintentional changes can be made to the schema. In this case, the Schema Managers just need to be given permissions to add and remove members of the Schema Admins group to enable any of the Schema Managers to add themselves to the Schema Admins group whenever changes are to be made to the Schema.

 If you are designing code that will modify some other organization's schema, then the documentation accompanying that code should make it explicitly clear exactly what classes are being created and why. The documentation also should explain that the code needs to be run with the privilege of a member of the Schema Admins group, since some organizations may have an Active Directory in which the Schema Admins group is empty most of the time, as mentioned earlier.

Note that the membership of OID Managers does not necessarily coincide with that of Schema Managers, although it is a possibility.

Thinking of Changing the Schema

Before you start thinking of changing the Schema, you need to consider the data your Active Directory will hold and not just the namespace. After all, if you know your data, you then can decide what changes you want to make and whom those change might impact.

Designing the Data

Your new Windows 2000 system is likely to fall into one or more of the following categories:

* A *plain vanilla* Windows 2000 system with no existing NT-based infrastructure

* An in-place upgrade of one or more previous NT domains to a Windows 2000 forest in a piecemeal fashion

* A migration to Windows 2000 from a different operating system

No matter where you're coming from, at some point you'll need to determine exactly what data you will add or migrate for the objects you create. Will you use the Physical-Delivery-Office-Name attribute of the user object? What about the Telephone-Pager attribute? Do you want to merge the internal staff office location list and telephone database during the migration? What if you really need to also know what languages each of your staff speaks or qualifications they hold? What about their shoe size, their shirt size, number of children, and whether they like animals? The point is that some of these will already exist in the Active Directory Schema and some won't. So at some point you need to design the actual data that you want to include.

If you're putting in a brand new plain vanilla installation, then you should be collating the data to put into Active Directory early on in the design. With a migration from a different operating system, you will be looking at the data that you wish to export from that system into the new Windows 2000 structure.

However, with an in-place upgrade, you are migrating existing NT user, group, and computer objects. These objects exist in Active Directory already, and when you migrate the objects over from Windows NT, a subset of the attributes will be populated with data. Since the subset of each attribute is not very large compared to the total number of attributes available for these objects in Active Directory, you need to work out exactly what data you wish to include.

During this analysis, you may come to consider what data you can actually get out of Active Directory by looking at the Schema; you may find that the schema is lacking an essential element.

Let's consider MyUnixCorp, a large organization that for many years has run perfectly well on a large mainframe system. The system is unusual in that the login process has been completely replaced in-house with a two-tier password system. A file called *additional-passwd* maintains a list of usernames and their second Unix password in an encrypted format. Your design for the migration for MyUnix-Corp's system has to take account of the extra login check. In this scenario, either MyUnixCorp accepts that the new Windows 2000 Kerberos security mechanism is secure enough for its site or has to add entries to the schema for the second password attribute and write a new Windows 2000 logon interface that incorporates both checks.

This example serves to outline that the data that is to be stored in Active Directory has a bearing on the schema structure and consequently has to be incorporated into the design phase.

To Change or Not to Change

When you identify a deficiency in the Schema for your own Active Directory, you have to look hard into whether modifying the Schema is the correct way forward. Finding that the Schema lacks a complete series of objects along with multiple attributes is a far cry from identifying that the Person-who-needs-to-refill-the-printer-with-toner attribute of the printer object is missing from the Schema. There's no rule, either, that says once you wish to create three extra attributes on an existing object, you should modify the Schema. It all comes down to choice.

 There is one useful guideline: you should identify all the data you wish to hold in Active Directory prior to considering your design. If you consider how to implement each change in Active Directory one at a time, you may simply lose sight of the overall picture.

To help you make that choice, you should ask yourself whether there are any other objects or attributes that you could use to solve your problem.

Let's say you were looking for an attribute of a user object that would hold a staff identification number for your users. You need to ask whether there is an existing attribute of the user object that could hold the staff ID number and that you are not going to use. This saves you from modifying the Schema if you don't have to. Take Leicester University as an example. While we had a large user base that we were going to register, we needed to hold a special ID number for our students. In Great Britain, every university student has a so-called University and Colleges Administration System number, more commonly known as the UCAS number, a unique alphanumeric string that UCAS assigns independent of a student's particular university affiliation. Students receive their UCAS numbers when they first begin looking into universities. The numbers identify students to their prospective universities, stay with students throughout their undergraduate careers, and are good identifiers for checking the validity of students' details. By default, there is no schema attribute called UCAS-Number, so we had two choices. We could find an appropriately named attribute that we were not going to use and make use of that, or we could modify the Schema.

Since we were only initially looking to store this piece of information in addition to the default user information, we were not talking about a huge change in any case. We simply looked to see whether we could use any other schema attributes to contain the data. We soon found the Employee-ID user attribute that we were not ever intending to use, and which seemed to fit the bill, so we decided to use that. While it isn't as appropriately named as an attribute called UCAS-Number would be, it did mean that we didn't have to modify the base Schema in this instance.

The important point here is that we chose not to modify the Schema, having found a spare attribute that *we were satisfied with.* We could just as easily have found no appropriate attributes and decided to go through making the schema changes using our own customized attributes.

There are also a set of attributes available to each class that store text strings. These are known as the *extension attributes* and have names like Extension-Attribute-1, Extension-Attribute-2, and so on. These are never used by the operating system and have been left in for you to use as you wish. There are around 20 created by default, thus giving you spare attribute capacity already in Active Directory. So if I wanted to store the number of languages spoken by a user, I could just store that value inside Extension-Attribute-1 if I chose. You can see how these attributes have been designed by using the Schema Manager.

Extension attributes and making use of unused attributes works well for a small number of cases. However, if there were 20, 30, or more complex attributes with a specific syntax or perhaps the need to store 20 objects with 30 attributes each, then you would have more difficulty. When you have data like that, you need to consider the bigger picture.

The Global Picture

So you have a list of all your data and suspect either that the Schema will not hold your data or that it will not do so to your satisfaction. You now need to consider the future of your organization's Schema and design it accordingly. The following questions should help you decide how to design for each new class-schema or attribute-schema object.

Q: Is this class-schema or attribute-schema object already held in the Schema in some form? In other words, does the attribute already exist by default or has someone already created it? If it doesn't exist, you can create it. If it does already exist in some form, can you make use of that existing attribute? If you can, you need to consider doing so. If you can't, you need to consider modifying the existing attribute to cope with your needs or creating a second attribute that essentially holds similar or identical data, which is wasteful. If the existing attribute is of no use, can you create a new one and migrate the values for the existing attribute to the new one and disable the old one? These are the sorts of questions you need to be thinking of.

Q: Is this a class-schema or attribute-schema object that is to be used only for a very specific purpose or could this object potentially be made of use (i..e., created, changed, and modified) by others in the organization? If the object is for only a specific purpose, the person suggesting the change should know what is required. If the object may impact others, care should be taken to ensure it is designed to cope with the requirements of all potential users. For example, that it can later be extended if necessary, without affecting the existing object instances at the moment the schema object is updated. For example, for an attribute, you should ask whether the attribute's syntax and maximum/minimum values (for strings or integers) are valid or whether they should be made more applicable to the needs of the many. Specifically, if you created a CASE_ INSENSITIVE_STRING of between 5 and 20 characters now and later you require that attribute to be a CASE_SENSITIVE_STRING of between 5 and 20, you may or may not have a problem depending on whether you care that the values for the case-insensitive strings are now case-sensitive. You obviously could write a script that goes through Active Directory and modifies each string appropriately, but what if you had changed the schema attribute to being a CASE_SENSITIVE_STRING of between 8 and 20? Then you have another problem if there are any strings of between 5 and 7 letters. These attributes would be invalid, since their contents are wrong. I think you can see the sort of problems that can occur.

Q: Are you modifying an existing object with an attribute? If so, would this attribute be better if it were not applied directly to the object, but instead added to a set of attributes within an auxiliary class class-schema object?

Q: Are you adding a mandatory attribute to an existing object that will suddenly make all existing instances invalid? Say you added a new mandatory attribute called languages-spoken to the User class. Since none of the existing users will have this attribute set initially, you will instantly make all of the users invalid. You have to make sure though, in this specific case, that you will never create users via Active Directory Users and Computers MMC, because this tool will not be aware of your new mandatory requirement and so cannot create valid users any more. You must be aware of the impact that your changes may have on existing tools and ones that you design yourself.

Basically, these questions boil down to four much simpler ones:

- Is the change that needs to be made valid and sensible for all potential uses and users of this object?

- Will my change impact any other changes that may need to be made to this and other objects in the future?

- Will my change impact anyone else now or in the future?

- Will my change impact any applications that people inside or outside the company are developing?

In a similar fashion to getting a valid OID namespace, I would make sure that the class-schema and attribute-schema objects are created with sensible names. These names really should have a unique company prefix for easy identification and be capitalized words separated by hyphens. For specific examples, see Chapter 19, *Extending the Schema and the GUI.*

The Schema Managers group needs to sit down with all groups of people who potentially would like to make changes to the schema and brief them on how the schema operates and attempt to identify the sorts of changes that would need to be made by these groups. If a series of meetings is not your style, consider creating a briefing paper, followed by a form to request schema updates, issued to all relevant department heads. If you allow enough time, you will be able to collate responses received and make a good stab at an initial design. You can find attributes that may conflict, ways of making auxiliary classes rather than modifications to individual attributes, and so on. This gives the Schema Managers a good chance to come up with a valid initial design for the schema changes prior to or during a rollout.

I never modify default system attributes, although the system does allow me to do so. It's a simple rule that I use. It makes sure that I never conflict with anything considered as *default* by the operating system, which might eventually cause problems when I upgrade. Adding extra attributes to objects is fine, but I personally never modify existing ones.

If I need a longer string for an existing attribute, or it needs to be of a slightly different type, I just create a new one with a similar name and the class I want.

Managing and Modifying the Schema

There are two ways to modify the Schema: through the Schema Manager MMC or via code that makes use of ADSI. I will not cover the use of the Schema Manager MMC very heavily here since it is fairly straightforward to use, although I will cover its use in managing the FSMO Schema Master role. I will, however, give an introduction to creating classes with ADSI. Before I start, you should know that it will not be possible to modify the Schema with either ADSI or the Schema Manager MMC unless you bypass certain safeguards.

Running the Schema Manager MMC for the First Time

The Schema Master MMC is not available by default with the standard tools. To make it available, you need to first register the Dynamic Link Library (DLL) file for the MMC snap-in. You do this by typing the following command at the command prompt:

```
regsvr32.exe schmmgmt.dll
```

You now can start the Schema Manager via the Resource Kit Tools console or by creating a custom MMC and adding the Active Directory Schema snap-in to it.

The latter is simply a matter of going to the Run menu from the Start button, typing MMC, and clicking OK. Then in the empty MMC, choose the Console menu and select to Add/Remove Snap-in. From here, you can click the Add button and select Active Directory Schema as the item. If you then click the Add button, followed by Close, and then the OK button, that will give you an MMC hosting the Schema Manager snap-in for you to use and later save as required.

Allowing Schema Changes to Take Place

There are two safeguards that you have to bypass in order for the system to allow you to modify the Schema with either the Schema Manager console or via ADSI. First, the user who is to make the changes has to be a member of the Schema Admins group, which exists in the forest root domain. Second, you need to make a change to the registry on the DC that you wish to make the changes on.

The fastest and probably best solution is to use the checkbox from the Schema Master MMC, shown later in the chapter.

Alternatively, on the DC itself, open up the registry using *REGEDT32.EXE* or *REGEDIT.EXE* and locate the following key:

HKEY_LOCAL_MACHINE\SYSTEM\CurrentControlSet\Services\NTDS\Parameters

Now, create a new REG_DWORD value called Schema-Update-Allowed and set the value to 1. That's all you need to do. You now can edit the Schema on that DC.

Another alternative method for making the change is to copy the following three lines to a text file with a REG extension and open it (i.e., execute it) on the DC where you wish to enable schema updates. This will automatically modify the registry for you without the need to open the registry by hand:

```
REGEDIT4
[HKEY_LOCAL_MACHINE\SYSTEM\CurrentControlSet\Services\NTDS\Parameters]
"Schema Update Allowed"=dword:00000001
```

Once you've modified the registry on a particular DC and placed the user account that is to make the changes into the Schema Admins group, any changes that you make to the Schema on that DC will be accepted. If you wish changes to be accepted on any DC, you need to correspondingly modify the registry on every DC.

The Schema Cache

Each Windows 2000 DC maintains a copy of the entire Schema in memory. This is known as the *schema cache*. It is used to provide a very rapid response when requesting a schema object OID from a name.

The schema cache is actually a set of hash tables of all the class-schema and attribute-schema objects known to the system along with specific indices (Attribute-ID and LDAP-Display-Name for attribute-schema objects and Governs-ID, LDAP-Display-Name, and Mapi-ID for class-schema objects) for fast searching.

The hash table sizes are dynamic in terms of the amount of memory that is allocated for the objects that are stored. Initially, the tables are set to a size capable of holding 2,048 attributes and 1,024 classes. The system keeps count of the number of attributes and classes in the Schema and is responsible for making sure that the table sizes are kept greater than twice the number of attributes (for the attribute hash tables) or twice the number of classes (for the class hash tables). If at any time the number of attributes or classes increases enough that the table sizes are not at least twice as big, as required, the cache table sizes are incremented in blocks of 2,048 or 1,024, as appropriate.

The objects are loaded into the schema cache when the DC is booted and then five minutes after an update. However, if you need the schema cache to be updated immediately for some reason, say after the creation of a new object or attribute class, you can force an immediate reload of the cache.

As I said, the system holds a copy in memory solely to aid in searches that require quick and regular access to the Schema. If the system were to keep both the cache and the actual Active Directory Schema in parity, it could be costly in terms of performance, since making changes to the Schema is an intensive process due to the significant checking and setting of object defaults involved by the system upon creation of new objects. Consequently, there is a time delay between changes made to the underlying Schema and the cached copy. Research by Microsoft has found that the Schema tends to be updated in bunches. This is likely to be due to applications creating multiple classes for their own purposes during an installation or even normal operation. If classes are still being created after five minutes, the system updates the cache in five-minute increments after the first five-minute update has completed. This continues for as long as schema class updates continue.

During the intervening five-minute period, when the underlying Schema has been modified but the cache has yet to be updated, instances of objects or attributes of the new classes cannot be created. If you try to create an object, the system will return an error. This is due to the fact that object creations refer to the cache and not the underlying Schema. To get around this problem, you can force an immediate reload of the cache by adding a special attribute to the schema container. I'll cover this later when I consider how to use the Schema Manager interface to create and delete classes. In a similar vein, if you mark an object as defunct, this will not take effect until the cache is reloaded.

While you cannot create new instances, since this would reference the schema cache, you can add new attributes or classes that you have created to other classes that you are creating. For example, if you create a new attribute, you can immediately add it to a new class. Why? Because the attribute or class is added using an OID, and the system thus doesn't need to do any lookups in the schema cache. While all system checks by Active Directory confirming that the data is valid (covered in detail a couple of sections later) will still be performed, the checks are performed on the Schema in Active Directory, not in the cache. If this weren't the case, you would have to wait for at least five minutes before any new attributes that you created could be added to new classes, and that would be unacceptable.

The FSMO Schema Master

The FSMO Schema Master is the server where changes to the Schema take place so that multiple users or applications cannot modify the Schema on two or more different domain controllers at the same time. When Windows 2000 is installed in an enterprise, the first server in the first domain in the forest (the forest root domain) becomes the nominated FSMO Schema Master. Later, if changes need to be made to the Schema, they can be made at the nominated master. However, if you start to make the changes on another domain controller using the Schema Manager console, the console will transparently contact the current FSMO Schema Master and request that the role be transferred to the one you are currently communicating from. Providing no problems occur, the role is transferred, and the new server becomes the current FSMO Schema Master.

Let's take two servers, Server A and Server B. Server A is the current FSMO Schema Master. When the role is to be transferred, Server A modifies the FSMO-Role-Owner attribute to represent Server B and then passes that attribute to Server B along with any other schema changes that Server B may not yet have seen. Server B then applies any schema changes it hasn't seen, including the FSMO-Role-Owner attribute and thus becomes the new FSMO Schema Master. This new role is replicated out when the Schema NC data is next replicated.

You can transfer the role from an existing Schema Master in three ways: via the Schema Manager MMC, via the NTDSUTIL tool, or via code that makes use of ADSI.

Using the Schema Manager MMC to make the changes is easy. First you need to connect to the server that is to be the new master (*moose.windows.mycorp.com*), and then you need to force the role to change to the server to which you are now connected. To start the process, simply run the MMC and right-click Active Directory Schema in the lefthand scope pane. From the context menu that drops down, select Change Domain Controller. A dialog box similar to Figure 11-1 then appears.

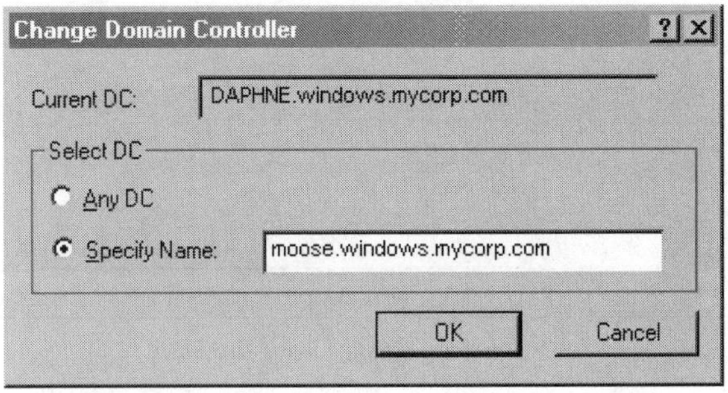

Figure 11-1. Changing the connected server

You now can select a new server to connect to. You should transfer any FSMO roles (not just the Schema Master) to a new server before shutting a server down for an extended period, such as for maintenance. You may just wish to transfer the role to any other server, rather than to a specific one, which is why there is an option to connect to any other server. Once that has been done, right-click on Active Directory Domains Schema in the scope pane and select Operations Master from the context menu. A dialog box will appear showing the current DC holding the FSMO Schema Master role as well as an option to change the role to the currently connected server. Figure 11-2 shows this dialog box.

Click the Change button and change the schema role. There is also an option to modify the registry on the DC you are currently connected to so that schema changes will be allowed on this new FSMO Schema Master.

If a server corruption or crash takes the FSMO Schema Master out of the enterprise, no server will automatically assume the role. In this situation, you can use similar methods to force the FSMO Schema Master role on a server. It is possible to force a server to assume the role, but this can cause data corruption if the old

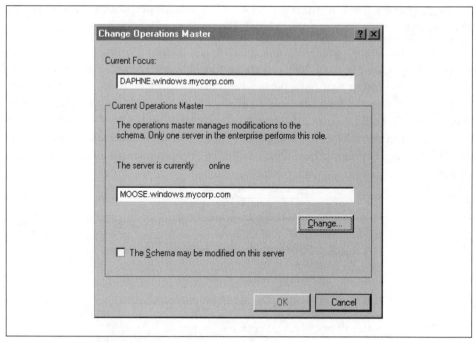

Figure 11-2. Changing the FSMO Schema Master from the MMC

server comes back online. This is covered later under the section entitled "Wreaking Havoc with Your Schema."

If you are writing ADSI scripts to manipulate the Schema, rather than worrying about checking to see if the server you wish to make the changes on is the FSMO Schema Master, just connect to the FSMO Schema Master directly and make the changes there. I'll show you how to do that later in the book.

Checks the System Makes When You Modify the Schema

When you create a new class or attribute, the system performs some basic checks within Active Directory to see if the data is valid, in addition to any checks you provide. The checks for attributes are shown in Table 11-1, and those for new classes are in Table 11-2.

Table 11-1. System Checks Made when Creating New Attributes

Attribute	System Check Performed
LDAP-Display-Name	Must be unique in Active Directory.
Attribute-Id	Must be unique in Active Directory.
Mapi-Id	If present, must be unique in Active Directory.

Table 11-1. System Checks Made when Creating New Attributes (continued)

Attribute	System Check Performed
Schema-ID-GUID	Must be unique in Active Directory.
Attribute-Syntax	Must correlate with OM-Syntax.
OM-Syntax	Must correlate with Attribute-Syntax.
Range-Lower	If Range-Upper is present as well, the following should be true: Range-Upper > Range-Lower.
Range-Upper	If Range-Lower is present as well, the following should be true: Range-Upper > Range-Lower.

Table 11-2. System Checks Made when Creating New Classes

Attribute	System Check Performed
LDAP-Display-Name	Must be unique in Active Directory.
Governs-Id	Must be unique in Active Directory.
Schema-ID-GUID	Must be unique in Active Directory.
Sub-Class-Of	Checks to make sure that the X.500 specifications are not contravened, (i.e., that an auxiliary class cannot inherit from a structural class, and an abstract class can *only* inherit from another abstract class). All classes defined in this attribute must already exist.
RDN-Att-ID	Must have a Unicode string as its syntax.
May-Contain	All classes defined in this attribute must already exist.
System-May-Contain	All classes defined in this attribute must already exist.
Must-Contain	All classes defined in this attribute must already exist.
System-Must-Contain	All classes defined in this attribute must already exist.
Auxiliary-Class	All classes defined in this attribute must already exist. All classes defined in this attribute must have an Object-Class-Category indicating either 88-Class or Auxiliary.
System-Auxiliary-Class	All classes defined in this attribute must already exist. All classes defined in this attribute must have an Object-Class-Category indicating either 88-Class or Auxiliary.
Poss-Superiors	All classes defined in this attribute must already exist. All classes defined in this attribute must have an Object-Class-Category indicating either 88-Class or Auxiliary.
System-Poss-Superiors	All classes defined in this attribute must already exist. All classes defined in this attribute must have an Object-Class-Category indicating either 88-Class or Auxiliary.

Making Classes and Attributes Defunct

It is not possible to delete objects from the schema in Windows 2000 because, in order to delete a class or an attribute, the system would have to perform a forest-wide cleanup operation to make sure that no instances of the object existed. This could take a very long time. So, for this first version of Active Directory, deletion of objects is not supported. Later versions of Active Directory will support object deletion.

If you create a class or attribute of some sort and decide that you don't want it any more, you simply make it *defunct*. This is achieved by setting the Is-Defunct attribute on the schema object to True. In order for this to succeed for an attribute, the system makes sure that the attribute is not a mandatory or optional attribute of any non-defunct class. In order for this to succeed for a class, the system makes sure that the class is not a parent of any other nondefunct class, is not an auxiliary class to any other nondefunct class, and is not a possible superior of any other nondefunct class. While an object is defunct, no changes can be made to it. If you then decide that you want to use the schema object again, set the value of Is-Defunct to False. The checks that occur when doing this are the same as for creating a new schema object of the appropriate type in the first place.

When a schema object is defunct, attempts to create instances of it fail as if it doesn't exist. The same applies to modifying existing instances, whether an attribute on an object or an object itself, as they will appear not to exist. Instances of defunct classes can, however, be deleted, as can objects that contain now-defunct attributes. Searches for defunct classes will happily succeed, as will searches on nondefunct classes that contain defunct attributes. All attributes, defunct or not, will be able to be read. This is all required to enable the administrator or application author to clean up and remove the now defunct object instances and all values from now defunct attributes.

Even though a schema object is defunct, it still exists in terms of its Distinguished-Name, Object-ID, and LDAP-Display-Name. You cannot create a second schema object that has these values.

Wreaking Havoc with Your Schema

There are a number of superb ways to totally corrupt your Active Directory via the Schema. I include them here so that you can be fully aware of the problems.

Let's start by considering the main base classes of Attribute-Schema, Class-Schema, and Top. Imagine I decide to add a new mandatory attribute to Top. As all classes derive from Top, then the mandatory attribute requirement is suddenly added to every class and attribute throughout the Schema in one go. Since none of the existing classes and attributes have this value, they all suddenly become marked as invalid. They still exist and can be used, but they cannot be modified at all. New timestamps cannot be added, USNs cannot be changed, replication stops, and effectively your Active Directory grinds to a halt. The reason that the objects cannot be modified is that Active Directory does a special check when existing instances of objects are modified to make sure that all mandatory attributes have been set. If they have not all been set, which they won't have been in this case, Active Directory will not allow any attribute changes from now on. The only solution is to remove the new mandatory attribute or set a value for the attribute on every single object in every NC in the entire forest.

There are also concurrent problems. Having a FSMO Schema Master is perfectly fine, but that doesn't necessarily stop members of Schema Admins from attempting to run two schema-modifying applications at the same time. Every time an application or piece of code attempts to write to the Schema, it automatically writes a special system attribute at the same time. Two system-attribute writes anywhere in Active Directory cannot occur simultaneously, so one will fail if this is the case. In the scenario of simultaneous applications executing, the changes to the schema may all be handled sequentially and the requests from both applications may be interleaved, but the two applications at some point may attempt to write together. At that point, one of them will fail. If the failed application is rerun, it must be coded to detect the existence of each object (i.e., the previous creation succeeded) prior to creating the object, or else the object-creation process will continually fail.

You can also make instances of objects invalid quite easily. For example, let's say that I define that new class I mentioned earlier called Finance-User, and create an instance of it called cn=SimonWilliams. If I then remove Languages-Spoken from Finance-User's mandatory attributes, the SimonWilliams user becomes invalid because the SimonWilliams instance has an attribute that is not now allowed in the schema definition for Finance-User. Again, it is up to the person or code that makes the Languages-Spoken attribute defunct to go through Active Directory and find all instances of Finance-User and modify them to remove the value in this now-defunct attribute. If this isn't done, any instances of Finance-User with the Languages-Spoken attribute defined (all, in this case, as it was mandatory) will remain invalid.

You cannot cause invalid instances by modifying existing attribute-schema objects, as all the key attributes are defined in system attributes. However, you can cause havoc with existing class-schema objects. Ways of doing this are:

- Removing classes as possible superiors; this can leave instances under invalid parent containers.

- Adding classes to the list of auxiliary classes; this can change what attributes are now considered mandatory.

- Removing classes from the list of auxiliary classes; this can change what attributes are now considered mandatory and optional and can thus leave instances with now non-existent attributes.

- Directly removing mandatory or optional attributes; this can leave instances with now-nonexistent attributes.

If the DC holding the FSMO Schema Master role unexpectedly disappears, you can force another to assume the role. But if the original DC ever comes back, then you have two FSMO Schema Masters, and you will need to rectify that by making sure only one server has the role. However, if the original server had some updates applied prior to its crash and you allow updates to be made on the new Schema Master, then the updates from the old DC will eventually propagate around the network. Your problems to be aware of in this scenario are twofold:

- If the new FSMO Schema Master created objects that conflict with some created on the original master prior to its departure, then some objects will be removed from Active Directory during the conflict-resolution process.

- If the two DCs are online and both believe that they are the FSMO Schema Master, both will accept schema updates equally.

A simple solution, if you can live with it, is either not to force a FSMO until the old DC returns and assumes its role or to force a FSMO temporarily and remove everyone from the Schema Admins group to prevent changes in the meantime. In the latter case, when the original DC comes back, force the FSMO role onto it.

Finally, the system itself will protect you from some forms of stupidity using the System-Only attribute and Access Control Lists (ACLs). These work together to prevent you from deleting the user or group object from Active Directory or removing the Security-Principal as an auxiliary class of both. While you may be aware of this already from my many examples of the use of the four system attributes, it bears mentioning one final time. For attribute-schema object classes, the Attribute-Id, Attribute-Syntax, and OM-Syntax are marked as system-only attributes and so cannot be changed or deleted. For class-schema objects, the Sub-Class-Of, Governs-Id, System-May-Contain, System-Must-Contain, System-Auxiliary-Class, and System-Poss-Superiors are marked as system-only attributes and so cannot be changed or deleted. Other very important classes and attributes cannot be deleted as their ACLs are locked to prevent this.

Summary

Carefully designing the changes that you make to the Active Directory Schema cannot be stressed highly enough for an Active Directory that is to encompass a large corporation. Selecting a team of Schema Managers and OID Managers and creating documentation to accompany and justify changes will smooth that process. Whether you are a small company or a large multinational, creating sensible structures should mean that you rarely make mistakes and almost never have to make objects defunct.

I hope that I have shown you not only the perils and pitfalls of modifying the Schema but also why the Schema is necessary and how it underpins the entire Active Directory. While you should be cautious when modifying Active Directory, a sensible administrator should have as little to fear from the Active Directory Schema as he does from the Windows Registry.

You now should have enough information from the previous chapters in this part to be able to make an effective design for your organization. The next two chapters take a look at how to implement that design and make it interoperable with any other systems that you may have.

12

Windows NT 4.0 Migration

Knowing how to design Windows 2000 Active Directories is very useful, but it's not the end of the story. You already may have an existing NetWare or Windows NT infrastructure and want to consider migrating to Windows 2000. Alternatively, you may have existing directories and networks that you would like Active Directory to complement rather than replace. One of the most important features of Active Directory is its ability to integrate with other directory services.

The next two chapters cover how to migrate from Windows NT 4.0 and how to integrate your Active Directory with other directories and data stores. In a book written during the beta cycle of a new product, there is no way to cover every possible combination of options thoroughly. Detailed information in this area also requires the author to have an in-depth knowledge of every possible option, which is something I'll readily admit that I don't have. I am going explain the technologies open to you now and in the near future so that you have a basic grounding in the available options.

Consolidating, Migrating, and Upgrading from NT

With the advent of Windows 2000 and its need for significantly fewer domains, consolidation of domains prior to or during upgrade is a sensible solution. In recent years there have been three respectable Independent Software Vendors (ISVs) that have developed tools to help administrators migrate users, groups, and computer accounts from one Windows NT domain to another. These vendors are:

- Mission Critical Software (*http://www.missioncritical.com*)

- Entevo (*http://www.entevo.com*)

- FastLane (*http://www.fastlanetech.com*)

These ISVs produce tools that enable administrators to plan and automate existing Windows NT domain and directory reconfigurations and to prepare Windows NT 4.0 domains for efficient transitions to Windows 2000. Mission Critical, Entevo, and FastLane provide products that offer benefits to users of Windows NT Server, including the following:

- The ability for administrators to delegate security privileges to simplify domain management and consolidation

- Enhanced auditing and reporting features to improve administrative control

- Ways to manage users and resources hierarchically in preparation for Active Directory and Windows 2000

- Features to enable customers to integrate and migrate servers running Novell's NDS to a Windows NT Server-centric management infrastructure

During the Windows 2000 beta program, many of the members told Microsoft that they wanted tools provided to help support various upgrade and consolidation scenarios with Windows NT 4.0. A number of sites were also requesting the ability to upgrade and consolidate existing domains in one step. To that end, rather than take the time and effort to reinvent the wheel, Microsoft decided to license one set of technologies for inclusion with Windows 2000 on release: the Domain Migrator product from Mission Critical Software, Inc. By providing a simple, task-based user interface, powerful preview and rollback capabilities, extensive reporting features, and prune and graft* support, Domain Migrator will help administrators accelerate their upgrades to Windows 2000 Server from Microsoft Windows NT Server 4.0.

As this is being written, the Domain Migrator tools are not yet available for Windows 2000, but Microsoft has indicated that it intends to deliver the Domain Migrator technologies as an MMC snap-in along with the full release of Windows 2000.

While there are tools to help users consolidate, integrate, and migrate from Novell's NDS and Windows NT 4.0, it's worth taking a look at the underlying methods or principles that you will be employing during an upgrade. This will give you a better understanding of the undertaking.

---

* The ability to cut sections of one tree (known as pruning) and paste them under other sections of the same or different trees (known as grafting).

The Principles of Upgrading Windows NT Domains

There are many reasons that you will want to upgrade your Windows NT domains to Windows 2000, not least of which is to make use of Active Directory and other features. It's possible to have significantly fewer domains in Windows 2000 because each domain can now store 1 to 2 million objects, and each forest can store more than 10 million objects. While fewer domains means less administration, the added benefit of using organizational units to segregate objects makes the Windows 2000 Active Directory represent a business more accurately, both geographically and organizationally, and is a significant step forward. Couple this with the ability to set ACLs on objects and their properties in Active Directory, and you get much more fine-grained control for administrative delegation than before. You also can start phasing out old services, such as Windows Internet Naming Service (WINS) and extraneous Windows NT Backup Domain Controller (BDC) servers, since the clients now make more efficient use of DCs via TCP/IP and the DNS. With all of these improvements, the goals of upgrading a domain are easy to state:

- Reduce the number of domains in use since it is easier to administer fewer domains

- Gain an extensible schema that allows much more corporate information to be stored than was previously possible

- Create a hierarchical namespace that as closely as possible mirrors the organizational structure of the business

- Gain much more fine-grained control over delegation of administration without needing to resort to the use of multiple domains

- Reduce network bandwidth use by DCs through both multimaster replication and a significantly more efficient set of replication algorithms

- Reduce the number of PDCs/BDCs to a smaller number of DCs through a more efficient use of DCs by clients

- Eliminate the need for reliance on WINS servers and move to the Internet-standard DNS for name resolution

 To get the maximum benefit from the new technologies, you really need to upgrade both clients and servers.

Let's start by looking at the core technology that Windows 2000 runs on: the DNS.

The DNS

Windows 2000 Active Directory requires DNS as the cornerstone of its operation. Without a DNS, you have no domain. That means your primary task before you can consider an upgrade is to see what choices you have for the DNS in your environment, and then implement one of them. As covered in Chapter 2, *Active Directory Overview*, you have three main situations:

- Allow Windows 2000 to host the DNS root of your company's domain, e.g., *mycorp.com*

- Use your organization's DNS to delegate a zone that Windows 2000's DNS will host as the Windows 2000 root

- Use a non-Windows 2000 DNS

Let's briefly reconsider each of these in turn.

Windows 2000 hosts the DNS root

This is a lot simpler for smaller companies than for larger ones, since by definition the larger companies will have more tools, scripts, and utilities and a much larger set of entries centered on their DNSs than smaller ones will. While this is arguably the best solution for Active Directory, it may not be the best solution for your organization. There also may be resistance to changing the entire DNS infrastructure solely for a new operating system; you may have more concerns with other operating systems and services that use the DNS than just Active Directory. Basically, this is the best solution to take advantage of native dynamic updates, support for Unicode DNS names, and integration of Active Directory with the DNS to allow multiple primary DNS servers, but it will require you to migrate or upgrade your existing DNS infrastructure and all of its management functionality.

Windows 2000 hosts a subdomain

This may be the next best choice and is one that I'm seeing adopted on a regular basis now. In this scenario, the main DNS servers continue to host the main zone but delegate a child zone as the root of the Windows 2000 service (e.g., *windows. mycorp.com* delegated from *mycorp.com*). This child zone is hosted by Windows 2000 DNS servers and is authoritative for all queries to that zone.

This solution requires no upgrade to existing DNS servers and allows you to maximize your use of Windows 2000–integrated technologies, such as dynamic update and Active Directory integration, without removing your existing DNS infrastructure. The only drawbacks to this scenario are the need to have more DNS servers than you had before (slightly increasing the management overhead),[*] possible

---

[*] Using dynamic update should keep this to a minimum.

registration of clients in existing zones as well as in the newly delegated zone, and longer names overall for the domains.

A non-Windows 2000 DNS hosts the Windows 2000 root

This solution is perfectly fine, but will require some testing to make sure that full compatibility is possible. The existing DNS servers must support SRV Resource Records (SRV RRs from RFC 2052) and dynamic DNS updates (RFC 2136) to be fully compliant. If the DNS does not support SRV RRs, you cannot host a Windows 2000 domain. Dynamic updates do not have to be supported, but they can significantly cut down on the administrative burden of registering data manually. If the DNS does not and will not support dynamic updates, you will have to make sure that every client is configured not to use dynamic updates by changing the registry. You also will have to make sure that you have an infrastructure in place to facilitate a rapid response to DNS registrations. Remember that every new server requires data to be added to the DNS, and this will have to be manually entered into the zone unless dynamic updates are turned on. You'll have to do some testing to make sure that not only will Windows 2000 and the third-party DNS work together, but also that the DNS team has the correct infrastructure in place in order to support the environment and number of updates that you'll require with Windows 2000.

Preparing for a Domain Upgrade

There are three important steps in preparing for a domain upgrade:

1. Test the upgrade on an isolated network segment set aside for testing.

2. Do a full backup of the SAM and all core data prior to the actual upgrade.

3. Set up a fallback position in case of problems.

I cannot stress strongly enough how enlightening doing initial testing on a separate network segment can be. It can show a wide variety of upgrade problems, show you areas that you never considered, and in cases in which you have considered everything, give you the confidence that your trial run did exactly what you expected. In the world of today's complex systems, some organizations still try to roll out operating system upgrades and patches without full testing; this is just plain daft. The first part of your plan should be for a test of your upgrade plans.

When you do the domain upgrade itself, it should go without saying that you should have full backups of the Windows NT SAM and the data on the servers. You would think this is obvious, but again I have seen a number of organizations attempt this without doing backups first.

The best fallback position is to have an ace up your sleeve, and in Windows NT upgrade terms that means you need a copy of the SAM somewhere safe. While backup tapes are good for this, there are better solutions for rapid recovery of a domain. These recipes for success require keeping a PDC or a BDC of your domain safely somewhere. In this context, by *safely* I mean off the main network. Your first option is to take the PDC off the network. This effectively stores it safely in case anything serious goes wrong. Next, as your domain now has no PDC, you need to promote a BDC to be the PDC for the domain. Once that has successfully promoted, and you've manipulated any other services that statically pointed at the old PDC, you can upgrade that new PDC with the knowledge that your old PDC is safe in case of problems. The second option is to make sure that an existing BDC is fully replicated and then take it offline and store it. Both solutions give you a fallback PDC in case of problems.

Forests and the Forest Root Domain

Remember that the first domain in a forest is a significant domain and cannot be deleted. That means you cannot create a test domain tree called *testdom.mycorp.com*, add a completely different noncontiguous tree called *mycorp.com* to the same forest, and subsequently remove *testdom.mycorp.com*. You have to make sure that the first domain that you ever upgrade is the major or root domain for the company. In Windows NT domain model terms, that means upgrading the master domains prior to the resource domains. The resource domains may end up being Organizational Units instead anyway now, unless political, cultural, or bandwidth reasons force you to want to keep them as domains.

Windows NT Domain Upgrades

Single Windows NT domains and complete trust domains can be upgraded with few problems. With a single domain, you have just one to convert, and with complete trust domains, every domain that you convert will still maintain a complete trust with all the others. However, when you upgrade master domains or multimaster domains, there are account and resource domains that need to be considered.[*] No matter how many master domains you have, the upgrade of these domains has to be done in a certain manner in order to preserve the trust relationships and functionality of the organization as a whole. I'll now explain the three broad ways to upgrade your master domain structure.

Let's assume that you have one or more single-master or multimaster domains that you wish to convert. Your first task will be to create the forest root domain. This

---

[*] See the "Windows NT Versus Windows 2000" section of Chapter 2 for more details on the four Windows NT domain models.

domain will act as your placeholder and allow you to join the rest of the domains to it. The forest root domain can be an entirely new domain that you set up, or you can make the first domain that you migrate the forest root domain.

Take a look at Figure 12-1, which shows a Windows NT multimaster domain. Each domain that holds resources trusts the domains that holds user accounts, allowing the users to log on to any of the resource domains and use the respective resources.

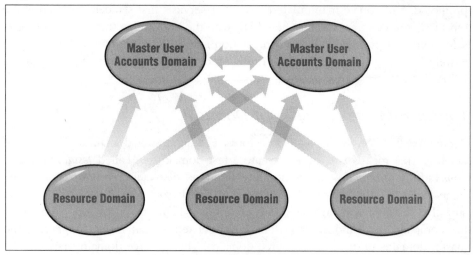

Figure 12-1. Windows NT multimaster domain prior to migration

There are three main ways to upgrade this domain. None of them is necessarily any better than the other, as each design would be based on choices that you made in your namespace design notes from Chapter 6.

Solution 1—Migration to a new forest root domain

First, the domains could all be joined as one tree under an entirely new root. Each master domain would represent a branch under the root with each resource domain joined to one of the masters. This is shown in Figure 12-2.

While it is conventional to think of the resource domains under the master domains, there is nothing to stop you from joining resource domains under resource domains if you like; it will make no difference for access to the resource domain's data.

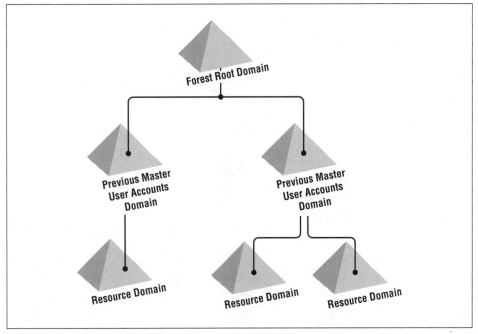

Figure 12-2. Migration to a new forest root domain

Solution 2—Migration with one domain as the domain-tree root

The second option is to aim toward making one of the master domains the root of the new tree. All resource domains then could join to either the root, one of the other master domains, or one of the resource domains. Figure 12-3 shows this in more detail. Two resource domains have been joined to one of the master domains, but the third resource domain can still go to one of three parents as indicated by the dashed lines.

Solution 3—Migration to separate domain trees in a forest

Finally, you could make each domain a separate tree. While the first master domain that you migrate will be the forest root domain, the rest of the master domains will simply be tree roots in their own right.

A Solution-Independent Migration Process

Let's now consider the process for migrating these domains. We must migrate the master account domains first, since they are the ones that the resource domains depend on. To start the process, convert any one of the master account domains over to Windows 2000 by upgrading the PDC of that master domain. If any of the trust relationships have been broken between this domain and the other master and resource domains during migration, reestablish them. Once the PDC is

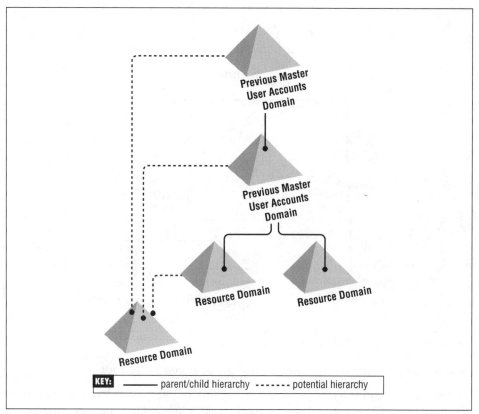

Figure 12-3. Migration with one domain as tree root

upgraded, then proceed to upgrade the other BDCs of that domain (or you can leave the domain running with Windows NT BDCs; it doesn't really matter to the rest of the migration).

The next step is to migrate the other master domains. You continue in the same manner as you did with the first domain until all master domains have been converted. Once each domain is converted, you need to re-establish only trust relationships with the existing Windows NT domains; the Windows 2000 domains in the forest will each have hierarchical and transitive trusts automatically anyway. So now you end up with a series of Windows 2000 master domains in a tree/forest and a series of Windows NT resource domains with manual trusts in place.

Once all the master domains are converted, you can start consolidating them (as discussed in the next section), or you can immediately convert the resource domains. Either way, once all domains are converted, you are likely to start a consolidation process in order to reduce the number of domains that you have in existence. Part of that consolidation will be to convert existing resource domains to Organizational Units. This is because resource domains by their very nature tend to fit in well as Organizational Units.* In order for that to happen, these future Organizational Units will need to be children of one of the migrated master or resource domains. It doesn't matter which master or resource domain acts as the parent, since there are consolidation tools available that allow you to move entire branches of the tree between domains. The process is simple: you take each resource domain in turn and convert it to a child domain of one of the existing Windows 2000 master or resource domains. Once they are all converted, you can really begin consolidation.

Consolidating Domains After the Move

Upgrading your domains is not the end of the story. Many administrators implemented multiple Windows NT domains to cope with the size constraints inherent in Windows NT domains. With Windows 2000, those constraints are lifted, and each domain in a forest can easily share resources with any other domain. This allows administrators to begin removing extraneous information from the directory that has become unnecessary in a Windows 2000 environment.

Mixed-mode and native-mode groups

When your final Windows NT 4.0 BDC for a domain has been taken out of service or upgraded, you are ready to convert the domain to native mode. After the conversion, you have some decisions to make about the groups you have in this domain. You can leave all groups as they are or start converting some or all groups to universal groups. With multiple domains in a single forest, you can consolidate groups from more than one domain together into one universal group. This allows you to combine resources and accounts from many domains into single groups.

There are two methods for bringing these groups online:

- Setting up parallel groups
- Moving existing groups

In a parallel group setup, the idea is that the administrator sets up groups that hold the same members as existing groups. In this way, users become members of both groups at the same time, and the old group and a user's membership can be removed in a calculated manner over time. The arguably easier solution is to move existing groups, but to do that you need to follow a series of steps. Take the following example, which leads you through what's involved.

---

* Resource domains were created because of Windows NT's inability to allow delegation of authority within a domain. Now Organizational Units provide that functionality, so separate resource domains are no longer required. Thus, old resource domains can become Organizational Units under Windows 2000 and still maintain all their functionality.

Three global groups—part_time_staff in *finance.windows.mycorp.com*, part_time_ staff in *mktg.windows.mycorp.com*, and part_time_staff in *sales.windows.mycorp. com*—need merging into one universal group, to be called part_time_staff in *windows.mycorp.com*. The following is the step-by-step procedure:

1. All part_time_staff global groups are converted to universal groups in their current domains.

2. To make the part_time_staff universal group names unique so that they can all exist in one domain, the group needs to be renamed with the domain element. That means finance\part_time_staff, mktg\part_time_staff, and sales\ part_time_staff become finance\finance_part_time_staff, mktg\mktg_part_ time_staff, and sales\sales_part_time_staff.

3. Then make use of the native-mode ability to move groups, and move the three groups to the *windows.mycorp.com* domain. This leaves you with windows\finance_part_time_staff, windows\mktg_part_time_staff, and windows\ sales_part_time_staff.

4. Now create a new universal group called part_time_staff in the *windows. mycorp.com* domain.

5. Finally, make the windows\finance_part_time_staff, windows\mktg_part_ time_staff, and windows\sales_part_time_staff groups members of the new windows\part_time_staff universal group.

You then can remove the three old groups as soon as it is convenient. Remember that, while this is an easy series of steps, there may be an entire infrastructure of scripts, servers, and applications relying on these groups. If that is the case, you will need either to perform the steps completely, modifying the infrastructure to look at the new single universal group after Step 5, or to modify the groups immediately after you complete Step 2 and then again after you complete Steps 3 to 5 in quick succession. I favor the former, since it requires that the work be done once, not twice.

 You should not underestimate the amount of work in analyzing what parts of the infrastructure make use of each group, planning the changes to that infrastructure, and ultimately implementing the changes. The preceding example was for one set of groups. If you have a significant number of groups, this is no small undertaking, and managers should be made aware of this fact.

Computers

When it comes to considering computer accounts, things are relatively straightforward. Under Windows NT, a computer could exist in only one domain at a time, since that computer and domain required a trust relationship to be established in order to allow domain users to log on to the domain at that client. You could set up bidirectional trust relationships manually between domains, allowing a client in Domain A to authenticate Domain B users to Domain B, but this was not common. With Windows 2000, all domains in a forest implicitly trust one another automatically. As long as the computer has a trust relationship with one domain, users from any other domain can log on to their domain via the client by default. The following is a rough list of items to consider:

- Moving computer accounts between domains to gain better control over delegation
- Joining computers to the domain
- Creating computer groups
- Defining system policies

In all of these, it is important to understand that the source domain does not have to be native mode in order to move computers to a new domain. In addition, administrators can use the NETDOM utility in the Windows 2000 Resource Kit[*] to add and remove domain computer objects/accounts; join a client to a domain, move a client between domains; verify, reset, and manage the trust relationship between domains; and so on.

While you may have had computer accounts in a series of domains before, you now can move these accounts anywhere you wish in the forest in order to aid your delegation of control. Group Policy Object processing also has a significant impact on where your computer accounts should reside. However, you now can work out what sort of Organizational Unit hierarchy you would ideally wish for your computer accounts and attempt to bring this about. Moving computers between domains is as simple as the following NETDOM command.

Here I want to move a workstation or member server, called *mycomputerorserver*, from the domain *sales.windows.mycorp.com* to the location LDAP://ou=computers, ou=finance, dc=windows, dc=mycorp, dc=com. I specifically want to use the *myDC* domain controller and the WINDOWS\JOINTODOMAIN account to do the move. Connection to the client will be done with the SALES\Administrator account, which uses an asterisk (*) in the password field to indicate to prompt for

---

[*] This may end up becoming the Enterprise Resource Kit after shipping.

the password. I could just as easily have used an account on the client itself. I also include a 60-second grace period before the client is automatically rebooted:

```
NETDOM MOVE mycomputerorserver /DOMAIN:windows.mycorp.com /OU:Finance/Computers
   /UserD:jointodomain /PasswordD:thepassword
   /Server:myDC
   /UserO:SALES\Administrator /PasswordO:*
   /REBOOT:60
```

This is actually the long-winded version, split up onto multiple lines for visibility; here's the short form:

```
NETDOM MOVE /D:windows.mycorp.com /OU:Finance/Computers /UD:jointodomain
   /PD:thepassword /S:myDC /UO:SALES\Administrator /PO:* /REB:60
```

Note that moving a Windows NT computer doesn't delete the original account, and moving a Windows 2000 computer just disables it in the source domain.

You also need to consider who will be able to add workstations to the domain. You can set up an account with join-domain privileges only, i.e., an account with the ability to make and break trust relationships for clients. I've used this approach myself with a lot of success, and it means that an administrator-equivalent user is no longer required for joining clients to a domain. Let's take the previous example, but this time we wish to both create an account and join a new computer to the domain with that account. This is the code to do that using NETDOM:

```
NETDOM JOIN mycomputerorserver /D:windows.mycorp.com /OU:Finance/Computers
   /UD:jointodomain /PD:thepassword /S:myDC /UO:SALES\Administrator /PO:* /REB:60
```

In all these NETDOM examples, I'm using a specially constructed account that only has privileges to add computer objects to this specific Organizational Unit. At Leicester we precreated all the computer accounts, and the jointodomain account was used only to establish trusts between existing accounts; it had no privilege to create accounts in any way.

You also need to be aware that workstation accounts under Windows NT could not go into groups. Under Windows 2000, that has all changed, and you can now add computers to groups. So when moving computers between domains for whatever purposes, you now can use hierarchical Organizational Unit structures to delegate administrative/join-domain control, as well as using groups to facilitate Group Policy Object (GPO) upgrades from system policies.

System policies themselves are not upgradable. However, as explained in Chapter 8, *Profiles and Group Policy Primer* and Chapter 9, *Designing Organization-Wide Policies*, you can use system policies with Windows 2000 clients and bring GPOs online slowly. In other words, you can keep your system policies going and then incrementally introduce the same functionality into GPOs. Since each part of each System Policy is included in the GPO, you can remove that functionality from the System Policy while still maintaining the policies application.

Ultimately, you will end up replacing all the functionality incrementally and the system policies will have no more policies left so can be deleted.

Users

When consolidating domains, you'll have a need at some point to move users around in order to better represent the organization's structure, to gain better control over delegation of administration, or for group policy reasons. Whichever of these it is, there are useful tools to help you move users between domains.

In order to be able to transfer users between domains, you need to have gone to native mode, and this will have ditched all your Windows NT BDCs. This allows a seamless transfer of the user object, including the password. A good method for transferring users and groups so that no problems occur is as follows:

1. The first stage is to transfer all the domain global groups that will be required to the destination domain. This maintains the links to all users within the source domain, even though the groups themselves have moved.

2. Now the users themselves are transferred to the destination domain. The domain global group memberships are now updated with the fact that the users have now joined the same domain.

3. You then can consolidate the domain global groups or move the domain global groups back out to the original domain again. This latter option is similar to Step 1, where you move the groups and preserve the existing links during the move.

4. Clean up the user's Access Control Lists to resources on local computers and servers, since they will need to be modified after the change.

If you do it this way, you may have fewer problems with group memberships during the transition. As for moving users: while you can use Active Directory Users and Computers MMC to move containers of objects from one domain to another, there are also two utilities—called MOVETREE and SIDWALK—in the Windows 2000 Resource Kit that can come in very handy.

MOVETREE allows you to move containers from one part of a tree in one domain to a tree in a completely different domain. For example, suppose I wish to move the branch of the tree under an Organizational Unit called Managers from the *sales.windows.mycorp.com* domain to the Organizational Unit called Sales-Managers on the *windows.mycorp.com* domain. The command I would use is something like the following to start the move, preceded by a full check:

```
MOVETREE /start /s sales.windows.mycorp.com /d windows.mycorp.com
  /sdn OU=Managers,DC=sales /ddn OU=Sales-Managers,DC=Windows
  /u SALES\Administrator /p thepassword
```

The SIDWALK utility is designed to support a three-stage approach to modifying ACLs. Each stage of changing ACLs can take a while to complete and verify, sometimes a day or more. It thus requires some amount of system resources and administrator time. The stages are:

Planning

> The administrator needs to determine what users have been granted access to resources (file shares, print shares, NTFS files, registry keys, and local group membership) on a particular computer.

Account mapping

> Based on who has access to what resources on the system, the administrator can chose to delete old, unused security identities, or replace them with corresponding new identities, such as new security groups.

Converting ACLs

> Using the information from the planning and mapping phases, the third stage is the conversion of security identities found anywhere on a system to corresponding new identities.

At the time of going to press, these utilities were not finalized, and still others were coming onto the scene.

Specifically, MOVETREE has been updated to make modifications to the SIDhistory attribute of security principals. A new set of "cloning" tools (e.g., ClonePrincipal) is to be made available to allow a user or group to be cloned from a Windows NT or Windows 2000 domain to a native-mode Windows 2000 domain *without* removing the source account.

Member servers and removing domains

After you've migrated, you may want to get rid of some old domains entirely, move member servers between domains, consolidate multiple servers together, or possibly even convert a member server to become a DC. Whatever you're considering, moving member servers and their data while maintaining group memberships and ACLs to resources can be done. Again, as with users and computers, taking the process in stages helps ensure that there is less chance of a problem.

If you're considering moving member servers between domains or removing domains in general, these are the steps that you need to consider:

1. Make sure that the source domain and the destination domain are in native mode.

2. Move all groups from the source domain to the target domain in order to preserve memberships.

3. Move the member servers to the destination domain.

4. Demote the DCs to member servers, removing the domain in the process.

5. Clean up the Access Control Lists to resources on local computers and servers, since they will need to be modified after the change.

Summary

This chapter focused on the principles behind the migration of existing Windows NT domains to Windows 2000. Microsoft has taken the time to properly think through a very scalable and stable directory service in its Active Directory implementation. It has in its own words "bet the barn on Windows 2000."

The next chapter takes a look at the potential for integrating Active Directory into a total directory service strategy.

13

Directory Interoperability

This chapter explains Microsoft's strategy for integration and interoperability; you can get some idea what you can do now and what you'll be able to do in the future. The chapter covers how to integrate other directory services, such as Novell Directory Services, Microsoft Exchange, and other X.500 directory services into your Windows 2000 network.

Microsoft has a number of initiatives underway to help you with integration and interoperability. To start with, many of the major Microsoft BackOffice products will soon start moving toward making Active Directory their primary storage medium for data. Some products will integrate to a larger extent than others. Take Exchange as the ultimate example. The Exchange Directory is the precursor to today's Active Directory, so if any component is likely to disappear, it's certainly the Exchange directory as it gets merged into Active Directory.

There is no real reason in the long term to want a set of valid user mailbox information in one LDAP-compliant database within Exchange if you can effectively mail-enable the data within Active Directory and thus store all the mail information as extended attributes of the individual users. Microsoft's successor to Exchange 5.5 is code-named Exchange Platinum. Under the new version, the Exchange directory is Active Directory; the Exchange user, contact, and group data is held as part of Active Directory. If you want to deploy Exchange, you will need Windows 2000's Active Directory in place to act as the backend directory service. This product is expected to ship around 90 days after the shipment of Windows 2000.

If you don't want to upgrade Exchange for a while and want to make use of Exchange 5.5 and Windows 2000, you can use the Windows 2000 Active Directory Connector (ADC). The ADC is a Windows 2000 service that can be used to regularly replicate data from the Exchange directory to Active Directory, from

Active Directory to the Exchange directory, or both. This enables you to keep your Windows 2000 and Exchange directories in synchronization without having to duplicate the effort of adding objects to both. It has been used very successfully at Leicester University for exactly these reasons. I'll go into the details of the ADC later in this section, since it is a very useful stopgap measure until Exchange 2000 is fully implemented by your business.

Exchange is the core part of BackOffice that integrates and is the easiest component to explain, because the LDAP-capable X.500-based Exchange directory service database was the original starting point for Active Directory. In the near future, though, you'll see a lot of other data integrated into Active Directory. Microsoft Site Server, which I expect to soon be renamed Microsoft E-commerce Server, will start integrating data into Active Directory. While Microsoft Systems Management Server 2.0 (SMS) stores its management data in a SQL Server database, moves are underway to start integrating the data that is automatically collected by SMS in Active Directory and keep the two in synchronization. If it is ultimately decided that the SMS database is to stay, then keeping synchronization will become the key aim. If the SMS data is to ultimately be stored in Active Directory, then the SMS database itself will ultimately die.

You also need to consider integrating with other operating systems and LDAP X.500-based directories. For example, there's NetWare and Unix to consider in the LAN server market. In the directory market, there is Netscape Commerce Server, ICL's I500 directory service, and so on. To enable you to coexist with these directory services, Microsoft is writing a number of tools collectively known as DirSync. As I write this chapter, NetWare DirSync already exists to enable Novell Directory Services (NDS) and Active Directory to coexist to some extent. While this tool is limited in scope at present, it does do the job it was made for very well. A more generalized version of the DirSync tool, known as General DirSync, is currently being developed. General DirSync will use LDAP and the X.500 standards to allow coexistence and bidirectional replication of information between disparate directories that support common standards.

Background to Interoperability with Other Directory Services

Microsoft's main thrust with Active Directory is to use it as a storehouse of a wide variety of data. When they set out on this route, they understood that organizations already had many application-specific repositories of data that held the same or similar information stored in a multitude of locations. Microsoft's idea was to create the *one* directory that would be powerful enough to hold all this information, yet still be fast enough for access to make it feasible to implement. This directory would hold all of the directory information required for network users, email, and white pages, coupled with extensibility in order to be able to include vendor-provided application-specific data. If this directory were to include so much disparate information, it also had to be easy to populate via integration with existing directories. That way, legacy directories could be migrated, and existing current directories could be made to interoperate with Active Directory.

The integration problems can be discussed in four main areas:

Data organization

Problems with data organization result because data may be stored in different hierarchies in different directories. If you have two directories that store data in different hierarchies, then you have to spend time working out how you will map objects and attributes in order to synchronize them.

Directory semantics

You also have issues with semantics that need to be overcome. You may update your Active Directory automatically from a user authorization database, such as an ERP system, but then this needs synchronizing with your email directory. You also may need to link in or include information from other directories or databases that you have, as well as to update various other catalogs or logs. In each case, you may be talking about small modules of work, but each one will probably require coding in a different way as the technologies to do each task differ.

Data integrity

Integrity is very important in directory services. When an object is deleted, you have to know it has been deleted and not left hanging around in some uncertain form. Integrity has to be maintained both within a directory and between directories. Within a directory, referential integrity between objects and attributes is paramount; between directories, you have to know that modifying an object at one location will force a ripple effect that cascades throughout the separate directories in order to synchronize the change.

Data ownership

Data ownership comes in two forms. If you have multiple directories hosting similar objects and attributes, each directory must know which attributes it is capable of updating itself and which objects it should passively receive from others. If two directories believe that they are in the dominant role for setting passwords, then conflicts can occur. The other form of ownership suggests that the applications that update the data should own the changes that they make. If a finance-user object is created and updated by an application, then that application should be responsible for properly cleaning up the relevant objects, attributes, and links in the directory relating to those objects.

Solutions for Interoperability with Other Directory Services

At the present time, I can see four major solutions to the preceding issues:

- Directory interface unification
- Directory synchronization
- Directory brokering
- Directory consolidation

Each of these relates to a direction that is being explored by Microsoft and other vendors and suppliers to help you move forward with migrating or integrating your directories. I'll consider each one in turn and then take one major example forward and explore it fully.

Directory Interface Unification

I speak throughout this book about the merits of Active Directory Services Interface (ADSI). Microsoft's technology has come a long way in the past two years and is now a robust and reliable suite of tools and technologies that enables scripters and developers alike to create and manage objects in a variety of directories. ADSI can be used to interface to Novell's Directory Services (NDS), Novell NetWare's bindery-based services, any other LDAP-compliant directory, and Windows NT, in addition to Active Directory. Novell also has started to produce two types of their own COM components as well: those that exist in place of ADSI and those that complement ADSI. Novell's entry to this arena signifies that it recognizes that this area of directory interfacing is an important one.

This common set of APIs allows you to simply and easily manage multiple directory services from your own suite of connectors or management applications. It doesn't matter whether Microsoft, Novell, or Netscape is providing general connectors or synchronization tools if you have the technology available to write applications that are customized to your environment. With ADSI and related technologies, it is simple and easy to maintain the authority and dominant relationships that I explained in the previous section.

Directory Synchronization

In Windows 2000's multimaster model, each DC synchronizes itself with its partner DCs using intrasite routes set up by the Knowledge Consistency Checker. The mechanism that replicates changes involves initiating a connection from the source to the target, identifying which objects and attributes the target requires, and then transferring the relevant data to the target DC. The mechanism for this entire process can be thought of as a connector. While this conceptual connector passes data between identical directories, actual connectors tend to pass data between directories that are structured in different ways.

All connectors have the following important features:

- They are directory-aware. Each connector understands how different object classes from one directory map to object classes from another directory.

- They have the capacity to schedule connectivity. There is no need for a connector that runs once to update the directory service; that is not very useful as a synchronization tool. What you actually want is a tool that can run according to a schedule you set and that can do object creations, deletions, and attribute changes.

- They are directional. Connectors can pass data unidirectionally or bidirectionally. A bidirectional connector by its very nature is actually a combination of two unidirectional connectors. A connector that is unidirectional from A to B has no need to know how to map objects and attributes from B to A; this functionality simply is not applicable to a unidirectional connector. So, a bidirectional connector requires twice the amount of knowledge.

- They are fast. In order to keep your directories in synchronization for the object-update levels that you have, the connector has to be able to keep up with the speed of changes that occur.

Bidirectional connectors used in a unidirectional manner are normally employed to keep an older directory in synchronization with a newer one, with all management and directory modifications being done on the newer directory. After the legacy directory is no longer required, it can be removed. Leicester University uses the Active Directory Connector (ADC) in a unidirectional mode, with the Windows 2000 directory as the source and the Exchange 5.5 directory as the target. The university uses the connector in this way to prepare for Exchange 2000, where the entire Exchange 2000, Directory will be held as extended attributes on objects that are part of Active Directory. In the meantime, to keep their Exchange 5.5 Directory in synchronization with the user objects in Active Directory, all Exchange 5.5 mailbox modifications such as quota limits are made on Windows 2000 and the ADC synchronizes the changes to Exchange 5.5. If not, the two directories will get out of synchronization, since the connector is not running bi-directionally.

The other connectors that Microsoft is exploring are collectively known as DirSync. These connectors are being developed under two headings at present:

- A General DirSync connector that enables connections with directory services

- A NetWare/NDS DirSync connector, also known as MS DirSync, that will replicate data to and from Novell's NDS

Both are still under heavy development at the time of writing. The General DirSync connector functionality may come as a single connector in its own right, it may be integrated with the existing ADC, or it may be integrated into other services that play specific roles. While it's difficult to say exactly what form the General DirSync connector will take, it's possible for me to briefly explain the thrusts of its intentions. For example, Netscape produces an LDAP-compliant directory service, and functionality will be provided to connect to that and replicate data bidirectionally. Release is intended for 90 days after launch of Windows 2000. Another example is Sun, which has a directory service product called NIS. A team is currently working on a product called Solar Coaster within Services for Unix that will allow connectivity. This is slated for release 60 days after Windows 2000's launch.

Finally, there are two forms of the MS DirSync connector on the horizon. The first will be the simpler connector of the two, as you would expect, intended to ship 60 days after launch of Windows 2000. The second currently has no release date. The big difference between the two is that the former is a unidirectional connector from Active Directory to NDS; the latter is a bidirectional connector.

The unidirectional connector is to include a number of features and restrictions:

- Replication of Organizational Unit, user, and group objects at the Organizational Unit level and below (i.e., not directly from a domain container) with the limitation that objects must have identical names on both systems. You also will be able to filter the contents that get replicated. However, you will not be able to select specific individual objects to replicate from a container. Instead, you will be able only to specify, for example, that all Finance Organizational Unit objects are replicated or use filters to replicate all users from the Finance Organizational Unit that match selection criteria.

- Password changes on Active Directory will be replicated as long as the password changes have occurred via one of two mechanisms: Active Directory Users and Computers MMC or users using the Ctrl-Alt-Del functionality of a Windows NT/2000 workstation.

- Administration via an MMC interface.

This feature list will grow over time as Microsoft extends the connector to full functionality.

Directory Brokering

The concept of brokering can be thought of as a middle tier of software that interfaces between the end-user applications and the directories themselves. This is the most complex of the four strategies to implement, since each piece of the software has to work with the whole so that each individual transaction updates each directory in an appropriate manner. The idea stems from the fact that you can actually implement business processes and rules as a set of modules, each of which individually understands a particular area of the business. Then you can bring these modules together within a single middle-tier structure to present a single interface to application developers who wish to access multiple and disparate directory services. The application developers need only to interface the applications to the modules and can leave the backend directory processing to the modules themselves.

As I said, this is the most complex of the four solutions, since it requires a team of experienced middle-tier-aware developers in order to develop not only the middle tier that interfaces to the directories but also the applications that interface with the middle tier. The benefits are worthwhile, though, because application developers can cut down on directory-specific code and get a single point of access to all directories. The benefits also come because the developed solution can encompass all types of data stores, not just directories. With this solution, you are looking more at information brokering than just directory brokering.

Microsoft's products in this area, such as Microsoft Transaction Server and Microsoft Message Queue Server, help toward producing the middle-tier software. Microsoft is also working with third-party vendors to enable Active Directory to be the store of all directory-related information. The two main vendors right now appear to be:

- Isocor and its MetaConnect software aim to allow interfacing with Active Directory. More information on Isocor and MetaConnect can be found on their web site at *http://www.isocor.com/products/Products.htm.*

- Zoomit with its VIA software was the recognized industry leader in directory interoperability and consolidation in 1999, when Microsoft purchased the company. The product is now available as Microsoft Metadirectory Services. More details can be found here: *http://www.microsoft.com/WINDOWS2000/guide/server/features/mms.asp.*

Directory Consolidation

Last comes the idea that it would be better to have one unified directory for all your main data. In Microsoft's eyes, this should be Active Directory due to the wide level of support, application interfaces, and connectors that it will be producing. Whether in time it does become the de facto standard directory is difficult to say, but it is unlikely to come away from the race as anything other than a significant player.

Obviously if you consolidate your directories together, you require no more synchronization with any other directories and can concentrate on using a single uniform access to your single-object organization. For this reality to come to pass, you will need support from all the application vendors that provide your organization's directory services. To this end, Microsoft has formed vendor partnerships to enable the vendors to Active Directory–enable their products. Two prominent examples of vendors that are working with Microsoft on this issue are Baan and Cisco.

The main contender for Active Directory is NDS. Therefore, Microsoft has asked Computer Associates to create a Directory Service Migration tool called DS Migrate for them. DS Migrate is used to migrate NDS accounts and files one way to Windows 2000 in a nondestructive and across-the-wire fashion. Users can be renamed during the migration, and files will maintain security access rights. However, at the time of writing, there are a number of limitations of which you need to be aware. DS Migrate does not migrate NDS login scripts or templates, schema extensions, MAC namespace files, or existing passwords. It also does not support migration for server-based NetWare Loadable Modules (NLMs), the Novell equivalent of NT services, or for client Novell/NetWare Application Launcher (NAL) application configurations.

Having now considered the four solutions, I'll delve deeply into one of Microsoft's main connectors to give you a detailed view of one implementation.

Exchange and the Active Directory Connector

The ADC is comprised of a service that does the work and an MMC console to manage the service. While the console can be installed on any client or server, the ADC service has to be installed onto a DC in order for it to work.

 In order to support connection to the ADC, you will need Microsoft Exchange 5.5 Service Pack 1 or above.

When you install the ADC for the first time in a forest, it modifies the schema to extend it to include new Exchange objects and attributes, as well as modifying existing Active Directory objects to include new Exchange-relevant attributes. The Exchange Schema also is modified if you intend to replicate Active Directory data to Exchange. For example, the User class object in the Active Directory Schema is directly modified to include three Exchange-relevant auxiliary classes in the

auxiliary-class attribute: `msExchMailStorage`, `msExchCustomAttributes`, and
`msExchCertificateInformation`. Auxiliary classes and Schema are discussed
more fully in Chapter 3, *Active Directory Schema*.

 Attributes on Exchange can be seen by using *ADMIN.EXE /r* to view
the directory in raw mode.

Once the Active Directory Schema is extended, Active Directory then can hold
mail attributes for groups, users, and contacts just as the Exchange directory can.
This means that the ADC now can replicate data bi-directionally, knowing that
either end can store the same data. This allows you to run the ADC in one of three
ways:

From Active Directory to Exchange
Every new creation of a user, distribution group, security group, or contact
object that is mail-enabled in a designated Organizational Unit will be copied
over to a designated Recipients container on Exchange. Every change to the
attributes of an existing mail-enabled object also will be passed. Deletions also
can be synchronized.

From Exchange to Active Directory
Every new creation of a user, mailing list, or contact object in Exchange auto-
matically creates a corresponding user account in a specified Organizational
Unit in Active Directory. Attribute changes also get passed, as do deletions.

Bidirectional replication
Changes at either end get replicated over to the other system.

If you choose to manage one-way replication, you must appreciate that you can
update the details only for those objects on the one-way source directory from that
time on. If you were to update the target directory, then the changes you made
could potentially be erased during the next update as the system realizes that the
target is no longer in synchronization with the source. To fully appreciate this and
see why bidirectional replication does not necessarily help you here, see the later
sections on "Mail-Enabling Objects via the GUI" and "Why Bidirectional Replication May Not Solve Your Problems."

There are other implications that need to be understood for these scenarios. When
passing information from Active Directory to Exchange, for example, you must
designate a set of specific Organizational Units that will contain the objects to be
replicated. Any Organizational Units that you do not list will never have objects
replicated, even if they are mail-enabled objects.

Once the ADC is installed, Active Directory Users and Computers MMC have three extra property pages available to it. Two of these pages are visible only if you choose the Advanced option from the View menu. One word of warning: in order to see the extra pages in Active Directory Users and Computers MMC on any server or workstation, you must have the ADC MMC installed onto that client first. Installing the MMC part of the ADC onto a client configures Active Directory User and Computers MMC with the extra snap-in options for these pages.

I'll now take a look at how to configure the ADC for your use and follow on with how to mail-enable a user using the GUI and ADSI.

Configuring the ADC

Once you've installed the ADC, you need to designate a DC to hold what's known as a connection agreement. This agreement is an Active Directory msExch-ConnectionAgreement object that will hold all of the information relating to the replication of the data you require. Specifically, when you set up an agreement, it adds an item to a part of the Configuration Naming Context with a path similar to this: cn=My Connection Agreement, cn=Active Directory Connections, cn=Microsoft Exchange, cn=Services, cn=Configuration, dc=windows, dc=mycorp, dc=com. The agreement stores all the data as attributes of the agreement object itself. Attributes hold information such as which direction replication will take place, when it will take place, what parts of Active Directory or Exchange actually hold the objects that you wish to replicate, and so on. For example, the attribute that holds Active Directory Organizational Units to replicate to Exchange is known as the msExchServer1ExportContainers attribute. Figure 13-1 shows a sample connection agreement running on a DC called *Mint* and connecting to an Exchange server called *Sumac*.

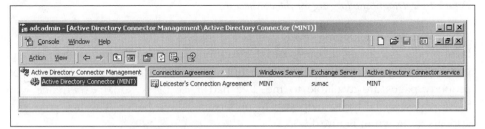

Figure 13-1. A connection agreement

 If you right-click the agreement in the display pane, then you can replicate the agreement immediately. You also can create new agreements from here as well.

If you have more than one Exchange site or multiple Windows 2000 domains that you wish to replicate to or from, you need more than one connection agreement. Similarly, if you have only one Exchange server, but you have a need to replicate differently for various parts of the service (e.g., the Finance Organizational Unit replicates once nightly to an Exchange container, the Sales Organizational Unit replicates hourly to an Exchange container, but the Marketing Exchange container replicates every 15 minutes back to Active Directory), then you will need more than one agreement in this case (three).

When you set a connector up and try to replicate objects and attributes back and forth, it's not surprising that there might be a few problems at first while you begin to understand how things work. To help with this, you can open up the properties of any connection agreement and specify a set of logging levels for various aspects of the agreement. Figure 13-2 shows these.

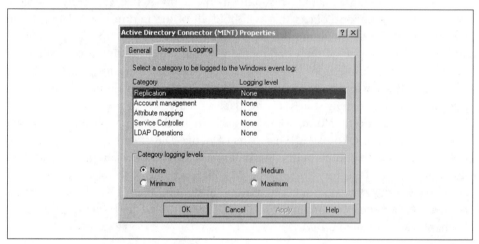

Figure 13-2. Diagnostic logging for the connector

When you select a logging level, events are logged to the event log. The highest level produces copious amounts of information and so is very useful when debugging. When I go to create a new connection agreement from the ADC MMC, seven property pages are available to me. I've had a lot of personal experience with these pages, so I'll try to help you to understand them better. The first page that appears is shown in Figure 13-3.

During the beta testing cycle, these screens have changed a number of times, and I wouldn't be surprised to find them changing again during the rest of the beta cycle and after the initial shipment of the full product.

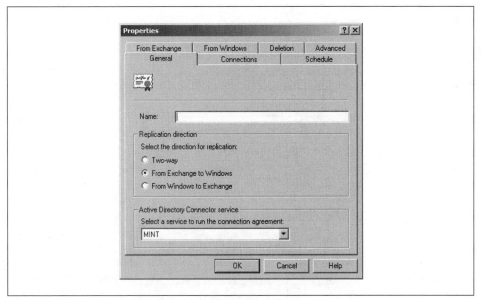

Figure 13-3. Properties of a new connection agreement

The agreement needs a name, which is what the screen is prompting for. The agreement is currently unidirectional from Exchange to Active Directory, and the ADC service is running on the DC called *Mint* at present. Depending on the replication direction that you choose, the From Windows and From Exchange tabs will be modified. Having typed in my name, I then need to tell the ADC what server is hosting the Exchange services and what server is hosting the ADC service. I do that from Figure 13-4 which is the Connections property page.

Here *Mint*, a DC in the domain CFS, is using Windows Challenge/Response authentication and connecting to the Exchange server *Sumac*, also in the CFS domain, as the Administrator user from the CFS domain. Any account can be used for connection; I've just chosen the standard account here for my test domain. The only requirement is that the account has full privilege in both directions in order to be able to replicate and update the required databases. Once this page is completed, I need to consider when I want the agreement to run. I do this from the Schedule property page shown Figure 13-5.

Figure 13-5 appears to show that I can specify the replication interval in 15-minute or hourly cycles. In fact, this isn't the case. While this screen allows you to see a weekly replication cycle in 15-minute or hourly slots, replication will occur once during every 15-minute slot. Figure 13-5 shows a replication schedule from 8 A.M. to 10 P.M. This means that replication will occur every 15 minutes between 8 A.M. and 10 P.M., i.e., 56 times. If I want the replication to occur once an hour, my only recourse is to switch to a 15-minute view and highlight the 15-minute time period

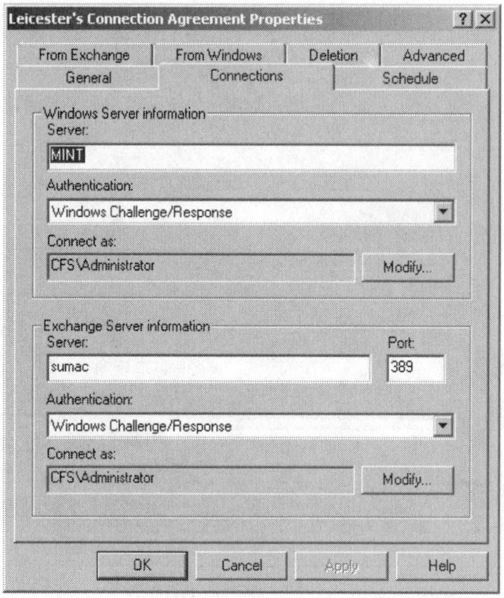

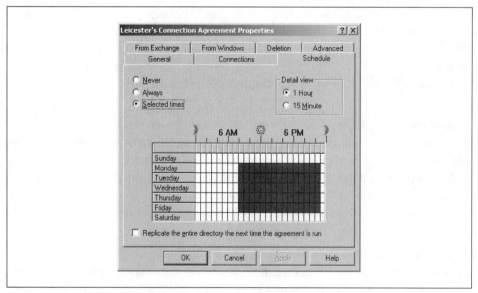

Figure 13-4. Connections property page

Figure 13-5. Schedule property page

when I want replication to take place. For example, I could switch to the 15 minute view and choose 08:45–09:00, 09:45–10:00, 10:45–11:00, and so on, making sure that no other 15-minute slots were enabled.

While I have chosen to replicate at the selected times on this screen, there are two other options available. The first is to never replicate the agreement. If you ever need to stop replicating this agreement, this is where you come to disable replication. The option called Always forces the agreement to constantly replicate with almost no breathing space. Almost as soon as the agreement has finished replicating, it starts the replication cycle over again. It is unlikely to be replicating a significant amount of data each time the agreement replicates, as there will have been so little time since the previous cycle. However, one or both databases will still be scanned to see whether any updates have occurred since last time, so it is important to realize that turning this on will produce a performance hit, however small. Only you will know how much traffic is likely to be replicated between the two databases for your organization, so testing is the only way to see if there is a problem with turning this setting to Always.

The last checkbox is very useful in fully updating one database or another, and I used it most during testing of the ADC. If you choose to replicate the entire directory, then every object in the target is fully updated by every object in the source. But hang on, you may be thinking, if all the items are replicated, what's the point in replicating the whole lot again? Consider that you're setting up the ADC on a new site, replicating from Exchange to Active Directory, and want to make sure that everything works correctly when the data is replicated to Active Directory. To that end, you decide to test-replicate a number of the Exchange Recipients containers to one Active Directory test Organizational Unit. Replication goes well the first time, but you want to do some more tests. You empty the test Organizational Unit of users in Active Directory and then open up the agreement to replicate the entire directory the next time replication takes place. You then can go back to the main agreement, Figure 13-1, and right-click the agreement to select Replicate Now. Then every object is immediately replicated again, just as if this were the first time that the agreement had ever been replicated.

Figure 13-6 shows the property page detailing the settings for replication from Exchange as the source to Active Directory as the target. You can specify for this agreement, mailboxes, custom recipients, and distribution lists will be copied from a series of Recipients containers to a single Organizational Unit in Active Directory.

Remember that you can have only one target for either direction of a connection agreement. If you want to replicate distribution lists from the Recipients container(s) to a specific Organizational Unit, custom recipients from the Recipients container(s) to another Organizational Unit, and mailboxes to a third Organizational Unit, then you need three agreements. Each agreement would replicate one type of source object from multiple recipient containers to a single target Organizational Unit.

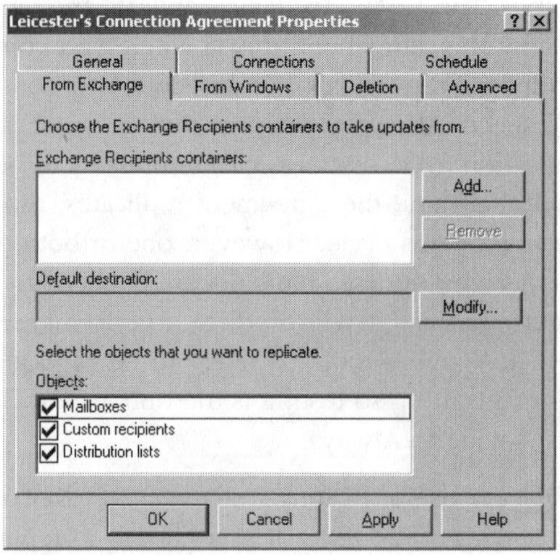

Figure 13-6. From Exchange property page

The property page relating to replication in the direction from Active Directory to Exchange is very similar, as shown in Figure 13-7. Here, instead, you specify multiple Organizational Units going to a single Recipients container. Again users, contacts, and groups can be specified as being copied during replication. In Figure 13-7, only users are being copied.

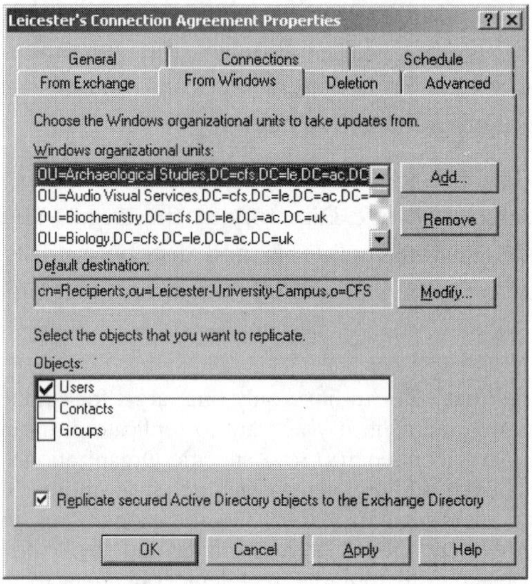

Figure 13-7. From Windows property page

The checkbox at the bottom of the screen is used to indicate whether you wish to use or ignore the Access Control Lists that are defined on user, contact, and group objects to filter the items that get replicated. While items that are not mailbox-enabled are never copied, neither are items whose ACL indicates that they should be filtered out if this checkbox is cleared.

Figure 13-8 indicates what should happen when you replicate through a deletion in either direction. When an Active Directory user is deleted, his mailbox can be removed immediately. Alternatively, the information can be stored in a Comma-Separated-Value (CSV) file for later action using the Bulk Import command in the Exchange Administrator or via a script. If you choose the CSV option, the system sets the Hide Mailbox flag on the object and writes information to a file in this location: *ADC Path\Connection Agreement Name\LocalToRemote\lra.csv.*

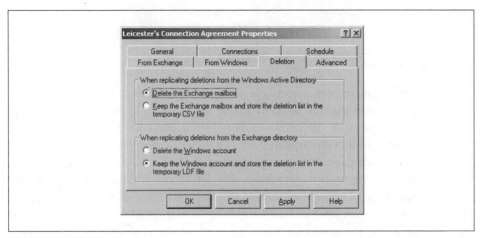

Figure 13-8. Deletion property page

The converse also is true. When an Exchange mailbox is deleted, Active Directory user also can be immediately deleted or the information kept in a CSV for later action. In the latter case, the system sets the Mail-Enabled attribute to False and records the deletion information into this file: *ADC Path\Connection Agreement Name\RemoteToLocal\lra.csv.* If you want to later delete the users using this CSV file, the file has to first be converted to an LDAP Data Interchange File Format (LDF), using the LDIF Directory Synchronization Bulk Import/Export tool found on a DC: *%systemroot%\system32\ldifde.exe.* The option that you choose really depends on your own environment and whether you wish to keep users that have no mailbox or mailboxes that have no corresponding user for a time period to comply with internal regulations.

The last property page, Advanced, shown in Figure 13-9, is really a selection of items that don't fit anywhere else.

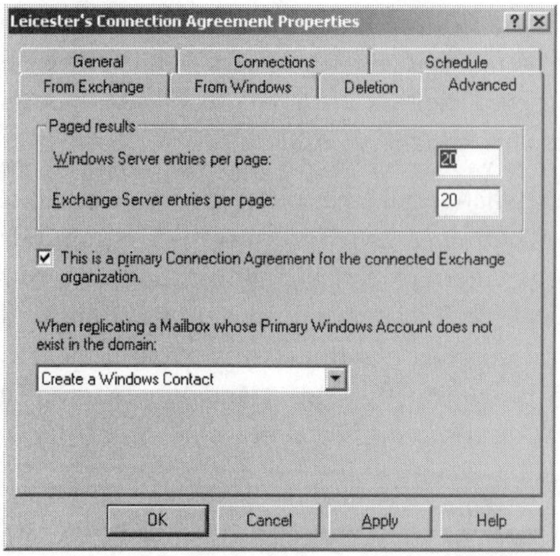

Figure 13-9. Advanced property page

There are certain times when so many changes have been made and need replicating in a single run that the memory needed to store and send them is too large for the DC to cope with. To combat this before it becomes a problem, the ADC can page results, so that the updates are placed on pages, each holding a certain set of updates. Each page is sent to Exchange; then the system waits for the page to complete updating before continuing. This slows down the process slightly but is much less likely to impede or cripple any systems. The Advanced page allows you to specify the number of entries that you wish to hold for each direction. In normal operations, there shouldn't be any need to alter these values. However, if you do have a lot of memory and believe that your system can cope with hundreds or thousands of updates in one go, then you can modify these values.

The simple Primary Connection Agreement checkbox tucked away here belies its importance. A primary connection agreement is one that can create objects in a target directory service; a secondary connection agreement can update only existing objects in a directory service. Here this agreement is a primary agreement, so it has full authority. I can create a number of secondary agreements on other DCs if I wish to enable fault tolerance and load balancing.

Finally, when a mailbox is replicated without an associated user, the system allows one of three options. A windows contact can be created, a disabled user can be created, or a fully specified user can be created and enabled. This covers the fact that certain mailboxes may be placeholders for external contacts that do not have associated user accounts and the ADC needs to know what you want to do with these sorts of replicated items.

The limitations of the ADC are that it is not possible from looking at the set of multiple agreements to see which agreements go in which direction and which containers are copied over in each direction. I think it would have been more useful to have a second tool that acts almost as a map, which says that agreement A replicates mailboxes only from these Active Directory Organizational Units to this Exchange container, and agreement B is bi-directional and replicates all objects in this single Exchange container to this Active Directory Organizational Unit, and vice versa. For complex Active Directory and Exchange organizations that will be slowly adopting Active Directory and Exchange 2000/Platinum, this would have been a useful addition. The only way to do this at present is to somehow incorporate this information into the name of the agreement. That's the only gripe I have, and compared to the usefulness of the tool, it's a very small one indeed.

*Mail-Enabling Objects via the GUI**

Now that the ADC is installed and configured, and the schemas have been modified, you can run up Active Directory Users and Computers tool on any client that has Active Directory Connector Management MMC installed on it and see extra property pages relating to the Exchange attributes of users. You will need to enable Advanced view from the View menu of the MMC in order to see all three pages.

 The extra property pages are not visible from a client that does not have Active Directory Connector Management MMC installed on it.

Figure 13-10 shows the Exchange General tab, the first of the three new property pages available to you. It allows you to configure various options that you used to need the Exchange Administrator program to do directly. Figure 13-11 allows you to set new email addresses in any of the available types that Exchange supports.

Figure 13-12 allows you to configure the less used and more advanced settings.

If we now went back to the Exchange General property page and clicked on the Storage Limits button, the screen shown in Figure 13-13 appears. I'm not going to go through every option in this manner, but Figure 13-3 serves to highlight an example of when you can get into problems.

Any Exchange mailbox can have a set of three custom limits for the private information store, the user's own mailbox. The Exchange service as a whole also can

---

* An example of mail-enabling objects using ADSI can be found in Chapter 16, *Users*.

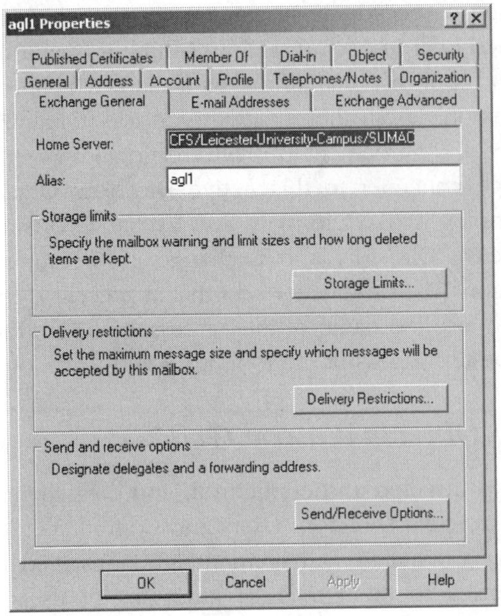

Figure 13-10. Exchange General property page

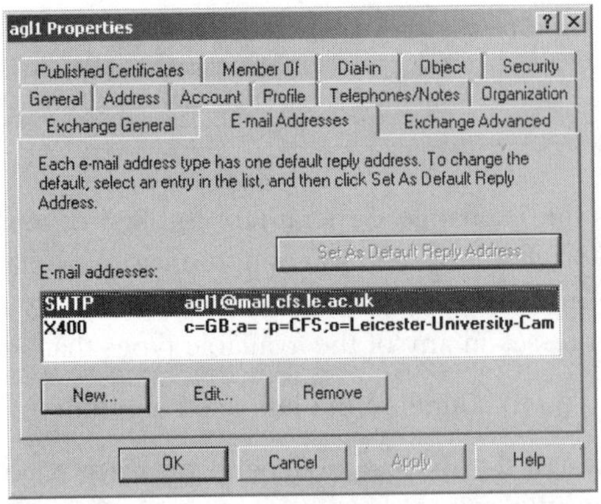

Figure 13-11. Exchange E-mail Addresses property page

have default limits defined; any users who have no custom limits defined get the defaults. These limits cause warnings to be issued to transgressors on a daily basis by default based on whether certain conditions have been met. In addition, as soon as the user exceeds the Prohibit Send limit, he can send mail no more. When he reaches the Prohibit Receive limit, he cannot receive mail any more, and all fur-

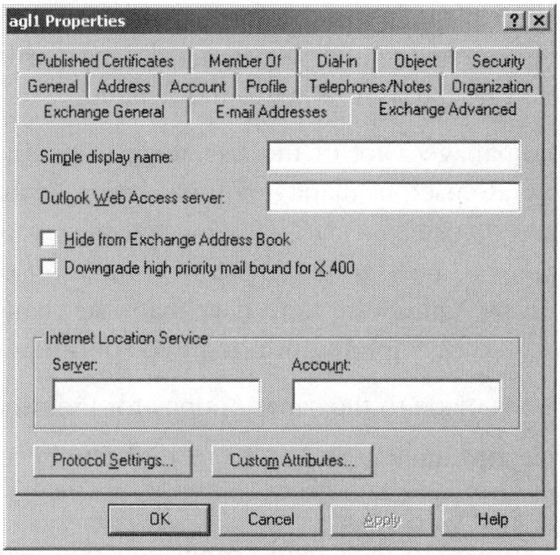

Figure 13-12. Exchange Advanced property page

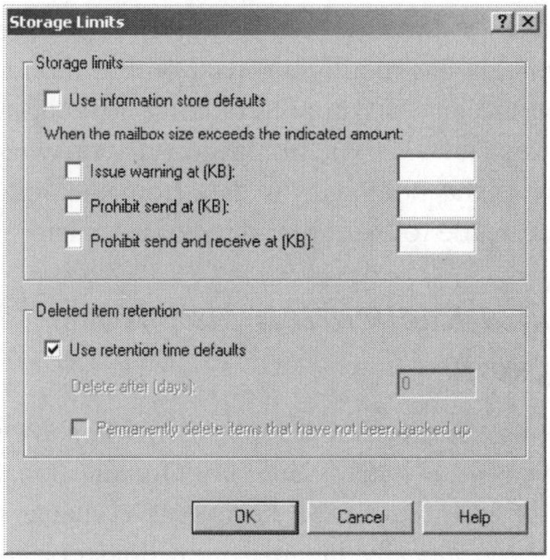

Figure 13-13. Storage Limits options

ther mail to that mailbox is returned to sender. Figure 13-13 shows that for this particular Active Directory user, the "Use information store defaults" checkbox is not checked but cleared. This means that this user is not using the Exchange information store default limits and instead will use the values indicated on the form. But hang on; there are no values on the form. None of the next three checkboxes been set. This means that you've told the Exchange system not to use its default limits and not to set any custom limits for this user either. In other words, the user has no limits defined for his mailbox. On the second part of the form, you can see that the Deleted Item Retention time, how long the system keeps messages after they have been deleted by the user, is set to the defaults.

It is now possible to manage a lot of the Exchange user functionality from these property pages. If you are used to managing this data on Exchange, and your ADC connection agreement(s) state that data is being transferred one way from Active Directory to Exchange, you need to get into a new mind-set of managing the data on Active Directory now. Otherwise, any data that you change on the Exchange server has the potential to be wiped out during two specific replication cycles:

- When any change is made to the same options for the user in Active Directory
- When the connection agreement is told to replicate all data during the next replication cycle

Of course, this also applies to data being replicated one way from Exchange to Active Directory.

If you have an agreement that replicates only one way (Active Directory to Exchange or Exchange to Active Directory), you should not modify the data on the replication target directory directly. This is very bad practice and liable to cause problems. Instead, you should modify the data on the replication source directory and let the data replicate across naturally or force a replication. This ensures the data in both directories stays in synchronization. If you were to modify only the target directory, there is the potential for data from the source directory to over-write any changes you made to the target directory at a later point in time.

Why Bidirectional Replication May Not Solve Your Problems

While you may think that bi-directional replication will solve the problems, in fact, it probably won't unless your Active Directory Organizational Unit structure tends to mirror the setup of your Exchange Recipients containers. While bidirectional replication appears to specifically link up individual objects in Active Directory with objects in the Exchange directory—so that whenever a change is made in one, the corresponding change is made in the other—isn't exactly true. In fact, as shown earlier, to replicate from Active Directory to Exchange, you have to designate one or more Organizational Units in Active Directory as the source and only one Recipient container in Exchange as the target. Then the data can be replicated from Active Directory objects in the source Organizational Units to the target container in Exchange. If you wish to have data going from Exchange to Active Directory, then you have to specify one or more Recipient containers in the Exchange directory as the source and one Organizational Unit in Active Directory as the target. The point is that you do not have a one-to-one mapping of the containers; you have a many-to-one mapping.

So no matter which direction one-way replication takes place, with only one target in either connection agreement I have the following problem best shown as an example. Let's say that I have Test as the only Organizational Unit in the one-way connection agreement as the source and a Recipients container as the target. If I want Exchange modifications to replicate back to Active Directory, then with a one-to-one mapping existing between containers in the agreement, I can simply set the agreement up bi-directionally. But what would happen if I add a second Organizational Unit to the one-way agreement, called Finance. Now a Test user's data gets replicated over to Exchange as before. But when you want any changes to that user's Exchange mailbox replicated back and set the agreement up bidirectionally, you have to tell the system that the single Recipients container that receives updates from Test and Finance now has to replicate its data back to one and only one Organizational Unit. This is a severe problem.

The only solution is to mirror the Organizational Unit structure that you use in your connection agreement with the same structure of Recipients folders in Exchange. I would need to set up two Exchange recipients containers that represented Test users and Finance users and then set up multiple one-to-one connection agreements in order to get proper bi-directional replication.

Obviously when Exchange 2000 comes along and uses Active Directory as its directory service rather than its own Exchange directory service, there will be no need to worry about the ADC and replication of data any more.

A Word About Windows 2000 and Unix

Microsoft released Services For Unix (SFU) version 1.0 for Windows NT at the beginning of 1999. SFU consists of a number of licensed third-party technologies that have been brought together with some of Microsoft's own functionality in an attempt to provide a complete package for Unix and Windows integration and interoperation. Windows 2000 will use and support version 2.0 of SFU, which is due early in 2000.

SFU version 1.0 functionality operates in four main areas:

- SFU allows Unix workstations to connect to Windows NT servers and vice versa. NFS server and client technology on the Windows NT machines achieves this. This code has been licensed from Intergraph.

- SFU supports a ksh (Korn Shell) environment within NT along with 25 other basic Unix commands. This technology, licensed from MKS, allows a full shell-scripting environment from Windows NT.

- SFU supports a fully featured Windows NT Telnet server and client, rather than the very basic ones that have been available in the past.

- SFU supports one-way password synchronization from Windows NT to Unix.

It's the last one that's important in the context of Active Directory. If you have one or more Unix workstations or servers, you can integrate the Unix account databases (*passwd/shadow passwd* and SAM) together. This allows you to remove any requirement to manage the Unix account database from a password point of view, at least if you use these services. To use this concept within SFU requires the account names to be identical across the two systems. If the account names are identical, any password changes on the NT/2000 systems are automatically transferred over to the corresponding Unix systems that have been linked up via SFU.

While integration in this manner is limited, it is a useful way forward. However, this isn't the only area to consider when integrating Unix and Windows 2000.

Windows 2000 uses Kerberos Version 5.0, an Internet standard, for its security and authentication. Unix has supported Kerberos for years, and it is likely that many organizations will already be supporting Kerberos for efficient and secure Unix security. If you don't use Kerberos security for Windows NT, now would be a good time to do an analysis of such a project. Because Windows 2000 provides valid Kerberos ticketing servers, implement Kerberos on the Unix machines that will integrate with the existing ticketing infrastructure hosted by Windows 2000. If you are already using Kerberos on Unix in your organization, you can ease management of these services by integrating the two sets of ticketing servers or removing one set to consolidate the management of the security infrastructure.

Summary

Microsoft would like everyone to use Active Directory as the one true directory service; just as Novell and Netscape/Sun/iPlanet would like you to use theirs. Microsoft is providing users with as much functionality as possible around the core directory service to enable network managers to make strategic recommendations on how to allow their current set of directories to integrate and interoperate. Creating and publishing ADSI allows all organizations to utilize the same interfaces that Microsoft has used to provide directory functionality. If an organization has one or more directories, administrators can come up with their own personal strategy for developing connectors, middle-tier brokering solutions, or tools for consolidation as required.

Active Directory will become widely adopted over the next few years; Microsoft has used its ability to work well with vendors in order to provide extra functionality that will make sure having Active Directory on your site is more than just having any directory service. Microsoft makes it simple to introduce the complexity of Active Directory into your organization and give you a benefit by empowering you to leverage this functionality to re-evaluate your core directory service strategy.

III

Scripting the Active Directory with ADSI

In the networks of today, companies can have tens of thousands of users on hundreds of servers in an organization that spans many sites. This is going to be especially true with Windows 2000 and the Active Directory. Managing complex systems like this can take a lot of time, and setting up the mechanisms to effect sensible management can be cumbersome. Migrating to the new system and deploying multiple client builds also requires a lot of preparation.

Windows 2000 provides the administrator with a variety of tools to manage the system. Unfortunately, they are no good for a variety of tasks that you may need to do en masse. No one in his right mind creates thousands of user accounts using User Manager for Domains under NT 4.0, for example, and this holds true under Windows 2000 as well. There is no need to manage users using only the Active Directory Users and Computers tool; you also can manage and manipulate the Active Directory objects using scripts, and very powerful scripts at that. You can write scripts to manipulate any object and its properties, and you can interface these scripts to web pages, allowing administration through a browser interface.

Before I start, I will state categorically that scripting the Active Directory is easy. You don't have to know complex code algorithms, pointer structures, object class inheritance, or any of the weird world of complex program languages. Here I'm using Microsoft's VBScript language, a very simple language both to use and to understand. You should have no problem coming to this section with zero knowledge and being able to understand and implement the concepts behind the chapters in the section.

- Chapter 14, *Scripting with ADSI*, introduces ADSI scripting by
  leading you through a step-by-step example involving groups.

- Chapter 15, *IADs and the Property Cache*, delves into the concept of the property cache used extensively by ADSI and shows you how to properly manipulate any attribute of any object within it.

- Chapter 16, *Users*, gives you the lowdown on how to rapidly create users, giving them whatever attributes you desire. I also show you how to create an Exchange mailbox programmatically at the same time you create a user.

- Chapter 17, *Manipulating Persistent and Dynamic Objects*, explains how other persistent objects such as services, shares, and printers may be manipulated, as well as looks at dynamic objects, like print jobs, user sessions, and resources.

- Chapter 18, *Permissions and Auditing*, describes how each object contains its own list of permissions and auditing entries that govern how it can be accessed and how that access is logged. The chapter then details how you can create and manipulate the entire lists or individual entries as you choose.

- Chapter 19, *Extending the Schema and the GUI*, covers how you can create new classes and attributes programmatically in the schema, and also how you can modify the existing Active Directory GUI tools that ship with Windows 2000.

- Chapter 20, *Enhancing ADSI via an ASP or VB Interface*, goes into how you can extend the scripts that have been written up to now by incorporating them into web pages or even converting them into simple VB programs.

- Chapter 21, *Scripting Fast Searches Using ADO*, demonstrates how to make use of a technology normally reserved for databases and now extended to allow rapid searching for any property of any object in the entire Active Directory.

14

Scripting with ADSI

This chapter covers the basics of VBScript, WSH, HTML, ASP, and ADO/RDS so that you can get a handle on how to write scripts even if you have no prior knowledge of VBScript. If you're coming from experience with another language, you'll be able to update your knowledge to include the basics of VBScript. I also include references to various web pages holding further information and free documentation, so that you can read around the subject or get more in-depth information should you need it.

What Are All These Buzzwords?

First, let's take a look at some of the underlying technologies. I'll see if I can help you to understand what they are and how they work.

ActiveX

ActiveX, the root or base component of a number of these technologies, enables software components to interact with one another in a networked environment, regardless of the language in which they were created. Think of ActiveX as the method developers can use to specify objects that the rest of us can then create and access with our scripts in whatever language we choose. Microsoft currently provides three hosts that run scripts to manipulate ActiveX objects: the Internet Information Server (IIS) web server, the Internet Explorer (IE) web browser, and the Windows Scripting Host (WSH). IIS allows scripts called from HTML pages to run on the host server where IIS resides; and IE runs scripts called from HTML pages on the client. WSH allows scripts to run directly on whichever host computer is running WSH without the need to wrap them into web pages first. WSH is an integral part of Windows 2000 and Windows 98 and is available to Windows NT 4.0 users through the free Option Pack.

Windows Scripting Host (WSH)

WSH is an important technology for a number of reasons:

- No new software needs to be bought or obtained to use scripting.

- It supports scripts without the need for web pages, which means that anyone can quickly write a script in the scripting language and execute it on Windows 98, Windows NT, or Windows 2000 without needing to know HTML.

- There is no requirement to learn a new development environment when you use WSH; your favorite text editor will do.

- WSH executes any script with a VBS or JS extension just by double-clicking the icon; those extensions are preloaded in the operating system when WSH installs.

- You can actually execute scripts from the command line, directing window output to that command line. This is possible because WSH has two interpreters, one called *WSCRIPT.EXE*, which interprets scripts in the 32-bit Windows environment and one called *CSCRIPT.EXE*, which interprets scripts in the command-line environment of a command-prompt window. By default, if you double-click a script called *MYSCRIPT.VBS*, the system passes that script to *WSCRIPT.EXE*, just as if you had manually typed: *WSCRIPT.EXE MYSCRIPT.VBS*. The default interpreter can be changed generally or on a per-script basis along with other settings.

- WSH comes with a series of procedures that allow you to script interactions with the host machine. There are procedures for running programs, reading from and writing to the registry, creating and deleting files and shortcuts, manipulating the contents of files, reading and writing environment variables, mapping and removing drives, and adding, removing, and setting default printers. These procedures are native to WSH, meaning that only scripts executing under WSH can access them. Being able to access these settings is very useful when configuring users' environments, since you can now write logon scripts using VBScript or JScript if you wish.

 WSH comes with Windows 2000 and Windows 98 but can be downloaded from *http://msdn.microsoft.com/isapi/gomscom.asp?TARGET=/ msdownload/vbscript/scripting.asp* and installed on Windows 95 and Windows NT 4.0 servers and workstations.

Active Server Pages (ASPs)

When VBScripts are wrapped inside HTML pages, they're called Active Server Pages (ASPs), because they can contain dynamic content. This means that the results of the web page displayed to the user will differ depending on the results of a script incorporated as part of that web page. Imagine a web server connected to a database. You can write ASPs to contain server-side scripts that query the database and return the information to the user. You also can include client-side scripts to gather information from the user to pass with the query. You can create an ASP in which a user fills in various settings for how he wants results of various database searches to be displayed; the client-side script then stores this information locally on the user's disk in one or more files known as *cookies*. Then by reading the cookie, you can display the results of the database query the way the user wants.

Active Directory Services Interface (ADSI)

In February 1997, Microsoft released a free set of generic interfaces, called the ADSI Software Development Kit (SDK), to access and manipulate different directory services. ADSI is a special series of procedures that allows developers using almost any language to access and manipulate objects on a server or in a directory service. Contrary to its name, it was written to be generic and extensible rather than specific to one operating system or directory. This means that developers can write code to access a variety of objects on various directories without the need to know vendor-specific library routines. ADSI is also extensible so developers of other directory services can write the underlying Dynamic Link Library (DLL) code that will allow ADSI to interact with their systems as well. This is possible because Microsoft publishes the exact specifications that a *Directory Service Provider* (a directory service to be supported by ADSI) must meet in order to work correctly with ADSI. This means that whenever you call an ADSI procedure or reference any object via ADSI against a valid provider, you can guarantee that the procedure will perform according to ADSI's formal documentation no matter who the provider is. While directory service provider-specific extensions are fine, ADSI supports the Lightweight Directory Access Protocol (LDAP) natively, and that changes everything.

LDAP is a network protocol that proposes a mechanism for accessing directory services over TCP/IP stacks and is becoming the de facto standard for directory service access on the Internet. A service provider simply has to support LDAP 2.0 or later, and ADSI can instantly access the directory service without a provider-specific DLL. Allowing access via LDAP means that the list of directory services that can be accessed is very large and includes the following:

- Windows 2000's Active Directory

- Microsoft Exchange Server

- Windows NT 4.0 and NT 3.51 systems

- NetWare 3.x's bindery-based system

- NetWare and IntraNetware 4.x's and 5.x's Novell Directory Service (NDS)

- Netscape Commerce Server

- Netscape Directory Server 1.0

- IBM Lotus Notes

- The objects and hierarchy stored in Microsoft's Web Based Enterprise Management (WBEM) implementation as the "WMI registry"

- Microsoft's Internet Information Server (IIS) objects

- Microsoft Commercial Internet System's (MCIS's) Address Book Server

- Microsoft Site Server

In June 1999, Microsoft released ADSI 2.5, which is included with Windows 2000. This release is a major leap forward because of its extra interfaces, bug fixes, and much improved documentation. In these chapters, use ADSI 2.5 for the examples.

ActiveX Data Objects (ADO)

In the same way that ADSI is a general set of interfaces for access to any directory service provider, ActiveX Data Objects (ADO) is a general technology that allows developers to write scripts and applications to access and manipulate data held in a database server. In order for a database server to work with ADO, the database server must be an *OLE DB Provider* so that an *OLE DB Connector* can be supplied to allow searching. If database server designers wish their database server to work with ADO, they must develop an OLE DB provider interface for their database server. Having an OLE DB connector for a database server means that the database server supports the ADO series of procedures and properties. This is relevant to Active Directory because Microsoft wrote an OLE DB Provider for ADSI. This allows developers to access Active Directory, or indeed any other directory service, via ADO using the ADSI OLE DB Connector. This provider effectively considers Active Directory a database to provide extremely fast and powerful searching capabilities. For example, using ADO you can search Active Directory for all computers whose names begin with *CF*, or all those users whose accounts are disabled and get back the ADsPath of each one. While it is possible to search and retrieve sets of records using standard ADSI calls, you would have to write your own set of routines to iterate through a directory service. When the developers of ADSI came to this requirement, they developed a provider so that the database searching algorithms that already existed in ADO could be leveraged for use by ADSI.

There is, however, one important caveat for ADO use with ADSI: the ADO OLE DB connector is currently read-only, so many of the useful ADO methods for updating data aren't available yet. Until this situation changes, you can use ADO for searching and retrieving only.

Remote Data Service (RDS)

The last technology I want to discuss in conjunction with ADSI and ADO is the Remote Data Service (RDS). RDS allows a technique known as *data remoting*, in which data is retrieved on a client from a server, updated or manipulated on that client, and then returned to the server in a single round-trip. I will not be discussing it in this book because the ADSI provider is *read-only*. However, in your investigations into ADO, you will see it mentioned because ADO and RDS are the two components of a technology called Microsoft Data Access Components (MDAC). Once the provider becomes *read/write*, then you will be able not only to use the update procedures in ADO but also to use RDS.

There are currently a variety of other providers for ADO/RDS such as ODBC, Oracle, Ingres, and MS Index Server. The techniques that I supply here will adequately work when accessing any SQL Server (or other ODBC) database server. That's the benefit of learning a generic object model.

By the end of this chapter you will be aware of how to use VBScript, VB, JScript, and to a small extent VC++ to access Active Directory using the procedures in ADSI. You will be able to write VBScript that can execute directly from the desktop or a command-line window using WSH technology. In Chapter 20 I cover how to add VBScript code to HTML web pages so that ADSI scripts can execute when buttons are clicked, passing results of those scripts to fields on a web page or directly to the page itself. In Chapter 21, *Scripting Fast Searches Using ADO*, I go on to show you how to use ADO to search Active Directory and retrieve sets of records back according to the powerful search conditions that you impose. Other chapters will take this knowledge and extend it so that you can manipulate other aspects of Windows 2000, such as permissions and auditing (Chapter 18, *Permissions and Auditing*), and modifying the schema (Chapter 19, *Extending the Schema and the GUI*).

Further Information on All the Technologies

This is by no means an in-depth discussion of the various technologies. For more information, you should look at the Microsoft Developer Network (MSDN) library documentation, which contains all of the documentation on how to develop using Microsoft's products, including VBScript, JScript, ADO, ADSI, and so on. There are two main ways to get hold of the MSDN library: you can purchase an MSDN library subscription from Microsoft and get quarterly CDs with all of the documentation, or you can access the documentation directly via the Internet.

MSDN online can be found at *http://msdn.microsoft.com/library/default.htm*. The first time that you access the library, Microsoft will want to register who you are for their records, but after that access is immediate.

Once you enter the MSDN library from the CD-ROM or the Web, you will see a list of content on the lefthand side. The items that are appropriate to these ADSI chapters are listed in the next section:

MSDN Locations

*   Tools and Technologies

    Active Server Pages

    > This area contains a large amount of information on ASPs. In addition to a component and object reference, it also contains a scripting guide and code examples. See the other ASP location further down in the list as well.

*   Platform SDK → Data Access Services → Microsoft Data Access 2.5 SDK

    Microsoft ActiveX Data Objects (ADO)

    > This is the location that I go to in order to look up the methods and properties.

*   Platform SDK → Component Services

    COM

    > This is an in-depth section for anyone who is interested in finding out more about the Component Object Model.

*   Platform SDK → Networking Services → Active Directory

    Active Directory

    > This contains full documentation on ADSI, including two programmer's guides, one to straight ADSI and one to ADSI for Exchange, as well as the entire set of interface definitions and some interesting interfaces on how to do replication with code.

- Backgrounders → Component Object Model (COM)

  ActiveX Controls
  A brief background discussion on ActiveX controls, which some readers may find useful.

  Component Object Model
  More information on COM.

- Backgrounders → Database and Messaging Services → Data Access

  OLE DB/ADO: Making Universal Data Access A Reality
  A brief paper on ADO, which may provide useful background reading.

  Microsoft Strategy for Universal Data Access
  Another brief paper on MDAC and ADO.

- Backgrounders → Web Development

  Active Server Pages
  A series of background papers on ASPs.

- Partial Books

  Professional Active Server Pages (WROX Press)
  Chapters 5 through 8 of this book are on ASPs. The chapters contained here are not very relevant except for Chapter 5, which covers ADO.

  Web Scripting with VBScript (MIS:Press)
  Two chapters on using and building ActiveX controls in VBScript to give you a taste of the book. This book was published in 1996, yet the concepts are still valid for ActiveX controls.

- Conference Papers → PDC 97 Conference Papers

  Windows NT Active Directory
  A series of early papers on Active Directory. You definitely should read these.

- Conference Papers → PDC 96 Conference Papers

  Microsoft Open Directory Services Interface: Active Directory
  A series of papers from the 1996 Professional Developers Conference. These are very early papers; you can tell as ADSI was called ODSI then. However, they do give insights into the makeup of Active Directory and are worth reading.

Useful Internet Sites

Microsoft's main scripting web site
http://msdn.microsoft.com/scripting/default.htm

Microsoft's main ADSI web site
http://www.microsoft.com/adsi/

MSDN Library root
http://msdn.microsoft.com/library/default.htm

ADSI start page in MSDN library
*http://msdn.microsoft.com/isapi/msdnlib.idc?theURL=/library/sdkdoc/adsi/
adsistartpage_7wrp.htm*

ADSI interface reference start page
*http://msdn.microsoft.com/isapi/msdnlib.idc?theURL=/library/sdkdoc/adsi/ds2_
ref_2x45.htm*

VBScript docs can be found here
*http://msdn.microsoft.com/scripting/default.htm?/scripting/vbscript/techinfo/
vbsdocs.htm*

WSH docs here
*http://msdn.microsoft.com/scripting/default.htm?/scripting/windowshost/docs/
reference/default.htm*

Microsoft's universal data access components site (including the official pages for
ADO)
http://www.microsoft.com/data/

A fantastic site for developers of ASP, ADSI, and ADO pages and scripts (including a superb ADSI mailing list)
http://www.15seconds.com/

A great set of resources to the Windows Scripting Host (including a WSH mailing
list)
http://wsh.glazier.co.nz/

O'Reilly's Windows and VB sites detailing its resources and books
http://windows.oreilly.com/
http://vb.oreilly.com/

The VBScripts.com site
http://www.vbscripts.com/

Clarence Washington's arguably best repository for scripting solutions on the
Internet
http://cwashington.netreach.net/

Wrox publishes books on ADSI, ADO, VB, and WSH (I highly recommend Dino Esposito's book on WSH)

http://www.wrox.com/

Windows 2000 Magazine is published monthly as is the Win32 Scripting Journal, dedicated to helping people learn more about scripting for the Win32 platform

http://www.win2000mag.com/
http://www.win32scripting.com/

Writing and Running ADSI Scripts Under Windows 2000

The third part of this book is dedicated to a technology that allows you to gain access to Active Directory using scripts. It not only contains a series of useful scripts that you will be able to adapt for use in your organization but also contains all the information you will need on how you can write your own scripts to access Active Directory to do whatever you need. Let's take a quick look at scripts, so I can show you how easy it is to script Active Directory, even for a scripting novice.

A Brief Primer on COM and WSH

Windows 2000 comes with a standard technology called the Windows Scripting Host, more commonly known as WSH, that allows scripts to execute directly on the client. These scripts can access files on disks, attach to network resources, automate Word and Excel to create reports and graphs, automate Outlook to manipulate email and news, change values in the registry, and so on. The reason these scripts can be so versatile is that WSH supports scripting access to all Component Object Model (COM) objects installed on the client.

COM is a Microsoft standard that allows both Microsoft or anyone else to automate and manipulate virtually any operations you require by defining individual items to be operated on as *objects*. When someone needs to create such operations, he creates what is known as an *interface*, which can be thought of as the definition of the object and the entire set of operations that can be performed on that object. Interfaces normally are stored in Dynamic Link Library (DLL) files.*

So, for example, if you want to manipulate a file, you actually need to manipulate a file COM object. The file COM object definition will be stored in an interface held in a DLL. The interface also will hold all of the operations, such as creating

---

* There are other file types, such as OCX controls that define graphical forms and windows you can use in your scripts, but they aren't worth going into here.

the file, deleting the file, writing to the file, and so on. The interface will also allow modifications to a series of properties of the object, such as the filename and owner. Procedures that operate on an object are known as *methods*, whereas the properties of an object are known simply as *properties*.

In addition to methods and properties provided by interfaces, each scripting language that you use will have a series of defined *functions*, such as writing to the screen or adding two numbers together.

You can write scripts that execute using WSH and access any COM objects available to you using the methods and properties defined in the interface for that object as well as any functions in your chosen scripting language. By default, you can use Microsoft VBScript or Microsoft JScript (Microsoft's version of JavaScript). WSH is fully extensible, so other language vendors can provide installation routines that update WSH on a client to allow support for other languages. A good example is PerlScript, the scripting language provided by the authors of Perl.

How to Write Scripts

Scripts are simple to write. Example 14-1 is a very simple one in VBScript called *SIMPLE.VBS*.

Example 14-1. SIMPLE.VBS

```
MsgBox "Hi World!"
```

All you have to do is open up your favorite text editor and add the commands in, one per line. You then save the file with a specific filename extension, VBS for VBScript and JS for Jscript. Then you can double-click the script and it will run using WSH. Figure 14-1 shows the output of that script; a simple dialog box with a text string in it. The script uses the VBScript **MsgBox** function.

Figure 14-1. Output from a very simple script

Now let's take a look at a slightly more complex script called *SIMPLE ADSI.VBS* (Example 14-2). This script makes use of the Active Directory Service Interfaces (ADSI), a set of COM interfaces that allow you to access and manipulate Active Directory.

Example 14-2. SIMPLE ADSI.VBS

```
Dim adsUser 'A variable representing my user

Set adsUser = _
  GetObject("LDAP://cn=Richard Lang,ou=Pre-Sales,ou=Sales,dc=mycorp,dc=com")

MsgBox adsUser.Description

Set adsUser = Nothing
```

The first line is a variable declaration. I am declaring that **adsUser** is a name for the variable in which I am going to store some information. The **Dim** keyword is used to declare a variable, and the apostrophe (') indicates that everything following it is a comment that should not be executed.

The second line is too long to print on the page, so I have broken it into two with an underscore (_) continuation character at the end of the line. It tells WSH interpreter that it should read the next line as if it were joined to the end of the first. The entire line, ignoring the underscore, uses the **adsUser** variable to hold a reference to a user object via an ADsPath. It uses the VBScript **GetObject** function to do this.

The third line simply uses the VBScript **MsgBox** function again to print out the description of the Richard Lang user object. The dot signifies that I am accessing a property or method available to me from ADSI for the specific type of object I am accessing, which in this case is a user.

The last line simply discards the reference to Richard Lang, and **adsUser** becomes empty again. Strictly speaking, at the end of a script, the system discards all references anyway, but including it shows completeness.

So, printing out properties of objects in Active Directory isn't very hard at all.

WSH 1.0 and WSH 2.0

Windows 98 shipped with WSH Version 1.0. Windows 2000 ships with WSH Version 2.0, which is backward-compatible with WSH Version 1.0. WSH is also available as a download for Windows 95 and Windows NT. The scripts in the two previous examples are WSH 1.0 scripts. WSH 2.0 scripts support a lot more features, but they appear a little more complex as well. With WSH 2.0, the actual WSH code is embedded inside a set of Extended Markup Language (XML) sections that actually describe the script.

The *SIMPLE.VBS* example from before looks like Example 14-3 under WSH 2.0.

Example 14-3. SIMPLE.WSF

```
<job>
<script language="VBScript">

MsgBox "Hello World"

</script>
</job>
```

Note that the filename is not now language-specific and just uses a .WSF exten-sion. Instead, the XML defines that the file contains a single script (a job) and that the script to be run is written in VBScript. At its simplest, to write WSH 2.0 scripts instead of WSH 1.0 scripts, all you have to do is prefix your code with the first two lines and end your code with the last two lines. In Example 14-4, *SIMPLE ADSI. VBS* becomes *SIMPLE ADSI.WSF* in WSH 2.0.

Example 14-4. SIMPLE ADSI.WSF

```
<job>
<script language="VBScript">

Dim adsUser 'A variable representing my user

Set adsUser = _
  GetObject("LDAP://cn=Richard Lang,ou=Pre-Sales,ou=Sales,dc=mycorp,dc=com")

MsgBox adsUser.Description

Set adsUser = Nothing

</script>
</job>
```

I recommend that you use WSH 2.0 for all the scripts in this book. I also encour-age you to find out all about the other features of WSH 2.0, such as building up a library of your own operations that you can reference in each script without hav-ing to keep redefining them. For more information on WSH 2.0's advanced ways of running scripts by describing the data using XML tags, check out Dino Esposito's WSH book published by Wrox Press (*http://www.wrox.com*), or Bob Wells "WSH 2000" article in *Windows NT/2000 Magazine*. Bob Wells' articles can be found at *http://www.winntmag.com/Articles/Index.cfm*.

ADSI

Before you can start writing scripts that use ADSI, you first need to understand the basic Component Object Model (COM) concept of interfaces as well as ADSI's concepts of namespaces, programmatic identifiers (ProgIDs), and ADsPaths.

Objects and Interfaces

A COM interface is a way of accessing specific functionality of a defined item, known as an *object*. It provides an entire suite of management functionality for that object. VBScript has a *scripting* object you can use, and WSH has a number of objects available to access the shell, network, and so on. ADSI is a standard that provides specifications for interfaces that each provider uses to allow access to their directory services. Each ADSI interface normally provides two types of information:

• Methods

• Properties (and property methods)

A *method* is a procedure or function defined on an object, which interacts with the object. So an interface to access Windows 2000 Group objects would have an Add and Remove method, so that members could be added or removed from a group. Methods are normally represented as *Interface::MethodName* when referenced, and this is the form I adopt in this book. Objects also have properties that are retrieved using the IADs::Get method and replaced using the IADs::Put method.

Each ADSI object supports an IADs interface that provides six basic pieces of information about that object:

• Name

• ADsPath

• GUID

• Schema class of the object

• ADsPath to the schema class of the object

• ADsPath to the parent object

If I wanted to retrieve the GUID property of an object, I would use a line of code like this:

```
strGUID = adsObject.Get("GUID")
```

You can see that I am calling the IADs::Get method on the object called adsObject; the dot (.) signifies the user of a method. The IADs::Get method takes one parameter, the property to retrieve, which in this case is the GUID, and passes it out to a variable that I have called strGUID. So that you do not have to use the IADs::Get method for the most common properties; certain interfaces define these common properties with *property methods*. In these specific cases, you use the dotted method notation to retrieve the property by using the property method of the same name. So in the previous GUID example, the GUID property has a property method of the same name (i.e., IADs::GUID). I could therefore retrieve the GUID with:

```
strGUID = adsObject.GUID
```

I don't want to go into the interfaces in any more depth here, I just want to give you a feel for the fact that methods and properties can be accessed on an object via ADSI interfaces. Although an object can support more than one interface without a problem, each object supports only the interfaces that are relevant to it. For example, the user object does not support the interface that works for groups. The other interfaces, of which there are around 40, begin with the prefix IADs. Interfaces can relate to many different types of objects, including objects that reside in directory services (e.g., IADsUser, IADsGroup), transient objects that don't exist in a directory service (e.g., IADsPrintJob), and objects that help ensure security (e.g., IADsOpenDSObject, IADsAccessControlList).

Because each directory service is slightly different, not every ADSI interface method and property works in every directory service. If you make a method call to a directory service that doesn't support that method, you'll receive a specific error message specifying that the provider doesn't support that method. This message is part of the ADSI specification. If a service provider supports ADSI, the provider must reject all inappropriate calls with the correct ADSI error message.

Namespaces, ProgIDs, and ADsPaths

To reference different types of servers (e.g., Windows NT 4.0, IntraNetWare, Exchange Server) with ADSI, use namespaces to distinguish between the different providers' directory services. ADSI uses a unique prefix called a *ProgID* to distinguish between these namespaces. Each ProgID is synonymous with a particular namespace.

In a script, you specify the ProgID to tell the ADSI method to which namespace you want to bind. For example, you specify WinNT:// to access individual Windows NT 3.51, Windows NT 4.0, or Windows 2000 systems while you use LDAP:// to access Active Directory itself. When ADSI encounters the ProgID, ADSI loads an appropriate ADSI-provider DLL to process the bind request.

ProgIDs are case-sensitive. `WinNT://` will work, whereas `WINNT://` will not.

Since each ProgID is synonymous with a particular namespace, the term ProgID normally is dropped. For example, individual Windows NT and Windows 2000 systems are accessed using the ProgID `WinNT:`. However, conventionally, this namespace is referred to as the *WinNT namespace* rather than the *WinNT ProgID*. This is the convention I adopt in this book.

Telling ADSI you want to bind via a particular namespace isn't enough. You also need to reference the object that you want to access in that namespace. A reference to an object via a namespace is an *ADsPath*. Each object has a unique ADs-Path. Take, for example, these WinNT namespace ADsPaths.

These two reference JoeB, a user in DOMAIN:

```
WinNT://DOMAIN/JoeB
WinNT://DOMAIN/JoeB, User
```

These two reference COMP12345, a computer in DOMAIN:

```
WinNT://DOMAIN/COMP12345
WinNT://DOMAIN/COMP12345, Computer
```

These two reference Users, a group in DOMAIN:

```
WinNT://DOMAIN/Users
WinNT://DOMAIN/Users, Group
```

This references JoeB, a user on computer MOOSE in DOMAIN:

```
WinNT://NT4DOMAIN/MOOSE/JoeB
```

This references JoeB, a user on computer MOOSE in WORKGROUP:

```
WinNT://WORKGROUP/MOOSE/JoeB
```

This references JoeB, a user on computer MOOSE:

```
WinNT://MOOSE/JoeB
```

As these examples show, you can reference each object by using only its name or, more properly, by using its name and type if two or three identically named objects with different types exist.

Each namespace has a unique format for the ADsPath string, so you need to make sure that you're using the correct ADsPath notation. For example, each of these ADsPaths reference a unique object.

This one references JoeB, a user in DOMAIN:

```
WinNT://DOMAIN/JoeB, User
```

This next one references JoeB, a user in the Finance Organizational Unit (OU) within the Mycorp organization of the IntraNetWare tree called MyNetWareTree:

```
NDS://MyNetWareTree/O=MYCORP/OU=FINANCE/CN=JoeB
```

This one references JoeB, a NetWare 3.x or 4.x (bindery services) user that exists on server MYSERVER:

```
NWCOMPAT://MYSERVER/JoeB
```

Finally, this one references the WWW service component of IIS running on the local host:

```
IIS://localhost/w3svc/1
```

In the preceding example, NDS: refers to IntraNetWare 5.x and 4.x. (Because intraNetWare 5.x is LDAP-compliant, you also can use LDAP paths with it.) NWCOMPAT: refers to NetWare 4.x, 3.2, 3.12, and 3.11 servers in bindery-emulation mode. IIS: refers to metabase paths on a host running IIS 3.0 or later.

One of the most commonly used namespaces is the LDAP namespace. You can use LDAP with ADSI to access a variety of directory services, including Windows 2000's Active Directory. Although you can use the WinNT namespace to access Active Directory, you need to use the LDAP namespace to fully utilize all of ADSI's methods and properties. Throughout this series, I'll primarily use the LDAP namespace.

You can use several formats to refer to LDAP directories. For example, all the following ADsPaths reference the Administrator object within the Users container of the *moose* directory server in the *mycorp.com* zone:

```
LDAP://cn=administrator,cn=users,dc=mycorp,dc=com
LDAP://moose.mycorp.com/cn=administrator,cn=users,dc=mycorp,dc=com
LDAP://moose/cn=administrator,cn=users,dc=mycorp,dc=com
LDAP://DC=com/DC=mycorp/CN=Users/CN=Administrator
LDAP://moose.mycorp.com/DC=com/DC=mycorp/CN=Users/CN=Administrator
```

In these examples, CN stands for common name and DC stands for domain controller. These examples show that you can specify the LDAP namespace ADsPath going down or up the hierarchical Directory Information Tree (DIT). You also can specify a fully qualified Domain Name System (DNS) server name after LDAP://, using a forward slash character (/) to separate the DNS server name from the rest of the path.

If a name includes some unusual characters, such as a forward slash or a comma, you can use double quotation marks ("/") or a single backslash (\) to specify that the character is to be interpreted as part of the ADsPath itself. For example, if you have a user called AC/DC on the server, then this is wrong:

```
LDAP://cn=ac/dc,cn=users,dc=windows,dc=mycorp,dc=com
```

This will interpret the path using **cn=ac** followed by **dc** followed by **cn=users** and so on. As **dc** on its own is not a valid part of the path, the ADsPath is invalid. Here are the correct paths:

```
LDAP://cn=ac\/dc,cn=users,dc=windows,dc=mycorp,dc=com
LDAP://"cn=ac/dc",cn=users,dc=windows,dc=mycorp,dc=com
```

Obviously, as the backslash is a special character, to use it in a name, you would need to do the following for an object called **cn=hot\cold**:

```
LDAP://cn=hot\\cold,cn=users,dc=windows,dc=mycorp,dc=com
LDAP://"cn=hot\cold",cn=users,dc=windows,dc=mycorp,dc=com
```

The first specifies that the following character is to be interpreted as part of the name, and the latter says to specify that the whole first name is a valid string.[*]

When to Use the LDAP and WinNT Namespaces

Contrary to popular belief, just because the WinNT namespace is used to access Windows NT servers, does not mean it is of little use to us here with Windows 2000. Actually, while the LDAP namespace is used to access Active Directory, the WinNT namespace is used to access users, groups, and other objects on individual computers. Active Directory only exists on DCs in your enterprise. If you have a server or a client that is a member of a workgroup or a domain running Windows NT or Windows 2000, that machine also will have objects on it. These could be local users, such as Administrator or Guest, printers, shares, and so on. Obviously, these objects are not part of Active Directory if they are unique to the machine. As individual machines do not support direct access via LDAP, you have to use another method, and that method is the WinNT namespace.

Security and Authentication

Now that you know how to use ADsPaths to distinguish between different namespaces, I'll demonstrate how to establish a connection to the server containing the directory you want to access. Authenticating a connection isn't always

---

[*] Unfortunately, the latter, while valid, will not work with VBScript's GetObject function due to the extra quotation marks ("/").

necessary; some directories, such as Windows 2000's Active Directory, allow read-only access to certain parts of the data from an anonymous connection. However, if you want to update information or access a restricted object or property in the directory, you may need to authenticate first. If authentication is not done, the default account's credentials are used.

If you don't want to specifically authenticate

If you just want to bind using the current account's credentials (also known as an *anonymous connection*) to a directory server to get a reference to an object, you use VBScript's `GetObject` function:[*]

```
Dim strPath        'path to the directory server
Dim adsMyObject    'root object of the directory

strPath = "LDAP://dc=windows,dc=mycorp,dc=com"

Set adsMyDomain = GetObject(strPath)
```

You begin by declaring two variables with VBScript `Dim` statements.[†] The first variable, `strPath`, is an ADsPath. The prefix `str` specifies that this ADsPath is a text string; I don't have to include it, but I tend to in order to make things easier to read. The second variable, `adsMyDomain`, is a pointer to the object in the directory that the path represents. The prefix `ads` specifies that the variable is an ADSI object. I use the prefix `ads` for all the ADSI objects in my scripts; however, you also can use other prefixes, such as `o` and `obj`. See the sidebar for more details.

Next, you assign the `strPath` variable to the path of the directory server you want to bind to, in this case, `"LDAP://dc=windows,dc=mycorp,dc=com"`. You need to enclose this path in quotation marks, because it's a text string.

Finally, you use VBScript's `Set` statement with the `GetObject` method to create a reference between the variable you declared and the existing object you want to interact with. In this case, you're creating a reference between `adsMyObject` and the existing object that the ADsPath `"LDAP://dc=windows,dc=mycorp,dc=com"` represents (i.e., the root object of the LDAP-enabled directory). After you've established this reference, you can use other interfaces to interact with that object.

---

[*] Visual Basic and JScript also have the `GetObject` function.

[†] For more information about `Dim` and other VBScript statements, Bob Wells' Scripting column from *Windows NT Magazine* can help. Bob has a variety of articles published on VBScript and WSH, including his excellent Scripting 101 series. You can find them all at *http://www.winntmag.com/Magazine/Author. cfm?AuthorID=101&Action=Author*.

Variable Prefix Conventions

You can use whatever name you like for a variable. However, the consensus is to use a prefix with a descriptive name. The prefix, which represents the type of data, typically contains one lowercase character or three lowercase characters. Commonly used three-character prefixes include:

- `str` = String
- `int` = Integer
- `bol` = Boolean
- `obj` = Object
- `ads` = ADSI object
- `app` = Application object
- `wsh` = WSH object
- `arr` = Array
- `ado` = ADO object
- `fso` = Folder system object
- `fil` = File object
- `fol` = Folder object
- `lgn` = Long integer
- `sgl` = Single precision value
- `dbl` = Double precision value

In the descriptive name, you capitalize the first letter of each word but don't put hyphens between words. Typically, variable names are case-insensitive. For example, you can name a string variable `strMyPassword`.

If you want to authenticate

To authenticate to a directory server, you use the `IADsOpenDSObject` interface, which contains only one method: `OpenDSObject`. `IADsOpenDSObject::OpenDSObject` takes four arguments:

- The ADsPath to authenticate to
- The username
- The password
- A security setting

The following listing shows how to use `IADsOpenDSObject::OpenDSObject` to authenticate to a directory server. You begin by declaring three string variables (`strPath`, `strUsername`, and `strPassword`) and two object variables (`adsNamespaceLDAP` and `adsMyObject`):

```
Dim strPath            'path to authenticate to in the directory service
Dim strUsername        'DN of the username
Dim strPassword        'plain text password
Dim adsNamespaceLDAP   'ADSI namespace object
Dim adsMyObject        'root object of the directory

strPath = "LDAP://dc=windows,dc=mycorp,dc=com"
strUsername = "cn=Administrator,cn=Users,dc=windows,dc=mycorp,dc=com"
strPassword = "the password goes here in plain text"

Set adsNamespaceLDAP = GetObject("LDAP:")
Set adsMyObject = adsNamespaceLDAP.OpenDSObject(strPath,strUsername,strPassword,0)
```

You then assign the `strPath`, `strUsername`, and `strPassword` variables the appropriate ADsPath, username, and password strings. The username string, which is also called the Distinguished Name (DN), references the username's exact location in the directory.

The `strPath` is used to authenticate to a specific point in Active Directory if you wish. This is used if the user authenticating does not have permission to work at the root, and has to authenticate further down the hierarchy.

Next, you use a `Set` statement with `GetObject` to create a reference for the variable called `adsNamespaceLDAP`. Notice that you're using `"LDAP:"` rather than `strPath` as an argument to `GetObject`. Using the LDAP namespace might seem unusual, but it is necessary so that, in the next line, you can call the `IADsOpenDSObject::OpenDSObject` method on the LDAP namespace that ADSI returns. The last `IADsOpenDSObject::OpenDSObject` argument is the security setting. This setting is typically 0, which denotes that the script will use neither encryption nor secure authentication.

Other values can also be used, such as:

- `ADS_SECURE_AUTHENTICATION`

- `ADS_USE_ENCRYPTION`

- `ADS_READONLY_SERVER`

These are just defined constants so that you do not have to remember the exact values for the fourth argument. You use them by adding them together—i.e., (`ADS_SECURE_AUTHENTICATION` + `ADS_USE_ENCRYPTION`) as they are only integer values. The entire set of values from the `ADS_AUTHENTICATION_ENUM` enumerated type can be found under the following MSDN location: Platform SDK →

Networking Services → Active Directory → Active Directory Service Interfaces Version 2.5 → ADSI Reference → ADSI Enumerations → ADS_AUTHENTICATION_ENUM. This equates currently to the following URL: *http://msdn.microsoft.com/isapi/msdnlib.idc?theURL=/library/sdkdoc/adsi/ds2_enum_760d.htm.*

> I should emphasize the importance of using encryption. If encryption is not used, anyone using a network sniffer like NetMon on the network might be able to see the information being passed including the name and password specified in the `IADsOpenDSObject::OpenDSObject` call.

Obviously, including an administrator's password in a script can compromise security. If you don't want to include plain-text passwords, you have several options. The first option is to assign a value to `strPassword` from the VBScript `InputBox` function. The following listing shows this:

```
Dim strPath              'path to authenticate to in the directory service
Dim strUsername          'DN of the username
Dim strPassword          'plain-text password
Dim adsNamespaceLDAP     'ADSI namespace object
Dim adsMyObject          'root object of the directory

strPath = "LDAP://dc=windows,dc=mycorp,dc=com"
strUsername = "cn=Administrator,cn=Users,dc=windows,dc=mycorp,dc=com"
strPassword = InputBox("Enter the Administrator password","Password entry box")

Set adsNamespaceLDAP = GetObject("LDAP:")
Set adsMyObject = adsNamespaceLDAP.OpenDSObject(strPath,strUsername,strPassword,0)
```

When you run the script, the `InputBox` prompts you to enter the administrator's password. However, the `InputBox` echoes the password in plain text into the password entry box, so this approach isn't too secure.

Three other options are secure. However, because VBScript doesn't natively support password retrieval boxes, you can't use these solutions without some work:

- One solution requires that you obtain a custom ActiveX component for VBScript to extend WSH's functionality that natively supports password dialog boxes. A link to one such ActiveX control by Dino Esposito can be found at *http://www.wrox.com/consumer/store/Download.asp?ISBN=1861002653.*

- The second solution is to write a script in a language other than VBScript that supports password boxes natively. For example, you use the Perl/Tk extension modules for ActiveState Perl and standard Perl to create an Entry widget with the -show parameter as an asterisk. For the Perl aficionados, this Entry widget would look like this:

```
$dlg->Entry(qw/-show * -width 35/)->pack(); # arbitrary width
```

- The third solution requires that you write the script from within Active Server Pages (ASP). You use the password field in an ASP form to retrieve the password.

If you want to authenticate a connection but already have logged on to the directory, you can use the default credentials for your existing connection. You simply use the VBScript vbNullString constant in both the username and password fields, as the following listing shows:

```
Dim strPath           'path to authenticate to in the directory service
Dim adsNamespaceLDAP  'ADSI namespace object
Dim adsMyObject       'root object of the directory

strPath = "LDAP://dc=windows,dc=mycorp,dc=com"

Set adsNamespaceLDAP = GetObject("LDAP:")
Set adsMyObject = adsNamespaceLDAP.OpenDSObject(strPath, vbNullString, _
   vbNullString,0)
```

 Note the use of the underscore (_) character on the second to last line. This tells VBScript that I have split this line with the next, but it should treat them as one long line. You can use multiple underscores to concatenate multiple lines together in this manner.

From now on, most of the scripts will use GetObject, but you can just as easily use IADsOpenDSObject::OpenDSObject if you need to without modifying any of the other code.

Simple Manipulation of ADSI Objects

Let's now take a look at simple manipulation of Windows 2000 Active Directory objects. While I am using Active Directory as the primary target for these VBScript scripts, the concepts are the same for any supported ADSI namespace and automation language. All the scripts use GetObject, assuming that you are logged in already with an administrator-equivalent account to the domain tree; if you aren't, you need to use IADsOpenDSObject::OpenDSObject.

The easiest way to show how to manipulate objects with ADSI is through a series of real-world examples, the sort of simple tasks that form the building blocks of everyday scripting. To that end, imagine that I want to perform the following tasks on my Windows 2000 *windows.mycorp.com* Active Directory tree:

1. Create an Organizational Unit called Sales under the domain root

2. Create a group called Managers in the Sales Organizational Unit

3. Create two users, Sue Peace and Keith Cooper, in the default Users container

4. Add both users to the Sales group

5. Remove both users from the group

6. Delete the group

7. Delete the Organizational Unit

In addition to those seven simple operations, I also would like to be able to perform the following two bonus tasks at various points during the script:

- Test membership of both users in the group

- List all members of the group

These are specific tasks for which there are corresponding methods, which is why I have included them in the list. This list of tasks is a great introduction to how ADSI works because you need to reference most of the major interfaces using these examples. Let's get started with the tasks.

Creating the OU

The creation process for the Sales Organizational Unit is the same as for any object. First you need to get a pointer to the container in which you want to create the object. You do that using this line of code:

```
Set adsContainer=GetObject("LDAP://dc=windows,dc=mycorp,dc=com")
```

This uses VBScript's `GetObject` function to create a pointer to the root of the domain tree.

 While VBScript and VB have the `GetObject` function, VC++ has no such built-in function. ADSI provides the `adsGetObject` function for use by those languages that need it.

This location in the tree is a container of other objects, rather than a leaf object; you can use the `IADsContainer` interface methods and properties on it. One of these is called `IADsContainer::Create`, and it works like this:

```
Set adsSalesOU = adsContainer.Create("organizationalUnit","ou=Sales")
```

Here you pass two arguments to `IADsContainer::Create`: the schema class name of the class of object you wish to create and the Relative Distinguished Name (RDN) of the object itself. Use the `ou=` prefix because the type of object is an Organizational Unit.

The IADsContainer interface enables you to create, delete, and manage other Active Directory objects directly from any container. Think of it as the interface that allows you to manage the directory hierarchy. A second interface called IADs goes hand in hand with IADsContainer, but while IADsContainer works only on containers, IADs will work on any object.

To create the object, you now have to execute this line of code:

```
adsSalesOU.SetInfo
```

ADSI implements a system in which the object to be created and its properties first are written to an area of memory called the *property cache* on the client executing the script. Each object has a property cache all its own, and each cache has to be explicitly written out to Active Directory using `IADs::SetInfo` in order for any creations or modifications to get physically written to Active Directory. This may sound counterintuitive but in fact makes sense for a number of reasons, mostly involved with cutting network traffic.

Each object has a number of properties, some mandatory and some optional. Mandatory properties have to be defined during the creation of an object and serve to uniquely identify it from its other class members. If you need to create an object with a large number of mandatory properties, it makes sense to write them all into a cache first and then write them out in one operation rather than perform a sequence of single operations.

If you look at the previous script, you also will notice that all it asks you for is a name. In fact, the Organizational Unit class has a number of mandatory properties. The reason you don't see the others is because they have default values that are assigned and placed in the property cache by the system when you use the `IADsContainer::Create` method. The five mandatory properties are written out in one block using the single `IADs::SetInfo` call, which cuts down on network traffic.

While the Organizational Unit example has no other mandatory properties, other objects will. User objects, for example, require `sAMAccountName` to be set in the cache before they can be written out successfully. In addition, you can always choose to set any of the optional properties before you use `IADs::SetInfo`.

Putting the three lines together, we have our first simple script:

```
Set adsContainer = GetObject("LDAP://dc=windows,dc=mycorp,dc=com")
Set adsSalesOU = adsContainer.Create("organizationalUnit", "ou=Sales")
adsSalesOU.SetInfo
```

Creating the Group

You got a pointer to a container in the directory (which happened to be the root domain), and then you created a new Organizational Unit in that container by first writing that Organizational Unit to the property cache and then writing that cache out to Active Directory itself.

To move on to the second task, you need to create a group called Managers. You already know how to create an object, and you use the same `IADsContainer::Create` method again to do what is required:

```
Set adsGroup = adsSalesOU.Create("group", "cn=Managers")
adsGroup.Put "sAMAccountName", "Managers"
adsGroup.SetInfo
```

The `IADs::Put` method is used here to set the SAM Account Name, a mandatory requirement with no default value. The SAM Account Name is the name of the group (or user) as it would have appeared in previous versions of NT and is used to communicate with older servers. It is still required because Windows 2000 supports mixed-mode domains as well as native-mode domains. The previous versions of NT stored their user and group data in part of the registry called the Security Accounts Manager (SAM). The `sAMAccountName` property is the name used when communicating with previous versions of NT.

I ought to point out that you can put your `IADs::SetInfo` commands much later in the script if you wish to. As long as they go in the right order (i.e., objects are created in a hierarchical fashion), then this will work:

```
Set adsContainer = GetObject("LDAP://dc=windows,dc=mycorp,dc=com")
Set adsSalesOU = adsContainer.Create("organizationalUnit", "ou=Sales")

Set adsGroup = adsSalesOU.Create("group", "cn=Managers")
adsGroup.Put "sAMAccountName", "Managers"

adsSalesOU.SetInfo
adsGroup.SetInfo
```

This works because the property cache is being updated by the earlier statements and not the underlying directory service. As the system does not have to check the legality of the LDAP ADsPaths or the properties until the `IADs::SetInfo` statement is called, you could feasibly do all your cache writes later. There is no special benefit to doing scripts this way, and it can lead to confusion if you believe properties exist in the underlying service during later portions of the script when they don't. In addition, if you bunch up cache writes and the server crashes, none of your writes will have gone through, which I suppose you could see as a good thing. However, I will not be using this method in my scripts; I prefer to flush my cache as soon as I'm ready to do so. Bunching caches to write at the end of a script only encourages authors to neglect proper error checking and progress logging to a file from within scripts.

Creating the Users

Having created the Organizational Unit and group, you now need to create the two users in the Users container. The principle is the same as before; get a pointer to the parent container, call the `IADsContainer::Create`, set the mandatory properties that do not have default values, and then call `IADs::SetInfo`:

```
Set adsUsersContainer = GetObject("LDAP://cn=Users,dc=windows,dc=mycorp,dc=com")

Set adsUser1 = adsUsersContainer.Create("user", "cn=Sue Peace")
adsUser1.Put "sAMAccountName", "SueP"
adsUser1.SetInfo

Set adsUser2 = adsUsersContainer.Create("user", "cn=Keith Cooper")
adsUser2.Put "sAMAccountName", "KeithC"
adsUser2.SetInfo
```

There are three pieces of information relating to a user that must be unique: the `cn`, the `sAMAccountName`, and the `userPrincipalName`. The `sAMAccountName`, also known as the *downlevel logon name* when using the GUI, represents the username as it would appear to an NT4 server when authenticating. The userPrincipalName or User Logon Name is the Windows 2000 username represented as *username@fully.qualified.domain.name*. The `cn` and `name` properties show the full name of the user as it appears in the directory manager window. The `cn` property of an object in a container must be different from the `cn` for all other members of the container. You can have more than one Chris Heaton user in the directory, as long as they are not in the same container. The `cn` and `name` properties are equivalent because they are inherited from different class definitions, which make up the User class in the Schema. The User class inherits from the Organizational-Person class among others, which in turn inherits from Person. Person has the `cn` property as a mandatory requirement. The Person class inherits from the Top class, which has a property called `name`, which is the object's RDN.

Adding the Users to the Group

The first three tasks are now completed. Adding a user to a group is done with the `IADsGroup::Add`, a simple method that takes the DN of the object to be added to the group:

```
adsGroup.Add("LDAP://cn=Sue Peace,cn=Users,dc=windows,dc=mycorp,dc=com")
adsGroup.Add("LDAP://cn=Keith Cooper,cn=Users,dc=windows,dc=mycorp,dc=com")
```

Tearing Down What Was Created

That seems simple enough, so let's continue and remove the users from the group. Here is the code:

```
adsGroup.Remove("LDAP://cn=Sue Peace,cn=Users,dc=windows,dc=mycorp,dc=com")
adsGroup.Remove("LDAP://cn=Keith Cooper,cn=Users,dc=windows,dc=mycorp,dc=com")
```

Now delete the users, the group and the Organizational Unit:

```
adsUsersContainer.Delete "user", adsUser2.Name
Set adsUser2 = Nothing
adsUsersContainer.Delete "user", adsUser1.Name
Set adsUser1 = Nothing

adsSalesOU.Delete "group", adsGroup.Name
Set adsGroup = Nothing

adsContainer.Delete "organizationalUnit", adsSalesOU.Name
Set adsSalesOU = Nothing
```

The parameters for each `IADsContainer::Delete` lines are not enclosed in parentheses because the `IADsContainer::Delete` method does not return a value. This is known in VBScript as a *subprocedure* or *sub*. If the method returned a value and required parameters, such as VBScript's `GetObject` function, then it would be a function and not a subprocedure and you would use parentheses around the parameters.

Each `IADsContainer::Delete` line uses the `IADs::Name` method that I have shown you before when talking about property methods. This is a property method on IADs that retrieves the names `cn=Sue Peace` and `cn=Keith Cooper` for `adsUser1` and `adsUser2`, respectively. `IADs::Name` is a method you will come to use often in your code.

The `Nothing` keyword in VBScript is used to disassociate an object variable from any object. This prevents you from being able to use it later in your code. Setting the value of each object to `Nothing` may seem less than worthwhile when the script is due to end soon. However, you must get into this habit, and I can't stress its importance enough. After you have deleted an object from the underlying directory service, the property cache for that object still exists. If you do not remove the reference to it, and use it again later, then it refers to data that no longer exists. Trying to do a `SetInfo` (or a `GetInfo`, covered later) on a deleted object's property cache generates a failure. I once spent hours on a script in which I had made this mistake; now I always dereference my variables.

The script is complete except for the bonus tasks. These can be achieved through `IADsGroup::IsMember` and `IADsGroup::Members`. `IADsGroup::IsMember` is easier, so I'll cover that one first.

If you attempt to delete a container object, such as an Organizational Unit, which still has objects contained within it, then the call will fail with an error that states "The directory service can perform the requested operation only on a leaf object." This does make sense and is intentional. If you want to delete a container, then you have to delete all of its children. If these children are containers with objects themselves, then you have to recursively delete these containers and their children before you can delete the parent.

If you attempt to delete a group that either has members or is itself a member of other groups, then this call will succeed. This is because the membership relationships are not true parent-child relationships within Active Directory.

Membership of Groups

The `IADsGroup` interface that operates on group objects supports four methods and one property* that are specific to the group object (Table 14-1).

Table 14-1. The IADsGroup Interface

IADsGroup Methods and Properties	Action
Add method	Adds users to the group as members
Remove method	Removes user members from the group
IsMember method	Tests to see if a user is a member of a group
Members method	Returns a list of all the members of the group
Description property	Returns the text describing the group
get/put_Description method	Retrieves the description a method interface used only by VC++

The `IADsGroup::IsMember` method takes one argument: the DN of the user to check, just as **Add** and **Remove** do. It returns a value called a Boolean, i.e., True or False. That allows you to use it in an if . . . **then** statement like this:

```
Set adsGroup = GetObject("LDAP://cn=Managers,ou=Sales," _
    & "dc=windows,dc=mycorp,dc=com")
If adsGroup.IsMember("LDAP://cn=Vicky Launders,ou=Sales," _
    & "dc=windows,dc=mycorp,dc=com") Then
    WScript.Echo "Is a Member!"
Else
    WScript.Echo "Is NOT a Member!"
End If
```

---

* Ignore the VC++ method for now. VC++ is explained briefly in the next chapter; I include it here only for completeness sake.

This should seem fairly obvious after the examples you've already gone through. Two lines are too long to fit on the page, so I'm using the VBScript underscore (_) character again to tell VBScript that it should treat the current line as continuous with the next line. However, when you use the underscore to separate long strings, you must enclose both strings in quotation marks and then use the ampersand character (&) to concatenate two strings together.

The `IADsGroup::Members` function, on the other hand, is different from all the other methods you have used up until now, as this one returns a pointer to an ADSI Members object. ADSI has this Members object in order to be able to create and manage sets of object references or pointers or when you want to create a list of pointers to user objects that represent the members of a group. When you call the `IADsGroup::Members` method, it creates a Members object, which itself has its own interface called IADsMembers. The one method I will be using from this interface for the moment is `IADsMembers::Count`.

IADsMembers, shown in Table 14-2, supports two properties specific to collections of ADSI objects, ADSI Group objects and ADSI Member objects.

Table 14-2. The IADsMembers Interface

IADsMembers Methods and Properties	Action
Count property	The number of items in the container. If there is a filter set, then only the number of items that match the filter are returned.
Filter property	A filter, consisting of an array of object class strings, which can restrict the number of objects returned during enumeration of the container.

I also use the `WScript.Echo` method to print output from the scripts in this and the following chapters. VBScript has a `MsgBox` function that I could use equally well to print GUI output. For example:

```
MsgBox "Hi There!"
```

However, if you were to run these scripts via the command-line WSH interpreter, *CSCRIPT.EXE*, then all output would end up appearing on the screen in separate GUI dialog boxes rather than being redirected to the command line. `WScript.Echo` redirects output to the GUI for the *WSCRIPT.EXE* interpreter and the command line for the *CSCRIPT.EXE* interpreter.

In both cases, `MsgBox` and the GUI version of `WScript.Echo` have a limit of 255 characters. When I start writing scripts that could potentially get close to this, I will start placing the results in files and automatically opening them with *NOTEPAD. EXE* instead.

Coming back to the script, there are a number of ways of enumerating the members of a group. The `for each . . . in . . . next` loop is the most common. This is how it works:

```
Set adsGroup = GetObject("LDAP://cn=Managers,ou=Sales," _
  & "dc=windows,dc=mycorp,dc=com")

WScript.Echo "Number of members of the group: " & adsGroup.Members.Count

For Each adsMember In adsGroup.Members
   WScript.Echo adsMember.Name
Next
```

This script opens a dialog box displaying the number of members and then opens successive dialog boxes for each member, displaying the member's name in the box. As the `for` loop executes, `adsMember` ends up holding a class of objects called Members. Remember that the string `ads` on the front of a variable indicates an ADSI object, so this isn't a standard count here.

The ability to use multiple methods is demonstrated well by the way the count is retrieved. The methods are resolved left to right, so `adsGroup.Members` is resolved to the ADSI Members object first. This Members object supports the `IADsMembers::Count` method of retrieving the `count` property, so that can be added to the end because `adsGroup.Members` is a pointer to that Members object. Think of it this way:

```
Set adsMembers = adsGroup.Members
WScript.Echo "Number of members of the group:" & adsMembers.Count
```

Both are equivalent, and I will be using the simpler short form as often as I can.

The Members object supports IADs as do all objects. This means that as we enumerate the members using a `FOR EACH` loop, we are able to obtain the `IADs::Name` from each object that we iterate past. A very neat solution.

Bringing It All Together

Example 14-5 shows a slightly more complex script encompassing all of the elements. Notice that the only explicit LDAP paths I provided were for the Users container and the root of the domain. Every other reference was using `IADs::ADsPath`. Names were retrieved using `IADs::Name`. Comments in the code are prefixed by an apostrophe (') character.

Example 14-5. Demonstrating the Methods and Properties of Groups

```
'**********************************************************************
'Force all variables to be declared so that we don't make any mistakes
'**********************************************************************
Option Explicit
```

Example 14-5. Demonstrating the Methods and Properties of Groups (continued)

```
'************************************************************************
'Declare all variables
'************************************************************************
Dim adsRootContainer  'Pointer to the root of the domain tree
Dim adsSalesOU        'Pointer to the Sales OU
Dim adsGroup          'Pointer to the Managers group
Dim adsUsersContainer 'Pointer to the Users container
Dim adsUser1          'Pointer to the Sue Peace user
Dim adsUser2          'Pointer to the Keith Cooper user
Dim adsMember         'Pointer to individual members of a group


'************************************************************************
'Get a pointer to the root domain
'************************************************************************
Set adsRootContainer = GetObject("LDAP://dc=windows,dc=mycorp,dc=com")


'************************************************************************
'Create the Sales OU
'************************************************************************
Set adsSalesOU = adsRootContainer.Create("organizationalUnit", "ou=Sales")
adsSalesOU.SetInfo


'************************************************************************
'Create the Managers group in the Sales OU
'************************************************************************
Set adsGroup = adsSalesOU.Create("group", "cn=Managers")
adsGroup.Put "sAMAccountName", "Managers"
adsGroup.SetInfo


'************************************************************************
'Display the number of users in the group. This will be 0.
'************************************************************************
WScript.Echo "Number of members of the group: " & adsGroup.Members.Count


'************************************************************************
'While this code should display the name and ADsPath of each
'member of the group in its own dialog box, there will be no
'members to display yet. So, it will be skipped.
'************************************************************************
For Each adsMember In adsGroup.Members
  WScript.Echo adsMember.Name & vbCrLf & adsMember.ADsPath
Next


'************************************************************************
'Get a pointer to the Users container
'************************************************************************
Set adsUsersContainer = GetObject("LDAP://cn=Users,dc=windows,dc=mycorp,dc=com")


'************************************************************************
'Create the two users
'************************************************************************
Set adsUser1 = adsUsersContainer.Create("user", "cn=Sue Peace")
```

Example 14-5. Demonstrating the Methods and Properties of Groups (continued)

```
adsUser1.Put "sAMAccountName", "SueP"
adsUser1.SetInfo
Set adsUser2 = adsUsersContainer.Create("user", "cn=Keith Cooper")
adsUser2.Put "sAMAccountName", "KeithC"
adsUser2.SetInfo

'***********************************************************************
'Add Sue to the group
'***********************************************************************
adsGroup.Add(adsUser1.ADsPath)

'***********************************************************************
'Test for Sue's membership of the group, which should succeed
'***********************************************************************
If adsGroup.IsMember(adsUser1.ADsPath) Then
  WScript.Echo adsUser1.Name & " is a Member of " & adsGroup.Name
Else
  WScript.Echo adsUser1.Name & " is NOT a Member of " & adsGroup.Name
End If

'***********************************************************************
'Test for Keith's membership of the group, which should fail
'***********************************************************************
If adsGroup.IsMember(adsUser2.ADsPath) Then
  WScript.Echo adsUser2.Name & " is a Member of " & adsGroup.Name
Else
  WScript.Echo adsUser2.Name & " is NOT a Member of " & adsGroup.Name
End If

'***********************************************************************
'Display the number of users in the group. This will be 1.
'***********************************************************************
WScript.Echo "Number of members of the group:" & adsGroup.Members.Count

'***********************************************************************
'Display each member of the group's name and ADsPath in its
'own dialog box
'***********************************************************************
For Each adsMember In adsGroup.Members
  WScript.Echo adsMember.Name & vbCrLf & adsMember.ADsPath
Next

'***********************************************************************
'Add Keith to the group
'***********************************************************************
adsGroup.Add(adsUser2.ADsPath)

'***********************************************************************
'Test for Sue's membership of the group, which should succeed
'***********************************************************************
If adsGroup.IsMember(adsUser1.ADsPath) Then
  WScript.Echo adsUser1.Name & " is a Member of " & adsGroup.Name
```

Example 14-5. Demonstrating the Methods and Properties of Groups (continued)

```
Else
  WScript.Echo adsUser1.Name & " is NOT a Member of " & adsGroup.Name
End If

'**********************************************************************
'Test for Keith's membership of the group, which should succeed
'**********************************************************************
If adsGroup.IsMember(adsUser2.ADsPath) Then
  WScript.Echo adsUser2.Name & " is a Member of " & adsGroup.Name
Else
  WScript.Echo adsUser2.Name & " is NOT a Member of " & adsGroup.Name
End If

'**********************************************************************
'Display the number of users in the group. This will be 2.
'**********************************************************************
WScript.Echo "Number of members of the group:" & adsGroup.Members.Count

'**********************************************************************
'Display each member of the group's name and ADsPath in
'its own dialog box
'**********************************************************************
For Each adsMember In adsGroup.Members
  WScript.Echo adsMember.Name & vbCrLf & adsMember.ADsPath
Next

'**********************************************************************
'Remove both users from the group
'**********************************************************************
adsGroup.Remove(adsUser1.ADsPath)
adsGroup.Remove(adsUser2.ADsPath)

'**********************************************************************
'Display the number of users in the group. This will be 0.
'**********************************************************************
WScript.Echo "Number of members of the group:" & adsGroup.Members.Count

'**********************************************************************
'While this code should display the name and ADsPath of
'each member of the group in its own dialog box, there will be
'no members to display any more. So, it will be skipped.
'**********************************************************************
For Each adsMember In adsGroup.Members
  WScript.Echo adsMember.Name & vbCrLf & adsMember.ADsPath
Next

'**********************************************************************
'Delete the two users, the group, and the Organizational Unit,
'removing the objects from memory with each one as we delete it.
'**********************************************************************
adsUsersContainer.Delete "user", adsUser2.Name
Set adsUser2 = Nothing
```

Example 14-5. Demonstrating the Methods and Properties of Groups (continued)

```
adsUsersContainer.Delete "user", adsUser1.Name
Set adsUser1 = Nothing

adsSalesOU.Delete "group", adsGroup.Name
Set  adsGroup = Nothing

adsRootContainer.Delete "organizationalUnit", adsSalesOU.Name
Set adsSalesOU = Nothing
```

Summary

I hope you've managed to come to grips with the basics of ADSI now. It's a very rewarding technology that allows you to interface to all aspects of both the Windows 2000 Active Directory and Windows NT/2000 individual servers. Even though the majority of this chapter covers Microsoft operating systems, the code does use the LDAP: namespace and is portable to many other directory services. That is ADSI's strength, its ability to communicate with a variety of directory services using either LDAP or a provider-specific namespace.

ADSI is also in a state of continuous development. New interfaces that I do not cover here in the book are being developed for accessing many other different objects and properties. However, if you know the basics of ADSI, moving forward with any of these new interfaces should be much easier.

15

IADs and the
Property Cache

Each object in a directory has a series of attributes, or properties, that uniquely define it. Although properties can vary from object to object, ADSI supports the manipulation of a core set of six properties common to all objects using the IADs interface. These properties are common to all objects because IADs is the most basic interface in ADSI.

The IADs Properties

The six core IADs properties represent the following information for an object:

Class
    The object's schema class

GUID
    The object's globally unique ID (GUID)

Name
    The object's name

ADsPath
    The ADsPath to the object in the current namespace

Parent
    The ADsPath to the object's parent

Schema
    The ADsPath to the object's schema class

Each core property has a corresponding property method in the IADs interface. You use the property method, which has the same name as the property to access that property's value. Accessing properties' values is fundamental in scripting. For example, if you want to add a user (i.e., a User object) to the Sales Organizational

Unit (i.e., an OrganizationalUnit container), you need to access the user object's properties. Example 15-1 contains code to display the six core properties of a user object.

Example 15-1. Using the Explicit Property Methods to Display the Six Core Properties

```
Dim adsUser 'An ADSI User object
Dim str     'A text string

Set adsUser=GetObject("WinNT://MYCORP/Administrator,User")
str = "Name: " & adsUser.Name & vbCrLf
str = str & "GUID: " & adsUser.GUID & vbCrLf
str = str & "Class: " & adsUser.Class & vbCrLf
str = str & "ADsPath: " & adsUser.ADsPath & vbCrLf
str = str & "Parent: " & adsUser.Parent & vbCrLf
str = str & "Schema: " & adsUser.Schema & vbCrLf & vbCrLf
Set adsUser = Nothing

Set adsUser=GetObject("LDAP://cn=Administrator,cn=Users,dc=mycorp,dc=com")
str = str & "Name: " & adsUser.Name & vbCrLf
str = str & "GUID: " & adsUser.GUID & vbCrLf
str = str & "Class: " & adsUser.Class & vbCrLf
str = str & "ADsPath: " & adsUser.ADsPath & vbCrLf
str = str & "Parent: " & adsUser.Parent & vbCrLf
str = str & "Schema: " & adsUser.Schema & vbCrLf & vbCrLf

WScript.Echo str

Set adsUser = Nothing
```

To begin, you declare two variables (i.e., `str` and `adsUser`); apply VBScript's `GetObject` method to create a reference, or pointer, to the User object; and set `adsUser` to that pointer. You then set the `str` variable to the string "Name:" and apply the `IADs::Name` property method (`adsUser.Name`) to retrieve the Name property's value (i.e., Administrator). The carriage-return line-feed constant (`vbCrLf`) specifies to move to the start of a new line. At this point, `str` represents the string "Name: Administrator."

In the next line, you use the `IADs::GUID` property method (`adsUser.GUID`) to retrieve the GUID property's value (i.e., {D83F1060-1E71-11CF-B1F3-02608-C9E7553}). The `str = str &` sets `str` to a new string that now represents the Name property value and the GUID property value. You continue this process until you retrieve all six core properties in both the WinNT and the LDAP namespaces.

You might be surprised to find out that enumerating properties in different namespaces produces different output, as Figure 15-1 shows. For example, the Name property under the LDAP namespace has the Common Name (CN) X.520 key prefix from Request for Comments (RFC) 1779, whereas the Name property under the WinNT namespace doesn't.

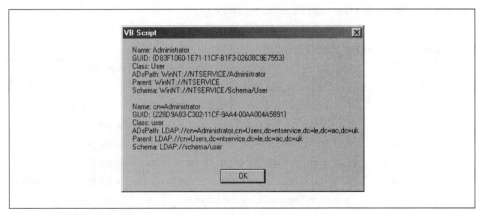

Figure 15-1. The IADs properties from the WinNT and LDAP namespaces

Both the code and the figure demonstrate another important point: The type of directory can affect the results. For example, using the `IADs::Parent` property makes sense when you're using the LDAP namespace to access a hierarchical directory, such as Active Directory, because you can see parent-child relationships (e.g., you can see that the Users container is the parent for the Administrator User object). However, using the `IADs::Parent` property to look at NT's Security Accounts Manager (SAM) doesn't make sense where domains are concerned because the contents are all in one flat namespace.

Using IADs::Get and IADs::Put

While you can use property methods to access an object's properties, you don't have to use a property method if you don't want to. Instead, you can use the IADs interfaces `IADs::Get` and `IADs::Put` methods.

In other words, the following two sets of statements are equivalent:

```
strName = adsUser.description
adsUser.description = strName

strName = adsUser.Get("description")
adsUser.Put "description", strName
```

However, using the `IADs::Get` and `IADs::Put` methods is more of a performance hit as it involves internally doing a search for the property specified. Compared to this, the direct use of a property is what is known as a *direct vtable binding* per the COM documentation and is the faster of the two. `IADs::Get` and `IADs::Put` should be used only when a generic browser or program is written to work with any ADSI object. See Table 15-1 for the full set of methods and property methods for the IADs interface.

Table 15-1. The Main IADs Methods and Properties

IADs Methods and Properties	Action
Get method	Retrieves a single item from the property cache
Put method	Sets a single item in the property cache
GetEx method	Retrieves a multi-valued item from the property cache
PutEx method	Sets a multivalued item in the property cache
GetInfo method	Retrieves all of an object's properties into the property cache
GetInfoEx method	Retrieves one or more of an object's properties into the cache
SetInfo method	Writes out all the items in the property cache to the directory
get_Name method	Gets the name of the object[a]
get_GUID method	Gets the GUID of the object
get_Class method	Gets the schema class name of the object
get_ADsPath method	Gets the ADsPath of the object
get_Parent method	Gets the parent ADsPath of the object
get_Schema method	Gets the ADsPath of the object's schema class
Class property	Represents the Schema class of the object
GUID property	Represents the GUID of the object
Name property	Represents the name of the object
AdsPath property	Represents the ADsPath of the object
Parent property	Represents the ADsPath to the parent of this object
Schema property	Represents the ADsPath of the object's schema class

a A VC++ method. I won't include these in the future interface definitions, but they do serve as an example that VC++ does not support setting properties in the same way as VBScript.

Why Microsoft couldn't have named IADs::SetInfo *PutInfo*, or renamed IADs::Put and IADs::PutEx *Set* and *SetEx* for consistency is beyond me.

For example, the next script shows how you use **IADs::Get** and **IADs::Put** to retrieve, change, and return the **mail** property. After you set the adsGroup variable to the pointer to the Managers group, you use the **IADs::Get** method (**adsGroup.Get**) with the **"mail"** argument to retrieve the mail property's value. The **WScript.Echo** method displays the results in a window.

Changing the value and returning it to the property cache is just as simple. You use the **IADs::Put** method with the argument **"mail"**. You don't put the argument in parentheses when you use the **IADs::Put** method as the method in a subprocedure and not a function, and it doesn't return a value. The string that follows the `IADs::Put` function contains the Managers group's new mail contact address. To write the new **mail** property to Active Directory, you use `IADs::` `SetInfo`:

```
Set adsGroup = GetObject("LDAP://cn=Managers,ou=Sales,dc=mycorp,dc=com")
WScript.Echo adsGroup.Get("mail")

adsGroup.Put "mail", "agl1@mycorp.com"
adsGroup.SetInfo
```

The Property Cache

Having looked at the properties and property methods, let's take a look at the property cache, the area of memory that stores properties for objects. Each object that you bind to has a personal property cache; the OS creates this cache the instant the bind succeeds. However, the OS doesn't immediately populate the cache with values.

When you use the `IADs::Get` method to retrieve an object's property, ADSI doesn't go to Active Directory to retrieve the value. Instead, ADSI reads the value from the property cache on the client executing the script. If ADSI doesn't find the property in the property cache when the call comes in, the system implicitly executes an `IADs::GetInfo` call to read all the properties for the current object into the cache. (You also can explicitly use the `IADs::GetInfo` method to populate the property cache with an object's properties.) The `IADs::Get` method then reads the appropriate value from that newly created cache.

Microsoft designed the property cache with efficiency in mind. The property cache lets you access an object's properties with a minimum number of calls, thereby minimizing network traffic. Retrieving all an object's properties with one `IADs::` `GetInfo` call is more efficient than individually retrieving each property. Similarly, the process of writing all an object's properties first to the cache and then to Active Directory with one `IADs::SetInfo` call is more efficient than writing each property individually to Active Directory.

Be Careful

The `IADs::GetInfo` and `IADs::SetInfo` methods are two of the most important methods you'll use. However, you need to be aware of two possible problems.

The first problem can arise if you try to access a property that doesn't have a value. For example, when you create a group object, the mail property doesn't automatically receive a value; you must provide a value, such as **agl1@mycorp.** **com**. When you use the `IADs::GetInfo` method, only those properties that have values appear in the property cache. Thus, if you don't give the mail property a

Accessing the Property Cache with Microsoft Visual C++

VC++ cannot use the same property method mechanism to get and set values in the property cache that automation languages like VBScript can use. Instead, Microsoft designed a variety of nonautomation interfaces, methods, and properties VC++ can make use of.

For example, when setting properties for a group, VC++ has access to the `IADs::Get` and `IADs::Put` methods in the same way that VBScript does. In addition, it also has access to the `IADsGroup::get_Description` and `IADs::put_Description` methods. This is because VC++ cannot use the `IADs::Description` property method. Code in VC++ would look like this using `IADs::Put`:

```
    Declare the variables
IADsGroup  *pGroup;
IADs       *pObject;

ADsGetObject(
   TEXT("LDAP://cn=Managers,ou=Sales,dc=windows,dc=mycorp,dc=com"),
   IID_IADsGroup,
   (void**) &pGroup);

    Set using IADs::Put method
pGroup->QueryInterface(IID_IADs,(void **) &pObject);
pObject->Put("Description",TEXT("My new group description goes here"))
pGroup->SetInfo;
```

Code in VC++ would look like this when using the `IADsGroup::put_Description` method.

```
    Declare the variables
IADsGroup  *pGroup;
IADs       *pObject;

ADsGetObject(
   TEXT("LDAP://cn=Managers,ou=Sales,dc=windows,dc=mycorp,dc=com"),
   IID_IADsGroup,
   (void**) &pGroup);

// Set using IADsGroup::put_Description property method
pGroup->put_Description(TEXT("My new group description goes here"));
pGroup->SetInfo;
```

value and you use `IADs::GetInfo`, the mail property value won't be in the property cache. If you try to access a property that doesn't exist in the cache, the script will give an empty value as the result.

Later on I talk about navigating the property cache. If you want to see a good example of how this actually works, try this: Create a new object of type group, which has about 21 properties set by the system by default. You then use IADs::GetInfo in a script and display the number of properties, and possibly their names, in a dialog box. Then set the description. Now when you rerun the script, you will find that you have one more property in the cache than you did before the description. In other words, the description does not appear in the cache until you do an IADs::GetInfo after it has been set.

Another problem can arise if you forget to use IADs::SetInfo after modifying a property. For example, suppose you want to change the Managers group's mail property value and you create the Example 15-2 script.

Example 15-2. Making the Mistake of Forgetting the SetInfo Call

```
Dim adsGroup   'An ADSI group object

Set adsGroup = GetObject("LDAP://cn=Managers,ou=Sales,dc=mycorp,dc=com")

'**********************************************************************
'Get and write the mail property value, which forces an
'implicit GetInfo call
'**********************************************************************
WScript.Echo adsGroup.Get("mail")

'**********************************************************************
'Set the new mail address in the cache
'**********************************************************************
adsGroup.Put "mail", "new-address@mycorp.com"

'**********************************************************************
'Use an explicit GetInfo call to again retrieve all items into the cache
'**********************************************************************
adsGroup.GetInfo

WScript.Echo adsGroup.mail
```

In this script, you set the **adsGroup** variable to the pointer to the Managers group. To display the current mail property value in a window, you use the WScript:: Echo method with the IADs::Get method, which forces an implicit IADs:: GetInfo call. You then set the new value for the **adsGroup**'s mail property, after which you use an explicit IADs::GetInfo call to again retrieve all the object's properties into the cache. Finally, you use the WScript.Echo method to display the results in a window.

When you run the script, two windows pop up. To your dismay, both windows state the original value of the mail property, which means that the system didn't write the new mail address to Active Directory. This cache write didn't occur because you need to explicitly call the `IADs::SetInfo` method to write out data from the cache to Active Directory. To fix the script, you need to insert the line:

```
objGroup.SetInfo
```

between the line setting the new mail address and the line making the explicit `IADs::GetInfo` call.

More Complexities of Property Access: IADs::GetEx and IADs::PutEx

Using the IADs interface's `IADs::Get` method works well for properties with one value. However, some properties have multiple values, such as a user with several telephone numbers. If a property stores multiple values, you need to use the IADs interface's `IADs::GetEx`[*] and `IADs::PutEx` methods to retrieve and return the values.

Using IADs::GetEx

The Example 15-3 script shows how to use `IADs::GetEx`. In this script, you pass the multiple-value property as an argument to the `IADs::GetEx` method. You then use a `for each...next` loop on the resulting list.

Example 15-3. Value Property

```
Dim adsUser        'An ADSI user object
Dim arrPhoneList   'An array of phone numbers
Dim strPhoneNumber 'An individual phone number

Set adsUser=GetObject("LDAP://cn=administrator,cn=Users,dc=mycorp,dc=com")

arrPhoneList = adsUser.GetEx("telephoneNumber")

For Each strPhoneNumber In arrPhoneList
  WScript.Echo strPhoneNumber
Next
```

When you make the `IADs::GetEx` call, the system makes an implicit `IADs::GetInfoEx` call rather than an implicit `IADs::GetInfo` call to Active Directory. You can use an explicit `IADs::GetInfoEx` call to get one or more properties if you don't want to use `IADs::GetInfo` to get all the property values. However, few scriptwriters use `IADs::GetInfoEx` for this purpose, because they typically

---

[*] You also can use *IADs::GetEx* for single-value properties.

use implicit calls or use `IADs::GetInfo` to read all values into the property cache. In addition, if you use `IADs::GetEx` for every property retrieval rather than using `IADs::GetInfo`, your underlying network traffic will increase. Instead of sending one request to the server for all the information, you'll be sending several requests for smaller amounts of information.

Although `IADs::GetInfoEx` isn't a good substitute for `IADs::GetInfo`, it works well for selectively reading properties into the property cache. Example 15-4 shows how to selectively retrieve only two properties.

Example 15-4. Using IADs::GetInfoEx to Selectively Read Properties into the Property Cache

```
Dim adsUser   'An ADSI user object
Dim arrProps 'An array of properties to return

Set adsUser=GetObject("LDAP://cn=administrator,cn=Users,dc=mycorp,dc=com")

'**********************************************************************
'Set the list of properties to return
'**********************************************************************
arrProps = Array("cn","ADsPath")

'**********************************************************************
'Get the specified properties
'**********************************************************************
adsUser.GetInfoEx arrProps, 0

WScript.Echo adsUser.cn & vbTab & adsUser.ADsPath
```

After you set the **adsUser** variable, you create an array containing the properties you want (i.e., **cn** and **ADsPath**). Next, you pass that array to the `IADs::GetInfoEx` method as the first parameter. (In ADSI 2.5, the second parameter must be 0 for all actions; however, this situation might change in a later version of ADSI.) Then, the last line uses the **WScript.Echo** method to print the **cn** and **ADsPath** attributes, separating them with a tab.

Using IADs::PutEx

To return multiple-value properties, you use the `IADs::PutEx` method. This is slightly more complicated than using `IADs::GetEx`. Suppose a property already has three values (e.g., pager numbers) and you want to put in two more. You must let `IADs::PutEx` know whether it needs to overwrite, update, or add to the existing values. You use the constants in Table 15-2 to tell `IADs::PutEx` what to do.

Table 15-2. The Constants for Updating the Property Cache with the PutEx Method

Constant Name	Value	Action
ADS_PROPERTY_CLEAR	1	Use when clearing all values
ADS_PROPERTY_UPDATE	2	Use when replacing all existing values
ADS_PROPERTY_APPEND	3	Use when adding to existing values
ADS_PROPERTY_DELETE	4	Use when deleting specific values

You use the constant name only if you're using VB. If you use VBScript with the WSH, you must either define the constants, as I've done in the Example 15-5 script, or use the values directly. The four values are fairly straightforward to use, as the example script shows.

Example 15-5. Adding Value Properties to the Property Cache

```
Const ADS_PROPERTY_CLEAR = 1
Const ADS_PROPERTY_UPDATE = 2
Const ADS_PROPERTY_APPEND = 3
Const ADS_PROPERTY_DELETE = 4

Dim adsUser   'An ADSI User object
Dim strPager 'A text string holding a phone number

Set adsUser=GetObject("LDAP://cn=Administrator,cn=Users,dc=mycorp,dc=com")

'***********************************************************************
'Set three telephone numbers for the Administrator account
'***********************************************************************
adsUser.PutEx ADS_PROPERTY_UPDATE, "pager", _
  Array("123-1234", "234-2345", "345-3456")
adsUser.SetInfo
adsUser.GetInfo
For Each strPager in adsUser.telephoneNumber
  WScript.Echo strPager
Next

'***********************************************************************
'Delete the first and last number
'***********************************************************************
adsUser.PutEx ADS_PROPERTY_DELETE, "pager", Array("123-1234", "345-3456")
adsUser.SetInfo
adsUser.GetInfo
For Each strPager in adsUser.telephoneNumber
  WScript.Echo strPager
Next

'***********************************************************************
'Add a new telephone number without deleting the remaining number
'***********************************************************************
adsUser.PutEx ADS_PROPERTY_APPEND, "pager", Array("456-4567")
adsUser.SetInfo
adsUser.GetInfo
```

Example 15-5. Adding Value Properties to the Property Cache (continued)

```
For Each strPager in adsUser.telephoneNumber
  WScript.Echo strPager
Next

'************************************************************************
'Delete all values
'************************************************************************
adsUser.PutEx ADS_PROPERTY_CLEAR, "pager", vbNull
adsUser.SetInfo
adsUser.GetInfo
For Each strPager in adsUser.telephoneNumber
  WScript.Echo strPager
Next
```

After you bind to the user object, you set three pager numbers for the Administrator account, wiping out any existing values. You then reload the property cache explicitly to make sure it contains the new values that you just set. Now, you use a for each...next loop to go through the newly set property to show the individual pager numbers. You then delete the first and last pager numbers of the new property in the cache and write that cache out to Active Directory.

At this point, Active Directory should contain only one pager number, which you verify by looping through the values again. You decide to append a number to the value held for that property in the cache and subsequently write it out to Active Directory, leaving two numbers in Active Directory for that property. Looping through the values again shows there are two numbers. Finally, you delete all the values in the property cache for that property and write the changes out to Active Directory. Using the for each...next loop one last time shows no values.

Knowing now that you can access all of an object's properties from the cache individually, it would make sense if there were a way to count the number of items, display their names as well as their values, and so on. For this purpose, Microsoft provided three interfaces: IADsPropertyList, IADsPropertyEntry, and IADsPropertyValue.

Manipulating the Property Cache

There will be times when you need to write a script that queries all the values that have been set in the underlying directory for a particular object. For example, suppose you're one of several systems administrators who work with your company's Windows 2000 Active Directory implementation. You need to write a script that queries all the property values that the administrators have set for a particular user.

Discovering the set property values for an object can be a long, tedious job. Fortunately, ADSI provides a quick method. If someone has set a value for a property, it must be in that object's property cache. So all you need to do is walk through the property cache, displaying and optionally modifying each item as you go.

In this section, I'll describe the property cache mechanics and show you how to write scripts that use several ADSI methods and properties to add individual values, add a set of values, walk through the property cache, and write modifications to the cache and to the directory. Although these examples access the Lightweight Directory Access Protocol (LDAP) namespace, you can just as easily substitute the WinNT namespace in any of the scripts and run them against Windows NT servers.

Details of the property cache interfaces can be found on the following MSDN location: Platform SDK → Networking Services → Active Directory → Active Directory Service Interfaces Version 2.5 → ADSI Reference → ADSI Interfaces → Property Cache Interfaces. This equates currently to the following URL: *http://msdn. microsoft.com/isapi/msdnlib.idc?theURL=/library/sdkdoc/adsi/if_prop_7bjn.htm.*

Property Cache Mechanics

Every object has properties. When you perform an explicit `IADsGetInfo` call (or an implicit `IADsGetInfo` call using `IADsGet`) on an object that you previously bound to, the OS loads all the properties for that specific object into that object's property cache. Consider the property cache as a simple list of properties. The `PropertyList` object represents this list. You can use several `IADsPropertyList` methods to navigate through the list and access items. For example, you can navigate the list and access each item, every nth item, or one particular item based on its name.

Each item in the property list is a property entry represented by the `PropertyEntry` object. You use the `IADsPropertyEntry` interface to access property entries.

A property entry can have one or more property values. The `PropertyValue` object represents a value. To access values in a property entry, you use the `IADsPropertyValue` interface.

To summarize, use `IADsPropertyList` to navigate through and access property entries in the property list. When you want to manipulate a property, use `IADsPropertyEntry`. To access the values of that property entry, use `IADsPropertyValue`.

Adding Individual Values

To show you how to add an individual value, I'll expand on one of the examples from the previous section: the pager property of the User object. The pager property is an array of text strings representing multiple pager numbers.

Consider that any property represents data. Data can take several forms, including a string, an integer, or a Boolean value. In the cache, each property has two attributes: one attribute specifies the type of data that property represents and the other attribute specifies the value of that datatype. So, for example, each pager property has two attributes: a Unicode string (the type of data) and the pager number (the value of that Unicode string). The User object's `lastLogon` property, which specifies the time the user last logged on, has the two attributes of LargeInteger (type of data) and a date/time stamp (the value of that LargeInteger).

The `pager` and lastLogon properties are instances of the `PropertyValue` object, so you manipulate them with the method and property methods of the `IADsPropertyValue` interface. For example, you use the `IADsPropertyValue::ADsType` property method to set the PropertyValue's type of data. Table 15-3 shows some of the corresponding constant names and values that you can set for the `IADsPropertyValue::ADsType` property.

Table 15-3. Constants for the IADsPropertyValue::ADsType Property

Constant Name	IADsPropertyValue Property Method (if Appropriate)	Value
ADSTYPE_INVALID	None	0
ADSTYPE_DN_STRING	IADsPropertyValue::DNString	1
ADSTYPE_CASE_EXACT_STRING	IADsPropertyValue::CaseExactString	2
ADSTYPE_CASE_IGNORE_STRING	IADsPropertyValue::CaseIgnoreString	3
ADSTYPE_PRINTABLE_STRING	IADsPropertyValue::PrintableString	4
ADSTYPE_NUMERIC_STRING	IADsPropertyValue::NumericString	5
ADSTYPE_BOOLEAN	IADsPropertyValue::Boolean	6
ADSTYPE_INTEGER	IADsPropertyValue::Integer	7
ADSTYPE_OCTET_STRING	IADsPropertyValue::OctetString	8
ADSTYPE_UTC_TIME	IADsPropertyValue::UTCTime	9
ADSTYPE_LARGE_INTEGER	IADsPropertyValue::LargeInteger	10
ADSTYPE_PROV_SPECIFIC	None	11
ADSTYPE_OBJECT_CLASS	None	12
ADSTYPE_CASEIGNORE_LIST	None	13
ADSTYPE_OCTET_LIST	None	14
ADSTYPE_PATH	None	15
ADSTYPE_POSTALADDRESS	None	16
ADSTYPE_TIMESTAMP	None	17
ADSTYPE_BACKLINK	None	18
ADSTYPE_TYPEDNAME	None	19
ADSTYPE_HOLD	None	20
ADSTYPE_NETADDRESS	None	21

Table 15-3. Constants for the IADsPropertyValue::ADsType Property (continued)

Constant Name	IADsPropertyValue Property Method (if Appropriate)	Value
ADSTYPE_REPLICAPOINTER	None	22
ADSTYPE_FAXNUMBER	None	23
ADSTYPE_EMAIL	None	24
ADSTYPE_NT_SECURITY_ DESCRIPTOR	IADsPropertyValue::SecurityDescriptor	25
ADSTYPE_UNKNOWN	None	26

Suppose you want to add a PropertyValue object with the value of "Hi There!" The two attributes are a case-sensitive string (i.e., the type of data, or `IADs-PropertyValue::ADsType` property) and "Hi There!" (i.e., the value of that case-sensitive string or the `IADsPropertyValue::CaseExactString` property). The constant for the `IADsPropertyValue::ADsType` of a case-sensitive string is ADSTYPE_CASE_EXACT_STRING, which has a numeric value of 2. As shown in Table 15-3, `IADsPropertyValue::CaseExactString` is one of a number of IADsPropertyValue property methods that exist, each relating to a specific datatype. It is the value in `IADsPropertyValue::ADsType` that determines which of the many property methods are actually used to get and set the data.

The following script shows how you create this new PropertyValue object. You begin by setting the ADSTYPE_CASE_EXACT_STRING constant to its numeric value (i.e., 2) and declaring the **adsPropValue** variable. As I mentioned earlier, if you use VBScript with the WSH, you must either define the constants, as the script does, or use the values directly:

```
Const ADSTYPE_CASE_EXACT_STRING = 2

Dim adsPropValue     'An ADSI PropertyValue object

Set adsPropValue = CreateObject("PropertyValue")
adsPropValue.ADsType = ADSTYPE_CASE_EXACT_STRING
adsPropValue.CaseExactString = "Hi There!"
```

I use VBScript's **CreateObject** method to create an instance of the Property-Value object and set it to the **adsPropValue** variable. You then assign the two attributes to the PropertyValue object. You use **adsPropValue**'s `IADs-PropertyValue::ADsType` property method to assign the property's datatype to the ADSTYPE_CASE_EXACT_STRING constant. You use **adsPropValue**'s `IADs-PropertyValue::CaseExactString` property method to assign the property's value to "Hi There!"

Adding Sets of Values

As I mentioned previously, some properties hold one value (e.g., lastLogon property); others hold multiple values in an array (e.g., pager property). The PropertyEntry object holds the entire set of values for a property, be it one value or many values.

However, the PropertyEntry object does more than store values. This object's properties dictate how you can manipulate those values. The PropertyEntry object supports the IADsPropertyEntry interface that has four property methods:

IADsPropertyEntry::Name

> The `IADsPropertyEntry::Name` property method sets the name of the property that you want to manipulate (e.g., pager).

IADsPropertyEntry::Values

> The `IADsPropertyEntry::Values` property method sets an array containing those values you want to manipulate (e.g., the pager numbers).

IADsPropertyEntry::ADsType

> The `IADsPropertyEntry::ADsType` property method determines the data type of those values (e.g., Unicode string).

IADsPropertyEntry::ControlCode

> The `IADsPropertyEntry::ControlCode` property method tells the cache whether to overwrite, update, or add to the property's existing values. You use the constants in Table 15-4 with the `IADsPropertyEntry::ControlCode` property. These constants are the same as the constants for the `IADs::PutEx` method described earlier. Because `IADsPropertyEntry::ControlCode` constants work the same way as the `IADs::PutEx` method constants, I won't go through them again here.

Table 15-4. The Constants for the IADsPropertyEntry::ControlCode Property Method

Constant Name	Value	Action
ADS_PROPERTY_CLEAR	1	Use when clearing all values
ADS_PROPERTY_UPDATE	2	Use when replacing all existing values
ADS_PROPERTY_APPEND	3	Use when adding to existing values
ADS_PROPERTY_DELETE	4	Use when deleting specific values

The next script shows how to create a PropertyEntry object from one property value:

```
Const ADSTYPE_CASE_IGNORE_STRING = 3
Const ADS_PROPERTY_UPDATE = 2

Dim adsPropValue 'An ADSI PropertyValue object
```

```
Dim adsPropEntry 'An ADSI PropertyEntry object

Set adsPropValue = CreateObject("PropertyValue")
adsPropValue.ADsType = ADSTYPE_CASE_IGNORE_STRING
adsPropValue.CaseIgnoreString = "0123-456-7890"

Set adsPropEntry = CreateObject("PropertyEntry")
adsPropEntry.Name = "pager"
adsPropEntry.Values = Array(adsPropValue)
adsPropEntry.ADsType = ADSTYPE_CASE_IGNORE_STRING
adsPropEntry.ControlCode = ADS_PROPERTY_UPDATE
```

The first part of the script is similar to the previous one. You begin by setting the constants to their numeric values and declaring the variables. Next, you create an instance of the PropertyValue object and set it to the **adsPropValue** variable. You then use the IADsPropertyValue::ADsType property method to assign the property's data type to the ADSTYPE_CASE_IGNORE_STRING constant and the IADsPropertyValue::CaseIgnoreString property method to assign the property's value to 0123-456-7890.

You begin the second part of the script by creating an instance of the PropertyEntry object and setting it to the **adsPropEntry** variable. Then you set all four PropertyEntry properties. For the IADsPropertyEntry::Values property, you must use the VBScript **Array( )** function to force the values into an array, even if you set only one value. For the IADsPropertyEntry::ControlCode property, you're replacing the existing values with the ones you're passing in.

Walking Through the Property Cache

For any object, the property cache consists of PropertyEntry objects that correspond to each property. When you use the IADs::Get method, it reads the cache's PropertyEntry for that particular property.

As I've previously mentioned, whenever you do a GetObject or an IADsOpenDSObject::OpenDSObject, the object that is returned can use the IADs interface in addition to any interface designed for that object. The IADsPropertyList interface also is directly available for any object. It is of no real use without a call to GetInfo first, or else the property cache will be empty. Once the cache is populated, however, the methods and properties come into their own. Table 15-5 lists the IADsPropertyList methods and properties.

Table 15-5. IADsPropertyList Methods and Properties

IADsPropertyList Methods and Properties	Action
Next method	Retrieves the value of the next item in the property list
Skip method	Skips a number of items in the property list

Table 15-5. IADsPropertyList Methods and Properties (continued)

IADsPropertyList Methods and Properties	Action
Reset method	Puts the pointer back to the beginning of the list
Add method	Adds a new property to the list
Remove method	Removes a property from the list
Item method	Gets an item from the property list
GetPropertyItem method	Gets an item in the property list
PutPropertyItem method	Puts an item in the property list
ResetPropertyItem method	Resets an item in the property list back to its original value
PurgePropertyList method	Deletes all items in the property list
PropertyCount property	The number of properties in the property list

The PropertyList object represents the entire set of properties for an object. You use the methods and property methods of the IADsPropertyList interface to manipulate the PropertyList object. Example 15-6 uses several of those methods and property methods to demonstrate three ways of walking through the property cache.

Example 15-6. Three Approaches for Walking Through the Property Cache

```
Option Explicit

'************************************************************************
'Force error checking within the code using the Err.Number property
'method in approaches 2 and 3
'************************************************************************
On Error Resume Next

'************************************************************************
'Declare the variables
'************************************************************************
Dim adsGroup      'The group whose property list you want to investigate
Dim txtStr        'A text string that displays results in one message box
Dim intPropCount  'The number of properties
Dim intIndex      'The index used while looping through the property list
Dim adsPropEntry  'An individual property entry used in a loop

Set adsGroup = GetObject("LDAP://cn=Managers,ou=Sales,dc=mycorp,dc=com")
adsGroup.GetInfo

intPropCount = adsGroup.PropertyCount
WScript.Echo "There are " & intPropCount & " values in the property cache."

'************************************************************************
'Approach 1: PropertyCount property method
'************************************************************************
txtStr = ""
```

Example 15-6. Three Approaches for Walking Through the Property Cache (continued)

```
For intIndex = 0 To (intPropCount-1)
  txtStr = txtStr & adsGroup.Item(intIndex).Name & vbTab _
  & adsGroup.Item(intIndex).ADsType & vbCrLf
Next
WScript.Echo txtStr


'*********************************************************************
'Approach 2: Next method
'*********************************************************************
txtStr = ""
Set adsPropEntry = adsGroup.Next
While (Not (IsNull(adsPropEntry)) And Err.Number = 0)
  txtStr = txtStr & adsPropEntry.Name & vbTab & adsPropEntry.ADsType
          & vbCrLf
  Set adsPropEntry = adsGroup.Next
Wend
WScript.Echo txtStr
Set adsPropEntry = Nothing


'*********************************************************************
'Approach 3: Next and Skip methods
'*********************************************************************
txtStr = ""
adsGroup.Reset
Set adsPropEntry = adsGroup.Next
While (Not (IsNull(adsPropEntry)) And Err.Number = 0)
  txtStr = txtStr & adsPropEntry.Name & vbTab & adsPropEntry.ADsType
          & vbCrLf
  adsGroup.Skip(2)
  Set adsPropEntry = adsGroup.Next
Wend
WScript.Echo txtStr
Set adsPropEntry = Nothing
```

The script begins by using VBScript's **Option Explicit** statement (which requires you to declare all variables before using them) and the **On Error Resume Next** statement (which enables an error-handling routine). Then, after declaring the variables, you use VBScript's **GetObject** method to bind to the group whose property cache you want to look at. In this case, you want to view the properties for the Manager group object and you bind that group to the **adsGroup** variable. Next, you explicitly use the **IADs::GetInfo** method to load the property cache for this group. As you won't be using the **IADs::Get** method in the script, the system won't implicitly use the **IADs::GetInfo** method to load the cache, so you have to explicitly load it in.

Each object in **adsGroup** has a PropertyList object, so you use the **IADsPropertyList::PropertyCount** property method to count each Property-List object. You store the count for later use by setting it to the **intPropCount** variable. You also use WSH's **Echo** method to print the count in a message box.

You now know how many properties that `adsGroup` has, but you need to find out the values of those properties. You can use one of three approaches to walk through the property cache to get this information.

Approach 1—Using the IADsPropertyList::PropertyCount property method

You begin this approach by setting the `txtStr` variable to a zero-length string ("/"). You'll be concatenating the string's value later as part of a loop, so you want to make sure that the initial value is a zero-length string.

You then walk through the property list by counting the items in the 0 through `intPropCount-1` index. You need to specify this index, because the property list index starts at 0 rather than 1. So, for example, a property list with 15 items has an index ranging from 0 to 14.

For each item in the index, you concatenate (`&`) two property methods to retrieve the property's `IADs::Name` and `IADsPropertyValue::ADsType`. The script processes concatenated statements from left to right, so it first uses the `IADsPropertyList::Item` method with the `intIndex` value as the item number to retrieve a property entry, to which it applies the `IADs::Name` property method to get the property's name. The script then uses the same process to retrieve the same property entry, to which it applies the `IADsPropertyValue::ADsType` property method to get the property's datatype. Forcing the script to process `IADsPropertyList::Item` twice is inefficient. I processed it twice only to illustrate how to walk through the property list. The concatenated code includes more than just the two property methods. The code also concatenates a tab (`vbTab`) between the two property methods and a carriage-return line-feed (`vbCrLf`), or hard return, after the second property method. But even more important, the code first concatenates the existing `txtStr` variable onto the front (i.e., `txtStr = txtStr & property method 1 & property method 2`), which means that, in the output, you're appending these property values to the existing `txtStr` string. As a result, the WSH displays all the property values in one message box if you use WSH's *wscript.exe* scripting engine to run the script. If you're using WSH's *cscript.exe* scripting engine, using this append technique makes no difference. If you don't concatenate the `txtStr` variable (i.e., `txtStr = property method 1 & property method 2`), WSH displays a separate message box for each property.

When the script finishes looping through the property list index, it prints the appended `txtStr` string in the message box. Aproaches 2 and 3 also use the append technique to display all their output in one message box.

Approach 2—Using the IADsPropertyList::Next method

You start this approach by resetting the txtStr variable to a zero-length string to ensure that no values from the previous approach are left in the string. You then call the IADsPropertyList::Next method to retrieve a copy of the first property entry and set the result to the adsPropEntry variable. Because you called the IADsPropertyList::Next method, you can use a while loop to iterate through the cache until you encounter a null value, which specifies that you're at the end of the list.

Providing that the first property entry isn't a null entry, you enter the while loop. The And Err.Number = 0 code designates a test to see whether an error has occurred. A value of 0 specifies no error; any other value specifies an error. If you retrieve a valid entry (i.e., not a null entry) and an error hasn't occurred (i.e., the error number is equal to 0), you enter the loop. Within the loop, you append the property name and data type to the txtStr string in a similar manner as before. To move to the next property entry in the property cache, you again call the IADsPropertyList::Next method. As long as this value isn't null and isn't generating an error code, this process continues until you hit a null entry, which means you're at the end of the list. The wend keyword signifies the end of the while loop. Finally, you print the results.

Approach 3—Using the IADsPropertyList::Next and IADsPropertyList::Skip methods

This approach's code is identical to the code you use in Approach 2, except for the addition of two lines. The IADsPropertyList::Reset property method sets the property list pointer to the first property entry in the cache. If you don't use the IADsPropertyList::Reset property method, the pointer will be at the end of the cache, which would generate a null entry. The IADsPropertyList::Skip code tells the IADsPropertyList::Next property method to skip the next two property entries. In other words, the IADsPropertyList::Next property method is retrieving every third property, so this approach returns only property entries 1, 4, 7, 10, and so on.

Writing the Modifications

Now that you can walk through the cache, I'll show you how to write the modifications to the cache and the directory. Example 15-7 illustrates these procedures. This script is an amalgam of the code in the earlier examples. As such, it shows you how to assemble the pieces of code into a usable script.

Example 15-7. Script to Write a New Property and Note the Changes in the Cache

```
Option Explicit

'**********************************************************************
'Force error checking within the code using the Err.Number property
'method in approaches 2 and 3
'**********************************************************************
On Error Resume Next

'**********************************************************************
'Declare the constants and variables
'**********************************************************************
Const ADSTYPE_CASE_IGNORE_STRING = 3
Const ADS_PROPERTY_UPDATE = 2

Dim adsPropValue    'An ADSI PropertyValue object
Dim adsPropEntry    'An ADSI PropertyEntry object
Dim adsUser         'The user whose property list you want to investigate
Dim txtStr          'A text string that displays results in one message box
Dim intPropCount    'The number of properties
Dim intIndex        'The index used while looping through the property list

Set adsUser = GetObject("LDAP://cn=AlistairGLN,ou=Sales,dc=mycorp,dc=com")
adsUser.GetInfo

'**********************************************************************
'Section A: Calculate the property count, and enumerate each
'property's name and datatype
'**********************************************************************
intPropCount = adsUser.PropertyCount
WScript.Echo "There are " & intPropCount _
  & " values in the property cache before adding the new one."

txtStr = ""
For intIndex = 0 To (intPropCount-1)
  txtStr = txtStr & adsUser.Item(intIndex).Name & vbTab _
    & adsUser.Item(intIndex).ADsType & vbCrLf
Next
WScript.Echo txtStr

'**********************************************************************
'Section B: Create a property entry, and write it to the cache
'**********************************************************************
Set adsPropValue = CreateObject("PropertyValue")
adsPropValue.ADsType = ADSTYPE_CASE_IGNORE_STRING
adsPropValue.CaseExactString = "0123-456-7890"

Set adsPropEntry = CreateObject("PropertyEntry")
adsPropEntry.Name = "pager"
adsPropEntry.Values = Array(adsPropValue)
adsPropEntry.ADsType = ADSTYPE_CASE_IGNORE_STRING
adsPropEntry.ControlCode = ADS_PROPERTY_UPDATE
```

Example 15-7. Script to Write a New Property and Note the Changes in the Cache (continued)

```
adsUser.PutPropertyItem(adsPropEntry)


'**********************************************************************
'Section C: Write out the cache to Active Directory and read the new
'cache explicitly back in from the object
'**********************************************************************
adsUser.SetInfo
adsUser.GetInfo


'**********************************************************************
'Section D: Recalculate the property count, and re-enumerate each
'property's name and datatype to see the changes
'**********************************************************************
intPropCount = adsUser.PropertyCount

WScript.Echo "There are " & intPropCount _
  & " values in the property cache before adding the new one."

txtStr = ""
For intIndex = 0 To (intPropCount-1)
  txtStr = txtStr & adsUser.Item(intIndex).Name _
    & vbTab & adsUser.Item(intIndex).ADsType & vbCrLf
Next
WScript.Echo txtStr
```

The script begins with `Option Explicit` and `On Error Resume Next`, after which it sets the constants, declares the variables, and binds the `adsUser` variable to the `AlistairGLN` user object. The script then divides into four sections:

Section A

Determines the User object's property count and lists each property's name and data type.

Section B

Creates a property entry and writes it to the cache. The last line uses the `IADsPropertyList::PutPropertyItem` method to write the new property entry for `adsUser` to the cache. However, you need to use the `IADs::SetInfo` method to write this entry to the directory.

Section C

Contains new code. The first line uses the `IADs::SetInfo` method to write the cache to the directory. The second line uses the explicit `IADs::GetInfo` method to read it back into the cache. Although the second line might not seem necessary, it is. If you don't use an explicit `IADs::GetInfo` call, you'll be accessing the same cache that you accessed before you added the new property entry. The explicit `IADs::GetInfo` call retrieves any new properties that anyone else has updated since your last implicit or explicit `IADs::GetInfo` call.

Section D

Recalculates the property count and renumerates each property's name and data type so that you can see the modifications. If you see the property count increase by one after you write the cache to the directory, the script has successfully executed.

Walking the Property Cache—The Solution

Example 15-8 is quite long. It walks through the property cache for an object and prints the name, data type, and values of each entry. Some of the properties are not printable strings, so printing them in a text format makes little sense. Thus, this script prints only the text strings.

The script also illustrates how you can use the WinNT: namespace rather than the LDAP: namespace in a script and how you can run the script against Windows NT domains and Windows NT/2000 individual servers rather than just Active Directory.

Example 15-8. Script to Walk Through the Property Cache for an Object and Display All Values

```
Option Explicit
'*********************************************************************
'Force error checking within the code using the Err.Number property
'method in approaches 2 and 3
'*********************************************************************
On Error Resume Next


'*********************************************************************
'Declare the constants and variables
'*********************************************************************
Const ADSTYPE_INVALID = 0
Const ADSTYPE_DN_STRING = 1
Const ADSTYPE_CASE_EXACT_STRING = 2
Const ADSTYPE_CASE_IGNORE_STRING = 3
Const ADSTYPE_PRINTABLE_STRING = 4
Const ADSTYPE_NUMERIC_STRING = 5
Const ADSTYPE_BOOLEAN = 6
Const ADSTYPE_INTEGER = 7
Const ADSTYPE_OCTET_STRING = 8
Const ADSTYPE_UTC_TIME = 9
Const ADSTYPE_LARGE_INTEGER = 10
Const ADSTYPE_PROV_SPECIFIC = 11
Const ADSTYPE_OBJECT_CLASS = 12
Const ADSTYPE_CASEIGNORE_LIST = 13
Const ADSTYPE_OCTET_LIST = 14
Const ADSTYPE_PATH = 15
Const ADSTYPE_POSTALADDRESS = 16
Const ADSTYPE_TIMESTAMP = 17
Const ADSTYPE_BACKLINK = 18
```

*Example 15-8. Script to Walk Through the Property Cache for an Object and Display
All Values (continued)*

```
Const ADSTYPE_TYPEDNAME = 19
Const ADSTYPE_HOLD = 20
Const ADSTYPE_NETADDRESS = 21
Const ADSTYPE_REPLICAPOINTER = 22
Const ADSTYPE_FAXNUMBER = 23
Const ADSTYPE_EMAIL = 24
Const ADSTYPE_NT_SECURITY_DESCRIPTOR = 25
Const ADSTYPE_UNKNOWN = 26

Const ADS_PROPERTY_CLEAR = 1
Const ADS_PROPERTY_UPDATE = 2
Const ADS_PROPERTY_APPEND = 3
Const ADS_PROPERTY_DELETE = 4

Dim adsPropValue   'An individual property value within a loop
Dim adsPropEntry   'An ADSI PropertyEntry object
Dim adsObject      'The object whose property list we wish to investigate
Dim txtStr         'A text string used to display results in one go
Dim intPropCount   'The number of properties in
Dim intIndex       'The index used while looping through the property list
Dim intCount       'Used to display property values in a numbered sequence

'***********************************************************************
'Uncomment one of these lines and modify it to your own environment.
'The first uses the LDAP namespace; the second uses the WinNT namespace.
'***********************************************************************
'Set adsObject = GetObject("LDAP://cn=Managers,ou=Sales,dc=mycorp,dc=com")
'Set adsObject = GetObject("WinNT://WINDOWS/Managers,Group")
adsObject.GetInfo

'***********************************************************************
'Write out the current property cache total to the string that is
'storing output
'***********************************************************************
intPropCount = adsObject.PropertyCount
txtStr = "There are " & intPropCount & " values in the property cache."
        & vbCrLf

'***********************************************************************
'The extra vbTabs used in the first loop are to space the results so
'that they are nicely formatted with the list of values in the second loop
'***********************************************************************
For intIndex = 0 To (intPropCount-1)

  Set adsPropEntry = adsObject.Item(intIndex)
  txtStr = txtStr & adsPropEntry.Name & vbCrLf

  If (adsPropEntry.ADsType = ADSTYPE_INVALID) Then
    txtStr = txtStr & vbTab & "Type:" & vbTab & vbTab & "INVALID"
            & vbCrLf
  ElseIf (adsPropEntry.ADsType = ADSTYPE_DN_STRING) Then
```

Example 15-8. Script to Walk Through the Property Cache for an Object and Display All Values (continued)

```
            txtStr = txtStr & vbTab & "Type:" & vbTab & vbTab & "DN_STRING"
                    & vbCrLf
        ElseIf (adsPropEntry.ADsType = ADSTYPE_CASE_EXACT_STRING) Then
            txtStr = txtStr & vbTab & "Type:" & vbTab & vbTab
                    & "CASE_EXACT_STRING" & vbCrLf
        ElseIf (adsPropEntry.ADsType = ADSTYPE_CASE_IGNORE_STRING) Then
            txtStr = txtStr & vbTab & "Type:" & vbTab & vbTab
                    & "CASE_IGNORE_STRING" & vbCrLf
        ElseIf (adsPropEntry.ADsType = ADSTYPE_PRINTABLE_STRING) Then
            txtStr = txtStr & vbTab & "Type:" & vbTab & vbTab
                    & "PRINTABLE_STRING" & vbCrLf
        ElseIf (adsPropEntry.ADsType = ADSTYPE_NUMERIC_STRING) Then
            txtStr = txtStr & vbTab & "Type:" & vbTab & vbTab & "NUMERIC_STRING"
                    & vbCrLf
        ElseIf (adsPropEntry.ADsType = ADSTYPE_BOOLEAN) Then
            txtStr = txtStr & vbTab & "Type:" & vbTab & vbTab & "BOOLEAN"
                    & vbCrLf
        ElseIf (adsPropEntry.ADsType = ADSTYPE_INTEGER) Then
            txtStr = txtStr & vbTab & "Type:" & vbTab & vbTab & "INTEGER"
                    & vbCrLf
        ElseIf (adsPropEntry.ADsType = ADSTYPE_OCTET_STRING) Then
            txtStr = txtStr & vbTab & "Type:" & vbTab & vbTab & "OCTET_STRING"
                    & vbCrLf
        ElseIf (adsPropEntry.ADsType = ADSTYPE_UTC_TIME) Then
            txtStr = txtStr & vbTab & "Type:" & vbTab & vbTab & "UTC_TIME"
                    & vbCrLf
        ElseIf (adsPropEntry.ADsType = ADSTYPE_LARGE_INTEGER) Then
            txtStr = txtStr & vbTab & "Type:" & vbTab & vbTab & "LARGE_INTEGER"
                    & vbCrLf
        ElseIf (adsPropEntry.ADsType = ADSTYPE_PROV_SPECIFIC) Then
            txtStr = txtStr & vbTab & "Type:" & vbTab & vbTab & "PROV_SPECIFIC"
                    & vbCrLf
        ElseIf (adsPropEntry.ADsType = ADSTYPE_OBJECT_CLASS) Then
            txtStr = txtStr & vbTab & "Type:" & vbTab & vbTab & "OBJECT_CLASS"
                    & vbCrLf
        ElseIf (adsPropEntry.ADsType = ADSTYPE_CASEIGNORE_LIST) Then
            txtStr = txtStr & vbTab & "Type:" & vbTab & vbTab & "CASEIGNORE_LIST"
                    & vbCrLf
        ElseIf (adsPropEntry.ADsType = ADSTYPE_OCTET_LIST) Then
            txtStr = txtStr & vbTab & "Type:" & vbTab & vbTab & "OCTET_LIST"
                    & vbCrLf
        ElseIf (adsPropEntry.ADsType = ADSTYPE_PATH) Then
            txtStr = txtStr & vbTab & "Type:" & vbTab & vbTab & "PATH"
                    & vbCrLf
        ElseIf (adsPropEntry.ADsType = ADSTYPE_POSTALADDRESS) Then
            txtStr = txtStr & vbTab & "Type:" & vbTab & vbTab & "POSTALADDRESS"
                    & vbCrLf
        ElseIf (adsPropEntry.ADsType = ADSTYPE_TIMESTAMP) Then
            txtStr = txtStr & vbTab & "Type:" & vbTab & vbTab & "TIMESTAMP"
                    & vbCrLf
        ElseIf (adsPropEntry.ADsType = ADSTYPE_BACKLINK) Then
```

Example 15-8. Script to Walk Through the Property Cache for an Object and Display
All Values (continued)

```
        txtStr = txtStr & vbTab & "Type:" & vbTab & vbTab & "BACKLINK"
            & vbCrLf
    ElseIf (adsPropEntry.ADsType = ADSTYPE_TYPEDNAME) Then
        txtStr = txtStr & vbTab & "Type:" & vbTab & vbTab & "TYPEDNAME"
            & vbCrLf
    ElseIf (adsPropEntry.ADsType = ADSTYPE_HOLD) Then
        txtStr = txtStr & vbTab & "Type:" & vbTab & vbTab & "HOLD"
            & vbCrLf
    ElseIf (adsPropEntry.ADsType = ADSTYPE_NETADDRESS) Then
        txtStr = txtStr & vbTab & "Type:" & vbTab & vbTab & "NETADDRESS"
            & vbCrLf
    ElseIf (adsPropEntry.ADsType = ADSTYPE_REPLICAPOINTER) Then
        txtStr = txtStr & vbTab & "Type:" & vbTab & vbTab & "REPLICAPOINTER"
            & vbCrLf
    ElseIf (adsPropEntry.ADsType = ADSTYPE_FAXNUMBER) Then
        txtStr = txtStr & vbTab & "Type:" & vbTab & vbTab & "FAXNUMBER"
            & vbCrLf
    ElseIf (adsPropEntry.ADsType = ADSTYPE_EMAIL) Then
        txtStr = txtStr & vbTab & "Type:" & vbTab & vbTab & "EMAIL" & vbCrLf
    ElseIf (adsPropEntry.ADsType = ADSTYPE_NT_SECURITY_DESCRIPTOR) Then
        txtStr = txtStr & vbTab & "Type:" & vbTab & vbTab
            & "NT_SECURITY_DESCRIPTOR" & vbCrLf
    ElseIf (adsPropEntry.ADsType = ADSTYPE_UNKNOWN) Then
        txtStr = txtStr & vbTab & "Type:" & vbTab & vbTab & "UNKNOWN"
            & vbCrLf
    End If

    '************************************************************************
    'Go through each property value in the property entry and use the AdsType
    'to print out the appropriate value, prefixed by a count (intCount), i.e.:
    '
    '   Value #1: Keith Cooper
    '   Value #2: Vicky Launders
    '   Value #3: Alistair Lowe-Norris
    '************************************************************************
    intCount = 1

    For Each adsPropValue In adsPropEntry.Values

        If (adsPropValue.ADsType = ADSTYPE_DN_STRING) Then
            txtStr = txtStr & vbTab & "Value #" & intCount & ":" _
                & vbTab & adsPropValue.DNString & vbCrLf
        ElseIf (adsPropValue.ADsType = ADSTYPE_CASE_EXACT_STRING) Then
            txtStr = txtStr & vbTab & "Value #" & intCount & ":" _
                & vbTab & adsPropValue.CaseExactString & vbCrLf
        ElseIf (adsPropValue.ADsType = ADSTYPE_CASE_IGNORE_STRING) Then
            txtStr = txtStr & vbTab & "Value #" & intCount & ":" _
                & vbTab & adsPropValue.CaseIgnoreString & vbCrLf
        ElseIf (adsPropValue.ADsType = ADSTYPE_PRINTABLE_STRING) Then
            txtStr = txtStr & vbTab & "Value #" & intCount & ":" _
                & vbTab & adsPropValue.PrintableString & vbCrLf
```

*Example 15-8. Script to Walk Through the Property Cache for an Object and Display
All Values (continued)*

```
    ElseIf (adsPropValue.ADsType = ADSTYPE_NUMERIC_STRING) Then
        txtStr = txtStr & vbTab & "Value #" & intCount & ":" _
            & vbTab & adsPropValue.NumericString & vbCrLf
    ElseIf (adsPropValue.ADsType = ADSTYPE_BOOLEAN) Then
        txtStr = txtStr & vbTab & "Value #" & intCount & ":" _
            & vbTab & CStr(adsPropValue.Boolean) & vbCrLf
    ElseIf (adsPropValue.ADsType = ADSTYPE_INTEGER) Then
        txtStr = txtStr & vbTab & "Value #" & intCount & ":" _
            & vbTab & adsPropValue.Integer & vbCrLf
    End If

    intCount=intCount+1

  Next
Next

WScript.Echo txtStr
```

This script displays every value in the property cache for an object. However, there may come a time when you wish to see the entire potential property cache for an object and list which of all possible values have been set. In order to do that, you need to query the formal schema class definition for the object. This leads us to the final section on the property cache.

Walking the Property Cache Using the Formal Schema Class Definition

There is one other way to walk the property list for a particular object: using its schema class details. Chapter 3, *Active Directory Schema*, explained how the Schema is the blueprint for objects that can exist in Active Directory. As each object schema class actually is held in Active Directory, you can navigate the object's properties by using IADsClass to display each individual item according to its formal name in the schema class. To do this, you first obtain a pointer to the object in the normal manner. You then obtain a pointer to the schema class for that object. You can do this using the **IADs::Schema** property method, which gives you the full ADsPath of the formal schema class. For example, the user object in the *mycorp.com* domain has the following schema ADsPath:

```
LDAP://cn=User,cn=Schema,cn=Configuration,dc=mycorp,dc=com
```

Then you can use the **IADsClass::MandatoryProperties** and **IADsClass:: OptionalProperties** methods to retrieve the appropriate properties. Example 15-9 nicely brings together **IADs::GetEx** for retrieving multiple properties and writing to a file, which is required due to the large number of properties.

This script uses On Error Resume Next on purpose as all properties may not display and the program will fail otherwise. The script also differs from the previous script; it lists all *possible* properties and if they've been set. The previous one listed those that had been set. The script is also generic; it will print out the property cache for any object class. Just change the ADsPath passed to GetObject.

Example 15-9. Complex Walk of the Property List for an Object Based on the Schema Definition for Its Class

```
Option Explicit
'**********************************************************************
'Force error checking within the code using the Err.Number property
'method in approaches 2 and 3
'**********************************************************************
On Error Resume Next

'**********************************************************************
'Declare the constants and variables
'**********************************************************************
Dim adsObject      'Active Directory object
Dim adsClass       'ADSI Class object
Dim adsProp        'An individual property
Dim intCount       'Incremental counter for display
Dim fileObject     'A FileSystemObject
Dim outTextFile    'A TextStream Object


'**********************************************************************
'Create a VBScript file object and use it to open a text file. The
'second parameter specifies to overwrite any existing file that exists.
'**********************************************************************
Set fileObject = CreateObject("Scripting.FileSystemObject")
Set outTextFile = fileObject.CreateTextFile("c:\out.txt", TRUE)

'**********************************************************************
'Bind to the object and get a pointer to the appropriate schema class,
'i.e., User in this case
'**********************************************************************
Set adsObject =
         GetObject("LDAP://cn=administrator,cn=Users,dc=mycorp,dc=com")
Set adsClass = GetObject(adsObject.Schema)

intCount = 1

'**********************************************************************
'Iterate through all the mandatory properties
'**********************************************************************
For Each adsProp in adsClass.MandatoryProperties
  EnumerateProperties adsProp, outTextFile, adsObject
  intCount=intCount+1
Next

'**********************************************************************
'Iterate through all the optional properties
```

Example 15-9. Complex Walk of the Property List for an Object Based on the Schema Definition for Its Class (continued)

```
'**********************************************************************
For Each adsProp in adsClass.OptionalProperties
  EnumerateProperties adsProp
  intCount=intCount+1
Next

outTextFile.Close

'**********************************************************************
'Subroutine EnumerateProperties
'**********************************************************************
Sub EnumerateProperties(ByVal adsProp, ByVal tsFile, ByVal adsObj)

  Dim adsProperty   'ADSI Property object
  Dim arrElement    'Array of elements

  '**********************************************************************
  'Get pointer to the schema property object
  '**********************************************************************
  Set adsProperty = GetObject("LDAP://Schema/" & adsProp)

  '**********************************************************************
  'Check whether property requires GetEx using IADsProperty::MultiValued
  '**********************************************************************
  If adsProperty.MultiValued Then
    tsFile.WriteLine intCount & ") " & adsProp & _
      " (" & adsProperty.Syntax & ") (MULTI-VALUED)"

    '**********************************************************************
    'Check whether array returned from GetEx is empty using VBScript
    'function
    '**********************************************************************
    If (IsEmpty(adsObj.GetEx(adsProp))) Then
      tsFile.WriteLine vbTab & "= " & "NO VALUES SET!"
    Else
      For Each arrElement in adsObj.GetEx(adsProp)
        tsFile.WriteLine vbTab & "= " & arrElement
      Next
    End If

  Else
    tsFile.WriteLine intCount & ") " & adsProp _
      & " (" & adsProperty.Syntax & ")"

    Err.Clear
    If Err=0 Then
      tsFile.WriteLine vbTab & "= " & adsObj.Get(adsProp)
    Else
      tsFile.WriteLine vbTab & "= " & "Not Set!"
    End If

  End If
End Sub
```

Checking for Errors in VBScript

It will be worthwhile to look at error handling in a little more detail now. Normally errors that occur in a script are termed *fatal errors*. This means that execution of the script terminates whenever an error occurs. When this happens, a dialog box opens up and gives you the unique number and description of the error. While this is useful, sometimes you may like to set errors to be nonfatal, so that execution continues after the error. To do this, you include the following line in your code:

```
On Error Resume Next
```

Once you have done this, any line with an error is ignored. This can cause confusion, as can be seen from the following code. Note the missing *P* in *LDAP*:

```
On Error Resume Next

Set adsGroup = GetObject("LDA://cn=Managers,ou=Sales,dc=mycorp,dc=com")

adsGroup.GetInfo
WScript.Echo adsGroup.Description
adsGroup.Description = "My new group description goes here"
adsGroup.GetInfo
WScript.Echo adsGroup.Description
```

This script fails to execute any of the lines after the **On Error Resume Next** statement, as the first LDAP call into the **adsGroup** variable failed. However, it will not terminate as usual with an error after the **GetObject** line, due to the **On Error** statement. To get around this, you should couple important lines with error checking. Here is a good example of error checking in a different script:

```
On Error Resume Next

'**********************************************************************
'Clear errors
'**********************************************************************
Err.Clear

'**********************************************************************
'Get a pointer to the Administrator account
'**********************************************************************
Set adsUser =
        GetObject ("LDAP://cn=Administrator,cn=Users,dc=mycorp,dc=com")
If Hex(Err.Number)="&H80005000" Then
  WScript.Echo "Bad ADSI path!" & vbCrLf & "Err. Number: " _
    & vbTab & CStr(Hex(Err.Number)) & vbCrLf & "Err. Descr.: " _
    & vbTab & Err.Description
  WScript.Quit
End If

'**********************************************************************
```

```
'Explicitly call GetInfo for completeness
'**********************************************************************
adsUser.GetInfo


'**********************************************************************
'Clear any previous errors
'**********************************************************************
Err.Clear


'**********************************************************************
'Try and get a pointer to the "moose" attribute of the user (which
'doesn't exist)
'**********************************************************************
x = adsUser.Get("moose")


'**********************************************************************
'Check for property does not exist error
'**********************************************************************
If Hex(Err.Number)="&H8000500D" Then
  WScript.Echo "No such property!" & vbCrLf & "Err. Number: " _
    & vbTab & CStr(Hex(Err.Number)) & vbCrLf & "Err. Descr.: " _
    & vbTab & Err.Description
End If
```

This is a simple example; the path does exist and the moose property does not exist for the user. ADSI errors start at 80005 in hexadecimal, and 8000500D is the error indicating that there is no such property. The ampersand H (&H) prefix indicates that the following string is a hexadecimal number. You must use the Err::Clear method from the Err interface to clear any existing error information, prior to making a call that could generate an error. If an error has occurred, then the value of Err.Number is nonzero; if Err.Number is 0, then no error occurred. If an error has occurred, Err.Description contains any description that has been set for that error.

I use the functions Hex and CStr in Example 15-9 one after the other in order to print out the hexadecimal string of the error number. I choose to do this as Microsoft specifies error numbers in hexadecimal, and if you are to easily look them up against Microsoft's documentation, you need to see the hexadecimal rather than getting out a calculator. The CStr function converts the newly converted hexadecimal value to a text string that can be printed out.

Since most calls to the Err interface will be to retrieve the Err::Number property, the Err::Number property is set as the default property method, meaning that you don't have to explicitly state it. For example, these two statements are equivalent:

```
If Hex(Err)="&H8000500D" Then
If Hex(Err.Number)="&H8000500D" Then
```

In addition, as Hex(0) is the same as 0, most sample code that you will see using VBScript looks like this:

```
On Error Resume Next

'Some_code_goes_here

Err.Clear
Set x = GetObject(something_goes_here)
If Err=0 Then
  'No error occurred
  Some_success_code_goes_here
Else
  'Error occurred
  Some_failure_code_goes_here
End If
```

Finally, to reset error checking back to the default as if the On Error Resume Next statement had not been included, you use the following code:

```
'The last character is a zero, not a capital "o"
On Error Goto 0
```

A full list of ADSI errors can be found in the following MSDN location: Platform SDK → Networking Services → Active Directory → Active Directory Service Interfaces Version 2.5 → ADSI Reference → ADSI Error Codes. This equates currently to the following URL: *http://msdn.microsoft.com/isapi/msdnlib.idc?theURL=/library/ sdkdoc/adsi/ds2_error_0t9v.htm.*

Summary

In the past two chapters, I've covered the interfaces that have methods and properties that manage the basic Active Directory objects:

- IADs
- IADsContainer (covered more fully later when dealing with services)
- IADsPropertyList
- IADsPropertyEntry
- IADsPropertyValue

I've also looked at how to supply credentials to authenticate to a directory service:

- IADsOpenDSObject

and how to manage group objects and their members:

- IADsGroup
- IADsMember

16

Users

In this chapter I show you how to automate two fundamental administrative tasks: creating and manipulating user accounts.

Although tools to create user accounts already exist (e.g., the *Microsoft Windows NT Server 4.0 Resource Kit's* Addusers utility), ADSI's versatility lets you quickly write a script that creates one standard or fully featured user account or a script that creates a thousand fully featured user accounts. You can even create a command-line utility that unlocks locked-out user accounts.

Creating a Standard User Account

You can quickly create a standard user account (i.e., a user account with minimal attributes) with the ADSI script in Example 16-1.

Example 16-1. Creating a Standard User Account in Windows NT and Windows 2000

```
Option Explicit

Dim adsDomain, adsUser

'Creating a user in a Windows NT domain
Set adsDomain = GetObject("WinNT://MYDOMAIN")
Set adsUser = adsDomain.Create("user","vlaunders")
adsUser.SetInfo

'Creating a local user on a local computer (valid for Windows 2000 or Windows NT)
Set adsComputer = GetObject("WinNT://MYCOMPUTER,Computer")
Set adsUser = adsComputer.Create("user","vlaunders")
adsUser.SetInfo

'Creating a user in a Windows 2000 domain
```

Example 16-1. Creating a Standard User Account in Windows NT and
Windows 2000 (continued)

```
Set adsDomain = GetObject("LDAP://cn=Users,dc=mywindowsdomain,dc=mycorp,dc=com")
Set adsUser = adsDomain.Create("user","cn=vlaunders")
adsUser.Put "sAMAccountName", "vlaunders"
adsUser.Put "userPrincipalName", "vlaunders@mycorp.com"
adsUser.SetInfo
```

Example 16-1 is composed of three sections. The first section uses the WinNT: namespace to create a user account in an NT domain. The second section creates a user account in a local SAM on a Windows NT or Windows 2000 workstation or member server. Using the WinNT: namespace, however, will not enable you to set all Active Directory attributes that a Windows 2000 account might require. Thus, in the third section, I use the LDAP: namespace to create a user account in a Windows 2000 domain. Creating a user account with ADSI is almost identical to creating a group. You first need to bind to the parent container, and then use the `IADsContainer::Create` method to create the user. Then set the properties and write the property cache out with `IADs::SetInfo`.

When you create standard users in a Windows 2000 domain, you need to be aware of two important User object attributes: sAMAccountName and userPrincipalName. The User object has several mandatory attributes. The system sets these mandatory attributes, except for one, sAMAccountName, which specifies the name that represents the user to NT clients and servers that are lower in the Windows 2000 hierarchy. You must set the sAMAccountName attribute before you call `IADs::SetInfo`. The userPrincipalName attribute isn't mandatory, but I recommend that you set this property value. If you include the userPrincipalName attribute, Windows 2000 users can log on with their fully qualified Request for Comments (RFC) 822 email address.*

Creating a Fully Featured User Account

Creating standard users is acceptable if you need to get the task done quickly. However, you probably want to create fully featured users (i.e., users for whom you set all applicable attributes). The approaches you use to create fully featured users in the NT and Windows 2000 environments differ slightly; Windows 2000 offers many more properties than NT offers, such as the office and home addresses of users, as well as lists of email addresses and pager, fax, and phone numbers.

You can manipulate User objects with a special interface called IADsUser. IADsUser's methods and property methods let you directly set many of the User

---

* For more information about RFC 822, go to *ftp://ftp.isi.edu/ innotes/rfc822.txt.*

object's property values. Tables 16-1 through 16-3 contain the methods, read-write property methods, and read-only property methods, respectively, for the IADs-User interface.

Table 16-1. IADsUser Methods for Windows NT and Windows 2000

Method	Description
IADsUser::ChangePassword	Changes the existing password.
IADsUser::SetPassword	Sets a new password without needing the old one.
IADsUser::Groups	Gets a list of groups of which the user is a member. You can use the IADsMembers interface to iterate through the list.

Table 16-2. IADsUser Read-Write Property Methods

Property Method	Available in NT?
IADsUser::AccountDisabled	Yes
IADsUser::AccountExpirationDate	Yes
IADsUser::Department	No
IADsUser::Description	Yes
IADsUser::Division	No
IADsUser::EmailAddress	No
IADsUser::EmployeeID	No
IADsUser::FaxNumber	No
IADsUser::FirstName	No
IADsUser::FullName	Yes
IADsUser::GraceLoginsAllowed	Yes (NDS: and NWCOMPAT: providers only)
IADsUser::GraceLoginsRemaining	Yes (NDS: and NWCOMPAT: providers only)
IADsUser::HomeDirDrive	Yes (WinNT: providers only)
IADsUser::HomeDirectory	Yes
IADsUser::HomePage	No
IADsUser::IsAccountLocked	Yes
IADsUser::Languages	No
IADsUser::LastName	No
IADsUser::LoginHours	Yes
IADsUser::LoginScript	Yes
IADsUser::LoginWorkstations	Yes
IADsUser::Manager	No
IADsUser::MaxLogins	Yes (NDS: and NWCOMPAT: providers only)
IADsUser::MaxStorage	Yes
IADsUser::NamePrefix	No

Table 16-2. IADsUser Read-Write Property Methods (continued)

Property Method	Available in NT?
IADsUser::NameSuffix	No
IADsUser::OfficeLocations	No
IADsUser::OtherName	No
IADsUser::PasswordExpirationDate	Yes (can't set via LDAP; must set via group policies)
IADsUser::PasswordMinimumLength	Yes (can't set via LDAP; must set via group policies)
IADsUser::PasswordRequired	Yes
IADsUser::Picture	No
IADsUser::PostalAddresses	No
IADsUser::PostalCodes	No
IADsUser::Profile	Yes
IADsUser::RequireUniquePassword	Yes (can't set via LDAP; must set via group policies)
IADsUser::SeeAlso	No
IADsUser::TelephoneHome	No
IADsUser::TelephoneMobile	No
IADsUser::TelephoneNumber	No
IADsUser::TelephonePager	No
IADsUser::Title	No

Table 16-3. IADsUser Read-Only Property Methods

Property Method	Available in NT?
IADsUser::BadLoginAddress	No (NDS: and NWCOMPAT: providers only)
IADsUser::BadLoginCount	Yes
IADsUser::LastFailedLogin	No
IADsUser::LastLogin	Yes
IADsUser::LastLogoff	Yes
IADsUser::PasswordLastChanged	No

For descriptions of the property methods, go to MSDN and then select Platform SDK → Network Services → Active Directory → Active Directory Service Interface Version 2.5 → ADSI Reference → ADSI Interfaces → Persistent Object Interfaces → IADsUser.

To be up to date on which properties WinNT doesn't support, select Platform SDK → Network Services → Active Directory → ADSI 2.5 → ADSI Reference → ADSI System Providers → ADSI WinNT Provider → WinNT User Object → Unsupported IADsUser Property Methods.

Let's apply some of this knowledge to two examples. Example 16-2 shows how to create a fully featured user in Windows NT, and Example 16-3 shows how to create a fully featured user in Windows 2000. Both contain user-specific scripts.

Creating a User with the WinNT Namespace

Example 16-2 uses several IADsUser property methods and several constant values to create a fully featured user in NT. The script sets several read-write properties for the User object, including HomeDirectory.

In NT, you can establish a home directory for a user one of two ways. You can specify an explicit local path that the system automatically maps during logon, or you can specify a Uniform Naming Convention (UNC) path to a remote share that you map to a drive letter. If you want to map to a local path (e.g., *C:*), don't set the HomeDirDrive property and use an explicit path for IADsUser::HomeDirectory. If you want to map a drive letter to a remote share, set the HomeDirDrive property to the drive letter you want to map to and use a UNC path for IADsUser::HomeDirectory.

Example 16-2. Creating a Full-Featured User Account in NT

```
Option Explicit

'*********************************************************************
'WshShell::Run constants
'*********************************************************************
Const vbMinimizedNoFocus = 6


'*********************************************************************
'Flag constants. See the later sidebar on "Boolean Arithmetic with
'Hexadecimal Values."
'*********************************************************************
Const UF_SCRIPT = &H1
Const UF_ACCOUNTDISABLE = &H2
Const UF_HOMEDIR_REQUIRED = &H8
Const UF_LOCKOUT = &H10
Const UF_PASSWD_NOTREQD = &H20
Const UF_PASSWORD_CANT_CHANGE = &H40
Const UF_ENCRYPTED_TEXT_PASSWORD_ALLOWED = &H80
Const UF_DONT_EXPIRE_PASSWD = &H10000

Dim adsDomain, adsUser, fso, intUserFlags, intNewUserFlags
Dim fldUserHomedir, wshShell

Set adsDomain = GetObject("WinNT://MYDOMAIN")
Set adsUser = adsDomain.Create("user","vlaunders")

'*********************************************************************
'Write the newly created object out from the property cache and read
'all the properties for the object, including the ones set by the
'system on creation
```

Example 16-2. Creating a Full-Featured User Account in NT (continued)

```
'**********************************************************************
adsUser.SetInfo
adsUser.GetInfo


'**********************************************************************
'Set the properties
'**********************************************************************
adsUser.AccountDisabled = False
adsUser.AccountExpirationDate = "02/05/01"
adsUser.Description = "My description goes here!"
adsUser.FullName = "Victoria Launders"
adsUser.IsAccountLocked = False
adsUser.LoginScript = "\\MYDOMAIN\DFS\Loginscripts\vlaunders.vbs"
adsUser.PasswordRequired = True
adsUser.Profile = "\\MYDOMAIN\DFS\Users\vlaunders\profile"
adsUser.HomeDirectory = "\\MYDOMAIN\DFS\Users\vlaunders"
adsUser.HomeDirDrive = "Z:"


'**********************************************************************
'Set all the properties for the user and read back the data, including
'any default so that you can set the flags
'**********************************************************************
adsUser.SetInfo
adsUser.GetInfo


'**********************************************************************
'Make sure the password never expires and the user can't change it
'**********************************************************************
intUserFlags = adsUser.Get("userFlags")
intNewUserFlags = intUserFlags Or UF_DONT_EXPIRE_PASSWD
intNewUserFlags = intNewUserFlags Or UF_PASSWORD_CANT_CHANGE
adsUser.Put "userFlags", intNewUserFlags
adsUser.SetInfo


'**********************************************************************
'Create the home directory
'**********************************************************************
Set fso = CreateObject("Scripting.FileSystemObject")
If Not fso.FolderExists("\\MYDOMAIN\DFS\Users\vlaunders") Then
    Set fldUserHomedir = fso.CreateFolder("\\MYDOMAIN\DFS\Users\vlaunders")
End If


'**********************************************************************
'Set full rights for the user to the home directory
'**********************************************************************
Set wshShell = WScript.CreateObject("Wscript.Shell")
wshShell.Run "cacls \\MYDOMAIN\DFS\Users\vlaunders /e /g vlaunders:F", _
  vbMinimizedNoFocus, True


'**********************************************************************
'Set the password
'**********************************************************************
adsUser.SetPassword "thepassword"
```

Most of the code in the script is self-explanatory, except for two areas: making sure the password never expires and setting full rights for the user to their new home directory.

You use two hexadecimal constants to explicitly force the new user account to have a password that never expires and that the user can't change. The code to set these password requirements might seem complicated, but the code involves simple arithmetic; the sidebar "Boolean Arithmetic with Hexadecimal Values" explains this arithmetic. If you prefer not to use hex constants, you might be able to use a User object property method. For example, you can use the `IADsUser::AccountDisabled` property method instead of the UF_ACCOUNTDISABLE constant to disable an account. Similarly, you can use the `IADsUser::IsAccountLocked` property method instead of the UF_LOCKOUT constant to lock an account. These IADs property methods hide the arithmetic within a simple Boolean value.

You create the directory by obtaining a reference to a FileSystemObject object and calling the `FileSystemObject::CreateFolder` method if the directory doesn't already exist. Set the permissions by running Windows NT/Windows 2000's *CACLS.EXE* command from within Windows Scripting Host (WSH) via the `WshShell::Run` method. You need to include three parameters. The first parameter is the command you want to execute; the second parameter can be any of the following constant values based on your needs:

```
Const vbHide = 0
Const vbNormalFocus = 1
Const vbMinimizedFocus = 2
Const vbMaximizedFocus = 3
Const vbNormalNoFocus = 4
Const vbMinimizedNoFocus = 6
```

The last parameter to the `WshShell::Run` method is True if you want the script to wait until CACLS finishes before continuing to the next line, which sets the password.

As an alternative to using CACLS to set permissions, you could write a script that makes use of the *ADSecurity.dll* provided with the full ADSI SDK to set the permissions. This DLL provides a different interface for managing Security Descriptors, ACLs, and ACEs as discussed in Chapter 18, *Permissions and Auditing*.

The User object has several read-write attributes that the script doesn't include but that you might want to set for NT users. Those attributes are PasswordExpired, PrimaryGroupID, ObjectSID, and Parameters.

Boolean Arithmetic with Hexadecimal Values

Assume that you want an attribute of an object (e.g., userFlags of the User object) to set eight values. You use an 8-bit binary number to represent those eight values. If you want the attribute to hold 11 values, you use an 11-bit binary number.

The binary system is a base-2 system in which 0 typically represents a false condition and 1 typically represents a true condition. In this example, 0 means the value isn't set, and 1 means the value is set. So, if you want to set only the third and eighth values of an eight-value attribute, you set the third and eighth bits of an 8-bit binary number to 1, or &B10000100. (You read binary numbers from right to left.) The prefix *&B* specifies that the number is binary.

However, attributes store data as decimal values. Thus, you need to convert the binary number into a decimal value, which is base-10. For example, the binary number &B10000100 translates into:

$$2^7 + 2^2 = 128 + 4 = 132$$

You use the Boolean AND operator to check whether a bit is set and the OR operator to set a bit. For example, suppose you want to see whether the fourth bit is set in an 8-bit binary number that has a decimal value of 132. You can check for the existence of this bit using the AND operator to compare the number to a binary mask indicating that the fourth bit is set. The equation to do this is:

```
&B10000100 AND &B00001000 = &B00000000
```

You solve this equation by resolving the AND operation for each bit individually. For example, the first bit in &B10000100 is 0, and the first bit in &B00001000 is 0: 0 AND 0 is 0. The second bit in &B10000100 is 0, and the second bit in &B00001000 is 0: 0 AND 0 is 0. The third bit in &B10000100 is 1, and the third bit in &B00001000 is 0; 1 AND 0 is 0. When you calculate all eight bits, the result is &B00000000. In other words, the fourth bit isn't set.

Suppose you want to test whether the third bit is set:

```
&B10000100 AND &B0000100 = &B00000100
```

Because the third bit in &B10000100 is 1, and the third bit in &B0000100 is 1, the resulting bit is 1 (1 AND 1 is 1), which specifies that the value for the third bit is set.

Let's translate this binary equation into decimal and hex equations:

```
&B10000100 AND &B0000100 = &B00000100
132 AND 4 = 4
&H84 AND &H4 = &H4
```

—Continued—

If the return value is 0 or &H0, the bit isn't set. If the return value is the bit's actual value (in this case, 4 or &H4), the bit is set.

Just like the AND operator, the OR operator works with binary, decimal, and hex systems. Taking the example just given, let's try to set the third bit, which happens to be already set:

```
&B10000100 OR &B0000100 = &B10000100
132 OR 4 = 132
&H84 OR &H4 = &H84
```

In other words, the result is the new value with that bit set. Because that bit was already set, nothing changes. Let's try setting the fourth bit, which isn't already set:

```
&B10000100 OR &B00001000 = &B10001100
132 OR 8 = 140
&H84 OR &H8 = &H8C
```

The result includes a newly set fourth bit. You can even set two bits at once. For example, here's how you set the fourth and fifth bits:

```
&B10000100 OR &B00011000 = &B10011100
132 OR 24 = 156
&H84 OR &H18 = &H9C
```

Although the Boolean mathematics is straightforward, luckily you don't have to include this code in a script. Instead, you typically use constants. For example, if you declare the constant:

```
Const UF_DONT_EXPIRE_PASSWD = &H10000
```

you just need to specify that constant in the script. To determine this bit's existence, use the code:

```
If intUserFlags And UF_DONT_EXPIRE_PASSWD = 0 Then
'UF_DONT_EXPIRE_PASSWD is not set
Else
'UF_DONT_EXPIRE_PASSWD is set
End If
```

You set bits in a similar fashion. For example, to set the &H10000 bit, use the code:

```
intUserFlags = intUserFlags Or UF_DONT_EXPIRE_PASSWD
```

The PasswordExpired attribute specifies if users must change their passwords the next time they log on. A value of 1 means users must change their passwords; a value of 0 means users don't have to change their passwords. The Primary-GroupID property holds the primary group ID as an integer, and the ObjectSID attribute holds security ID (SID) data. The Parameters attribute holds a host of extra user data relating to other Microsoft products, such as NT Server 4.0 Terminal Server Edition and File-and-Print-for-NetWare data.

The Parameters attribute illustrates how Windows 2000's Active Directory is much better than NT's SAM. Previously, the only way to add extra property data into the static SAM was through the Parameters attribute method. With Active Directory, you can extend the User object to hold whatever properties you need. Thus, if you need a Languages Spoken attribute on the User object, you create it and then use IADs::Get and IADs::Put to get and set the attribute.

Creating a User with the LDAP Namespace

Example 16-3 shows how to create the same user in Windows 2000's Active Directory. This script is similar to the last one, with one major difference: the property name userFlags changes to userAccountControl for the extended settings. Other minor differences exist, such as the use of more constants and property methods. Windows 2000 lets you set many property values for users, including multivalue properties that you set via an array. For example, you can list several telephone numbers for the TelephoneNumber, TelephoneMobile, and TelephoneHome properties. Through the use of constants, you can even set up Active Directory to let users log on with smart cards.

Example 16-3. Creating a Full-Featured User Account in Windows 2000

```
Option Explicit

'*********************************************************************
'WshShell::Run constants
'*********************************************************************
Const vbMinimizedNoFocus = 6

'*********************************************************************
'Flag constants. See the later sidebar on "Boolean Arithmetic with
'Hexadecimal Values."
'*********************************************************************
Const UF_SCRIPT = &H1
Const UF_ACCOUNTDISABLE = &H2
Const UF_HOMEDIR_REQUIRED = &H8
Const UF_LOCKOUT = &H10
Const UF_PASSWD_NOTREQD = &H20
Const UF_PASSWORD_CANT_CHANGE = &H40
Const UF_ENCRYPTED_TEXT_PASSWORD_ALLOWED = &H80
Const UF_DONT_EXPIRE_PASSWD = &H10000
Const UF_MNS_LOGON_ACCOUNT = &H20000
Const UF_SMARTCARD_REQUIRED = &H40000
Const UF_TRUSTED_FOR_DELEGATION = &H80000
Const UF_NOT_DELEGATED = &H100000

Const ADS_PROPERTY_UPDATE = 2

Dim adsDomain, adsUser, fso, intUserFlags, intNewUserFlags
Dim fldUserHomedir, wshShell
```

Example 16-3. Creating a Full-Featured User Account in Windows 2000 (continued)

```
Set adsDomain = GetObject("LDAP://cn=Users,dc=windows,dc=mycorp,dc=com")
Set adsUser = adsDomain.Create("user","cn=vlaunders")
adsUser.Put "sAMAccountName", "vlaunders"
adsUser.Put "userPrincipalName", "vlaunders@mycorp.com"

'**********************************************************************
'Write the newly created object out from the property cache and read
'all the properties for the object, including the ones set by the
'system on creation
'**********************************************************************
adsUser.SetInfo
adsUser.GetInfo

'**********************************************************************
'Set the properties
'**********************************************************************
adsUser.AccountDisabled = False
adsUser.AccountExpirationDate = "02/05/01"
adsUser.Description = "My description goes here!"
adsUser.IsAccountLocked = False
adsUser.LoginScript = "\\MYDOMAIN\DFS\Loginscripts\vlaunders.vbs"
adsUser.Profile = "\\MYDOMAIN\DFS\Users\vlaunders\profile"
adsUser.PasswordRequired = True
adsUser.TelephoneHome = Array("0123-555-7890")
adsUser.PutEx ADS_PROPERTY_UPDATE, "otherHomePhone", _
  Array("0123 555 7891", "0123 555 7892")
adsUser.TelephoneNumber = Array("0123 555 7890")
adsUser.PutEx ADS_PROPERTY_UPDATE, "otherTelephone", _
  Array("0123 555 7891", "0123 555 7892")
adsUser.TelephoneMobile = Array("0123 555 7890")
adsUser.PutEx ADS_PROPERTY_UPDATE, "otherMobile", _
  Array("0123 555 7891", "0123 555 7892")
adsUser.NamePrefix = "Ms."
adsUser.FirstName = "Victoria"
adsUser.LastName = "Launders"
adsUser.DisplayName = "Victoria Launders"

'**********************************************************************
'Set the drive that you'll map to
'**********************************************************************
adsUser.HomeDirectory = "\\MYDOMAIN\DFS\Users\vlaunders"
adsUser.Put "homeDrive", "Z:"

'**********************************************************************
'Set all the properties for the user and read back the data, including
'any defaults, so that you can set the flags
'**********************************************************************
adsUser.SetInfo
adsUser.GetInfo

'**********************************************************************
'Make sure the password never expires and the user can't change it
```

Example 16-3. Creating a Full-Featured User Account in Windows 2000 (continued)

```
'************************************************************************
intUserFlags = adsUser.Get("userAccountControl")
intNewUserFlags = intUserFlags Or UF_DONT_EXPIRE_PASSWD
intNewUserFlags = intNewUserFlags Or UF_PASSWORD_CANT_CHANGE
adsUser.Put "userAccountControl", intNewUserFlags
adsUser.SetInfo


'************************************************************************
'Create the home directory
'************************************************************************
Set fso = CreateObject("Scripting.FileSystemObject")
If Not fso.FolderExists("\\MYDOMAIN\DFS\Users\vlaunders") Then
    Set fldUserHomedir = fso.CreateFolder("\\MYDOMAIN\DFS\Users\vlaunders")
End If


'************************************************************************
'Set full rights for the user to the home directory
'************************************************************************
Set wshShell = WScript.CreateObject("Wscript.Shell")
wshShell.Run "cacls \\MYDOMAIN\DFS\Users\vlaunders /e /g vlaunders:F", 1, True


'************************************************************************
'Set the password
'************************************************************************
adsUser.SetPass word "bibble"
```

Creating Many User Accounts

User-specific scripts work well if you have to create only a few user accounts. If you need to create many user accounts at one time or if you create new accounts often, using a universal script with an input file is more efficient. The input file includes the user data so that you can use the script to create any user account. For example, the output shown in Example 16-4 represents the *users-to-create.txt* input file that provides the user data for the universal script that follows. Although this input file includes only four data sets, you can include as many data sets as you want. You include a data set for each user account that you want to create:

```
vlaunders:12/09/01:The description:Victoria Launders:onebanana
aglowenorris:08/07/00:Another user:Alistair Lowe-Norris:twobanana
kbemowski:03/03/03:A third user:Karen Bemowski:threebanana
jkellett:08/09/99:A fourth user:Jenneth Kellett:four
```

As the output shows, each data set goes on a separate line. A data set can contain as many values as you want. The data sets in the *users-to-create.txt* file have five values: username, expiration date, description, full name, and password. You use colons to separate the values.[*]

---

[*] While comma-separate-value (CSV) files are the norm for this sort of thing, the comma is more often used in properties that will be added for users, so I use the colon here instead.

Example 16-4. Using a Text File to Create Many User Accounts in Windows 2000

```
Option Explicit

Const ForReading = 1

Dim adsDomain, adsUser, fso, tsInputFile, strLine, arrInput
Dim fldUserHomedir, wshShell

Set adsDomain = GetObject("LDAP://cn=Users,dc=mywindowsdomain,dc=mycorp,dc=com")
Set fso = CreateObject("Scripting.FileSystemObject")

'************************************************************************
'Open the text file as a text stream for reading.
'Don't create a file if users-to-create.txt doesn't exist
'************************************************************************
Set tsInputFile = fso.OpenTextFile("c:\users-to-create.txt", ForReading, False)

'************************************************************************
'Execute the lines inside the loop, even though you're not at the end
'of the file
'************************************************************************
While Not tsInputFile.AtEndOfStream

    '************************************************************************
    'Read a line, and use the Split function to split the data set into
    'its separate parts
    '************************************************************************
    strLine = tsInputFile.ReadLine
    arrInput = Split(strLine, ":")

    Set adsUser = adsDomain.Create("user","cn=" & arrInput(0))
    adsUser.Put "sAMAccountName", & arrInput(0)
    adsUser.Put "userPrincipalName", arrInput(0) & "@mycorp.com"

    '************************************************************************
    'Write the newly created object out from the property cache
    'Read all the properties for the object, including
    'the ones set by the system on creation
    '************************************************************************
    adsUser.SetInfo
    adsUser.GetInfo

    '************************************************************************
    'Set the properties
    '************************************************************************
    adsUser.AccountDisabled = False
    adsUser.AccountExpirationDate = arrInput(1)
    adsUser.Description = arrInput(2)
    adsUser.IsAccountLocked = False
    adsUser.LoginScript = "\\MYDOMAIN\DFS\Loginscripts\" & arrInput(0) & ".vbs"
    adsUser.Profile = "\\MYDOMAIN\DFS\Users\" & arrInput(0) & "\profile"
    adsUser.PasswordRequired = True
    adsUser.DisplayName = arrInput(3)
```

Example 16-4. Using a Text File to Create Many User Accounts in Windows 2000 (continued)

```
'**********************************************************************
'Set the drive that you'll map to
'**********************************************************************
adsUser.HomeDirectory = "\\MYDOMAIN\DFS\Users\" & arrInput(0)
adsUser.Put "homeDrive", "Z:"
adsUser.SetInfo

'**********************************************************************
'Create the home directory
'**********************************************************************
If Not fso.FolderExists("\\MYDOMAIN\DFS\Users\" & arrInput(0)) Then
  Set fldUserHomedir = fso.CreateFolder("\\MYDOMAIN\DFS\Users\" & arrInput(0))
End If

'**********************************************************************
'Set full rights for the user to the home directory
'**********************************************************************
Set wshShell = WScript.CreateObject("Wscript.Shell")
wshShell.Run "cacls \\MYDOMAIN\DFS\Users\" & arrInput(0) _
  & " /e /g " & arrInput(0) & ":F", 1, True

'**********************************************************************
'Set the password
'**********************************************************************
adsUser.SetPassword arrInput(4)

'**********************************************************************
'Stop referencing this user
'**********************************************************************
Set adsUser = Nothing
Wend

'Close the file
tsInputFile.Close
```

The universal script reads in the user data to create the user accounts. As the script shows, you use FileSystemObject (FSO) and TextStream (TS) objects to manipulate the user data. For information about FSO and TS objects, go to the MSDN Scripting web site at *http://msdn.microsoft.com/scripting/default.htm?/scripting/vbScript/doc/vbsfsotutor.htm.* After you create a reference to an FSO object and assign that reference to the `fso` variable, apply the `FileSystemObject::OpenTextFile` method to open the *users-to-create.txt* file, setting the user data to the `tsInputFile` TS variable. Then use a `while` loop with the `TextStream::AtEndOfStream` method to loop through each line in `tsInputFile` until the end of the file. Once you reach the end of the file, use the `TextStream::Close` method to end the script.

The `while` loop is the heart of the script. Begin the `while` loop by applying the `TextStream::ReadLine` method to read in one line of `tsInputFile` at a time. The `strLine` string variable holds the retrieved data from that line, which you pass to VBScript's `Split` function. Using the colon as the separator, this function splits the data set into its five parts, assigning the data to the `arrInput` array variable. This array has index values that correspond to the five parts: 0 represents the username, 1 represents the expiration date, 2 represents the description, 3 represents the full name, and 4 represents the password.

The code in the middle of the `while` loop is similar to the code used earlier. After you create a reference to an ADSI User object and assign that reference to the `adsUser` variable, set that user's property values (including the home drive). Then use `IADs::SetInfo`, create the home directory, set the directory permissions, and set the password. However, instead of specifying each user's username, expiration date, description, full name, and password in the code, specify the appropriate array index value. For example, for those property values in which you need to specify the username, you specify `arrInput(0)` instead of vlaunders, aglowenorris, kbemowski, or jkellett.

The `while` loop ends with setting `adsUser` to nothing. You need to clear `adsUser` because you use this variable again when the `TextStream::ReadLine` method reads in the next line from `tsInputFile` to create the next user account.

Instead of reading in user data from a text file, you can read in data from other sources, such as a web-based form, Microsoft Word document, Excel spreadsheet, Access database, or specially formatted Microsoft Outlook email message. You also can use command-line arguments to pass in user data, as Example 16-5 shows.

Creating an Account Unlocker Utility

Imagine that you need a utility that quickly enables and unlocks an NT or Windows 2000 user account that was locked because the password was entered incorrectly too many times in succession or because the account exceeded its expiration date. Writing a user-specific script is inefficient if you have many users. Using an input file to pass in the needed user data to a universal script also is inefficient. You'd have to create the input file just before running the universal script because you can't predict whose account you need to unlock. The best approach is to use command-line arguments to pass in the user data as you need it.

Examples 16-5 and 16-6 use this approach to enable and unlock NT and Windows 2000 user accounts, respectively. If you have a mixed NT and Windows 2000 network, you can even combine these two utilities into one script. You can run the scripts from a command window or from the Start menu's Run option.

Windows NT

Example 16-5 implements an unlocker in the WinNT: namespace.

Example 16-5. Windows NT Account Unlocker

```
'***********************************************************************
'How to unlock and enable a Windows NT user via arguments to this script
'
'Parameters should be <domain> <username>
'***********************************************************************
Option Explicit

Dim wshArgs, adsUser, strOutput

On Error Resume Next

'***********************************************************************
'Get the arguments
'***********************************************************************
Set wshArgs = Wscript.Arguments

'***********************************************************************
'If no arguments passed in, then quit
'***********************************************************************
If wshArgs.Count = 0 Then
  WScript.Echo "ERROR: No arguments passed in." & vbCrLf & vbCrLf _
    & "Please use NTUNLOCK <domain> <username>" & vbCrLf & vbCrLf
  WScript.Quit
End If

'***********************************************************************
'Error checking of the arguments could go here if we were bothered
'***********************************************************************

'***********************************************************************
'Attempt to bind to the user
'***********************************************************************
Set adsUser = GetObject("WinNT://" & wshArgs(0) & "/" & wshArgs(1) & ",user")
If Err Then
  Wscript.Echo "Error: Could not bind to the following user: " & vbCrLf _
    & vbCrLf & "WinNT://" & wshArgs(0) & "/" & wshArgs(1) & vbCrLf & vbCrLf
  WScript.Quit
Else
  strOutput = "Connected to user WinNT://" & wshArgs(0) & "/" & wshArgs(1) _
    & vbCrLf
End If

'***********************************************************************
'Attempt to enable the user (but don't quit if you fail)
'***********************************************************************
Err.Clear
adsUser.AccountDisabled = False
adsUser.SetInfo
```

Example 16-5. Windows NT Account Unlocker (continued)

```
If Err Then
  strOutput = strOutput & vbTab & "Error: Could not enable the user account." _
    & vbCrLf
Else
  strOutput = strOutput & vbTab & "User account enabled." & vbCrLf
End If

'*********************************************************************
'Attempt to unlock the user
'*********************************************************************
Err.Clear
adsUser.IsAccountLocked = False
adsUser.SetInfo
If Err Then
  strOutput = strOutput & vbTab & "Error: Could not unlock the user account." _
    & vbCrLf
Else
  strOutput = strOutput & vbTab & "User account unlocked." & vbCrLf
End If

WScript.Echo strOutput
```

You pass in two arguments, *domain* and *username*, to the script. Use the `Wscript::Arguments` property method to retrieve the arguments. The `Wscript::Arguments` property method stores the arguments as a collection, indexing them from 0 to the number of arguments minus 1. The `wshArgs` collection in the script includes the argument `wshArgs(0)`, which represents the *domain*, and `wshArgs(1)`, which represents the *username*.

You use the `WshArguments::Count` method to count the number of arguments. If the count is 0, the script sends an error message and then quits. I recommend that you use the `Wscript.Echo` method to display the error message so that you can use *cscript.exe* or *wscript.exe* to run the script. If you use the VBScript `MsgBox` function (which displays messages as dialog boxes) in a script that you run from *cscript.exe*, the error messages will be illegible in the command window.

Next, use the `GetObject` method to try to connect to the user account. Instead of specifying the actual ADsPath to the User object (which would make the script user-specific), concatenate (&) the following elements in this order: `"WinNT://"` (i.e., the provider), `wshArgs(0)` (i.e., the domain name), `"/"` (i.e., the slash that separates the domain name and username), `wshArgs(1)` (i.e., the username), and `",user"` (i.e., a comma and the object class).

If the connection attempt fails, the script writes an error message and then quits. If the attempt succeeds, the script puts the output from that attempt into the `strOutput` text string variable. That way, if you're running *wscript.exe* rather than *cscript.exe*, the results appear in one dialog box.

The next two sections attempt to enable and unlock the user account. However, the script doesn't quit if an attempt fails. The `Err::Clear` method, which works only if you enable `On Error Resume Next`, clears the error object so that you can detect the next error.

Whether an attempt succeeds or fails, the output goes to the `strOutput` string variable where it's appended to any existing text. The `vbTab` constant and the `vbCrLf` constant ensure that any new text that you concatenate appears in separate indented lines underneath the user's ADsPath. Finally, use the `WScript::Echo` method to print the results in `strOutput`.

This script is simple but powerful. You can easily add to the script to perform other tasks, such as changing passwords and account expiration dates.

Windows 2000

Because Windows 2000's Active Directory supports the WinNT: namespace, you can use the previous listing to enable and unlock Windows 2000 user accounts. However, I recommend that you instead use the script that follows in Example 16-6, because accessing Active Directory via the LDAP: provider is a more elegant and efficient approach.

Example 16-6. A Windows 2000 Account Unlocker (WIN2K-UNLOCK.VBS)

```
'*********************************************************************
'How to unlock and enable a Windows 2000 user via arguments to this script
'
' Parameters should be <domain> <username>, where domain specifies
' a fully qualified windows 2000 domain like dc=windows,dc=mycorp,dc=com
'*********************************************************************
Option Explicit

Const adStateOpen = 0' Used to specify an unsuccessful ADO connection

Dim adoConnection, adoRecordset, wshArgs, adsUser, strOutput

On Error Resume Next

'*********************************************************************
'Get the arguments
'*********************************************************************
Set wshArgs = Wscript.Arguments

'*********************************************************************
'If no arguments passed in, then quit
'*********************************************************************
If wshArgs.Count = 0 Then
  WScript.Echo "ERROR: No arguments passed in." & vbCrLf & vbCrLf _
    & "Please use WIN2K-UNLOCK <domain> <username>" & vbCrLf & vbCrLf
  WScript.Quit
```

Example 16-6. A Windows 2000 Account Unlocker (WIN2K-UNLOCK.VBS) (continued)

```
End If

'***********************************************************************
'Error checking of the arguments could go here if we were bothered
'***********************************************************************


'***********************************************************************
'Use SearchAD function from the end of Chapter 21 to scan the entire
'Active Directory for this user and return the ADsPath. If the search
'failed for whatever reason, then quit
'***********************************************************************
If Not SearchAD("LDAP://" & wshArgs(0), _
  "((objectClass=User)(cn=" & wshArgs(1) & "))", _
  "SubTree", "ADsPath", arrSearchResults) Then

  WScript.Echo "ERROR: No users found." & vbCrLf & vbCrLf
  WScript.Quit
Else
  '***********************************************************************
  'Attempt to bind to the first ADsPath specified in the array
  '(as there should be only one)
  '***********************************************************************
  Set adsUser = GetObject(arrSearchResults(0,0))
  If Err Then
    Wscript.Echo "Error: Could not bind to the following user: " & vbCrLf _
      & vbCrLf & arrSearchResults(0,0) & vbCrLf & vbCrLf
    WScript.Quit
  Else
      strOutput = "Connected to user " & arrSearchResults(0,0) & vbCrLf
  End If

  '***********************************************************************
  'Attempt to enable the user (but don't quit if you fail)
  '***********************************************************************
  Err.Clear
  adsUser.AccountDisabled = False
  adsUser.SetInfo
  If Err Then
    strOutput = strOutput & vbTab & "Error: Could not enable the user." & vbCrLf
  Else
    strOutput = strOutput & vbTab & "User enabled." & vbCrLf
  End If

  '***********************************************************************
  'Attempt to unlock the user
  '***********************************************************************
  Err.Clear
  adsUser.IsAccountLocked = False
  adsUser.SetInfo
  If Err Then
    strOutput = strOutput & vbTab & "Error: Could not unlock the user." & vbCrLf
  Else
```

Example 16-6. A Windows 2000 Account Unlocker (WIN2K-UNLOCK.VBS) (continued)

```
    strOutput = strOutput & vbTab & "User unlocked." & vbCrLf
  End If

  WScript.Echo strOutput
End If
```

Although more elegant and efficient, using the LDAP: provider is a little tricky because users can exist in any container anywhere in a domain tree. Thus, you can't immediately attempt to bind to the user account because you don't know the ADsPath. You first must conduct an ADSI search to obtain the ADsPath.

At the end of Chapter 21, *Scripting Fast Searches Using ADO*, I show you how to use ADO to construct the Active Directory search routine SearchAD that I use here to search Active Directory for the user's ADsPath and store it in **arr-SearchResults(0,0)**. The search is executed using a set of arguments including **wshArgs(0)** and **wshArgs(1)**. If you put the individual filters on separate lines and substitute the domain and username for **wshArgs(0)** and **wshArgs(1)**, the set of arguments looks something like this:

```
    LDAP://dc=windows,dc=mycorp,dc=com
    ((objectClass=User)(cn=vlaunders))
    ADsPath
    SubTree
    arrSearchResults
```

If the search fails, the script displays an error message and then quits. If the search succeeds, the script attempts to bind to the ADsPath. The rest of the script proceeds similarly to the one for Windows NT.

Automatically Creating Exchange Mailboxes for Users

The script in this section demonstrates how to automatically mail-enable a user. Mail-enabling makes sense only when you wish to link your Active Directory to Exchange via the Microsoft Active Directory Connector (ADC). When you create your users in Active Directory using ADSI, you also can indicate to the ADC that the user's mail properties should be replicated over to Exchange; a mailbox for the user is then automatically created and linked to the account. If you are creating hundreds of users with ADSI via a script, you don't want to have to go into the GUI and mail-enable each one.

In order for you to mail-enable an account, you need to be using Exchange 5.5 Service Pack 1 or above, and you need to have installed and configured the ADC as discussed in Chapter 13, *Directory Interoperability*. The ADC modifies the Schema on both Exchange and Active Directory so that both directories can store equivalent attributes. When you've done this, you can use the extra property pages and context menus available from Active Directory Users and Computers MMC tool to mail-enable users, groups, and contacts. You now can use ADSI to add values to certain new properties that now exist in the Schema for the object so that the ADC can recognize that the object should be replicated through to Exchange.

> You need to be using at least unidirectional replication from Active Directory to Exchange. The other alternative is to use ADSI to manipulate recipients on Exchange via LDAP, which is not covered here.

The following script was developed by making use of the scripts for walking the property cache in the previous chapter. I simply took a new user* that I had created and walked the property cache before and after I mail-enabled it. That gave me two sets of output that I could compare in order to identify what changes had been made to properties of the user account.

> While the script is currently functional, Microsoft may make some changes to the properties when Windows 2000 ships and afterward, so there is a chance that the script will not work as is. If that is the case, you should be able to walk the property cache as I did to identify the discrepancies.

You need to understand Exchange to properly make use of the following script since it contains settings that only Exchange can properly use. This script creates a new user called myuser in the Finance Organizational Unit within the *windows. mycorp.com* domain. The script sets the core properties via ADSI in order to mail-enable an Active Directory user such that the ADC would copy the user over to Exchange. Obviously this script copies users over only if the Finance Organizational Unit is set up as a source container in the ADC.

The corresponding Exchange server in the destination is called EXCHANGESERV-ERNAME in the script. This server hosts Exchange 5.5, running the LDAP service (or you won't be able to replicate over LDAP anyway), and has the Internet Mail Service running on it. This can be seen when I set the proxyAddresses attribute.

---

* In this section, I'm concerned with the idea of mail-enabling only users, although the techniques can be applied to group and contact objects as well.

The server's configuration is an organization called MYCORP with a site Organizational Unit called Main-Site. All the objects are stored in the default Recipients container:

```
Const ADS_PROPERTY_UPDATE = 2

'Bind to the Organizational Unit
Set adsDeptOU = GetObject("LDAP://ou=Finance,dc=windows,dc=mycorp,dc=com")

'Create the user
Set adsUser = adsDeptOU.Create("user", "cn=myuser")
adsUser.Put "sAMAccountName", "myuser"
adsUser.Put "userPrincipalName", "myuser@mycorp.com"
adsUser.SetInfo

'Now set the mail enabled options
adsUser.GetInfo
adsUser.Put "mail", "myuser@mycorp.com"
adsUser.Put "legacyExchangeDN", "/o=MYCORP/ou=Main-Site/cn=Recipients/cn=myuser"

'Set up X.400 and Internet Mail Service accounts
adsUser.PutEx ADS_PROPERTY_UPDATE, "proxyAddresses", _
   Array("X400:c=GB;a= ;p=MYCORP;o=Main-Site;s=myuser;", "SMTP:myuser@mycorp.com")

'Add user to the "All Users" and "GAL" address books in Active Directory
adsUser.PutEx ADS_PROPERTY_UPDATE, "showInAddressBook", _
   Array("CN=All Users,CN=Address Lists,CN=Microsoft Exchange,CN=Services," _
   & "CN=Configuration,DC=windows,DC=mycorp,DC=com", _
   "CN=Global Address List,CN=Address Lists,CN=Microsoft Exchange,CN=Services," _
   "CN=Configuration,DC=windows,DC=mycorp,DC=com")

adsUser.Put "textEncodedORAddress", "c=GB;a= ;p=MYCORP;o=Main-Site;s=myuser;"
adsUser.Put "autoReplyMessage", "/"
adsUser.Put "msExchHomeServerName", _
   "cn=EXCHANGESERVERNAME,cn=Servers,cn=Configuration,ou=Main-Site,o=MYCORP"
adsUser.Put "mailNickname", "myuser"
'Tell Exchange to use the default database quota limits
adsUser.Put "mDBUseDefaults", True
adsUser.Put "garbageCollPeriod", 0
adsUser.Put "securityProtocol", "x00 x00 x00 x00"
adsUser.Put "msExchHomeServerName", _
   "/o=MYCORP/ou=Main-Site/cn=Configuration/cn=Servers/cn=MYSERVER"

'Get SD from Security Template User
Set adsSecTempUser = GetObject("LDAP://CN=SecurityTemplateUser,DC=mycorp,DC=com")
Set adsTemplateUserSD = adsSecTempUser.Get("msExchMailboxSecurityDescriptor")
Set adsTemplateDACL = adsTemplateUserSD.DiscretionaryAcl
For Each adsACE In adsTemplateDACL
   'Set trustee to this user
   adsACE.Trustee = "mycorp\myuser"
Next

adsUser.Put "msExchMailboxSecurityDescriptor", adsTemplateUserSD
adsUser.SetInfo
```

Many other Exchange attributes also can be set from here, such as whether to hide a user from the Global Address List and Exchange Administrator program by default. For example, if I want to hide a user from the Global Address List, I include the following code:

```
adsUser.Put "msExchHideFromAddressLists", True
```

However, if I want to show an already-hidden user in the Global Address List, I include the following code:

```
adsUser.Put "msExchHideFromAddressLists", False
```

Some of the attributes may seem confusing, even to Exchange administrators. For example, mDBUseDefaults relates to the checkbox "Use information store defaults" shown in Figure 13-13. If the attributes are confusing, I suggest you use the GUI tools to set up a user, mail-enable it and set properties, and then look at the raw results in Active Directory (using *ADSIEDIT*) and Exchange (using the Exchange Administrator program in raw mode—**ADMIN.EXE /r**) and walk the property cache.

Slightly confusing are the modifications to the DACL and Security Descriptor.* Basically, the new Exchange mailbox needs a set of permissions for the new mailbox contained within a Security Descriptor (SD). To set up an SD simply, I have created a user account in Active Directory called Template User, which is disabled and not assigned to anyone for use. I then use the GUI to properly configure a mailbox for that user, which will then create the SD properly. I then can read that specific Exchange SD from the template user and copy it to other users as required. Obviously, each permission will relate to permissions for the template user, so I need to go through the DACL prior to copying it and set the trustee of each ACE to MYCORP\myuser.

Summary

In this chapter, we looked at how to create and manipulate properties of a user account object in Active Directory and Windows NT SAM. I used this knowledge to show how to create a script to create thousands of users from a set of data in a file or from a database easily. I then showed how to create simple tools, such as an account unlocker, that you can use in your day-to-day management of Windows 2000. Finally, I showed how to automatically create an Exchange mailbox at the same time you create a user.

---

* See Chapter 10, *Active Directory Security: Permissions and Auditing* and Chapter 18, *Permissions and Auditing* for more on Security Descriptors, Discretionary ACLs, and Access Control Entries.

17

Manipulating Persistent and Dynamic Objects

The future of automating systems management–related tasks lies with a technology called Windows Management Instrumentation. WMI is an implementation of the Desktop Management Task Force's (DMTF's) Web-Based Enterprise Management (WBEM) initiative, which provides standards for accessing and sharing management information in an enterprise environment. WMI has unique schema, classes, and interfaces. As part of the WBEM/WMI initiative, Microsoft intends to provide an ADSI-WMI bridge that will transparently expose data regardless of the underlying provider. Thus, WMI will likely become the primary technology that you'll use for systems management–related tasks.

In the meantime, you can use ADSI directly to accomplish some of those same tasks. ADSI provides a host of interfaces that you can use to manipulate persistent objects and dynamic objects in the Windows 2000 Active Directory or Windows NT SAM. Persistent objects are permanent parts of a directory, such as computer shares and services. Dynamic objects aren't permanent parts of a directory but instead are things like sessions (i.e., connections to a machine) and print jobs that users initiate.

ADSI's extra interfaces let you operate the dynamic parts of an OS and manipulate the permanent parts of a directory. In other words, ADSI lets you:

- Dynamically start, stop, and manage services and manipulate the permanent attributes of those services

- Dynamically manipulate shares, creating and deleting them as required

- Dynamically manipulate computers' open resources and users' active sessions and manipulate the permanent objects representing those computers and users

- Dynamically manipulate print jobs and manipulate the permanent queues

I'll go through each of these types of operation in this chapter.

The Interface Methods and Properties

Rather than describe the various interface methods and properties as I've done with the earlier interfaces, I'll concentrate on how to use those methods and properties in scripts. You can find complete descriptions of the interface methods and properties on the MSDN Library CD-ROM or web site. To access the descriptions on the MSDN web site, navigate to Platform SDK → Networking Services → Active Directory → Active Directory Service Interfaces Version 2.5 → ADSI Reference → ADSI Interfaces. From this point, you can navigate to:

Core Interfaces
> Include the descriptions for IADs or IADsContainer

Persistent Object Interfaces
> Include the descriptions for IADsCollection, IADsFileShare, IADsService, IADsPrintJob, and IADsPrintQueue

Dynamic Object Interfaces
> Include the descriptions for IADsServiceOperations, IADsComputerOperations, IADsFileServiceOperations, IADsResource, IADsSession, IADsPrintJobOperations, and IADsPrintQueueOperations

---

This ADSI documentation, however, leaves out three important quirks of the IADsSession and IADsResource interfaces. First, the WinNT: provider doesn't currently support the `IADsSession::UserPath`, `IADsSession::ComputerPath`, and `IADsResource::UserPath` property methods. Second, although the ADSI documentation states that the `IADsSession::ConnectTime` and `IADsSession::IdleTime` property methods return results in minutes, they actually return results in seconds. Finally, the `IADsSession::Computer` property method returns NetBIOS names for Windows NT and Windows 9x clients but returns TCP/IP addresses for Windows 2000 clients.

Manipulating Services with ADSI

Suppose you want to identify all the services on a Windows 2000 or NT computer. You can use several approaches to list the services. The simplest is to bind to the parent computer and print all the permanent objects. As Example 17-1 shows, the script binds to the server object with the following path:

```
WinNT://mydomainorworkgroup/mycomputer, computer
```

The trailing, **computer** parameter ensures that you retrieve a computer object with that name in case a user or group called **mycomputer** exists.

Example 17-1. Script to List All Objects on a Computer (show-objects.vbs)

```
Option Explicit

'***********************************************************************
'Sets the domain or workgroup where the servers or workstations reside.
'Also sets the computer name.
'***********************************************************************
Const strDomainOrWorkGroupName = "MYDOMAIN"
Const strComputerName = "MYCOMPUTER"

Dim adsComputer, adsObject, strOutput, intCount

On Error Resume Next

Set adsComputer = GetObject("WinNT://" & strDomainOrWorkGroupName _
    & "/" & strComputerName & ",computer")

If Err Then
  WScript.Echo "Failed to connect to: \\" & strDomainOrWorkGroupName _
      & "\" & strComputerName
Else
  strOutput = "The objects contained on " & adsComputer.ADsPath _
      & " are: " & vbCrLf & vbCrLf

  intCount = 0

  For Each adsObject in adsComputer
    intCount = intCount + 1
    strOutput = strOutput & intCount & ") " & adsObject.Name & ", " _
        & adsObject.Class & vbCrLf
  Next

  WScript.Echo strOutput
End if
```

Whether you're connecting to a Windows 2000 or NT machine, you must always use the WinNT: provider because you're connecting to the machine's OS, not its directory service.

The script then uses the **IADs::ADsPath** property method to print the computer's full path and the **IADs::Name** and **IADs::Class** property methods to print the names and schema classes of the objects in that computer. Because the list of objects will be long and `MsgBox` has a size limit, the script uses the `WScript::Echo` function to print out the text. This allows you to use the WSH command-line processor, *cscript.exe,* to run the script. For a script called *show-services.vbs,* type the following from the command line:

```
CSCRIPT show-services.vbs | MORE
```

When the script runs, the `MORE` command forces the text to scroll by in a command-line window a page at a time. If you don't include the `MORE` command, you can increase the output buffer size for *cmd.exe* (Windows 2000 or NT) or *command.exe* (Windows 9x) so that you can get more than 25 lines in the buffer.

To increase the output buffer size, open the properties window for the shortcut that you use to start a command prompt. If you're using Win9x, select the Screen tab. As Figure 17-1 shows, use the drop-down list to set Initial Size to the number of lines you want the window to display.

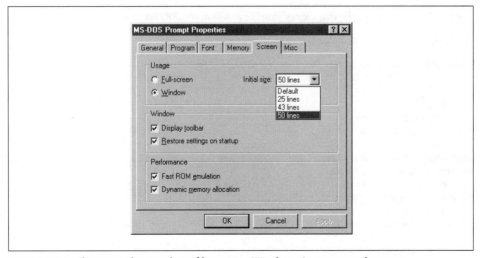

Figure 17-1. Changing the number of lines in a Windows 9x command prompt

You have more options if you're using NT or Windows 2000. As Figure 17-2 shows, the Layout tab lets you set the window's width (measured in characters) and height (measured in lines). You also can set the screen's buffer size. The buffer displays and holds the output so that you can scroll back through it.

An example of the first 47 lines output from the script is in Example 17-2. A couple of extra touches in the script make its output easier to read. First, the script uses the VBScript Err interface, which lets you see whether the binding failed to start with. Second, a simple integer-counting variable (`intCount`) numbers each line.

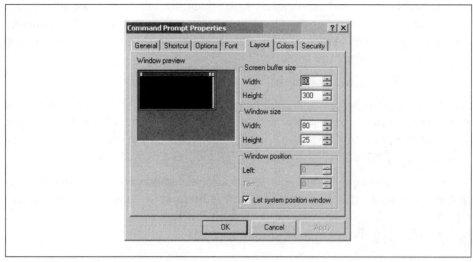

Figure 17-2. Changing the number of lines in a Windows 2000 command prompt

Example 17-2. Output from show-objects.vbs

```
Microsoft (R) Windows Scripting Host Version 5.1 for Windows
Copyright (C) Microsoft Corporation 1996-1998. All rights reserved.

1) Admin, User
2) Administrator, User
3) IUSR_PRTACC1, User
4) Guest, User
5) SQLExecutiveCmdExec, User
6) Account Operators, Group
7) Administrators, Group
8) Backup Operators, Group
9) Guests, Group
10) Print Operators, Group
11) Replicator, Group
12) Server Operators, Group
13) Users, Group
14) Domain Admins, Group
15) Domain Guests, Group
16) Domain Users, Group
17) Printstations, Group
18) upper_floor, PrintQueue
19) room_717, PrintQueue
20) outside_plan, PrintQueue
21) Alerter, Service
22) ASDiscoverySvc, Service
23) Browser, Service
24) Client Agent for ARCserve, Service
25) ClipSrv, Service
26) CPQMgmt, Service
27) DbaRpcService, Service
28) dbWebService, Service
```

Example 17-2. Output from show-objects.vbs (continued)

```
29) DHCP, Service
30) EventLog, Service
31) LanmanServer, Service
32) LanmanWorkstation, Service
33) LicenseService, Service
34) LmHosts, Service
35) LPDSVC, Service
36) Messenger, Service
37) MSDTC, Service
38) MSExchangeDS, Service
39) MSExchangeIMC, Service
40) MSExchangeIS, Service
41) MSExchangeMTA, Service
42) MSExchangeSA, Service
43) MSFTPSVC, Service
44) MSSQLServer, Service
45) NetDDE, Service
46) NetDDEdsdm, Service
47) NetLogon, Service
```

Although the *show-objects.vbs* script prints the service objects, it also prints all
other objects. You can adapt this script so that it prints only the services if you
replace the code in the **Else** statement in *show-objects.vbs* with the code section
in Example 17-3.

Example 17-3. Replacement Code to List Only Services

```
For Each adsObject in adsComputer
  intCount = intCount + 1

  If adsObject.Class = "Service" Then
    strOutput = strOutput & intCount & ") " & adsObject.Name & ", " & adsObject.Class
& vbCrLf
  End If
Next
```

However, you can use a more efficient approach to list a computer's services: the
IADsContainer::Filter property method filters the objects for you. Here's how
this approach works. Each object in a container (i.e., the computer) has a schema
class that you can retrieve with the **IADs::Class** property method. As the output
from *show-objects.vbs* shows, these classes have names such as User, Group, Service, and PrintQueue. If you pass an array of these classes to the **IADs-
Container::Filter** property method, the **IADsContainer::Filter** property
method allows only the classes of objects that you passed to be seen in the container. The **IADsContainer::Filter** property method also affects the **IADs-
Container::Count** property method, which counts only those objects matching
the filter (see Table 17-1).

Table 17-1. IADsContainer Methods and Properties

IADsContainer Methods and Properties	Action
Create method	Creates an object in the container
Delete method	Deletes an object in the container
CopyHere method	Copies an object to the container
MoveHere method	Moves an object to the container
GetObject method	A way of enumerating the contents of a container
Count property	The number of objects in the container
Filter property	Consists of an array of object class strings; restricts the number of objects returned during enumeration of the container

You use the VBScript **Array** function to create the filter. So, for example, to create a filter that returns objects of the class Service, use the following code:

```
adsComputer.Filter = Array("service")
```

If you want to filter for more than one item, then you simply use a comma-separated list of items as follows:

```
adsComputer.Filter = Array("service","printQueue")
```

If you want to remove the filter, you use the VBScript **Empty** keyword to specify an empty property:

```
adsComputer.Filter = Empty
```

Example 17-4 uses this code to filter out only the service objects.

Example 17-4. Code to Filter Out Service Objects (show-services.vbs)

```
Option Explicit

'***********************************************************************
'Sets the domain or workgroup where the servers or workstations reside.
'Also sets the computer name.
'***********************************************************************
Const strDomainOrWorkGroupName = "MYDOMAIN"
Const strComputerName = "MYCOMPUTER"

Dim adsComputer, adsObject, strOutput, intCount

On Error Resume Next

Set adsComputer = GetObject("WinNT://" & strDomainOrWorkGroupName _
   & "/" & strComputerName & ",computer")

If Err Then
  WScript.Echo "Failed to connect to: \\" & strDomainOrWorkGroupName _
    & "\" & strComputerName
Else
```

Example 17-4. Code to Filter Out Service Objects (show-services.vbs) (continued)

```
adsComputer.Filter = Array("service")

strOutput = "The services contained on " & adsComputer.ADsPath _
  & " are: " & vbCrLf & vbCrLf

intCount = 0

For Each adsService in adsComputer
  intCount = intCount + 1
  strOutput = strOutput & intCount & ") " & adsService.Name & vbCrLf
Next

WScript.Echo strOutput
End if
```

Using ADSI to retrieve the names of a machine's services is helpful, but you can use ADSI to accomplish a lot more. For example, you can use ADSI to dynamically manipulate services as illustrated in the next section.

Creating a Service Utility

Let me use an example to illustrate how to dynamically manipulate a service. I'd like to create a command-line utility that binds to the computer, connects to the service on that computer, and uses IADsServiceOperations to interact with the service. The service utility's format will be the same as that of the command-line account unlocker utility I discussed in Chapter 16, *Users*. I'll go through *service-utility.vbs* section by section so that you can see how it functions, and then I'll show you the whole script.

service-utility.vbs takes three parameters that specify the domain or workgroup, the computer, and the service you want to connect to. If you pass only these three parameters, the utility returns the service's current status. You can pass in additional parameters that tell the utility to complete a specific task, including starting, stopping, pausing, or continuing the service, as well as changing the service password.

To create the service utility, I first declared the constants that describe the status of the service. Remember that although VB defines the names of constants, VBScript doesn't. I declared eight constant names and set their values. For example, the constant to specify that a service has stopped is:

```
Const ADS_SERVICE_STOPPED = 1
```

When the utility runs, it returns a constant's value rather than its name. To make the utility more user friendly, I used the **arrServiceText** array to translate the returned values into descriptive text, so, for example, the utility now returns the message "The service has stopped" instead of the value 1.

I used the constants as the indexes of the descriptive text array, but because arrays always start with an index number of 0, I had to subtract 1 from every constant to get the correct index. For example, the code to prompt the utility to return the message "The service has stopped" is:

```
arrServiceText(ADS_SERVICE_STOPPED - 1) = "The service has stopped."
```

Although I could've just used an index of 0, this approach ensures that the text and constant names match up when I'm writing the script. And if I make a mistake in my code, this approach minimizes the chance of me chasing the wrong error message.

After declaring the constants and variables, I included code that forces the script to quit if you don't pass any parameters. Before the script quits, it prints a message detailing how to use the utility.

If you pass at least one parameter, the utility initializes the output text string:

```
strOutput = ""
```

It then binds to the server object:

```
'*************************************************************************
'Try to bind to the computer
'*************************************************************************
Err.Clear
Set adsComputer = GetObject("WinNT://" & wshArgs(0) & "/" & wshArgs(1) _
   & ",computer")

If Err Then
  Wscript.Echo "Error: Could not bind to the following path: " & vbCrLf _
     & vbCrLf & vbTab & "WinNT://" & wshArgs(0) & "/" & wshArgs(1) & ",computer"
  WScript.Quit
Else
  strOutput = strOutput & "Connected to " & adsComputer.ADsPath & vbCrLf
End If
```

Next it sets the result to adsComputer:

```
'*************************************************************************
'Get the service indicated by the third parameter
'*************************************************************************
Err.Clear
Set adsService = adsComputer.GetObject("Service", wshArgs(2))

If Err Then
  Wscript.Echo "Error: Could not get the service called: " & vbCrLf _
     & vbTab & wshArgs(2) & vbCrLf & "on the following server: " & vbCrLf _
     & vbTab & adsComputer.ADsPath & vbCrLf
  WScript.Quit
Else
  strOutput = strOutput & "Looking at Service: " & adsService.Name _
     & vbCrLf & vbCrLf
End If
```

The utility then uses the `IADsContainer::GetObject` method to retrieve an object of class Service from that computer and sets the result to the **adsService** variable. The `IADsContainer::GetObject` method differs from VBScript's `GetObject` function in that `IADsContainer::GetObject` lets you specify valid classes.

I could've bypassed using the adsComputer object and bound directly to the service object with code. However, because I used the adsComputer object, the utility checks the validity not only of the service name but also of the computer name.

After the utility successfully binds to the service, it checks to see whether you've supplied any more parameters. If you pass in three or fewer parameters, the script uses the `IADsServiceOperations::Status` property method to check against the existing constants and print the relevant text from the **arrServiceText** array. If you pass in more than three parameters, the script uses a `Select Case` statement, which acts like a multiple `If...Then...Else` statement to compare the fourth parameter to the six cases listed. Before the `Select Case` statement makes these comparisons, though, it uses the VBScript `LCase` function to convert the fourth parameter to lowercase.

The first four cases are fairly straightforward. They use the `IADsServiceOperations::Start`, `IADsServiceOperations::Stop`, `IADsServiceOperations::Pause`, and `IADsServiceOperations::Continue` methods, respectively, to start, stop, pause, or continue the service. This is the code for the "stop" case:

```
Case "stop"
  If adsService.Status = ADS_SERVICE_RUNNING Then
    adsService.Stop
    strOutput = strOutput & "An attempt has been made to stop the service." _
    & vbCrLf
  Else
    strOutput = strOutput _
    & "The service is not currently started so it cannot be stopped." & vbCrLf
  End If
```

The fifth case uses the `IADsServiceOperations::SetPassword` method to set a service password. As the following excerpt shows, you specify the password you want as the fifth parameter, and it must match the account password in the SAM or Active Directory; otherwise, the service will fail with a logon error the next time the service tries to start. When the script runs, the utility checks to see whether a fifth parameter exists. If the password exists, the utility sets it; if the password doesn't exist, the utility sets a blank password:

```
Case "setpassword"
  If wshArgs.Count = 5 Then
    adsService.SetPassword wshArgs(4)
```

```
            strOutput = strOutput & "The password has been set to: " & wshArgs(4) _
              & vbCrLf
        Else
          adsService.SetPassword ""
          strOutput = strOutput & "The password has been set to a blank string." _
            & vbCrLf
        End If
```

The last case is the **Case Else** statement. Similar to the **Else** condition's role in an **If...Then...Else** statement, the optional **Case Else** statement catches all invalid parameters and generates error messages. The **Case Else** statement always goes last in a list of case statements.

The entire utility is shown in Example 17-5.

Example 17-5. Command-Line Service Utility (Service-Utility.vbs)

```
'***********************************************************************
'The Command-Line Service Utility for NT or Win2K Computers
'***********************************************************************

Option Explicit

Const ADS_SERVICE_STOPPED = 1
Const ADS_SERVICE_START_PENDING = 2
Const ADS_SERVICE_STOP_PENDING = 3
Const ADS_SERVICE_RUNNING = 4
Const ADS_SERVICE_CONTINUE_PENDING = 5
Const ADS_SERVICE_PAUSE_PENDING = 6
Const ADS_SERVICE_PAUSED = 7
Const ADS_SERVICE_ERROR = 8

Dim wshArgs, strOutput, arrServiceText(8), adsComputer, adsService

'***********************************************************************
'Populate the array with descriptive text
'***********************************************************************
arrServiceText(ADS_SERVICE_STOPPED - 1) = "The service has stopped."
arrServiceText(ADS_SERVICE_START_PENDING - 1) = _
  "The service is currently attempting to start."
arrServiceText(ADS_SERVICE_STOP_PENDING - 1) = _
  "The service is currently attempting to stop."
arrServiceText(ADS_SERVICE_RUNNING - 1) = "The service is running."
arrServiceText(ADS_SERVICE_CONTINUE_PENDING - 1) = _
  "The service is currently attempting to continue after a pause operation."
arrServiceText(ADS_SERVICE_PAUSE_PENDING - 1) = _
  "The service is currently attempting to pause."
arrServiceText(ADS_SERVICE_PAUSED - 1) = "The service is paused."
arrServiceText(ADS_SERVICE_ERROR - 1) = "The service has an error."

On Error Resume Next

'***********************************************************************
'Get the parameters
```

Example 17-5. Command-Line Service Utility (Service-Utility.vbs) (continued)

```
'**********************************************************************
Set wshArgs = Wscript.Arguments


'**********************************************************************
'If you don't pass in any parameters, the script quits with a usage message
'**********************************************************************
If wshArgs.Count = 0 Then
  WScript.Echo "ERROR: No arguments passed in." & vbCrLf & vbCrLf & "Please " _
    & "use: service-utility <domain|workgroup> <computer-name> <service-name> " _
    & "[Start|Stop|Pause|Continue|SetPassword <new-password>]" & vbCrLf _
    & vbCrLf & "If <service-name> or <computer-name> contains multiple " _
    & "words enclose them in quotation marks" & vbCrLf & "If you specify " _
    & "only the first 3 parameters then the script will return the status " _
    & "of the service" & vbCrLf
  WScript.Quit
End If


'**********************************************************************
'Error checking of the arguments can go here if you want
'**********************************************************************


'**********************************************************************
'Initialize the text string that will represent the output text to a
'blank string
'**********************************************************************
strOutput = ""


'**********************************************************************
'Try to bind to the computer
'**********************************************************************
Err.Clear
Set adsComputer = GetObject("WinNT://" & wshArgs(0) & "/" & wshArgs(1) _
  & ",computer")

If Err Then
  Wscript.Echo "Error: Could not bind to the following path: " & vbCrLf _
    & vbCrLf & vbTab & "WinNT://" & wshArgs(0) & "/" & wshArgs(1) & ",computer"
  WScript.Quit
Else
  strOutput = strOutput & "Connected to " & adsComputer.ADsPath & vbCrLf
End If


'**********************************************************************
'Get the service indicated by the third parameter
'**********************************************************************
Err.Clear
Set adsService = adsComputer.GetObject("Service", wshArgs(2))

If Err Then
  Wscript.Echo "Error: Could not get the service called: " & vbCrLf _
    & vbTab & wshArgs(2) & vbCrLf & "on the following server: " & vbCrLf _
    & vbTab & adsComputer.ADsPath & vbCrLf
```

Example 17-5. Command-Line Service Utility (Service-Utility.vbs) (continued)

```
  WScript.Quit
Else
  strOutput = strOutput & "Looking at Service: " & adsService.Name _
    & vbCrLf & vbCrLf
End If

If wshArgs.Count = 3 Then
  '************************************************************************
  'Only 3 parameters specified, so return status of the service
  '************************************************************************
  strOutput = strOutput & "Current status: " _
    & arrServiceText(adsService.Status - 1) & vbCrLf
Else
  '************************************************************************
  'More than 3 parameters specified, so select a task based on the
  'fourth parameter (after converting to lowercase)
  '************************************************************************
  Select Case LCase(wshArgs(3))

    Case "start"
      If adsService.Status = ADS_SERVICE_STOPPED Then
        adsService.Start
        strOutput = strOutput _
          & "An attempt has been made to start the service." & vbCrLf
      Else
        strOutput = strOutput _
          & "The service is not currently stopped so it cannot be started." _
          & vbCrLf
      End If

    Case "stop"
      If adsService.Status = ADS_SERVICE_RUNNING Then
        adsService.Stop
        strOutput = strOutput & "An attempt has been made to stop the service." _
          & vbCrLf
      Else
        strOutput = strOutput _
          & "The service is not currently started so it cannot be stopped." _
          & vbCrLf
      End If

    Case "pause"
      If adsService.Status = ADS_SERVICE_RUNNING Then
        adsService.Pause
        strOutput = strOutput _
          & "An attempt has been made to pause the service." & vbCrLf
      Else
        strOutput = strOutput _
          & "The service is not currently started so it cannot be paused." _
          & vbCrLf
      End If
```

Example 17-5. Command-Line Service Utility (Service-Utility.vbs) (continued)

```
   Case "continue"
     If adsService.Status = ADS_SERVICE_PAUSED Then
       adsService.Continue
       strOutput = strOutput _
         & "An attempt has been made to continue the paused service." & vbCrLf
     Else
       strOutput = strOutput _
         & "The service is not currently paused so it cannot be continued." _
         & vbCrLf
     End If

   Case "setpassword"
     If wshArgs.Count = 5 Then
       adsService.SetPassword wshArgs(4)
       strOutput = strOutput & "The password has been set to: " & wshArgs(4) _
         & vbCrLf
     Else
       adsService.SetPassword ""
       strOutput = strOutput & "The password has been set to a blank string." _
         & vbCrLf
     End If

   Case Else
     WScript.Echo "ERROR: The parameter (" & wshArgs(3) _
       & ") that you specified is invalid." & vbCrLf & vbCrLf & "Please use: " _
       & "service-utility <domain|workgroup> <computer-name> <service-name> " _
       & "[Start|Stop|Pause|Continue|SetPassword <new-password>]" & vbCrLf _
       & vbCrLf & "If <service-name> or <computer-name> contains multiple " _
       & "words enclose them in quotation marks" & vbCrLf & "If you specify " _
       & "only the first 3 parameters then the script will return the status " _
       & "of the service" & vbCrLf
     WScript.Quit
   End Select
End If

WScript.Echo strOutput
```

You now know how to identify and manipulate the services on an Windows 2000 or NT computer. You can use this knowledge to create scripts that perform similar tasks. For example, you can transfer the knowledge to write a script that creates and manipulates the shares on a Windows 2000 or NT computer.

Creating and Manipulating Shares with ADSI

Example 17-6 shows how easily you can create shares with ADSI.

Example 17-6. Script to Create a Share

```
Dim adsComputer, adsFileShare

Set adsComputer = GetObject("WinNT://mydomainorworkgroup/mycomputer/LanmanServer")

Set adsFileShare = adsComputer.Create("FileShare", "MyNewShare")
adsFileShare.Path = "c:\mydirectory"
adsFileShare.Description = "My new Share"
adsFileShare.MaxUserCount = 8
adsFileShare.SetInfo
```

After you declare your **adsComputer** and **adsFileShare** variables, you bind to the LanmanServer object on the computer on which you want to create the shares. LanmanServer is the object name of the server service that runs on all Windows NT and Windows 2000 computers. You bind to this object because NT's predecessor was LAN Manager. This former OS introduced the shares you're likely to be familiar with.

Next, you use the **IADsContainer::Create** method to create an object of class FileShare and apply the IADsFileShare property methods to set the path, description, and maximum number of users. On an NT or Windows 2000 server, you can grant all users access to a share or limit access to as many users as you want. On an NT or Windows 2000 workstation, you can grant all users access to a share or limit access to between 1 and 10 users at a time. The latter restriction is due to the 10-connection limit that the OS imposes. The values that the **IADsFileShare::MaxUserCount** method accepts are -1 (which grants all users access), any numerical value between 1 and 10 on workstations, and within reason, any numerical value on the server family of OSs.

Finally, you end the script with **IADs::SetInfo**, which writes the information from the cache to the directory.

Enumerating existing shares is just as easy as creating them. Example 17-7 shows how to enumerate normal shares.[*]

---

[*] Hidden shares aren't shown due to their very nature.

Example 17-7. Script to Enumerate Existing Shares

```
Dim adsService, adsFileShare, strOutput

strOutput = ""

Set adsService = GetObject("WinNT://workgroup/vicky/LanmanServer")

For Each adsFileShare In adsService
  strOutput = strOutput & "Name of share : " & adsFileShare.Name & vbCrLf
  strOutput = strOutput & "Path to share : " & adsFileShare.Path & vbCrLf
  strOutput = strOutput & "Description : " & adsFileShare.Description & vbCrLf

  If adsFileShare.MaxUserCount = -1 Then
    strOutput = strOutput & "Max users : No limit" & vbCrLf
  Else
    strOutput = strOutput & "Max users : " & adsFileShare.MaxUserCount & vbCrLf
  End If

  strOutput = strOutput & "Host Computer : " _
    & adsFileShare.HostComputer & vbCrLf & vbCrLf
Next

WScript.Echo strOutput
```

This code is similar to that in the previous script for creating a share. This is a sample of the output:

```
Name of share : NETLOGON
Path to share : C:\WINNT35\system32\Repl\Import\Scripts
Description   : Logon server share
Max users     : No limit
Host Computer : WinNT://WORKGROUP/VICKY

Name of share : Add-ins
Path to share : C:\exchsrvr\ADD-INS
Description   : "Access to EDK objects"
Max users     : No limit
Host Computer : WinNT://WORKGROUP/VICKY

Name of share : Logs
Path to share : C:\exchsrvr\tracking.log
Description   : "Exchange message tracking logs"
Max users     : No limit
Host Computer : WinNT://WORKGROUP/VICKY

Name of share : Resources
Path to share : C:\exchsrvr\RES
Description   : "Event logging files"
Max users     : No limit
Host Computer : WinNT://WORKGROUP/VICKY

Name of share : Drivers
Path to share : C:\WINNT\system32\spool\drivers
```

```
Description    : Printer Drivers
Max users      : No limit
Host Computer  : WinNT://WORKGROUP/VICKY

Name of share  : Clients
Path to share  : C:\clients
Description    : Network Client Distribution Share
Max users      : No limit
Host Computer  : WinNT://WORKGROUP/VICKY
```

Enumerating Sessions and Resources

I now want to show you how to use ADSI to:

- Enumerate a client's sessions and resources

- Show which users currently are logged on to a server and count all the logged-on users across a domain's PDCs, BDCs, and other servers

Windows NT and Windows 2000 host two kinds of dynamic objects that you can use with ADSI to gain read-only access: sessions (i.e., instances of users connected to a computer) and resources (i.e., instances of file or queue access on a computer). When users connect to a file or a share on a computer, that instance creates both a session and a resource object. When the user disconnects, these dynamic objects cease to exist.

You can access dynamic objects by connecting directly to the Windows 2000 or NT service, which is called a *server service*. Although each server service has a user-friendly display name that appears in the Computer Management console in Windows 2000 or the Services applet in Control Panel in NT, each server service also has an ordinary name that you use when connecting to it with ADSI. For example, Server is the display name of the service that has the ordinary name of LanManServer. If you enumerate all the services on a machine, you can use `IADsService::DisplayName` to print the display name and `IADs::Name` to print the ordinary name.

LanManServer is an object of type FileService. FileService objects are responsible for maintaining the sessions and resources in their jurisdictions. You can use the IADsFileServiceOperations interface to access information about these sessions and resources. This simple interface has two methods: `IADsFileServiceOperations::Sessions` and `IADsFileServiceOperations::Resources`. Both methods return collections of objects that you can iterate through with a `For Each...Next` loop. When you're iterating through a collection in this manner, the system is using `IADsCollection::GetObject` to retrieve each item from the collection. As a result, you can use the same `IADsCollection::GetObject` method to retrieve a specific session or resource object. You then can use the IADsSession or IADsResource interface to manipulate that session or resource object's properties to access information. For example, if you retrieve a session object, you can access such information as the username of the user who is logged on and how long that user has been logged on.

Identifying a Machine's Sessions

Example 17-8 is a script that uses IADsSession to iterate through all the sessions on a particular machine.

Example 17-8. Script to Identify a Machine's Sessions

```
On Error Resume Next

Dim adsComputer, adsSession, strOutput

strOutput = ""

Set adsComputer = GetObject("WinNT://mydomainorworkgroup/mycomputer/LanManServer")

For Each adsSession In adsComputer.Sessions
   strOutput = strOutput & "Session Object Name : " & adsSession.Name & vbCrLf
   strOutput = strOutput & "Client Computer Name: " & adsSession.Computer & vbCrLf
   strOutput = strOutput & "Seconds connected   : " _
     & adsSession.ConnectTime & vbCrLf
   strOutput = strOutput & "Seconds idle         : " & adsSession.IdleTime & vbCrLf
   strOutput = strOutput & "Connected User       : " & adsSession.User & vbCrLf
   strOutput = strOutput & vbCrLf
Next

WScript.Echo strOutput
```

The script is straightforward. It uses the `IADs::Name` property method and IADsSession property methods to retrieve data about the session. The `IADs::Name` property method displays the object name, which is the name that you would use with `IADsCollection::GetObject` to individually retrieve the specific session. As Figure 17-3 shows, the object name always follows the format <user>\<COMPUTER>. In some sessions, the underlying system rather than a person is connecting to the computer. Here, the object name follows the format \<COMPUTER>.

You can use IADsSession property methods to retrieve the individual components of the object name. The `IADsSession::Computer` property method retrieves the computer component (e.g., `COMPUTER1`). The Connected User and Client Computer Name fields in Figure 17-3 contain the results of these property methods. The `IADsSession::User` property method retrieves the user component of the object name (e.g., `user1`).

The next line highlights an important consideration when you're specifying WinNT: provider paths in a script:

```
    Set adsComputer = GetObject("WinNT://mydomainorworkgroup/mycomputer/LanManServer")
```

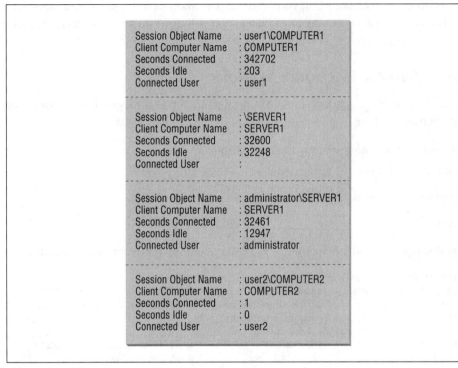

```
Session Object Name      : user1\COMPUTER1
Client Computer Name     : COMPUTER1
Seconds Connected        : 342702
Seconds Idle             : 203
Connected User           : user1


Session Object Name      : \SERVER1
Client Computer Name     : SERVER1
Seconds Connected        : 32600
Seconds Idle             : 32248
Connected User           :


Session Object Name      : administrator\SERVER1
Client Computer Name     : SERVER1
Seconds Connected        : 32461
Seconds Idle             : 12947
Connected User           : administrator


Session Object Name      : user2\COMPUTER2
Client Computer Name     : COMPUTER2
Seconds Connected        : 1
Seconds Idle             : 0
Connected User           : user2
```

Figure 17-3. The sessions on a computer

If you use only the computer name in the path with code such as this, your script will execute slowly because the system must locate the machine and its workgroup.

```
WinNT://MYCOMPUTER,computer
```

However, if you include the workgroup in the path, your script will execute significantly faster because the system can immediately access the machine.

```
WinNT://MYDOMAIN/MYCOMPUTER,computer
```

Identifying a Machine's Resources

The Example 17-9 script enumerates the resources in use on a machine.

Example 17-9. Script to Identify a Machine's Resources

```
On Error Resume Next

Dim adsComputer, adsSession, strOutput

strOutput = ""

Set adsComputer = GetObject("WinNT://mydomainorworkgroup/mycomputer/LanManServer")
```

Example 17-9. Script to Identify a Machine's Resources (continued)

```
For Each adsResource In adsComputer.Resources
   strOutput = strOutput & "Resource Name: " & adsResource.Name & vbCrLf
   strOutput = strOutput & "User         : " & adsResource.User & vbCrLf
   strOutput = strOutput & "Path         : " & adsResource.Path & vbCrLf
   strOutput = strOutput & "Lock count   : " & adsResource.LockCount & vbCrLf
   strOutput = strOutput & vbCrLf
Next

WScript.Echo strOutput
```

Figure 17-4 shows the output, which lists those files that each user has open. The Microsoft Excel spreadsheet that `user3` has open is locked.

> If you want to see locks in action, have one user open up a shared document and have another user try to open it.

```
Resource Name : 11237
User          : USER1
Path          : H:\dir1\folder1\Internet Explorer\Temporary Internet Files\Content.IE5\index.dat
Lock Count    : 0
- - - - - - - - - - - - - - - - - - - - - - - - - - - - - - - - - - - - - - - - - - - - - - - - - - - - - - - - -
Resource Name : 11239
User          : USER1
Path          : H:\dir1\folder1\Internet Explorer\History\History.IE5\index.dat
Lock Count    : 0
- - - - - - - - - - - - - - - - - - - - - - - - - - - - - - - - - - - - - - - - - - - - - - - - - - - - - - - - -
Resource Name : 59403
User          : USER2
Path          : K:\dir1\folder1\My Documents
Lock Count    : 0
- - - - - - - - - - - - - - - - - - - - - - - - - - - - - - - - - - - - - - - - - - - - - - - - - - - - - - - - -
Resource Name : 11765
User          : USER3
Path          : E:\dir2\folder1\default.xls
Lock Count    : 3
```

Figure 17-4. The resources on a computer

A Utility to Show User Sessions

You can use ADSI to write a script that displays which users are currently logged on to a server and counts all the logged-on users across a domain. For simplicity, suppose that you have only two servers in your domain. You want to determine and display the maximum number of simultaneous sessions on each server, the total number of sessions across the domain, the total number of unique connected users on the domain, and an alphabetized list of usernames. Users can simultaneously connect to both servers from their computers. However, you want to count these users only once.

You can use the session object to construct *ShowUsers.vbs*, a useful utility that runs from your desktop and determines and displays this user session information. What follows is an overview of how the *ShowUsers.vbs* utility obtains, manipulates, and displays the data. I heavily commented this script to show how it works line by line. The script follows the discussion of how it works.

Obtaining the data

ShowUsers.vbs begins by iterating through all your servers. To specify the servers you want to scan, you can either hardcode the server information in the script or have the script dynamically retrieve this information.* I've hardcoded the server information in *ShowUsers.vbs*.

When the utility iterates through all the servers, it ignores any empty usernames (which specify interserver connections) and usernames with a trailing dollar sign (which denote users that are actually computers connecting to one another). For each valid session, the script records the username and increments the session count by one.

The script uses a dynamic array (**arrResults**) to store the username data because the number of usernames in the array will change each time you run the utility.

The script uses a multidimensional array (**arrServerResults**) to store the servers' names and maximum number of connected sessions:

```
'***********************************************************************
'Sets up multidimensional array to hold server names and user counts
'***********************************************************************
arrServerResults(0,0) = "server1"
arrServerResults(1,0) = "server2"
arrServerResults(0,1) = 0
arrServerResults(1,1) = 0
```

---

* For Windows 2000, a domain's DCs are always in the Domain Controllers Organizational Unit off the root of the domain. Member servers will be in the Computers container by default.

The `arrServerResults` array stores this information in a simple table, putting the server names in the first column, the counts in the second column, and the data in the rows. To access data in `arrServerResults`, you include the indexes of first and second dimensions, respectively, in parentheses. For example, `arrServerResults(0,1)` accesses the data in the first row (0), second column (1). Thus, your server names are in `arrServerResults(0,0)` and `arrServerResults(1,0)`. The corresponding session counts are in `arrServerResults(0,1)` and `arrServerResults(1,1)`.

The script can iterate through the servers by using a `For` loop to go from 0 to `UBound(arrServerResults)`. The VBScript `UBound` function retrieves the upper array bound for an array and takes two parameters: the array to check and the dimension to count the upper bound of.

Note that `UBound`'s second parameter specifying the dimension starts from 1, not 0 as the actual array does.

If the second parameter is left off, the first dimension is used; these are equivalent:

```
UBound(arrServerResults,1)
UBound(arrServerResults)
```

Manipulating the data

After the script iterates through every server, you have a list of server session counts and a list of the usernames of those users who were connected to the servers at that time. This section of code achieves this:

```
For Each adsSession In adsFSO.Sessions
    If (Not adsSession.User = "") And (Not Right(adsSession.User,1) = "$") Then
        arrResults(UBound(arrResults)) = adsSession.User & vbCrLf
        ReDim Preserve arrResults(UBound(arrResults) + 1)
        arrServerResults(intIndex,1) = arrServerResults(intIndex,1) + 1
    End If
Next
```

Note the use of `ReDim` to preserve the existing contents of the array, while expanding the array's upper bound by one. So, if the upper bound is 12, you can increase the array to 13 elements with the following code:

```
ReDim Preserve arrResults(13)
```

Using the upper bound of the existing array as the parameter makes the code generic. The following line is used to increase the count of the users by one in the second dimension of the array:

```
arrServerResults(intIndex,1) = arrServerResults(intIndex,1) + 1
```

Because some of the users might have been connected to both servers and hence might appear in the username list twice, the script uses two subprocedures to manipulate the data. One subprocedure sorts the usernames; the other subprocedure removes duplicate usernames.

The sort subprocedure

You likely remember having to perform bubble sorts and shell sorts from your college days. Although including a general-purpose quick sort like the bubble or shell sort in VBScript would've made sense, Microsoft failed to do so. Fortunately, I found the Quicksort algorithm in the article "Sorts of All Types: VBA Algorithms for Getting Things in Order" (*Microsoft Office and VBA Developer*, March 1998, *http://msdn.microsoft.com/library/periodic/period98/html/ovbad0398sorting.htm*). The Quicksort algorithm is for Visual Basic for Applications (VBA), but I easily adapted the code for VBScript.

The `Quicksort` subprocedure takes in an array indexed from 0 to `UBound(array)` and sorts the values in the array between the two indexes you pass in as arguments. For example, if you specify the following code, `Quicksort` sorts elements 7 through 19 in `arrMyArray`:

```
Quicksort(arrMyArray, 7, 19)
```

I maintained `Quicksort`'s ability to sort between two indexes in case I ever want to reuse the procedure in another script that needs that functionality. However, in *ShowUsers.vbs*, you need to sort the whole array of usernames between indexes 0 and `UBound(array)`.

The duplicate-removal subprocedure

After `Quicksort` sorts the username list, the `RemoveDuplicates` subprocedure removes any duplicate usernames. Like `Quicksort`, `RemoveDuplicates` takes in an array and two indexes as arguments.* When `RemoveDuplicates` enumerates through a sorted list, it ignores items with the same name as the next item in the list and then passes the remaining elements to a new array. For example, let's say that a sorted list reads as follows:

```
bill, bill, bill, sandy, sandy, steve
```

`RemoveDuplicates` reads the list as:

```
<ignore>, <ignore>, bill, <ignore>, sandy, steve
```

This enumerates to:

```
bill, sandy, steve
```

---

* When I created this subprocedure, I gave it the ability to work between two indexes so that `RemoveDuplicates` and `Quicksort` are comparable.

Then `RemoveDuplicates` passes the remaining elements to a new array because placing the results into a second array is faster than manipulating the existing array.

Displaying the data

I have used the `WScript.Echo` or `MsgBox` functions to display data. I actually do that very rarely when large output is involved. While I have showed you how to use `WScript.Echo` to send data to the command prompt, that display method is out of date for today's Win32 platform. Instead, the script writes the data to a file.

Here are the constants that I use for setting the location of the temporary file and for opening it for write:

```
Const TEMPFILE = "C:\SHOWUSERS-TEMP.TXT"
Const ForWriting = 2
```

I then open the temporary text file for writing by creating a FileSystemObject and using the `FileSystemObject::OpenTextFile` method to open it. The third parameter states if the text file already exists, it should be overwritten:

```
Set fso = CreateObject("Scripting.FileSystemObject")
Set ts = fso.OpenTextFile(TEMPFILE, ForWriting, True)
```

I then use the `TextStream::WriteLine` and `TextStream::Write` functions to write out the data to the file and ultimately use the `TextStream::Close` method to close it.

Having the file written is only half the battle. I now want to display the file automatically using Notepad, maximize the window, display the results, and delete the file, again automatically, when I close Notepad. This is actually simply accomplished as follows:

```
Set objShell = CreateObject("WScript.Shell")
intRC = objShell.Run ("notepad.exe " & TEMPFILE, vbMaximizedFocus, TRUE)
fso.DeleteFile(TEMPFILE)
```

The `Shell::Run` method allows you to open and use an application such as Notepad synchronously or asynchronously with a script. The first parameter uses the temporary file as a parameter to Notepad, so that Notepad opens the file. The second parameter is one of the VBScript constants that came up before while setting rights to home directories for newly created users. The third parameter indicates whether to run the command synchronously (True) or asynchronously (False). In this case, the script pauses execution when Notepad is open and doesn't start up again until you close Notepad. The script effectively stops executing until you close Notepad. When that happens, a return code is placed into the variable `intRC`. This is to accommodate applications and commands that return a value that you may require. In this case, you don't care about a value being returned, so when Notepad is closed, the script deletes the file.

The script is in Example 17-10.

Example 17-10. The ShowUsers.vbs Utility

```
'*********************************************************************
'The ShowUsers.vbs Utility
'*********************************************************************
Option Explicit

On Error Resume Next

'*********************************************************************
'Maximizes the Notepad screen when started
'*********************************************************************
Const vbMaximizedFocus   = 3

'*********************************************************************
'The domain or workgroup in which the servers or workstations reside
'*********************************************************************
Const strDomainOrWorkGroupName = "MYDOMAIN"

'*********************************************************************
'Sets the location of the temporary file
'*********************************************************************
Const TEMPFILE = "C:\SHOWUSERS-TEMP.TXT"

'*********************************************************************
'Opens a file and lets you start writing from the beginning of the
'file
'*********************************************************************
Const ForWriting = 2

'*********************************************************************
'Declare all variables. As arrResults will be continually increased
'in size as more results are fed in, you have to initially declare it
'as an unbounded array
'*********************************************************************
Dim objShell, adsFSO, adsSession, arrServerResults(1,1), arrResults()
Dim arrResults2(), fso, ts, intRC, intMaxSessions, intIndex, strItem

'*********************************************************************
'Sets up multidimensional array to hold server names and user counts
'*********************************************************************
arrServerResults(0,0) = "server1"
arrServerResults(1,0) = "server2"
arrServerResults(0,1) = 0
arrServerResults(1,1) = 0

'*********************************************************************
'Redimensions arrResults to one element to start with
'*********************************************************************
ReDim arrResults(0)

'*********************************************************************
```

Example 17-10. The ShowUsers.vbs Utility (continued)

```
'Iterates through the array, connecting to the server service of
'each server and looks at each session on that server
'
'If the session has an empty user (is an interserver connection) or
'the user is a computer (the trailing character is a dollar sign), the
'script ignores that session and proceeds to the next session
'
'If the session is valid, the script adds the username to the last
'element of the arrResults array and expands the array by one element
'to cope with the next result when it arrives. The script also
'increments the session count for the corresponding server by one
'**********************************************************************
For intIndex = 0 To UBound(arrServerResults)
  Set adsFSO = GetObject("WinNT://" & strDomainOrWorkGroupName & "/" _
    & arrServerResults(intIndex,0) & "/LanmanServer")

  For Each adsSession In adsFSO.Sessions
    If (Not adsSession.User = "") And (Not Right(adsSession.User,1) = "$") Then
      arrResults(UBound(arrResults)) = adsSession.User & vbCrLf
      ReDim Preserve arrResults(UBound(arrResults) + 1)
      arrServerResults(intIndex,1) = arrServerResults(intIndex,1) + 1
    End If
  Next

  Set adsFSO = Nothing
Next

'**********************************************************************
'Sorts the entire arrResults array and then removes duplicates from
'it, placing the results in arrResults2
'**********************************************************************
Quicksort arrResults, 0, UBound(arrResults)
RemoveDuplicates arrResults, 0, UBound(arrResults), arrResults2

'**********************************************************************
'Opens the temporary text file for writing. If the text file already
'exists, overwrite it.
'**********************************************************************
Set fso = CreateObject("Scripting.FileSystemObject")
Set ts = fso.OpenTextFile(TEMPFILE, ForWriting, True)

'**********************************************************************
'Counts the max sessions by iterating through each server and adding
'up the sessions count in the second column of each row of the
'multidimensional array
'
'Writes out the user sessions for each server to the temporary file
'as the script iterates through the list. When the script finishes
'counting, it writes out the max sessions to the file as well.
'**********************************************************************
intMaxSessions = 0
For intIndex = 0 To UBound(arrServerResults)
```

Example 17-10. The ShowUsers.vbs Utility (continued)

```
  ts.WriteLine "Total User Sessions on " & arrServerResults(intIndex,0) _
    & ": " & arrServerResults(intIndex,1)
  intMaxSessions = intMaxSessions + arrServerResults(intIndex,1)
Next
ts.WriteLine "Total User sessions on CFS: " & intMaxSessions
ts.WriteLine

'*********************************************************************
'Writes out the total number of unique users connected to the domain,
'followed by each username in alphabetic order
'*********************************************************************
ts.WriteLine "Total Users on CFS: " & UBound(arrResults2)
ts.WriteLine
For Each strItem in arrResults2
  ts.Write strItem
Next
ts.Close

'*********************************************************************
'Sets the third parameter of the Shell::Run method to TRUE, which
'allows the script to open up the file in Notepad and maximize the
'screen. The script stops executing until you close Notepad, which
'places a return code into intRC. When Notepad is closed, the script
'deletes the file.
'*********************************************************************
Set objShell = CreateObject("WScript.Shell")
intRC = objShell.Run ("notepad.exe " & TEMPFILE, vbMaximizedFocus, TRUE)
fso.DeleteFile(TEMPFILE)

'*********************************************************************
'Subroutine Quicksort
'
'Sorts the items in the array (between the two values you pass in)
'*********************************************************************
Sub Quicksort(strValues(), ByVal min, ByVal max)

  Dim strMediumValue, high, low, i

  '*******************************************************************
  'If the list has only 1 item, it's sorted
  '*******************************************************************
  If min >= max Then Exit Sub

  '*******************************************************************
  'Pick a dividing item randomly
  '*******************************************************************
  i = min + Int(Rnd(max - min + 1))
  strMediumValue = strValues(i)

  '*******************************************************************
  'Swap the dividing item to the front of the list
  '*******************************************************************
```

Example 17-10. The ShowUsers.vbs Utility (continued)

```
  strValues(i) = strValues(min)

'**********************************************************************
'Separate the list into sublists
'**********************************************************************
low = min
high = max
Do
  '********************************************************************
  'Look down from high for a value < strMediumValue
  '********************************************************************
  Do While strValues(high) >= strMediumValue
    high = high - 1
    If high <= low Then Exit Do
  Loop

  If high <= low Then
    '******************************************************************
    'The list is separated
    '******************************************************************
    strValues(low) = strMediumValue
    Exit Do
  End If

  '********************************************************************
  'Swap the low and high strValues
  '********************************************************************
  strValues(low) = strValues(high)

  '********************************************************************
  'Look up from low for a value >= strMediumValue
  '********************************************************************
  low = low + 1
  Do While strValues(low) < strMediumValue
    low = low + 1
    If low >= high Then Exit Do
  Loop

  If low >= high Then
    '******************************************************************
    'The list is separated
    '******************************************************************
    low = high
    strValues(high) = strMediumValue
    Exit Do
  End If

  '********************************************************************
  'Swap the low and high strValues
  '********************************************************************
  strValues(high) = strValues(low)
Loop 'Loop until the list is separated.
```

Example 17-10. The ShowUsers.vbs Utility (continued)

```
'************************************************************************
'Recursively sort the sublists
'************************************************************************
Quicksort strValues, min, low - 1
Quicksort strValues, low + 1, max

End Sub


'************************************************************************
'Subroutine RemoveDuplicates
'
'Removes duplicate items in the strValues array (between the two
'values you pass in) and writes the results to strNewValues()
'************************************************************************
Sub RemoveDuplicates(ByVal strValues(), ByVal min, ByVal max, strNewValues() )

  Dim strValuesIndex, strNewValuesIndex

  ReDim strNewValues(0)
  strNewValuesIndex = 0

  For strValuesIndex = min To max-1
    If Not strValues(strValuesIndex) = strValues(strValuesIndex+1) Then
      strNewValues(strNewValuesIndex) = strValues(strValuesIndex)
      ReDim Preserve strNewValues(strNewValuesIndex + 1)
      strNewValuesIndex = strNewValuesIndex + 1
    End If
  Next
  strNewValues(strNewValuesIndex) = strValues(max)

End Sub
```

Room for improvement

Although *ShowUsers.vbs* is useful, this utility is lacking in one area: users can legitimately use two connection slots if their `IADsSession::Computer` names are different, but the utility counts the user only once. For example, `user1` might log on to the domain twice, once on COMPUTER1 and once on SERVER1, but my script counts `user1` only once because of the `RemoveDuplicates` subprocedure. If you want to make the script even better, you can create an extension to the utility that remedies this situation. For example, the extension might log all user counts to a file every five minutes for later analysis.

Manipulating Print Queues and Print Jobs

I've now shown you how to use ADSI to manipulate persistent and dynamic objects such as services, shares, sessions, and resources. Now I'm going to conclude looking at these types of objects by examining printer queues and jobs. In this section, I'm going to lead you through creating the following scripts:

- Identifying print queues in Active Directory

- Binding to a print queue* and accessing its properties

- Listing the print jobs in a print queue and manipulating them

 All the code in these scripts for managing printers is done using the WinNT: provider, so it will work on Windows NT as well as Windows 2000. The LDAP searches will not work on Windows NT.

One point before I go on: at the end of Chapter 21, *Scripting Fast Searches Using ADO*, I detail a function called `SearchAD`. I used it earlier in the chapter, and I need to use it now to search Active Directory for the printer's ADsPath and store it in `arrSearchResults(0,0)`.

Identifying Print Queues in Active Directory

List-Print-Queue.vbs in Example 17-11 is a heavily commented script so it should make quite a lot of sense.

Example 17-11. A Utility to List Print Queues in Active Directory (List-Print-Queue.vbs)

```
Option Explicit
On Error Resume Next

'************************************************************************
'Active Directory path to start the search from
'************************************************************************
Const strDomainToSearch = "LDAP://dc=mycorp,dc=com"

'************************************************************************
'Maximizes the Notepad screen when started
'************************************************************************
Const vbMaximizedFocus    = 3
```

---

* Print queues are logical ADSI names for printers installed on a computer.

Example 17-11. A Utility to List Print Queues in Active Directory
(List-Print-Queue.vbs) (continued)

```
'***********************************************************************
'Sets the location of the temporary file
'***********************************************************************
Const TEMPFILE = "C:\PRINTERLIST-TEMP.TXT"


'***********************************************************************
'Opens a file and lets you start writing from the beginning of the file
'***********************************************************************
Const ForWriting = 2

Dim arrPaths(), fso, ts, strItem, intRC, objShell, intIndex

If Not SearchAD(strDomainToSearch,"(objectClass=printQueue)","SubTree",arrPaths) Then
  MsgBox "Printer listing failed!"
Else
  '*********************************************************************
  'Opens the temporary text file for writing. If the text file already
  'exists, overwrite it.
  '*********************************************************************
  Set fso = CreateObject("Scripting.FileSystemObject")
  Set ts = fso.OpenTextFile(TEMPFILE, ForWriting, True)


  '*********************************************************************
  ' Writes out the printer ADsPaths
  '*********************************************************************
  ts.WriteLine "Total printers in Active Directory: " & UBound(arrPaths)+1
  ts.WriteLine
  For intIndex=0 To UBound(arrPaths)
    ts.WriteLine arrPaths(intIndex,1)
    ts.WriteLine vbTab & arrPaths(intIndex,0)
  Next
  ts.Close


  '*********************************************************************
  'Sets the third parameter of the Shell::Run method to TRUE, which
  'allows the script to open up the file in Notepad and maximize the
  'screen. The script stops executing until you close Notepad, which
  'places a return code into intRC. When Notepad is closed, the script
  'deletes the file.
  '*********************************************************************
  Set objShell = CreateObject("WScript.Shell")
  intRC = objShell.Run ("notepad.exe " & TEMPFILE, vbMaximizedFocus, TRUE)
  fso.DeleteFile(TEMPFILE)
End If
```

The script uses the search function to search Active Directory for all objects of class printQueue, writes their ADsPath and cn attributes out to a temporary file, displays the file for you in Notepad, and then erases the file when Notepad is closed. The code for opening and closing files and displaying them with Notepad is the same as in the *ShowUsers.vbs* script earlier in the chapter. Here is an example of the output from this program:

```
Total printers in Active Directory: 3

DC1-ph_stores_hp4000
   LDAP://CN=DC1-stores_hp4000,CN=DC1,OU=Domain Controllers,DC=mycorp,DC=com
SS-0001-Alex&Mark
   LDAP://CN=COMPUTER-0789-Alex&Mark,CN=COMPUTER-0789,OU=Finances, _
      OU=Finance Clients,OU=Clients,DC=mycorp,DC=com
ZZ-NT0089-HP LaserJet 4M Plus
   LDAP://CN=ZZ-0089-HP LaserJet 4M Plus,CN=ZZ-0089,OU=Finances, _
      OU=Finance Clients,OU=Clients,DC=mycorp,DC=com
```

The lines are too long to fit on the page, so I have broken them up with underscores as I would do if this were a script. They normally would be unbroken.

Let's take a look at the output for a moment. The first PrintQueue object is called "DC1-stores_hp4000" and is held within the DC1 domain controller, as if that DC were itself a container object. Computer objects are a special case and can act as containers and hold other objects beneath them. The computer called DC1 (actually a Windows 2000 domain controller) is actually the parent of this printQueue object. Now I could go through listing the properties of the PrintQueue objects for you in a script, but this is very easy and to save this chapter from getting any bigger, you can find the print queue properties yourself on MSDN.

Binding to a Print Queue

Unfortunately, I cannot connect to this printQueue object and list the jobs because this Active Directory object that I have connected to is only the advertisement or publication that such a queue exists; to connect to the printer object that holds the jobs and can be manipulated, I need to use the WinNT: namespace.

While I could provide a simple piece of code to connect to a queue, I'd like to modify the previous script to show you how that could be accomplished. I'll list the queues as before, but this time in addition I'll bind to the *first* queue that I find (and only the first) and print out some properties.

To see what I need to do, let's take a look at the first queue in the previous output. The actual printer path that I need to connect to is:

```
WinNT://MYCORP/DC1/stores_hp4000
```

So I need to massage the data returned by the **SearchAD** function to produce the information about the computer name and the printer name. *List-Print-Queue-2. vbs* is the result, a modified version of *List-Print-Queue.vbs* with two extra sets of information provided. The first is a new constant to define the workgroup or domain; the second I'll go through after the script shown in Example 17-12.

Example 17-12. A Second Generation Utility to List Print Queues in Active Directory (List-Print-Queue-2.vbs)

```
Option Explicit
On Error Resume Next

'*********************************************************************
' Sets the domain or workgroup that the servers or workstations reside in
'*********************************************************************
Const strDomainOrWorkGroup = "MYCORP"

'*********************************************************************
'Active Directory path to start the search from
'*********************************************************************
Const strDomainToSearch = "LDAP://dc=mycorp,dc=com"

'*********************************************************************
'Maximizes the Notepad screen when started
'*********************************************************************
Const vbMaximizedFocus   = 3

'*********************************************************************
'Sets the location of the temporary file
'*********************************************************************
Const TEMPFILE = "C:\PRINTERLIST-TEMP.TXT"

'*********************************************************************
'Opens a file and lets you start writing from the beginning of the file
'*********************************************************************
Const ForWriting = 2

Dim arrPaths(), fso, ts, strItem, intRC, objShell, intIndex, strComputer
Dim strPrinter, adsPrinter

If Not _
  SearchAD(strDomainToSearch,"(objectClass=printQueue)","SubTree",arrPaths) Then
    MsgBox "Printer listing failed!"
Else
  '*********************************************************************
  'Opens the temporary text file for writing. If the text file already
  'exists, overwrite it
  '*********************************************************************
  Set fso = CreateObject("Scripting.FileSystemObject")
  Set ts = fso.OpenTextFile(TEMPFILE, ForWriting, True)

  '*********************************************************************
  ' Writes out the printer ADsPaths
```

Example 17-12. A Second Generation Utility to List Print Queues in Active Directory (List-Print-Queue-2.vbs) (continued)

```
'***********************************************************************
ts.WriteLine "Total printers in Active Directory: " & UBound(arrPaths)+1
ts.WriteLine
For intIndex=0 To UBound(arrPaths)
  ts.WriteLine arrPaths(intIndex,1)
  ts.WriteLine vbTab & arrPaths(intIndex,0)
Next
ts.WriteLine


'***********************************************************************
'Bind to the first printer and list the properties
'***********************************************************************
strComputer = Split(arrPaths(0,0),",")(1)
strComputer = Right(strComputer,Len(strComputer) - 3)
strPrinter = Right(arrPaths(0,1),Len(arrPaths(0,1)) - Len(strComputer) - 1)
Set adsPrinter = GetObject("WinNT://" & strDomainOrWorkGroup & "/" _
  & strComputer & "/" & strPrinter)
ts.WriteLine "Name        : " & adsPrinter.Name
ts.WriteLine "Status      : " & adsPrinter.Status
ts.WriteLine "Model       : " & adsPrinter.Model
ts.WriteLine "Location    : " & adsPrinter.Location
ts.WriteLine "PrinterPath : " & adsPrinter.PrinterPath
ts.Close


'***********************************************************************
'Sets the third parameter of the Shell::Run method to TRUE, which
'allows the script to open up the file in Notepad and maximize the
'screen. The script stops executing until you close Notepad, which
'places a return code into intRC. When Notepad is closed, the script
'deletes the file.
'***********************************************************************
Set objShell = CreateObject("WScript.Shell")
intRC = objShell.Run ("notepad.exe " & TEMPFILE, vbMaximizedFocus, TRUE)
fso.DeleteFile(TEMPFILE)
End If
```

To bind to the printer and list the properties, the script first splits the entire LDAP path of the first array element using the comma as the delimiter. It then immediately retrieves the second item (indexed as 1 because item numbers start at 0) and adds it to **strComputer**. You use VBScript's **Split** function like this:

```
arrResults = Split("Moose 1,Moose 2,Penguin,Banana,Squirrel,Hamster",",")
```

This results in **arrResults(0)** containing "Moose 1" and **arrResults(5)** containing "Hamster." Instead of passing the results out to an array, I can directly retrieve one value from that array by passing the index value to the **Split** function. To retrieve and print "Squirrel" from the preceding string, I use the following code:

```
MsgBox Split("Moose 1,Moose 2,Penguin,Banana,Squirrel,Hamster",",")(4)
```

You can see that here I don't need **arrResults** at all. That's how **Split** works in the previous code.

The first item returned is "CN=DC1." I can then use the VBScript **Right** function to take the righthand part of that string ignoring the first three characters, i.e. DC1, and put the result back into the **strComputer** variable. I now need the printer name. This is done by taking the righthand part of the **cn** attribute returned (DC1-stores_hp4000) and ignoring the number of characters equal to the length of the computer name. That yields "stores_hp4000." I then can assemble all the pieces and bind to the printer object on that computer. I finally print out five attributes (**IADs::Name**, **IADsPrintQueueOperations::Status**, **IADsPrintQueue::Model**, **IADsPrintQueue::Location**, **IADsPrintQueue::PrinterPath**) of that printer to confirm that the printer exists.

IADsPrintQueueOperations and Print Queues

Having successfully connected to a print queue, you then can use the IADsPrint-QueueOperations interface to its full extent. This interface has methods with names like Pause, Resume, and Purge that you should recognize; they correspond to specific print queue functions. There is one important property status that is also available and allows you to query the status of the printer. While *List-Print-Queue-2.vbs* just prints out this value as an integer, *Display-Print-Queue-Status.vbs* (Example 17-13) is a script that binds to the same printer and uses a **Select Case** statement to print the status out using the **MsgBox** function.

Example 17-13. Display the Status of a Specific Printer
(Display-Print-Queue-Status.vbs)

```
'**********************************************************************
'IADsPrintQueueOperations::Status values
'**********************************************************************
Const ADS_PRINTER_PAUSED = &H00000001
Const ADS_PRINTER_PENDING_DELETION = &H00000002
Const ADS_PRINTER_ERROR = &H00000003
Const ADS_PRINTER_PAPER_JAM = &H00000004
Const ADS_PRINTER_PAPER_OUT = &H00000005
Const ADS_PRINTER_MANUAL_FEED = &H00000006
Const ADS_PRINTER_PAPER_PROBLEM = &H00000007
Const ADS_PRINTER_OFFLINE = &H00000008
Const ADS_PRINTER_IO_ACTIVE = &H00000100
Const ADS_PRINTER_BUSY = &H00000200
Const ADS_PRINTER_PRINTING = &H00000400
Const ADS_PRINTER_OUTPUT_BIN_FULL = &H00000800
Const ADS_PRINTER_NOT_AVAILABLE = &H00001000
Const ADS_PRINTER_WAITING = &H00002000
Const ADS_PRINTER_PROCESSING = &H000040000
Const ADS_PRINTER_INITIALIZING = &H00008000
Const ADS_PRINTER_WARMING_UP = &H00010000
```

Example 17-13. Display the Status of a Specific Printer
(Display-Print-Queue-Status.vbs) (continued)

```
Const ADS_PRINTER_TONER_LOW = &H00020000
Const ADS_PRINTER_NO_TONER = &H00040000
Const ADS_PRINTER_PAGE_PUNT = &H00080000
Const ADS_PRINTER_USER_INTERVENTION = &H00100000
Const ADS_PRINTER_OUT_OF_MEMORY = &H00200000
Const ADS_PRINTER_DOOR_OPEN = &H00400000
Const ADS_PRINTER_SERVER_UNKNOWN = &H00800000
Const ADS_PRINTER_POWER_SAVE = &H01000000


'**********************************************************************
' Bind to the printer
'**********************************************************************
Set adsPrinter = GetObject("WinNT://MYCORP/DC1/stores_hp4000")


'**********************************************************************
' Print out the queue status
'**********************************************************************
Select Case adsPrinter.Status
  Case 0
    MsgBox "On line"
  Case ADS_PRINTER_PAUSED
    MsgBox "Paused"
  Case ADS_PRINTER_PENDING_DELETION
    MsgBox "Pending deletion"
  Case ADS_PRINTER_ERROR
    MsgBox "Printer error"
  Case ADS_PRINTER_PAPER_JAM
    MsgBox "Paper jam"
  Case ADS_PRINTER_PAPER_OUT
    MsgBox "Out of paper"
  Case ADS_PRINTER_MANUAL_FEED
    MsgBox "Manual feed pending"
  Case ADS_PRINTER_PAPER_PROBLEM
    MsgBox "Paper trouble"
  Case ADS_PRINTER_OFFLINE
    MsgBox "Offline"
  Case ADS_PRINTER_IO_ACTIVE
    MsgBox "I/O active"
  Case ADS_PRINTER_BUSY
    MsgBox "Printer busy"
  Case ADS_PRINTER_PRINTING
    MsgBox "Printing"
  Case ADS_PRINTER_OUTPUT_BIN_FULL
    MsgBox "Output bin full"
  Case ADS_PRINTER_NOT_AVAILABLE
    MsgBox "Not available"
  Case ADS_PRINTER_WAITING
    MsgBox "Waiting"
  Case ADS_PRINTER_PROCESSING
    MsgBox "Processing"
  Case ADS_PRINTER_INITIALIZING
```

```
   MsgBox "Initializating"
 Case ADS_PRINTER_WARMING_UP
   MsgBox "Warming up"
 Case ADS_PRINTER_TONER_LOW
   MsgBox "Toner low"
 Case ADS_PRINTER_NO_TONER
   MsgBox "Without toner"
 Case ADS_PRINTER_PAGE_PUNT
   MsgBox "Page punt"
 Case ADS_PRINTER_USER_INTERVENTION
   MsgBox "User intervention required"
 Case ADS_PRINTER_OUT_OF_MEMORY
   MsgBox "Out of memory"
 Case ADS_PRINTER_DOOR_OPEN
   MsgBox "Door open"
 Case ADS_PRINTER_SERVER_UNKNOWN
   MsgBox "Server unknown"
 Case ADS_PRINTER_POWER_SAVE
   MsgBox "Power save"
 Case Else
   MsgBox "UNKNOWN"
End Select
```

The final important IADsPrintQueueOperations method that is available to you is
`IADsPrintQueueOperations::PrintJobs`, which returns a collection of print
jobs that you can interact with using IADsCollection. Let's take a look at how you
use that.

Print Jobs

The `IADsPrintQueueOperations::PrintJobs` method allows you to obtain a
collection object that you then can use in a **For Each...Next** loop. You then can
pause and resume the jobs using methods of the same name from the IADsPrint-
JobOperations interface. In addition, as the collection represents the underlying
print jobs, you also can use the `IADsCollection::Add` and `IADsCollection::`
`Remove` methods to add and remove print jobs from the collection. The Add
method is not of much use here, but the Remove method is, since this allows you
to delete jobs from the queue. Assuming I had bound successfully to the queue as
before, then this section of code would purge the queue manually. The following
code gives you some idea of what you can do:

```
For Each adsJob in adsPrinter.PrintJobs
   adsPrinter.PrintJobs.Remove (adsJob.Name)
Next
```

Example 17-14 demonstrates that each job has a number of attributes from IADsPrintJob and IADsPrintJobOperations you can print. This is not the definitive list, and I urge you to check out MSDN for the full set.

Example 17-14. Print Job Properties and Status

```
'***********************************************************************
'IADsPrintJobOperations::Status values
'***********************************************************************
Const ADS_JOB_PAUSED = &H00000001
Const ADS_JOB_ERROR = &H00000002
Const ADS_JOB_DELETING = &H00000004
Const ADS_JOB_PRINTING = &H00000010
Const ADS_JOB_OFFLINE = &H00000020
Const ADS_JOB_PAPEROUT = &H00000040
Const ADS_JOB_PRINTED = &H00000080
Const ADS_JOB_DELETED = &H00000100


'***********************************************************************
' Bind to the printer
'***********************************************************************
Set adsPrinter = GetObject("WinNT://MYCORP/DC1/stores_hp4000")


'***********************************************************************
'Print out some properties and the status of each job
'***********************************************************************
For Each adsJob in adsPrinter.PrintJobs
  str = "Name: " & adsJob.Name & vbCrLf
  str = str & "Position: " & adsJob.Position & vbCrLf
  str = str & "Size: " & adsJob.Size & vbCrLf
  str = str & "Total Pages: " & adsJob.TotalPages & vbCrLf
  str = str & "Pages Printed: " & adsJob.PagesPrinted & vbCrLf
  Select Case adsJob.Status

    Case 0
      str = str & "Status : " & "OK"
    Case ADS_JOB_PAUSED
      str = str & "Status : " & "Paused"
    Case ADS_JOB_ERROR
      str = str & "Status : " & "Error"
    Case ADS_JOB_DELETING
      str = str & "Status : " & "Deleting"
    Case ADS_JOB_PRINTING
      str = str & "Status : " & "Printing"
    Case ADS_JOB_OFFLINE
      str = str & "Status : " & "Offline"
    Case ADS_JOB_PAPEROUT
      str = str & "Status : " & "Paper Out"
    Case ADS_JOB_PRINTED
      str = str & "Status : " & "Printed"
    Case ADS_JOB_DELETED
      str = str & "Status : " & "Deleted"
    Case Else
      str = str & "Status : " & "Unknown"
```

Example 17-14. Print Job Properties and Status (continued)

```
  End Select

  MsgBox str
Next
```

Again, just as in *Display-Print-Queue-Status.vbs*, the `IADsPrintJobOperations::` `Status` property method has a defined set of constants that can be used to tell you about a job. One thing to note is that `IADsPrintJobOperations::Position` is a read/write value so you can use this to move jobs around in the queue print sequence. Actually, a number of IADsPrintJob property methods are also read/ write: `IADsPrintJob::StartTime` and `IADsPrintJob::UntilTime` (to set a future time before which the job can be printed), `IADsPrintJob::Priority`, `IADsPrintJob::Description`, and `IADsPrintJob::Notify`, plus `IADsPrint-` `Job::NotifyPath` (the user is contacted when the job is printed).

Summary

While the future of automating systems management–related tasks lies with WMI and the WBEM initiative, for now you can use ADSI very effectively to accomplish a number of key tasks. In this chapter, I took a look at how you can use ADSI to manipulate persistent objects (like a computer's shares and services) and dynamic objects (computers' open resources, users' active sessions, and print jobs that users initiate) in the Windows 2000 Active Directory or Windows NT SAM.

18

Permissions and Auditing

SDs, ACLs, and ACEs have been used for files and directories on NTFS for years. While the information in this chapter relates to using ADSI interfaces to access objects and properties in an Active Directory, the principles of creating an SD that contains a DACL and SACL can map exactly over to NTFS drives as well. Most administrators need to perform only a few simple operations on their Access Control Lists. In its simplest form, they need to know how to manipulate the access that a user or group has to a particular object or property. For example, a printer published in Active Directory will have a single Security Descriptor listing, among other items, the owner of the object, the group to which the owner belongs, an ACL representing a collection of ACEs for audit purposes, and an ACL representing a collection of ACEs for permissions purposes.

ADSI provides three main interfaces you will need to use:

IADsAccessControlEntry
    Manipulates individual ACEs that represent access or audit permissions for specific users or groups to objects and properties in Active Directory.

IADsAccessControlList
    Manages collections of ACEs for an object.

IADsSecurityDescriptor
    Manages the different sets of ACLs to an object.

All the ADSI security interfaces can be found online at *http://msdn. microsoft.com/isapi/msdnlib.idc?theURL=/library/sdkdoc/adsi/if_sec_ 5g6r.htm.*

Microsoft released a new DLL (*ADSecurity.dll*) provided with the full ADSI 2.5 SDK that contains extra interfaces that you can use to manage security. This DLL provides extra interfaces for managing Security Descriptors, ACLs, and ACEs. It isn't covered in this chapter as it doesn't ship as standard with Windows 2000, but I encourage you to check it out and take a look at the example source code that comes with it for more information. Remember that the DLL will need to be installed and registered using *REGSVR32.EXE ADSecurity.dll* on every client in order for it to be used on that client.

How to Create an ACE Using ADSI

Microsoft has a habit of calling a shovel a ground insertion earth management device. The contents of the five properties of the ACE object are not all immediately obvious from the names. In addition, as Microsoft uses the ACE for both system-audit and permissions entries, a number of values that can go into the properties make sense only in a particular context. To complicate matters further, one property (AceFlags) is a catchall area that currently is the location for two completely different sets of information.

Creating an ACE is a simple matter. In order to set up an ACE, you need the following basic pieces of information:

AccessMask
What permissions you want to set

AceType
Whether you are setting allow/deny permissions or auditing for an object or property

Trustee
Who to apply the permissions to

AceFlags
What inheritance options you want and, if it is an audit entry, whether you are monitoring successes or failures

Flags, ObjectType, InheritedObjectType
What the ACE applies to if not just the entire object

Let's start with the simple example: giving a user full control permissions to an Organizational Unit. That means the information in Table 18-1 gets stored as an ACE on the SD of the Organizational Unit itself.

Table 18-1. Contents of the ACE Properties When Giving a User Full Control Permissions to an Organizational Unit

Name of the Property	Value to be Stored
Trustee	Names the user who is to have the permission.
AccessMask	Gives full control (i.e., give every permission).
AceType	This is an allow permission.
AceFlags	The permission applies to this object. Child objects inherit this ACE.
Flags	Neither ObjectType nor InheritedObjectType is set.
ObjectType	Null.
InheritedObjectType	Null.

So the user (trustee) is allowed (AceType) full control (AccessMask) to the current object and all objects down the tree (AceFlags). The last three are not used here as the permission is a simple one to an entire object.

If I were auditing successful and failed modifications to the entire Organizational Unit by the user, the contents of the audit ACE on the Organizational Unit would look like Table 18-2.

Table 18-2. Contents of the ACE Properties When Auditing Successful Modifications to an Organizational Unit and All Children by a User

Name of the Property	Value to be Stored
Trustee	Names the user who is to be audited.
AccessMask	Gives full control (i.e., audit every action).
AceType	This is an audit ACE.
AceFlags	The auditing applies to this object. Child objects inherit this ACE. This ACE audits successes and failures.
Flags	Neither ObjectType nor InheritedObjectType is set.
ObjectType	Null.
InheritedObjectType	Null.

I am auditing (AceType) successful and failed (AceFlags) modifications of all types (AccessMask) by a user (trustee) for this object and all children (AceFlags).

Note the changes to AceFlags as compared to the previous permissions entry. While a permissions entry uses AceType to indicate whether it is allow or deny, an auditing entry uses AceFlags to indicate whether it is auditing successes or failures.

Let's take a look at the more complex example: giving the same user the ability to set the password for user objects within the entire branch beneath an Organizational Unit as shown in Table 18-3. Again, this ACE is set on the SD of the Organizational Unit, yet it doesn't actually apply to the Organizational Unit itself. This ACE applies to passwords of user objects, so the Organizational Unit acts only as a carrier. The ACE is inherited down the tree by all containers that could ever contain users. As soon as a user is created in one of those containers, the ACE is instantly added as an ACE on the SD of the user via inheritance rules.

Table 18-3. Contents of the ACE Properties for a More Complex Example

Name of the Property	Value to be Stored
Trustee	Names the user who is to have the permission.
AccessMask	Gives write access to a specific property.
AceType	This is an allow permission.
AceFlags	The permission is inherited only and does not apply to this object. Child objects inherit this ACE.
Flags	Both ObjectType and InheritedObjectType are set.
ObjectType	This is the GUID of the userpassword attribute.[a]
InheritedObjectType	This is the GUID of the User class.[a]

[a] Globally Unique Identifiers (GUIDs) are used in the Schema to distinguish objects and object attributes uniquely across your forest. Specifying that a GUID is used somewhere means that you are using a unique identifier for that item.

The user (trustee) is allowed (AceType) write access (AccessMask) to a specific attribute of a specific object class (Access Mask and Flags), namely, the password (ObjectType) of user objects (InheritedObjectType). The ACE does not apply to the current object (AceFlags), and so the current object is acting only as a propagator of the ACE down the tree (AceFlags).

If I were auditing successful and failed modifications to the passwords of user objects within the entire branch beneath an Organizational Unit, the contents of the audit ACE on the Organizational Unit would look like Table 18-4.

Table 18-4. Contents of the ACE Properties When Auditing Successful Modifications to an Organizational Unit and All Children by a User

Name of the Property	Value to be Stored
Trustee	Names the user who is to be audited.
AccessMask	Gives write access to a specific property.
AceType	This is an audit ACE.
AceFlags	The auditing is inherited only and does not apply to this object. Child objects inherit this ACE. This ACE audits successes and failures.
Flags	Both ObjectType and InheritedObjectType are set.
ObjectType	This is the GUID of the userpassword attribute.
InheritedObjectType	This is the GUID of the User class.

I am auditing (AceType) successful and failed (AceFlags) write access (Access-Mask) to a specific attribute of a specific object class (Access Mask and Flags) by a user (trustee), namely, the password (ObjectType) of user objects (InheritedObjectType). The ACE does not apply to the current object (AceFlags), and so the current object is acting only as a propagator of the ACE down the tree (AceFlags).

Each ACE property uses a set of values that indicate the text populating the tables. In the last example, AceFlags is held by the system as the integer 202 that is interpreted as a bit flag.* As you saw in Chapter 16, *Users*, bits in specified positions on an integer represent each of the flags.

Many companies and programmers that publish sets of values like these do not always keep the sequences as simple as this. Sometimes the values make no sense as binary values. For example, under the later section "AceType," I'll show you that Microsoft has values of 0,1,2,5,6, and 7. This may seem daft, since you won't know if the integer 7 represents 7 on its own or 5+2. Not only that, but surely every value can include 0, so how do you check for it? The simple answer is that in this case, each integer represents one and only one value at any one time, so there is no need to check for multiple bits.

Let's take the time to consider each of the properties of an ACE in turn in order to examine the values that can be stored within.

---

* I'm using flags here as a general term (*lowercase*) to distinguish it from the ACE property called Flags (*uppercase*).

Trustee

The *trustee* is the group or user receiving the permissions defined in the Access-Mask and AceType fields or the user or group that is being audited. The trustee can take any of the following forms:

Domain accounts
> These are the logon names used in previous versions of Windows NT in the form <domain>\<useraccount> where <domain> is the name of the Windows NT domain that contains the user and <useraccount> is the sAMAccountName property of the specified user. An example is windows\jsmith. This is still valid for Windows 2000 domains.

Well-known security principals
> These represent special identities defined by the Windows NT/Windows 2000 security system, such as Everyone, Authenticated Users, System, Creator Owner, etc. The objects representing the security principals are stored in the WellKnown Security Principals container beneath the Configuration container.

Built-in groups
> These represent the built-in user groups defined by the Windows NT security system. They have the form BUILTIN\<groupname> where <groupname> is the name of the built-in user group. The objects representing the built-in groups are stored in the Builtin container beneath the domain container. An example is BUILTIN\Administrators.

Security Identifiers (SIDs)
> These are specified in string format and represent the objectSID property of the specified user or group in Active Directory. An example is S-1-5-99-427-9.

Distinguished Name (DN)
> The distinguishedName property of the specified user or group in Active Directory. An example is cn=Tracy Poodles,ou=Finance,dc=mycorp,dc=com.

AccessMask

The *AccessMask* specifies the single or multiple permissions you are setting or auditing for the ACE. Note that this property does not determine whether you are allowing or denying the permission or whether you are auditing successful or failed access, only what the permission is.

 If you are applying the permissions to a specific object or property, you also need to specify the relevant GUID of the object or property that you are giving rights to in the ObjectType or InheritedObjectType properties.

The largest set of values applies to the AccessMask, which is probably what you would expect. See Table 18-5.

Table 18-5. AccessMask Constants

ADSI Name	Decimal Value	Hex Value	Description
ADS_RIGHT_GENERIC_READ	2,147,483,648	&H80000000	Right to read from the Security Descriptor, to examine the object and its children, and to read all properties
ADS_RIGHT_GENERIC_WRITE	1,073,741,824	&H40000000	Right to write all properties, write to the DACL, and add/remove the object from the tree
ADS_RIGHT_GENERIC_EXECUTE	536,870,912	&H20000000	Right to list children of the object
ADS_RIGHT_GENERIC_ALL	268,435,456	&H10000000	Right to create/delete children, delete the tree, read/write properties, examine the object and its children, add/remove the object from the tree, and read/write with an extended right
ADS_RIGHT_ACCESS_SYSTEM_SECURITY	16,777,216	&H1000000	Right to get or set the SACL in the SD of the object
ADS_RIGHT_SYNCHRONIZE	1,048,576	&H100000	Right to use the object for synchronization (see ADSI documentation for more information)
ADS_RIGHT_WRITE_OWNER	524,288	&H80000	Right to assume ownership of the object; no right to grant ownership to others (User must be a trustee of the object)
ADS_RIGHT_WRITE_DAC	262,144	&H40000	Right to write to the DACL of the object
ADS_RIGHT_READ_CONTROL	131,072	&H20000	Right to read from the security descriptor of the object
ADS_RIGHT_DELETE	65,536	&H10000	Right to delete the object

Table 18-5. AccessMask Constants (continued)

ADSI Name	Decimal Value	Hex Value	Description
ADS_RIGHT_DS_CONTROL_ACCESS	256	&H100	Right to perform an application-specific extension on the object (GUID=extended right)
ADS_RIGHT_DS_LIST_OBJECT	128	&H80	Right to examine the object (if this is missing, the object is hidden from the user)
ADS_RIGHT_DS_DELETE_TREE	64	&H40	Right to delete all children of this object, regardless of the permission on the children
ADS_RIGHT_DS_WRITE_PROP	32	&H20	Right to write properties of the object (GUID=specific property; no GUID=all properties)
ADS_RIGHT_DS_READ_PROP	16	&H10	Right to read properties of the object (GUID=specific property; no GUID=all properties)
ADS_RIGHT_DS_SELF	8	&H8	Right to modify the group membership of a group object
ADS_RIGHT_ACTRL_DS_LIST	4	&H4	Right to examine children of the object
ADS_RIGHT_DS_DELETE_CHILD	2	&H2	Right to delete children of the object (GUID=specific child object class; no GUID=all child object classes)
ADS_RIGHT_DS_CREATE_CHILD	1	&H1	Right to create children of the object (GUID=specific child object class; no GUID=all child object classes)
No name defined	-1	&HFFFFFFFFFFFFFF	Full control

These values were taken from the ADSI 2.5 documentation for the ADS_RIGHTS_ENUM enumerated type at: *http://msdn.microsoft.com/isapi/msdnlib.idc?theURL=/library/sdkdoc/adsi/ds2_enum_16el.htm.*

The value in the first column is the constant name that Microsoft defined for ADSI. This works fine if you are programming in VB or VC++ or scripting in a language that can make use of the available ADSI libraries, but with VBScript these constants do not immediately exist. In other words, you have to define them in each script you use. To save you time, just copy the **Const** definitions from any of the ACE scripts provided on the O'Reilly web site for this book. I've included the values in decimal and in hex for two reasons. First, I'm going to be using hex in my scripts; the decimal values are there in case you want to use them for your own preference. Second, Microsoft defines all their constants in hexadecimal, so that is what you will see in the ADSI help documentation. *&H* is the prefix for a hex number in VBScript, and so if you want to specify that a group can list, create, and delete all children, you would use the value &H7, consisting of the rights ADS_RIGHT_ACTRL_DS_LIST + ADS_RIGHT_DS_DELETE_CHILD + ADS_RIGHT_DS_CREATE_CHILD.

The last value has no name and is what you use if you want to define full control permissions. Note that in this case most programmers tend to use the integer value -1 even if they have used hex elsewhere.

The GUIDs relating to properties and children are discussed further under the ACE Flags property.

AceType

This property dictates whether the ACE denies permissions, allows permissions, or audits use of permissions (whether success or failure is defined in AceFlags). The values set here depend on whether the ACE applies to a specific object/property or just applies generally. See Table 18-6.

 Only one value can be set at any one time. This is why the values are not 1, 2, 4, 8, and so on.

Table 18-6. AceType Constants

ADSI Name	Decimal Value	Hex Value	Description
ADS_ACETYPE_SYSTEM_AUDIT_OBJECT	7	&H7	This is a system-audit entry ACE using a GUID
ADS_ACETYPE_ACCESS_DENIED_OBJECT	6	&H6	This is an access-denied ACE using a GUID
ADS_ACETYPE_ACCESS_ALLOWED_OBJECT	5	&H5	This is an access-allowed ACE using a GUID

Table 18-6. AceType Constants (continued)

ADSI Name	Decimal Value	Hex Value	Description
ADS_ACETYPE_SYSTEM_ AUDIT	2	&H2	This is a system-audit entry ACE using a Windows NT Security Descriptor
ADS_ACETYPE_ACCESS_ DENIED	1	&H1	This is an access-denied ACE using a Windows NT Security Descriptor
ADS_ACETYPE_ACCESS_ ALLOWED	0	&H0	This is an access-allowed ACE using a Windows NT Security Descriptor

These values were taken from the ADSI 2.5 documentation for the ADS_ ACETYPE_ENUM enumerated type at this location: *http://msdn.microsoft.com/ isapi/msdnlib.idc?theURL=/library/sdkdoc/adsi/ds2_enum_7nal.htm.*

Those ACEs that have a GUID in ObjectType or InheritedObjectType use the top three _OBJECT values. Any ACEs that do not refer to a specific GUID use the bottom three.

AceFlags

This catchall location stores two sets of information: inheritance and auditing. First it stores whether this ACE can be inherited by its children, whether the ACE applies to this object or if it is only acting as a propagator to pass it on to other objects, and whether the ACE is itself inherited. Secondly, for system-audit ACEs, this property indicates whether audit events are generated for success, failure, or both of the AccessMask permissions. See Table 18-7.

Table 18-7. AceFlags Constants

ADSI Name	Decimal Value	Hex Value	Description
ADS_ACEFLAG_FAILED_ACCESS	128	&H80	Used in the SACL only; indicates to generate audit messages for failed access attempts.
ADS_ACEFLAG_SUCCESSFUL_ ACCESS	64	&H40	Used in the SACL only; indicates to generate audit messages for successful access attempts.
ADS_ACEFLAG_VALID_INHERIT_ FLAGS	31	&H1F	Indicates whether the inherit flags for this ACE are valid (set only by the system).

Table 18-7. AceFlags Constants (continued)

ADSI Name	Decimal Value	Hex Value	Description
ADS_ACEFLAG_INHERITED_ACE	16	&H10	Indicates whether this ACE was inherited. (set only by the system).
ADS_ACEFLAG_INHERIT_ONLY_ ACE	8	&H8	Indicates an inherit-only ACE that does not exercise access controls on the object to which it is attached.
ADS_ACEFLAG_NO_ PROPAGATE_INHERIT_ACE	4	&H4	Child objects will not inherit this ACE.
ADS_ACEFLAG_INHERIT_ACE	2	&H2	Child objects will inherit this ACE.

These values were taken from the ADSI 2.5 documentation for the ADS_ ACEFLAG_ENUM enumerated type at this location: *http://msdn.microsoft.com/ isapi/msdnlib.idc?theURL=/library/sdkdoc/adsi/ds2_enum_2xbb.htm.*

There are three unusual aspects to this property:

- The two SACL flags should surely be in AceType not AceFlags, since AceType already indicates the allow or deny aspects of a DACL ACE. Strangely, they are here instead.

- The ADS_ACEFLAG_INHERIT_ONLY_ACE indicates that the object that this ACE is attached to is acting only as a carrier for the object, rather than being affected by the ACE itself. This normally applies to containers, where the container acts as a placeholder for the ACE and applies it to whatever specific objects it is targeted to when they are created. If appropriate, the ACE will be propagated to containers below so they can act as carriers themselves.

- Flags of this nature in ADSI normally are intended to indicate the presence or absence of something. Either the flag is set or it is not, giving us two states for whatever the flag refers to. Take a look at the latter two flags. The ADS_ ACEFLAG_INHERIT_ACE flag indicates that the ACE will be propagated down to child objects throughout the section of the tree below this object. If the ADS_ACEFLAG_INHERIT_ACE flag is set, then ADS_ACEFLAG_NO_PROP- AGATE_INHERIT_ACE will not be set. If ADS_ACEFLAG_NO_PROPAGATE_ INHERIT_ACE is set, ADS_ACEFLAG_INHERIT_ACE is not, and this prevents the ACE from being inherited by subsequent generations of objects. Don't try and set both at the same time.

Flags, ObjectType, and InheritedObjectType

In order for the ACE to know whether it contains an *ObjectType* or *InheritedObjectType* field, it contains a *Flags* property. This can have only four values. If the value is 0, neither object is present in the ACE. The other three values (1, 2, and 3) are made up from two constants displayed in Table 18-8.

Table 18-8. Flag Type Constants

ADSI Name	Decimal Value	Hex Value	Description
ADS_FLAG_ INHERITED_OBJECT_ TYPE_PRESENT	2	&H2	Indicates that an InheritedObjectType is present in the ACE and that an Object-Type is not present
ADS_FLAG_OBJECT_ TYPE_PRESENT	1	&H1	Indicates that an ObjectType is present in the ACE and that an InheritedObject-Type is not present

These values were taken from the ADSI 2.5 documentation for the ADS_ FLAGTYPE_ENUM enumerated type at this location: *http://msdn.microsoft.com/ isapi/msdnlib.idc?theURL=/library/sdkdoc/adsi/ds2_enum_99rb.htm.*

The ObjectType and InheritedObjectType fields store GUIDs or null values that indicate what the ACE actually applies to. Table 18-9 explains it much better.

Table 18-9. How to Use ObjectType and InheritedObjectType

ACE Requirement	AceFlags	Flags	ObjectType	InheritedObjectType
Permissions are to apply to entire current object.	Effective on current object; not inherited by child objects	Neither	Null (ignored but still set)	Null (ignored but still set)
Permissions are to apply to a specific attribute of the current object.	Effective on current object; not inherited by child objects	ObjectType only	schemaID-GUID of the attribute-Schema object that defines the attribute in the schema	Null (ignored but still set)
Permissions are to apply to all child objects.	Not effective on current object; inherited by children	ObjectType only	Null[a]	Null (ignored but still set)

Table 18-9. How to Use ObjectType and InheritedObjectType (continued)

ACE Requirement	AceFlags	Flags	ObjectType	InheritedOb-jectType
Permissions are to apply to child objects that are of a specific class.	Not effective on current object; inherited by children	ObjectType only	schemaID-GUID of the classSchema object that defines the class in the schema	Null (ignored but still set)
Permissions are to apply to a specific attribute of specific child objects.	Not effective on current object; inherited by children	Both	schemaID-GUID of the attribute-Schema object that defines the attribute in the schema	schemaID-GUID of the classSchema object that defines the class in the schema

[a] Setting null for the ObjectType field in the third entry signifies that this ACE applies to all child objects; this is the only time that you do not use a GUID in this property. The system understands that a null value for a required ObjectType field is the same as providing the GUIDs for every possible child object all at once.

Null items that are ignored do not need to be set by you; they will be set to null by the system on creation of the ACE.

Note that Flags, ObjectType, and InheritedObjectType have defaults of 0, null, and null, respectively.

A Simple ADSI Example

All of the seven ACE properties are set using property methods of the same names as those in an ADSI interface called IADsAccessControlEntry. The ACEs that are created using this then are modified using IADsAccessControlList and IADsSecurityDescriptor.

Let's go through an example now so you can see how it all fits together. Example 18-1 shows a section of VBScript code that creates an ACE that allows ANewGroup full access to the myOU organizational unit and all its children.

Example 18-1. Creating an ACE .

```
'************************************************************************
'Declare constants
'************************************************************************
Const FULL_CONTROL = -1
Const ADS_ACETYPE_ACCESS_ALLOWED = 0
Const ADS_FLAG_INHERITED_OBJECT_TYPE_PRESENT = 2


'************************************************************************
'Declare variables
'************************************************************************
Dim adsObject       'Any object
Dim adsSecDesc      'SecurityDescriptor
Dim adsDACL         'AccessControlList
Dim adsNewACE'AccessControlEntry


'************************************************************************
'Create the new ACE and populate it
'************************************************************************
Set adsNewACE = CreateObject("AccessControlEntry")
adsNewACE.Trustee = "WINDOWS\ANewGroup"
adsNewACE.AccessMask = FULL_CONTROL
adsNewACE.AceType = ADS_ACETYPE_ACCESS_ALLOWED
adsNewACE.AceFlags = ADS_FLAG_INHERITED_OBJECT_TYPE_PRESENT


'************************************************************************
'Add the new ACE to the object and write it to the AD
'************************************************************************
Set adsObject = GetObject("LDAP://ou=myOU,dc=windows,dc=mycorp,dc=com")


'************************************************************************
'Use IADs::Get to retrieve the SD for the object
'************************************************************************
Set adsSecDesc = adsObject.Get("ntSecurityDescriptor")


'************************************************************************
'Use IADsSecurityDescriptor:: DiscretionaryAcl to retrieve the existing DACL
'************************************************************************
Set adsDACL = adsSecDesc.DiscretionaryAcl


'************************************************************************
'Use IADsAccessControlList::AddACE to add an ACE to an existing DACL
'************************************************************************
adsDACL.AddAce adsNewACE


'************************************************************************
'Use IADsSecurityDescriptor:: DiscretionaryAcl to put back the modified DACL
'************************************************************************
adsSecDesc.DiscretionaryAcl = adsDACL


'************************************************************************
'Use IADs::Put to replace the SD for the object
'************************************************************************
```

Example 18-1. Creating an ACE (continued).

```
adsObject.Put "ntSecurityDescriptor", Array(adsSecDesc)

'**********************************************************************
'Write out the property cache using IADs::SetInfo
'**********************************************************************
adsObject.SetInfo
```

First I create the new ACE. This requires use of a **CreateObject** function call to create a new empty instance of an ACE object. I then have to set the four fields that I need. The **trustee** is the user or group that will have the permission to the myOU object. The **AccessMask** value set to -1 indicates that full permission is being set. In order to say whether the full permissions are allowed or denied, I use a 0 in the **AceType** field, which indicates that the ACE is a permissions-allowed ACE. Finally, the **AceFlags** field is set to 2 so that child objects will inherit this ACE. This means that the ACE now allows ANewGroup full access to the myOU organizational unit and all its children.

I then go through binding to the object to get the security descriptor and ultimately the DACL so that I can add the new ACE to the DACL. Once that is done, I reverse the steps and set the security descriptor for the object, writing out the property cache as the last step.

A Complex ACE Example

Example 18-2 shows two further ACEs being created. This time I have included all the constants, whether I needed them or not. This example sets the following ACEs on myOU:

- No permissions to even see the object for members of DenyGroup.

- Ability to create, delete, and examine all children of the object for AllowChild-Group.

- Ability for user Vicky Launders to assume ownership of the Organizational Unit only and not any children.

- Permission for the user Lee Flight to read and write this OU's description.

- Permission for the Chris Heaton account to read and write all users' passwords

- Generation of audit messages for failed access by Everyone to delete the object itself.

- Generation of audit messages for all modifications to Active Directory by Brian Kerr below this Organizational Unit, but not including this Organizational Unit.

Example 18-2. Creating Two More Complex ACEs

```
'***************************************************************************
'AccessMask constants
'***************************************************************************
Const ADS_RIGHT_GENERIC_READ = &H80000000
Const ADS_RIGHT_GENERIC_WRITE = &H40000000
Const ADS_RIGHT_GENERIC_EXECUTE = &H20000000
Const ADS_RIGHT_GENERIC_ALL = &H10000000
Const ADS_RIGHT_SYSTEM_SECURITY = &H1000000
Const ADS_RIGHT_SYNCHRONIZE = &H100000
Const ADS_RIGHT_WRITE_OWNER = &H80000
Const ADS_RIGHT_WRITE_DAC = &H40000
Const ADS_RIGHT_READ_CONTROL = &H20000
Const ADS_RIGHT_DELETE = &H10000
Const ADS_RIGHT_DS_CONTROL_ACCESS = &H100
Const ADS_RIGHT_DS_LIST_OBJECT = &H80
Const ADS_RIGHT_DS_DELETE_TREE = &H40
Const ADS_RIGHT_DS_WRITE_PROP = &H20
Const ADS_RIGHT_DS_READ_PROP = &H10
Const ADS_RIGHT_DS_SELF = &H8
Const ADS_RIGHT_ACTRL_DS_LIST = &H4
Const ADS_RIGHT_DS_DELETE_CHILD = &H2
Const ADS_RIGHT_DS_CREATE_CHILD = &H1
Const FULL_CONTROL = -1


'***************************************************************************
'AceType constants
'***************************************************************************
Const ADS_ACETYPE_SYSTEM_AUDIT_OBJECT = &H7
Const ADS_ACETYPE_ACCESS_DENIED_OBJECT = &H6
Const ADS_ACETYPE_ACCESS_ALLOWED_OBJECT = &H5
Const ADS_ACETYPE_SYSTEM_AUDIT = &H2
Const ADS_ACETYPE_ACCESS_DENIED = &H1
Const ADS_ACETYPE_ACCESS_ALLOWED = &H0


'***************************************************************************
'AceFlags constants
'***************************************************************************
Const ADS_ACEFLAG_FAILED_ACCESS = &H80
Const ADS_ACEFLAG_SUCCESSFUL_ACCESS = &H40
Const ADS_ACEFLAG_VALID_INHERIT_FLAGS = &H1F
Const ADS_ACEFLAG_INHERITED_ACE = &H10
Const ADS_ACEFLAG_INHERIT_ONLY_ACE = &H8
Const ADS_ACEFLAG_NO_PROPAGATE_INHERIT_ACE = &H4
Const ADS_ACEFLAG_INHERIT_ACE = &H2


'***************************************************************************
'Flags constants
'***************************************************************************
Const ADS_FLAG_INHERITED_OBJECT_TYPE_PRESENT = &H2
Const ADS_FLAG_OBJECT_TYPE_PRESENT = &H1


'***************************************************************************
```

Example 18-2. Creating Two More Complex ACEs (continued)

```
'Constants representing paths to classes and attributes in the schema
'***************************************************************************
Const USER_PASSWORD_ADSPATH = _
  "LDAP://cn=User-Password,cn=Schema,cn=Configuration,dc=mycorp,dc=com"
Const DESCRIPTION_ADSPATH = _
  "LDAP://cn=Description,cn=Schema,cn=Configuration,dc=mycorp,dc=com"
Const USER_ADSPATH = "LDAP://cn=User,cn=Schema,cn=Configuration,dc=mycorp,dc=com"


'***************************************************************************
'Declare general variables
'***************************************************************************
Dim adsObject                  'The Organizational Unit to bind to
Dim adsSecDesc                 'SecurityDescriptor
Dim adsDACL                    'AccessControlList object containing permission ACEs
Dim adsSACL                    'AccessControlList object containing audit ACEs
Dim adsNewACE                  'AccessControlEntry
Dim adsAttributeSchemaObject 'An object representing an attribute in the schema


'***************************************************************************
'Get a handle to the DACL of the OU
'***************************************************************************
Set adsObject = GetObject ("LDAP://ou=myOU,dc=mycorp,dc=com")
Set adsSecDesc = adsObject.Get("ntSecurityDescriptor")
Set adsDACL = adsSecDesc.DiscretionaryAcl
Set adsSACL = adsSecDesc.SystemAcl


'***************************************************************************
'Set no permission to view the object for members of DenyGroup
'***************************************************************************
Set adsNewACE = CreateObject("AccessControlEntry")
adsNewACE.Trustee = "WINDOWS\DenyGroup"
adsNewACE.AccessMask = ADS_RIGHT_DS_LIST_OBJECT
adsNewACE.AceType = ADS_ACETYPE_ACCESS_DENIED
adsNewACE.AceFlags = ADS_ACEFLAG_INHERIT_ACE
adsDACL.AddAce adsNewACE
Set adsNewACE = Nothing


'***************************************************************************
'Ability to create, delete, and examine all children of the object for
'AllowChildGroup
'***************************************************************************
Set adsNewACE = CreateObject("AccessControlEntry")
adsNewACE.Trustee = "WINDOWS\AllowChildGroup"
adsNewACE.AccessMask = ADS_RIGHT_ACTRL_DS_LIST + ADS_RIGHT_DS_DELETE_CHILD _
  + ADS_RIGHT_DS_CREATE_CHILD
adsNewACE.AceType = ADS_ACETYPE_ACCESS_ALLOWED
adsNewACE.AceFlags = ADS_ACEFLAG_INHERIT_ACE
adsDACL.AddAce adsNewACE
Set adsNewACE = Nothing


'***************************************************************************
'Ability for user Vicky Launders to assume ownership of the Organizational
```

Example 18-2. Creating Two More Complex ACEs (continued)

```
'Unit only and not any children
'*************************************************************************
Set adsNewACE = CreateObject("AccessControlEntry")
AdsACE.Trustee = "cn=Vicky Launders,cn=Users,dc=windows,dc=mycorp,dc=com"
adsNewACE.AccessMask = ADS_RIGHT_WRITE_OWNER
adsNewACE.AceType = ADS_ACETYPE_ACCESS_ALLOWED
adsNewACE.AceFlags = ADS_ACEFLAG_NO_PROPAGATE_INHERIT_ACE
adsDACL.AddAce adsNewACE
Set adsNewACE = Nothing


'*************************************************************************
'Allowing the Lee Flight account to read and write this OU's description
'*************************************************************************
Set adsNewACE = CreateObject("AccessControlEntry")
AdsACE.Trustee = "cn=Lee Flight,cn=Users,dc=windows,dc=mycorp,dc=com"
adsNewACE.AccessMask = ADS_RIGHT_DS_WRITE_PROP + ADS_RIGHT_DS_READ_PROP
adsNewACE.AceType = ADS_ACETYPE_ACCESS_ALLOWED_OBJECT
adsNewACE.AceFlags = ADS_ACEFLAG_NO_PROPAGATE_INHERIT_ACE
adsNewACE.Flags = ADS_FLAG_OBJECT_TYPE_PRESENT
'*************************************************************************
'Retrieve the GUID of the Description class from the schema and place the
'result in the ObjectType property
'*************************************************************************
Set adsAttributeSchemaObject = GetObject(DESCRIPTION_ADSPATH)
adsNewACE.ObjectType = adsAttributeSchemaObject.GUID

adsDACL.AddAce adsNewACE
Set adsNewACE = Nothing


'*************************************************************************
'Allowing the Chris Heaton account to read and write users' passwords
'*************************************************************************
Set adsNewACE = CreateObject("AccessControlEntry")
adsNewACE.Trustee = "WINDOWS\Chris Heaton"
adsNewACE.AccessMask = ADS_RIGHT_DS_WRITE_PROP + ADS_RIGHT_DS_READ_PROP
adsNewACE.AceType = ADS_ACETYPE_ACCESS_ALLOWED_OBJECT
adsNewACE.AceFlags = ADS_ACEFLAG_INHERIT_ACE + ADS_ACEFLAG_INHERIT_ONLY_ACE
adsNewACE.Flags = ADS_FLAG_OBJECT_TYPE_PRESENT _
  + ADS_FLAG_INHERITED_OBJECT_TYPE_PRESENT
'*************************************************************************
'Retrieve the GUID of the User-Password class from the schema and place
'the result in the ObjectType property
'*************************************************************************
Set adsAttributeSchemaObject = GetObject(USER_PASSWORD_ADSPATH)
adsNewACE.ObjectType = adsAttributeSchemaObject.GUID
'*************************************************************************
'Retrieve the GUID of the User class from the schema and place the result
'in the InheritedObjectType property
'*************************************************************************
Set adsAttributeSchemaObject = GetObject(USER_ADSPATH)
adsNewACE.InheritedObjectType = adsAttributeSchemaObject.GUID
```

Example 18-2. Creating Two More Complex ACEs (continued)

```
adsDACL.AddAce adsNewACE
Set adsNewACE = Nothing


'**************************************************************************
'Generation of audit messages for failed access by Everyone to delete the
'object itself
'**************************************************************************
Set adsNewACE = CreateObject("AccessControlEntry")
adsNewACE.Trustee = "WINDOWS\Everyone"
adsNewACE.AccessMask = ADS_RIGHT_DELETE
adsNewACE.AceType = ADS_ACETYPE_SYSTEM_AUDIT
adsNewACE.AceFlags = ADS_ACEFLAG_FAILED_ACCESS _
  + ADS_ACEFLAG_NO_PROPAGATE_INHERIT_ACE
adsSACL.AddAce adsNewACE
Set adsNewACE = Nothing


'**************************************************************************
'Generation of audit messages for successful and failed modifications by
'Brian Kerr to Active Directory below this Organizational Unit, but
'not including this Organizational Unit
'**************************************************************************
Set adsNewACE = CreateObject("AccessControlEntry")
AdsACE.Trustee = "cn=Brian Kerr,cn=Users,dc=windows,dc=mycorp,dc=com"
adsNewACE.AccessMask = FULL_CONTROL
adsNewACE.AceType = ADS_ACETYPE_SYSTEM_AUDIT_OBJECT
adsNewACE.AceFlags = ADS_ACEFLAG_FAILED_ACCESS + ADS_ACEFLAG_SUCCESSFUL_ACCESS _
  + ADS_ACEFLAG_INHERIT_ONLY_ACE + ADS_ACEFLAG_INHERIT_ACE
adsNewACE.Flags = ADS_FLAG_OBJECT_TYPE_PRESENT
adsNewACE.ObjectType = vbNull
adsSACL.AddAce adsNewACE
Set adsNewACE = Nothing


'**************************************************************************
'Write the newly expanded DACL and SACL to the SD and then out to the AD
'**************************************************************************
adsSecDesc.DiscretionaryAcl = adsDACL
adsSecDesc.SystemAcl = adsSACL
adsObject.Put "ntSecurityDescriptor", Array(adsSecDesc)
adsObject.SetInfo
```

Note that the last two items modify the SACL and not the DACL as they are audit
ACEs and not permissions ACEs. Also you can see that I have chosen to use DNs
and domain accounts for the trustees in the script. Both are valid for Windows
2000. Again as usual in these scripts, there is no error handling. As the SD is not
being written until the end of the code, an error causes the entire script to fail.

Creating Security Descriptors

If you are creating an object from scratch and you don't want it to get the default DACL and SACL that would be applied to objects normally created at that location in the tree due to inheritance, you can write your own DACL and SACL for an object. As you would expect, there are a number of properties associated with Security Descriptors and ACLs that you need to set. SDs and ACLs can be manipulated with the IADsAccessControlList (see Table 18-10) and IADsSecurityDescriptor (see Table 18-11) interfaces. I'll go through these briefly now and then move on to some more examples.

Table 18-10. IADsAccessControlList Methods and Properties

IADsAccessControlList Methods and Properties	Action
AddAce method	Adds an ACE to an ACL
RemoveAce method	Removes an ACE from an ACL
CopyAccessList method	Copies the current ACL
AclRevision property	Shows the revision of the ACL (always set to 4; see later text)
AceCount property	Indicates the number of ACEs in the ACL

The revision level is a static version number for every ACE, ACL, and SD in Active Directory. It is defined in the ADS_SD_REVISION_ENUM enumerated type which contains a single constant definition as follows:

```
Const ADS_SD_REVISION_DS = 4.
```

Having a revision allows Active Directory to know which elements of an ACE could exist. Later if new properties and concepts are added to the ACE so that it has a more extended definition, the revision would increment. Then Active Directory would know that old revision-4 ACEs could not support the new extensions and could upgrade them or support them with lesser functionality.

Table 18-11. IADsSecurityDescriptor Methods and Properties

IADsSecurityDescriptor Methods and Properties	Action
CopySecurityDescriptor method	A copy of an existing SD.
Revision property	The revision of the SD (always set to 4, as noted earlier).
Control property	A set of flags indicating various aspects of the SD (see later text).
Owner property	The SID of the owner. If this field is null, then no owner is set.

Table 18-11. IADsSecurityDescriptor Methods and Properties (continued)

IADsSecurityDescriptor Methods and Properties	Action
OwnerDefaulted property	A Boolean value indicating whether the owner is derived by the default mechanism when created (i.e., assembled out of all the inherited ACEs passed down by its parents) rather than explicitly set by the person or application that created the SD in the first place.
Group property	The SID of the object's primary group if appropriate. If this field is null, then no primary group exists.
GroupDefaulted property	A Boolean value indicating that the group is derived by the default mechanism rather than explicitly set by the person or application that created the SD in the first place.
DiscretionaryAcl property	The discretionary ACL that holds permissions ACEs. The SE_DACL_PRESENT flag must be set in the Control property if a DACL exists. If the flag is set and yet this field is null, this indicates full access is allowed to everyone.
DaclDefaulted property	A Boolean value indicating that the DACL is derived by the default mechanism rather than explicitly set by the person or application that created the SD in the first place. This is ignored unless SE_DACL_PRESENT is set.
SystemAcl property	The system ACL that holds auditing ACEs. The SE_SACL_PRESENT flag must be set in the Control property if a SACL exists.
SaclDefaulted property	A Boolean value indicating that the SACL is derived by the default mechanism rather than explicitly set by the person or application that created the SD in the first place. This is ignored unless SE_SACL_PRESENT is set.

The Control property can take a number of flags that help to define the properties of an SD. See Table 18-12 for a full description.

Table 18-12. Control Constants

ADSI Name	Decimal Value	Hex Value	Description
ADS_SD_CONTROL_SE_ OWNER_DEFAULTED	1	&H1	This Boolean flag, when set, indicates that the SID pointed to by the Owner field was provided by the default mechanism rather than set by the person or application that created the SD in the first place. This may affect the treatment of the SID with respect to inheritance of an owner.

Table 18-12. Control Constants (continued)

ADSI Name	Decimal Value	Hex Value	Description
ADS_SD_CONTROL_SE_ GROUP_DEFAULTED	2	&H2	This Boolean flag, when set, indicates that the SID in the Group field was provided by the default mechanism rather than explicitly set by the person or application that created the SD in the first place. This may affect the treatment of the SID with respect to inheritance of a primary group.
ADS_SD_CONTROL_SE_ DACL_PRESENT	4	&H4	This Boolean flag, when set, indicates that the security descriptor contains a DACL. If this flag is set and the DiscretionaryAcl field of the SD is null, then an empty (but present) ACL is explicitly being specified.
ADS_SD_CONTROL_SE_ DACL_DEFAULTED	8	&H8	This Boolean flag, when set, indicates that the DiscretionaryAcl field was provided by the default mechanism rather than explicitly set by the person or application that created the SD in the first place. This may affect the treatment of the ACL with respect to inheritance of an ACL. This flag is ignored if the SE_DACL_PRESENT flag is not set.
ADS_SD_CONTROL_SE_ SACL_PRESENT	16	&H10	This Boolean flag, when set, indicates that the security descriptor contains a SACL.
ADS_SD_CONTROL_SE_ SACL_DEFAULTED	32	&H20	This Boolean flag, when set, indicates that the ACL pointed to by the SystemAcl field was provided by the default mechanism rather than explicitly set by the person or application that created the SD in the first place. This may affect the treatment of the ACL with respect to inheritance of an ACL. This flag is ignored if the SE_SACL_PRESENT flag is not set.
ADS_SD_CONTROL_SE_ DACL_AUTO_INHERIT_ REQ	256	&H100	The DACL of the SD must be inherited.
ADS_SD_CONTROL_SE_ SACL_AUTO_INHERIT_ REQ	512	&H200	The SACL of the SD must be inherited.
ADS_SD_CONTROL_SE_ DACL_AUTO_ INHERITED	1,024	&H400	The DACL of the SD supports auto-propagation of inheritable ACEs to existing child objects.

Table 18-12. Control Constants (continued)

ADSI Name	Decimal Value	Hex Value	Description
ADS_SD_CONTROL_SE_ SACL_AUTO_ INHERITED	2,048	&H800	The SACL of the SD supports auto-propagation of inheritable ACEs to existing child objects.
ADS_SD_CONTROL_SE_ DACL_PROTECTED	4,096	&H1000	The DACL of the SD is protected and will not be modified when new rights propagate through the tree.
ADS_SD_CONTROL_SE_ SACL_PROTECTED	8,192	&H2000	The SACL of the SD is protected and will not be modified when new rights propagate through the tree.
ADS_SD_CONTROL_SE_ SELF_RELATIVE	32,768	&H8000	The SD is held in a contiguous block of memory.

These values were taken from the ADSI 2.5 documentation for the ADS_SD_ CONTROL_ENUM enumerated type at this location: *http://msdn.microsoft.com/ isapi/msdnlib.idc?theURL=/library/sdkdoc/adsi/ds2_enum_290t.htm.*

 In your ADSI scripting code, it is possible for you to specify that the DACL or SACL is either null or empty. While in both cases each ACL contains no ACEs, there is a big difference between the effects of each setting. Specifically, any ACL that has been set to null (vbNull) grants full permissions to everyone while an ACL that exists but contains no ACEs (i.e., is empty) grants no permissions to anyone at all.

Now I have enough information to be able to create my own SD. Example 18-3 does exactly that. While I have defined only all of the SD constants, to save space I have defined only the ACE constants that I am using. Also note that this code is not 100% complete; I have not included the object creation in the code.

Example 18-3. Creating an SD

```
'*********************************************************************
'AccessMask constants
'*********************************************************************
Const ADS_RIGHT_DS_LIST_OBJECT = &H80


'*********************************************************************
'AceType constants
'*********************************************************************
Const ADS_ACETYPE_ACCESS_DENIED = &H1


'*********************************************************************
'AceFlags constants
'*********************************************************************
```

Example 18-3. Creating an SD (continued)

```
Const ADS_ACEFLAG_INHERIT_ACE = &H2


'**************************************************************************
'Security Descriptor constants
'**************************************************************************
Const ADS_SD_CONTROL_SE_OWNER_DEFAULTED = &H1
Const ADS_SD_CONTROL_SE_GROUP_DEFAULTED = &H2
Const ADS_SD_CONTROL_SE_DACL_PRESENT = &H4
Const ADS_SD_CONTROL_SE_DACL_DEFAULTED = &H8
Const ADS_SD_CONTROL_SE_SACL_PRESENT = &H10
Const ADS_SD_CONTROL_SE_SACL_DEFAULTED = &H20
Const ADS_SD_CONTROL_SE_DACL_AUTO_INHERIT_REQ = &H100
Const ADS_SD_CONTROL_SE_SACL_AUTO_INHERIT_REQ = &H200
Const ADS_SD_CONTROL_SE_DACL_AUTO_INHERITED = &H400
Const ADS_SD_CONTROL_SE_SACL_AUTO_INHERITED = &H800
Const ADS_SD_CONTROL_SE_DACL_PROTECTED = &H1000
Const ADS_SD_CONTROL_SE_SACL_PROTECTED = &H2000


'**************************************************************************
'Security Descriptor Revision
'**************************************************************************
Const ADS_SD_REVISION_DS = 4


'**************************************************************************
'Declare general variables
'**************************************************************************
Dim adsObject                    'The object to bind to
Dim adsSecDesc                   'SecurityDescriptor
Dim adsDACL                      'AccessControlList object containing permission ACEs
Dim adsSACL                      'AccessControlList object containing audit ACEs
Dim adsNewACE                    'AccessControlEntry
Dim adsAttributeSchemaObject 'An object representing an attribute in the schema


'**************************************************************************
'Create the adsObject first [this code is not included here]
'**************************************************************************


'**************************************************************************
'Set no permission to view the object for members of DenyGroup
'**************************************************************************
Set adsNewACE = CreateObject("AccessControlEntry")
AdsACE.Trustee = "cn=VickyLaunders,cn=Users,dc=windows,dc=mycorp,dc=com"
adsNewACE.AccessMask = ADS_RIGHT_DS_LIST_OBJECT
adsNewACE.AceType = ADS_ACETYPE_ACCESS_DENIED
adsNewACE.AceFlags = ADS_ACEFLAG_INHERIT_ACE


'**************************************************************************
'Create a new DACL and add the ACE as the sole entry
'**************************************************************************
Set adsDACL = CreateObject("AccessControlList")
adsDACL.AceCount = 1
adsDACL.AclRevision = ADS_SD_REVISION_DS
```

Example 18-3. Creating an SD (continued)

```
adsDACL.AddAce adsNewACE
Set adsNewACE = Nothing


'***********************************************************************
'Create the SD for the object. Set the SD to use the DACL supplied rather
'than the default one. Set the SD to use the default SACL that will be
'generated from all the inherited ACEs from parents further up the hierarchy.
'***********************************************************************
Set adsSecDesc = CreateObject("SecurityDescriptor")
adsSecDes.Revision = ADS_SD_REVISION_DS
adsSecDes.Control = ADS_SD_CONTROL_SE_SACL_PRESENT _
  + ADS_SD_CONTROL_SE_SACL_PRESENT + ADS_SD_CONTROL_SE_SACL_DEFAULTED _
  + SE_OWNER_DEFAULTED + SE_GROUP_DEFAULTED
adsSecDes.OwnerDefaulted = True
adsSecDes.GroupDefaulted = True
adsSecDes.DiscretionaryAcl = adsDACL
adsSecDes.DaclDefaulted = False
adsSecDes.SaclDefaulted = True


'***********************************************************************
'Assign the SD to the existing object
'***********************************************************************
adsObject.Put "ntSecurityDescriptor", adsSecDes
ads Object.SetInfo
```

Listing ACEs to a File for All Objects in an OU and Below

A good example of a useful real-world task is when you are curious to see what ACEs have been set on all objects below a container, such as a domain or Organizational Unit. Example 18-4 is a piece of code that I used as the basis of checking through my initial Windows 2000 Active Directory for irregularities.

This code also could be used on the root of Active Directory when dealing with the problem outlined in "Bringing Order Out of Chaos" in Chapter 10, *Active Directory Security: Permissions and Auditing*. The code is fairly simple but very long, due to the fact that it has to check every constant for both the SACL and DACL of each object.

Example 18-4. Checking for ACEs on Objects Below a Container

```
On Error Resume Next


'***********************************************************************
'If the GUID corresponds to a schema object or attribute, then print the
'schema attribute/object name and the GUID. Otherwise just print the GUID.
'***********************************************************************
Sub PrintGUID(ByVal objType)
```

Example 18-4. Checking for ACEs on Objects Below a Container (continued)

```
  Dim strACEGUID, bolFound, intIndex

  '*************************************************************************
  'Convert a GUID that starts and ends with {} and has dashes within to a
  'simple string of text
  '*************************************************************************
  strACEGUID = Replace(Mid(objType,2,Len(objType)-2),"-","")

  '*************************************************************************
  'Scan the array of schema values for a matching GUID (after converting both
  'GUIDs to uppercase first). If a GUID is found, the name is printed.
  '*************************************************************************
  ts.WriteLine vbTab & vbTab & "GUID: " & objType
  For intIndex=0 To UBound(arrSchema,2)
    If (UCase(strACEGUID) = UCase(arrSchema(0,intIndex))) Then
      ts.WriteLine vbTab & vbTab & "Name: " & arrSchema(1,intIndex)
    End If
  Next
End Sub

'*************************************************************************
'This function checks to see if the first integer value contains the constant
'passed in as the second integer value. If it does, then the third parameter
'is written out to the file, and the first value is decremented by the amount
'of the constant.
'*************************************************************************
Sub CheckValue(ByRef lngValueToCheck, ByVal lngConstant, ByVal strConstantName)
  If ((lngValueToCheck And lngConstant) = lngConstant) Then
    ts.WriteLine vbTab & strConstantName
    lngValueToCheck = lngValueToCheck Xor lngConstant
  Else
    lngValueToCheck = lngValueToCheck
  End If
End Sub

'*************************************************************************
'AccessMask constants
'*************************************************************************
Const ADS_RIGHT_GENERIC_READ = &H80000000
Const ADS_RIGHT_GENERIC_WRITE = &H40000000
Const ADS_RIGHT_GENERIC_EXECUTE = &H20000000
Const ADS_RIGHT_GENERIC_ALL = &H10000000
Const ADS_RIGHT_SYSTEM_SECURITY = &H1000000
Const ADS_RIGHT_SYNCHRONIZE = &H100000
Const ADS_RIGHT_WRITE_OWNER = &H80000
Const ADS_RIGHT_WRITE_DAC = &H40000
Const ADS_RIGHT_READ_CONTROL = &H20000
Const ADS_RIGHT_DELETE = &H10000
Const ADS_RIGHT_DS_CONTROL_ACCESS = &H100
Const ADS_RIGHT_DS_LIST_OBJECT = &H80
Const ADS_RIGHT_DS_DELETE_TREE = &H40
Const ADS_RIGHT_DS_WRITE_PROP = &H20
```

Example 18-4. Checking for ACEs on Objects Below a Container (continued)

```
Const ADS_RIGHT_DS_READ_PROP = &H10
Const ADS_RIGHT_DS_SELF = &H8
Const ADS_RIGHT_ACTRL_DS_LIST = &H4
Const ADS_RIGHT_DS_DELETE_CHILD = &H2
Const ADS_RIGHT_DS_CREATE_CHILD = &H1
Const FULL_CONTROL = -1


'***************************************************************************
'AceType constants
'***************************************************************************
Const ADS_ACETYPE_SYSTEM_AUDIT_OBJECT = &H7
Const ADS_ACETYPE_ACCESS_DENIED_OBJECT = &H6
Const ADS_ACETYPE_ACCESS_ALLOWED_OBJECT = &H5
Const ADS_ACETYPE_SYSTEM_AUDIT = &H2
Const ADS_ACETYPE_ACCESS_DENIED = &H1
Const ADS_ACETYPE_ACCESS_ALLOWED = &H0


'***************************************************************************
'AceFlags constants
'***************************************************************************
Const ADS_ACEFLAG_FAILED_ACCESS = &H80
Const ADS_ACEFLAG_SUCCESSFUL_ACCESS = &H40
Const ADS_ACEFLAG_VALID_INHERIT_FLAGS = &H1F
Const ADS_ACEFLAG_INHERITED_ACE = &H10
Const ADS_ACEFLAG_INHERIT_ONLY_ACE = &H8
Const ADS_ACEFLAG_NO_PROPAGATE_INHERIT_ACE = &H4
Const ADS_ACEFLAG_INHERIT_ACE = &H2


'***************************************************************************
'Security Descriptor constants
'***************************************************************************
Const ADS_SD_CONTROL_SE_OWNER_DEFAULTED = &H1
Const ADS_SD_CONTROL_SE_GROUP_DEFAULTED = &H2
Const ADS_SD_CONTROL_SE_DACL_PRESENT = &H4
Const ADS_SD_CONTROL_SE_DACL_DEFAULTED = &H8
Const ADS_SD_CONTROL_SE_SACL_PRESENT = &H10
Const ADS_SD_CONTROL_SE_SACL_DEFAULTED = &H20
Const ADS_SD_CONTROL_SE_DACL_AUTO_INHERIT_REQ = &H100
Const ADS_SD_CONTROL_SE_SACL_AUTO_INHERIT_REQ = &H200
Const ADS_SD_CONTROL_SE_DACL_AUTO_INHERITED = &H400
Const ADS_SD_CONTROL_SE_SACL_AUTO_INHERITED = &H800
Const ADS_SD_CONTROL_SE_DACL_PROTECTED = &H1000
Const ADS_SD_CONTROL_SE_SACL_PROTECTED = &H2000


'***************************************************************************
'Flags constants
'***************************************************************************
Const ADS_FLAG_INHERITED_OBJECT_TYPE_PRESENT = &H2
Const ADS_FLAG_OBJECT_TYPE_PRESENT = &H1


'***************************************************************************
'Two example paths. You need to specify your own path here in the constant or
```

Example 18-4. Checking for ACEs on Objects Below a Container (continued)

```
'obtain it from an argument to the script or an InputBox.
'****************************************************************************
'Const LDAP_PATH = "LDAP://cn=Mike Felmeri,ou=Sales,dc=windows,dc=mycorp,dc=com"
'Const LDAP_PATH = "LDAP://dc=windows,dc=mycorp,dc=com"
Const SCHEMA_ROOT="LDAP://cn=Schema,cn=Configuration,dc=windows,dc=mycorp,dc=com"


' ****************************************************************************
' Opens a file, and lets you start writing from the beginning of the
' file.
' ****************************************************************************
Const ForWriting = 2


' ****************************************************************************
' Sets the location of the temporary file
' ****************************************************************************
Const TEMPFILE = "C:\SD-LIST-TEMP.TXT"


'****************************************************************************
'Declare the variables
'****************************************************************************
Dim adsUser, adsSecDesc, adsSecDescControl, adsACE, adsDACL
Dim adsSACL, adsACEAccessMask, adsACEAceType, adsACEAceFlags
Dim lngBeforeChange, intCount, fso, ts, strCriteria, adsObject
Dim arrSchema(), adsSchema, intIndex


'****************************************************************************
'Fill an array with GUIDs and CNs from all the objects in the schema. As we
'don't know the maximum number of elements in advance, the array is gradually
'redimensioned (i.e., has its size increased) each time we wish to add a new value.
'
'So, if there are 4,000 values in the schema, then the array will look like
'this:
'
'  arrSchema(0,0) = 1st schema object GUID
'  arrSchema(1,0) = 1st schema object cn
'  arrSchema(0,1) = 2nd schema object GUID
'  arrSchema(1,1) = 2nd schema object cn
'  arrSchema(0,2) = 3rd schema object GUID
'  arrSchema(1,2) = 3rd schema object cn
'     etc.
'  arrSchema(0,3999) = 4,000th schema object GUID
'  arrSchema(1,3999) = 4,000th schema object cn
'
'UBound(arrSchema,1) gives the max-size of the first dimension (i.e., 1)
'UBound(arrSchema,2) gives the max-size of the second dimension (i.e., 3999)
'****************************************************************************
Set adsSchema = GetObject(SCHEMA_ROOT)
intIndex = 0
For Each adsObject in adsSchema
   'Increase the size of the array while preserving values
   ReDim Preserve arrSchema(1,intIndex)
   arrSchema(0,intIndex) = adsObject.GUID
```

Example 18-4. Checking for ACEs on Objects Below a Container (continued)

```
    'Set the name to be everything except the "cn=" on the front
    arrSchema(1,intIndex) = Right(adsObject.cn, Len(adsObject.Name)-3)
    intIndex = intIndex + 1
Next


'***********************************************************************
'Opens the temporary text file for writing. If the text file already
'exists, overwrite it.
'***********************************************************************
Set fso = CreateObject("Scripting.FileSystemObject")
Set ts = fso.OpenTextFile(TEMPFILE, ForWriting, True)


'***********************************************************************
'Get the security descriptor of the object
'***********************************************************************
Set adsObject = GetObject(LDAP_PATH)
Set adsSecDesc = adsObject.Get("nTSecurityDescriptor")


'***********************************************************************
'Write out the SD general information
'***********************************************************************
ts.WriteLine "----------------------------------------------------------------"
ts.WriteLine "SD revision is: " & adsSecDesc.Revision
ts.WriteLine "SD Owner is: " & adsSecDesc.Owner
ts.WriteLine "SD Group is: " & adsSecDesc.Group
ts.WriteLine "SD GroupDefaulted is: " & adsSecDesc.GroupDefaulted
ts.WriteLine "SD OwnerDefaulted is: " & adsSecDesc.OwnerDefaulted
ts.WriteLine "SD DaclDefaulted is: " & adsSecDesc.DaclDefaulted
ts.WriteLine "SD SaclDefaulted is: " & adsSecDesc.SaclDefaulted
ts.WriteLine "----------------------------------------------------------------"


'***********************************************************************
'Write out the SD control flags
'***********************************************************************
ts.WriteLine "SD Control is: "
adsSecDescControl = adsSecDesc.Control
CheckValue adsSecDescControl, ADS_SD_CONTROL_SE_SELF_RELATIVE, _
    "The SD is held in a contiguous block of memory."
CheckValue adsSecDescControl, ADS_SD_CONTROL_SE_SACL_PROTECTED, "The SACL of " _
    & "the SD is protected and will not be modified when new rights propagate " _
    & "through the tree."
CheckValue adsSecDescControl, ADS_SD_CONTROL_SE_DACL_PROTECTED, "The DACL of " _
    & "the SD is protected and will not be modified when new rights propagate " _
    & "through the tree."
CheckValue adsSecDescControl, ADS_SD_CONTROL_SE_SACL_AUTO_INHERITED, "The SACL" _
    & " of the SD supports auto-propagation of inheritable ACEs to existing " _
    & " child objects."
CheckValue adsSecDescControl, ADS_SD_CONTROL_SE_DACL_AUTO_INHERITED, "The DACL" _
    & " of the SD supports auto-propagation of inheritable ACEs to existing " _
    & "child objects."
CheckValue adsSecDescControl, ADS_SD_CONTROL_SE_SACL_AUTO_INHERIT_REQ, "The " _
    & "SACL of the SD must be inherited."
```

Example 18-4. Checking for ACEs on Objects Below a Container (continued)

```
CheckValue adsSecDescControl, ADS_SD_CONTROL_SE_DACL_AUTO_INHERIT_REQ, "The " _
  & "DACL of the SD must be inherited."
CheckValue adsSecDescControl, ADS_SD_CONTROL_SE_SACL_DEFAULTED, "The ACL " _
  & "pointed to by the SystemAcl field was provided by the default mechanism " _
  & "rather than explicitly set by the person or application that created the " _
  & "SD in the first place."
CheckValue adsSecDescControl, ADS_SD_CONTROL_SE_SACL_PRESENT, "The security " _
  & "descriptor contains a SACL."
CheckValue adsSecDescControl, ADS_SD_CONTROL_SE_DACL_DEFAULTED, "The " _
  & "DiscretionaryAcl field was provided by the default mechanism rather than " _
  & "explicitly set by the person or application that created the SD in the " _
  & "first place."
CheckValue adsSecDescControl, ADS_SD_CONTROL_SE_DACL_PRESENT, "The security " _
  & "descriptor contains a DACL."
CheckValue adsSecDescControl, ADS_SD_CONTROL_SE_GROUP_DEFAULTED, "The SID in " _
  & "the Group field was provided by the default mechanism rather than " _
  & "explicitly set by the person or application that created the SD in the " _
  & "first place."
CheckValue adsSecDescControl, ADS_SD_CONTROL_SE_OWNER_DEFAULTED, "The SID " _
  & "pointed to by the Owner field was provided by the default mechanism " _
  & "rather than set by the person or application that created the SD in the " _
  & "first place."

'************************************************************************
'Write out the DACL general information
'************************************************************************
Set adsDACL = adsSecDesc.DiscretionaryAcl    'Permissions List

ts.WriteLine "-----------------"
ts.WriteLine "-----------------"
ts.WriteLine "Discretionary ACL"
ts.WriteLine "-----------------"
ts.WriteLine "-----------------"
ts.WriteLine "There are " & adsDACL.AceCount & " ACEs in the DACL."
ts.WriteLine "DACL revision is: " & adsDACL.AclRevision

intCount = 1
For Each adsACE In adsDACL
  ts.WriteLine "----------------------------------------------------------------"
  ts.WriteLine "ACE Trustee " & intCount & " of " & adsDACL.AceCount & " is: " _
    & adsACE.Trustee

  '************************************************************************
  'Write out the ACEType details
  '************************************************************************
  adsACEAceType = adsACE.AceType
  ts.WriteLine "AceType: "

  If (adsACEAceType <> 0) Then
    CheckValue adsACEAceType, ADS_ACETYPE_SYSTEM_AUDIT_OBJECT, "This is a " _
      & "System Audit Entry ACE using a GUID"
    CheckValue adsACEAceType, ADS_ACETYPE_ACCESS_DENIED_OBJECT, "This is an " _
```

Example 18-4. Checking for ACEs on Objects Below a Container (continued)

```
                 & "Access Denied ACE using a GUID"
        CheckValue adsACEAceType, ADS_ACETYPE_ACCESS_ALLOWED_OBJECT, "This is an " _
                 & "Access Allowed ACE using a GUID."
        CheckValue adsACEAceType, ADS_ACETYPE_SYSTEM_AUDIT, "This is a System " _
                 & "Audit Entry ACE using a Windows NT Security Descriptor."
        CheckValue adsACEAceType, ADS_ACETYPE_ACCESS_DENIED, "This is an Access " _
                 & "Denied ACE using a Windows NT Security Descriptor."
    Else
        ts.WriteLine vbTab & "This is an Access Allowed ACE using a Windows NT " _
                 & "Security Descriptor."
    End If

    '************************************************************************
    'Write out the AccessMask details
    '************************************************************************
    adsACEAccessMask = adsACE.AccessMask
    ts.WriteLine "Access Mask: "

    If adsACEAccessMask = FULL_CONTROL Then
        ts.WriteLine vbTab & "Full Control"
    ElseIf (adsACEAccessMask <> 0) Then
        CheckValue adsACEAccessMask, ADS_RIGHT_GENERIC_READ, "Right to read from " _
                 & "the security descriptor, to examine the object and its children, and " _
                 & "to read all properties."
        CheckValue adsACEAccessMask, ADS_RIGHT_GENERIC_WRITE, "Right to write all " _
                 & "properties and write to the DACL. User can also add/remove the " _
                 & "object from the tree."
        CheckValue adsACEAccessMask, ADS_RIGHT_GENERIC_EXECUTE, "Right to list " _
                 & "children of the object."
        CheckValue adsACEAccessMask, ADS_RIGHT_GENERIC_ALL, "Right to " _
                 & "create/delete children, delete the tree, read/write properties, " _
                 & "examine the object and its children, add/remove the object from the " _
                 & "tree, and read/write with an extended right."
        CheckValue adsACEAccessMask, ADS_RIGHT_ACCESS_SYSTEM_SECURITY, "The right " _
                 & "to get or set the SACL in the SD of the object."
        CheckValue adsACEAccessMask, ADS_RIGHT_SYNCHRONIZE, "The right to use the " _
                 & "object for synchronization."
        CheckValue adsACEAccessMask, ADS_RIGHT_WRITE_OWNER, "Right to assume " _
                 & "ownership of the object; no right to grant ownership to others. " _
                 & "[User must be a trustee of the object]."
        CheckValue adsACEAccessMask, ADS_RIGHT_WRITE_DAC, "Right to write to the " _
                 & "DACL of the object."
        CheckValue adsACEAccessMask, ADS_RIGHT_READ_CONTROL, "Right to read from " _
                 & "the security descriptor of the object."
        CheckValue adsACEAccessMask, ADS_RIGHT_DELETE, "Right to delete the object."

        lngBeforeChange = adsACEAccessMask
        CheckValue adsACEAccessMask, ADS_RIGHT_DS_CONTROL_ACCESS, "Right to " _
                 & "perform an application specific extension on the object."
        If (adsACEAccessMask <> lngBeforeChange) Then
            PrintGUID adsACE.ObjectType
        End If
```

Example 18-4. Checking for ACEs on Objects Below a Container (continued)

```
CheckValue adsACEAccessMask, ADS_RIGHT_DS_LIST_OBJECT, "Right to examine " _
  & "the object. [If this is missing the object is hidden from the user]."
CheckValue adsACEAccessMask, ADS_RIGHT_DS_DELETE_TREE, "Right to delete " _
  & "all children of this object, regardless of the permission on the " _
  & "children."

lngBeforeChange = adsACEAccessMask
CheckValue adsACEAccessMask, ADS_RIGHT_DS_WRITE_PROP, "Right to write " _
  & "properties of the object."
If (adsACEAccessMask <> lngBeforeChange) Then
  If adsACE.ObjectType = "" Then
    ts.WriteLine vbTab & vbTab & "All properties can be written."
  Else
    PrintGUID adsACE.ObjectType
  End If
End If


lngBeforeChange = adsACEAccessMask
CheckValue adsACEAccessMask, ADS_RIGHT_DS_READ_PROP, "Right to read " _
  & "properties of the object."
If (adsACEAccessMask <> lngBeforeChange) Then
  If adsACE.ObjectType = "" Then
    ts.WriteLine vbTab & vbTab & "All properties can be read."
  Else
    PrintGUID adsACE.ObjectType
  End If
End If


CheckValue adsACEAccessMask, ADS_RIGHT_DS_SELF, "Right to modify the " _
  & "group membership of a group object."
CheckValue adsACEAccessMask, ADS_RIGHT_ACTRL_DS_LIST, "Right to examine " _
  & "children of the object."

lngBeforeChange = adsACEAccessMask
CheckValue adsACEAccessMask, `ADS_RIGHT_DS_DELETE_CHILD, "Right to delete " _
  & "children of the object"
If (adsACEAccessMask <> lngBeforeChange) Then
  If adsACE.ObjectType = "" Then
    ts.WriteLine vbTab & vbTab & "All Children inherit this right."
  Else
    PrintGUID adsACE.ObjectType
  End If
End If


lngBeforeChange = adsACEAccessMask
CheckValue adsACEAccessMask, ADS_RIGHT_DS_CREATE_CHILD, "Right to create " _
  & "children of the object"
If (adsACEAccessMask <> lngBeforeChange) Then
  If adsACE.ObjectType = "" Then
    ts.WriteLine vbTab & vbTab & "All Children inherit this right."
  Else
    PrintGUID adsACE.ObjectType
```

Example 18-4. Checking for ACEs on Objects Below a Container (continued)

```
      End If
    End If

  Else
    ts.WriteLine vbTab & "ACE Access Mask is 0, therefore no permissions " _
      & "exist for this ACE!"
  End If

  '****************************************************************************
  'Write out the ACEFlags details
  '****************************************************************************
  adsACEAceFlags = adsACE.AceFlags
  ts.WriteLine "ACEFlags: "

  If (adsACEAceFlags <> 0) Then
    CheckValue adsACEAceFlags, ADS_ACEFLAG_FAILED_ACCESS, "SACL: Generates " _
      & "audit messages for failed access attempts."
    CheckValue adsACEAceFlags, ADS_ACEFLAG_SUCCESSFUL_ACCESS, "SACL: " _
      & "Generates audit messages for successful access attempts."
    CheckValue adsACEAceFlags, ADS_ACEFLAG_VALID_INHERIT_FLAGS, "Indicates " _
      & "whether the inherit flags are valid. [Set only by the system]."
    CheckValue adsACEAceFlags, ADS_ACEFLAG_INHERITED_ACE, "Indicates whether " _
      & "or not the ACE was inherited. [Set only by the system]."
    CheckValue adsACEAceFlags, ADS_ACEFLAG_INHERIT_ONLY_ACE, "Indicates an " _
      & "inherit-only ACE that does not exercise access controls on the " _
      & "object to which it is attached."
    CheckValue adsACEAceFlags, ADS_ACEFLAG_NO_PROPAGATE_INHERIT_ACE, "Child " _
      & "objects will not inherit this ACE."
    CheckValue adsACEAceFlags, ADS_ACEFLAG_INHERIT_ACE, "Child objects will " _
      & "inherit this ACE."
  Else
    ts.WriteLine vbTab & "ACE is not inherited by children."
  End If

  '****************************************************************************
  'Write out the Flags details
  '****************************************************************************
  ts.WriteLine "Flags: "

  If (adsACE.Flags = 0) Then
    ts.WriteLine vbTab & "Object Type and Inherited Object Type aren't present."
  ElseIf (adsACE.Flags = ADS_FLAG_INHERITED_OBJECT_TYPE_PRESENT) Then
    ts.WriteLine vbTab & "Inherited Object Type present: "
    PrintGUID adsACE.InheritedObjectType
  ElseIf (adsACE.Flags = ADS_FLAG_OBJECT_TYPE_PRESENT) Then
    ts.WriteLine vbTab & "Object Type present: "
    PrintGUID adsACE.ObjectType
  ElseIf (adsACE.Flags = (ADS_FLAG_OBJECT_TYPE_PRESENT + _
    ADS_FLAG_INHERITED_OBJECT_TYPE_PRESENT)) Then
    'Both present, so print the GUIDs

    ts.WriteLine vbTab & "Inherited Object Type present: "
```

Example 18-4. Checking for ACEs on Objects Below a Container (continued)

```
    PrintGUID adsACE.InheritedObjectType

    ts.WriteLine vbTab & "Object Type present: "
    PrintGUID adsACE.ObjectType
  End If

  intCount = intCount + 1
Next


'*************************************************************************
'Write out the SACL general information
'*************************************************************************
Set adsSACL = adsSecDesc.SystemAcl      'System Auditing List

ts.WriteLine "----------"
ts.WriteLine "----------"
ts.WriteLine "System ACL"
ts.WriteLine "----------"
ts.WriteLine "----------"
ts.WriteLine "There are " & adsSACL.AceCount & " ACEs in the SACL."
ts.WriteLine "SACL revision is: " & adsSACL.AclRevision

intCount = 1
For Each adsACE In adsSACL
  ts.WriteLine "-----------------------------------------------------------"
  ts.WriteLine "ACE Trustee " & intCount & " of " & adsSACL.AceCount & " is: " _
    & adsACE.Trustee

  '*************************************************************************
  'Add the ACEType, AccessMask, ACEFlags, and Flags code here from the preceding.
  'The code has been cut to save wasting space by duplicating it in the book.
  'You could even move the entire section of code to a Sub rather than including
  'it twice.
  '*************************************************************************

  intCount = intCount + 1
Next

ts.WriteLine "-----------------------------------------------------------"
ts.Close

MsgBox "End!"
```

Adding Many USER Groups to DRUP Groups

In the section on "Restricting Users in an Organizational Unit from Viewing Properties of Users Outside That Organizational Unit" (Chapter 10), I described the requirement to add many user groups as members of many permission groups. Example 18-5 is the code to implement the group add. It scans for all groups prefixed with USER_ and DRUP_. It then adds all the USER groups to each DRUP

group, except for the group where the suffix matches. In other words, all USER_
groups except USER_Finance are added to DRUP_Finance. This was why the
names were set up in this way.

 The searches in Example 18-5 make use of the ADO search function-
called `SearchAD` from Chapter 21, *Scripting Fast Searches Using
ADO.*

Example 18-5. Adding Groups

```
'*************************************************************************
'Search the entire AD for all groups starting USER_ and return the cn
'and AdsPath variables in the following structure
'
'  arrUSERGroup(0,index) = cn attributes
'  arrUSERGroup(1,index) = ADsPath attribute
'
'where index goes from 0 to (the maximum number of results returned -1)
'*************************************************************************
If SearchAD( _
  "LDAP://dc=mycorp,dc=com", "(&(objectClass=group)(cn=USER_*))", _
  "SubTree", "cn,ADsPath", arrUSERGroup) Then

  '*********************************************************************
  'As above but for DRUP_ groups
  '*********************************************************************
  If SearchAD( _
    "LDAP://dc=mycorp,dc=com", "(&(objectClass=group)(cn=DRUP_*))", _
    "SubTree", "cn,ADsPath", arrDRUPGroup) Then

    '*******************************************************************
    'Set up an index to allow us to iterate through the USER_ groups. The
    'Ubound function here counts the maximum number of elements in the
    'array's second dimension of values (the first dimension has only two
    'values, "cn" and "ADsPath")
    '*******************************************************************
    For intUSERGroupIndex = 0 To Ubound(arrUSERGroups,2)
      '*****************************************************************
      'As above but for DRUP_ groups
      '*****************************************************************
      For intDRUPGroupIndex = 0 To Ubound(arrDRUPGroups,2)
        '***************************************************************
        'Extract the portion of the name that corresponds to all letters after
        'the "cn=USER_" or "cn=DRUP_" parts (i.e., eight  letters)
        '***************************************************************
        txtUSERGroupSuffixName = Right(arrUSERGroup(0,intUSERGroupIndex), _
          Len(arrUSERGroup(0,intUSERGroupIndex))-8)
        txtDRUPGroupSuffixName = Right(arrDRUPGroup(0,intDRUPGroupIndex), _
          Len(arrDRUPGroup(0,intDRUPGroupIndex))-8)
```

Example 18-5. Adding Groups (continued)

```
      '************************************************************************
      'If the two extracted strings are not the same, then add the USER group
      'to the DRUP group
      '************************************************************************
      If Not txtUSERGroupSuffix = txtDRUPGroupSuffix Then
        Set adsDRUPGroup = GetObject(arrDRUPGroup(1,intDRUPGroupIndex))
        adsDRUPGroup.Add(arrUSERGroup(1,intUSERGroupIndex))
      End If
    Next
  Next
  End If
End If
```

You should note, by the way, that the For loop evaluates the UBound condition every time it completes a loop. To speed up the code, you really should put the result of the UBound in a variable and use the For loop with that directly.

Summary

This chapter took a very detailed look at the three main interfaces that you can use to manipulate permissions and auditing entries for objects and properties in your organization:

• IADsAccessControlEntry

• IADsAccessControlList

• IADsSecurityDescriptor

19

Extending the Schema and the GUI

This chapter takes a look at two different areas: ways you can programmatically extend the Schema and expand the functionality of the Windows 2000 GUI tools. While these could be considered separate topics, they share the common thread of storing and presenting information beyond that which Active Directory is configured to hold by default. In the first half, I take a look at how you can manipulate the Schema to include new attributes and classes. In the second half, I move on to looking at the 15 so-called user-definable extension attributes that exist on each object in Active Directory for storing extra information. I then use the extension attributes in an example in which I modify the existing Active Directory Users and Computers tool to include my own menus in its GUI.

Modifying the Schema with ADSI

I've shown you how the schema works in Chapter 3, *Active Directory Schema*, and how to design for it in Chapter 11, *Designing Schema Changes*. Now let's take a look at how to modify and manipulate it using ADSI. In this chapter, I'm assuming that when I connect to a server and modify Active Directory, the Schema safeguards against accidental modification have already been taken care of, as explained in Chapter 11.

IADsClass, IADsProperty, and IADsSyntax

ADSI comes with three main interfaces for manipulating objects and properties in the Schema: IADsClass, IADsProperty, and IADsSyntax. Each of these has a variety of useful methods and property methods to allow you to set mandatory properties for classes, optional properties for classes, maximum values for attributes, and so on. If you look at these interfaces, you will see that they are very simple to

understand. However, to give you a bit more grounding in what goes on underneath, I have chosen to directly access the properties themselves. Here are
excerpts from two separate scripts:

```
adsAttribute.Put "isSingleValued", False
adsAttribute.Put "attributeId", "1.3.6.1.4.1.999999.1.1.28"

arrMustContain = adsSchemaClass.Get("mustContain")
arrMayContain = adsSchemaClass.Get("mayContain")
```

When you come to write schema scripts with ADSI, take a look at the three main
interfaces, and you will find that you can actually write the code like this:

```
adsAttribute.MultiValued = True
adsAttribute.OID = "1.3.6.1.4.1.999999.1.1.28"

arrMustContain = adsSchemaClass.MandatoryProperties
arrMayContain = adsSchemaClass.OptionalProperties
```

This makes use of the following property methods: `IADsProperty::Multi-`
`Valued`, `IADsProperty::OID`, `IADsClass::MandatoryProperties`, and `IADs-`
`Class::OptionalProperties`. As you can see, it's not hard to convert the code.
However, I feel that including code that directly modifies the properties themselves gives you some idea of what you are actually changing and helps you to
refer back to the definitions presented in Chapter 3.

The three interfaces can be found in MSDN at Platform SDK → Networking Services → Active Directory → Active Directory Service Interfaces → ADSI Reference →
ADSI Interfaces → Schema Interfaces. You can find them online at *http://msdn.
microsoft.com/isapi/msdnlib.idc?theURL=/library/sdkdoc/adsi/if_schem_6437.htm.*

Creating Attributes and Classes

Let's now look at how easy it is to create an attribute with ADSI.

Creating an attribute and creating an object are both very easy with
ADSI. Due to this ease and the fact that once you change the
Schema and create an attribute or object you cannot delete it later, I
caution you to make sure that your code is thoroughly tested in a
test forest first. Note that it must be a test forest and not just a test
domain as the Schema is a forest-wide NC.

I need to set the following mandatory attributes:

Common-Name (cn)   OM-Syntax (oMSyntax)

Attribute-ID (attributeID)   LDAP-Display-Name
                                    (lDAPDisplayName)

Attribute-Syntax (attribute-   Is-Single-Valued
Syntax)   (isSingleValued)

The following mandatory attributes will be set automatically by the system:

Schema-ID-GUID   Attribute-Security-GUID

Extended-Chars-Allowed   System-Only

Object-Class   NT-Security-Descriptor

Instance-Type

The system will either generate an appropriate value or use the default value for an attribute, if appropriate. For example, a unique GUID for Schema-ID-GUID will be generated automatically by the system when the object is created, System-Only will be set to the default of False, the NT-Security-Descriptor will be set to the default for new objects in the schema container, and Object-Class will be Attribute-Schema as specified when you create the object.

Creating the Mycorp-Languages-Spoken attribute

The attribute I wish to create will be called Mycorp-Languages-Spoken; it is an attribute that I really wish to know about all the finance users. It's actually so important that I wish to index it in Active Directory for rapid searching, but not so important that it is to go in the GC and be visible throughout the forest. The name is prefixed with Mycorp; it is obvious that Mycorp created the attribute. It is to be a multivalued indexed attribute that can hold an array of case-sensitive strings of between 1 and 50 characters.

Mycorp's Schema Manager has decided that the OID for this attribute is to be 1.3.6.1.4.1.999999.1.1.28. This is worked out as follows:

- Mycorp's root OID namespace: 1.3.6.1.4.1.999999.

- Mycorp's new attributes use this: 1.3.6.1.4.1.999999.1.1.xxxx (where xxxx increments from 1).

- Mycorp's new classes use this: 1.3.6.1.4.1.999999.1.2.xxxx (where xxxx increments from 1).

- The attribute is to be the 28th new attribute created by Mycorp.

This is the code to create such an attribute:

```
Dim adsAttribute
Dim adsSchemaContainer

Set adsSchemaContainer = _
```

```
GetObject("LDAP://cn=Schema,cn=Configuration,dc=windows,dc=mycorp,dc=com")

Set adsAttribute = adsSchemaContainer.Create("attributeSchema", _
  "cn=Mycorp-Languages-Spoken")

'Write out mandatory attributes
adsAttribute.Put "cn", "Mycorp-Languages-Spoken"
adsAttribute.Put "attributeId", "1.3.6.1.4.1.999999.1.1.28"
adsAttribute.Put "oMSyntax", 20
adsAttribute.Put "attributeSyntax", "2.5.5.3"
adsAttribute.Put "isSingleValued", False
adsAttribute.Put "lDAPDisplayName", "mycorpLanguagesSpoken"

'Create the attribute
adsAttribute.SetInfo

'Write out optional attributes
adsAttribute.GetInfo
adsAttribute.Description = "Indicates the languages that a user speaks"
adsAttribute.Put "rangeLower", 1
adsAttribute.Put "rangeUpper", 50
adsAttribute.Put "searchFlags", True
adsAttribute.SetInfo
```

That seems fairly straightforward. Remember to change the Attribute-ID to correspond to your own OID namespace if you use the code. The preceding Attribute-ID is not a valid one. Figure 19-1 shows the newly created attribute using the Schema Manager.

Creating the Finance-User class

Let's now take a look at creating a new object. There are eight mandatory attributes, but again some will be set by the system on creation.

I need to set the following mandatory attributes:

Common-Name (cn)	Governs-ID (governsID)
Object-Class-Category (objectClassCategory)	Sub-Class-Of (subClassOf)

The following mandatory attributes will be set automatically by the system:

Schema-ID-GUID	Instance-Type.
Object-Class	NT-Security-Descriptor

This new object class called MycorpFinanceUser is to be a structural class so that others can create instances of it within containers (although this part is inherited from User). It is to have the new Mycorp-Languages-Spoken as an attribute, as

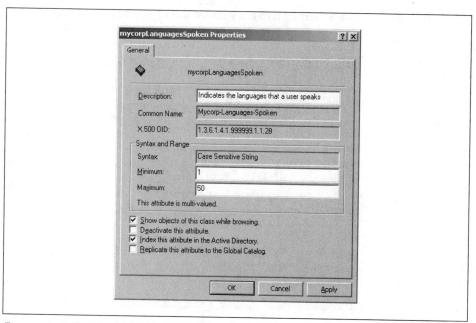

Figure 19-1. The Mycorp-Languages-Spoken attribute viewed using the Schema Manager MMC

well as inheriting from the User class. It is the fourth class to be created, so its OID is 1.3.6.1.4.1.999999.1.2.4, as shown in the following script:

```
Const ADS_PROPERTY_APPEND = 3

Dim adsAttribute
Dim adsSchemaContainer

Set adsSchemaContainer = _
   GetObject("LDAP://cn=Schema,cn=Configuration,dc=windows,dc=mycorp,dc=com")

Set adsClass = adsSchemaContainer.Create("classSchema","cn=Mycorp-Finance-User")

'Write out mandatory attributes
adsClass.Put "cn", "Mycorp-Finance-User"
adsClass.Put "governsId", "1.3.6.1.4.1.999999.1.2.4"
adsClass.Put "objectClassCategory", 1 'Structural Class
adsClass.Put "subClassOf", "user"
adsClass.Put "lDAPDisplayName", "mycorpFinanceUser"

'Create the class
adsClass.SetInfo

'Write out optional attributes
adsClass.GetInfo
adsClass.Description = "Indicates a Financial User"
adsClass.Put "mustContain", "1.3.6.1.4.1.999999.1.1.28"
adsClass.SetInfo
```

Figure 19-2 displays the Schema Manager view of the Mycorp-Finance-User class.

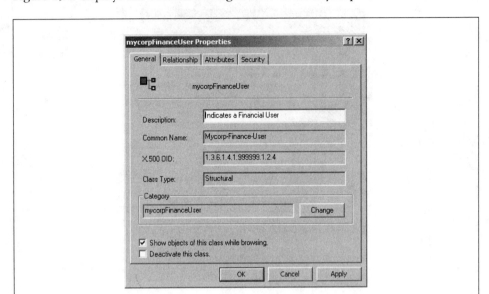

Figure 19-2. The Mycorp-Finance-User class viewed using the Schema Manager MMC

Creating instances of the new schema classes

Finally, if I want to create a new **MycorpFinanceUser** object, I have to get a reference to the container that is to be the parent and create the object with all the mandatory attributes. This is what the code would look like:

```
Dim adsContainer
Dim adsMycorpFinanceUser

Set adsContainer = _
  GetObject("LDAP://ou=Finance Users,dc=windows,dc=Mycorp,dc=com")

'Create the new Mycorp-Finance-User object
Set adsMycorpFinanceUser = adsContainer.Create("Mycorp-Finance-User", _
  "cn=SimonWilliams")

'Set the mandatory properties
adsMycorpFinanceUser.Put "sAMAccountName", "SimonWilliams"
adsMycorpFinanceUser.Put "userPrincipalName", "SimonWilliams@mycorp.com"
adsMycorpFinanceUser.Put "Mycorp-Languages-Spoken", _
  Array("English", "French", "German")

'Write the object to the AD
adsMycorpFinanceUser.SetInfo
```

Note that the mandatory properties include the one on the `MycorpFinanceUser` class and the one on the User class that the `MycorpFinanceUser` class inherits from.

Modifying the Schema with ADSI When You Do Not Know the Domain Name or FSMO Schema Master

Knowing that the Schema exists as a container under the Configuration container within all the domains in a forest is great if you know the name of the domain. However, if you are writing code to modify the Schema on potentially any domain (say a program that is to be distributed around the world to multiple organizations with different directories), then you need to know how to reference the schema container relative to the current domain without knowing its name. You also need to know how to find out which server is currently the FSMO Schema Master so that you can make changes directly to it.

The solution is to use code similar to the following to find the full path to the schema container:

```
Dim adsRootDSE
Dim adsSchemaContainer
Dim txtSchemaPath

'Get the Root DSE from a random DC
Set adsRootDSE = GetObject("LDAP://RootDSE")

'Get the Schema NC path for the domain
txtSchemaPath = adsRootDSE.Get("schemaNamingContext")

'Connect to the schema container on a random DC
Set adsSchemaContainer = GetObject("LDAP://" & txtSchemaPath)
```

The first line retrieves an object that points to the root of the Directory Services Environment (DSE, i.e., the list of all the NCs that are available within the forest on a random DC). From here it is a simple matter to obtain the ADsPath of the Schema NC and to pass that to a `GetObject` (or the `IADsOpenDSObject::OpenDSObject` method if you prefer to authenticate) and retrieve a reference to the schema container on a random DC.

If you want to make changes without forcing the FSMO role to your currently connected server, then you need to change that last line to connect to the server holding the schema master. This actually requires a bit more code:

```
Set adsSchemaContainer = GetObject("LDAP://" & txtSchemaPath)
txtFSMORoleOwner = adsSchemaContainer.Get("fSMORoleOwner")

'Split the line up into an array (indexed from 0) with elements
'corresponding to the items separated by commas
```

```
arrComponents = Split(txtFSMORoleOwner, ",")

'Grab the portion of the server name that follows the cn= text
txtServerIPName = Right(arrComponents(1),Len(arrComponents(1))-3)

'Concatenate to the existing name (with dots) any array parts that
'start dc= (removing the dc= parts from the string). These parts
'will start from index 6 onward due to the other preceding parts
'of the path.
For intIndex = 6 To Ubound(arrComponents)-1
  If Left(arrComponents(intIndex),3) = "dc=" Then
    txtServerIPName = txtServerIPName _
      + Right(arrComponents(intIndex),Len(arrComponents(intIndex))-3)
  End If
Next

'Connect to the schema container on the server holding the FSMO Schema
'Master role
Set adsSchemaContainer = _
  GetObject("LDAP://" & txtServerIPName & "/" & txtSchemaPath)
```

The **fSMORoleOwner** attribute of the schema container actually contains a string similar to "cn=NTDS Settings, cn=MOOSE, cn=Servers, cn=Main-Headquarters-Site, cn=Sites, cn=Configuration, dc=windows, dc=mycorp, dc=com." From this you can easily get hold of the server's name and use it to connect to the FSMO Schema Master as shown.

Note that the resulting value of **txtServerIPName** from the sample string in the preceding paragraph would be *moose.windows.mycorp.com*, which is what I then use to connect to a specific server.

Transferring the FSMO Schema Master Role

If I want to transfer the FSMO Schema Master role to a specific server (*niles. windows.mycorp.com*), all I have to do is set the **becomeSchemaMaster** attribute to 1 on the RootDSE at that server. The moment I write out the property cache, the proposed master contacts the current master and requests the role and any updates to the Schema NC that it has yet to see:

```
Const DC_TO_TRANSFER_FSMO_TO = "niles.windows.mycorp.com"

Dim adsRootDSE
Dim adsSchemaContainer
Dim txtSchemaPath

'Get the Root DSE from a random DC
Set adsRootDSE = GetObject("LDAP://" & DC_TO_TRANSFER_FSMO_TO & "/RootDSE")

'Request a Schema Master transfer
adsRootDSE.Put "becomeSchemaMaster", 1
adsRootDSE.SetInfo
```

At this point, the transfer has been requested. I now need to connect to the Schema NC and wait until the **fSMORoleOwner** attribute points to my new server:

```
'Get the Schema NC path for the domain
txtSchemaPath = adsRootDSE.Get("schemaNamingContext")

'Connect to the schema container on my DC
Set adsSchemaContainer = GetObject("LDAP://" & DC_TO_TRANSFER_TO _
   & "/" & txtSchemaPath)

'Initialize the while loop by indicating that the server is not the one
'I am looking for
txtServerIPName = ""

'While the Server IP Name is not the one we are looking for, keep searching
While Not txtServerIPName = DC_TO_TRANSFER_FSMO_TO
   'Get the FSMO Role Owner attribute
   txtFSMORoleOwner =  adsSchemaContainer.Get("fSMORoleOwner")

   'Split the line up into an array (indexed from 0) with elements
   'corresponding to the items separated by commas
   arrComponents = Split(txtFSMORoleOwner, ",")

   'Grab the portion of the server name that follows the cn= text
   txtServerIPName = Right(arrComponents(1),Len(arrComponents(1))-3)

   'Concatenate to the existing name (with dots) any array parts that
   'start dc= (removing the dc= parts from the string). These parts
   'will start from index 6 onwards due to the other preceding parts
   'of the path.
   For intIndex = 6 To Ubound(arrComponents)-1
     If Left(arrComponents(intIndex),3) = "dc=" Then
       txtServerIPName = txtServerIPName _
          + Right(arrComponents(intIndex),Len(arrComponents(intIndex))-3)
     End If
   Next

   'Make the path lowercase (for comparison purposes)
   txtServerIPName = Lcase(txtServerIPName)
Wend

'At this point in the code, the role has been transferred, so I can continue
```

You shouldn't use the code exactly as written here because I am doing no error trapping. Without error trapping, there is no guarantee that the original writing of the **becomeSchemaMaster** attribute actually worked. There is also no guarantee that the attachment to the DC_TO_TRANSFER_FSMO_TO server actually worked, either. So if either of these or anything else went wrong, I may never exit the **while** loop. Even if both of these conditions worked, I may set the value, and my DC may attempt to contact the current FSMO Schema Master to find that it is unavailable. Again, I go into an infinite loop and my code never terminates. You certainly should include a timeout value as a second condition to the **while** loop to trap an occurrence of this problem.

Forcing a Reload of the Schema Cache

If you need to reload the schema cache, Microsoft recommends that you do so once you've finished all your writes. While the cache is being reloaded, any new queries are served from the old cache and will continue to be served by the old cache until the new one comes online. Microsoft specifically states that working threads that are referencing the old cache once a reload is finished will continue to reference the old cache. Only new threads will reference the new cache. As a worst case (and really daft) scenario, if you were to create 100 new attributes, start a process that queried the schema cache, and then reload the schema cache before continuing on to the next attribute, you potentially have 101 sets of schema caches (the original plus 100 new ones) being maintained by the DC acting as the Schema Master. This would cause the DC to have 101 times the amount of normal schema cache memory in use for caching. This is likely to cause a drain on your DC. In this scenario, things will only improve as the working threads cease referencing the old caches on the DC, allowing it to free up the memory.

Reloading the cache using ADSI is very simple. All you have to do is set the **schemaUpdateNow** attribute to 1 on the schema container of a DC. Here's an example:

```
Dim adsRootDSE
Dim adsSchemaContainer
Dim txtSchemaPath

'Get the Root DSE from a random DC
Set adsRootDSE = GetObject("LDAP://RootDSE")

'Get the Schema NC path for the domain
txtSchemaPath = adsRootDSE.Get("schemaNamingContext")

'Connect to the schema container on a random DC.
Set adsSchemaContainer = GetObject("LDAP://" & txtSchemaPath)

'Reload the cache on that DC
adsSchemaContainer.Put "schemaUpdateNow", 1
```

Note that just because you have requested a change doesn't mean it's going to happen instantaneously, although your code will continue executing. You should check the Schema to see if your new objects are there, and if they are not, wait until they are before proceeding.

Finding Which Attributes Are in the GC for an Object

In Chapter 3, I describe a desire to programmatically query all attributes directly defined on an object class in the Schema to find out which ones are in the GC. It now should be possible to see how simple it is to write this code. First, you know that you can find out which attributes a Class-Schema object can have by looking in the May-Contain, System-May-Contain, Must-Contain, and System-Must-Contain attributes.

Once you have the entire list of attributes, you can use the LDAP-Display-Name that you will have retrieved to reference the Attribute-Schema class in the schema container. Lastly, you need to check to see whether each Attribute-Schema object has an attribute called Is-Member-Of-Partial-Attribute-Set. Here's the code:

```
'Check the User class, via the administrator user
Const OBJECT_TO_CHECK = _
    "LDAP://cn=administrator, cn=Users, dc=windows, dc=Mycorp, dc=com"

Dim adsObject, adsSchemaClass, arrMustContain, arrMayContain
Dim txtListOfAttributesinGC, adsAttribute, txtAttribute

'Connect to object and get IADs::Schema on an object instance
Set adsObject = GetObject(OBJECT_TO_CHECK)

Set adsSchemaClass = GetObject(adsUser.Schema)

'Get May-Contain and Must-Contain attributes directly on the class
arrMustContain = adsSchemaClass.Get("mustContain")
arrMayContain = adsSchemaClass.Get("mayContain")

'Initialize the output string
txtListOfAttributesinGC = "The list of attributes for the class: " & vbCrLf _
    & vbCrLf & vbTab & adsUser.Schema & vbCrLf & vbCrLf & "is:"_
    & vbCrLf & vbCrLf

'Use the array of LDAP names to connect to each attribute in turn
'and read whether it is in the GC or not. If it is, then add it to the string
For Each txtAttribute In arrMustContain
    Set adsAttribute = GetObject("LDAP://" & txtAttribute & _
      ",cn=Schema,cn=Configuration,dc=windows,dc=Mycorp,dc=com")
    If adsAttribute.Get("isMemberOfPartialAttributeSet") Then
      txtListOfAttributesinGC = txtListOfAttributesinGC & txtAttribute & vbCrLf
    End If

    'Stop referencing the current attribute
    Set adsAttribute = Nothing
Next

For Each txtAttribute In arrMayContain
    Set adsAttribute = GetObject("LDAP://" & txtAttribute & _
```

```
            ",cn=Schema,cn=Configuration,dc=windows,dc=Mycorp,dc=com")
        If adsAttribute.Get("isMemberOfPartialAttributeSet") Then
            txtListOfAttributesinGC = txtListOfAttributesinGC & txtAttribute & vbCrLf
        End If

        'Stop referencing the current attribute
        Set adsAttribute = Nothing
    Next

        Wscript.Echo txtListOfAttributesinGC
```

This will print out a list of all attributes that are held in the GC and defined directly on the object. Of course, to be very thorough and find every attribute that the Class-Schema object could have in the GC, you also would need to look inside Auxiliary-Class, System-Auxiliary-Class, and Sub-Class-Of to retrieve any class names and then iterate back up the tree to find the May-Contain, System-May-Contain, Must-Contain, and System-Must-Contain from any inherited objects.

Extending Active Directory GUI to Meet Business and Organizational Needs

Windows NT came with a tool known as User Manager that you're familiar with. This tool allowed the user to manipulate the properties of users and groups within a GUI application. In Windows 2000, a Microsoft Management Console (MMC) snap-in called the Active Directory Users and Computers (ADUC) tool has brought the concept up to date.

While the ADUC is built to manage users and groups as the previous User Manager was, the tool actually allows you to manage all the objects in any domain. You can create an entire domain hierarchy of Organizational Units, user accounts, computer accounts, groups, volumes, and so on. The tool, however, is limited. You can manage users very well indeed, since the tool has been hardcoded with all the information about users, as ahown in Figure 19-3.

You see can in Figure 19-3 that all the tabs appear in ADUC on a Domain Controller after turning on Advanced view and installing the Active Directory Connector. That's a lot of detail and includes tabs for Terminal Server, Exchange mailbox properties, and security permissions and auditing. Now compare this to Figure 19-4, which takes a look at a computer object.

Figure 19-4 contains many fewer property pages. A computer object inherits its schema class structure (its own blueprint) from the User class before adding a few attributes of its own, so if a computer potentially has more attributes that can be set, the management of most of the attributes that are part of a computer object will never need modifying by an administrator using the GUI, if they need modifying at all. The description property of computer objects seems to be the most important item.

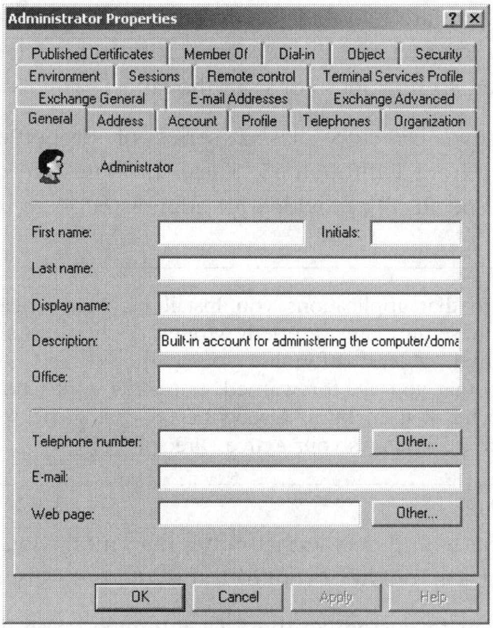

Figure 19-3. The many property pages for a user object

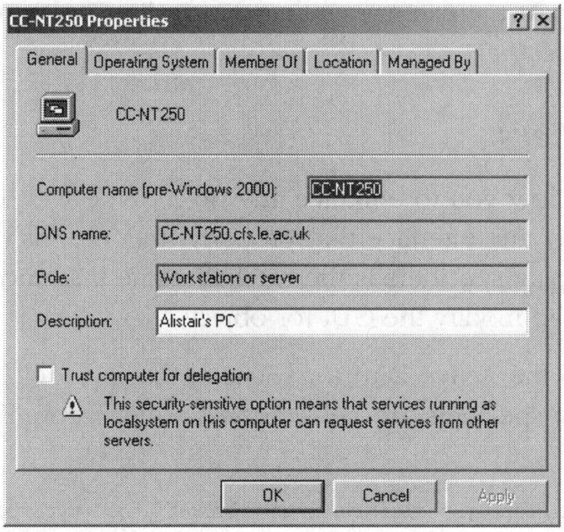

Figure 19-4. The few property pages for a computer object

So the ADUC is only good at managing the properties that it specifically knows about. But that can cause problems. Let me give you a couple of examples. Let's say that you decide that you want to store the languages all employees can speak in Active Directory. This attribute does not exist in Active Directory by default, so what do you do? There are two solutions. The first is to create a new attribute in the Active Directory Schema and the second is to use the extension attributes. I've addressed the former, so now let's consider the latter.

Each object in Active Directory has a series of properties called extension attributes, numbered from 1 through 15. These attributes are not used by the system and have been specifically provided for administrators to use.

Be aware that applications you install may have been written to modify these attributes. Properly written applications should not do this without at least informing you in the *README* or installation notes so that you are forewarned, but some application developers may not be so thoughtful. Always be on your guard with new software that manipulates your Active Directory.

I look at these attributes and decide that rather than modifying the schema, I'll add the data into the **Extension-Attribute-1** attribute on every user object instead.

Microsoft enables you to customize the GUI interface using scripts. These scripts don't have to be complex, as I hope you'll see by the end of this chapter. In fact, Microsoft has allowed extensions to Active Directory that mean any properly written GUI interface to Active Directory (such as all the tools that Microsoft provides) will be able to support the extensions that you make. This is all due to something known as *display specifiers.*

Display Specifiers

Display specifiers allow you to enhance any object type with information that will be read and used by any interface that properly understands the display specifier. In other words, display specifiers is the catchall name that encompasses the different ways that you can modify the GUI for objects.

Each object class in the Active Directory Schema has a set of display specifiers set for it. These display specifiers are held in the Configuration Naming Context, in a path similar to this:

```
LDAP://cn=409,cn=DisplaySpecifiers,cn=Configuration,dc=mycorp,dc=com
```

The preceding container signifies the display specifiers for the U.S./English locale of 409. If you wanted to create or manage display specifiers for a different locale, you just create a new container with the relevant hexadecimal code for the locale and populate it with the relevant Display-Specifier's objects. For example, 409 in hex represents 1,033 in decimal, and 1,033 is the U.S./English locale. If I created 809 (2,057 in decimal) I would get the U.K./English locale, and if I created 40C (1,036 in decimal) I would get the French locale. The currently installed locale values can be found at this location in the registry: HKLM\SYSTEM\Current-ControlSet\Control\ContentIndex\Language. Supporting different locales allows you to have different display specifiers for the different locales, so Active Directory objects can have different names, property pages, and menus depending on which locale and language settings a user has installed.

The preceding container holds a series of objects of the Display-Specifiers class. So, the user class has one called User-Display, the computer class has one called Computer-Display, and so on. In order to extend the interface for an object class for a particular language, you just need to modify the appropriate attributes on the Display-Specifier object that represents the class in this container.

Here's a simple example. The Class-Display-Name attribute exists on all Display-Specifier objects. Let's say I use the ADSIEDIT tool from the Windows 2000 Resource Kit to open up the Group-Display object and change this attribute from Group to Moose. If I right-click on any container in the ADUC tool, then normally a context menu appears which allows me to create a new User, Group, or Organizational Unit (among other things). Instead, it allows me to create a new User, Moose, or Organizational Unit. I changed the way that the Group class was displayed in the interface. Just the name used to display that class has changed. If I wanted to change the display specifier for the French locale as well as or instead of the U.S./English locale, I create the 40C container and apply my change to a newly created Group-Display Display-Specifiers object in the 40C container.

Let's now go into what you actually can do to the interface.

Property Pages

You can see the array of property pages that exist for two objects in Figures 19-3 and 19-4. You can add property pages to these and display your own here. In order for this to work, though, the property page has to exist as a Component Object Model (COM) object that supports the IShellExitInit and IShellPropSheetExt interfaces. This means that the property page has to be created first in Visual Basic, Visual C++, or something similar.

Creating the object is the hardest part. Actually telling the system to use it is easy. Once the property page COM object exists, it will have a Universally Unique Identifier (UUID) to uniquely identify it. You then use ADSIEDIT to go to the display specifier object representing the class that you wish to modify and alter the Admin-Property-Pages or Shell-Property-Pages attributes. These attributes are multivalued and store data in the following form:

```
2, {AB4909C2-6BEA-11D2-B1B6-00C04F9914BD}
1, {AB123CDE-ABCD-1122-ABAB-00CC4DD11223}
```

The first item represents the order number in which the sheets should appear. The second represents the UUID. A third optional parameter can be used to store extended information, such as passing data to the property page as it is displayed.

To add your own property page to a class, you edit either the Shell or Admin property page attribute, depending on whether you want the shell or administrator UI to be modified and add in a line like the preceding form. It really is that simple. You can even modify the existing pages, if any exist, and resequence them to your liking.

Icons

When you look at a container of objects in the ADUC tool, it shows you an icon for each object appropriate to the specific object class for that object. The icons for Organizational Units look different than those for containers, users, and printers, for example. The icon can actually be used to represent different states of that object. For example, if you disable a user or computer object, then the icon is changed to indicate that the object is disabled. All in all, 16 different state icons can be defined for any object class. The first three represent the states closed (the default state), open, and disabled; the last 13 are currently undefined and left for your own use.

To modify the icon for an object class, simply use the Icon-Path attribute to store multivalued data of the following form:

```
0, c:\winnt\system32\myicon.ico
1, c:\winnt\system32\myicons.dll, 0
2, c:\winnt\system32\myicons.dll, 2
3, c:\winnt\system32\myicons.dll, 7
```

This sets the first four icon values. Remember that 0 is closed, 1 is open, and 2 is disabled; 3 through 15 are undefined. The first one uses a proper icon file with an ICO extension and so doesn't need a third parameter. The last three use the first (0), third (2), and eighth (7) icons from *MYICONS.DLL* using an index for the set of icons held in the DLL, starting at 0. The icon path has to exist on the local machine for any client to properly display the icon. Remember to take that into account, since you may need to deploy the icon files to all clients in an enterprise if they are to properly display the icons.

Class and Attribute Names

As shown earlier, you can alter the way that both class and attribute names appear within a GUI. If you want to change the class name, change the text in the Class-Display-Name property of the relevant Display-Specifier object. If you want to change what attributes names appear as, then you need to modify the multivalued attribute Attribute-Display-Names. Attribute values take the form of a comma-delimited string as follows:

```
mobile,Mobile Number
physicalDeliveryOfficeName,Office Location
extensionAttribute1,My First Extended Attribute
```

The first value is the LDAP name corresponding to the attribute in the schema, and the second is the name that it is to be displayed as. Note that you shouldn't insert a space between the comma and the second value unless you want the name to be preceded by a space.

Leaf or Container

When you view objects in the ADUC, some display as containers and some display as leaf objects. Most objects that you see every day actually act as containers, even if you see them displayed as leaf objects. Take a printer on a computer, for example. If that printer is published as a Print-Queue object to Active Directory, the object is located as a leaf object within the Computer object that it is published on. The Computer object acts as a container for any print queues that it publishes. User, Computer, and Group objects by default do not display themselves as containers. The ADUC tool in fact has an option on the View menu to change this, called "View users, groups, and computers as containers." However, all objects get treated in this fashion, and you can modify any object's default setting by going to the Display-Specifier and changing the Boolean value of Treat-As-Leaf to True or False as required.

Object Creation Wizard

When you create a user, group, or Organizational Unit, the system presents a simple wizard to allow you to specify the relevant data for that object. It is possible for administrators to modify the default behavior in one of two ways. Administrators can replace the existing wizard entirely, if one exists, or they can just add extra pages to the wizard. Only one wizard can ever exist, so you either create a new one or modify the existing one. Let's say that you decided that the Languages-Spoken for a user was a mandatory attribute of the User class. This forces you to define a value for Languages-Spoken for all new users on creation. As the existing User creation wizard does not allow data to be input for this attribute, you can replace the entire wizard with a new one of your own, or you can place a new page into the wizard to receive data on this attribute. Since with property pages, I need to create new wizards or creation wizard extensions (extra pages to existing wizards) as COM objects that support the IDsAdminWizExt interface. New wizards that replace the default wizards in use by the system are known as *primary extensions*, and replace the core set of pages that would be used to create the object.

Primary extensions support creation wizard extensions; you can define a primary extension for all users, for example, and later add a couple of extra pages using a creation wizard extension if you require.

The COM object UUID is used to denote the items in Active Directory. If you are replacing the wizard entirely with a primary extension, you modify the Creation-Wizard attribute of the relevant Display-Specifier object to hold the UUID of the COM object. If you are just providing creation wizard extensions, then you specify the order that the pages should appear, followed by the UUID in the Create-Wizard-Ext multivalued attribute. The format is the same as for property pages.

Context Menus

When you right-click an object in the ADUC tool, a context menu pops up. You can add your own entries to this context menu. Menu items for this menu are held in the Admin-Context-Menu attribute on the Display-Specifier object. You also can add entries to the context menus that appear in the shell for end users. These items are held in the Shell-Context-Menu attribute on the Display-Specifier object. Items that should appear in both go into the Context-Menu attribute.

The items that you add to the context menus can launch an application or create an instance of a COM object. The data takes the following form in the relevant attributes:

```
1,Extra &Data..., E:\MYPROG.EXE
2,&Extended Attributes...,C:\MYSCRIPT.VBS
3,{DB4909C2-6BEA-11D2-B1B6-00C04F9914BD}
```

You can see that the last item is a COM object. It is denoted by its UUID. The COM object must have been created to support the IShellExtInit and IContext-Menu interfaces. Extra data can be passed to the COM object by including it as a third parameter on the line. The former two items are much more important to administrators. Here you can see that I am adding two extra items to the menu. These items are an executable program and a VBScript script. Any type of application is valid. The second parameter is the string you want to appear on the context menu. Use of an ampersand (&) character before a letter denotes that letter as the menu selector. So, when the menu is being displayed, typing d selects the first option, and e selects the second.

Being able to add scripts and programs to a context menu is a significant step forward. Couple these scripts and programs with Active Directory Services Interface (ADSI) and you have a way of offering new functionality directly from the GUI. For example, let's say that you wish to extend the schema and include a new optional Languages-Spoken attribute for the User class. You can go to the User-Display Display-Specifier object and modify the Context-Menu attribute (so it is available to both users and administrators) to include an ADSI script that displays the languages spoken for that user in a message box on screen:

```
Set wshArgs = WScript.Arguments

Set adsUser = GetObject(wshArgs(0))
MsgBox adsUser.extensionAttribute1,,"Languages Spoken"
```

The script does nothing more than bind to the object's ADsPath that is passed in as an argument to the program, and print out the attribute in a MsgBox with an appropriate title, as shown in Figure 19-5.

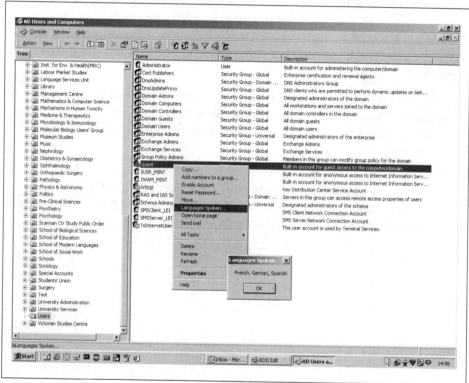

Figure 19-5. Looking at the languages spoken for a user

I have right-clicked on the Guest user to pop up a context menu that includes Languages Spoken. You can see that it is actually the string "&Languages Spoken..." being displayed if you look hard at the text in the bottom lefthand corner of the window. When I click the item or press the L key, a dialog box generated by the script is displayed on the screen. Normally the dialog box and the context menu would not be displayed together, but I have done so in this screen to show you the process.

You also could write a script or program that allowed you to modify the Languages-Spoken attribute and have it appear only on the administrator's context menus. Then you can use the ADUC tool to manage your users and this extra attribute, without ever needing to actually develop an entirely new interface if you don't want to.

Summary

You can extend Active Directory by programmatically modifying the schema to include your own classes and attributes or use the existing extension attributes whenever you think that an easier or more sensible option. You also can enhance the Windows 2000 GUI with your own personal customizations. If you want to find out more, check out the following information in the Microsoft Developer Network (MSDN) Library:

- Platform SDK → User Interface Services → The Windows Shell → Shell Programmers Guide → Shell Extension Handlers. You can find this online at *http://msdn.microsoft.com/isapi/msdnlib.idc?theURL=/library/sdkdoc/shellcc/shell/shellext.htm*.

- Platform SDK → Networking Services → Active Directory → Active Directory Programmer's Guide → Extending the User Interface for Directory Objects. You can find this online at *http://msdn.microsoft.com/isapi/msdnlib.idc?theURL=/library/sdkdoc/adsi/gldispl1_06pf.htm*.

20

Enhancing ADSI via an ASP or VB Interface

Two important features of Active Directory require administrators to create their own tools:

- The ability to extend the Active Directory Schema with your own classes and attributes

- The ability to delegate control of administration of Active Directory in a very detailed manner

If you take advantage of these, there is a large chance that you will want to provide customized tools for administration of that system.

Consider that you decide that a group of users is to manage only certain properties of certain objects, say which users can go into a group. There is no point in giving them Active Directory Users and Computers tool; that's like using a sledgehammer to crack a nut. Why not quickly create a tool of your own that only allows them to manipulate the values that they have permission to. If you then incorporate logging into a file or database within this application, you have a customized audit trail as well.

Tools of this nature do not lend themselves to VBscript since they tend to require a much more enhanced GUI interface. Consequently, you are left with three choices:

- Write code in a compiled language like Visual Basic that supports complex GUI routines

- Write code with an HTML interface using Active Server Pages (ASPs)

- Write code in another scripting language such as Perl that supports complex graphical controls

I will concentrate on the first two in this chapter.

VBScript Limitations and Solutions

Using ADSI from within the WSH is very useful, but it does have certain limitations. For one thing, you cannot display output on screen in anything other than a MsgBox or request information from users without using the InputBox. It is easy to show how these are lacking. Consider that I wish to write a general script that adds a user to a single group selected from a list. If I wrote this under the WSH, I would have to list all the groups to the screen in a large MsgBox (or via a file using Notepad) with incremental numbers so that each group could be identified. Then the person running the script would have to remember the number and type it into an InputBox later so that the request could be serviced. If I had more than a few dozen groups in my Active Directory, the person running the script would have to go through a number of screens of groups before being able to see them all. It would be much simpler if I could just display a drop-down list box of all groups and get the user to select one. This is not possible under the WSH using VBScript, but it is possible under VB and Active Server Pages (ASPs).

VB provides a full programming environment for your ADSI applications. ASP provides VBScript with the user-interface facilities that HTML allows, effectively making your scripts more user friendly. While I tend to use VB whenever I want to roll out a more complex interface to users, ASP is also a valid solution. ASPs are useful for two important reasons. First, there is a single copy maintained in the organization. Hence, if the single copy is updated, everyone gets the latest copy on the next use. This also saves you from a version hell of multiple versions of a program floating around. Second, no runtime or design-time licenses are required in the development of such pages, as would be the case when you develop VB applications.

Also, if I publish the web pages on an internet server rather than an intranet server, I can make the scripts available to anyone who has the correct privilege to the script whether he is on my local network or not. At present you may find it hard to see a need for being able to manipulate Active Directory from outside the organization. As Active Directory becomes a larger store for complex objects, you may find yourself writing pages to interrogate company databases for certain information as well as Active Directory, bringing both sets of information forward to the user. Web pages also allow you to prototype or identify a need for a future application. If you find that your users are making heavy use of the web interface, perhaps it is time to consider rolling out a proper application. It all depends on what sort of mechanism you prefer to let your users access your Active Directory.

This chapter will enable you to create ASPs effectively using HTML and ADSI and to create simple VB applications from your VBScript scripts.

While incorporating ADSI scripts into ASPs via HTML is fairly easy, anyone who is considering using VBScript with HTML pages needs to go and do some background reading. This chapter alone barely scratches the surface and in no way covers HTML in any real depth. I just want to give you a taste of what you need to do so that you can see just how simple this is.

How to Avoid Problems When Using ADSI and ASP

If you want to make proper use of these examples, there are a few minimum requirements that you should be aware of. You will need a combination of Microsoft Internet Explorer 3.02 (IE) and Microsoft Internet Information Server 3.0 (IIS) or above with ASP to run VBScript. As both IE and IIS are free, I would highly recommend upgrading to the latest version available to run your scripts. I have used only IE 5.0 served from IIS 5.0 (the Windows 2000 defaults) to test these examples.

The Two Largest Pitfalls with ASP and ADSI

There is one very large pitfall with ADSI scripts under ASP, and I have fallen for it again and again. I kick myself every time it happens as it is so obvious a mistake, yet it does happen and it may well happen to you. ADSI scripts running under ASP work only when served from IIS. This is because IIS understands ADSI, and IE on its own does not. So whenever you want to test-run an ASP incorporating an ADSI script, make sure that you are obtaining it from the server. This problem tends to occur in two main ways:

- When developing scripts on the machine that IIS is running on
- When developing scripts on a machine that has a drive mapped to the directory on IIS where you are storing the scripts

In both of these cases, it is just as easy to open a file called *C:\INETPUB\ WWWROOT\MYTEST.ASP* as it is to open *http://www.mycorp.com\mytest.asp* from within IE. Both files will open correctly, but only the IIS-served page will correctly work with ADSI. If you start getting unexplained errors, with code that you know should be working, just check the URL of the ASP that you are opening.

The second annoying pitfall occurs when you are constantly updating pages, testing them with a browser, and then updating them again. If you are developing in this cycle, remember to keep refreshing the page. It becomes really annoying to find that the bug you have been trying to solve is due to the fact that your browser thoughtfully cached a page 15 minutes ago, and you have been forgetting to depress the Shift key when clicking the Refresh button.*

Combining VBScript and HTML

HTML pages are written as text files in the same way that VBScripts are. Each HTML page displays information according to a series of *tags*, which you use to turn certain formatting on and off. The tags you normally would use to construct a basic page looks like this:

```
<HTML>

<HEAD>
<TITLE>Hello World Page</TITLE>
</HEAD>

<BODY>
Hello World
<P>Hello again
</BODY>

</HTML>
```

The <HTML> tag denotes it as an HTML document. The <HEAD> and </HEAD> pair denote everything within those tags as belonging to the header description part of the document. The <TITLE> tag denotes the start of the page title and </TITLE> turns it off again. The <BODY> tag denotes the main part of the page, which contains a simple text string, a newline or paragraph marker <P>, and then another line of text. This is the bare bones of writing HTML documents. You can create lists, set colors, make and populate tables, display images, and so on. However, you do not need to go into all of that in order to demonstrate incorporating ADSI VBScripts into HTML pages. You only need to be aware of the following major sets of tags: <FORM>. . .</FORM>, <OBJECT>. . .</OBJECT>, <%. . .%>, and <SCRIPT>. . .</SCRIPT>.

Incorporating Scripts into Active Server Pages

Two sorts of scripts can be created within ASPs: client-side scripts and server-side scripts. Client-side scripting is used to access all the objects in a web page, (e.g., text, images, tags, etc.), browser objects (e.g., frames, windows, etc.), and local ActiveX components. Server-side scripting is used to dynamically create a web page via parameters, forms, and code that is then passed to a browser.

---

* Another option if you are using Internet Explorer is to open up the Internet Options from the Tools menu and set the Temporary Internet Files to check for newer versions of stored pages on every visit to the page.

Because the two types of scripts are executed at different locations, each has a separate set of interfaces. You place your ADSI scripts in server-side scripting, not client-side scripting. I'll go through the major differences now so that you will be less likely to make annoying mistakes.

Client-side scripting

You can use the <SCRIPT> tags to add client-side VBScript code to an HTML page. Whenever the browser encounters the tags, the enclosed script is executed as if it were being issued from the client. You can use blocks of scripting in both the BODY and HEAD sections of an ASP if you want to. If you put your code in the HEAD section, it will be read and executed before any item in the BODY section is accessed. As an example, here is a procedure to display a line of text:

```
<SCRIPT LANGUAGE="VBScript">
  Document.Write "This is a line of text<P>"
</SCRIPT>
```

The LANGUAGE attribute indicates that this is VBScript rather than one of the other languages. As this is not running under the WSH, you do not have a VBS or JS extension to denote the language. The `Document::Write` method writes the line to the web page. It is only one of a number of properties and methods from interfaces available to you as an ASP developer. You also can use MsgBox and InputBox within client-side scripts.

The important thing about client-side scripts from this chapter's point of view is that ADSI functions and methods cannot be included in these scripts. This is an important limitation, one that I will show you how to get around later.

Server-side scripting

You also can use the SCRIPT tags to denote server-side scripting in ASPs. In order to distinguish server-side SCRIPT tags from client-side tags, you use the RUNAT attribute as follows:

```
<SCRIPT LANGUAGE="VBScript" RUNAT="SERVER">
Set adsGroup = GetObject("LDAP://cn=Managers,ou=Sales," _
  & "dc=windows,dc=mycorp,dc=com")

  Response.Write adsGroup.Description
</SCRIPT>
```

The `RUNAT="SERVER"` tag is used as is. It does not require you to substitute an actual server name.

Server-side scripting also can go in either the BODY or HEAD sections. As you can see from the example, server-side scripting can include ADSI calls without any problem. The `Response::Write` method is used to write lines of text out to a page by code that is processed on the web server. You cannot use `Document::Write` in server-side scripts as the Document interface is unavailable to the server; it is available only to the browser.

There is also another and more common short form to denote server-side scripting, the <% . . .%> tags. Any code between this set of tags is automatically treated as server-side scripting code. Here is the previous example again, using these tags:

```
<%
  Set adsGroup = GetObject("LDAP://cn=Managers,ou=Sales," _
    & "dc=windows,dc=mycorp,dc=com")

  Response.Write adsGroup.Description
%>
```

Throughout the rest of the book, I will use the <%. . .%> tags to indicate server-side scripting and the SCRIPT tag to indicate client-side scripting. The <%. . .%> tags allow you to create quite complex scripts that switch back and forth between HTML on every line if you like. For example, here is a simple server-side script:

```
<%
  If myCondition = True Then
    Response.Write "The Condition is TRUE<P>"
  Else
    Response.Write "The Condition is FALSE<P>"
  End If
%>
```

Here is the same script again using the <%. . .%> tags more heavily so that I can make use of HTML whenever I want to:

```
<% If myCondition = True Then %>
    The Condition is TRUE<P>
<% Else %>
    The Condition is FALSE<P>
<% End If %>
```

ActiveX Controls and ASPs

Anyone who has developed ASPs before or who reads any ASP book will find out about embedding ActiveX controls into web pages. The OBJECT tag is used to add extra functionality to an HTML document by allowing the insertion of various ActiveX controls onto web pages. Included in these are items such as buttons you can press, drop-down list boxes from which you can select items, text entry and display fields, and so on. When you insert an object into your web page using the OBJECT tag, you can specify its initial contents, its position, its caption, its color,

Setting the Default Language

If you choose to use the <%. . .%> tags, you can change the primary scripting language for a single page by adding a command line to the beginning of your ASP. The syntax for this command is the following if you are using JScript, VBScript, or any other language that supports `Object.Method` syntax:

```
<%@ LANGUAGE="VBSCRIPT" %>
<%@ LANGUAGE="JSCRIPT" %>
```

You should make this line the first line of the ASP and make sure that you have a blank space between the @ character and the LANGUAGE keyword.

If you are writing ASPs using VBScript as your language, you can omit this line from all your ASPs, as VBScript is set as the default language anyway.

and so on. Most people who create web pages using ActiveX controls do not type all this data in by hand. Instead, developers normally use a tool to select from the available options when creating the tag.

If you wanted to buy a tool, you could use Microsoft FrontPage, which was designed for people who are not used to scripting and would prefer an Office type interface. Alternatively, you could use Microsoft InterDev which was designed to have the same interface as all of Microsoft's other development products such as VB. Various other free web development tools also exist to edit web pages that will insert these tags.

Alternatively, if you just want to get hold of a free tool in order to get started, you can download the ActiveX Control Pad from Microsoft. It is a very rough-and-ready tool, requiring you to know what object you want to insert, but it does get the job done. The ActiveX Control Pad can be downloaded from *http://msdn.microsoft.com/workshop/c-frame.htm#/workshop/misc/cpad/default.asp.*

Here is the code for a command button that you would click on in a web page:

```
<HTML>
<HEAD>
<TITLE>Simple Command Button</TITLE>
</HEAD>
<BODY>

<OBJECT ID="CommandButton1" WIDTH=93 HEIGHT=33
  CLASSID="CLSID:D7053240-CE69-11CD-A777-00DD01143C57">
    <PARAM NAME="ForeColor" VALUE="2147483670">
    <PARAM NAME="BackColor" VALUE="2147483668">
    <PARAM NAME="VariousPropertyBits" VALUE="23">
    <PARAM NAME="Caption" VALUE="Click me!">
    <PARAM NAME="Size" VALUE="2469;882">
    <PARAM NAME="MousePointer" VALUE="1">
```

```
    <PARAM NAME="FontCharSet" VALUE="0">
    <PARAM NAME="FontPitchAndFamily" VALUE="2">
    <PARAM NAME="ParagraphAlign" VALUE="3">
    <PARAM NAME="FontWeight" VALUE="0">
</OBJECT>

</BODY>
</HTML>
```

ActiveX controls are very useful, but they do have their limits with respect to ADSI. For example, the object specified in the preceding script is a client-side ActiveX control. So if you wanted to attach an event to it, say a procedure that is executed when the button is pressed, you couldn't use ADSI code within that procedure. For example, while this looks like great code, it will not work:

```
<SCRIPT LANGUAGE="VBScript">
Sub CommandButton1_Click()
    Set adsGroup = GetObject("LDAP://cn=Managers,ou=Sales," _
      & "dc=windows,dc=mycorp,dc=com")

    Document.Write adsGroup.Description
</SCRIPT>
```

You can, however, easily populate list boxes and other controls with the results of ADSI calls. This is great for display purposes, but you can't manipulate the contents. Let me lay out an example to show you the problem.

Let's say that I have an ASP with two list box ActiveX controls. When the page is loaded, I can trigger the population of the first list box with all the users in Active Directory. I can do the same for the second list box with all the groups in Active Directory. I now can click and select values from each of the list boxes, although nothing happens when I do so. Now I decide that I wish to add a command button ActiveX control to the ASP. I wish to attach an event to that button so that an ADSI call is made that attempts to add the user to the group and print out the result. Unfortunately, I can't do that, since the ActiveX control event procedure is client-side and ADSI code must be server-side.

While ActiveX controls may be very powerful, they can't incorporate ADSI directly from triggered events; I will not be making use of them in this chapter.

Forms

If ActiveX control events are not available, you can use HTML forms to create simple ASPs. Here is an example:

```
<FORM ACTION = "simple_form_demo.asp" METHOD = "POST">
    <P>A simple input field: <INPUT NAME = "myfield1" SIZE = 48>
    <P>Here is a list of all the users in the default Users container:
    <SELECT NAME = "user">
        <% Set adsUsers = GetObject("LDAP://cn=Users,dc=windows,dc=mycorp,dc=com")
```

```
        For Each adsObject in adsUsers
            If adsObject.Class = "user" Then %>
                <OPTION><% = adsObject.Name %>
        <%   End If
           Next %>
    </SELECT>
    <P><INPUT TYPE = SUBMIT>
    </FORM>
```

This form incorporates an alphanumeric input field, a list box populated by users from the default Users container and a button entitled Submit Query. The list box is populated via the OPTION tag between a <SELECT>. . .</SELECT> tag pair. Clever use of server-side scripts here between the SELECT tag pair means that you can populate the list box using ADSI calls.

More importantly, once the form is submitted, server-side scripts can retrieve the values typed into the input fields by passing the name of the form to the `Request::Form` method. If the previous form were submitted, you could retrieve the value selected in the list box by using the following code:

```
Request.Form("user")
```

One important point needs noting here. It is possible to attach scripts to form-field events, such as clicking a button or tabbing out of a field. Unfortunately, as the form is client-side, the script attached to the event has to be client-side. That precludes the use of ADSI in these sort of scripts. Here is an example:

```
<HTML>
<HEAD>
<TITLE>Display Description</TITLE>
</HEAD>
<BODY>
<FORM NAME="Form1">
    <INPUT TYPE="Button" NAME="Button1" VALUE="Click me for Description!">
    <SCRIPT FOR="Button1" EVENT="onClick" LANGUAGE="VBScript">
      MsgBox "Clicked!"
    </SCRIPT>
</FORM>
</BODY>
</HTML>
```

Since the scripts are only client-side I will not be using these type of scripts within this chapter.

Binding to Objects via Authentication

Whenever I need to access the properties of an object in Active Directory, I bind to it using VBScript's `GetObject` function or the ADSI method `IADs-OpenDSObject::OpenDSObject`. The circumstances in which I use each method of accessing Active Directory is very clear-cut but deserves to be outlined here as it will be important whenever you construct ASPs.

When to Use VBScript's GetObject Function

By default, many of the objects and properties within Active Directory can be read by anyone whether they authenticate or not. If you issue a `GetObject` call on an LDAP namespace, then the LDAP provider DLL is loaded and a TCP/IP port 389 connection is made to the remote directory service in order to process the request. Provided that Active Directory has not been specifically restricted from this sort of access, the LDAP path can be properly resolved, and the port is accessible on that remote server from the machine making the connection, you will gain access to Active Directory.

As an example, here is some code to connect to an Organizational Unit called Sales under the root of the domain. This code works under the WSH:

```
Set adsSalesOU = GetObject("LDAP://ou=Sales,dc=windows,dc=mycorp,dc=com")
Wscript.Echo adsSalesOU.Description
```

Here is the same script incorporated into an ASP:

```
<HTML>
<HEAD>
<TITLE>Binding to an existing Organizational Unit</TITLE>
</HEAD>

<BODY>
<%
   Set adsSalesOU = GetObject("LDAP://ou=Sales,dc=windows,dc=mycorp,dc=com")
   Response.Write "The Sales OU description is: " & adsSalesOU.Description
%>
</BODY>
</HTML>
```

This mechanism works perfectly when you wish to have read-only access to properties of objects that can be read without authentication. Using `GetObject` is not appropriate in the following cases:

- If you wish to force authentication to the tree

- If you ever want to write back properties to the object

- If the object you are attempting to bind to has restrictive permissions prohibiting nonauthenticated access

- If you wish to access any of the object's properties that are themselves restricted due to permissions denying nonauthenticated access

While it may make little sense, it is perfectly feasible to restrict read access to the description of the Sales Organizational Unit, or more commonly the Sales Organizational Unit itself. If the Sales Organizational Unit is restricted, a `GetObject` will fail to bind to it. If only the description is restricted, a `GetObject` will successfully bind to the Sales Organizational Unit, but access to the description property will be denied.

To gain access in any of the four preceding cases, authentication must be used.

When to Use IADsOpenDSObject::OpenDSObject

Here is a simple Organizational Unit creation script which works under the WSH when an administrator is logged in:

```
Set adsRoot=GetObject("LDAP://dc=windows,dc=mycorp,dc=com")

Set adsSalesOU = adsRoot.Create("organizationalUnit","ou=Sales")
adsSalesOU.Description = "My new description!"
adsSalesOU.SetInfo
```

I cannot transfer the script to an ASP as it stands. To make the script work, I must use the `IADsOpenDSObject::OpenDSObject` method, which does allow authentication. Here is the same example using authentication within an ASP:

```
<HTML>
<HEAD>
<TITLE>Successful Organizational Unit Creation</TITLE>
</HEAD>

<BODY>
<%
   strPath = "LDAP://dc=windows,dc=mycorp,dc=com"
   strUsername = "cn=Administrator,cn=Users,dc=windows,dc=mycorp,dc=com"
   strPassword = "my-admin-password"

   Set adsNamespace = GetObject("LDAP:")
   Set adsRoot = adsNamespace.OpenDSObject(strPath, strUsername, strPassword, 0)

   Set adsSalesOU = adsRoot.Create("organizationalUnit","ou=Sales")
   adsSalesOU.Description = "My new description!"
   adsSalesOU.SetInfo

   Response.Write "The Sales OU has been created in the " & strPath & " domain."
%>
</BODY>
</HTML>
```

If I wanted to manipulate any of the properties of the new Sales Organizational Unit during that script, I could continue to use the adsSalesOU variable to do so. If I write a new script that needs to access that Organizational Unit and to print the description, I now can use either `GetObject` or authenticate directly to that Organizational Unit in the same way as I did to the root of the tree:

```
<HTML>
<HEAD>
<TITLE>Binding to an existing Organizational Unit</TITLE>
</HEAD>

<BODY>
```

```
<%
   adsOUPath = "LDAP://ou=Sales,dc=windows,dc=mycorp,dc=com"
   strUsername = "cn=Administrator,cn=Users,dc=windows,dc=mycorp,dc=com"
   strPassword = "my-admin-password"

   Set adsNamespace = GetObject("LDAP:")
   Set adsSalesOU = adsNamespace.OpenDSObject(adsOUPath,strUsername,strPassword,0)

   Response.Write "The Sales OU description is: " & adsSalesOU.Description
%>
</BODY>
</HTML>
```

What may seem strange is that you can authenticate to the root of the tree and access objects there but still need to authenticate again to other areas of the tree if you need to bind to them. One authentication to a point in the tree does not allow you to use GetObject happily throughout the rest of the script for all objects and containers below that point. If you need authentication, for whatever reason, to access objects in disparate areas of the tree, you need to authenticate each binding separately. As an example, this next script creates the Organizational Unit again and then sets the description for a user named Ian Harcombe in the Users container. In this example, both need authentication because I wish to update properties in both cases:

```
<HTML>
<HEAD>
<TITLE>Example use of Complex Authentication</TITLE>
</HEAD>

<BODY>
<%
   strRootPath = "LDAP://dc=windows,dc=mycorp,dc=com"
   strUserPath = "LDAP://cn=Ian Harcombe,cn=Users,dc=windows,dc=mycorp,dc=com"
   strUsername = "cn=Administrator,cn=Users,dc=windows,dc=mycorp,dc=com"
   strPassword = "my-admin-password"

   Set adsNamespace = GetObject("LDAP:")
   Set adsRoot = adsNamespace.OpenDSObject(strRootPath,strUsername,strPassword,0)

   Set adsSalesOU = adsRoot.Create("organizationalUnit","ou=Sales")
   adsSalesOU.Description = "My new description!"
   adsSalesOU.SetInfo

   Set adsUser = adsNamespace.OpenDSObject(strUserPath,strUsername,strPassword,0)
   adsUser.Description = "My new description!"
   adsUser.SetInfo
%>
</BODY>
</HTML>
```

I ought to state at this point that it is quite valid to authenticate with null credentials to the `IADsOpenDSObject::OpenDSObject` method. Doing so is effectively equivalent to using `GetObject`:

```
adsOUPath = "LDAP://ou=Sales,dc=windows,dc=mycorp,dc=com"

Set adsNamespace = GetObject("LDAP:")
Set adsSalesOU = adsNamespace.OpenDSObject(adsOUPath,vbNullString,vbNullString,0)
```

When to Use IADsContainer::GetObject

I've shown that I cannot use the VBScript `GetObject` function to authenticate a connection to objects in Active Directory from an ASP. However, there is a method called `IADsContainer::GetObject` that can be used to bind to objects from a container using the pre-existing authenticated connection for the container. While both GetObjects have identical names and similar functions, to save confusion, I will use the fully qualified `IADsContainer::GetObject` when talking about the method and `GetObject` when talking about VBScript's function.

The `IADsContainer::GetObject` method is used to retrieve items from a container. It takes two parameters, the class of the object to retrieve and the object's RDN. The fact that `IADsContainer::GetObject` retrieves objects using the RDN means that you do not have to bind to individual objects below a container. This saves authenticating a connection to each object if you need to work on multiple objects in a container. If my Sales Organizational Unit now has three users below it, I can authenticate to the container and then use the `IADsContainer::GetObject` method to manipulate the three users. Here is an example:

```
<HTML>
<HEAD>
<TITLE>Use of IADsContainer::GetObject</TITLE>
</HEAD>

<BODY>
<%
    adsOUPath = "LDAP://ou=Sales,dc=windows,dc=mycorp,dc=com"
    strUsername = "cn=Administrator,cn=Users,dc=windows,dc=mycorp,dc=com"
    strPassword = ""

    Set adsNamespace = GetObject("LDAP:")
    Set adsSalesOU = adsNamespace.OpenDSObject(adsOUPath,strUsername,strPassword,0)

    Set adsUser1 = adsSalesOU.GetObject("User","cn=Simon Williams")
    Set adsUser2 = adsSalesOU.GetObject("User","cn=Markie Newell")
    Set adsUser3 = adsSalesOU.GetObject("User","cn=Jason Norton")

    Response.Write "Simon Williams' description is: " & adsUser1.Description
    Response.Write "Markie Newell's description is: " & adsUser2.Description
    Response.Write "Jason Norton's description is: " & adsUser3.Description
```

```
%>
</BODY>
</HTML>
```

This works under the WSH in exactly the same way as it does here. However, it is something that you may make much more use of in an ASP to save you from a lot of unnecessary authentication. If the class is null with `IADsContainer::Get-Object`, the first item matching the RDN of any class is returned.

Authenticating from Passwords Input via Forms

When you need to force authentication in a script, the last thing you will want to do is hardcode a password into the script as I have been doing previously.

That's not to say that the ASP isn't secure; it is. The script is visible only to users of the computer in which IIS is running and not to web client users, because it is parsed before being displayed. Also, if the permissions are secured, even this is not visible. However, you have to keep in mind that you will have to change the embedded password in all the ASPs every time the real password is changed. The simplest solution is to use an HTML form with a field for the password in your ASP and prompt for a password from the user. An example would look like this:

```
<HTML>
<HEAD>
<TITLE>Authentication Request</TITLE>
</HEAD>

<BODY>
<FORM ACTION="restricted.asp" METHOD=POST>

  <P>Name <BR><INPUT
    NAME="Name"
    TYPE=TEXT
    VALUE="cn=Administrator,cn=Users,dc=windows,dc=mycorp,dc=com"
    SIZE="60">

  <P>Password<BR><INPUT
    TYPE="PASSWORD"
    NAME="Password">

  <P><INPUT TYPE="SUBMIT" VALUE="OK"><INPUT TYPE="RESET" VALUE="Reset">
</FORM>

</BODY>
</HTML>
```

This eliminates the problem of having to embed the username and password in a script. The <INPUT TYPE="PASSWORD"> tag places asterisk (*) characters in the field whenever a character is entered. In this instance, the username and password are passed from this authentication page to your page entitled *restricted.asp*, which will use the credentials to perform the authentication and continue on.

However, it is still extremely cumbersome for you to have to type in the full DN you want to authenticate with. What would be much better would be for it to accept the simple username (i.e., Administrator), in the username box. For this script to do that, it would need to use ADO to search Active Directory for the user object with the RDN that would be made up of the prefix CN= and the username. You know it is CN= as all users use this prefix, and you only authenticate to the tree with user objects. This example will be left until Chapter 21, *Scripting Fast Searches Using ADO*.

A Simple Password Changer

A simple ASP example to show both server-side ADSI scripts and the use of the password attribute of the FORM tag is a password changer. Users load the page, type their usernames along with their old and new passwords into a form, and click the Submit button. Submitting the form triggers an authentication access to the user object supplied, using the user object itself and the old password. Provided that the user successfully authenticated to the user's own object, the password is then changed using the IADsUser::ChangePassword method.

This script consists of two parts: the form itself, which sits in the body of the page, and the code that interprets the submission of the form, which is located in the header. Let's start with the makeup of the form, which needs six fields:

- A text input field for the name
- A password input field for the current password
- A password input field for the new password
- A password input field to confirm the new password
- A Submit button
- A Reset button that sets all the input fields back to their default values

Here is the form:

```
<FORM ACTION="psw_changer1.asp" METHOD=POST>

  <P>Name <BR><INPUT
    NAME="Name"
    TYPE=TEXT
    VALUE="cn=xxxxx,cn=Users,dc=windows,dc=mycorp,dc=com"
    SIZE="60">

  <P>Old Password<BR><INPUT
    TYPE="PASSWORD"
    NAME="OldPassword">

  <P>New Password<BR><INPUT
    TYPE="PASSWORD"
```

```
  NAME="NewPassword1">
<P>Confirm Password<BR><INPUT
  TYPE="PASSWORD"
  NAME="NewPassword2">

<P><INPUT TYPE="SUBMIT" NAME="SetPass" VALUE="Change Password!">
<INPUT TYPE="RESET" VALUE="Reset">
</FORM>
```

The username field has been given a default value that will appear in the entry box to save on typing. Obviously this would be much improved if the user could just type his username and an ADO search was initiated.

Whenever the Submit button is clicked, the page is reloaded according to the value associated with the ACTION parameter. In addition, the form's fields have been set. This differs from the normal loading of a page when the fields will be empty. In the server-side code, I need to make sure that the code is triggered only when the page is loaded via the submission of the form. To do this, I can surround the code with the following section:

```
<%
  On Error Resume Next
  If Request.Form("SetPass") = "Change Password!" Then
    'Code goes here
  End If
%>
```

Once the form is submitted, the value of the SetPass button will be the button's label. Until that happens, the value is blank. This is a good way to check for the submission of a form.

Assuming that this code is being executed properly after submission, I need to check that the new passwords match. I will be using only one of the values to set the new password, so I have to make sure that both passwords are as the user intended. To do that, I can use **Request::Form** again to check both passwords like this:

```
<%
  On Error Resume Next
  If Request.Form("SetPass") = "Change Password!" Then
    If Request.Form("NewPassword1") = Request.Form("NewPassword2") Then
      'code goes here
    Else
      Response.Write "The two new passwords do not match. Please try again."
    End If
  End If
%>
```

I am now ready to fill in the rest of the code, which is fairly straightforward. First, I need to authenticate to the user, and if that is successful, I can attempt to change the password. Here is the completed ASP code incorporating the ADSI calls, which have been highlighted:

```
<HTML>
<HEAD>
<TITLE>Simple Password Changer</TITLE>
<%
  On Error Resume Next
  If Request.Form("SetPass") = "Change Password!" Then
    If Request.Form("NewPassword1") = Request.Form("NewPassword2") Then

      strUsername = "LDAP://" & Request.Form("Name")
      Set adsNamespace = GetObject("LDAP:")

      'Attempt to authenticate to the user object in the tree using
      'the username and the current password
      Err.Clear
      Set adsUser = adsNamespace.OpenDSObject(strUsername, _
        Request.Form("Name"), Request.Form("OldPassword"), 0)

      If Err=0 Then

        'Attempt to change the password
        Err.Clear
        adsUser.ChangePassword CStr(Request.Form("OldPassword")), _
          CStr(Request.Form("NewPassword1"))

        If Err=0 Then
          Response.Write "Password has been changed."
        Else
          Response.Write "Error: the Password has not been changed."
        End If
      Else
        Response.Write "Unable to authenticate. Password or Username incorrect."
      End If
    Else
      Response.Write "The two new passwords do not match. Please try again."
    End If
  End If
%>
</HEAD>

<BODY>
<FORM ACTION="psw_changer1.asp" METHOD=POST>

  <P>Name <BR><INPUT
    NAME="Name"
    TYPE=TEXT
    VALUE="cn=xxxxx,cn=Users,dc=windows,dc=mycorp,dc=com"
    SIZE="60">

  <P>Old Password<BR><INPUT
    TYPE="PASSWORD"
    NAME="OldPassword">
```

```
<P>New Password<BR><INPUT
   TYPE="PASSWORD"
   NAME="NewPassword1">
<P>Confirm Password<BR><INPUT
   TYPE="PASSWORD"
   NAME="NewPassword2">

<P><INPUT TYPE="SUBMIT" NAME="SetPass" VALUE="Change Password!">
<INPUT TYPE="RESET" VALUE="Reset">
</FORM>
</BODY>
</HTML>
```

As you can see, this is not particularly difficult. You also could add an **ELSE** clause and print out `Hex(Err.Number)` and `Err.Description` if you wished.

Adding Users to Groups

A password changer is a good example for a simple form, but more complex forms can sometimes be necessary. In this example, I want to populate two list boxes with users and groups from the default Users container. If I select a user and a group from the two list boxes and enter a username/password that has permissions, I should be able to click the Submit button to add the user to the group.

Once again, like most ADSI ASPs that use forms, this page is split into two parts: the form itself and the server-side script. The form is a fairly simple extension of the one that I outlined earlier. Population of the list boxes is done using two sets of server-side scripts that enumerate all values in the Users container and add any items to the list box of the appropriate class. The important population code is emphasized:

```
<FORM ACTION = "userlist2.asp" METHOD = "POST">
  <P>Users:
  <SELECT NAME = "user">
<%  Set adsUsersContainer = _
      GetObject("LDAP://cn=Users,dc=windows,dc=mycorp,dc=com")
    For Each adsObject in adsUsersContainer
      If adsObject.Class = "user" Then %>
        <OPTION><% = adsObject.Name %>
<%    End If
    Next %>
  </SELECT>
  Groups:
  <SELECT NAME = "group">
<%  For Each adsObject in adsUsersContainer
      If adsObject.Class = "group" Then %>
        <OPTION><% = adsObject.Name %>
<%    End If
    Next %>
  </SELECT></P>
```

```
    <P>Username: <INPUT
      NAME="Name"
      TYPE=TEXT
      VALUE="cn=Administrator,cn=Users,dc=windows,dc=mycorp,dc=com"
      SIZE="60">

    <P>Password<INPUT
      TYPE="PASSWORD"
      NAME="Password">

    <P><INPUT TYPE=SUBMIT NAME="Submit" VALUE="Add User To Group!">
  </FORM>
```

The server-side script that interprets the results needs to make sure that the script is executed only when the form has been submitted. Once that condition is true, the script has to attempt to authenticate to the selected group using the username and password supplied in the form. Here is the whole script with the major ADSI calls in the server-side script emphasized:

```
<HTML>
<HEAD>
<TITLE>Adding Users to Groups from the default Users Container</TITLE>

<%
  On Error Resume Next
  If Request.Form("Submit") <> "" Then
    strGroupPath = "LDAP://" & Request.Form("group") _
      & ",cn=Users,dc=windows,dc=mycorp,dc=com"
    strUserPath = "LDAP://" & Request.Form("user") _
      & ",cn=Users,dc=windows,dc=mycorp,dc=com"

    Set adsNamespace = GetObject("LDAP:")
    Err.Clear
    Set adsGroup = adsNamespace.OpenDSObject(strGroupPath, _
      CStr(Request.Form("Name")),CStr(Request.Form("Password")),0)

    If Err=0 Then
      If adsGroup.IsMember(strUserPath) Then
        Response.Write "User is already a member of the group"
      Else
        Err.Clear
        adsGroup.Add(strUserPath)

        If Err=0 Then
          Response.Write "User is now a member of the group"
        Else
          Response.Write "An error occurred when adding the user to the group."
        End If
      End If
    Else
      Response.Write "Authentication failed."
    End If
  End If
```

```
%>
</HEAD>

<BODY>
<P>
<FORM ACTION = "userlist2.asp" METHOD = "POST">
  <P>Users:
  <SELECT NAME = "user">
<%  Set adsUsersContainer = _
      GetObject("LDAP://cn=Users,dc=windows,dc=mycorp,dc=com")
    For Each adsObject in adsUsersContainer
      If adsObject.Class = "user" Then %>
        <OPTION><% = adsObject.Name %>
<%    End If
    Next %>
  </SELECT>
  Groups:
  <SELECT NAME = "group">
<%  For Each adsObject in adsUsersContainer
      If adsObject.Class = "group" Then %>
        <OPTION><% = adsObject.Name %>
<%    End If
    Next %>
  </SELECT></P>

  <P>Username: <INPUT
    NAME="Name"
    TYPE=TEXT
    VALUE="cn=Administrator,cn=Users,dc=windows,dc=mycorp,dc=com"
    SIZE="60">

  <P>Password<INPUT
    TYPE="PASSWORD"
    NAME="Password">

  <P><INPUT TYPE=SUBMIT NAME="Submit" VALUE="Add User To Group!">
</FORM>
</BODY>
</HTML>
```

I checked to see if the user was a member just so that the script is more user friendly. You also can see in this script that I use the `GetObject` function to populate the initial list boxes, but then I switch to `IADsOpenDSObject::OpenDSObject` as soon as I need to update Active Directory.

Migrating Your ADSI Scripts from VBScript to VB

If you've been writing scripts for a while and decide that you need a larger application that incorporates manipulating the properties of any Active Directory object, it is time to start thinking about coding in a different language. VB is a simple language with great complexity. The VB language itself is very similar to VBScript, so you can port code very quickly from your existing scripts. However, there is so much that you can do with VB that the bewildering array of interfaces and methods can easily get confusing. The simplest solution to this is to get a book on VB. There are many dozens of books that already exist on the complexities of writing VB, and I do not intend to do much of an introduction to it here. If you are seriously considering writing in VB, I strongly suggest you pick one of the books up.

This section covers what you need to do in order to write ADSI code with VB after having written ADSI code in VBScript. This includes a brief look at the major differences between VBScript and VB, the options that need to be set, and the ADSI SDK, which you will need for your code to compile. I also briefly cover a series of examples that are available from the O'Reilly web site. The notes that I present in this section are with respect to Microsoft Visual Basic Professional Version 6.0. You can, however, extrapolate my notes to previous or future versions of VB.

The ADSI Software Development Kit

In order to code in ADSI, you need to be able to reference the appropriate component of the Microsoft Platform Software Development Kit (SDK) in your code. You can either download the appropriate component or obtain the full SDK, which includes all components.

The full SDK provides developers with a single, easy-to-use location from which to download current and emerging Microsoft technologies and includes tools, headers, libraries, and sample code. The Platform SDK is the successor to the SDKs of Win32 and includes components that have been distributed separately in the Win32 SDK, BackOffice, ActiveX/Internet Client, and DirectX.

You can get the full SDK build environment or just the ADSI component in a number of ways:

- If you purchase an MSDN Professional-level subscription, you will be shipped all of the SDKs that you require.

- If you purchase an MSDN Enterprise-level subscription, you will be shipped all of the SDKs and all of the Visual Studio products, which includes Microsoft Visual Basic Enterprise Edition as well.

- If you purchase Visual Basic 6.0 Enterprise Edition, you receive the full MSDN set of CDs and the SDK build environment.

- You can download the ADSI component of the build environment for the platform SDK by following links from this page: *http://www.microsoft.com/adsi/*.

If you wish to make use of ADO from the next chapter, then you need Microsoft Data Access Components (MDAC) as well. You can download these from the Downloads section of the Universal Data Access site: *http://www.microsoft.com/data/download.htm.*

Once the SDK has been downloaded and installed, start VB and in any new project that you write make sure that you go to Project → References and check items according to Table 20-1.

Table 20-1. When to Use Relevant References in VB

Reference	To Use
Active DS Type Library	ADSI
Microsoft ActiveX Data Objects 2.5 Library	ADO

You can see the References window in Figure 20-1, with both items checked.

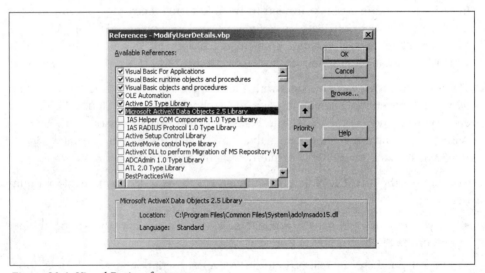

Figure 20-1. Visual Basic references

The Differences Between VB and VBScript

There are many differences between VBScript and VB, but the three major ones that you will come into contact with when porting your scripts can be quickly explained.

Screen functions

As the code will not be executing under the WSH any more, `Wscript.Echo` is not appropriate. While `MsgBox` still works, these lines should be replaced either by `Debug.Print` or by directly passing results into `TextBox` controls.

Variables

In VBScript, every variable is of the type Variant and does not have to be declared. In VB, every variable must be declared at the beginning, just as if you were using `Option Explicit` in VBScript. In addition, each variable must be declared to be of a particular type. Here are some examples for VB:

```
'VB code
Dim adsUser as IADsUser
Dim adsRoot as IADsContainer
Dim adsMember as IADsMember
```

In addition, `CreateObject` is not needed. Instead, you use the `New` keyword and declare the object created prior to the main code:

```
'VBScript code
Set adoConnection = CreateObject("ADODB.Connection")
```

This is replaced with the following code in VB:

```
'VB code
Dim adoConnection as New ADODB.Connection
```

For another important point, look at these declarations:

```
'VB code
Dim adsUser as IADsUser
Dim adsUser2 as IADs
```

If I want to use the IADsUser methods and properties, I have to use the variable `adsUser`. If I want to use the IADs methods and properties, I have to use `adsUser2`. This is how it works:

```
'VB code
Dim adsUser as IADsUser
Dim adsUser2 as IADs

Set adsUser = GetObject("LDAP://cn=Administrator,cn=Users,dc=mycorp,dc=com")
Set adsUser2 = adsUser
Debug.Print adsUser.Description
Debug.Print adsUser2.Class
```

The first `Debug::Print` statement prints the `IADsUser::Description` property, and the second prints the `IADs::Class` property. I have to include the second `Set` command to make sure that `adsUser2` points to the same object as `adsUser`.

Loop constructs

The syntax for loops changes slightly. Here, for example, are two loops in VBScipt:

```
'VBScript code
While (condition)
   'Do something
Wend

For Each adsMember In adsGroup.Members
   WScript.Echo adsMember.Name & vbCrLf & adsMember.ADsPath
Next
```

Here they are again in VB:

```
'VB code
While (condition) Do
   'Do something
Wend

For Each adsMember In adsGroup.Members
   Debug.Print adsMember.Name & vbCrLf & adsMember.ADsPath
Next adsMember
```

I now can move on to some proper VB coding.

Getting Help from VB When Coding in ADSI

When you begin to code in VB, the interface tries to help you code by providing you with the appropriate methods and properties for the object you are manipulating.

For example, if I started declaring a variable in VB, then as soon as I had stated something like this:

```
'Declare use variable
Dim adsUser As
```

the interface would pop-up a box displaying all the variable types so I could pick one. I'll say that I chose IADsUser from the list at this point. Now in my code I wish to use a method on the object, so I start typing:

```
'Declare use variable
Dim adsUser As IADsUser

'Use IADsUser method
adsUser.
```

As soon as I have typed the dot, VB knows I wish to use a method, so it pops up all the possible methods that I could use at this point. This is a great help, so that you do not have to try and remember the names of the methods and properties all the time.

You also can use View → Object Browser (or use the F2 key), which shows you all the possible methods and properties available in any SDKs that are currently included as references to your project.

A Simple Password Changer in VB

This is a variation on the password changer I introduced earlier. This changer is for use by a help desk to set a user's password and automatically unlock the account if it is locked. All the users are presumed to be in the Users container for this simple project, which makes use of one form, shown in Figure 20-2.

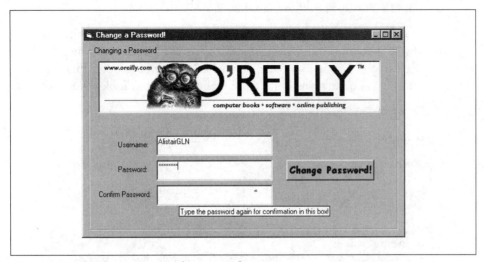

Figure 20-2. The change password script result

 The entire project can be downloaded from the O'Reilly web site.

The form (the window) contains the following controls (objects that sit on the window):

- One `PictureBox` control, the O'Reilly logo
- Three `Label` controls, the text fields that cannot be edited
- Three `TextBox` controls (`txtUsername`, `txtPass1`, and `txtPass2`), the three data entry fields
- One `CommandButton` control (`cmdChangePassword`), the Change Password button

Some of the properties for fields have been set as follows:

- To make sure that using the Tab key cycles properly through the three Text-Box and the CommandButton controls, the `TabIndex` property is set for each control in the order that the Tab key is to cycle through, e.g., `txt-Username=1`, `txtPass1=2`, `txtPass2=3`, `cmdChangePassword=4`.

- The two password boxes have the `PasswordChar` property set to `"*"` so that the password is not displayed in plain text on the form.

- The `ToolTipText` property specifies the text that will appear when the cursor hovers over each TextBox and CommandButton. The text for the second password field is displayed in Figure 20-2.

The command button needs some code to tell it what to do when the button is clicked. This is known as an *event procedure*, as it is triggered when an event (clicking the button) occurs. No code is attached to anything other than the command button. The code that sits behind the command button looks like this:

```
Private Sub cmdChangePassword_Click()

Dim adsUser As IADsUser

If txtUsername.Text <> "" Then
  If txtPass1.Text = txtPass2.Text Then
    Set adsUser = GetObject("LDAP://cn=" + txtUsername.Text _
      + ",cn=Users,dc=windows,dc=mycorp,dc=com")

    adsUser.SetPassword txtPass1.Text
    adsUser.pwdLastSet = 0
    If adsUser.IsAccountLocked Then adsUser.IsAccountLocked = False

    adsUser.SetInfo

    'Reset everything
    txtUsername.Text = ""
    txtPass1.Text = ""
    txtPass2.Text = ""

    MsgBox "Password changed!"
  Else
    MsgBox "Passwords are not the same, please try again!"
  End If
Else
  MsgBox "A username must be specified!"
End If
```

You can see that I am using the text typed into the `TextBox::Text` property for each `TextBox` control as necessary. I don't declare these controls as I do with variables, as the very fact that they're on the form is enough to declare them.

There is a procedure that is attached to the `CommandButton` called `cmd-ChangePassword`, and it is executed when a single-click event occurs on that button. When that button is clicked, I check that the `txtUsername` field has had a username typed in and if it has, then I check that the two passwords are the same. If they are, I concatenate the username with the domain string and get a handle to the user object. I then use the `IADsUser::SetPassword` method with one of the two passwords as the parameter and also set the `pwdLastSet` property to 0 to indicate that the password is expired. This means the user has to change it when he next logs on. I then unlock the account if it was locked, because otherwise the user will be unable to make use of the new password. I then write out the property cache. You also can see that I'm not checking that either the password was set properly or later that the other properties were set. It would be simple to put in if desired.

The ModifyUserDetails Program in VB

Let's take one more example by extending the previous one to modify a variety of user details. Take a look at Figure 20-3.

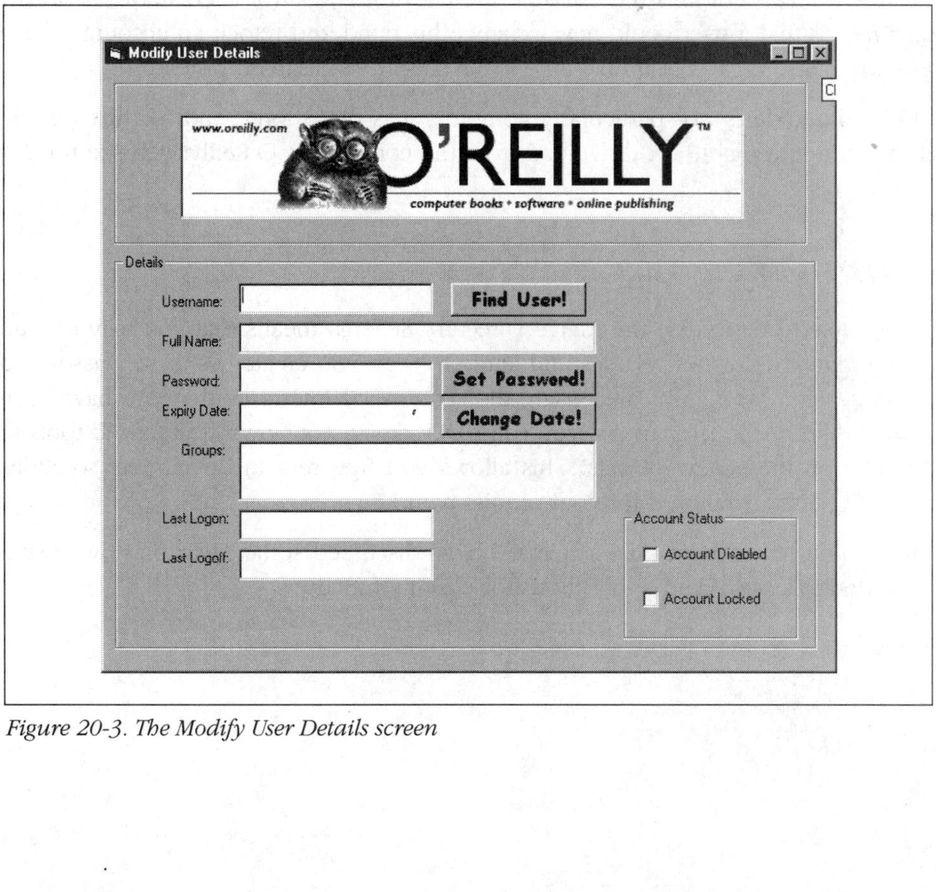

Figure 20-3. The Modify User Details screen

Figure 20-3 is another simple user querying and modification tool. This one has a number of different features. To start with, the username is typed into the top TextBox. When the user clicks on the Find User! command button, an ADO search function (to be discussed in Chapter 21) goes and retrieves the full ADsPath of the user. This ADsPath then is used to bind to the user and to retrieve the full name, the expiry date, the group memberships, the last logon and last logoff times, and whether the account is disabled or locked. The group membership's TextBox automatically displays vertical scrollbars if the results cannot be displayed in the space available.

The administrator then can use the Set Password! button to set the password. This time, no confirmation is requested; the password is just accepted as is. The Change Date! button can set the expiration date. The two account status checkboxes in the bottom right can enable/disable the account or unlock it if it gets locked.

Actually, the unlock checkbox should never give the option to lock an account; instead, it should be grayed out (disabled) by default. Then it can be enabled only when an account is locked. Clicking the checkbox on a locked account would unlock the account and then disable the checkbox again immediately. Obviously this means that a user could never change his mind and relock an account, which is fairly nonsensical, but in that case it can simply be disabled instead.

While the code is not particularly complex, it is quite long, and for that reason, I've made it available for download from the companion O'Reilly web site for this book.

Summary

Being able to customize the Active Directory Schema means that you may end up using a number of new classes and attributes that you create. As these classes and attributes can be manipulated using the same ADSI interfaces that you have seen used in the previous chapters, you can easily create your own customized tools to operate on these new objects. This allows you free rein in developing solutions that are perfectly tailored for your requirements.

In addition to extending the schema, I have discussed some ideas on how easy it is to deploy customized applications for existing functions.

21

Scripting Fast Searches
Using ADO

Microsoft's ADO technology features fast algorithms that let you quickly scan for database objects that match certain criteria, conduct database searches, and retrieve the results of searches (i.e., resultsets). These same fast algorithms also let you update the retrieved data and return it to the database. Because Microsoft created an ADO database connector for ADSI (the ADO OLE DB connector), you can use ADO's database query technology on valid ADSI providers, such as Lightweight Directory Access Protocol (LDAP) and Novell Directory Services (NDS).*

However, the ADO OLE DB connector is currently read-only, so many of the useful ADO methods for updating data aren't available yet. Until this situation changes, you can use ADO only for searching and retrieving. Despite the read-only limitation, using ADO technology is still a boon. It is significantly faster to search Active Directory using ADO than it is to use ADSI to bind to each object recursively down a branch. Even using IADsContainer::Filter, shown in Chapter 9, *Designing Organization-Wide Policies,* is slow in comparison. So if you need to rapidly search Active Directory for attributes matching criteria you provide, ADO is exactly what you should use. The ADO object model consists of nine objects (Command, Connection, Error, Field, Parameter, Property, Record, Recordset, and Streams) and four collection objects (Errors, Fields, Parameters, and Properties). However, some of these objects aren't useful if you're using the ADO OLE DB connector, as they are more often used for accessing full-fledged database services. For example, the Parameter object lets you pass parameters to stored procedures, but this object is of little use because the ADSI provider doesn't support stored procedures.

---

* The WinNT: provider does not support ADO searching. This means that you cannot use ADO to search Windows NT servers.

The objects that are appropriate to ADSI in a read-only environment are the Command, Connection, Error, Field, Property, and Recordset objects. I use them to show you how to perform complex searches. For a full description of the ADO object model and the available functions, check here: *http://msdn.microsoft.com/ isapi/msdnlib.idc?theURL=/library/sdkdoc/dasdk/mdao2of9.htm.**

> If you wish to make use of the tools in this chapter in a VB project rather than a VBScript script, you need to include the "Microsoft ActiveX Data Objects 2.x" library from the Reference item on the Project menu of the Visual Basic Environment before you can do so.

One point to note before I continue. As ADO is written to work with all types of databases, there are a large number of ways of doing exactly the same thing. I will attempt to cover examples of each different way as they crop up so that you will be able to choose whatever suits you best or whatever you are familiar with.

The First Search

The easiest way to explain basic searching using ADO is with an example. Here I'll build an ADO query to search and display the ADsPaths of all users in the AD. You can create a simple script to do this search in six steps.

Step 1—Define the Constants and Variables

For this script, you need to define one constant and three variables. The constant is `adStateOpen`, which you set to 1. If you're using Visual Basic Script (VBScript), you use this constant later to determine whether you made a successful connection to the database. If you're using Visual Basic (VB), you don't have to include this constant because VB has already defined it. The two main variables are `adoConnection` (an ADO Connection object that lets you connect to the AD database) and `adoRecordset` (an ADO Recordset object that lets you hold the retrieved resultset). The third variable holds the output of the resultset, as shown in the following example:

```
Option Explicit

Const adStateOpen = 1
```

---

* If this URL ever fails to work, navigate to MSDN and open the online MSDN Library up with a browser. Then drill-down through the headings Platform SDK → Data Access Services → Microsoft Data Access 2.5 SDK → Microsoft ActiveX Data Objects (ADO) → Microsoft ADO Programmers Reference → ADO API Reference.

```
Dim adoConnection    'ADO Connection object
Dim adoRecordset     'ADO Recordset object
Dim str              'The output of the search
```

The `Option Explicit` statement at the beginning of the script is optional, but I recommend that you include it. This statement forces the script to declare variables, so you can quickly spot errors.

Step 2—Establish an ADO Database Connection

To perform an ADO query, you need to establish an ADO connection, whether or not you already have an ADSI connection implicitly or via `IADsOpenDSObject::OpenDSObject`. Before you can establish this connection, you must create an ADO Connection object to use. You create this object the same way you create a file system object: you use VBScript's `CreateObject` method, with `"ADODB.Connection"` as a parameter. You use the ADODB prefix to create all ADO objects, and Connection is the top-level object in the ADO object model:

```
Set adoConnection = CreateObject("ADODB.Connection")
```

Just as you use different programmatic identifiers (ProgIDs) (e.g., WinNT:, LDAP:) to tell ADSI which directory to access, you use different OLE DB providers to tell ADO which query syntax to use. (An OLE DB provider implements OLE DB interfaces so that different applications can use the same uniform process to access data.) ADSI's ADO OLE DB supports two forms of syntax: the SQL dialect and the ADSI dialect. Although you can use the SQL dialect to query the ADSI namespace, most scriptwriters use the ADSI dialect because Microsoft defined it specifically for ADO queries to directory services. However, the default for the Connection object's read/write property, `adoConnection.Provider`, is MSDASQL, which specifies the use of the SQL syntax. Because you want to use the ADSI provider, you need to set `adoConnection.Provider` to `"ADsDSOObject"`, which specifies the use of the ADSI syntax. By setting this specific provider, you force the script to use not only a specific syntax but also a specific set of arguments in the calls to the Connection object's methods:

```
adoConnection.Provider = "ADSDSOObject"
```

Step 3—Open the ADO Connection

You open a connection to the directory by calling the `Connection::Open` method. When describing the methods and property methods of COM interfaces in text, the established notation is to use a double colon (::) separator. So, for example, `Connection::Open` specifies the Open method of the Connection object, as shown in the following example:

```
adoConnection.Open _
    "", "CN=Administrator,CN=Users,DC=windows,dc=mycorp,dc=com", ""
```

As the code shows, the `Open` method takes three parameters. The first parameter is the `Connection::ConnectionString` parameter, which contains information that the script needs to establish a connection to the data source. The second and third parameters contain authentication information.

In this code, you're authenticating with a username DN (the second parameter) and that username's password (the third parameter). You can leave the first parameter blank. Here's why: In ADO, you can perform the same task many ways because the Command, Connection, and Recordset objects heavily interrelate. If you set the properties of one object, you can use those same properties to open the connection of another object as long as you're not setting any new options. Such is the case in the preceding section of code; you're opening the connection without setting any new options. You then use an `If...Then...Else` statement to see whether the `Open` call worked. If the call succeeded (i.e., the connection state has a value of 1), the script prints the message "Authentication Successful" and proceeds to the query. If the call didn't work (i.e., the connection state has a value of 0), the script prints the message "Authentication Failed" and quits, setting the returned error code to 1:

```
If adoConnection.State = adStateOpen Then
  WScript.Echo "Authentication Successful!"
Else
  WScript.Echo "Authentication Failed."
  WScript.Quit(1)
End If
```

Step 4—Execute the Query

You use the `Connection::Execute` method to perform the query. You pass `Connection::Execute` a string containing four arguments separated by semicolons:

```
Set adoRecordset = adoConnection.Execute _
  ("<LDAP://dc=windows,dc=mycorp,dc=com>;(objectClass=User);" _
  & "Name,ADsPath;SubTree")
```

If the string contains spaces before or after the semicolons, the code will fail. It's easy to forget this, and it's very annoying to try and debug, as the error just states that a parameter is invalid. You must also remember to enclose the parameter in parentheses because you're passing the `Execute` method's result to a variable.

The four arguments for any LDAP query you want to execute are:

Search base (also known as root)
> The search base/root argument specifies the point in the directory from which the search is to start. You must use a full ADsPath to specify the search base and enclose the ADsPath in angle brackets (< >). In this script, you're starting from the directory's root (i.e., LDAP://dc=windows,dc=mycorp,dc=com).

Filter
> The filter argument defines which objects match the query. You must enclose this argument in parentheses. You also must use a special format that Request for Comments (RFC) 1960 defines. (I'll cover this format in great detail later, in the "Understanding Search Filters" section.) The script specifies that you're looking for the object class of users.

Attributes
> The attributes argument is a comma-delimited list of attributes to return. You must specify each attribute individually. Unlike the IADs::Get method, which executes an implicit GetInfo call to obtain all attributes, this ADO search returns only the specified attributes in the resultset. In this case, the ADO search will return the Name and ADsPath attributes. The ADsPath is a useful attribute to retrieve because it lets you use ADSI to bind to that object. You then can perform an explicit GetInfo to obtain all the attributes for that object.

Scope
> The optional scope argument is important only in hierarchical directories, where you can specify how far down from the query's starting point you want to search. You can specify one of three string constants: Base, OneLevel, or Subtree. If you set scope to Base, the ADO search checks only objects directly within that container. If you set scope to OneLevel, the ADO search checks any object directly under the root and any objects directly under containers within the root. If you set scope to Subtree, as this script does, the ADO search checks every container in the tree.

Step 5—Navigate Through the Resultset

The adoRecordset variable holds the resultset. Recordset objects have a table-like structure. The structure's columns are *fields*, and the rows are *records*. Fields correspond to the attributes you want to return and assume the titles of those attributes (e.g., Name or ADsPath). ADO also numbers the fields from left to right, starting with 0. Thus, you can access fields using attribute names or index numbers. Records correspond to the values of those attributes.

To manage the members of **adoRecordset**, the simplest approach is to use the `Recordset::MoveNext` method (which navigates to the next record in the result-set) with the `Recordset::EOF` (end-of-file) property method (which tests whether you're at the end of the resultset):

```
str = ""
While Not adoRecordset.EOF
   str = str & adoRecordset.Fields.Item("Name").Value _
      & vbCrLf & adoRecordset.Fields.Item("ADsPath").Value
   adoRecordset.MoveNext
Wend
WScript.Echo str
```

As this section of code shows, you're using these two methods in a simple **WHILE** loop to move through each record. If `Recordset::EOF` returns a value of *false* (i.e., you're not at the end of the resultset), the script stores the contents of the record for each field into the output variable and moves on to the next record. If `Recordset::EOF` returns a value of *true* (i.e., you're at the end of the resultset), the script exits the **WHILE** loop. Finally, I print the string.*

The script can look complicated at first glance. You're using **adoRecordset. Fields**, which is a Fields collection object. As with all collections, Fields has a method called Item. The **Fields::Item** method takes an argument that equates to either the name of the field or its index number. The **Fields::Item** method returns a Field object. You then use that object's Value property method to return the value of the record for that field. In other words, the code:

```
adoRecordset.Fields.Item("Name").Value
```

is telling the script to return the value of the individual field called Name from the collection of all possible fields in the recordset. I'll come back to this more in the later examples on navigating resultsets.

Step 6—Close the ADO Connection

You use the `Connection::Close` method to close the connection to the directory. You then set the Recordset object to nothing to make sure you don't mistakenly reuse it. This line isn't mandatory because you've finished the script. However, I recommend that you use it. That way, if you later add code to the end of the script, you can't mistakenly reuse the now-defunct adoRecordset variable without reinitializing it first:

```
adoConnection.Close
Set adoRecordset = Nothing
```

---

* The GUI WScript.Echo method has a limit of 256 characters, just like MsgBox. The box is likely to become full very quickly, so using techniques from Chapter 17 to redirect the output to a temporary file, opening that file automatically, and then deleting the file when finished would be a better solution.

The Entire Script for a Simple Search

Example 21-1 is the entire script.

Example 21-1. A Simple ADO Search

```
Option Explicit

Const adStateOpen = 1

Dim adoConnection   'ADO Connection object
Dim adoRecordset    'ADO Recordset object
Dim str             'The output of the search

Set adoConnection = CreateObject("ADODB.Connection")
adoConnection.Provider = "ADSDSOObject"
adoConnection.Open "", "CN=Administrator,CN=Users,DC=windows,dc=mycorp,dc=com", ""
If adoConnection.State = adStateOpen Then
  WScript.Echo "Authentication Successful!"
Else
  WScript.Echo "Authentication Failed."
  WScript.Quit(1)
End If

Set adoRecordset = adoConnection.Execute _
  ("<LDAP://dc=windows,dc=mycorp,dc=com>;(objectClass=User);" _
  & "Name,ADsPath;SubTree")

str = ""
While Not adoRecordset.EOF
  str = str & adoRecordset.Fields.Item("Name").Value _
    & vbCrLf & adoRecordset.Fields.Item("ADsPath").Value
  adoRecordset.MoveNext
Wend
WScript.Echo str

adoConnection.Close
Set adoRecordset = Nothing
```

While I have opened and closed the connection within the short script in Example 21-1, I could keep the connection open for every query if I had many queries to execute. This is how ADO normally is used.

Other Ways of Connecting and Retrieving Results

As mentioned earlier, there are a number of ways of authenticating a connection to the AD. The simplest is the way outlined in the simple example search in Example 21-1, using the `Connection::Provider` set with the username and password as second and third arguments:

```
Set adoConnection = CreateObject("ADODB.Connection")
adoConnection.Provider = "ADSDSOObject"
adoConnection.Open "", "CN=Administrator,CN=Users,DC=windows,dc=mycorp,dc=com", _
    "mypass"
```

Because ADO is designed for databases, it often is necessary to specify a number of other requirements when opening a connection. These include a different provider, a different server, or a specific database. All of these items can be set prior to opening the connection. However, none of these make any difference to the AD provider. If you wish to open a connection by setting these values in the ConnectionString property, then do so like this:

```
Set adoConnection = CreateObject("ADODB.Connection")
adoConnection.Provider = "ADSDSOObject"
adoConnection.ConnectionString = _
    "DSN=;UID=CN=Administrator,CN=Users,DC=windows,dc=mycorp,dc=com;PWD=mypass"
adoConnection.Open
```

The arguments are separated by semicolons, with the expected DataSourceName (DSN) specified as empty at the start of the string.

One important point: do not authenticate at both places. The following script is wrong:

```
Set adoConnection = CreateObject("ADODB.Connection")
adoConnection.Provider = "ADSDSOObject"
adoConnection.Open _
    "DSN=;UID=CN=Administrator,CN=Users,DC=windows,dc=mycorp,dc=com;PWD=mypass", _
    "CN=Administrator,CN=Users,DC=windows,dc=mycorp,dc=com", "mypass"
```

So is this one:

```
Set adoConnection = CreateObject("ADODB.Connection")
adoConnection.Provider = "ADSDSOObject"
adoConnection.ConnectionString = _
    "DSN=;UID=CN=Administrator,CN=Users,DC=windows,dc=mycorp,dc=com;PWD=mypass"
adoConnection.Open "", "CN=Administrator,CN=Users,DC=windows,dc=mycorp,dc=com", _
    "mypass"
```

Retrieving Results Using SQL

You can retrieve resultsets in a variety of ways and achieve exactly the same values. Both of the ways discussed here, using the Command object and using the `Recordset::Open` call, allow you to use SQL-formatted queries to retrieve resultsets if you so desire. SQL is a complex query language that allows selection of results from database tables. I do not propose to go through the basics of SQL here, but I will cover some examples for those who may already be familiar with SQL and would find using it to be a more comfortable way of querying Active Directory.

Using the Connection::Execute method

You can pass a SQL select statement to a connection like this:

```
Set adoConnection = CreateObject("ADODB.Connection")
adoConnection.Provider = "ADSDSOObject"
adoConnection.Open "", "CN=Administrator,CN=Users,DC=windows,dc=mycorp,dc=com", ""

Set adoRecordset = adoConnection.Execute "Select Name, AdsPath" _
   & " FROM 'LDAP://dc=windows,dc=mycorp,dc=com' where objectClass = 'User'"

adoConnection.Close
Set adoRecordset = Nothing
```

Using the Recordset::Open method

The first script sets the `Recordset::ActiveConnection` and `Recordset::Source` properties before the `Recordset::Open` method is called; the second passes values directly to the `Recordset::Open` method.

Setting the properties first:

```
Set adoConnection = CreateObject("ADODB.Connection")
adoConnection.Provider = "ADSDSOObject"
adoConnection.Open "", "CN=Administrator,CN=Users,DC=windows,dc=mycorp,dc=com", ""

'Open a recordset based on a SQL string by presetting the properties

Set adoRecordset = CreateObject("ADODB.Recordset")
adoRecordset.ActiveConnection = adoConnection
adoRecordset.Source = "Select Name, AdsPath FROM " _
   & "'LDAP://dc=windows,dc=mycorp,dc=com' where objectClass = 'User'"
adoRecordset.Open

adoRecordset.Close
adoConnection.Close
```

Passing values directly:

```
Set adoConnection = CreateObject("ADODB.Connection")
adoConnection.Provider = "ADSDSOObject"
```

```
adoConnection.Open "", "CN=Administrator,CN=Users,DC=windows,dc=mycorp,dc=com", ""

'Open a recordset based on a SQL string

'Set the SQL search string
strSource = "Select Name, AdsPath FROM 'LDAP://dc=windows,dc=mycorp,dc=com' " _
  & "where objectClass = 'User'"

'Pass what will become the Source and ActiveConnection properties to
'the Recordset::Open call
adoRecordset.Open strSource, adoConnection

adoRecordset.Close
adoConnection.Close
```

Executing a specific command

You can use the Command object's methods and properties to pass a complete command to an already-open connection:

```
Set adoConnection = CreateObject("ADODB.Connection")
adoConnection.Provider = "ADSDSOObject"
adoConnection.Open "", "CN=Administrator,CN=Users,DC=windows,dc=mycorp,dc=com", ""

'Opening a recordset based on a command object

Set adoCommand = CreateObject("ADODB.Command")
Set adoCommand.ActiveConnection = adoConnection
adoCommand.CommandText = "Select Name, AdsPath FROM" _
  & " 'LDAP://dc=windows,dc=mycorp,dc=com' where objectClass = 'User'"

Set adoResultset = adoCommand.Execute()

adoConnection.Close
Set adoRecordset = Nothing
```

Or you can do this:

```
Set adoConnection = CreateObject("ADODB.Connection")
adoConnection.Provider = "ADSDSOObject"
adoConnection.Open "", "CN=Administrator,CN=Users,DC=windows,dc=mycorp,dc=com", ""

'Opening a recordset based on a Command object

Set adoCommand = CreateObject("ADODB.Command")
Set adoCommand.ActiveConnection = adoConnection

Set adoResultset = adoCommand.Execute "Select Name, AdsPath FROM" _
  & " 'LDAP://dc=windows,dc=mycorp,dc=com' where objectClass = 'User'"

adoConnection.Close
Set adoRecordset = Nothing
```

> ## *Controlling How a Search Is Conducted*
>
> When conducting a search, the Command object can take a number of extra parameters. For example, parameters can dictate how many results are returned (`Page Size`), how long in seconds the command can take before it fails (`Timeout`), how far to search in the database (`searchscope`), and whether the resultset is cached in memory for faster access at a later date. These four values are shown in the following code section. For more information, consult the Command object in the ADO object model:
>
> ```
> Const ADS_SCOPE_SUBTREE = 2
> Set adoCommand = CreateObject("ADODB.Command")
> adoCommand.Properties("Page Size") = 10000
> adoCommand.Properties("Timeout") = 60
> adoCommand.Properties("searchscope") = ADS_SCOPE_SUBTREE
> adoCommand.Properties("Cache Results") = False
> ```

The Command object and Recordset::Open

You can even combine both like this:

```
Set adoConnection = CreateObject("ADODB.Connection")
adoConnection.Provider = "ADSDSOObject"
adoConnection.Open "", "CN=Administrator,CN=Users,DC=windows,dc=mycorp,dc=com", ""

Set adoCommand = CreateObject("ADODB.Command")
Set adoCommand.ActiveConnection = adoConnection
adoCommand.CommandText = ""Select Name, AdsPath FROM" _
    & " 'LDAP://dc=windows,dc=mycorp,dc=com' where objectClass = 'User'"

'Pass what will become the Source and ActiveConnection properties to
'the Recordset::Open call
adoRecordset.Open adoCommand, adoConnection

adoRecordset.Close
adoConnection.Close
```

Understanding Search Filters

When you use ADO to conduct a search, you need to specify a filter as the second parameter. The previous script uses a simple filter, (`objectClass=User`), to select every object with the user class in the Windows 2000 Active Directory. The word `objectClass` is the Lightweight Directory Access Protocol (LDAP) name for classes in the AD, and `User` is the LDAP name of the user class, as shown in the following example:

```
(objectClass=User)
```

You can use a filter on any property of any object, thus you can conduct powerful searches. For example, you can search for any object that has a description matching a specified substring. The only requirement is that the filter must match text attributes only. You can't match long integers and other nontext datatypes. In addition, the filter must follow a format laid down in Request for Comments (RFC) 1960. For example, the format dictates that you must not have any spaces within a string in a filter, that filters are case-sensitive, that you enclose each filter in parentheses, and that you use semicolons with no spaces before or after to separate filters.

 You can download the text of RFC 1960 from *ftp://ftp.isi.edu /in-notes/rfc1960.txt.*

Although filters let you conduct powerful searches, working with filters can seem complex because of the format. To make it easier to understand, I have divided the discussion into two parts: items within a filter and items connecting filters.

Items Within a Filter

Within a filter, you can have three types of items:

Operators
   A filter can include one of four operators. The equal-to (=) operator checks for exact equivalence. An example is (`name=vicky`). The approximately-equal-to (~=) operator checks for approximate equivalence. An example is (`size~=10`). The greater-than-or-equal-to (>=) and less-than-or-equal-to (<=) operators check for compliance to a range. Examples are (`size>=5`) and (`size<=20`).

Attributes
   You can include attributes in filters when you want to determine whether an attribute exists. You simply specify the attribute, followed by the = operator and an asterisk (*). For example, the (`mooseHerderProperty=*`) filter searches for objects that have the mooseHerderProperty attribute.

Substrings
   You can include substrings in filters when you want to search for objects with specific strings. Test for substrings by placing the attribute type (e.g., `cn` for common name, `sn` for surname) to the left of the = operator and the substring you're searching for to the right. Use the * character to specify where that substring occurs in the string. The (`cn=Keith*`) filter searches for common name (CN) strings that begin with the substring "Keith"; the (`cn=*Cooper`) filter searches for CN strings that end with the substring "Cooper".

You can place several substrings together, using an * character several times. For example, the `(cn=Kei*Coo*)` filter searches for two substrings in the string: the first substring begins with "Kei", followed by the second substring that begins with "Coo". Similarly, the `(cn=*ith*per)` filter searches for strings that have two substrings: the first substring ends in "ith" followed by the second substring that ends in "per".

The resultset of a substring search might contain objects that you don't want. For example, if you use the filter `(cn=Kei*Coo*)` to search for the object representing "Keith Cooper", your resultset might contain two objects: one representing "Keith Cooper" and another representing "Keith Coolidge".

Items Connecting Filters

Now that you know what can go inside a filter, you can combine filters to perform more powerful searches. You can use the ampersand (&), the vertical bar (|), and the exclamation mark (!) to combine filters.

Let's start by creating a filter to find all groups whose common name begins with the letter *a*. The following is the filter for this search:

    (&(objectClass=Group)(cn=a*))

This filter actually consists of two filters: `(objectClass=Group)` and `(cn=a*)`, but because you're enclosing the filters in parentheses, you're treating them as one filter. The & prefix specifies the use of the logical AND operator. In other words, you're searching for objects that are in the Group object class and have a CN that begins with the letter *a*.

You can add additional filters to narrow the search. Suppose that in groups whose CN begins with the letter *a*, you want to find only those users whose surnames begins with the letter *d*. To perform this search, you use the filter:

    (&(objectClass=Group)(cn=a*)(sn=d*))

You also can widen a search. Instead of using the & operator, you use the | prefix, which specifies the logical OR operator. For example, if you want to find all group or user objects, you use the filter:

    (|(objectClass=Group)(objectClass=User))

You can nest sets of filters, as long as each filter conforms to the correct notation. For example, if you want to find all groups whose CN begins with the letter *a* or whose description begins with the substring "Special groups", you use the filter:

    (&(objectClass=Group)(|(cn=a*)(description=Special groups*)))

So far, you've been searching for objects that have a certain characteristic. You can also search for objects that don't have a certain characteristic. You use the ! prefix, which specifies the **NOT**, or negation, operator. For example, you can search for all objects that aren't users with the filter:

```
(!(objectClass=User))
```

By combining the &, |, and ! operators, you can perform powerful searches. For example, consider the following query:

```
(&
   (|(objectClass=container)(objectClass=organizationalUnit))
   (!(MyCorpSpecial=*))
   (|(cn=*cor*)(cn=J*))
)
```

This query has been split onto multiple lines to fit onto the page. It is *not* valid as it stands, as it is not a single long string.

This query is searching for any container or organizational unit (OU) that doesn't contain the MyCorpSpecial property and whose CN contains the letters *cor* or starts with the letter *J*. Here's how to include this filter in a script:

```
filterStr = _
   "(&(|(objectClass=container)(objectClass=organizationalUnit))" & _
     "(!(MyCorpSpecial=*))" & _
     "(|(cn=*cor*)(cn=J*))" & _
   ")"
```

There are no spaces in the string, yet the quotation marks do not overly detract from the formatting.

As you can see, this is a very powerful specification.

If a value must contain an asterisk or parenthesis, the character must be preceded by a backslash (\).

Filtering an Existing Resultset

Imagine that you have returned a resultset containing a large number of items. It is possible to select particular items from that resultset by using the `Recordset::Filter` property. Once the `Recordset::Filter` property has been set, you can access only the items in the resultset that match the filter. Properties such as the `Recordset::RecordCount` return only the number of items that match the filter.

If you then set the filter back to an empty string, the whole resultset is available to you again. As filtering an existing resultset relies on already-existing data, you can only filter using the Fields object and its values. For example, if my initial resultset was returned using the following filter in the execute statement, then I must specify CN in the list of attributes to return in that resultset if I want to filter it later via the `Recordset::Filter` property:

```
(&(objectClass=User)(cn=Kei*))
```

If I do not return cn as a field, there is no way I can filter on it later.

Being able to filter an existing resultset is a useful tool but only in certain situations. It tends to make sense only when performing another search for a more restricted resultset does not. These situations do not occur regularly. In my experience, it is useful in only three main situations in which you do not want to impact Active Directory performance:

- When you do not want to impact Active Directory performance as you need to conduct multiple searches every few seconds

- When you do not want to impact Active Directory performance as the resultset being returned contains a huge number of objects

- When you do not want to impact Active Directory performance as the resultset execution filter is very complex

Let's consider a contrived example where use of the `Recordset::Filter` makes some sense. I decide that I wish to count how many usernames begin with each of the 26 letters of the alphabet. The fastest method is probably to execute 26 ADO searches and record the `Recordset::RecordCount` property. However, this will hit Active Directory with 26 separate searches. Now I expand my requirement and decide that I require these 26 totals recorded continually in a file every minute or so. By now, I may be unwilling to keep hitting Active Directory with this sort of traffic. I have another alternative; I could execute a single search for all users and loop through the resultset using `Recordset::MoveNext`, updating an array of 26 counts as I go. This hits Active Directory only once, but it iterates through every item. This process is fast for a moderate number of users, but for a really large number of users, it will be much slower. If your resultset will return, say, 20 thousand users in a single search, you will need to use `Recordset::Filter`.

To solve the problem, I write a piece of code that executes one search and then sets 26 separate filters, recording the `Recordset::RecordCount` value at each stage. Here is the sample code, from which the values are written to the *C:\out.txt* file:

```
Option Explicit

Const adStateOpen = 1
```

```
Dim fso            'A FileSystemObject
Dim filOutput      'A TextStream Object
Dim adoConnection 'An ADO Connection object
Dim adoRecordset  'An ADO Recordset object
Dim intCount       'An integer

'******************************************************************************
'Create the file if it doesn't exist or truncate it if it does exist
'******************************************************************************
Set fso = CreateObject("Scripting.FileSystemObject")
Set filOutput = fso.CreateTextFile("c:\out.txt", TRUE)

'******************************************************************************
'Write out the current time and date using the VBScript 'Now' function
'******************************************************************************
filOutput.WriteLine "Starting..." & Now

Set adoConnection = CreateObject("ADODB.Connection")
adoConnection.Provider = "ADSDSOObject"
adoConnection.Open "", "CN=Administrator,CN=Users,DC=windows,dc=mycorp,dc=com", ""
If adoConnection.State = adStateOpen Then
  filOutput.WriteLine "Authentication Successful!"
Else
  filOutput.WriteLine "Authentication Failed."
  WScript.Quit(1)
End If

Set adoRecordset = adoConnection.Execute _
  ("<LDAP://dc=windows,dc=mycorp,dc=com>;(objectClass=User);cn;SubTree")

'******************************************************************************
'Loop through the ASCII characters letters Asc("a") to Asc("z")
'where Asc("a") = 97 and Chr(97) = "a"
'******************************************************************************
For intCount = 97 To 122
  adoRecordset.Filter = "cn LIKE '" & Chr(intCount) & "*'"
  filOutput.WriteLine(Chr(intCount) & " = " & adoRecordset.RecordCount)
Next

adoConnection.Close
Set adoRecordset = Nothing


filOutput.Close
```

The filter property is not using RFC 1960 notation. Instead, it uses a notation similar to that of SQL queries in order to filter the data. If you want to use this property, you need to learn a new filter notation. Luckily the notation is fairly simple to use. The string can be either an empty string ("") thats removes the current filter, a criteria string, or an array of bookmarks.

Using a criteria string

The criteria string can take a number of different forms, which basically can be broken down to:

```
Field-name          operator          value-to-check
```

Here are some simple examples:

```
Name = vicky   'Checks for exact equivalence (=)
size < 10        'Checks for less-than (<)
size > 10         'Checks for greater-than (>)
size >= 5        'Checks greater-than-or-equal-to (>=)
size <= 20        'Checks less-than-or-equal-to (<=)
size <> 10        'Checks for not-equal-to (<>)
```

Dates are simple to check if you surround them with pound signs (#):

```
Date = #12/12/99#
```

You also can use the keyword **LIKE**:

```
cn LIKE 'a*'          'Checks for all cn's beginning with "a"
cn LIKE 'ca%'          'Checks for all three-letter cn's beginning with "ca"
cn LIKE '*eithCoo*'
```

You can also use **AND** and **OR**:

```
size > 10 AND size < 20
cn LIKE 'a*' OR cn LIKE 'b*'
```

However, there is a strict rule to follow if you want to group a criteria string containing OR with another string using AND. Again, this is sloppy, and Microsoft should look to fixing it in a later release:

```
(cn LIKE 'a*' OR cn LIKE 'b*') AND (size <> 10)              'This is WRONG!
(cn LIKE 'a*' AND size <> 10) OR (cn LIKE 'b*' AND size <> 10) 'This is CORRECT!
```

That is all you need to know for setting the search filter.

Using bookmarks

Each object in a resultset has a bookmark associated with it. You can always obtain the bookmark for the current record and store it for later use by retrieving the value of **ResultSet::Bookmark**. After recording the bookmark, you can instantly jump to that record in the resultset at any time by writing the recorded value back to the bookmark property. For example:

```
'Record the bookmark for the current record
adoBookmark = adoRecordset.Bookmark

'Do something

'Now return the current record to the record indicated by the bookmark
adoRecordset.Bookmark = adoBookmark
```

If you read up about the ADO object model on the Microsoft Developer Network site, you will come across the `Recordset::Clone` method for cloning a resultset. Cloning a resultset will clone bookmarks. However, each recordset's bookmarks can be used only with its own resultset.

Incorporating Searches into Active Server Pages

In order to demonstrate how searches work, I thought it would be different if I showed you how to use VBScript within an ASP to display resultsets in a very simple web page. So, in this section, I lead you through a set of ASPs that ultimately end up with a displayed resultset that can be navigated through using a set of First, Last, Next, Previous, and Filter buttons.

Populating an HTML Table by Navigating a Simple Resultset

ADO searches can easily be incorporated into Active Server Pages using the information laid down in the previous chapter. The most common requirement with a returned recordset is to navigate through it. In this first example, I will navigate through a resultset using server-side scripts in order to populate a table that I create dynamically.

To make it easier to understand, Figure 21-1 is what the final result should look like for a new server with very few users.

This ASP includes all its code in the body of the web page. To begin with, I must retrieve the resultset as usual:

```
<%
   Set adoConnection = CreateObject("ADODB.Connection")
   adoConnection.Provider = "ADSDSOObject"
   adoConnection.Open "", _
     "CN=Administrator,CN=Users,DC=windows,dc=mycorp,dc=com", ""

   Set adoRecordset = adoConnection.Execute _
     ("<LDAP://dc=windows,dc=mycorp,dc=com>;" _
       & "(objectClass=User);Name,ADsPath;SubTree")
%>
```

Having done this, I can now begin to create the table. The table definition must include the number of columns. Even though I know that I am retrieving two columns, to extend this page later, I include the value returned from the query rather

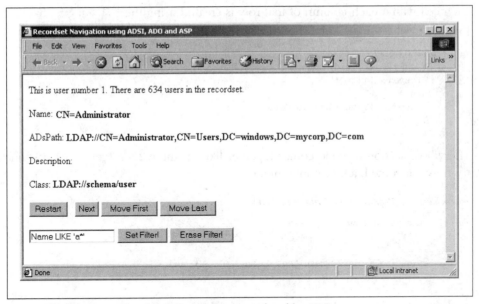

Figure 21-1. A navigable table on a web page populated by ADO

than hardcoding a value of 2 into the table. The table definition then looks like this:

```
<TABLE BORDER=1 COLS=<% = adoRecordset.Fields.Count%>>
```

Now I need to include column headings. Again, if I take these directly from the query, then I can expand the query much more easily later:

```
<TR>
    <% For Each adoField In adoRecordset.Fields %>
        <TH> <% = adoField.Name %> </TH>
    <% Next %>
</TR>
```

Now I can navigate through the actual resultset and populate the table. Each row is created via the <TR.../TR> pair of tags by navigating through the resultset using a Do While...Loop construct. As soon as I go past the end of the loop, the table closing tag is sent. I populate each individual row using a For...Each loop:

```
<% Do While Not adoRecordset.EOF %>
    <TR>
        <% For Each adoField In adoRecordset.Fields %>
            ' Populate the cells here
        <% Next
        adoRecordset.MoveNext %>
    </TR>
<% Loop %>
</TABLE>
```

Each cell within each column of that row is created using the <TD> tag within that
For loop like so:

```
<TD ALIGN=LEFT>
<% If IsNull(adoField) Then
     Response.Write ""
   Else
     Response.Write adoField.Value
   End If %>
</TD>
```

The whole section of code comes together like Example 21-2. Ignore the first line
for now; I'll come back to it in a minute.

Example 21-2. Populating a Table via ADO

```
<!--#include file="adovbs.inc" -->
<html>
<HEAD>
<TITLE>Navigating a simple resultset using ADSI, ADO and ASP</TITLE>
</HEAD>

<BODY>
<%
  On Error Resume Next

  Set adoConnection = CreateObject("ADODB.Connection")
  adoConnection.Provider = "ADSDSOObject"
  adoConnection.Open "", _
    "CN=Administrator,CN=Users,DC=windows,dc=mycorp,dc=com", ""

  Set adoRecordset = adoConnection.Execute _
    ("<LDAP://dc=windows,dc=mycorp,dc=com>;" _
      & "(objectClass=User);Name,ADsPath;SubTree")
%>

<TABLE BORDER=1 COLS=<% = adoRecordset.Fields.Count%>>
  <TR>
    <% For Each oField In adoRecordset.Fields %>
        <TH> <% = oField.Name %> </TH>
    <% Next %>
  </TR>
  <% Do While Not adoRecordset.EOF %>
    <TR>
      <% For Each oField In adoRecordset.Fields %>
          <TD ALIGN=LEFT>
          <% If IsNull(oField) Then
               Response.Write " "
             Else
               Response.Write oField.Value
             End If %>
          </TD>
      <% Next
      adoRecordset.MoveNext %>
```

Example 21-2. Populating a Table via ADO (continued)

```
    </TR>
  <% Loop %>
</TABLE>

<%
  adoConnection.Close
  Set adoRecordset = Nothing
%>

</BODY>
</HTML>
```

While this looks complicated at first due to the use of the <%. . .%> tags, it really is fairly simple code. Continue to ignore the first line for now, I'll cover it soon.

ASP Searches Allowing User Navigation of a Resultset

I'll now go through a rather more complex example so that you can see how to allow users to navigate through a resultset. This example came from a need to be able to display the name, description, and ADsPath of every object in the tree in a simple fashion on a web page. The most obvious solution was to use an ADO resultset with Move First, Move Last, Previous, and Next buttons to step through it. Once the simple example is assembled, I will expand it to include a demonstration of filters.

The ASP is split up as usual between the server-side script and the HTML of the web page itself. The resultset is retrieved as part of the server-side script and looks identical to those we considered earlier:

```
<%
    Set adoConnection = CreateObject("ADODB.Connection")
    adoConnection.Provider = "ADSDSOObject"
    adoConnection.Open "", _
      "CN=Administrator,CN=Users,DC=windows,dc=mycorp,dc=com", ""

    Set adoRecordset = adoConnection.Execute _
      ("<LDAP://dc=windows,dc=mycorp,dc=com>;(objectClass=User);ADsPath;SubTree")
%>
```

 You may need to add either MDAC (Microsoft Data Access Components) or ADO components to the installation of IIS that you have before IIS will accept ADO on web pages. If you find that you are getting continual errors with simple ADO queries, you may have forgotten to install the relevant components so that IIS can interpret ADO code.

I'll leave the server-side script for now and concentrate on the HTML elements. The web page needs to display the name, description, and ADsPath of the user. To do that, I need to bind to the user via the ADsPath of the current record of the resultset. I will use `IADsOpenDSObject::OpenDSObject` here, although `Get-Object` will do just as well:

```
<%
    strUsername = "cn=Administrator,cn=Users,dc=windows,dc=mycorp,dc=com"
    strPassword = ""

    Set adsNamespace = GetObject("LDAP:")
    Set adsUser = adsNamespace.OpenDSObject(adoRecordset("ADsPath"), _
      strUsername,strPassword,0)

    Response.Write "Name: <B>" & adsUser.Name & "</B><P>"
    Response.Write "ADsPath: <B>" & adsUser.ADsPath & "</B><P>"
    Response.Write "Description: <B>" & adsUser.Description & "</B><P>"
%>
```

For the form itself, I've made sure that the Previous button is not displayed at the first resultset record and that the Next button is not displayed at the final resultset record. This prevents the resultset from going out of range and is simple to do using server-side scripting within the HTML code by checking the `Recordset::AbsolutePosition` and `Recordset::RecordCount` properties:

```
<FORM METHOD="POST" ACTION="rs_demo.asp">
  <% If adoRecordset.AbsolutePosition = adoRecordset.RecordCount Then %>
    <INPUT TYPE="SUBMIT" NAME="Previous" VALUE="Previous">
  <% ElseIf adoRecordset.AbsolutePosition = 1 Then %>
    <INPUT TYPE="SUBMIT" NAME="Next" VALUE="Next">
  <% Else %>
    <INPUT TYPE="SUBMIT" NAME="Previous" VALUE="Previous">
    <INPUT TYPE="SUBMIT" NAME="Next" VALUE="Next">
  <% End If %>

  <INPUT TYPE="SUBMIT" NAME="First" VALUE="Move First">
  <INPUT TYPE="SUBMIT" NAME="Last" VALUE="Move Last">
</FORM>
```

This is essentially it for the client HTML code. Before looking at the server-side code, there is one HTML line I have to add for ADO prior to anything else on the page:

```
<!--#include file="adovbs.inc" -->
```

This line is known as a *Server-side Include* (SSI) and is used to include all of the ADO constants you may wish to use in your ASP without having to redeclare them yourself. This file is installed with the ADO component of IIS in the *Program Files\Common Files\System\ado* directory as a text file so you can easily open it and look through the constants that are available to you. If you are using JScript, you need to use *adojavas.inc* instead.

After including the code to retrieve the resultset, I now need to include the code to navigate that resultset according to which buttons are clicked on the form. However, at this point I have a problem. As the page reloads the resultset every single time, the current record will always be the first no matter what button I select. For this web page to properly navigate a resultset, I will have to maintain some sort of indicator to the current record between refreshes of each page. This is very easy to do using the HIDDEN attribute of fields on the existing form. All I need to do is set up an extra entry anywhere on the form that includes a reference to the current record. I can simply do this using the `Recordset::AbsolutePosition` of the resultset:

```
<INPUT TYPE="HIDDEN" NAME="AbsPosition"
   VALUE="<% = adoRecordset.AbsolutePosition %>">
```

If I do this, whenever the form is submitted, the current record's position is transmitted with the form.

 There is one problem with using `Recordset::AbsolutePosition` in this example: the resultset may not be static throughout every query. If users are being created and deleted while the page is being accessed, there is a chance, however small, that the current record may disappear between page refreshes or that a navigation moves to a new record that did not previously exist. Solutions to this problem are discussed later in the chapter.

Assuming that I do this, I can navigate through the new resultset using the following code:

```
<%
   If Request.Form("Next") <> "" Then
      adoRecordset.AbsolutePosition = Request.Form("AbsPosition") + 1
   ElseIf Request.Form("Previous") <> "" Then
      adoRecordset.AbsolutePosition = Request.Form("AbsPosition") - 1
   ElseIf Request.Form("First") <> "" Then
      adoRecordset.MoveFirst
   ElseIf Request.Form("Last") <> "" Then
      adoRecordset.MoveLast
   End If
%>
```

At this point, the code is essentially complete. Example 21-3 shows it in its entirety.

Example 21-3. Navigable ADO Resultset

```
<!--#include file="adovbs.inc" -->
<%
   Set adoConnection = CreateObject("ADODB.Connection")
```

Example 21-3. Navigable ADO Resultset (continued)

```
    adoConnection.Provider = "ADSDSOObject"
    adoConnection.Open "", _
      "CN=Administrator,CN=Users,DC=windows,dc=mycorp,dc=com", ""

    Set adoRecordset = adoConnection.Execute _
      ("<LDAP://dc=windows,dc=mycorp,dc=com>;(objectClass=User);ADsPath;SubTree")

    If Request.Form("Next") <> "" Then
      adoRecordset.AbsolutePosition = Request.Form("AbsPosition") + 1
    ElseIf Request.Form("Previous") <> "" Then
      adoRecordset.AbsolutePosition = Request.Form("AbsPosition") - 1
    ElseIf Request.Form("First") <> "" Then
      adoRecordset.MoveFirst
    ElseIf Request.Form("Last") <> "" Then
      adoRecordset.MoveLast
    End If
%>

<! Start the main page>
<html>
<HEAD>
<TITLE>Recordset Navigation using ADSI, ADO and ASP</TITLE>
</HEAD>

<BODY>
<%
  strUsername = "cn=Administrator,cn=Users,dc=windows,dc=mycorp,dc=com"
  strPassword = ""

  Set adsNamespace = GetObject("LDAP:")
  Set adsUser = adsNamespace.OpenDSObject(adoRecordset("ADsPath"), _
    strUsername,strPassword,0)

  Response.Write "Name: <B>" & adsUser.Name & "</B><P>"
  Response.Write "ADsPath: <B>" & adsUser.ADsPath & "</B><P>"
  Response.Write "Description: <B>" & adsUser.Description & "</B><P>"
%>
<FORM METHOD="POST" ACTION="rs_demo.asp">
  <INPUT TYPE="HIDDEN" NAME="AbsPosition"
    VALUE="<% = adoRecordset.AbsolutePosition %>">
  <% If adoRecordset.AbsolutePosition = adoRecordset.RecordCount Then %>
    <INPUT TYPE="SUBMIT" NAME="Previous" VALUE="Previous">
  <% ElseIf adoRecordset.AbsolutePosition = 1 Then %>
    <INPUT TYPE="SUBMIT" NAME="Next" VALUE="Next">
  <% Else %>
    <INPUT TYPE="SUBMIT" NAME="Previous" VALUE="Previous">
    <INPUT TYPE="SUBMIT" NAME="Next" VALUE="Next">
  <% End If %>
```

Example 21-3. Navigable ADO Resultset (continued)

```
  <INPUT TYPE="SUBMIT" NAME="First" VALUE="Move First">
  <INPUT TYPE="SUBMIT" NAME="Last" VALUE="Move Last">
</FORM>

</BODY>
</HTML>
```

Enhancing the User Navigation ASP

There are a number of enhancements that you can make to the code, not only to make it more user friendly but also in order to demonstrate the use of filtering an existing resultset. I'll deal with these enhancements individually and then combine them all at the end into an expanded ASP incorporating all of the enhancements.

Empty resultsets

Occasionally, you will write an ASP that will generate an empty resultset. While this is almost impossible when scanning Active Directory for users, I will be using filters later that could restrict the resultset to be effectively empty. If that is the case, I should make sure that the page handles this properly. If this occurs, I could print a simple message to that effect and stop processing the page any further. In addition, I could provide a Restart button that could reload the page from scratch if desired. Here is the section of code to accomplish this:

```
<%
  If adoRecordset.EOF Then
     Response.Write("No users found!")
%>
     <FORM METHOD="POST" ACTION="rs_demo.asp">
       <INPUT TYPE="SUBMIT" NAME="Restart" VALUE="Restart">
     </FORM>
<%
     adoConnection.Close
     Set adoRecordset = Nothing
     Set adoConnection = Nothing
     Response.End
  End If
%>
```

Starting from scratch

Occasionally, it would be nice to wipe the resultset clean and start again from scratch at the first item. This is easy to achieve using another button on the form:

```
<INPUT TYPE="SUBMIT" NAME="Restart" VALUE="Restart">
```

If the page is opened using the Restart button, I reload the page from scratch by using the trick of redirecting the browser to the page. This triggers the browser to get a new copy of the page, clearing all the values set by the form on previous pages. The server-side code looks like this:

```
<%
  If Request.Form("Restart") = "Restart" Then
    Response.Redirect("rs_demo.asp")
    Response.End
  End If
%>
```

Filters

In order to include filters on an existing resultset, I need to monitor two extra values when the form is submitted. First, I need to know that a filter is being applied to the resultset, so that I can reapply it when the page is refreshed after the submission of a form. Second, I need to keep a copy of the actual filter itself. The first is easily taken care of by another hidden field in the form:

```
<INPUT TYPE="HIDDEN" NAME="IsFilterOn" VALUE="<% = bolFilter %>">
```

In order to set this value, I need to include some server-side code to cope with the fact that the value will not be set for the first-ever access to the page. I can do it like this:

```
<%
  If Request.Form("IsFilterOn") = "FALSE" Then
    bolFilter = "FALSE"
  ElseIf Request.Form("IsFilterOn") = "TRUE" Then
    bolFilter = "TRUE"
  Else
    bolFilter = "FALSE"
  End If
%>
```

I could just as easily use an **INPUT** field of type CHECKBOX here if desired. This is a Boolean input and would work just as well.

The second requirement can be taken care of by an **INPUT** field on the form:

```
<INPUT TYPE="TEXT" NAME="FilterText" VALUE= "<% = strFilter %>">
```

I also would like to include a default value for this filter, so `strFilter` needs to be set somewhere prior to the form itself. After the page has been accessed once, the value of this field entry will have been set. From then on, I should be able to use the existing value of this field as the base for the input field. Here is the code:

```
<%
  If CStr(Request.Form("FilterText")) = "" Then
    strFilter = "Name LIKE 'a*'"
  Else
    strFilter = CStr(Request.Form("FilterText"))
  End If
%>
```

I also need some way of being able to set and remove the filter on the resultset. As there will always be a value in the filter field, I cannot use this to trigger the addition of a filter to the resultset. Once again, the simplest solution is to use two more buttons on the form:

```
<INPUT TYPE="SUBMIT" NAME="SetFilter" VALUE="Set Filter!">
<INPUT TYPE="SUBMIT" NAME="EraseFilter" VALUE="Erase Filter!">
```

I now can write the code that actually applies and removes the filter using these two buttons:

```
ElseIf Request.Form("SetFilter") <> "" Then
   adoRecordset.Filter = CStr(Request.Form("FilterText"))
   bolFilter = "TRUE"
ElseIf Request.Form("EraseFilter") <> "" Then
   adoRecordset.Filter = adFilterNone
   bolFilter = "FALSE"
```

There is still one small piece of code missing. While I can set a filter using the appropriate button, as soon as I begin to navigate the filtered resultset, I will be clicking other buttons. I need to make sure that the filter is applied while the `IsFilterOn` field is True. To do this, I add an extra line to the code that sets `bolFilter`, which I laid out earlier. The code should now look like this:

```
If Request.Form("IsFilterOn") = "FALSE" Then
   bolFilter = "FALSE"
ElseIf Request.Form("IsFilterOn") = "TRUE" Then
   adoRecordset.Filter = CStr(Request.Form("FilterText"))
   bolFilter = "TRUE"
Else
   bolFilter = "FALSE"
End If
```

This makes sure that the filter is always applied after it has been initially set.

Displaying the location of individual records

I will add two other lines of code to the ASP. While they are not strictly necessary, these two lines serve to demonstrate how resultsets work:

```
This is user number <% = adoRecordset.AbsolutePosition %>.
There are <% = adoRecordset.RecordCount %> users in the recordset.<P>
```

The last line will always tell you how many records you can *currently navigate through* in the resultset. If there are 12 records and you have no filter, the result will be 12. If you have 12 records but have a filter that limits it to 4, the result will be 4. Conversely, the first line always refers to the record number out of the entire recordset total, regardless of whether a filter has been set.

This means that including the following code can lead to some undesired results:

```
<P>This is user <% = adoRecordset.AbsolutePosition %> out of a total of
<% = adoRecordset.RecordCount %> users in the recordset.</P>
```

If a filter were applied to a resultset that limited the resultset to the entries 1, 3, 8, and 9, when you navigated between the four results, you would receive the following responses:

```
This is user 1 out of a total of four users in the recordset.
This is user 3 out of a total of four users in the recordset.
This is user 8 out of a total of four users in the recordset.
This is user 9 out of a total of four users in the recordset.
```

It is important to understand this distinction.

The enhanced ASP search

Example 21-4 is the code for the enhanced version of the ASP ADO search.

Example 21-4. Navigable ADO Resultset

```
<!--#include file="adovbs.inc" -->
<%
  ' If the page is opened using the Restart button then reload the page
  ' from scratch by redirecting to the page itself
  If Request.Form("Restart") = "Restart" Then
    Response.Redirect("rs_demo.asp")
    Response.End
  End If


  ' Retrieve the Resultset
  Set adoConnection = CreateObject("ADODB.Connection")
  adoConnection.Provider = "ADSDSOObject"
  adoConnection.Open "", _
    "CN=Administrator,CN=Users,DC=windows,dc=mycorp,dc=com", ""

  Set adoRecordset = adoConnection.Execute _
    ("<LDAP://dc=windows,dc=mycorp,dc=com>;(objectClass=User);ADsPath;SubTree")

  If Request.Form("IsFilterOn") = "FALSE" Then
    bolFilter = "FALSE"
  ElseIf Request.Form("IsFilterOn") = "TRUE" Then
    adoRecordset.Filter = CStr(Request.Form("FilterText"))
    bolFilter = "TRUE"
  Else
    bolFilter = "FALSE"
  End If


  If Request.Form("Next") <> "" Then
    adoRecordset.AbsolutePosition = Request.Form("AbsPosition") + 1
  ElseIf Request.Form("Previous") <> "" Then
    adoRecordset.AbsolutePosition = Request.Form("AbsPosition") - 1
  ElseIf Request.Form("First") <> "" Then
    adoRecordset.MoveFirst
  ElseIf Request.Form("Last") <> "" Then
    adoRecordset.MoveLast
  ElseIf Request.Form("SetFilter") <> "" Then
    adoRecordset.Filter = CStr(Request.Form("FilterText"))
```

Example 21-4. Navigable ADO Resultset (continued)

```
      bolFilter = "TRUE"
  ElseIf Request.Form("EraseFilter") <> "" Then
      adoRecordset.Filter = adFilterNone
      bolFilter = "FALSE"
  End If


  ' If no results were returned, then end the session
  ' but provide a restart button
  If adoRecordset.EOF Then
      Response.Write("No users found!")
%>
      <FORM METHOD="POST" ACTION="rs_demo.asp">
        <INPUT TYPE="SUBMIT" NAME="Restart" VALUE="Restart">
      </FORM>
<%
      adoConnection.Close
      Set adoRecordset = Nothing
      Set adoConnection = Nothing
      Response.End
  End If
%>


<! Start the main page>
<html>
<HEAD>
<TITLE>Recordset Navigation using ADSI, ADO and ASP</TITLE>
</HEAD>

<BODY>
This is user number <% = adoRecordset.AbsolutePosition %>.
There are <% = adoRecordset.RecordCount %> users in the recordset.<P>

<%
  If CStr(Request.Form("FilterText")) = "" Then
      strFilter = "Name LIKE 'a*'"
  Else
      strFilter = CStr(Request.Form("FilterText"))
  End If
  strUsername = "cn=Administrator,cn=Users,dc=windows,dc=mycorp,dc=com"
  strPassword = ""

  Set adsNamespace = GetObject("LDAP:")
  Set adsUser = adsNamespace.OpenDSObject(adoRecordset("ADsPath"), _
      strUsername,strPassword,0)

  Response.Write "Name: <B>" & adsUser.Name & "</B><P>"
  Response.Write "ADsPath: <B>" & adsUser.ADsPath & "</B><P>"
  Response.Write "Description: <B>" & adsUser.Description & "</B><P>"
  Response.Write "Class: <B>" & adsUser.Schema & "</B><P>"
%>

<FORM METHOD="POST" ACTION="rs_demo.asp">
```

Example 21-4. Navigable ADO Resultset (continued)

```
<INPUT TYPE="SUBMIT" NAME="Restart" VALUE="Restart">
<INPUT TYPE="HIDDEN" NAME="AbsPosition"
    VALUE="<% = adoRecordset.AbsolutePosition %>">
<INPUT TYPE="HIDDEN" NAME="IsFilterOn" VALUE="<% = bolFilter %>">

<% If adoRecordset.AbsolutePosition = adoRecordset.RecordCount Then %>
    <INPUT TYPE="SUBMIT" NAME="Previous" VALUE="Previous">
<% ElseIf adoRecordset.AbsolutePosition = 1 Then %>
    <INPUT TYPE="SUBMIT" NAME="Next" VALUE="Next">
<% Else %>
    <INPUT TYPE="SUBMIT" NAME="Previous" VALUE="Previous">
    <INPUT TYPE="SUBMIT" NAME="Next" VALUE="Next">
<% End If %>

<INPUT TYPE="SUBMIT" NAME="First" VALUE="Move First">
<INPUT TYPE="SUBMIT" NAME="Last" VALUE="Move Last">
<P>
<INPUT TYPE="TEXT" NAME="FilterText" VALUE= "<% = strFilter %>">
<INPUT TYPE="SUBMIT" NAME="SetFilter" VALUE="Set Filter!">
<INPUT TYPE="SUBMIT" NAME="EraseFilter" VALUE="Erase Filter!">
</FORM>

</BODY>
</HTML>
```

Problems with this example

As mentioned earlier, there is the problem that the resultset may not be static throughout every query. One way around this would be to pass the ADsPath of the user back in a hidden field, and once the query is executed, confirm that the current record of the new query is the same current record of the old query prior to performing any actions from the buttons. If there were a problem, you could pop up a MsgBox or write some text to the screen to that effect.

I have not used this code to demonstrate the use of bookmarks, as Microsoft specifically warns against moving to a record in a resultset using a bookmark from another query. Because the query is executed again each time the page is loaded, the use of bookmarks is not appropriate. While the bookmarks for the ADSI OLE DB provider are currently only a copy of the Recordset::AbsolutePosition field, it would be wise to follow Microsoft's advice in case they change the format in the future.

Other Ideas for Expansion

There are many other ways that you could extend the look and functionality of the existing code. For example, you could place Previous and Next buttons on each page even if you were at the first or last record. If you did this, you could use the following section of code to cycle around the resultset. If you click Next from the

last record, you will go to the first; if you click Previous from the first you will get
to the last:

```
If Request.Form("Next") <> "" Then
  adoRecordset.AbsolutePosition = Request.Form("AbsPosition") + 1
  If adoRecordset.EOF Then
    adoRecordset.MoveFirst
  End If
ElseIf Request.Form("Previous") <> "" Then
  If Request.Form("AbsPosition") = 1 Then
    adoRecordset.MoveLast
  Else
    adoRecordset.AbsolutePosition = Request.Form("AbsPosition") - 1
  End If
End If
```

You actually can modify the descriptions on the buttons themselves using a script
if you wish. For example, you could replace Next and Previous with Move to
Record 2 and Move to Record 4 while you were on record 3.

While I bound to Active Directory using the administrator username and password, you could easily adapt the username and password authentication examples from the previous chapter so that the web page had fields for both of these.
That removes the authentication details from the ASP. In addition, as I have
authenticated to Active Directory, you could use this fact to extend this page to
manipulate the existing Active Directory information. For example, instead of displaying the description for a user as text, you could make the current description
the default value for a text INPUT field in the existing form. Then you could modify this description and click another button that you included, which would write
that new description back to Active Directory.

If you wanted to use the ASP to display every attribute for every mandatory and
optional property that user objects have, then you could use Example 15-9 from
Chapter 15, *IADs and the Property Cache*, to walk the property list based on the
schema class definition and write the results to a web page rather than a file. This
is easily achieved using the IADs::Schema property (i.e., adsUser.Schema).

You could modify what happens when you get an empty resultset due to an incor-
rect filter. Instead of just providing a Restart button and ending the session, you
could put up the three filter fields and allow people to see and correct their mistakes.

Obviously, you also could expand and extend the search so that it could search
for any classes of objects, possibly via a list box within a form.

Even though the HTML code on the ASPs is dynamically generated and sent to the
client by server-side scripts, the HTML is static once it has been generated. This
means that for a new set of data to be sent to the client, a new page has to be

opened. As the data on the page returned to the client has to change each time a button is pressed, the web page is therefore reloaded with every button click. This means that the query is executed again and the resultset is retrieved afresh with every click of the button. The only way to alter the HTML code that exists on the client after it has been generated is to use Dynamic HTML or DHTML. This recent update to HTML does exactly what it says; it allows HTML to be dynamically updated on the client. While you could use DHTML here, it lies outside the scope of this book.

The point is that there are quite a few things that you can do with ADO searches of Active Directory within Active Server Pages. I hope this discussion has helped to show you some of them.

A Significant Problem

Imagine the scenario in which you want to connect to Active Directory in order to manipulate it in some manner. Specifically, this time you want to authenticate the connection as the user that is currently running the script. All of my previous authenticated examples have included the user's DN and the password in the code or prompted for the user's DN and password. Even so, with a specific ADSI authentification using `IADsOpenDSObject::OpenDSObject`, I still require the full DN of the user to authenticate. So, how do I retrieve the DN of the user?

First of all, I must ask the user for his username (i.e., CN). This value is the one that the user was created with in Active Directory. I also need to ask for the user's password, and finally, I need to know the LDAP path in the tree that the user wishes to authenticate at, because the user may be able to read only the data from a branch of Active Directory and not have privilege to do so for the entire tree.

Remembering that the namingProperty of a user account according to RFC 1779 is CN, I prefix the username with the string **CN=** to make up the RDN for the user account. I then connect to Active Directory via ADO's Connection object so that I can execute a search for the ADsPath of the user that matches. The trick is to use a null string constant called vbNullString instead of a username and password for the connection. After all, if everyone has read-only access to Active Directory by default, I should be able to anonymously search in the same way that I can use `GetObject`, as shown in the following example:

```
Const adStateOpen = 1

'****************************************************************************
'Assume strUsername, strPassword and strLDAPPath have been correctly retrieved
'****************************************************************************

strUserRDN = "CN=" & strUsername
```

```
Set adoConnection = CreateObject("ADODB.Connection")
adoConnection.Provider = "ADSDSOObject"
adoConnection.Open "", vbNullString, vbNullString
If adoConnection.State = adStateOpen Then
  WScript.Echo "Authentication Successful!"
Else
  WScript.Echo "Authentication Failed."
  WScript.Quit(1)
End If
```

Having connected, I now should be able to construct a search filter to restrict the result of my search to one result, the user's account. The filter looks like this:

```
strFilter = "(&(objectClass=User)(" & strUserRDN & "))"
```

I now need to set the base of the first search for the user's ADsPath to the root of the domain, as the user could be anywhere in the hierarchy:

```
strBase = "<LDAP://dc=windows,dc=mycorp,dc=com>"
```

I then can execute the query and record the resulting ADsPath. This allows me to close the ADO connection and remove the resultset reference as soon as I've finished using it.

```
Set adoRecordset = adoConnection.Execute _
  (strBase & ";" & strFilter & ";ADsPath;SubTree")
If adoRecordset.EOF  Then
  Wscript.Echo "The user was not found in Active Directory."
  WScript.Quit(1)
End If

strADsPath = adoRecordset.Fields.Item("ADsPath").Value

adoConnection.Close
Set adoRecordset = Nothing
```

Remember that I need to authenticate using the ADsPath without the namespace progID. Attempting to authenticate with a user account with an LDAP:// prefix may look all right, but it will fail. To remove it, I use VBScript's Mid function to retrieve a substring by ignoring the first seven letters.

```
strUserDN = Mid(strADsPath, 8)
```

I then can go on and authenticate to Active Directory using this account and the previously recorded password:

```
Set adsNamespace = GetObject("LDAP:")

Err.Clear
Set adsUser = adsNamespace.OpenDSObject(strLDAPPath,strUserDN,strPassword,0)

If Err=0 Then
  WScript.Echo "Authentication Successful!"
Else
```

```
        WScript.Echo "Authentication Failed."
        WScript.Quit(1)
    End If
```

It is as simple as that.

A More Advanced Search Function—SearchAD

Understanding how to anonymously search our Active Directory suggests the ability to specify the most advanced VBScript search function that we will probably ever need. SearchAD can be included in any VBScripts that need a search in the /future and used immediately as is.

SearchAD takes in five parameters and returns a Boolean indicating whether it succeeded or failed in the search. You should recognize most of these parameters.

*   The root LDAP path to start the search from

*   A valid ADO criteria string

*   The depth that you wish to search, represented by one of the exact strings: **Base**, **OneLevel**, or **SubTree**

*   The comma-separated list of attributes that is to be returned

*   A variable that will hold the returned results of the search in an array

The last parameter does not have any values when passed in, but if SearchAD is successful, the array contains the resultset.

Here is an example use of SearchAD:

```
    bolIsSuccess = SearchAD("LDAP://ou=Finance,dc=windows,dc=mycorp,dc=com", _
        "(cn=a*)", "Base", "cn,description", arrSearchResults)
```

Or how about using it as part of an **If...Then** condition:

```
    If SearchAD("LDAP://dc=mycorp,dc=com", "(description=moose)", "SubTree", _
        "ADsPath,cn,description", arrSearchResults) Then
        'success code using arrSearchResults
    Else
        'failure code
    End If
```

The array that is returned is a two-dimensional array of attributes that match the criteria. So, if there were 12 results returned for the preceding query, then this is how you access the results:

```
    arrSearchResults(0,0) 'ADsPath of first result
    arrSearchResults(0,1) 'CN of first result
    arrSearchResults(0,2) 'Description of first result
    arrSearchResults(1,0) 'ADsPath of second result
```

```
arrSearchResults(1,1)  'CN of second result
arrSearchResults(1,2)  'Description of second result
arrSearchResults(2,0)  'ADsPath of third result
arrSearchResults(2,1)  'CN of third result
arrSearchResults(2,2)  'Description of third result
arrSearchResults(3,0)  'ADsPath of fourth result
arrSearchResults(3,1)  'CN of fourth result
arrSearchResults(3,2)  'Description of fourth result
.
.
.

arrSearchResults(11,0)  'ADsPath of 11th result
arrSearchResults(11,1)  'CN of 11th result
arrSearchResults(11,2)  'Description of 11th result
```

You can loop through these values in your own code using VBScript's built-in function **UBound** to find the maximum upper bound of an array:

```
UBound(arrSearchResults,1)  'This results in a value of 11
UBound(arrSearchResults,2)  'This results in a value of 2
```

The first **UBound** gives the upper bound of the array's first dimension, and the second gives the upper bound of the second dimension. Thus you can loop through an index from 0 to these values to iterate through the array. For example:

```
'Iterate through the entire set of records
For i=0 To UBound(arrSearchResults,1)
  'Now for each record iterate through the list of that record's values
  For j=0 To UBound(arrSearchResults,2)
    'Do something with arrSearchResults(i,j), e.g., the next line
    MsgBox arrSearchResults(i,j)
  Next
Next
```

So, without further ado, here is the SearchAD function:

```
'************************************************************************
'SearchAD Function (returns Boolean success or failure)
'************************************************************************
Function SearchAD(ByVal strLDAPBase, ByVal strCriteria, ByVal strDepth, _
  ByVal strAttributeList, ByRef arrResults())

  Dim adoConnection, adoCommand, adoRecordset, intArrayIndex, arrAttributes
  Dim intAttributeArrayIndex

  On Error Resume Next

  '************************************************************************
  'Used to specify an unsuccessful ADO connection
  '************************************************************************
  Const adStateClosed = 0

  '************************************************************************
  'Defined in ADS_SCOPEENUM (in the ADSI documentation) for a full
  'subtree search starting at the defined root
  '************************************************************************
```

```
Const ADS_SCOPE_SUBTREE = 2

Set adoConnection = CreateObject("ADODB.Connection")
Set adoCommand = CreateObject("ADODB.Command")
Set adoRecordset = CreateObject("ADODB.Recordset")

adoConnection.Provider = "ADSDSOObject"
adoConnection.Open "", vbNullString, vbNullString

'**********************************************************************
'If connection failed, then return FALSE
'**********************************************************************
If adoConnection.State = adStateClosed Then
  SearchAD = False
  Exit Function
End If

'**********************************************************************
'Link the now-open connection with the empty command object
'**********************************************************************
Set adoCommand.ActiveConnection = adoConnection

'**********************************************************************
'Populate the command object in order to execute a query through the
'linked connection. Set the text of the query command (i.e., the search),
'the max number of results to return, the timeout in seconds to wait
'for the query, and whether the results are to be cached.
'**********************************************************************
adoCommand.CommandText = "<" & strLDAPBase & ">;" & strCriteria & ";" _
  & strAttributeList & ";" & strDepth
adoCommand.Properties("Page Size") = 10000
adoCommand.Properties("Timeout") = 60
adoCommand.Properties("searchscope") = ADS_SCOPE_SUBTREE
adoCommand.Properties("Cache Results") = False

'**********************************************************************
'Execute the command through the linked connection
'**********************************************************************
Err.Clear
Set adoRecordset = adoCommand.Execute
'**********************************************************************
'If there was an error, then return FALSE
'**********************************************************************
If Err Then
  adoConnection.Close
  Set adoRecordset = Nothing
  SearchAD = False
Else
  '**********************************************************************
  'If we're pointing at the end of the resultset already (EOF) then there
  'were no records returned (although the query did search the AD), so
  'return FALSE
  '**********************************************************************
  If adoRecordset.EOF Then
    adoConnection.Close
    Set adoRecordset = Nothing
```

```
            SearchAD = False
      Else
         '*********************************************************************
         'Count number of attributes passed in by splitting the attributes up
         'using commas as separators into an array of elements. Then we can use
         'that array to find the upper bound (i.e., number of attributes).
         '*********************************************************************
         arrAttributes = Split(strAttributeList,",")


         '*********************************************************************
         'Now in order to place all the resulting attributes into the array that
         'we'll pass back out, we need to redimension the array so that it is
         'large enough to hold the records. The array is multidimensional in
         'order to hold all the attribute fields.
         '*********************************************************************
         ReDim arrResults((adoRecordset.RecordCount - 1),UBound(arrAttributes))


         '*********************************************************************
         'Loop through the newly redimensioned array, starting at zero, and add
         'each field to the array
         '*********************************************************************
         intArrayIndex = 0
         While Not adoRecordset.EOF
            For intAttributeArrayIndex = 0 To UBound(arrAttributes)
               arrResults(intArrayIndex,intAttributeArrayIndex) = _
                  adoRecordset.Fields.Item(arrAttributes(intAttributeArrayIndex)).Value
            Next
            intArrayIndex = intArrayIndex + 1
            adoRecordset.MoveNext
         Wend


         '*********************************************************************
         'Close the connection and return TRUE
         '*********************************************************************
         adoConnection.Close
         Set adoRecordset = Nothing
         SearchAD = True
      End If
   End If
End Function
```

Summary

If Active Directory is going to live up to its name as an information store for hundreds of thousands of objects, technologies have to exist to enable you to rapidly script queries to the directory. ADO is that technology and I hope I've shown you that scripting with it can be simple, yet powerful.

While ADO is powerful now, it is still a read-only solution. When Microsoft updates ADO with a technology called Remote Data Service (RDS), you can retrieve a resultset, modify it, and return it in a single transaction. When that happens, the use of ADO/RDS with Active Directory will be a significant leap forward.

Index

About the Author

Alistair G. Lowe-Norris is currently an enterprise program manager for Microsoft U.K., although during the writing of this book he worked for Leicester University as the project manager and technical lead of the Rapid Deployment Program for Windows 2000. During his time there, Leicester was part of both Microsoft's U.K. and U.S. Rapid Deployment Programs for Windows 2000, and he was responsible for rolling out what turned out to be one of the world's largest deployments of Windows 2000 prior to release of the final product.

He is the technical editor of the *Win32 Scripting Journal*, for which he writes a monthly article, as well as the technical consultant for the U.K.-based *Windows NT Explorer* magazine. He has contributed articles for *Windows 2000 Magazine* (formerly *Windows NT Magazine*). He also writes for the Motley Fool U.K. investment site (*http://www.fool.co.uk*) as TMFAlistair, helping to lay bare the complexities of investing in simple terms. He is a Microsoft Certified Systems Engineer and has been using Windows 2000 daily since October 1997.

Colophon

Our look is the result of reader comments, our own experimentation, and feedback from distribution channels. Distinctive covers complement our distinctive approach to technical topics, breathing personality and life into potentially dry subjects.

The animal on the cover of *Windows 2000 Active Directory* is a domestic cat (felis silvetris) and her kitten. The domestic cat is a descendant of the African wild cat, which first inhabited the planet almost a million years ago. Other early forerunners to the cat existed as many as 12 million years ago.

The domestic cat is one of the most popular house pets in the world. There are hundreds of breeds of domestic cats, which weigh anywhere from five to thirty pounds, with an average of twelve pounds. The cat is slightly longer than it is tall, with its body typically being longer than its tail. Domestic cats can be any of eighty different colors and patterns. They often live to be fifteen to twenty years old; ten years for a human life is about equal to sixty years for a cat.

The cat's gestation period is approxiately two months, and each litter may contain three to seven kittens. Mother cats teach their kittens to eat and to use litter boxes. Kittens can leave their mother's side ideally at the age of twelve weeks, and are considered full-grown at the age of about three years.

Maureen Dempsey was the production editor and proofreader for *Windows 2000 Active Directory*. Norma Emory was the copyeditor. Colleen Gorman and Jane Ellin provided quality control. Sebastian Banker and Anna Snow provided production support. Ellen Troutman-Zaig wrote the index.

Hanna Dyer designed the cover of this book, based on a series design by Edie Freedman. The cover image is a 19th-century engraving from the Dover Pictorial Archive. Kathleen Wilson produced the cover layout with QuarkXPress 3.32 using Adobe's ITC Garamond font.

Alicia Cech designed the interior layout based on a series design by Nancy Priest. Mike Sierra implemented the design in FrameMaker 5.5. The text and heading fonts are ITC Garamond Light and Garamond Book. The illustrations that appear in the book were produced by Robert Romano and Rhon Porter using Macromedia FreeHand 8 and Adobe Photoshop 5. This colophon was written by Nicole Arigo.

Whenever possible, our books use RepKover™, a durable and flexible lay-flat binding. If the page count exceeds RepKover's limit, perfect binding is used.

 # More Titles from O'Reilly

Windows 2000 Administration

Managing the Windows 2000 Registry

By Paul Robichaux
1st Edition August 2000
558 pages, ISBN 1-56592-943-8

The Windows 2000 Registry is the repository for all hardware, software, and application configuration settings. *Managing the Windows 2000 Registry* is the system administrator's guide to maintaining, monitoring, and updating the Registry database. A "must-have" for every 2000 system manager or administrator, it covers what the Registry is and where it lives on disk, available tools, Registry access from programs, and Registry content.

Windows 2000 Administration in a Nutshell

By Mitch Tulloch
1st Edition February 2001
798 pages, ISBN 1-56592-713-3

Anyone who installs Windows 2000, creates a user, or adds a printer is a 2000 system administrator. This book covers all the important day-to-day administrative tasks, and the tools for performing each task are included in a handy easy-to-look-up alphabetical reference. What's the same and what's different between the Windows 2000 and Windows NT platform? Has the GUI or the networking architecture changed, and if so, how? *Windows 2000 Administration in a Nutshell* addresses the problems associated with bridging the gap between the Windows NT and Windows 2000 platforms.

Securing Windows NT/2000 Servers for the Internet

By Stefan Norberg
1st Edition November 2000
200 pages, ISBN 1-56592-768-0

In recent years, Windows NT and 2000 systems have emerged as viable platforms for Internet servers, but securing Windows for internet use is a complex task. This concise guide simplifies the task by paring down installation and configuration instructions into a series of security checklists for security administration, including hardening servers for use as "bastion hosts," performing secure remote administration with OpenSSH, TCP Wrappers, VNC, and the new Windows 2000 Terminal Services.

DHCP for Windows 2000

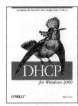

By Neall Alcott
1st Edition January 2001
288 pages, ISBN 1-56592-838-5

DHCP for Windows 2000 is custom-designed for system administrators who are responsible for configuring and maintaining networks with Windows 2000 servers. It explains the DHCP protocol and how to install and manage DHCP on both servers and clients – including client platforms other than Windows 2000.

O'REILLY®

TO ORDER: **800-998-9938** • **order@oreilly.com** • **http://www.oreilly.com/**
OUR PRODUCTS ARE AVAILABLE AT A BOOKSTORE OR SOFTWARE STORE NEAR YOU.
FOR INFORMATION: **800-998-9938** • **707-829-0515** • **info@oreilly.com**

How to stay in touch with O'Reilly

1. Visit Our Award-Winning Web Site

http://www.oreilly.com/

★ "Top 100 Sites on the Web" —*PC Magazine*
★ "Top 5% Web sites" —*Point Communications*
★ "3-Star site" —*The McKinley Group*

Our web site contains a library of comprehensive product information (including book excerpts and tables of contents), downloadable software, background articles, interviews with technology leaders, links to relevant sites, book cover art, and more. File us in your Bookmarks or Hotlist!

2. Join Our Email Mailing Lists

New Product Releases

To receive automatic email with brief descriptions of all new O'Reilly products as they are released, send email to:
ora-news-subscribe@lists.oreilly.com
Put the following information in the first line of your message (*not* in the Subject field):
subscribe ora-news

O'Reilly Events

If you'd also like us to send information about trade show events, special promotions, and other O'Reilly events, send email to:
ora-news-subscribe@lists.oreilly.com
Put the following information in the first line of your message (*not* in the Subject field):
subscribe ora-events

3. Get Examples from Our Books via FTP

There are two ways to access an archive of example files from our books:

Regular FTP

- ftp to:
  ftp.oreilly.com
  (login: anonymous
  password: your email address)
- Point your web browser to:
  ftp://ftp.oreilly.com/

FTPMAIL

- Send an email message to:
  ftpmail@online.oreilly.com
  (Write "help" in the message body)

4. Contact Us via Email

order@oreilly.com
To place a book or software order online. Good for North American and international customers.

subscriptions@oreilly.com
To place an order for any of our newsletters or periodicals.

books@oreilly.com
General questions about any of our books.

software@oreilly.com
For general questions and product information about our software. Check out O'Reilly Software Online at **http://software.oreilly.com/** for software and technical support information. Registered O'Reilly software users send your questions to: **website-support@oreilly.com**

cs@oreilly.com
For answers to problems regarding your order or our products.

booktech@oreilly.com
For book content technical questions or corrections.

proposals@oreilly.com
To submit new book or software proposals to our editors and product managers.

international@oreilly.com
For information about our international distributors or translation queries. For a list of our distributors outside of North America check out:
http://www.oreilly.com/distributors.html

5. Work with Us

Check out our website for current employment opportunites:
http://jobs.oreilly.com/

O'Reilly & Associates, Inc.
101 Morris Street, Sebastopol, CA 95472 USA
TEL 707-829-0515 or 800-998-9938
       (6am to 5pm PST)
FAX 707-829-0104

Titles from O'Reilly

PROGRAMMING

C++: The Core Language
Practical C++ Programming
Practical C Programming, 3rd Ed.
High Performance Computing, 2nd Ed.
Programming Embedded Systems in C and C++
Mastering Algorithms in C
Advanced C++ Techniques
POSIX 4: Programming for the Real World
POSIX Programmer's Guide
Power Programming with RPC
UNIX Systems Programming for SVR4
Pthreads Programming
CVS Pocket Reference
Advanced Oracle PL/SQL
Oracle PL/SQL Guide to Oracle8i Features
Oracle PL/SQL Programming, 2nd Ed.
Oracle Built-in Packages
Oracle PL/SQL Developer's Workbook
Oracle Web Applications
Oracle PL/SQL Language Pocket Reference
Oracle PL/SQL Built-ins Pocket Reference
Oracle SQL*Plus: The Definitive Guide
Oracle SQL*Plus Pocket Reference
Oracle Essentials
Oracle Database Administration
Oracle Internal Services
Oracle SAP
Guide to Writing DCE Applications
Understanding DCE
Visual Basic Shell Programming
VB/VBA in a Nutshell: The Language
Access Database Design & Programming, 2nd Ed.
Writing Word Macros
Applying RCS and SCCS
Checking C Programs with Lint
VB Controls in a Nutshell
Developing Asp Components, 2nd Ed.
Learning WML & WMLScript
Writing Excel Macros
Windows 32 API Programming with Visual Basic
ADO: The Definitive Guide

USING THE INTERNET

Internet in a Nutshell
Smileys
Managing Mailing Lists

SOFTWARE

WebSite Professional™ 2.0
Polyform™
WebBoard™ 4.0

WEB

Apache: The Definitive Guide, 2nd Ed.
Apache Pocket Reference
ASP in a Nutshell, 2nd Ed.
Cascading Style Sheets
Designing Web Audio
Designing with JavaScript, 2nd Ed.
DocBook: The Definitive Guide
Dynamic HTML: The Definitive Reference
HTML Pocket Reference
Information Architecture for the WWW
JavaScript: The Definitive Guide, 3rd Ed.
Java and XML
JavaScript Application Cookbook
JavaScript Pocket Reference
Practical Internet Groupware
PHP Pocket Reference
Programming Coldfusion
Photoshop for the Web, 2nd Ed.
Web Design in a Nutshell
Webmaster in a Nutshell, 2nd Ed.
Web Navigation: Designing the User Experience
Web Performance Tuning
Web Security & Commerce
Writing Apache Modules with Perl and C

UNIX

SCO UNIX in a Nutshell
Tcl/Tk in a Nutshell
The Unix CD Bookshelf, 2nd Ed.
UNIX in a Nutshell, System V Edition, 3rd Ed.
Learning the Unix Operating System, 4th Ed.
Learning vi, 6th Ed.
Learning the Korn Shell
Learning GNU Emacs, 2nd Ed.
Using csh & tcsh
Learning the bash Shell, 2nd Ed.
GNU Emacs Pocket Reference
Exploring Expect
TCL/TK Tools
TCL/TK in a Nutshell
Python Pocket Reference

USING WINDOWS

Windows Millenium: The Missing Manual
PC Hardware in a Nutshell
Optimizing Windows for Games, Graphics, and Multimedia
Outlook 2000 in a Nutshell
Word 2000 in a Nutshell
Excel 2000 in a Nutshell
Paint Shop Pro 7 in a Nutshell
Windows 2000 Pro: The Missing Manual

JAVA SERIES

Developing Java Beans
Creating Effective JavaHelp
Enterprise Java Beans, 2nd Ed.
Java Cryptography
Java Distributed Computing
Java Enterprise in a Nutshell
Java Examples in a Nutshell, 2nd Ed.
Java Foundation Classes in a Nutshell
Java in a Nutshell, 3rd Ed.
Java Internationalization
Java I/O
Java Native Methods
Java Network Programming, 2nd Ed.
Java Performance Tuning
Java Security
Java Servlet Programming
Java ServerPages
Java Threads, 2nd Ed.
Jini in a Nutshell
Learning Java

GRAPHICS & MULTIMEDIA

MP3: The Definitive Guide
Photoshop 6 in a Nutshell, 3rd Ed.
Director in a Nutshell
Lingo in a Nutshell
FrontPage 2000 in a Nutshell

X WINDOW

Vol. 1: Xlib Programming Manual
Vol. 2: Xlib Reference Manual
Vol. 4M: X Toolkit Intrinsics Programming Manual, Motif Ed.
Vol. 5: X Toolkit Intrinsics Reference Manual
Vol. 6A: Motif Programming Manual
Vol. 6B: Motif Reference Manual, 2nd Ed.

PERL

Advanced Perl Programming
CGI Programming with Perl, 2nd Ed.
Learning Perl, 2nd Ed.
Learning Perl for Win32 Systems
Learning Perl/Tk
Mastering Algorithms with Perl
Mastering Regular Expressions
Perl Cookbook
Perl in a Nutshell
Programming Perl, 3rd Ed.
Perl CD Bookshelf
Perl Resource Kit – Win32 Ed.
Perl/TK Pocket Reference
Perl 5 Pocket Reference, 3rd Ed.

MAC

AppleScript in a Nutshell
AppleWorks 6: The Missing Manual
Crossing Platforms
iMovie: The Missing Manual
Mac OS in a Nutshell
Mac OS 9: The Missing Manual
Photoshop Cookbook
REALbasic: The Definitive Guide

LINUX

Building Linux Clusters
Learning Debian GNU/Linux
Learning Red Hat Linux
Linux Device Drivers
Linux Network Administrator's Guide, 2nd Ed.
Running Linux, 3rd Ed.
Linux in a Nutshell, 3rd Ed.
Linux Multimedia Guide

SYSTEM ADMINISTRATION

Practical UNIX & Internet Security, 2nd Ed.
Building Internet Firewalls, 2nd Ed.
PGP: Pretty Good Privacy
SSH, The Secure Shell: The Definitive Guide
DNS and Bind, 3rd Ed.
The Networking CD Bookshelf
Virtual Private Networks, 2nd Ed.
TCP/IP Network Administration, 2nd Ed.
sendmail Desktop Reference
Managing Usenet
Using & Managing PPP
Managing IP Networks with Cisco Routers
Networking Personal Computers with TCP/IP
Unix Backup & Recovery
Essential System Administration, 2nd Ed.
Perl for System Administration
Managing NFS and NIS
Volume 8: X Window System Administrator's Guide
Using Samba
Unix Power Tools, 2nd Ed.
DNS on Windows NT
Windows NT TCP/IP Network Administration
DHCP for Windows 2000
Essential Windows NT System Administration
Managing Windows NT Logons
Managing the Windows 2000 Registry

OTHER TITLES

PalmPilot: The Ultimate Guide, 2nd Ed.
Palm Programming: The Developer's Guide

O'REILLY®

TO ORDER: **800-998-9938** • *order@oreilly.com* • *http://www.oreilly.com/*

OUR PRODUCTS ARE AVAILABLE AT A BOOKSTORE OR SOFTWARE STORE NEAR YOU.

FOR INFORMATION: **800-998-9938** • **707-829-0515** • *info@oreilly.com*

International Distributors

http://international.oreilly.com/distributors.html

UK, EUROPE, MIDDLE EAST AND AFRICA (EXCEPT FRANCE, GERMANY, AUSTRIA, SWITZERLAND, LUXEMBOURG, AND LIECHTENSTEIN)

INQUIRIES

O'Reilly UK Limited
4 Castle Street
Farnham
Surrey, GU9 7HS
United Kingdom
Telephone: 44-1252-711776
Fax: 44-1252-734211
Email: information@oreilly.co.uk

ORDERS

Wiley Distribution Services Ltd.
1 Oldlands Way
Bognor Regis
West Sussex PO22 9SA
United Kingdom
Telephone: 44-1243-843294
UK Freephone: 0800-243207
Fax: 44-1243-843302 (Europe/EU orders)
or 44-1243-843274 (Middle East/Africa)
Email: cs-books@wiley.co.uk

FRANCE

INQUIRIES & ORDERS

Éditions O'Reilly
18 rue Séguier
75006 Paris, France
Tel: 1-40-51-71-89
Fax: 1-40-51-72-26
Email: france@oreilly.fr

GERMANY, SWITZERLAND, AUSTRIA, LUXEMBOURG, AND LIECHTENSTEIN

INQUIRIES & ORDERS

O'Reilly Verlag
Balthasarstr. 81
D-50670 Köln, Germany
Telephone: 49-221-973160-91
Fax: 49-221-973160-8
Email: anfragen@oreilly.de (inquiries)
Email: order@oreilly.de (orders)

CANADA (FRENCH LANGUAGE BOOKS)

Les Éditions Flammarion ltée
375, Avenue Laurier Ouest
Montréal (Québec) H2V 2K3
Tel: 00-1-514-277-8807
Fax: 00-1-514-278-2085
Email: info@flammarion.qc.ca

HONG KONG

City Discount Subscription Service, Ltd.
Unit A, 6th Floor, Yan's Tower
27 Wong Chuk Hang Road
Aberdeen, Hong Kong
Tel: 852-2580-3539
Fax: 852-2580-6463
Email: citydis@ppn.com.hk

KOREA

Hanbit Media, Inc.
Chungmu Bldg. 210
Yonnam-dong 568-33
Mapo-gu
Seoul, Korea
Tel: 822-325-0397
Fax: 822-325-9697
Email: hant93@chollian.dacom.co.kr

PHILIPPINES

Global Publishing
G/F Benavides Garden
1186 Benavides Street
Manila, Philippines
Tel: 632-254-8949/632-252-2582
Fax: 632-734-5060/632-252-2733
Email: globalp@pacific.net.ph

TAIWAN

O'Reilly Taiwan
1st Floor, No. 21, Lane 295
Section 1, Fu-Shing South Road
Taipei, 106 Taiwan
Tel: 886-2-27099669
Fax: 886-2-27038802
Email: mori@oreilly.com

INDIA

Shroff Publishers & Distributors Pvt. Ltd.
12, "Roseland", 2nd Floor
180, Waterfield Road, Bandra (West)
Mumbai 400 050
Tel: 91-22-641-1800/643-9910
Fax: 91-22-643-2422
Email: spd@vsnl.com

CHINA

O'Reilly Beijing
SIGMA Building, Suite B809
No. 49 Zhichun Road
Haidian District
Beijing, China PR 100080
Tel: 86-10-8809-7475
Fax: 86-10-8809-7463
Email: beijing@oreilly.com

JAPAN

O'Reilly Japan, Inc.
Yotsuya Y's Building
7 Banch 6, Honshio-cho
Shinjuku-ku
Tokyo 160-0003 Japan
Tel: 81-3-3356-5227
Fax: 81-3-3356-5261
Email: japan@oreilly.com

SINGAPORE, INDONESIA, MALAYSIA AND THAILAND

TransQuest Publishers Pte Ltd
30 Old Toh Tuck Road #05-02
Sembawang Kimtrans Logistics Centre
Singapore 597654
Tel: 65-4623112
Fax: 65-4625761
Email: wendiw@transquest.com.sg

ALL OTHER ASIAN COUNTRIES

O'Reilly & Associates, Inc.
101 Morris Street
Sebastopol, CA 95472 USA
Tel: 707-829-0515
Fax: 707-829-0104
Email: order@oreilly.com

AUSTRALIA

Woodslane Pty., Ltd.
7/5 Vuko Place
Warriewood NSW 2102
Australia
Tel: 61-2-9970-5111
Fax: 61-2-9970-5002
Email: info@woodslane.com.au

NEW ZEALAND

Woodslane New Zealand, Ltd.
21 Cooks Street (P.O. Box 575)
Waganui, New Zealand
Tel: 64-6-347-6543
Fax: 64-6-345-4840
Email: info@woodslane.com.au

ARGENTINA

Distribuidora Cuspide
Suipacha 764
1008 Buenos Aires
Argentina
Phone: 5411-4322-8868
Fax: 5411-4322-3456
Email: libros@cuspide.com

O'REILLY®

TO ORDER: **800-998-9938** • **order@oreilly.com** • **http://www.oreilly.com/**
OUR PRODUCTS ARE AVAILABLE AT A BOOKSTORE OR SOFTWARE STORE NEAR YOU.
FOR INFORMATION: **800-998-9938** • **707-829-0515** • **info@oreilly.com**